Praise for

AUTHOR

"The definitive book about presidenti.... .....ing."
—Alex Shepard, *The New Republic*

"Credit to Craig Fehrman for the compendiousness, readability, and general exuberance of his *Author in Chief*."
—James Parker, *The Atlantic*

"Fehrman examines the writing by every United States president, situating each within his historical context—and revealing vanities, insecurities, and intrigues along the way. Taking us on a journey from a bygone era when books were peddled on the back of a wagon rolling through the undeveloped countryside, to the modern rise of the eight-figure blockbuster book deal, Fehrman reveals that presidents and their words are as subject to history as they are shapers of it."
—Andrew Heisel, *The Yale Review*

"Fehrman offers a decade of painstaking research boiled down into a supremely engaging narrative about presidents and their relationship to reading and writing."
—Rebecca Rego Barry, *Fine Books & Collection*

"Fehrman discovered that one of the best ways to understand a nation's history is to read the books their leaders penned. . . . *Author in Chief*, a compelling history of presidential books, is perhaps more accurately described as a love letter to the power of the written word."
—Caleb Gotthardt, BookBub

"*Author in Chief* is an absolutely absorbing read. . . . It's a years-long undertaking packed with an incredible depth of research and thoughtful analysis, all of it devoted to exploring the literary output of our presidents. Fehrman walks us through the entirety of American history . . . The combination of exceptionally detailed research and well-crafted prose results in a truly engaging work of nonfiction. It's a fascinating look at American history that isn't quite like anything you've read before, a chance to view the men who have led this country through a different and very specific lens."
—Allen Adams, *The Maine Edge*

"Entertaining and illuminating . . . Fehrman's deep research delivers a wealth of intriguing tidbits (Jimmy Carter leased a $12,000 word processor to compose *Keeping the Faith*; the Committee to Boycott Nixon's *Memoirs* sold T-shirts and bumper stickers with the slogan 'Don't Buy Books by Crooks'), which are complemented by a generous selection of illustrations. Bibliophiles and presidential history buffs alike will relish this gratifying deep dive into an underappreciated genre."
—*Publishers Weekly* (starred review)

"From the very beginnings of America's experiment in republican government, its chief executives, both actual and aspiring, have put pen to paper (nowadays fingers to keyboard) in attempts to justify themselves and inspire others. Here, Fehrman records such literary efforts back to Jefferson and Adams. . . . Both history buffs and politics enthusiasts will relish this."
—*Booklist* (starred review)

"A lively account of the literary achievements (and failures) of America's presidents. . . . The author covers a great deal of ground that even major biographers have skipped over in favor of 'sexier' storylines, yet to the book lover, these stories will be unquestionably enticing. Even the footnotes, appendix, and sources offer bookish gems. Fehrman's illuminating blend of presidential and publishing history with literary criticism will appeal to amateur historians and bibliophiles alike."
—*Kirkus Reviews*

"Conversational, engaging, and compelling, backed by extensive research and appendices . . . Bookworms, lovers of history, and political junkies will find a lot to like here."
—*Indianapolis Monthly*

"[An] eye-opener of a read . . . For both the scholar and the casually curious, there is a lot to learn about our presidents. . . . There are the predictable standouts—Washington, Jefferson, Lincoln, Grant, Roosevelt, and Kennedy—and some outstanding surprises, such as Coolidge, Truman, and Reagan."
—*BookPage*

"Original, illuminating, and entertaining—as good history can be—Craig Fehrman's *Author in Chief* is a book that should have been written, and should surely be read. By looking at presidents through the prism of their published writings, Fehrman throws new light on what John F. Kennedy—himself an author-president—called 'the vital center of action.' "
—Jon Meacham, author of *The Soul of America*

"Craig Fehrman takes us from Thomas Jefferson—a president who happened also to be the best prose stylist around—to the age of the obligatory campaign biography, on to the modern blockbuster. Along the way we meet revisionists, ghost writers (Truman went through four), runaway bestsellers (it seems there *was* a sport at which Calvin Coolidge excelled), surprising flops. We learn that the Civil War turned the occasional authorial impulse into a flood of literature; that Nathaniel Hawthorne quietly wrote a campaign biography; that the most literate presidents can meet with the worst reviews. Shapely, original, and brimming in anecdote, *Author in Chief* expertly illuminates, amid much else, how history finds its way into the books."
—Stacy Schiff, author of *The Witches*

"CAUTION: This book contains material highly addictive to history lovers. From its account of Thomas Jefferson's monumental efforts to bring out his *Notes on the State of Virginia*, to the description of John Kennedy's fraudulent claims about writing *Profiles in Courage*, Craig Fehrman's *Author in Chief* achieves what every original thesis should. The accumulated myths that we call our history are shattered by the recovery of the true facts. I'm annoyed right now that I didn't write this disciplined, enormously engaging narrative myself."
—Rinker Buck, author of *The Oregon Trail*

"*Author in Chief* takes the reader into the hearts and minds of America's presidents as they seek to define their legacies through literature. From Lincoln and Kennedy to Bush and Obama, Fehrman brings these men to life and allows us to see their struggles and revel in their successes. It offers an entirely new perspective into what it feels like to be president and how critical self-expression is to the study of American history."
—Kate Andersen Brower, author of
The Residence, *First Women*, and *First in Line*

"This engrossing and delightful work offers a fresh lens on famous presidents and a new understanding of obscure ones. Fehrman explains how the uneven written work of presidents—original and ghost-written—reveals the curious intersection of power and publishing."
—Jonathan Alter, author of *The Promise*

Craig Fehrman is a journalist and historian who's written for the *New York Times*, the *Washington Post*, and the *Wall Street Journal*, among others. He lives in Indiana with his wife and children. He is the editor of the book *The Best Presidential Writing: From 1789 to the Present*.

AUTHOR IN CHIEF

THE UNTOLD STORY OF OUR PRESIDENTS
AND THE BOOKS THEY WROTE

CRAIG FEHRMAN

AVID READER PRESS

New York   London   Toronto   Sydney   New Delhi

AVID READER PRESS
An Imprint of Simon & Schuster, Inc.
1230 Avenue of the Americas
New York, NY 10020

First Avid Reader Press trade paperback edition February 2021

AVID READER PRESS and colophon are trademarks of Simon & Schuster, Inc.

For information about special discounts for bulk purchases,
please contact Simon & Schuster Special Sales at 1-866-506-1949
or business@simonandschuster.com.

The Simon & Schuster Speakers Bureau can bring authors to your live event.
For more information or to book an event, contact the Simon & Schuster Speakers Bureau
at 1-866-248-3049 or visit our website at www.simonspeakers.com.

Manufactured in the United States of America

1   3   5   7   9   10   8   6   4   2

Library of Congress Cataloging-in-Publication Data has been applied for.

ISBN 978-1-4767-8639-1
ISBN 978-1-4767-8658-2 (pbk)
ISBN 978-1-4767-8659-9 (ebook)

To Candice, Henry, and Maisie,
the best readers (or soon-to-be readers)
I know

Everyone else connected with Washington has written a book. I am certainly not going to compound the felony.

—Bess Truman

Books are good company. Nothing is more human than a book.

—Marilynne Robinson

A NOTE ON QUOTATIONS

"The English language so far as spelling goes was created by Satan," Harry Truman once wrote to Bess. "I can honestly say I admire Roosevelt for his efforts to make people spell what they say. He really ought to begin on his own name." Truman was right, and things get only worse in a book that spans several centuries. In the following pages, I have silently standardized the spelling and punctuation of all quotations—with the one exception being a letter by Davy Crockett, on page 124.

Contents

PART IV:
HARRY S. TRUMAN TO DONALD TRUMP

Introduction

Jack Kennedy didn't need to worry—not like this, at least. When the National Book Awards announced that the senator would deliver the keynote address at its 1956 ceremony, the book trade hummed with excitement. The awards had an aura of glamour: the Commodore Hotel in midtown Manhattan, the tables piled high with cocktails and canapés. But Kennedy was *actually* glamorous. He'd be easy to spot among the older, dowdier authors. In fact, John F. Kennedy, thirty-eight years old, hair brushed back, slim suit buttoned, would be the biggest star in the room. Besides, it was just a speech. The senator had given plenty of those.

And yet sitting there, looking at his draft, Kennedy continued to fret. He knew he had to deliver the keynote in front of America's best writers. (The nominees that year included Flannery O'Connor, Richard Hofstadter, W. H. Auden, and Eudora Welty.) Then again, he was a writer himself—and, lately, a very successful one. His *Profiles in Courage* had just started its multiyear run on the best-seller lists. The book singled out eight senators who, at key times in American history, had demonstrated true courage, and reviewers were spotting that same quality—and that same historic potential—in its author. "That a United States Senator . . . produced this study," the *Christian Science Monitor* marveled, "is as remarkable as it is hopeful."

So there was no good reason for Kennedy to worry about this speech— finally, honestly, because as a US senator he had better things to worry about. That's why he normally let his staff handle his speeches, after which he might skim them (sometimes) and tweak them (lightly). That process had produced Kennedy's other recent addresses, at colleges and churches and the Massachusetts Farm Bureau Federation Convention.

To the senator, however, speaking at the National Book Awards mattered more. He picked up a pen and went to work, crossing out lines, toying with tenses, and considering the smallest word choices. He scratched out "political action" and replaced it with "political events."

1

He added an obscure historical allusion. He made changes in his tiny, tilted handwriting, then sent the text to his aides for further revision. By the time Kennedy and his staff had finished, there were edits all over the draft's eleven pages. The only thing they hadn't fussed with, it seemed, was the title: "The Politician and the Author: A Plea for Greater Understanding."

On the day of the National Book Awards, the Commodore Hotel pulsed with cheery enthusiasm. About a thousand literary types filed in, past the famous lobby, with its functioning waterfall, to the Grand Ballroom. The editors wore red carnations, the authors wore white, and everyone was making predictions.

Once the awards were handed out—the big winner was Auden—it was time for the keynote. Kennedy had made even more edits, tightening his case for why authors and politicians could form a respectful alliance. The senator indulged in easy jokes. ("The only fiction to which many modern politicians turn their hand is the party platform.") But he also spoke with an idealism that, four years later, would define his presidential campaign. In America, he pointed out, writers and elected officials shared a "common ancestry," starting with polymaths like Thomas Jefferson and extend-

After the National Book Awards, Kennedy chatted with the winners:
W. H. Auden, John O'Hara, and Herbert Kubly (left to right).

ing to politically vigilant scribes like Harriet Beecher Stowe. They shared similar goals—defending free speech, of course, but baser ones as well. "The politician and the author," Kennedy said, "are motivated by a common incentive—public approval. 'How many books will I sell?' asks the author. 'How many votes will I get?' asks the politician."

Today, the link between political success and best-seller status seems more intimate than ever. In fact, "How many books will I sell?" has become one of the better answers to "How many votes will I get?" Writing a book before a presidential run, or writing a book after a presidency has ended, is now mandatory in American politics. These books stir up as much excitement as most compulsory entertainment. They generate eye rolls. They feel at once modern and exhausted.

This reaction is wrong, for several reasons. First, it's trite. (The *New York Times* was rolling its eyes back in 1936: "The brave words spoken by presidential candidates, even by those who aspire to be candidates, have a habit of drawing together to form a book.") Second, it flattens a rich tradition of forgotten books and, just as much, forgotten consequences. Presidents have written books that won long-shot campaigns, that made or remade political images, that legitimized America to its most worldly critics, that critiqued America to its most patriotic supporters, that revealed the White House's deepest secrets—all while creating reliable media frenzies. Present-day pundits, biographers, and historians have, for the most part, ignored these books and their impact.

Contemporary readers didn't, and that's another problem with the eye rolling: it erases a durable and distinctly American desire to know more about one's politicians, past and present. For decades, international surveys have shown that Americans outpace the residents of other democracies in terms of discussing politics, joining political organizations, and contacting elected officials—what political scientists call America's "attitudinal advantage."*

These behaviors are the external side of democracy; reading is the internal side. Before participation, before organization, before the ballot, there comes an opportunity to learn about leaders and ideas. That's the theory, at least, a theory stated again and again in the diaries and letters and book margins of America's readers: a commitment to self-improvement

---

*Where America trails those democracies is turnout, which lags because of the onerous and intentional structure of its elections. The rules that make it harder to vote—many of them passed in the last few years—overwhelm this "attitudinal advantage." America's voting system is now one of the least American things about it.

and self-education, each as a step toward self-government; a didactic taste for facts; a nation of nonfiction. Books have been the best way to do this. They're a medium that's both personal, in their bond between author and reader, and egalitarian, in their portable uniformity. Richard Nixon recorded a lot of things in the White House, and one of them was a list of resolutions he jotted on a legal pad. In addition to noting his need for more exercise and more optimism, Nixon wrote: "Need for more reading."

America's passion for sensible books extends to (and helps explain) its passion for history and biography. The custom of reading obsessively about the founders—and of wanting to read them in their own words—started soon after the Constitution went into effect in 1789. A love of American history is as old as America itself, and each generation has tried to define its values, and to sell its policies, by citing that history. It's another national specialty—what a British historian once called "the peculiarly American version of the space-time continuum." Americans like to collapse the past and the present, to read for serious ideas and for hero worship. They read books that grapple with the meaning of "all men are created equal"; they read books that deify the man who wrote that phrase.

That tension itself feels rather American, and not just because it leads to more participation, more lessons, more books. The importance of reading and reasoning has been preached during the nation's founding and frequently during its defense: the Civil War, World War I, World War II. During the Cold War, the editor of *Time* declared, "A good citizen is a good reader." The reverse is also true, with the most bookish Americans being 31 percent more likely to vote than their peers. In other words, a good reader is also a good citizen.

This book tells the story of how, when, and why America's presidents began writing books—and why Americans have been so consistently drawn to reading them. The modern idea of an author (powerful and isolated, reaching a national audience) is a new one. So is the modern idea of a president (powerful and isolated, setting the national agenda). These ideas grew up together, but it took time. In 1859, when Abraham Lincoln was planning his presidential bid, he wrote an autobiographical sketch to shape the early coverage. Journalists and partisans usually adapted such sketches; publishing a candidate's own words would make him seem disqualifyingly vain. Just to be sure, though, Lincoln attached a cover letter to his sketch: "Of course it must not appear to have been written by myself."

Today, it's the opposite: politicians insist the books they don't write appear to have been written by themselves. This shift occurred slowly, across two rough categories. The first is the legacy book, which typically appears near the end of a career, recapitulating a life and rebutting one's critics. While these works have a rich and global history, they fit snugly with America's literary preferences. William Dean Howells once called memoir the "most democratic province of the republic of letters," by which he meant at least two things: that anyone could write one, regardless of "sex, creed, class, or color," and that the genre's modern flourishing depended on the visibility of the individual, on "the importance of each to all."

The second category fits America even better, probably because Americans invented it. The campaign book appears before a run for office, usually with the intent of influencing a campaign, though sometimes an older title resurfaces instead. These books became broadly popular in the nineteenth century, first as campaign biographies, which share some surprising overlaps with today's campaign books, and then as speech collections and other hybrid forms. Each variety thrived in America—perhaps because it expanded its electorate earlier than most other democracies, or perhaps because its presidential system put still more emphasis on the individual. Either way, the books worked. In 1928, when an editor was trying to recruit a governor named Franklin Roosevelt, he reminded his potential author that he'd edited the book that made Calvin Coolidge's national career. "A message in book form," the editor wrote, "carried a great deal more weight than a message in news print."

To chart the categories of legacy and campaign, this book zooms in on important presidents and important books. It does not examine every chief executive. (Rutherford B. Hayes partisans should prepare for one more disappointment.) Sometimes its chapters move forward or backward in time to trace the full literary arc of a particular president. But there's a payoff to this method. Examining presidents as they write means examining them at their most human. It reveals how they think and what they fear; it catches them at their most ambitious and their most reflective; it slows them down. Even someone as confident as Theodore Roosevelt became vulnerable with a pen in his hand. ("I struggle and plunge frightfully," he once admitted. "When written, my words don't express my thought.") These insights can burn through even the fog of ghostwriting. The most interesting thing about Kennedy as an author isn't that he got help with *Profiles* but that he worked so hard to cover up that help— that he was desperate to impress literary audiences, at the National Book Awards and anywhere else.

Much has changed since the time of Kennedy, and of Lincoln. Presidents have become more powerful. Political authors have become more wealthy. The old Commodore Hotel has been renovated into a glassy Grand Hyatt by a developer named Donald Trump.

There's been one constant through all of it: readers. Sometimes these readers have been presidents themselves—Adams reading Jefferson, Grant reading Lincoln, Reagan reading Coolidge, each a reminder of these books' cultural significance. More often, they've been regular Americans, and the following pages contain a number of their stories. The eighteenth-century teacher living in the shadow of Monticello; the nineteenth-century New Yorker addicted to biographies; the twentieth-century library lover moving to Ohio as part of the Great Migration: each of them had to find different ways to acquire books. For most of America's history, it turns out, books have not been as egalitarian as they may seem in the age of Amazon.

Yet these readers shared important similarities with each other and with readers today. There are still many such readers. According to the National Endowment for the Arts, 68 million Americans read at least one volume of history, biography, or memoir in 2017. This book is, among other things, an attempt to show these readers the history of themselves.

PART I

GEORGE WASHINGTON
TO
JAMES MONROE

CHAPTER ONE

In and Out of Control: Thomas Jefferson and the First Campaign Book

John Adams was in a fine mood—quite an accomplishment for any eighteenth-century traveler. It was the spring of 1785, and Adams, his wife, Abigail, and their daughter, Nabby, had spent the past few months in Paris, with John serving as a diplomat for that strange new entity, the United States of America. The Adamses had loved their time in Paris, going to ballets and balloon ascents and lively dinner parties with Thomas Jefferson, America's minister to France. Now Congress had appointed Adams the nation's first minister to England, and that meant moving the family from Paris to London—six days of jouncing in a cramped and dusty carriage, then pitching in a cramped and soggy boat.

The weather made the trip even worse, as France was suffering through a terrible drought. "The country is a heap of ashes," Adams wrote from the road. There was no grass in the fields, no vegetables at the inns. Outside the carriage, he counted skeletal sheep. Inside, however, Adams found something to keep his family merrily distracted. Before they'd left Paris, Jefferson had presented them with a copy of his new book, *Notes on the State of Virginia*, which had arrived from the printer only days before. The travelers couldn't stop reading Jefferson's book aloud to each other. "It is our meditation all the day long," Adams wrote to Jefferson. "The passages upon slavery are worth diamonds." Abigail and Nabby chimed in with favorite passages of their own, but on one thing they all agreed: Jefferson's *Notes*, Adams predicted, "will do its author and his country great honor."

Adams was only half right. *Notes* did bring great honor to Jefferson's country. It wasn't just the first book written by a future president—it was one of the two most important titles written by *any* eighteenth-century American, along with Benjamin Franklin's *Autobiography*. At a time when

America's literary culture was anemic, when new books were expensive and rare, Jefferson's *Notes* offered a vivid, original, and internationally acclaimed portrait of his new nation. "The American states," one author observed, "are, in a literary view, no more than a province of the British empire." Jefferson's book defended his province to readers around the world, making its case through its arguments and its very existence.

Jefferson was the perfect person to write such a book. Once, when a doctor visited him at the White House, he noticed the president had left three books on a fireplace mantle: an Enlightenment encyclopedia, in French; a volume of Tacitus, in Latin; and an edition of Plato, in Greek. Jefferson loved and relied on books more than perhaps any other president. And yet, bizarrely enough, Jefferson has never received full credit for the book he actually wrote. *Notes* took a twisted path to publication, beginning as a private document and debuting in a semipirated French translation. By the end of his life, Jefferson claimed the process had always appalled him, and his biographers have nodded along. But that's not true. Jefferson worked on *Notes* for years and fought to control its tiniest details. He wanted to publish his book, which provides his most polished statements on politics, religion, art, war, and, yes, slavery and race.

The trouble came when his book collided with his presidential ambitions. Despite Adams's happy forecast and the book's enormous success, *Notes* ultimately brought its author not honor but misery. Without intending to, Jefferson wrote what would become America's first campaign book. He also inaugurated a second tradition—that of politicians being haunted by their past, especially by anything they were foolish enough to preserve in print.

SEDUCTION! REVOLUTION! MURDER! BOOKS!

Thomas Jefferson was born in 1743, the son of a prosperous Virginia planter. Shadwell, the Jeffersons' plantation, had a library of forty or fifty books, and according to family lore, Jefferson had read every one of them by the time he turned five. Stories like that show Jefferson was exceptional not just in his ability but in his access to books. Even a library of fifty books would have been one of the biggest in the county, and it was radically larger than the average American's. To appreciate Jefferson's literary passion— and to understand his nation's literary origins—it makes sense to start not with him but with a forgotten American named Devereux Jarratt.

Jarratt was born a decade before Jefferson, and like him, he was a tall, thin, ambitious, Virginian. Yet Jarratt seemed different in every other way. His father died when he was six, and while Jarratt's older brother, a carpenter, sent him to a plain, one-room schoolhouse, he also kept him home whenever the family needed help—and pulled him out for good after their mother died. At twelve or thirteen, Jarratt was finished with formal schooling. He didn't know how or even what to continue studying on his own. "Philosophy, rhetoric, logic," he later recalled, "there were no books on such subjects among us."

Jarratt finally tracked down a book of arithmetic, and every afternoon, while the horse he plowed with was grazing, he would peruse it for an hour or two. He soon earned a reputation for his skill with numbers, and a man from Albemarle County—the same county where the Jeffersons lived—offered to set Jarratt up as a teacher, in a plain, one-room school-house of his own. Even there, books remained precious. The new teacher rode six miles and crossed a river just to borrow a single book about the New Testament. "As I had no candle," he wrote, "my custom was in an evening to sit down flat on the hearth, erect the volume on the end of a chest which stood near, and by the light of the fire read till near midnight."

Devereux Jarratt's experiences were far more typical than Thomas Jefferson's. In the eighteenth century, each stop on the literary supply chain—the person who wrote the book, the people who printed it, the people who distributed it, and, finally, the person who read it—came with its own trials and contradictions.

Religion organized everyday life in colonial America, which meant it also organized what people read. The best sellers were Bibles, sermon collections, exegetical texts. Even the secular hits focused on self-discipline and self-improvement—and rarely indulged in something as extravagant as fiction. "I myself used to have too great a hankering after those amusing studies," James Madison admitted to an old friend. "But I began to discover that they deserve but a moderate portion of a mortal's time." Instead, mortals like Madison sought out pious textbooks (the *New England Primer*) and practical guides (*The Advantages and Disadvantages of a Married Life*). Benjamin Franklin, who originally made his name as a Philadelphia printer, published *Every Man His Own Doctor*, then followed it up with *Every Man His Own Lawyer*. The next entry, Franklin joked, would be *Every Man His Own Priest*.

No other book summed up this period's tastes better than the humble almanac. In fact, colonial Americans bought more almanacs than they did of every other volume combined. Almost every farmhouse featured one hanging from a length of rope near the fireplace, where its inhabitants could track upcoming eclipses, look up postage rates, or survey the schedules of local churches and courts. Each year, Franklin donned his playful pseudonym, Richard Saunders, and wrote clever essays and proverbs for his *Poor Richard's Almanack*. ("Early to bed and early to rise . . .") But the reference materials were what made his volume sell—12,000 copies annually, plus 2,000 more in the pocket edition, a total that today would be the equivalent of selling nearly 4 million books per year.*

Clearly, America offered plenty of readers. In 1765, a decade before the battles of Lexington and Concord, John Adams argued that "a native of America who cannot read and write is as rare . . . as a comet or an earthquake." While Adams exaggerated, he did so in service of a vital American ideal: that his fellow citizens were widely literate, widely rational, and widely ready for a government of their own. In truth, the percentage of readers dipped somewhat lower in the South and on the frontier than it did in Adams's New England. Even close to home, it lagged for women— something Abigail reminded him of when she protested "the trifling narrow contracted education of the females of my own country." Still, the most pressing problem for Americans was not literacy but the price of books. Someone from the working class, someone like Devereux Jarratt's brother, the carpenter, would need to work two full days in order to buy a single novel. With that same money, he could purchase two pounds of sugar, plus a pair of leather shoes.

Books didn't cost this much because colonial printers were getting rich—something one could confirm with a quick peek inside any printer's shop, which often doubled as the printer's home. The space would be noisy, messy, and crowded, with a team of workers setting and inking the type for each line of text, then feeding the sheets of paper to the printer, his right arm visibly overmuscled from pulling the press.

It was essentially the same method Gutenberg had used centuries

---

*In 1750, the colonies' population was around 1.2 million, which means Franklin sold one book for every eighty-six people. Apply that rate to America's current population of 328 million, as estimated by the Census in 2019, and it comes to 3.8 million books sold. This is of course an extraordinarily rough statistic—a statistic that doesn't account for, among other variables, the Census's historically indifferent approach to counting black Americans. Adjusting for inflation across the centuries can be similarly rough, but both measures are useful because they demonstrate the consistent popularity of presidential titles. This book will frequently cite adjusted sales and adjusted dollar figures, always calculated with 2019 data.

before, and the labor, the equipment, the kegs of ink, and the paper made from white rags kept prices high. Most printers made their money from smaller orders: lottery tickets, advertisements, legal documents for local governments. The longer a book took to make, the more it cost in time, money, and risk. When Jonathan Edwards's family tried to publish his posthumous *A History of the Work of Redemption*—a book of nearly four hundred pages—they ended up frustrated by "the difficulty of getting any considerable work printed in this infant country."

Printers often squeezed a bookstore into their homes as well, in a street-facing room staffed by a family member or two. In Providence, Rhode Island, readers knew to look for the house whose sign displayed a bust of Shakespeare; far more common for the country's bookstores, though, were signs that featured Bibles. Mathew Carey became one of the period's most successful printers, an Irishman who hid his demanding stare behind a pair of bushy eyebrows—and who personally opened his Philadelphia shop every day for twenty-five years. Yet his early selection remained sparse. "My store," he remembered, "was of very moderate dimensions; but, small as it was, I had not full-bound books enough to fill the shelves."

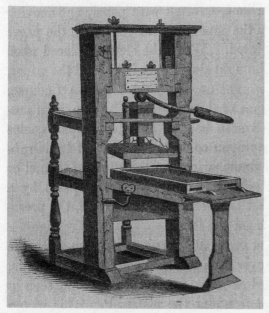

A nineteenth-century engraving depicted Benjamin Franklin's famous printing press.

Carey and his fellow printers filled those shelves—and kept their businesses afloat—by selling everything but books. Customers could flip through newspapers or brisk political pamphlets, buy stationery or sealing wax, pick out a new quill pen (the best ones came from geese and swans), even purchase dry goods like pickled sturgeon or Spanish snuff. Customers could also buy books, but given the problems with both supply and demand, most printers preferred to import already finished volumes from England, a few at a time. Even when they did gamble on printing a book in-house—in an edition of, say, five hundred copies—American printers often chose to produce their own versions of popular British books. There was no copyright, international or otherwise, so colonial printers banked on already established hits.

All of this contributed to a constricted literary culture—and even that culture was available only to the few who lived in big cities, with their print shop–bookstores and sporadic circulating libraries. Most Americans lived far outside those cities, in farms, on frontiers, or near slapdash county seats. Since the postal service mostly declined to deliver something as heavy as a book, rural access to literature came in the occasional visits of traveling booksellers, people like Mason Weems.

Short, bald, a quill pen stuck in his hat, Weems traveled the countryside in a book-laden wagon he dubbed the Flying Library. Whenever he pulled into a town, he hollered out: "Seduction! Revolution! Murder!" It was a strange thing for a former Episcopalian minister to say, but Weems now worked for Mathew Carey, and the solemn printer and his spastic salesman made for a delightfully mismatched team. It wasn't easy to transport books from city to city, which added one more challenge to selling five hundred copies of a new edition. So Weems would fill his Flying Library with an assortment of Carey's titles, then drift from New York to North Carolina, from the Pennsylvania mountains to the Georgia coast. In addition to the books in his wagon, the parson would sell subscriptions to other titles. Subscription bookselling—of upcoming titles and hard-to-move stock, of luxury editions and everyday volumes—became a phenomenon in America, with sellers like Weems taking the order now and figuring out the payment and delivery later.

It made for a difficult life, as Weems explained in one of his frequent letters to Carey: "Roused from sweet sleep at one o'clock in the morning . . . my ears startled with female screams . . . [my] whole sense stunned with rattling wheels, cracking whips, splashing water." But Weems always found the energy to sell. (Indeed, in his letter he was selling Carey on upping his commission.) To ensure the largest crowds, Weems timed his visits with local events—horse races, agricultural fairs, even election days. One time, while he and his wagon were stopped at a Virginia tavern, a fellow clergyman spotted a copy of Thomas Paine's *Age of Reason*, an atheistic urtext. The man began waving the book at Weems, demanding to know how he could sell such filth. "Behold," Weems said, "the antidote"—and handed him another available title, a noted minister's rebuttal.

Weems spent decades traveling, selling, and penning his dispatches from the frontlines of capitalism. What drove him, besides his zeal for profits, was his belief in the potential of a national reading culture. Weems wanted to provide books that appealed to (and were affordable to) regular readers. "Our country," he wrote to Carey, "is made up of that small fry." American literature could not yet reach those readers; it was too sober, too pricey, too diffuse. The best the country could offer were strange characters and small innovations—Ben Franklin and his proverbs, Mason Weems and his wagon, Devereux Jarratt and his book of math.

There's one last link in the literary supply chain: the author. In the eighteenth century, however, this link seemed the least important of all. Authorship, as an idea, still owed more to the age of manuscripts than to

A traveling bookseller, illustrated here in a nineteenth-century engraving, offered a volume for sale while a sack of others sat on the ground beside him.

the age of print—to a time when texts circulated among small, elite audiences; when poets relied on patrons or personal wealth; when the ideal authorial pose was one of befuddled modesty. The Enlightenment was changing this, but slowly. Descartes's *Discourse on Method*, Hume's *Treatise of Human Nature*, Locke's *Two Treatises on Government*: each of these seminal works appeared at first without their authors' names.

Authorship felt even more suspect in a republican government like America's. "No man is a true republican," declared one pamphleteer, "[who] will not give up his single voice to that of the public." America wanted to be a nation defined by the many, not the few—a place animated by ideas, not identities. For that reason, many of its writers chose to play up their humility and to publish under pseudonyms. Today the *Federalist Papers* is seen as the timeless work of James Madison, Alexander Hamilton, and John Jay. When those essays appeared in the 1780s—first in a series of newspapers, then as a two-volume book—the author was listed only as "Publius." Political insiders knew and cared about the men behind the pseudonym. Inside his personal copy, Jefferson made note of the numbers written by "Mr. Jay" and "Mr. Madison," then added "the rest of the work by Alexander Hamilton." But individual fame and daring creativity were not, or not supposed to be, the point.

It was easy for authors to be modest when they considered their legal and economic reality. While Royall Tyler worked as a lawyer in Vermont, he also wrote some of America's most significant early books. After he published one of the nation's first novels, *The Algerine Captive*—anonymously, of course—Tyler decided to write something that might actually sell: a practical textbook. A Boston printer promised him $250, until, in the middle of the project, he slashed that offer to some free copies of the final book. Printers were constantly abusing their writers—not just by cutting their pay, of which there was little to begin with, but by rewriting their words or mangling their layouts or simply lifting and reprinting their work. The author was rarely consulted about any of this. "If writing for the public is attended with no more profit," Tyler wrote, "I had rather . . . explain unintelligible law to Green Mountain jurors."

And yet a few Americans were beginning to see the value in creating a class of full-time writers. As the Revolutionary War wound down, Joel Barlow, someone who, like Tyler, was a professional who scribbled on the side, urged Congress to pass a national copyright law. "We have few gentlemen of fortune," Barlow wrote, "sufficient to enable them to spend a whole life in study." His goal wasn't fairness. He believed a new nation needed authors because it needed advocates. There was a reason Europeans didn't take Americans very seriously. "America has convinced the world of her importance in a political and military line," Barlow wrote. But that wasn't enough. "A literary reputation," he wrote, "is necessary in order to complete her national character."

HOW JEFFERSON READ

Thomas Jefferson spent his whole life as one of Barlow's "gentlemen of fortune." While he had enough wealth to experiment with authorship, Jefferson chose to focus on an equally unstable career: politics. His heart still belonged to books. At Monticello, his plantation of five thousand acres and more than a hundred slaves, visitors marveled at his ever-evolving library—a collection that, at its peak, included nearly seven thousand volumes spilling across several rooms. Jefferson's idiosyncratic architecture gave those rooms high arches and short, angled walls, and that meant custom-built pine bookcases, each one nine feet high. "I cannot live without books," Jefferson famously wrote to Adams. But he couldn't work without them either. While books could provide pleasure or connect readers, Jefferson saw them above all as tools, just like the hammer and plane used to build those pine bookcases.

A gentleman of fortune could count on a good education. Growing up, Jefferson studied with a series of fine teachers. ("A correct classical scholar," he remembered of one.) In 1760, he headed to the College of William and Mary in Williamsburg, immersing himself in the Enlightenment's best books and ideas before turning to an apprenticeship in law. Eventually Jefferson returned to Albemarle County to practice, and in 1768, its voters made him a member of Virginia's House of Burgesses.

A few years later, Jefferson married Martha Wayles Skelton, a frail but graceful widow. Martha also loved books—she was "a constant reader," remembered a family member—and the couple shared an affection for Laurence Sterne's novel *Tristram Shandy*. Jefferson had been keeping a commonplace book since he was a teenager, copying out his favorite passages from Homer, Virgil, Shakespeare, and others. At some point he added a passage from Sterne's novel to his commonplace book, a passage that captured the intensity of the newlyweds' love. It began: "Time wastes too fast . . ."

Jefferson bought all kinds of books, keeping in ardent contact with printers like Mathew Carey. One time, a traveling bookseller, a man try-ing to find subscribers for a new history of Greece, knocked on Monti-cello's front door. He was shocked when Jefferson answered it himself. "I told him of my work," the seller remembered, "and he said it was a very bad work." When it came to books, though, Jefferson usually said yes. On the wall of his library, he nailed a piece of paper listing the twelve catego-ries he used to organize his shelves, including ethics, mathematics, and modern history. The list was for guests; Jefferson created an even more intricate system for himself. Organizing books alphabetically, he believed, might hobble his work when he forgot an author's name, and Jefferson liked to control every variable as both a writer and a reader. "After using a book," he told a visitor, "it will be better to leave them on a table in the room." He didn't want to risk a volume being misplaced.

Over the years, Jefferson and Martha hosted many fellow readers at Monticello. A good example was François-Jean de Chastellux, a prominent Frenchman. Chastellux kept a careful diary, and he started his account of Monticello with a continental cheap shot: Jefferson, he quipped, must be "the first American who has consulted the fine arts to know how he should shelter himself from the weather." Yet the visitor was clearly charmed by owner and home. While at first he found Jefferson a bit cold, they soon fell into an intense and bookish rhythm—something that was part dance and part duel, that, as Chastellux put it, "made four days pass away like so many minutes." Their conversations would leap from politics to phi-losophy to the mechanics of English verse. One night, after Martha had gone to bed, they landed on a Scottish poet, and Jefferson and Chastellux started volleying their favorite passages, back and forth, until Jefferson sent for his copy of the poet's works. A bowl of punch had also materi-alized, and Jefferson opened the book next to the bowl. "By their mutual aid," Chastellux wrote, "the night far advanced imperceptibly upon us."

Despite his impossibly varied interests, Jefferson relied on his library to direct him—to help him concentrate and refine his ideas. One of his many paradoxes was that he was a disciplined dilettante. He didn't buy hulking folios that looked good on the shelf; he bought octavo-sized vol-umes that fit his hands, what he called "books of a handy size." Books, after all, were tools. "Sometimes," one of Jefferson's slaves remembered, "[he] would have twenty of them down on the floor at once."

Politics left less time for reading, family, and friends. The relationship between Britain and its colonies had always been one-sided, and now it was becoming strained. In 1773, some Massachusetts colonists hosted the Boston Tea Party; in 1774, the Continental Congress met for the first time. A few weeks before, Virginia's legislators assembled in Williamsburg to choose their delegates. On his way to that meeting, Jefferson came down with dysentery and had to turn back—but not before he sent ahead a document he'd been drafting, a list of potential resolutions to guide Virginia's delegates.

While Jefferson had written other bills and resolutions in the House of Burgesses, this text was different. It ran to nearly seven thousand words and demonstrated a new degree of polish and ambition. The colonists, he argued, could claim certain natural rights, regardless of what the king or British Parliament said. "The God who gave us life," he wrote, "gave us liberty at the same time." Though he was only thirty-one years old, the writing revealed Jefferson's mature style—at once elegant and aggressive, proceeding with lawyerly precision until it paused for a memorable line.

His colleagues liked it so much they published it as a pamphlet, *A Summary View of the Rights of British America*. Had Jefferson made it to Williamsburg, he might have resisted or demanded time to revise; years later, he was still dismissing the pamphlet ("a very hasty production"). But he was also reminding people that he had neither picked its title nor approved its preface. Jefferson often seemed torn between his era's two models of authorship—between the old one, with its modesty and deference, and the new one, with its individuality and control.

Once *A Summary View* was printed—by a Williamsburg woman named Clementina Rind, who'd taken over her husband's shop after his death—the Virginia delegates carried copies to Philadelphia and shared them with the other members of congress. The pamphlet was quickly reprinted in that city and twice more in London. Each time it appeared anonymously, with the title page saying only that it was written "by a Native, and Member of the House of Burgesses." But the political class knew the author. Adams noticed, with not a little envy, that the other delegates were passing around Jefferson's pamphlet and praising its "peculiar felicity of expression." When George Washington recorded his payment for several copies, he called it "Mr. Jefferson's Bill of Rights."

In 1775, the Continental Congress convened again. This time Jefferson was in attendance—and this time he had a reputation. "Yesterday, the famous Mr. Jefferson [arrived]," a delegate from Rhode Island observed. "I have not been in company with him yet, [but] he looks like a very sensible, spirited, fine fellow and by the pamphlet which he wrote last summer he certainly is one." During the sessions, Jefferson lived up to his pamphlet,

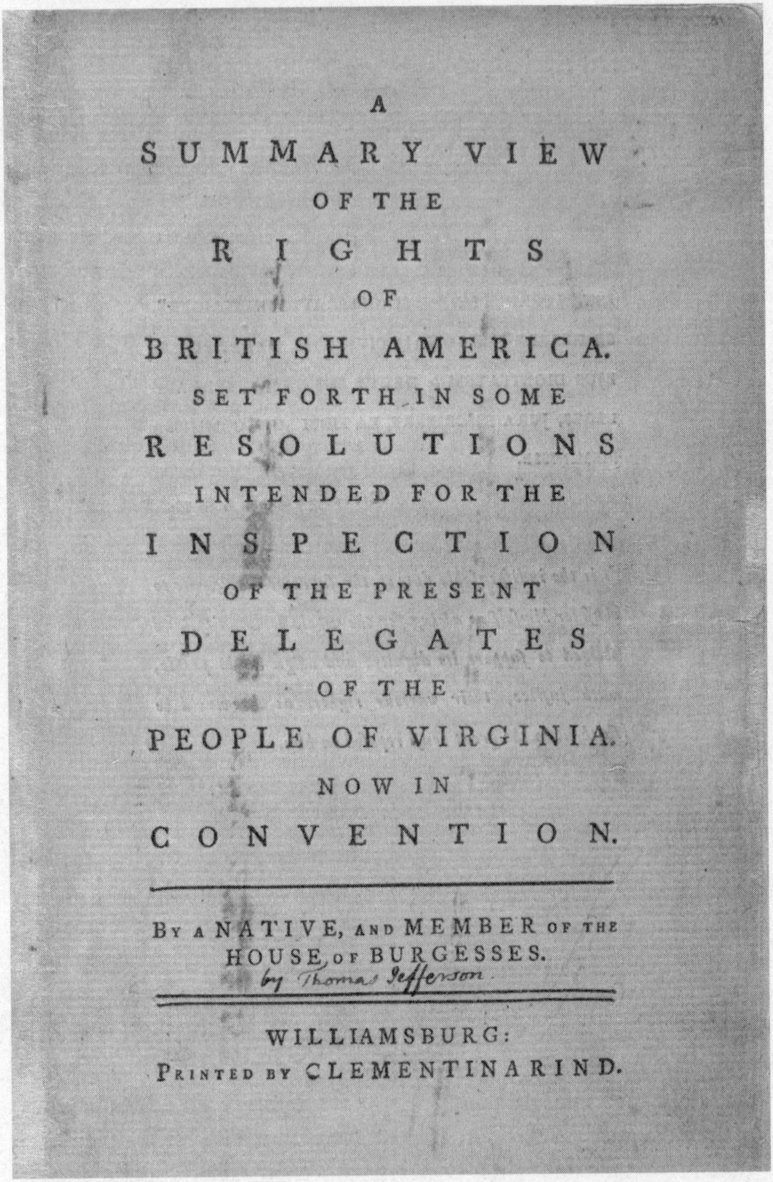

A

SUMMARY VIEW

OF THE

RIGHTS

OF

BRITISH AMERICA.

SET FORTH IN SOME

RESOLUTIONS

INTENDED FOR THE

INSPECTION

OF THE PRESENT

DELEGATES

OF THE

PEOPLE OF VIRGINIA.

NOW IN

CONVENTION.

BY A NATIVE, AND MEMBER OF THE
HOUSE, OF BURGESSES.

by Thomas Jefferson.

WILLIAMSBURG:
PRINTED BY CLEMENTINA RIND.

On his personal copy of *A Summary View*, which was published
anonymously, Jefferson wrote, "by Thomas Jefferson."

though he also found time to patronize Philadelphia's bookstores. One year later, when the congress formed a committee to draft what would become the Declaration of Independence, the Virginian was an obvious choice.

It was a five-person committee, with Jefferson joined by Franklin, Adams, and two others. One of them needed to write a first draft. "You shall do it," Adams told Jefferson. Jefferson protested. Adams insisted. Why? Jefferson asked.

"Reasons enough," Adams replied. Jefferson hailed from the largest colony, for one. Jefferson was popular. Finally: "You can write ten times better than I can."

Jefferson wrote the draft in his rented rooms on the edge of town—on the second floor of a plain brick building, working on a lap desk he'd designed himself. The committee made plenty of edits. (Where Jefferson had written, "We hold these truths to be sacred and undeniable," Franklin suggested a simpler finish: "We hold these truths to be self-evident.") The full congress made even more. Jefferson sat and listened to his colleagues' suggestions—"mutilations," he called them.* He hated ceding even a sliver of authorial control. Still, he and the other delegates were proud of and terrified by the text he'd written.

That text, and Jefferson's political ascent, was shaped by his reading. It wasn't just that he drew ideas from Enlightenment and American sources—so that Locke's "life, liberty, and estate" joined with George Mason's "life and liberty and pursuing and obtaining happiness" to become "life, liberty, and the pursuit of happiness." Jefferson's library created his celebrated style, first in *Summary View* and then in the Declaration. The author liked to tell a story about Patrick Henry, his fellow Virginian. Henry once borrowed two volumes of Hume, promising Jefferson he'd read them over the winter. In the spring, Henry returned the books, having made it no further than page thirty in the first volume. "I have often been astonished at his command of proper language," Jefferson would say of Henry, still not quite believing it. "He read nothing, and had no books." Jefferson needed books to think, legislate, and persuade. To him, the tools of a writer and the tools of a politician were the same.

On July 4, the congress approved the final Declaration. A Philadelphia

---

*Franklin tried to distract the author by telling him an old story from his time as printer. One of his friends, a hatmaker, had drawn up an elaborately descriptive sign for his shop. He decided to ask their circle for feedback, only to watch them nitpick the sign until all that was left were the friend's name and a picture of a hat.

printer worked late into the night, producing about two hundred copies as a poster-sized broadside—the first public version of the Declaration's text, the one most people would see in newspapers, read outside courthouses, or hear recited aloud. The only names on the broadside were John Hancock, the congress's president; Charles Thomson, its secretary; and John Dunlap, the printer. While the war with Britain lumbered forward, Jefferson's authorial act stayed behind, a secret of those Philadelphia sessions. It would be many years before regular Americans knew who actually wrote the Declaration. In 1789, for instance, a new book, *A History of the American Revolution*, described the Declaration as an "act of the united colonies"; it made no mention of Jefferson. If he wanted a literary triumph instead of a political one, he would need to try again.

HOW JEFFERSON WROTE

In the fall of 1780, a French official named François Barbé-Marbois sent a questionnaire to America and its new states. The queries were a blend of tourism bureau and chamber of commerce. What plants and fruit flourish in your region? How many seaports do you have? How did you set up your laws and courts? France was aiding America in its war against Britain and, naturally enough, wanted to know more about its ally. Most of the thirteen states ignored the questionnaire; a few sent perfunctory replies. But when Jefferson learned of Marbois's request, he realized it could provide cover for something else he'd been mulling: an ambitious project that would survey his country and its strengths. He would spend parts of the next five years on his manuscript, plus another two getting it published— years that overlapped with some of the most important and infamous moments of his life.

First, he needed to finish his term as governor of Virginia. It was a chaotic time, with Washington's Yorktown victory still a year in the future, but Jefferson was already starting his research. From Richmond, the state capital, he described his early efforts to a friend: "I am at present busily employed for Monsieur Marbois without his knowing it and have to acknowledge to him the mysterious obligation for making me much better acquainted with my own country than I ever was before." A few weeks later, Benedict Arnold and a British army captured Richmond, forcing Jefferson to flee.

It was hardly a writer's life, and Jefferson planned to retire from politics—

to devote more time to Martha and their children and also to keep work-ing on his answers to the questionnaire. At Monticello, he could peruse his books and his papers, a collection he called "most rare and valuable . . . especially of what relates to America." The writing went slowly. (The family had to flee Monticello briefly as well.) But on December 20, 1781, Jefferson sent Marbois about forty pages of material. That same day, he sent a second copy to Charles Thomson, still the congress's secretary, asking for advice on how the text might be "more fully handled." Jefferson was already planning to expand and, it seemed, to share.

Jefferson's early retirement frustrated his friends. "The present," James Monroe wrote in an acerbic letter, "is generally conceived to be an impor-tant era." But Jefferson saw his literary project as its own kind of polit-ical act. While his earliest drafts do not survive, he ultimately wrote a book of twenty-three chapters that, following the questionnaire, he titled "Queries." This structure preserved an air of modesty, of obligation, and *Notes on the State of Virginia* does cover the basics of its titular state. Yet Jefferson also revised Marbois's queries, shuffling them silently and even inventing new ones until the format allowed him to write a sprawling book about his sprawling enthusiasms.

By far the longest chapter, Query VI, centered on animals, a topic never mentioned in the questionnaire. One of Marbois's countrymen, the comte de Buffon, had popularized a theory that animals in the New World were smaller, weaker, "degenerated," in part because their climate was wetter and colder than Europe's. Buffon's boosters took his idea fur-ther. After all, they reasoned, if America's climate was hurting its animals, it must be hurting its humans too. This belief in American inferiority appeared everywhere. One time, Franklin, who was serving as a diplo-mat to France, went to dinner with a mix of local and American guests. As they sat around the table, a French intellectual began declaiming about degeneracy. Franklin listened, then proposed an experiment. "Let both parties rise," he said, knowing his compatriots were on the tall side, "and we will see on which side nature has degenerated."

While Franklin could win a dinner party, America needed a more last-ing response. Jefferson began collecting data on American wildlife for his book. He made long lists comparing the elk to the caribou. He compiled a table of every known bird in Virginia. He drafted a questionnaire of his own—sixteen queries on the past and present of the American moose. Jefferson wrote to the country's best hunters and explorers, telling them he would pay whatever it took for them to ship him promising samples.

He began receiving letters like this: "I killed a bear, not fat, which weighed 410 lb. after he was quartered, and have seen much larger." One day, while strolling past a shop, Jefferson spotted a freakishly big panther skin. He marched in and bought it on the spot.

Jefferson used this material to dismantle the theory of degeneracy, working through Buffon's claims in a series of logical steps. He continued to write about other topics for other queries, researching flood levels and personally inspecting Native American burial mounds. "All prospects of future happiness," he explained to Chastellux, could come from "domestic and literary objects." On May 8, 1782, Martha gave birth to the couple's sixth child. It had been a difficult pregnancy, and afterward Martha's health turned even worse. As spring faded into summer, then fall, Jefferson hovered over his bedridden wife, feeding her meals and giving her medicine. "He was never out of calling," one of their daughters remembered. "When not at her bed side he was writing in a small room, which opened immediately at the head of her bed."

That writing was almost certainly pages from *Notes*, and it's possible Jefferson showed them to his wife. Theirs had always been a literary marriage. At some point during her illness, Martha asked for Jefferson's old commonplace book. Perhaps the couple paged through it together; perhaps she turned to a particular page on her own. Either way, as her strength faded, Martha began copying their lines from *Tristram Shandy* in a faint hand: "Time wastes too fast . . ." She stopped midsentence—because of exhaustion, or emotion, or her death on September 6. Eventually Jefferson finished the passage. In a firmer hand but with a broken heart, he wrote, "And every time I kiss thy hand to bid adieu, every absence which follows it, are preludes to that eternal separation which we are shortly to make!"

Jefferson had discovered a new use for books—as a tool for grieving. After his wife's passing, he isolated himself for weeks, "as dead to the world," he admitted, "as she was whose loss occasioned it." Slowly, however, the widower returned to life, in part because he returned to his book.

Notes can feel strange and messy to modern readers. There are a *lot* of lists and tables, each one a selling point in the Age of the Almanac. Freed from the more narrowly political purview of works like *A Summary View*, Jefferson roamed among his interests. He wrote about literature, rebutting the idea—French, of course—that America hadn't developed enough poets. Since Jefferson's network of bear hunters didn't have many reports on local authors, he turned analytical instead. How long, he wondered, had Greece existed before it produced a Homer? (How long, for that mat-

ter, had France existed before it produced a Voltaire?) Jefferson then pivoted beyond poetry. "In war, we have produced a Washington," he wrote.
"In physics, we have produced a Franklin." Finally, he cited America's
population, which lagged well behind those of the Franklin-less England
and France. "Of the geniuses which adorn the present age," Jefferson concluded, "America contributes its full share."

In Query IV, on mountains, Jefferson actually attempted to write literature. He knew he wasn't a creative writer. (As he put it, "Nature had not
formed me for a continuator of Sterne.") But while revising his manuscript,
Jefferson decided to draw on his literary reading to describe the spot where
the Potomac and Shenandoah Rivers came together, a scene, he wrote,
"worth a voyage across the Atlantic." On a sheet of paper that he would paste
into his text, Jefferson used the second person to transport his reader: "You
stand on a very high point of land." To your right, the Shenandoah; to your
left, the Potomac—and up ahead, the notch they slowly sawed into the Blue
Ridge Mountains, through which you can glimpse "a small catch of smooth
blue horizon." It would become one of the book's most beloved passages.

What held the various queries together was their approach. *Notes*

One of the most celebrated passages in *Notes* described the confluence
of the Shenandoah and Potomac Rivers, depicted here in a nineteenth-
century engraving.

was a book that demonstrated how Jefferson thought as much as what he thought. "Nature has hidden from us her *modus agendi*," he wrote. "Our only appeal on such questions is to experience." Experience was a crucial concept for him, an information-gathering stage that preceded interpretation. He believed this rational two-step—experience, then interpretation—could untangle the most complex issues.

One such issue was slavery, which resurfaced again and again in his book. In Query VIII, Jefferson condemned it as a "great political and moral evil."* In Query XVIII, he reflected on slavery's repercussions: "I tremble for my country when I reflect that God is just: that his justice cannot sleep for ever." When Adams, who was staunchly antislavery, told Jefferson that his book's "passages upon slavery are worth diamonds," these were the passages he meant.

There was a second set of passages. In Query XIV, Jefferson proposed a solution to this evil: emancipate America's slaves and then expatriate them to a new colony somewhere else. Black people, he wrote, must be "removed beyond the reach of mixture." Jefferson carefully recorded the observations that had led him to this grim fix. Compared to whites, black people appeared to have good morals but weak imaginations. They slept less, grieved less, secreted more from the skin—"which gives them a very strong and disagreeable odor," he wrote, in a passage made only more revolting by its posture of reason. "I advance it therefore as a suspicion only," he concluded, "that the blacks are inferior to the whites in the endowments both of body and mind."

In a book obsessed with conditions and causes—Was America degenerated or not, and why?—Jefferson hypothesized that black people's ostensible inferiority flowed from their nature and not their circumstances. In arguing this, he slipped into a series of contradictions that, in another writer or on another subject, he would have dissected himself. To isolate the impact of circumstance, Jefferson examined the slave in antiquity, remarking that Romans treated their (fair-skinned) slaves far worse than Americans treated theirs. Yet Jefferson never got around to considering the actual lives of American slaves. In a blinding bit of irony, he dwelled on the slave owner's experiences but not on those of his property. ("The parent storms," Jefferson wrote, explaining why generations of whites had

---

*Jefferson made a similar point in his draft of the Declaration, trying to blame Britain for the rise of slavery at home and abroad. The king, Jefferson wrote, "has waged cruel war against human nature itself, violating its most sacred rights of life and liberty." The Continental Congress chose to edit this line out.

passed on their cruelty. "The child looks on, catches the lineaments of wrath, puts on the same airs in the circle of smaller slaves.") It was an unintentional reminder that "experience" can only be as rational as the person deciding what—or who—counts as worthy of analysis. In *Notes*, Jefferson doesn't reveal reason's power. He reveals its limits.

On January 16, 1784, Jefferson updated Chastellux on his book. "I have lately had a little leisure to revise," he wrote with typical understatement. "They are swelled nearly to treble bulk." That same year, Congress sent Jefferson to work alongside Franklin in France. He arrived in Paris with little more than his luggage, his panther skin, and his manuscript of *Notes*.

Jefferson had to scramble to buy the essentials—linens, furniture, a dress sword for his appearances at court. Still, it felt like he was *au paradis*. Jefferson loved everything about the French, other than their comprehensive climate theories, and in Paris he began frequenting the salon circuit. He joined in lively discussions at the spacious, sun-filled library of the abbé André Morellet, a well-regarded wit whom Voltaire had nicknamed L'abbé Mord-les, or "the Abbot Bite-them." Even better, Jefferson began shopping at the famous cluster of printers and booksellers on the Left Bank of the Seine. "I devoted every afternoon I was disengaged," he later remembered, "in examining all the principal bookstores, turning over every book with my own hands." Jefferson's time in France was his most important as a book collector. In five years there, he bought more than eighteen hundred volumes.

Jefferson toured the Left Bank not just as a reader but as a potential author. Before heading to France, he'd tried at least twice to print a private edition of *Notes*, only to find that American printers were too slow and too expensive. Paris, like London, offered a booming and highly centralized book trade. Jefferson quickly found a printer who could do his edition for a quarter of the American price, and on May 10, 1785, he received the two hundred copies he'd ordered. The man who'd purchased thousands of volumes could now, for the first time, pick up and turn over a book of his own.

The next day, Jefferson wrote Madison a giddy letter explaining that the book was finished—and that he could expect a volume shortly. "Answer me soon and without reserve," the new author begged. (At the end of the letter, he begged again: "Answer me immediately.") While Jefferson wanted his friend's feedback, he also wanted his advice. Jefferson told Madison he was sending out only five copies and would wait on those readers' counsel. Jefferson knew that circulating any book could open him to accusations of arrogance; he also worried about this book's content, especially its discussion of emancipation and expatriation. To James Monroe, who received one of the five initial copies, Jefferson confessed, "I fear the terms in which I speak of slavery . . . [may] do more harm than good."

The vagaries of transatlantic communication meant Madison did not reply until November. He adored the book and urged Jefferson to distribute it, though he understood his concerns about slavery. (Madison disguised part of his letter in a careful code.) But he was too late, as Jefferson's enthusiasm had overwhelmed his patience. The author had already fired off more than a dozen additional copies to readers in England, Italy, and France. Inside each volume, he wrote a humble inscription. In Franklin's copy of Notes, Jefferson downplayed "the circumstances under which they were written, and the talents of the writer"; he implored him "to put them into the hands of no person on whose care and fidelity he cannot rely." But Jefferson was clearly excited—and now he had knowingly put his book (and its author) on a trajectory toward publication.

The evidence of his excitement is conclusive. It started with his decision to privately print two hundred copies—a bold figure in an era when five hundred copies of an original book made for a solid run. It continued with his promiscuous circulation, with Jefferson handing out at least twenty-nine copies by the end of 1785. His friends, who lacked Jefferson's self-deprecating discipline, talked about publication as a given. When Adams shared his early copy of Notes with another friend, he described it as "not yet to be published." Even Jefferson admitted he liked the idea of excerpts appearing in French periodicals. "Make any extracts you please," he told Chastellux, who'd also received an early copy and said it reminded him of their crackling conversations at Monticello. Jefferson's letters from this period don't contain doubts or fears, except in regard to a few specific topics like slavery; instead, they shine with possibility. Should he send Notes to America's best college students? Jefferson wondered. Should he have his book discussed at Parisian salons? (The French were already doing that on their own.) Should he circulate it with the American Philosophical Society? Stock it at the public library in Philadelphia? Publish it—really publish it, after all?

Before Jefferson could decide on this final step, he lost control, briefly, of his book. In the fall of 1785, one of Notes' recipients died. Pierre-Théophile Barrois, a respected French publisher, pounced on the dead man's copy and began plotting a speedy translation. It wasn't the fairest move, but given the period's literary conventions (and given Jefferson's celebrity), it was a predictable one. Jefferson fretted at the thought of his prose in the hands of Barrois's "hireling translator." An old friend offered to bail him out. The abbé Morellet, whom Jefferson had also sent an early copy of *Notes*, suggested he might step in as translator. While Jefferson remained nervous about publication, he was grateful and even honored by Morellet's proposition, and the two went to work.

As an old man, Jefferson liked to complain about this translation—"mutilated," he called it, the same word he used to describe the edits to his Declaration. During 1786 and 1787, though, he threw himself into each step of the edition, exercising an astonishing degree of supervision for an eighteenth-century author. He fussed over the paper, the binding, even the size of the type. He reviewed Morellet's translations, line by line. He ordered an innovative and fabulously detailed map of Virginia that would fold out of the finished book. The finest engravers lived in London, and Jefferson personally hired one of the city's best. Still, no one could care as much as Jefferson cared himself. "I have got through about two thirds of the map," he wrote to his British contact, after receiving an early version, "and have a list of 172 errors. . . . I reckon only those which are material. Small and immaterial changes of orthography I do not correct."

London was on Jefferson's mind for other reasons. He knew another enterprising printer might translate the forthcoming French edition back into English. "I am now at a loss what to do as to England," he wrote to Madison. "Every thing, good or bad, is thought worth publishing there." Madison pushed him to issue *Notes* in its original form, and Jefferson agreed to an edition of one thousand copies with John Stockdale, a printer from whom he frequently bought books. The author remained just as demanding, reminding Stockdale that there should not be "a tittle altered, added, nor omitted."

By the summer of 1787, Jefferson and Stockdale were finishing their final details, including the author's compensation, which mostly amounted to some free copies of the book. While Jefferson was waiting on those volumes, he welcomed one of his daughters to live with him in Paris. She was accompanied by one of the family's slaves, a fourteen-year-old named Sally Hemings. Thanks to DNA testing and careful scholarly work, it now seems clear that during their time in Paris, Jefferson began sleeping with Hemings and impregnated her. Hemings and Jefferson eventually had at least six children. Many years later, one of them would describe her as "Mr. Jefferson's concubine."

Both of Jefferson's editions appeared in 1787 as *Notes on the State of*

Virginia, Written by Thomas Jefferson, and as *Observations sur la Virginie, par M. J.* (though everyone understood it was Jefferson). The author carefully tracked their sales and reviews. At a time when American books struggled to make an impact in America, much less abroad, *Notes* reached all the right European readers. In Germany, a periodical translated and published much of the text. In Britain, Stockdale advertised *Notes* in more than seventy newspapers. One of the country's most prominent magazines, the *Monthly Review*, praised the book and its "ingenious author" for "vindicating . . . North America against the depreciations of Buffon."

Buffon's homeland remained the key audience. How gratifying it must have been, then, for Jefferson to open the first June issue of *Le Mercure de France*, Paris's leading journal, and discover a long and ecstatic review. Jefferson, the critic wrote, had produced "one of the small number of truly instructive books." His critique of Buffon was "a model of good logic and excellent discussion." The review ranked Jefferson alongside the beloved Franklin. "I end," the critic wrote, "by allowing the author himself to speak with eloquence." He then quoted an extended passage from *Notes*, a passage announcing America's postwar readiness to thrive on the international stage. "Our interest will be to throw open the doors of commerce," Jefferson promised, "giving perfect freedom to all persons for the vent of whatever they may choose to bring into our ports, and asking the same in theirs."

THE FIRST CAMPAIGN BOOK

A few months after *Notes* appeared in England and France, Jefferson joined the many other authors who'd watched the New World pirate their books. Jefferson and Stockdale had talked about shipping hundreds of copies to America, but the author began receiving updates from home: his book was being cited by the *Federalist Papers*, excerpted in periodicals across the country, and celebrated for its debunking of America's European critics. ("We are flattered," Joel Barlow admitted to Jefferson, "with the idea of seeing ourselves vindicated.") Soon an American printer brought out *Notes* in an unauthorized edition, and it continued to be widely read. When George Washington replied to a Scotsman who was thinking about immigrating, he directed him to Jefferson's book: "*Notes on Virginia* will give the best idea of this part of the continent," Washington promised. *Notes* had done well in Europe, but in America it became a smash hit, going through at least nineteen editions in Jefferson's lifetime, an astounding run for a book of original nonfiction. While it's difficult to find sales numbers from this period, scholars estimate that *Notes* had sold at least twenty thousand copies by 1832—the equivalent of well over a half a million books today.

Jefferson might have preferred fewer sales, at least during election years. In fact, the nature of America's earliest campaigns ensured that *Notes* would cause lots of problems for its author, even if those problems were also one more way to gauge the book's impact.

America's first president didn't need to run since Washington was drafted—dragged, really—into the office in 1789. Washington's reluctance created a useful bearing for his fellow politicians. Campaigning was seen as ungentlemanly and gauche, usually for the same reasons authorship was seen as conceited. "Attempting to gain the affections or votes of the people," argued one congressman, "has oftener produced tyrants or dema-

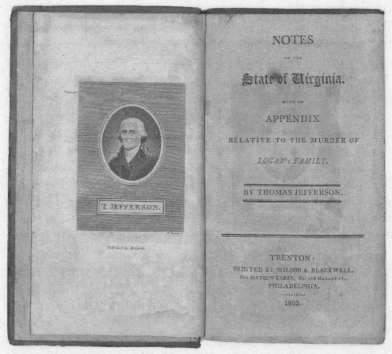

Notes went through many American editions. This one—published by Mathew Carey in 1803—featured a portrait of the president as its frontispiece.

gogues . . . than patriots and good government." Candidates, and above all presidential candidates, did not go out and grubbily seek votes.

Washington's distrust of political parties proved less influential. As president, he worked not only with Adams, his vice president, and Hamilton, his secretary of the treasury, but with their ideological opponent in Jefferson, whom Washington asked to serve as his secretary of state. But this nonpartisan spirit did not last. When the president declined to seek a third term, it set up a clear battle of parties and ideas. The horse race metaphors appeared immediately. Washington's decision, an insider predicted, would be "a signal, like the dropping of a hat, for party racers to start." In the election of 1796, Adams faced off with Jefferson. It was just as true, however, to say that the Federalists faced off with the Democratic-Republicans.

Both candidates marooned themselves at home, avoiding even the appearance of active campaigning. At the state and local levels, their supporters canvassed on horseback and organized rowdy outdoor speeches; the pamphleteers picked sides. The electorate was limited almost entirely to white male taxpayers and landowners, and that was only the first anti-populist filter. Across much of the country, state legislatures chose the electors, who then chose the president. This secretive process stretched on for months, all in the hopes of curbing partisanship. It didn't work. "Party spirit is busy but not fiery," Adams wrote to his son, John Quincy. "The scribblers must have their itching scratched. Poor Jefferson is tortured as much as your better acquaintance. If he feels as little, he will not mind."

Adams and the Federalists won, barely. After four years in office—plenty of time for those scratches to fester—he met Jefferson again in a louder, meaner rematch. The election of 1800 featured more voters, more money, and more outrage. Things grew so heated that Hamilton decided to break with tradition by campaigning on behalf of the Federalists. "Hamilton harangues the astonished group," shuddered one newspaper, though of course newspapers had become as partisan as everything else. While Adams and Jefferson again stayed home, the incumbent's supporters sought his advice. Jefferson went a bit further, not just strategizing with allies but selecting and circulating his preferred pamphlets. But those actions had to occur stealthily. "Do not let my name be connected with the business," Jefferson insisted to Monroe.

Jefferson's official silence caused at least one unintended consequence: it turned his popular book into his proxy, something his critics could mine for damning details. With so many accusations hurtling around, what could an honest voter believe? "Happily for truth and for us," a Federalist sneered, "Mr. Jefferson has written; he has printed."

The Federalists started by blasting Jefferson for writing a book in the first place. It proved he was too arrogant and intellectual to be a good president. One newspaper suggested that Jefferson wrote *Notes* merely "to theorize about government. All the ideas which were derived from experience were hooted at." This was utterly false, as Jefferson professed to build everything on a foundation of experience. But the attacks didn't need to be honest in order to work.

The biggest vulnerability in *Notes*—and the biggest issue in the campaign—was Jefferson's views on religion. In Query XVII, which he'd devoted to the topic, Jefferson made a careful, rational case for separating church and state. He believed a person's faith should be a private issue. Besides, the government had no real basis to intrude. "The legitimate powers of government extend to such acts only as are injurious to others," Jefferson wrote. "But it does me no injury for my neighbor to say there are twenty gods, or no god. It neither picks my pocket nor breaks my leg."

In 1800, this line exploded into one of America's first modern sound bites—a phrase ripped from its context and refashioned into a bludgeon. In one popular (and anonymous) pamphlet, a pro-Adams preacher singled the passage out for "the most serious attention." "It is true that a mere opinion of my neighbor will do me an injury," the minister wrote, "but let my neighbor once persuade himself that there is no God, and he will soon pick my pocket, and break not only my leg but my neck." Other Adams supporters made similar points, uncovering in the passage terrifying hints of a Jefferson presidency. "Ponder well this paragraph," another best-selling pamphlet urged. "Ten thousand impieties and mischiefs lurk in its womb."

Smart booksellers like Mason Weems pushed their *Notes* inventory during the election. Jefferson's supporters also tried to appeal to the book. At an ugly town meeting in Maryland, a Democratic-Republican brandished his copy. He alternated between reading passages aloud, including Jefferson's discussion of slavery and divine justice, and supplying his own analysis. "Could a man of those principles," he asked, "be devoid of religion?" But *Notes* had so many moments that begged for an atheistic gloss—Jefferson's math-driven argument for the impossibility of Noah's flood, or his suggestion that schools teach young people history instead of the Bible since "their judgments are not sufficiently matured for religious enquiries." Federalists hit Jefferson on all of them. There were too many openings, each one pried apart by the silent candidate's carefully chosen words.

Jefferson won the election, but that meant governing a divided nation—a nation where, after he was sworn in, Federalists urged each other to bury their Bibles in gardens or to lower them down wells, in case the infidel executive tried to take them away. Jefferson found the presidency to be exhausting, though he managed to have some fun with the partisan climate. During his first term, a gullible supporter came to Washington and asked Jefferson about the spot in the Blue Ridge Mountains where the Shenandoah and Potomac merged. How, asked this dedicated reader of *Notes*, could he locate the very place where Jefferson had stood? "He told me the place no longer existed," the supporter told his wife, "for during the reign of Federalism under Adams's administration, the spot . . . had been industriously blown up and destroyed by gunpowder!"

In 1804, Jefferson won reelection, though *Notes* again became an issue.* By the time his second term was finished, he was desperate to return to Monticello and a life of reading, farming, and family. The best description of his departure from Washington is still Henry Adams's, in his masterful history of the Jefferson and Madison administrations. "On horseback," John Adams's great-grandson wrote, "over roads impassable to wheels, through snow and storm, he hurried back to Monticello to recover in the quiet of home the peace of mind he had lost in the disappointments of his statesmanship. He arrived at Monticello on March 15, and never again passed beyond the bounds of a few adjacent counties."

"BOOKS WERE AT ALL TIMES HIS CHOSEN COMPANIONS"

A few months after Jefferson had settled in at Monticello, he received a letter from a printer in New York. *Notes*, the printer informed him, had become an American classic—"one of the standing stock books among booksellers." It was true. Jefferson's book could crop up in the libraries of a farmer in Missouri and a Revolutionary War veteran in Indiana. The nation's magazines and newspapers were still arguing with and excerpting it. Had Jefferson, the printer asked, ever considered a revised edition?

The ex-president admitted that he had. He'd saved one of his copies of the London edition, and he often found himself going back to it, collect-

*Clement Clarke Moore, better known for his poem "The Night Before Christmas," wrote a pamphlet lamenting that a book so evil "should have been extensively circulated in a Christian country for nearly twenty years."

ing more materials, adding long marginal notes, and pondering a return to authorship. Jefferson heard from plenty of printers who wanted to try an updated *Notes* or even a prestigious set of his complete prose. In the end, he always turned them down. But the author stood by his work. "Experience," he explained to another printer, "has not altered a single principle."

Jefferson's second retreat from politics was more permanent. Late one night, near the end of the War of 1812, one of his grandsons rushed into Monticello, grasping a fresh newspaper. The Americans, led by a general named Andrew Jackson, had defeated the British in the Battle of New Orleans. The grandson knocked on Jefferson's bedroom door to see if the old man wanted to read the news. He declined. The victory could wait for breakfast.

The War of 1812 gave Jefferson another way to influence America's literary culture. In 1814, during their assault on Washington, British soldiers torched the Library of Congress. Given the wartime conditions on the Atlantic, and given the underdeveloped state of American publishing, the library seemed impossible to replace. But Jefferson had an idea. "You know my collection," he wrote to a government official. "I have been fifty years making it." Jefferson proposed selling his library to Congress at whatever price it deemed fair, and he enclosed a new catalogue he'd been designing, a rich intellectual atlas that organized his volumes into forty-four "chapters." Congress approved the purchase after some partisan squabbling, and in 1815 the first wagons left Monticello for Washington, creaking under the weight of the books. The Library of Congress decided to retain a modified version of the catalogue, and the chief librarian sent a copy to Jefferson. "You ask how I like the arrangement of the chapters," he replied. "Of course, you know, not so well as my own."

Jefferson's other big project from this period was a work now known as *The Jefferson Bible*. Proving his Federalist antagonists wrong, or maybe proving them right, Jefferson had long been fascinated with sifting the historical parts of Jesus's narrative from the supernatural ones. In the White House, he tried to make a reading copy of the Gospels that separated these strains, and he returned to the idea in retirement. He took a sharp blade and sliced up stacks of New Testaments, pasting the results in a new book on facing pages: Greek and Latin on the left, French and English on the right. It would be hard to overstate how scrupulous Jefferson was in this—how careful, how in control. When he came to Matthew 19:2, to take a small example, he saw this sentence: "And great multitudes followed him, and he healed them there." Jefferson carefully cut out the miracle, *and he healed them there*, leaving behind the *him* and a hanging comma.

When Mathew Carey heard rumors about the project, he tried to make an offer. "Do you intend it for publication?" the printer asked. "Certainly not," Jefferson replied. "I write nothing for publication, and last of all things should it be on the subject of religion." The former president was easing into a routine of literary puttering. His famous red hair had faded to sandy, then gray. "I write now slowly, laboriously, painfully," he admitted. He spent his time reading alongside his grandchildren, sometimes pausing to share a favorite passage aloud, sometimes asking them what they were enjoying. Jefferson started assembling his last library. "Books," one granddaughter recalled, "were at all times his chosen companions."

It's a wonderful image—Jefferson surrounded by his books, still using them to work and to learn, the way he'd done his entire life. But it is static in another sense. Jefferson's life was saturated by slavery. His literary life was too. A slave, Sally Hemings's brother, had built Jefferson's custom pine bookcases. A slave had brought the bowl of punch Jefferson shared with Chastellux. When the traveling bookseller knocked on Monticello's door, it was only after a slave had intercepted him and escorted him there. While Jefferson liked to attack the idea of slavery, to denounce it as a "political and moral evil," it was not just an intellectual issue for him. Slavery was something that he saw—and experienced—every single day.

And yet, as Jefferson told one of those inquiring printers, experience had not moved him to change a single thing in his book, not even his dehumanizing descriptions of black people. Jefferson left behind a complex and frustrating record on slavery, one where biographers and historians can weigh his public actions and private statements. But he also left behind a book. In *Notes*, more than anywhere else, Jefferson said exactly what he wanted to say. His words are enough. Judge him by those. Mr. Jefferson has written; he has printed.

CHAPTER TWO

Autobiography's Founding Father: John Adams and the First Legacy Book

I t was a December–December romance, with the seventy-six-year-old
John Adams and the sixty-eight-year-old Thomas Jefferson setting
aside their grudges, picking up their pens, and jump-starting their epis-
tolary friendship. In letter after letter, the ex-presidents reminisced about
their families, their favorite books, and their remarkable shared history.
It was this final topic that occupied Adams when he sat down to write in
the summer of 1815. He liked to write at a folding desk in his escritoire, a
beautiful piece of furniture he'd acquired in France while a diplomat; now
it filled a corner in his home in Quincy, Massachusetts, the estate he called
Peacefield. Adams stored paper and ink in the escritoire's countless cub-
bies, and after locating some of each, he began. "Who shall write the history of the American Revolution?" he asked Jefferson skeptically. "Who
can write it? Who will ever be able to write it?"

Once he finished the missive, Adams mailed it off and waited. Even as
an old man, he hated this part. No one wrote as quickly, as passionately, as
impulsively as John Adams. ("I have never copied, nor corrected," he once
said of revising. "I understand it not.") During their late-life correspondence, Adams contributed more than twice as many letters as Jefferson,
and by the time the Virginian got to his partner's posterity-minded query,
he had three other letters to answer. "On the subject of the history of the
American Revolution," Jefferson replied, "who ever will be able to write it?
Nobody, except merely its external facts." Most of the participants hadn't
taken careful notes, and for that reason, Jefferson considered it impossible
to capture what had really happened inside the Pennsylvania State House.

It was a fair answer to a fair question. But Adams had not been entirely
honest with his friend. After all, he knew at least one person who'd nar-

rated those famous events—Adams himself, who, more than a decade earlier, had tried to recount them not as a historian but as something far
more radical: an autobiographer.

Adams left this work, more than four hundred pages in his hurried
handwriting, unfinished and unpublished at the time of his death. Even
today, his innovative autobiography remains largely overlooked, though
Adams would say this is true of most of his prose. He could be an aston-
ishingly productive writer once he found a proper goal. To meet the
deadline for his *Defense of the Constitutions of Government of the United
States of America*, the most important book he published in his lifetime,
Adams worked long and lonely days, straight through Christmas. Abigail, his wife, finally went to a friend's for the holidays, where she worried
her husband would forget to keep a fire going in the library. (On Christmas Day, he wrote to allay her fears. "If I am cold in the night," the busy
author promised, "I will take a virgin to bed with me," with "virgin" being
his nickname for their hot-water bottle.) Yet Adams could also be undis-
ciplined. He could be distracted. As soon as any criticism appeared, he
knew he'd get caught up in rebutting it. He couldn't help himself.

When it came to writing an autobiography, these weaknesses turned into
strengths. Adams told almost no one about his book, which he began soon
after losing the presidency in 1800. As he revisited his past—confronting
what he called, in a very Adamsean line, "the torment of a perpetual vol-
cano of slander, pouring on my flesh all my life"—he found that his emotions were pulling him to places much grimmer than he'd expected. Adams
ended up writing a book that, by the standards of his time and even by
the standards of today, is extraordinarily personal and pathologically petty.
Hunched over that escritoire, he went to war with his enemies, marshaling
a nasty intimacy that any score settler could admire—and, along the way,
becoming the first president to try writing his own legacy.

BY FAITH, ALONE

Human beings have been writing autobiographically for centuries—
something one can confirm in the works of Greece's Aratus, Rome's Julius
Caesar, and Christianity's Saint Augustine. During the Renaissance, European aristocrats wrote a smattering of courtly memoirs. But these were
exceptions. It wasn't until the seventeenth and eighteenth centuries that
autobiography began to develop into a wobbly genre, and America quickly

staked its claim, in part through the success of Franklin's *Autobiography*.*
When Franklin's book first appeared, after his death in 1790, it became a
transatlantic sensation. Still, Franklin had help. Autobiography, with its
emphasis on self-invention and self-improvement, seemed ideally suited
to America and its readers. It also provided the first genre in which American authors could compete on an international scale.

Early autobiographies were not as personal or revealing as their modern counterparts. Still, they were firmly democratic, especially in their
range of authors. An explorer like John Smith could tell his story, and in *A
General History of Virginia* he remembered (and perhaps embellished) the
time he was saved by a princess named Pocahontas. Yet a Native American like Samson Occom could tell his story too. So could a Massachusetts
woman like Mary Rowlandson and a black slave like Briton Hammon.
Some of these titles—and there were scores more—became big sellers.
Others did not appear until many years later, after their authors were
dead. Either way, in America an autobiography was a book anyone could
write and anyone could read.

What united most of these authors was their commitment to the Christian
faith. No one did more to nurture a tradition of autobiography than the Puritans of New England. Puritan churches often required each person to apply
for membership, and that meant fidgeting in front of the entire congregation
and testifying about how God had moved in your heart. One seventeenth-
century minister described the task like this: "Thus I was humbled, then thus
I was called, then thus I have walked, though with many weaknesses since."
It might sound formulaic, and it often was. But it still forced people to craft
public and psychological stories about their lives: Thus *I* . . .

This impulse hummed everywhere in Puritan culture. In their diaries,
men and women wrote about seeing God's majesty all around them, in the
clouds of a thunderstorm or in a field of rippling grass. They saw their failures
there too. One diarist recorded how, while feeding his chickens, he became
overwhelmed with "what need I stood in of spiritual food." Thankfully, dia-

---

*One way to watch the genre wobble was in its terminology. The word *autobiography*
did not become popular until the nineteenth century, and Franklin called his work-in-
progress *Memoirs* and *History of My Life*, among other titles. Even when *autobiography*
did enter the language, it meant something different than it does now. People who wrote
"memoirs" wrote something more formal, a stately summation of their external careers;
people who wrote "autobiographies," by contrast, wrote something more internal and literary. Today, these meanings have basically flipped, and since this book's terminology can't
help but be retrospective, it will use the words interchangeably.

ries also created a space for self-scrutiny, for growth, and Puritans scribbled down lists and rules and resolutions to aid them in their spiritual journey.

Printing offered another potential tool. The Puritans began publishing spiritual autobiographies, longer and more carefully crafted testimonies that turned on big, salvific epiphanies. One of the most popular examples came from the British preacher George Whitefield, whose sermons made him famous during the Great Awakening and who also wrote a number of autobiographical works. On his first voyage to America, in 1739, he completed *A Brief and General Account of the Life of the Reverend Mr. Geo. Whitefield . . . Written by Himself.* "Some may think this had been as well deferred till after my death," he wrote, "or written by some other person." But Whitefield believed that only he could reveal his soul's grisly before and redemptive after—"what I was by nature, as well as what I am by Grace." In a spiritual autobiography, the author, even one as celebrated as Whitefield, didn't strive to be an individual. He aimed to be an illustration of God's grace.

Whitefield preached several times in Philadelphia, and Benjamin Franklin wrote about one of them in a classic scene in his own *Autobiography.* Franklin's faith, like Jefferson's, leaned more toward the complicated than the devout, and he was unconvinced when Whitefield announced his plan to raise money for a new orphanage. "I silently resolved he should get nothing from me," Franklin wrote. "I had in my pocket a handful of copper money, three or four silver dollars, and five pistoles in gold." And yet, as Whitefield began to preach, Franklin was surprised by how much the sermon moved him—the copper, the silver, finally even the gold clinked into the collection plate.

Franklin made his money back and then some by publishing a few of Whitefield's best sellers, including *A Brief and General Account.* But secular autobiographers—and more and more authors were experimenting with the form, including Laurence Sterne, David Hume, and Edward Gibbon—encountered an additional problem. Puritan culture teemed with sermon titles like "The Sin and Dangers of Self-Love," and the danger increased dramatically once the author started writing outside a shared religious framework. Even more than running for political office or attempting a different, less personal book, writing an autobiography raised the specter of vanity. After all, if you weren't writing for God, who would get the glory? Other, that is, than you? Readers reacted skeptically to works like Jean-Jacques Rousseau's *Confessions.* When a translation hit America in 1796, even a Rousseau supporter called it "an unnatural compound of vanity, meanness, and contemptible self-love."

As the most famous man in America, Franklin seemed especially vulnerable to these attacks. Thanks to his scientific discoveries and earlier writings, Franklin had become an international celebrity. His face adorned watches, bowls, medallions, and rings; you could find his picture hanging in French and American homes. Even Adams, who often counted Franklin as one of his many foes, had to admit that "there was scarcely a peasant or a citizen . . . who was not familiar with him and who did not consider him as a friend to humankind." This reputation would make it easy to smear any achievement-stuffed autobiography. Franklin, always the inventor, developed an ingenious counter to the vanity scolds: first, construct a clever and self-aware character for the book, a "Benjamin Franklin"; and second, connect that character to a new higher calling— not the Grace of God, but the Ascent of America.

Franklin began his *Autobiography* in a rare moment of peace. It was 1771, and he was engaged in yet another round of European diplomacy, this time in England. For two weeks, though, he managed to escape to a quiet village and the home of a friend, and there he wrote his *Autobiography*'s first part. Although he initially framed it as a letter to his son, a common strategy for early autobiographers, he clearly hoped his book would reach many, many readers. (In fact, he read fresh passages aloud to his host.) In the book's opening, Franklin even confessed that a big reason he wrote was to "gratify my own vanity." Then he turned that shamelessness into a virtue: "I scarce ever heard or saw the introductory words, 'Without vanity I may say,' etc., but some vain thing immediately followed."

This winking humor popped up constantly in the *Autobiography*, though the target was often the author himself—in the Whitefield episode, or in the iconic moment where he ambled down a Philadelphia street, toting "three great puffy rolls." Franklin had read his Puritans, and he used their techniques to give his book a larger point. In another famous episode, where he drafted a list of thirteen virtues, then drew a chart to track his progress in keeping them, he could have been tearing a literal page from one of those pious, list-filled diaries. Franklin called it his "plan for self-examination," a very Puritan phrase, but it was also a plan for readers, and in this and many other places, the *Autobiography* turned into a self-help book, a guide for a sturdy citizenry.

While it took Franklin thirteen years to resume his *Autobiography*— self-made men tend to stay busy—he finished four parts. As the pages piled up, his friends and fans began to gossip about the project. Mathew Carey asked to read an early version. Adams inquired about it in a letter.

Jefferson visited Franklin at home, telling him how excited he was for the rumored book. "I cannot say much of that," the old man replied, before directing his grandson to hand Jefferson a stack of pages. "But I will give you a sample of what I shall leave."

Franklin died a few weeks later, and his book's afterlife (juicy excerpts, pirated translations) resembled that of Jefferson's *Notes*. Franklin's book sold even better, going through well over a hundred editions in its first few decades. At a time when autobiographies were especially tricky for public figures—for, say, a president, writing about his time in office— Franklin realized he could parallel his personal triumphs with his nation's. He made himself into a secular example, and when his friends read early passages, they praised precisely this quality. Franklin liked one of their letters so much he decided to include it in his text: "All that has happened to you," the reader marveled, "is also connected with the detail of the manners and situation of a rising people."

ADAMS VERSUS JEFFERSON

No one ever described Adams as a writer better than Adams did himself. In another letter to Jefferson, he summed up his style by alluding to a lush mountain in *The Iliad*: "Whenever I sit down to write to you," the author confided, "I am precisely in the situation of the woodcutter on Mount Ida: I cannot see wood for trees. So many subjects crowd upon me that I know not with which to begin." So Adams, as both a writer and a reader, would wander, chopping for a while on this tree, then trimming a branch on that one, then deciding to plant a sapling in the clearing up ahead.

The results often lacked polish and focus, and that's one reason Adams has never received enough credit for his literary talents. The bigger reason is Jefferson's shadow. Both men moved in a literary world that was incredibly small, sharing the same printers and bookstores and friends.* The club of ex-presidents was smaller still, and Adams's bookish side, while

---

*How small was the literary world? So small that Adams's daughter, Nabby, was briefly engaged to Royall Tyler, the Vermont novelist and lawyer. At the time, Adams was living alone in Paris, and Abigail informed him of the news in a letter (and admitted that when Tyler was a younger man, he had spent a few years in a "dissipated state"). Adams replied grumpily to both the engagement and the potential groom's profession: "My child is too young for such thoughts," the father fumed, "and I don't like your word 'dissipation' at all. . . . I am not looking out for a poet, nor a professor of belle letters."

extraordinary, would never measure up to Jefferson's. Adams was smart enough to see this. When writing to Jefferson, he sometimes changed the return address from "Peacefield" to "Montezillo"—a word, he explained, that conveyed not a large mountain ("Monticello") but a small hill.

The outline of Adams's early life can seem fairly standard for a New England striver. He was born in Massachusetts in 1735, and he could trace a branch of his family tree back to the *Mayflower* Pilgrims. But he was also the son of a farmer-slash-shoemaker, a boy with few connections who had to scrap as a student at Harvard, then as a small-town schoolteacher, and finally as a small-town lawyer. His appearance didn't stand out. (No one has described that better than Adams, either: America's second president, he wrote, looked "like a short, thick, fat Archbishop of Canterbury, seated at the table with a pen in his hand.") And yet what did stand out from the very beginning was Adams's startling ambition, his dissatisfaction with life's outline thus far—and his desire to write a bigger, better ending.

This came through clearest in Adams's diary. One day while he was still at Harvard, he folded a few sheets of paper and stitched them together with thread. It was a simple start to an incredible document he would keep, off and on, for decades, and his early entries bristled with the guilt and tabulations of a good Puritan. At twenty, he wrote, "I am now entering on another year, and I am resolved not to neglect my time." A few years later: "Another year is now gone and upon recollection, I find I have executed none of my plans." And again: "I am just entered on the twenty-sixth year of my life, and I think it is high time for a reformation." Adams could be relentless in his self-criticism, ridiculing himself for sleeping too late, for fretting about his clothes, for being socially awkward. Yet his motivating standard was not God and His plans but something more earthly—Adams's own lust for money, success, and fame. "Vanity," he wrote in another entry, "is my cardinal vice."

In his diary, Adams stoked and analyzed his ambitions with an honesty that no other founder can match. While his peers were practicing a pose of detachment (or, in Franklin's case, dancing cleverly behind that pose), Adams stared vanity in the face. Do authors, he once wondered in an essay, write books because of their "sense of duty" or "love of truth"? Hardly. "The universal object and idol of men of letters is reputation," Adams argued. "It is the notoriety, the celebration, which constitutes the charm."

This theory of literary motivation is worth keeping in mind since Adams's diary was fast evolving into the diary of a young writer. He'd long been a diligent reader, and on trips to nearby Boston, he would stop at shops like the London Bookstore, a cosmopolitan outlet that also imported Irish linens and bottles of British beer. Despite his earnest efforts, Adams was not yet a wealthy man. But he started building a library that would eventually top three thousand volumes—still short of Jefferson's, of course, but one of the largest private collections in America. As Adams conceded to Abigail, whom he married in 1764, "I have spent an estate in books."

Adams got into arguments even with his books. In their margins, he would scribble quick judgments like "Sensible!" or "Curious! Curious!" He would go on extended rants, adding more than ten thousand handwritten words to his copy of a book by the early feminist Mary Wollstonecraft. Adams also planned to direct his energy outward, toward readers. "A pen is certainly an excellent instrument to fix a man's attention and to inflame his ambition," he admitted in his diary, and alongside his other entries he began making notes and drafting essays on the problem with

Adams liked to shop at the London Bookstore, which would have resembled this other Boston bookstore, illustrated in an eighteenth-century engraving. Note the quill pens hanging for sale on the doorpost, along with the bottles of ink in the window.

taverns and the best behavior for young ladies, the last of which was staunchly pro-bundling.

Tensions between Britain and its colonies would soon present Adams with more serious subjects. The political climate was darkening. (In 1769, a group of angry Bostonians ran the owner of the London Bookstore out of town.) Adams started a second literary habit that, like his diary, would persist for decades—writing brash pamphlets and essays, sometimes under pseudonyms like "Humphrey Ploughjogger."

In this, he parted ways with Jefferson. Although the Virginian had built his reputation on a well-received pamphlet, he mostly avoided the messy public sphere, where newspapers and magazines would steal each other's essays and print them next to news that took weeks or months to circulate. Jefferson, always worried about control, compared this environment to the chaotic sport of bear baiting, calling the colonial media "a bear-garden scene into which I have made it a point to enter on no provocation." Jefferson preferred to lure his allies into the arena, where they could battle for him. Adams did his own fighting. He engaged in real time with works like Thomas Paine's *Common Sense*, a king-bashing pamphlet that sold tens of thousands of copies—and seemed to incite an equal number of newspaper spats.

Once the Revolutionary War ended—and once Adams finished his adventures in diplomacy with Franklin and Jefferson in France—he and his family headed to London, where he would serve as the minister to England. In 1785, the Adamses moved into an elegant stone house on the corner of Grosvenor Square, where they spent their evenings reading together, with John and Abigail in easy chairs and Nabby by the fire. Their favorite distractions were always letters from home, and Adams would divvy up the latest packet. "Here is one for you, my dear," he said to his wife one night, "and here is another. And here, Miss Nabby, are four, five, upon my word, six, and more yet for your momma." Adams looked down at what was left. "Well, I fancy I shall come off but slenderly. One only for me."

Before long, Adams found himself too busy for leisure reading and letters. In the spring of 1786, Jefferson came to London to see the Adamses and to make a frosty appearance at the British court. During the visit, Adams told his friend he'd been thinking about writing a book on the best forms of government. Jefferson, still reveling in his own recent authorship of *Notes*, urged his friend to do it. Within a few months, Adams was working on his first book—what would ultimately grow into the three-volume *Defense of the Constitutions of Government of the United States of America*.

firm feat in her dominions to affift her. She has vainly endeavoured, indeed, to make the fweet flowers of liberty grow under the poifonous fhade of defpotifm; giving the ruffians a falfe tafte for the luxuries of life before the attainment of it's conveniences. And this hafty attempt to alter the manners of a people has produced the worft effect on their morals: mixing the barbarifm of one ftate of fociety, deprived of it's fincerity and fimplicity, with the voluptuoufnefs of the other, void of elegance and urbanity, the two extremes have prematurely met.

Thus purfued and miftaken, liberty, though ftill exifting in the fmall ifland of England, yet continually wounded by the arbitrary proceedings of the britifh miniftry, began to flap her wings, as if preparing for a flight to more aufpicious regions—And the angloamericans having carried with them to their place of refuge the principles of their anceftors, fhe appeared in the new world with renovated charms, and fober matron graces.

Freedom is, indeed, the natural and imprefcriptible right of man; without the enjoyment of which, it is impoffible for him to become either a reafonable or dignified being.

Freedom

England

America

*I thank you
Miss Wollsto—
We long enjoy
your esteem.*

Adams filled his copy of Mary Wollstonecraft's *Historical and Moral View of the Origin and Progress of the French Revolution*, eventually writing close to 10,000 words in its margins.

Freedom he enjoys in a natural state, in it's full extent: but formed by nature for a more intimate society, to unfold his intellectual powers, it becomes necessary, for carrying into execution the main objects, which induces men to establish communities, that they should surrender a part of their natural privileges, more effectually to guard the most important. But from the ignorance of men, during the infancy of society, it was easy for their leaders, by frequent usurpations, to create a despotism, which choking up the springs that would have invigorated their minds, they seem to have been insensible to the deprivations under which they lived; and existing like mere animals, the tyrants of the world have continued to treat them only as machines to promote their purposes.

In the progress of knowledge, which however was very tardy in Europe, because the men who studied were content to see nature through the medium of books, without making any actual experiments themselves, the benefits of civil liberty began to be better understood: and in the same proportion we find the chains of despotism becoming lighter. Still the systematizing of pedants, the ingenious

5

[marginal annotations:]

one Man alone would be free, but give him a wife and Children and they must all loose a Part of their Liberty.

These Leaders were generally as ignorant as their followers, and both leaders and followers or still as ignorant as ever of the form of Gov't is indispensible to preserve liberty in rich commercial States — and neither will learn.

it would be quite as correct to say that the Progress of Navigation & Commerce and Manufactures necessitated Men to agree to fixed Laws of Property and from that Laws knowledge and liberty have increased. And

in the Course Commerce and wealth have destroy'd the Institutions & preserved Morals as well as Property and now all Nations and all Parties, except a very few Individuals appear to be ignorant of the political organizations and Equiponses necessary to Pursue Liberty Property Life or any Thing.

It was an odd title since Adams included little about America's state or federal systems. He attempted a grander argument instead. French philosophers and populists like Paine had been clamoring for simple, centralized governments. Adams didn't trust humanity enough to sign up for that. History, to him, was cyclical—just as every writer (every person) chased the same ambitions, so every nation followed the same dangerous patterns. Those patterns suggested that the most durable governments were the most complex: a house of commoners, a house of aristocrats, and a powerful executive to mediate between the two.

To support this theory, Adams's book surveyed dozens of governments from the classical, medieval, and contemporary periods. That required a staggering workload, and he retreated to his library and barricaded himself with books. Careful, considered writing did not come easily to Adams—he described the process as "painful and distressing . . . almost like a blow on the elbow or the knee"—and he knew his topic was timely. He chose a style that, to modern readers, can seem strange and even unethical. For each case study, Adams would copy long passages from other books, then quilt them together with his shorter riffs. In fact, the first volume of *Defense* lifted three-quarters of its prose straight from other writers, often without credits or quotation marks.

It's important to remember that in Adams's time "plagiarism" was as flexible an idea as "authorship." Besides, he was tracking down rare foreign titles and synthesizing their most important ideas. In a world where books were precious, his approach had the potential to provide real value. And it still demanded lots of work. "I tell him he will ruin himself in publishing his books," Abigail wrote to her sister that fall. "He says they are for the benefit of his country, and he always expected to be ruined in her service."

Defense's first volume appeared in early 1787—and under Adams's real name. The reactions arrived that spring. Britain's *Monthly Review*, the same outlet that had praised Jefferson's *Notes*, ran a brutal notice. "Had the book been written by a youth with a view to obtain some academical prize," the anonymous critic observed, "we should have said that it afforded indications of an active mind, . . . but that the young man [was] too eager to discover the extent of his reading." Yet *Defense* had come not from some student but from the well-known Adams. It was an embarrassment—confusing, superficial, and sloppily assembled.

The review, which was reprinted in several American newspapers, was devastating. Abigail admitted that the night after reading it, she couldn't sleep. In his diary, Adams considered various conspiracy theories on who might have influenced the critic. "The spirit of Franklin," he noted, "is to me very discernible."

The review was also fair. *Defense* was certainly too specialized for regular readers.* Political buffs also struggled with the book. Adams saw himself as a bold but objective tour guide, someone who was willing to point out where, say, monarchies had actually succeeded. This nuance didn't come through—because of careless readers who assumed Adams was simply defending those kings, but also because of his deluge of research and his waterlogged prose. *Defense* remained a significant work of political theory, going through several editions in America and in Europe, in addition to supplying lots of fresh meat for the media bear garden. But it also suffered from Adams's haste and stubbornness. When Abigail had read the manuscript, she warned him that Americans would take it to be pro-monarchy. The author ignored her advice.

The upside to stubbornness, of course, is not knowing when to quit. Adams finished two more volumes of *Defense*, each one longer than the last. In the spring of 1788, he and his family finally returned to America and to their new home, Peacefield. No sooner had they settled in—it took the young John Quincy Adams nearly a week to unpack his father's library—than Adams was chosen as America's first vice president.

The new role didn't slow his pen. One day in the capital, he bumped into a French diplomat. "I see well that I will have to make another trip to France," Adams blustered, "in order to explain to them my book." The vice president had already launched a new project, "Discourses on Davila," a series of essays that extended *Defense*'s themes. "Discourses" would trigger only more trouble—including the end of his friendship with Jefferson.

It all started with Thomas Paine. In 1791, Jefferson read his latest pamphlet, *Rights of Man*, then sent it to a printer who was planning an American edition. Jefferson included a short note saying he was "extremely pleased" since this new work would counter "the political heresies which have sprung up among us." The printer, in a clever bit of marketing, quoted Jefferson's letter in a preface to his edition. The comments pinged around the nation's newspapers, with readers everywhere understanding that the "heresies" Jefferson meant were Adams's latest pro-monarchy ramblings.

Jefferson quickly wrote to Adams, promising that he'd never meant for

---

*Mathew Carey sent some copies to Mason Weems, to sell on the road, and it earned the printer a predictably feverish reply. Weems claimed there was no chance he could move Adams's book, which was so poorly written that "the commonest carpenter might 'saw and plane' [something better] out of a maple slab of pine."

the letter to be published (true enough) and that the "heresies" weren't Adams's (a bald lie). Adams knew better, but accepted the apology icily. "My unpolished writings," he admitted to Jefferson, "have not been read by great numbers. Of the few who have taken the pains to read them, some have misunderstood them and others have willfully misrepresented them." What hurt Adams the most, it seemed, was being misunderstood by a reader as careful as Jefferson.

Their relationship began to cool just as America's partisan fires began to kindle. Before long, they were facing each other in the bitter contests of 1796 and 1800. In each election, Adams's opponents would dig through his writings in order to bend his words against him. "Do you ask me for proofs that he is a monarchist?" crowed an anonymous pamphleteer. "Read his *Defense*." Yet the candidate never took as many hits from his book as Jefferson did from his. Even on this miserable count, Adams trailed his rival.

SQUINTING TOWARD THE PRESIDENCY

Before Jefferson or Adams or even George Washington could become president, America had to invent the role itself. This was no simple task. On May 25, 1787, twelve states sent delegates back to the Pennsylvania State House, this time for the Constitutional Convention. Philadelphia, with its crowds, its soggy heat, its pre-sewer smells, did not feel as welcoming as it once had. Many Americans saw the convention as an uncertain experiment, and one of its biggest variables was the national executive. Actually, no one even knew how many executives there should be. Did America need a president or a board of presidents? No one even knew that "president" was the right term.

The convention turned to these questions near the end of its first full week. A delegate from Pennsylvania proposed a single executive, someone who could act quickly in crisis. A delegate from South Carolina seconded. Then came a long and nervous silence—"a considerable pause," in the words of James Madison, who was taking scrupulous notes. The delegates' anxiety stemmed in part from the presence of Washington, whom they'd made president of the convention and who would surely serve as America's first executive. But the delegates were also fretting about the idea of any executive at all. They'd just spent years—and, more important, lives—defeating a powerful monarch. No one wanted a system that would lead to similar mistakes.

So the silence stretched on, dilating, until Franklin broke in. He didn't offer an opinion—like Washington's, his was a distorting presence—but he did push the other delegates to debate. Slowly, they did, devoting more humid afternoons to defining the nature of executive power. While several delegates had written Adams to compliment him on his *Defense*, the book was not a major factor in the debates. By the time the convention closed in September, the delegates had designed a president who could veto legislation, issue pardons, appoint officials, negotiate treaties, and serve as commander in chief. Other than administrative tasks and a few smaller issues, that was pretty much it—the presidency was an office that would take shape largely through the actions of its occupants.

Even this seemed too much for many Americans. The states still needed to ratify the Constitution, and critics keyed on the executive. "It

In this ad, which ran in the summer of 1788, a New York bookstore promoted Adams's *Defense* alongside Jefferson's *Notes*.

squints toward monarchy," argued Patrick Henry. "Does this not raise indignation in the breast of every American?"

Washington neutralized those fears when he became president in 1789, mostly through the power of his example. After the war, the famous general could have demanded any reward he wanted. Instead, he retreated to Mount Vernon, planting crops, taking walks, and fixing his house's stubbornly leaky roof. Washington didn't lust after the presidency; he saw it as one final duty. "I feel," he told a friend, "very much like a man who is condemned to death does when the time of his execution draws nigh."

Reluctance turned out to be one of Washington's most durable presidential precedents. The other founders had national reputations and natural charisma, though not to Washington's degree. And yet they followed his tone, emphasizing that they didn't need or love power—that they were reluctantly called to serve. They exhibited the same restraint as presidents that they did as presidential candidates.

They were playing a part, at least during the campaign stage. When Jefferson bowed out as secretary of state, Adams diagnosed the real reason: "Jefferson thinks by this step to get a reputation as an humble, modest, meek man, wholly without ambition or vanity," he wrote to John Quincy. "He may even have deceived himself into this belief." Still, their presidencies and postpresidencies reflected their modest rhetoric. America's early executives did not boldly lead their parties. They did not position themselves as the voice of the people, and they did not try to dictate a national agenda. "In republican government," Madison had written in the *Federalist Papers*, "the legislative authority necessarily predominates."* Presidents deferred to that authority. The State of the Union address wasn't a chance to stump for their preferred policies; it was a chance to provide a progress report, which Jefferson emphasized by delivering it each year not as a ceremonial speech but as a simple piece of writing that a clerk would read aloud.

None of this made the presidency easy. When Adams followed Washington as president in 1797, he found himself in a tricky position—handicapped by a tiny margin of victory, beset by Britain and a feisty Napoleon Bonaparte, isolated by his decision to ask Washington's cabinet members to stick around. The job itself was isolating. "A peck of troubles

---

*These words, of course, came not from Madison but from "Publius." Yet the *Federalist Papers'* pseudonym provided one more example of this period's anxiety toward executives: Publius Valerius Publicola was an ancient Roman famous for his antimonarchical beliefs.

in a large bundle of papers, often in a handwriting almost illegible, comes every day," he wrote halfway through his first term. "No company. No society. Idle, unmeaning ceremony."

Adams didn't bother with organizing a newspaper to defend his administration, as other early presidents did. He decided, as always, to do the writing himself, firing off dozens of public letters that were reprinted around the country. He became only more isolated, including from some of his fellow Federalists, and he lost to Jefferson in 1800. But Adams left office with the same passion he'd felt while entering it. "I am weary of the game," he'd confessed to Abigail a few years before. "Yet I don't know how I could live out of it."

ADAMS VERSUS THE WORLD

America had never had a losing president before, which meant it was Adams's turn to set some precedents. For twenty-five years, he'd been a constant presence in national politics. Now he chose to retreat to Peacefield—to write only a handful of letters and to see only a handful of people outside his family. Those who did meet with Adams noted his despair. He tried distracting himself by reading authors like the French intellectual Madame de Staël. "The mind which devotes itself to the pleasures of ambition," she'd written, "renders itself incapable of any other mode of existence." When Adams read this passage, he jotted a feeble protest in the margin: "Books and agriculture may fill the mind."

De Staël was right—someone with Adams's ambition could not rest. His private life had reached new levels of comfort. During his presidency, Abigail had surprised him by converting part of a farmhouse near their home into a special place for his books, the best library he'd ever had. She also doubled the size of the home itself, and in a new wing Adams set up a study, complete with cozy rugs, trunks for his papers, and tall windows that let in plenty of light. But Adams also put his escritoire in that room, and before long, he was unfolding its desk and reaching for his pen. The energy that had driven his political life—and his political writings, if one could even untangle the two—had to spill out somewhere. In the fall of 1801, he began researching his family history. By 1802, he was ready to start writing his autobiography.

The genre had always appealed to Adams, who read both spiritual autobiographies and secular ones. On his first trip to France, he'd bought a shelf's worth of courtly memoirs; he also owned more recent attempts by Gibbon and Hume. These authors usually tried to build a wall between the public and the private, two potent words in this period, and readers usually found themselves stranded on the public side. Early autobiographers might relate dry genealogies, for instance, but most wouldn't delve into family lives or romantic pasts. When Gibbon came to "the delicate subject of my early love," he refused to say more; the subject, he wrote, "less properly belongs to the memoirs of an individual than to the natural history of the species."

As a reader, Adams loved it when authors revealed their private lives, even if it wasn't always intentional. "From the memoirs of individuals," he explained to Benjamin Rush, one of his closest remaining friends, "the true springs of events and the real motives of actions are to be made known to posterity."

As a writer, though, he decided to be conventional. At the top of a clean sheet of paper, he wrote out "John Adams" in large letters and began. "The lives of philosophers, statesmen, or historians written by themselves have generally been suspected of vanity," he wrote. "My excuse is that having been the object of much misrepresentation, some of my posterity may probably wish to see in my own handwriting a proof of the falsehood of that mass of odious abuse of my character with which newspapers, private letters, and public pamphlets and histories have been disgraced for thirty years." Adams's plan had been to avoid the charge of vanity by mentioning his family; he ended up picking a fight instead. He was trying, and failing, to be a good autobiographer, and the failures were what would make his book so fun.

Adams clearly hoped that his legacy book would appear after his death, and that it would revive his reputation. The manuscript captures him at his best: the earthy wit, the precise observations, the insight into human nature—all of the qualities that make him, sentence for sentence, detail for detail, the most entertaining writer among the founders. He described the childhood he passed in a small saltbox house, less than two miles from where he was now writing in Peacefield. He admitted that he struggled in school—to the point that his father, a kind man who hoped to send his son to college, began to fret. After several conversations, Adams told his father he wasn't going. "What would you do, child?" his father replied.

"Be a farmer."

"A farmer? Well, I will show you what it is to be a farmer."

Early the next morning, the father marched his son through the tough-

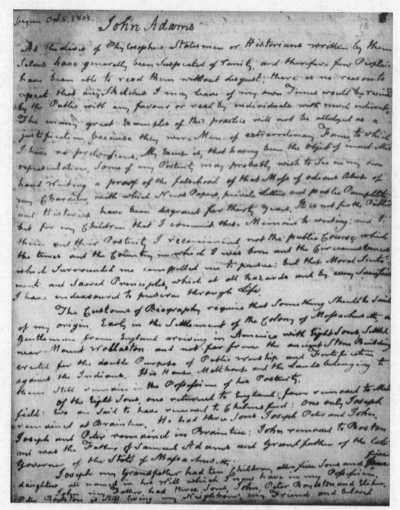

Adams's *Autobiography*, with the first page pictured here,
eventually expanded to 440 pages.

est, muddiest work he could find. It lasted all day, and that night he asked
the would-be agriculturalist what he'd learned: "Well, John, are you satisfied with being a farmer?"

"I like it very well, sir," Adams said.

"Ay, but I don't like it so well," his father replied. "So you shall go to
school."

This anecdote is one of many in which Adams's book blinks and breathes and quivers with life. It's impressive, even today, but in Adams's time, it was astonishing for a memoirist to indulge in this much private detail. He didn't banish his love life to the study of natural history, as Gibbon had. "I was of an amorous disposition," Adams wrote, "and very early, from ten or eleven years of age, was very fond of the society of females." He stressed his mature love for Abigail, calling their marriage "a connection which has been the source of all my felicity." Once Adams started a topic, though, he could rarely resist adding one more line. "My children," he wrote, "may be assured that no illegitimate brother or sister exists." It may have been a gibe at Jefferson or Franklin or one of Adams's other philandering peers. Even if it wasn't, it was striking that an early autobiographer would write such a sentence at all.

Adams's narrative was approaching the years when he actually met Franklin and Jefferson, and that seemed like the spot to pivot from a private story to a public one, or at least to bridge the two, as Franklin had so ably done. But Adams decided to stick with his own perspective while writing about the Continental Congress and the Revolutionary War. It felt even bolder than documenting the moment he first noticed young women—felt bolder, in fact, than even Franklin's approach.

The best way to compare these authors is in their competing accounts of, well, vegetarianism.* In another classic scene from the *Autobiography*, Franklin described his quest to give up meat. The benefits were obvious, starting with more money for books. But one day he ran into someone frying up fresh cod. Franklin decided that since the cod survived by eating smaller fish, it made sense to eat it himself. "So convenient a thing it is to be a reasonable creature," he concluded, "since it enables one to find or make a reason for everything one has a mind to do."

Franklin loved this strategy—present a sincere guide for self-improvement, then tweak it with humor that nodded toward a broader point. The broader points never arrived in Adams's version of going meat

---

*One reason this is the best comparison is that it's silly. Another is that Franklin never got to write about his own crucial role in the Revolutionary War. When he started working on his *Autobiography*, Franklin drafted a list of future topics. It was skeletal—for his stories about George Whitefield, he wrote simply "Whitefield"—but it mentioned events like the Stamp Act and wrapped up with "To France, Treaty, &c." Franklin's health problems ensured that his final narrative ended decades before that point. Had he reached his political material, he might have written a masterful legacy book. And yet, given Franklin's careful alignment of his early life and America's defining themes, perhaps he did that anyway.

free. After a long trip on horseback, during which he became quite sick, a doctor prescribed Adams a fad diet of milk, vegetables, and bread. He followed it for more than a year, though it gave him terrible indigestion. "My excellent father," Adams wrote, "at last by his tender advice at some times and a little good humored ridicule at others, converted me again to the use of a little meat." The story didn't end with some nation-building lesson. Instead, it offered another intimate glimpse of his family. It helped readers see the world the way Adams saw it.

The same thing happened when his autobiography turned political, though the view was rarely so serene. Indeed, the closer the book got to 1776, the tougher it got to read. That's in part because it got tougher to write. Adams worked on his autobiography for five years, though that span included plenty of stops and starts and bizarre authorial choices. He didn't think to dig out his old diary until he'd written many pages; once he had it, Adams revived his method from *Defense*, copying long passages from the diary and adding present-day commentary. Sometimes the results were incoherent, and Adams hinted at his authorial burden in a letter to John Quincy. Writing about his political life, Adams confessed, "would set me on fire" so reliably that "I should have occasion for a bucket of water constantly by my side, to put it out."

Adams wrote that letter during one of his more productive periods as a memoirist. Bitterness animated his book and its most delightful attacks. Adams introduced Thomas Paine as "a star of disaster"—until he crossed it out and went with "a disastrous meteor." (When it came to insults, at least, Adams made time to revise.) He came down even harder on Alexander Hamilton. Hamilton had recently died, after a scandalous duel with Aaron Burr, but Adams didn't care. He would not, he wrote, "suffer my character to lie under infamous calumnies because the author of them, with a pistol bullet through his spinal marrow, died a penitent."

A little spleen goes a long way. Adams continued cataloguing his grievances, never realizing that the increasingly drowsy reader would be the one who needed to be doused with a bucket of water. The autobiography became more needy and more preachy. Its narrative sputtered.

Through it all, though, the book remained profoundly personal. One of its best scenes—a scene Adams wrote from memory, relying on only a sliver of diary—came after he arrived in Paris in 1778 to work with Franklin and the other diplomats. Although Adams didn't speak much French, he found himself sucked into a confusing, exhausting routine of decadent parties and wine-soaked dinners. ("Franklin kept a hornbook always in his pocket in which he minuted all his invitations to dinner," Adams wrote, "the only thing in which he was punctual.") He remembered sitting there during a particularly stimulating evening, the din of foreign conversation all around. For once, Adams preferred silence.

Eventually a young woman approached with a question: "Mr. Adams, by your name I conclude you are descended from the first man and woman," she said through an interpreter. Then she asked Adams to clarify a bit of family lore: "How [did] the first couple find out the art of lying together?"

The descendant of a Puritan admitted that he blushed. He tried to recover with a delicately metaphorical reply, something about "a physical quality in us resembling the power of electricity" drawing Adam and Eve together "like two objects in electric experiments."

His interlocutor was ready: "Well, I know not how it was," she said, "but this I know, it is a very happy shock."

While the French woman got the final word, Adams got to convey what troubled him about her culture. His autobiography revealed his personality, his values, and his vendettas—all of them authorized not by God or Nation but by Adams's personal decision to write.

Yet there were things even Adams could not disclose. His other writings had returned again and again to the relationship between people and vanity. "To be wholly overlooked," he once wrote, "and to know it, are intolerable." Somehow, in 440 pages of autobiography, Adams never got around to discussing *his* ego, much less to dwelling on his mistakes. The man who, from his earliest days as a diarist, had been brutally self-critical, had eventually encountered enemies who were more critical still. Adams responded by turning his anger outward, by girding himself with certainty. He wasn't just the first president to write a legacy book. He was the first to write a legacy book that stumbled when it came to being self-aware.

PEACE AT PEACEFIELD

Adams's autobiography never made it out of France. During another discussion of diplomacy, he alluded to his years as president and vice president before adding, "More, much more of this after." At some point in 1807, however, Adams abandoned his narrative, this time for good. "You advise me to write my own life," he noted a couple years later, in a letter to Benjamin Rush. "I have made several attempts, but it is so dull an employment that I cannot endure it. I look so much like a small boy in my own eyes that with all my vanity I cannot endure the sight of the picture." It was the most honest thing a selectively honest man ever wrote.

The ex-president remained angry and articulate. He launched another series of newspaper essays in 1809, eventually publishing more than a hundred entries by "the late President Adams"—one last cocktail of transcribed documents and combative riffs. Adams tried to defend his older writings, often with absurd results. While perusing a book of French history, he read that the Thirty Years' War had ended "for reasons which no one could anticipate." Adams headed to the margins: "The Constitution of U.S. of 1787 was concluded in the same manner by the arrival of a ship with the first volume of the *Defense*." And yet elsewhere he described his epochal volume as "a book that has been misunderstood, misrepresented, and abused more than any other, except the Bible." Did *Defense* change the world, or did it fly over everyone's head? The truth was that no one seemed to care. The publishers who were pestering Jefferson to reprint *Notes* never bothered Adams. While he mulled a few ideas for a new book, he knew he didn't have the money to fund an edition of his own.

So he worked in his garden and on his farm. He kept enough projects going that Abigail complained about every room in the house being cluttered by papers and books. He began writing more and more letters—a manageable expense thanks to the privilege of franking, which meant that instead of postage, an ex-president needed only to sign his name and write "free" on the outside of any letter. The Adamses leaned heavily on this perk. "I have no scruples," Abigail sniffed, "as it is the only gratuity his country ever bestowed upon him."

Some of those letters went to Monticello. When Adams finally contacted Jefferson in 1812, after years of mutual silence, he knew he needed to charm his former friend. He also knew the perfect strategy: give him a book. Adams anxiously packed up a copy of *Lectures on Rhetoric and Oratory*, the new two-volume title by John Quincy, and sent it out. "As you are a friend to American manufactures," Adams wrote in a separate letter, "I take the liberty of sending you by the post a packet containing two pieces of homespun lately produced in this quarter." It was a deft pun on the state of American authorship, a subject dear to Jefferson's heart, but the difficulty of shipping books ensured that the letter arrived before the package. Jefferson, just as anxious as Adams, replied quickly and literally with a letter on the state of fabrics in the South. ("We consider a sheep for every person in the family as sufficient to clothe it.") The book arrived two days later, and Adams and Jefferson chuckled at the confusion. With that, their correspondence resumed.

In this portrait of Adams, completed in 1788, Jefferson's *Notes* appeared in the background, with its spine reading *Jefferson Hist. of Virginia.*

The letters did more than heal a friendship. They gave Adams a tangible reminder that his peers recognized and appreciated his political contributions. He finally started to mellow. It helped that he was getting older. Adams moved a bed into his study to allow for more rest; he started wearing cotton caps to ward off the cold; he made time for a steady trickle of visitors. One day, a young man named Ralph Waldo Emerson dropped by. "The world does not know how much toil, anxiety, and sorrow I have suffered," Adams told his guest. After an hour-long visit, though, Emerson left Peacefield with a sense of Adams's optimism for his country's future.

In his autobiography, Adams had written about his mother living to the age of eighty-nine—about how her presence had given him "inexpressible comfort." Now, as he neared that number himself, Adams spent time with his children and grandchildren. While his eyesight was going bad, his family read him the latest books—some poetry, even some novels, but above all, anything posthumous and autobiographical written by a member of the Revolutionary generation. During this period, Adams finally read Franklin's *Autobiography*. His younger self would have pivoted instantly to drafting a rebuttal. The older Adams decided to marvel at Franklin's accomplishments instead. The prose left Adams dazzled; the narrative left him reflecting on the arc of his own life. "I should be ashamed to read it," he admitted, "though written by a Franklin."

History was coming for Adams just as surely as it had come for Franklin. He began organizing his papers, sorting through trunks and boxes and drawers, some of which had been locked for so long that the keys had disappeared. He made plans to leave his library to the town of Quincy. But Adams wasn't dead yet. One day, he received a letter from a stranger named Charles Holt. Holt had edited a newspaper during Adams's presidency and, like so many others, had accused him of being a monarchist. Now, as he'd grown older himself, Holt had gone back and read Adams's books more carefully. He realized he'd been unfair, and in his letter he said he was sorry.

Adams wrote back, thanking Holt for the note and assuring him that he'd absorbed so many attacks he'd stopped feeling them long ago. And yet somewhere in Adams, a Puritan still lurked. "The just always rejoice," the autobiographer wrote, "over every sinner that repenteth."

CHAPTER THREE

Primed and Cocked:
American History Finds
Its Readers

O ne day in the summer of 1804, Alexander Hamilton dropped by the office of Egbert Benson, an old friend. The office was empty. Benson, his nephew explained, had just departed to spend a few days on the road. Hamilton wandered over to a bookcase and began inspecting it—normal behavior for a man who, as his son would later recall, was "a lover of books." But then Hamilton did something strange. He pulled down a volume by a Roman author, Pliny, opened it, closed it, and replaced it. When he was finished, Hamilton walked past the nephew and slipped out the door. Two days later, he would duel with Aaron Burr.

Hamilton had left a powerful secret in a place he thought Benson, a lifelong fan of the classics, would find it. Inside the Pliny, there now rested a list that itemized who had written which *Federalist Papers*. Those eighty-five essays were no longer the work of "Publius" or even the collective "Hamilton, Madison, and Jay." Hamilton, knowing he might die in two days' time, decided to shore up his literary legacy. It was something all of the founders were considering, though usually under less pressing circumstances. Adams, always an innovator in taking credit, had already made a list of his anonymous writings. (Actually, he'd done it twice.) Once they finished their presidencies, Jefferson, Madison, and Monroe also began organizing their documents and experimenting with autobiographies. Each act of writing or editing forced them to make choices, to divide their lives and their papers between public and private.

The founders did this in secret, of course, trusting their heirs to protect their words and to share them when the time was right. But publication turned out to be a trickier process than anyone had anticipated. America was still saddled with a lackluster book industry and a healthy inferiority complex, and the founders' families brought their own baggage—gambling addictions, devastating debts, alcoholic stepsons, even juicy rumors of ghostwriting that trailed Hamilton and George Washington, the most famous founder of all. Despite these obstacles, the documents got out. There was simply too much at stake. "American history," Madison observed in 1823, "may be expected to contain more truth, and lessons certainly not less valuable, than that of any country or age."

America's readers certainly agreed. Once the families and printers and a few semipro historians solved their issues, they discovered that a large and diverse audience had been waiting all along. American history became a big business, as readers sought intimate, authentic connections to their presidents. In fact, in the first decades of the nineteenth century, Americans became obsessed with the founders and their writings—even if the readers and the writers could never quite agree on what was private, what was public, and what was too scandalous to share.

FUR TRADERS, AUTOGRAPH HOUNDS, AND HISTORIANS

Hiram Harwood grew up on a farm his grandfather had carved out of the Vermont wilderness. He was a quiet, clumsy boy, then a quiet, clumsy man, especially around the women in his small community. In the fall of 1811, just before his twenty-third birthday, he was invited to an apple paring, a festive event where people would peel bushels of fruit, then string them up to dry for the winter ahead. There'd be lots of neighbors, probably some singing, surely some cider and ale. It sounded like a promising evening for a friendly bachelor, but Harwood spent the whole time thinking about other lovers—namely, the ones in the British novel he was reading, *Coelebs in Search of a Wife*. Later, in his diary, he admitted that he "wished I had been at home with *Coelebs*. Ah—that book I do like."

Harwood liked nonfiction even better. One time he went to fetch water, for his family's morning tea, and on the way to the brook he stopped to read and ended up forgetting his task. When his father found him, he snatched the bucket to fill it himself, though not before loosing a "tide of anger" on his son. Books did that to Harwood. He couldn't be picky, given how hard it was to find reading material in rural Vermont, so he devoured everything: atlases, medical texts, almanacs, novels. But he always seemed to be in the middle of at least one book of history, particularly about the Revolution.

America's recent past fascinated him. When an older man came to the farm to buy some rye, Harwood ended up quizzing him about his service at Bunker Hill. Another time, on the Fourth of July, Harwood and his father rode their horses to the nearby site of 1777's Battle of Bennington. There was no big event that year, but it didn't matter. Harwood had read so much history that he could point to the tree lines and the steep hills, re-creating the movements of the British and American armies from memory.

Harwood, who was born in 1788, might be called a member of the post-Revolution baby boom—except that America was now booming everywhere, all the time. The nation had exploded in both size (the Louisiana Purchase in 1803) and population (more than 7 million people in 1810). There was even a boom in history readers, especially in Harwood's generation, though it took a while for the literary industry to catch up.

The nation's authors received a small boost when Congress, led in part by Madison, passed a domestic copyright law in 1790. Now any citizen or resident could register a fourteen-year copyright and a fourteen-year extension. Mercy Otis Warren was the first female author to register a title, a book of her poems. "I have nothing else I can so properly call my own," she noted with pride, even though many writers didn't bother registering their books. Their biggest threat wasn't being pirated by an American printer but being overwhelmed by cheap British reprints, and the law did nothing to curb that.

There weren't many British authors looking to write American history, and that opened the genre up to natives. In a country still defined in many ways by its plucky states, the most popular books were local histories, like *The History of New Hampshire* and *The Natural and Civil History of Vermont*. There were also histories of the Revolution itself, including one by Mercy Otis Warren. (In her preface, she granted that politics and war were the "peculiar province of masculine strength"—then charged ahead and wrote three long volumes herself.) Still, convincing American printers to put out a war history or a local title or, really, anything original remained difficult. "I long to see the day," wrote one historian, "when an author will at least be on an equal footing with a tailor or shoemaker in getting his living."

That day had still not arrived, and most historians made their living as tailors or shoemakers—or, more realistically, as doctors or ministers, doing their writing and research on the side. And yet across all classes and professions, readers were becoming passionate about the past. It started in the classroom. States were pushing their schools to be more democratic, not just in their makeup but in their curriculum. "Every child in America," argued Noah Webster, who assembled best-selling textbooks, in addition to his distinctly American dictionary, "should be acquainted with his own country. . . . He should lisp the praise of liberty."

This spirit thrived long after its compulsory period. One could see it in the subscription-based libraries sprouting up around the country. In 1790, America had about 150 libraries; by 1820, that number had quadrupled. These libraries featured tiny selections and volunteer staffs; they depended on local merchants agreeing to host the books in their shops, which led to irregular hours. But readers were thrilled to sign up. Hiram Harwood patronized several libraries in Vermont, and similar institutions were opening everywhere, even on the expanding frontier. In southern Ohio, one township voted to form a library in 1803. Many locals paid for their memberships by bringing in furs from animals they'd trapped, and once the township collected enough payments, it dispatched a leading resident

No. *190*

VILLAGE LIBRARY.

Beauties in vain their pretty eyes may roll;
Charms strike the sense, but merit wins the soul.

Libraries often marked their books with custom bookplates—as in this nineteenth-century example, from a library in Farmington, Connecticut.

in a wagon packed with furs, to make the long journey to Boston. There, he cashed in his cargo and spent $73.50 on fifty-one books, with the list weighted heavily toward history. A frontier library was born. Its youngest subscriber, a boy of thirteen, had turned in ten raccoon skins to join.

This blend of patriotism and curiosity popped up in the strangest corners of American culture. Periodicals were devoting a third of their pages to historical content. History buffs were hunting for autographs, with the top prize being a complete set of the fifty-six signers of the Declaration of Independence. ("I laugh at my own mania on this subject," a collector confessed, "but really I cannot get rid of it, and would not if I could.") Historical societies were forming—volunteer-driven organizations that foraged for obscure pamphlets, important documents, and caches of private papers. By 1840, America boasted more than thirty of these societies, with many of them producing small batches of their own magazines and books.

With this much archival energy, America's authors, printers, and booksellers needed only to harness it. No one did that better than Jared Sparks. Sparks was not a wealthy gentleman who dabbled in history as a side gig. He was a bastard, born to an unmarried couple in 1789. After stints as a carpenter and a schoolteacher, Sparks finally enrolled at Harvard at the age of twenty-two. Like most other colleges, Harvard specialized in religious topics and the classics, and Sparks seemed set for a career in the ministry. He became America's first famous historian instead, earning a reputation as someone who, in the words of an admiring Edgar Allan Poe, stayed "very busy among a great pile of books."

Poe was only partly right. Early historians needed a sense of adventure, and in the 1820s, Sparks ditched the office and trekked across America, sifting through private collections, meeting with local historical societies, and interviewing important sources. Eventually he returned to Harvard—this time as the first professor of secular history America had ever seen.

One of Sparks's great achievements was editing the Library of American Biography, a popular and wide-ranging series of twenty-five books. Readers loved learning about the personal lives of famous politicians. One South Carolina library owned seven American biographies in 1811; by 1835, that number had jumped to fifty-two.

The most frequent muse for early biographers was George Washington, with the most popular Washington title coming from none other than Mason Weems. A few weeks after Washington's death, in 1799, Weems wrote to his old partner, Mathew Carey, and the traveling salesman didn't even try to hide his excitement: "I've something to whisper in your lug.

Washington, you know, is gone! Millions are gaping to read something about him. I am very nearly primed and cocked for 'em." Weems confessed that he'd recently started working on a biography of Washington, but in a sense he'd been working on it even longer, using his wagon as a rolling focus group where he could interact with readers and discover what they wanted.

What they wanted was Washington's private side. Weems unloaded anecdote after anecdote, starting with the ex-president's childhood and almost always ending with some kind of lesson. There was the time, for instance, when Washington's father forced him to share an apple; the next year, God blessed the family with a terrific orchard haul. Weems based these parable-like stories on interviews with people who'd grown up alongside Washington. The apple one came from "an aged lady," and she supplied another one involving Washington, a cherry tree, and that famous phrase: "I can't tell a lie."

There was plenty to make readers skeptical, starting with the fact that this source's stories all seemed to discover moral truths in fruit trees. With the cherry tree, Weems did the winking himself. "The following anecdote," he wrote, "is too valuable to be lost, and too true to be doubted." But the biographer and his readers didn't seem too worried as long as the story humanized Washington—as long as it showed his private victories leading to his public ones. "It is not," Weems wrote, "in the glare of public but in the shade of private life that we are to look for the man."

Weems kept expanding and perfecting his book, and it became an unprecedented hit. If you combine the adaptations for textbooks, the Sunday school readers, and the cheap periodicals, Weems's Washington really did reach millions of nineteenth-century readers, and other authors were quick to copy his techniques, if not always his research methods. The list of presidential biographies expanded rapidly—and most of those books shared the goal, in the words of Jefferson's best early chronicler, of getting their subjects "down off the statesman's stilts . . . [to] see him as the every day man."

ONLY THE PUBLIC (AND ONLY IN PRIVATE)

Thomas Jefferson told anyone who asked that he would never write an autobiography. Requests arrived regularly—from a friend, for instance, who'd devoured Franklin's *Autobiography* and then written the ex-president in the hope that Americans would one day see "the same kind of work from yourself." As Jefferson explained to another correspondent, "Writing the history of my whole life . . . nothing could be more repugnant to my feelings." Yet he also saw the surge in historical interest and the need for books that would defend the Democratic-Republican agenda. He tried tempting would-be authors with access to his papers—"very voluminous, very full," he cooed to Madison—but they all let him down.

So Jefferson began organizing what is now called the *Anas*, three fat notebooks that contained materials from his years as secretary of state, including letters, memos, and catty notes from closed-door meetings. ("A.H. condemning Mr. A's writings," read one, "and most particularly 'Davila.' ") Like Adams, Jefferson understood that someday this material would reach the public, and he wrote a passive-aggressive preface to accompany it. "We are not to suppose," he told his future readers, "that everything found among Gen. Washington's papers is to be taken as gospel truth."

In 1821, Jefferson started another project to reinforce his legacy: the autobiography he swore he'd never write. Before long, four of America's first five presidents would try writing their life stories—quite a contrast to, say, the more reticent prime ministers of Britain. At just under a hundred pages, Jefferson's narrative was much shorter than Adams's, but it was every bit as hard on its author. Jefferson reviewed his correspondence and made notes to refresh his memory. He settled on an opening: "At the age of 77, I begin to make some memoranda and state some recollections of dates and facts concerning myself, for my own more ready reference and for the information of my family." Like Adams, he tried using his family as a shield.

Jefferson spent six months on his autobiography, off and on, and as predicted, it wore on him. Sometimes the work went well—more than a thousand words written on a Tuesday. By Wednesday, though, the author was back to annoyed. "I am already tired of talking about myself," he wrote midnarrative, and he eventually gave up while discussing the events of 1790, a decade short of his presidency.

Thankfully, Jefferson had already written the key sentence for understanding his legacy book. It came just after Virginia elected him governor: "Being now, as it were, identified with the Commonwealth itself, to write my own history during the two years of my administration would be to write the public history of that portion of the revolution." Jefferson directed his readers to *The History of Virginia*, a popular book on his state; other than that, he skipped his time as governor. He saw no distinction between "public history" and "my own history," or at least between "public history" and the history he was willing to share. It was the old wall between public and private, and outside of a few flickers of the familiar—a sentence on his wife's death, in which he called her "the cherished companion of my life"—Jefferson put very little of his personal life in the autobiography. His book sided not with Adams and his radical intimacy but with more conventional memoirs. Jefferson could tell long, behind-the-scenes stories, including his accounts of writing *A Summary View* and *Notes*. (The proud author even reproduced his own pre-"mutilation" draft of the Declaration.) But those stories always circled back to his civic role. He chose to focus on his public self and his published writings—and even then, he did so in secret, confident nothing would appear until after his death.

This same caution guided the presidential memoirs of Madison and Monroe, two Jefferson acolytes who followed him as America's fourth and fifth executives. Madison, as his contributions to the Constitution suggest, was a fine stylist. (Henry Clay ranked him as America's "first political writer.") He was also an excellent storyteller. In his retirement, he liked to spend mornings on the portico of Montpelier, his home, from which he could see the soft dark shapes of the Blue Ridge Mountains. There, as the sun slowly filled the sky, Madison would chat about books and politics and people. "He gave me the private history of many important transactions," recalled a visitor named James Kirke Paulding. "His small bright blue eyes would twinkle most wickedly when lighted up by some whimsical conception."

Paulding was a writer himself, and he'd been planning a history of the Revolutionary generation. In 1831, he asked Madison to compose a sketch of his life, something Paulding could build on in his own volume. It seemed like an easy request for a person with the ex-president's talents and interests. Montpelier featured the library of a true book lover, with four thousand volumes filling the shelves, covering the floor, and swallowing many pieces of furniture. Madison had written important essays and pamphlets and even pondered a book of his own—"a chronicle, or rather a history, of our present Constitution," as he put it back in 1804.* While Madison never wrote that book, he'd already finished a major work

---

*Madison also wrote poetry while a student at Princeton. Out of respect to the presidency, it will be confined to a footnote:

> When sleep had closed my slumbering eyes
> I spurned the earth and pierced the skies.
> Through unknown tracts of air I flew
> And passed by worlds of various hue.

in his journals from the Constitutional Convention, a work he continued to expand and revise in his retirement.

When it came to writing about his own life, though, Madison struggled. "I feel the awkwardness of attempting 'a sketch of the principal incidents of my life,'" he confessed to Paulding. The ex-president managed about fifteen pages in a stilted third person. His memoir went even skimpier than Jefferson's on the personal details, and while it technically reached Madison's presidency, it revealed little. Like Jefferson, Madison thought either that his private experiences weren't valuable or that they weren't anyone else's business. "The biography of an author must be a history of his writings," he wrote near the end of his text. "So must that of one whose whole life has in a manner been a public life be gathered from his official transactions and his manuscript papers on public subjects."

James Monroe spent most of his adult life as a soldier, a diplomat, and a statesman—one of America's first career politicians. He was a student at William and Mary when the Revolutionary War began, and soon he was fighting next to General Washington and wintering at Valley Forge. After the war, Monroe started his long political career. By the time he rose to president, in 1817, the country had changed in many ways. Men now sported shorter hairstyles and longer pants, but Monroe, the final founder, still opted for a powdered wig and breeches. He assembled a library of about three thousand volumes at his Virginia plantation; he cultivated a love, with Jefferson's encouragement, of French culture.

After his second term as president, Monroe needed money. All the time away from home—and all the expenses incurred as a diplomat—had left him nearly bankrupt. Monroe believed his country owed him compensation, something he stated in testimony before Congress and in a short pamphlet titled *The Memoir of James Monroe*. This pamphlet, which also ran in a Washington, DC, newspaper, wasn't a memoir in any real sense; it targeted Monroe's time as a diplomat and reprinted pages and pages of insider-y documents. But it succeeded, as Congress eventually gave the ex-president thirty thousand dollars.

In his retirement, Monroe continued to write, working on a book that, like Adams's *Defense*, would compare modern government to its predecessors in antiquity. Monroe called it *The People, the Sovereigns*, and once he finished a few pages, he showed them to a friend. "I think your time could have been better employed," the friend admitted. "A history of your life and times, written by yourself, would really be interesting."

Monroe seemed to agree. He abandoned his first book for his second, which would incorporate his previous *Memoir* while telling his full life story. He wrote nearly four hundred pages. "My pursuits at home are interesting," he told the marquis de Lafayette in 1829. "A review of past occurrences in which I have acted, and of which I have been a witness, occupies a large portion of my time."

Monroe knew his legacy book would reach "the public," and he even seemed open to that occurring "during my life." Still, his narrative stopped well short of his presidency. Like Madison, he stuck to the third person; like Jefferson, he concentrated on his public self. The best moments came from Monroe's time as a soldier in the Revolutionary War, especially his descriptions of the famous Christmas crossing of the Delaware River. "The night was tempestuous," Monroe wrote, "and made more severe by a heavy fall of snow." Monroe, still a teenager, volunteered to fight with a smaller unit that would cross ahead of Washington and the main army. The next morning, the unit encountered two enemy cannons—big brass guns that would maul the troops coming up behind. So the Americans charged, and when their captain went down, it was Monroe who stepped in to lead. The soldiers took the cannons, though Monroe was wounded critically. He carried the musket ball in his shoulder as an old man, working on his unfinished book.

JEFFERSON'S (SECOND) BEST SELLER

Jeremy Bentham seemed ready to go on a New World binge. The British philosopher had asked a friend to track down some American books he'd seen in a catalogue, including *The History of New Hampshire*. But Bentham wanted to know something about one of the titles, *Memoirs of the Honorable Thomas Jefferson*: "Is this self-written?"

It was not—*Memoirs* was yet another biography—but Bentham's question made sense. The same readers who were gobbling up all sorts of history were starting to prioritize something more specific: prose written by the founders themselves. Benjamin Franklin's *Autobiography* was becoming only more popular. The newest editions of the *Federalist Papers* broke their contents down by author, in the spirit of the note Hamilton had written before his duel. After years of not caring who wrote the Declaration, Americans were making extravagant Fourth of July toasts to Jefferson and "the hand that drew the Declaration." Authorship was emerging as a viable idea in America's culture, and that meant authorship was being discov-

By the time this photograph was taken, in 1857, the building where Jefferson had written the Declaration of Independence had become a tourist attraction. Note the decorative awning, which read "Birth Place of Liberty." The white vertical lines show the building's footprint in Jefferson's time.

ered in America's past. It wasn't just that people had started referring to the Pennsylvania State House in Philadelphia as "Independence Hall"—it was that they had started making pilgrimages to that city to see the house where Jefferson had written his famous document.

This enthusiasm peaked in 1829 with the publication of Jefferson's writings. For the first time, a president's private documents became public, in four fat volumes stuffed with history and gossip. It was a stunning success. "These volumes," promised one critic, "will prove to the American reader the most delicious literary treat that their own country has ever afforded." Yet the impetus behind it was neither literary nor patriotic. When it came to actually publishing legacy books and presidential prose, money mattered from the very start.

The first step toward publication, of course, was Jefferson's death, which occurred on the same day as John Adams's in 1826. Jefferson left behind a series of devastating debts, inflated by his diplomatic service, his poor financial instincts, and his desire to keep up appearances (and to keep buying books). The person tasked with fixing it was his grandson and executor, Thomas Jefferson Randolph. Jefferson had adored Randolph and helped raise him; he was the grandson who'd knocked on the door with news of Andrew Jackson and New Orleans. As an adult, Randolph shared his grandfather's height but not his face—Randolph's was rounder, rosier, more open. He wasn't as restless as Jefferson, but he was diligent and loyal and better with money. He would need each of those qualities to pull off the first edition of Jefferson's prose.

Randolph started out in Virginia, auctioning off his grandfather's furniture, farm equipment, and slaves. ("The negroes," the newspaper notice read, "are believed to be the most valuable for their number ever offered at one time in the state of Virginia.") None of it generated enough cash. The next plan was to rush out a stand-alone version of Jefferson's autobiography, something to capitalize on the overwhelming mix of grief and reverence that had greeted his and Adams's deaths. Randolph decided the autobiography should be a small and handy volume, like the ones Jefferson had preferred. He convinced Madison to read the manuscript and to write a preface, in which he praised its "perfect authenticity . . . all in the hand writing of [Jefferson]."

A mere four months after Jefferson's death, Randolph headed north to meet with potential printers. They couldn't reach a deal on the autobiography, in part because America's book trade couldn't guarantee the sale (or distribution) of enough copies to make a dent in Jefferson's debts. Madison grumbled about the printers' "backwardness" and urged Randolph to print his own edition, financed by subscriptions. They began to think bigger—not one but four volumes, filled with letters, state documents, and selections from the *Anas*, with the memoir as the centerpiece.

Randolph recruited his family members to help. He would serve as editor, selecting the volumes' contents, he explained, "almost exclusively with a view to promote their sale." The Jefferson women would handle the much harder task of producing legible copies of the original prose. Sometimes Randolph's sisters had to hold the faded documents up to the noonday sun just to read them; sometimes, when the ink had faded completely, they used a magnifying glass to examine the back of a page, where the pen marks still showed. In the words of Randolph's mother, it would be "treason" to "alter or add to the writings of Thomas Jefferson."

While the family labored over the prose, anticipation for the project began to grow. One of the most widely reprinted Jefferson eulogies had hinted that he'd written a "considerable memoir on his own life and times." The announcement of a four-volume edition created even more excitement; the ex-president's writings would, one newspaper believed, be "sought by every class of readers." Randolph made a second trip north, meeting with printers in Philadelphia and Boston. They again failed to agree to terms. Randolph decided to print six thousand sets in Charlottes-ville, in an old house where four presses operated on the first floor while compositors set the type on the second. Even at a price of ten dollars per set, Randolph sold five hundred subscriptions in Tennessee, a thousand in Alabama, fifteen hundred in Jefferson's beloved Virginia. There was national demand, even if there wasn't national distribution. When a frus-trated Philadelphian didn't subscribe fast enough, his bookseller told him the only way he'd get a copy was if one of the subscribers died before the volumes were finished.

On January 17, 1829, not quite three years after his grandfather's death, Randolph registered the copyright for *Memoir, Correspondence, and Miscellanies, from the Papers of Thomas Jefferson*. The first volume, which included the autobiography, went out that spring. There were some predictable criticisms, including the claim that it was too soon to reveal Jefferson's most intimate thoughts. The book, claimed one detractor, "exploded so near his grave that it only mutilated the monument."

Most readers, however, responded with elation. In fact, the four-volume set became one of the most widely discussed American titles to come out before the Civil War. People praised the prose, with the volumes frequently appearing in bookstore ads and library listings as simply *The Writings of Thomas Jefferson*. They praised the memoir. ("We are friendly to autobiography," one reviewer admitted, "and were glad to find this nar-rative of a considerable part of Mr. Jefferson's life from his own pen.") The edition marked the first time, outside of Franklin's *Autobiography*, that Americans could dig deep into the personal life and ideas of one of the founders—not through the mediation of biographers or historians but in the subject's own words.

Randolph's copies quickly sold out, at which point a Boston printer finally agreed to help, offering the family a considerable sum in order to bring out another edition. A New York edition soon followed, along with ones in London and Paris, where the volumes drew as much notice as Jefferson's *Notes* once had. (The *Westminster Review* proclaimed them "one of the most important publications ever presented to the world.") In America alone, the family sold more than nine thousand sets, a number that translates today into well over two hundred thousand sales. "It is a luxury," marveled one reviewer, "to be able to accompany a great man in the relaxation of his private hours, to be admitted under his roof when he is relieved from the cares of office."

Reactions like that oversold the edition, at least a bit. Randolph's editing had emphasized Jefferson's public side, with many of the buzziest selections coming from the *Anas*, a text that suggested Jefferson didn't mind private history as long as it centered on someone other than himself. Still, the volumes felt so thrilling and fresh that only the most careful readers registered any frustration.

One such reader was John Quincy Adams. During the first weeks of 1831, in a winter he called "unusually severe," Adams passed many hours in front of the fire, browsing and reflecting on the four volumes of Jefferson's prose. He started with the autobiography and, after his first night of reading, recorded his reactions in his diary. "There are no confessions," Adams complained. "Jefferson, by his own narrative, is always in the right. This is not uncommon to writers of their own lives. Dr. Franklin was more candid."

Adams finished the memoir on the second night, then returned to his diary to make another entry. He felt the autobiography had captured at least a piece of its author, a man he'd grown up around, a man in whom he saw both good and bad. Yet Adams also felt let down. His disappointment, he decided, stemmed from the story stopping in 1790, more than a decade before Jefferson's presidency. "There it ends," Adams wrote. "And there, as a work of much interest to the present and future ages, it should have begun."

FIRST IN THE HEARTS OF HIS READERS

Out of Jefferson's financial disaster emerged an international literary event—and an inspiration to other presidential editors. At Peacefield, Charles Francis Adams, John Quincy's son, began sifting through his family's enormous cache of papers. He would eventually assemble the *Works of John Adams*, with two of its ten volumes containing excerpts from the author's *Autobiography*. ("No one can doubt that Mr. Adams faithfully depicts himself in his autobiography," wrote one reviewer. "It is the original all over.") But Charles decided to start with Abigail, and in 1840 he published *Letters of Mrs. Adams, the Wife of John Adams*. The book sold so well that the printer started a second edition a few weeks later. While *Letters of John Adams, Addressed to His Wife* appeared the next year, it never could catch up to Abigail's book—the first of many instances where a first lady outsold her husband.

Meanwhile, at Montpelier, Dolley Madison faced an easier task in editing her husband's papers. He had arranged them meticulously before his death, especially his journal of the Constitutional Convention. The problems came from her son, an alcoholic and a gambling addict who started hawking the best documents in order to pay his creditors. With the government's help, Dolley was able to rescue most of the papers. She published them along with Madison's journal in a popular three-volume edition that, as one newspaper wrote, would appeal to "every lover of his country."

Yet the most sales, and the most intrigue, accompanied the founder who seemed the least bookish of all: Washington. In truth, Washington wrote all the time. He kept a diary, sometimes scribbling entries in the blank pages of his *Virginia Almanac*.* As a young soldier, serving in the buildup to the French and Indian War, he prepared a detailed report from the frontier; his superiors published it as a pamphlet, *The Journal of Major George Washington*. During the Revolutionary War, his speeches appeared constantly in newspapers on both sides of the Atlantic. Washington dealt with sack after sack of mail—"letters of compliment," he complained to one friend, "as unmeaning perhaps as they are troublesome, but which must be attended to."

Washington also knew how to delegate. Whatever the format, he maintained what's best described as a military style: clipped, concrete, active. Given his prose output—and given his tendency to take on demanding day jobs—he often enlisted aides to help him keep up. "They ought," he once wrote, "to possess the soul of the general; and, from a single idea given to them, to convey his meaning in the fullest and clearest manner." It was a fine definition of ghostwriting, though that exact term would not appear until well into the twentieth century, and Washington's aides showed remarkable skill at capturing his literary style.

One of those aides was a former schoolteacher (and current poet) named David Humphreys. In the summer of 1784, after the war had finally lurched to a close, he urged Washington to write his memoirs. "I have not leisure to devote my time and thoughts to commentaries," the busy general replied. He also added a second reason: "I am conscious of a defective education and want of capacity to fit me for such an undertaking." This was not mere modesty. While Washington loved reading

---

*Washington added poetry to his youthful diary, though biographers can't agree on whether he composed it or copied it from an unknown source. Either way, it also belongs in the footnotes:

Ah! Woe's me that I should love and conceal,
Long have I wished, but never dare reveal,
Even though severely love's pains I feel. . . .

Washington frequently used the blank pages in his almanac as a diary,
a common practice among colonial readers.

history and biography, he lacked the collegiate polish of a Madison or a
Jefferson.

When Humphreys offered to write the book himself, Washington
invited him to Mount Vernon, where the writer could consult his papers
and interview him at length. The general even reviewed an early draft
and gave Humphreys eleven pages of handwritten comments. Some were
minor corrections. (Humphreys said his subject went hunting once a
week; Washington admitted the true number might be a touch higher.)
Others were vivid bursts of narrative. ("They then, from every little rising tree, stump, stone, and bush, kept up a constant galling fire upon us.")
It's the closest Washington ever came to narrating his own life, and he
attached the following warning to his comments: "Earnestly requested,
that after Colonel Humphreys has extracted what he shall judge necessary,
and given it in his own language, that the whole of what is here contained
may be returned to George Washington, or committed to the flames."

This was an extreme version of the era's public-private unease—and
another instance of Washington's reluctant authorship. Humphreys failed

to destroy the pages. (He also failed to finish the book.) But Washington returned to his collaborative approach as president, though he upgraded his assistants. James Madison helped write Washington's First Inaugural, in 1789. Madison also wrote Congress's reply to the speech—and then ghostwrote the president's letter thanking them for it. Political insiders understood and respected Washington's reliance on others. "If I could persuade my friend Rush," Adams observed, "or perhaps my friend Jefferson, to write such a thing for me, I know not why I might not transcribe it, as Washington did so often. Borrowed eloquence, if it contains as good stuff, is as good as own eloquence."

Washington stuck with his method for his best-known speech, the Farewell Address. Technically, the address wasn't an address; it was an essay. In the spring of 1792, when the president was thinking about retiring after one term, Madison suggested he announce it in the newspapers himself—"a direct address to the people." Washington liked the idea, which would leverage the power of the occasion (and of his celebrity) to bolster his most cherished causes: upholding the Constitution, avoiding partisan squabbles, and maintaining national unity.

Madison went to work, writing a short draft that summer. With a few others, he also convinced Washington to stay for a second term. The president returned to the address in 1796, and this time he asked for Hamilton's help. Hamilton had resigned from Washington's cabinet the year before, to return to his life as a lawyer in New York, and it was there that Washington sent a copy of Madison's draft, along with new material that the president had written himself. Washington trusted Hamilton to choose between revising those texts and composing something new, but it was always clear who was in charge. "If you form one anew," the president insisted, it should follow "the sentiments contained in the enclosed paper." Washington even specified the tone: "a plain style."

Hamilton worked on the address during slow spells at his office, sometimes calling in his wife, Eliza, to listen to passages as he read them aloud. "You must be to me," he told her, "what Molière's old nurse was to him." He made a detailed outline, then completed a revision of the Madison-Washington material while also attempting his own original take. Washington, after some thought and a few tweaks of his own, chose Hamilton's version. All told, the two spent nearly four months getting the address right.

In the fall of 1796, Washington asked an editor named David Claypoole if he would print the address in his newspaper. Claypoole was honored, and he set the type from Washington's final copy, which the president had written out himself. When they finished, Claypoole asked if he could keep the manuscript—"a precious treasure," he called it. The president smiled and agreed.

The address became an instant classic, appearing in Claypoole's paper and then in virtually every other American outlet. From the start, it was extolled in literary language. A New Jersey paper praised "its illustrious author"; a Massachusetts paper promised its "sentiments will be written on our hearts." Readers sent Washington letter after letter, telling him how moved they were by his prose and by his willingness to step down. A young man in Baltimore—a student at Washington College, which had been named after the president—admitted the address had made him weep. "May God," the student wrote, "when you die receive you in His blessed mansion. But yet I pray that He may prolong your life to give advice to those that fill your place."

The address grew only more popular after Washington was gone. Each year on Washington's birthday—a national holiday that would eventually evolve into Presidents Day—the address was read aloud by schoolchildren and US senators alike. Savvy printers sold it as a pamphlet. Mason Weems appended it to his biography—"the last letter," he murmured, "of a once-loved father now in his grave." Washington was becoming more famous in death than he'd ever been in life. Yet Americans were celebrating him for something he'd never claimed for himself: the intimacy of authorship. And that's where the trouble began.

While the nation was venerating Washington and his address, Hamilton never forgot his own contribution. One night, while strolling down Broadway, he'd bought one of those pamphlet editions from a Revolutionary War veteran. "That man does not know he has asked me to purchase my own work," Hamilton said to Eliza. Still, he never took steps to disclose that role, as he'd done with the *Federalist Papers* and his pre-duel note.

After her husband's death in 1804, Eliza dedicated herself to revealing the true author of the address. The origins of the pro-Hamilton whispers remain fuzzy, as with rumors they often do, but soon enough the idea that Hamilton wrote the speech was everywhere in elite circles: discussed during house calls, gossiped about after dinner, muttered between puffs of pipe smoke. Eliza and her supporters recruited a series of biographers to dig for the real story. They also pushed the rumors, which ricocheted from New York to Philadelphia to Boston. It didn't take much pushing. "Fondness for revealing secrets," grumbled a Washington supporter, "is one reason for its circulation buzzingly."

Eventually the uproar reached the other founders. Madison seemed confused. "It was never understood," he wrote to Jefferson, "that Washington valued himself on his writing talent." At the same time, insiders like Madison and John Jay didn't want to tell the whole story because they didn't want to diminish Washington's character or causes. What Hamilton's supporters needed was proof.

That proof existed: the outline, the drafts, and the letters, all in Hamilton's hand. The problem was that those documents belonged to Nathaniel Pendleton. Pendleton was a close friend of the Hamiltons—so close, in fact, that he'd served as Alexander's second at the duel with Burr. Now he was one of the dead man's executors. Pendleton was also a supporter of Washington, and the rumors about the address worried him. "If I had it in [Hamilton's] handwriting," another Washington ally admitted, "I would burn it." Pendleton couldn't go that far. But in 1810 he gathered the most important documents, bundled them up, and sealed them shut with wax.

Pendleton gave the bundle to Rufus King, another friend of the Hamiltons who was friendlier still to Washington's legacy. Perhaps Pendleton feared Eliza would target him since he was an executor; at the very least, he urged King to keep the documents from "falling into the hands of [Hamilton's] family."

King kept the bundle safe, which meant the scandal continued to simmer behind the scenes. It boiled over a few years later. One day, James Hamilton, one of Eliza's adult children, ran into Pendleton on a steamboat. For reasons that remain unclear, the aging man confessed that documents in Hamilton's handwriting did exist and that he'd given them to King. (Pendleton died soon after.) The news delighted Eliza, who'd finally located proof for her explosive claim. She begged James to track King down, and in the spring of 1825, he went to King's house in New York. James acted casually at first, but as soon as the two were alone, he told King he knew about the bundle and asked for it to be returned to the family. King declined to discuss it, saying only that he and his heirs would never hand anything over.

Eliza was determined. A few days later, another of her adult children, John Hamilton, dropped by King's home—and quickly it became clear that the family had settled on a good son–bad son strategy. When John finally left, King drafted a furious letter to James that accused the Hamiltons of trying "to menace me in my own house."

King still refused to release the bundle, so the Hamiltons decided to menace him in court. The family sued for the documents, which catapulted the issue into the public record. Newspapers around the country began covering the controversy feverishly; they dubbed it "the Hamilton papers."

Journalists analyzed the address's sentiments and style to prove it was indisputably Washington's. One magazine did a story on the old printer, Claypoole, and his treasured manuscript, though it withheld Claypoole's name to protect him from getting sucked into the growing scandal. Almost everyone denounced the Hamiltons. "It is a vile impeachment of the integrity of our political father," wrote one critic, "to suppose that he would ever have claimed the credit of the address, had he not been the author of it."

The drama stemmed partly from a desire to keep Washington a hero, an image that now included the role of heroic author. It stemmed partly from a fear that the address might lose, in Madison's words, "the charm of the name subscribed to it." It stemmed partly from the fact that many Americans did not grasp the complex realities of ghostwriting. At a time when authorship itself was an evolving concept—something one could see by looking at the contents page in two different editions of the *Federalist Papers*, published only a few years apart—it made sense that ghostwriting was not yet fully intelligible, either.

Clarity seemed possible once the experts arrived. In 1826, the Historical Society of Pennsylvania, one of the country's most prominent such societies, formed a special committee to investigate the address. They conducted interviews and examined documents, but they never bothered to contact a single Hamilton. In the end, the society succumbed to the power of Washington's memory, issuing a report that depicted Hamilton as a mere secretary who'd copied the address to save the president some time.

The society's report effectively ended the "Hamilton papers" uproar. Given the cover provided by the report and the still-pending lawsuit, King gave the bundle to the family. After years of searching and being publicly shamed, they broke the seal and thumbed through the documents. The bundle didn't prove Hamilton was the sole author—nor did it prove he wasn't. Instead, it hinted at a complex partnership and suggested more answers might exist in Washington's papers. As it happened, the president's heirs were about to start working with the famous historian Jared Sparks on a Jefferson-like edition of Washington's prose. But Sparks and the Hamiltons couldn't agree on how to share their documents, and when the twelve-volume *Writings of George Washington* began appearing, in 1834, Sparks still downplayed Hamilton's role.

The Washington edition sold more than six thousand pricey sets—plus another nineteen thousand stand-alone copies of the biography Sparks had written to go with it. Throughout the nineteenth century, Washington's name sold a staggering number of books: short biographies, long biographies,

biographies aimed at women, biographies aimed at children, and that's to say nothing of the many Washington-themed novels and poems and plays. The market for First-in-the-Hearts lit grew so heated that even Washington's grandson, a child so fat and lazy his grandfather had nicknamed him "Washtub," managed to cash in by writing a few essays about his celebrated relation.

In 1859, Horace Binney added one more Washington book to the pile: *An Inquiry into the Formation of Washington's Farewell Address*. Binney, a retired congressman, had finally convinced both the Washingtons and the Hamiltons to grant access to their papers. In his widely discussed book, Binney detailed the real drama behind the speech, a drama with two leading actors. The Farewell Address, he wrote, "speaks the very mind of Washington." And yet it was just as true that Hamilton was its "composer and writer." Thanks in part to Binney's work, Americans began to understand the process and value of ghostwriting—the way a president could authorize a document without authoring it.

Of course, there were those who chose not to understand. The belief that Washington wrote the Farewell Address—and the belief that suggesting otherwise was treasonous—persisted across many decades and in countless examples. Here's a presidential one. In 1906, when Woodrow Wilson was still an academic, he delivered a lecture on Washington's birthday. The topic: "George Washington as Ideal American Citizen." Wilson spoke to a crowd of about five hundred, and one of his texts was the Farewell Address. While explicating it, Wilson couldn't resist adding a cheeky aside: ". . . which he did not write."

Six years later, when Wilson was a Democratic candidate for president, a newspaper decided to attack him for being snobby and sneering. "A majority of citizens revere the memory of Washington," the paper noted. But not Wilson, an elitist who looked down on America's first president, and on anyone patriotic enough to call him a great man. As evidence, the paper resurrected Wilson's old aside: "He goes so far as to deny that Washington even wrote his own Farewell Address."

The idea of Washington-the-author would not die. It had been more than a century since Hamilton had helped Washington assemble his speech—and more than fifty years since Horace Binney had shown just how that help had worked. But "I can't use a ghost" had become as durable a myth as "I can't tell a lie," and many readers had decided they liked the myth just fine. They finally had the private story, but all it did was make them realize they preferred the public one instead.

PART II

JOHN QUINCY ADAMS
TO
ULYSSES S. GRANT

CHAPTER FOUR

The Poet, the President
Who Couldn't Spell, and
the Campaign Biography

Like most college students, Nathaniel Hawthorne needed to write home more often. It was the spring of 1821, and Hawthorne would soon enroll at Bowdoin, a tiny college in Maine. He was already on his own, preparing with a tutor, and his mother was asking for updates. "I have not yet concluded what profession I shall have," the seventeen-year-old finally wrote. It was a common problem for bright students; in his auto-biography, John Adams recalled fretting about whether to "study divinity, law, or physic." Now, in his letter, Hawthorne cycled through those same options, and one could already see glimmers of his mature style—dark, dry, self-deprecating. Hawthorne ruled out minister right away. ("I should not think," he teased his mother, "that even you could desire me to choose so dull a way of life.") There was such a glut of lawyers that half of them, he calculated, "are in a state of actual starvation." Doctors, for their part, made a living on the suffering of others.

As Hawthorne continued, it became clear he was warming his mother up for a more daring suggestion. "What do you think," he wrote, "of my becoming an author, and relying for support upon my pen?"

The 1820s was the first time an American could ask this question some-what seriously. During that decade, American literature began to emerge as a discrete and vibrant category. "American author" began to sound like a plausible part-time career. While the country continued to grow rapidly, the number of readers grew more rapidly still, and those readers sought out not just British novels and American histories but all sorts of native books. A few of America's most popular writers became famous, and their fans developed intimate attachments. ("I feel as if I knew you," one wrote to the novelist Susan Warner, "and you were my personal friend.") A few

85

of them even produced the nation's first literary classics, including novels like *The Scarlet Letter*, where Hawthorne showed that the life of a minister could be anything but dull.

The 1820s also saw an enormous shift in America's democratic process. General elections began to change—from the founders' deliberately detached system, where many states let their legislatures chose the electoral delegates, to one where voters could choose those delegates directly. Only 108,000 Americans voted in the presidential election of 1820, as James Monroe sauntered to his second term. In 1824, when Andrew Jackson challenged John Quincy Adams, that number tripled. When Jackson and Adams clashed again in 1828, more than a million Americans cast a vote.

To reach that many people, candidates needed new forms of campaigning—or, to use the era's more skeptical term, of *electioneering*. Having those candidates write books might seem like an obvious answer. What politician, after all, could resist a chance to emulate authors like Susan Warner and become a reader's "personal friend"? But most contenders remained anxious about picking up their pens or electioneering in public. "Candidates for president," argued Martin Van Buren, "ought not to say one word on the subject of the election. Washington, Jefferson, and Madison were silent as the grave when they were before the American people for this office."

The campaign biography provided the perfect solution. In a campaign biography, the writer could devote several hundred pages to rehearsing the life and résumé of the desired candidate, all while maintaining a buffer between the candidate and the book itself. It didn't matter that the candidates frequently handpicked their writers and fed them facts, or that their supporters frequently bought and circulated the books. The genre slipped just enough cover between the politician and the book—and in that way shaped elections through the Civil War and beyond, with a fresh batch of biographies appearing every four years and in the most popular cases selling tens of thousands of copies.

The campaign biography did something more. It created space for a new style of politics, one that prioritized personalities and narratives over policies and ideas. A good campaign biography didn't merely recount a life—it attempted to spin one. These books transformed their subjects into a series of symbols, plot points, and signs of "character": the humble start, the self-made success, the outsider with a desire to clean up Washington. Those clichés, of course, guide America's politics to this day. But there is one twist in the story of the campaign biography, and it involves the protagonist. The first candidate to harness this genre wasn't someone like John Quincy Adams, a bookish man who flirted more lustily with an authorial career than any previous president. Instead, it was his opponent and his opposite: the hot-blooded, undereducated, rabble-pleasing (and yet remarkably savvy) General Andrew Jackson.

FERTILE LITERARY SOIL

Before authors like Hawthorne could truly thrive—and before politicians like Jackson could leverage their talents in secret—America needed to confront Europe and its stubborn prejudices. Thanks to books like Jefferson's *Notes on the State of Virginia*, those prejudices had shifted. It was no longer trendy to criticize the New World's climate or its inferior citizenry. Instead, Europeans pointed to its absentee culture. In 1820, the year before Hawthorne enrolled at Bowdoin, a British writer gloated about this deficiency in the pages of the *Edinburgh Review*. America had its founders, the writer conceded, but they were "born and bred subjects of the King of England." As an independent nation, it had offered no history, no tradition, no inspiration for the artist working today. "In the four quarters of the globe," he wrote, "who reads an American book?"

That question was political as much as literary, and America's authors tried to answer it. They got help from people like Mathew Carey. While Carey's bookstore had started as one small room, carrying sundries as well as books, he now welcomed readers into a four-story building on a prominent street corner, a Philadelphia landmark that also housed his healthy wholesale operation. Carey had started organizing book fairs where printers and booksellers from around the country could swap inventory and form partnerships. These meetings hadn't solved the puzzle of national distribution, a puzzle that grew more intricate with each new territory and state. But they did encourage a new class of literary operatives: book publishers, or entrepreneurs who, instead of relying on authors or subscribers to prepay for books, were financing it themselves. In the first part of the nineteenth century, Carey's firm became the most powerful publisher in America.

The key figure in this rise wasn't Mathew but his son, Henry. Henry Carey had worked at his father's fairs since he was eight years old. (Charmed customers had dubbed him "the bookseller in miniature.") Now at full size, Henry tried to tweak the family business. Where Mathew had preferred semisafe bets like the Bible or British reprints, Henry wanted to

Mathew and Henry
Carey's upgraded
bookstore emerged as a
Philadelphia landmark.

take risks. "There is nothing on earth worse than an old stock of books," he explained to his father. So he proposed a different model: more novels, more new titles, and, most of all, more books written by Americans.

Some of Carey's countrymen still saw novels as a vice. (One treatise, *On Diseases Peculiar to Women*, warned that promiscuously reading fiction would "hasten the development of the nervous system and the phenomena of puberty.") But more and more of them were devouring novels—especially the novels of Scotland's literary superstar, Sir Walter Scott. America and Europe still hadn't forged an international copyright, and that meant any American publisher could pirate any of Scott's novels at any time. Speed was the only way to stand out, so the Careys hired a London insider to help them get the latest copies of Scott's work. One of their competitors countered by dispatching a rowboat to intercept its own Scott-laden ship before it docked, with the rowboat then rushing the pages to crews of typesetters and printers. When that novel went on sale, not even twenty-four hours after the ship had crossed into American waters, readers crushed against each other as they tried to enter the winning store.

A wave of Scott imitators soon followed. No one expected the best of them to hail from America. Washington Irving was a wealthy New Yorker with a roundish face and inquisitive gray eyes, and he spent his twenties experimenting in the pages of American magazines and newspapers. After the War of 1812, he moved to Britain to try saving his family's mercantile business. He also continued to write, and when the business finally failed a few years later, he was ready to release *The Sketch Book of Geoffrey Crayon*, a multipart collection that included "The Legend of Sleepy Hollow" and other stories. Irving knew what he was up against as an American crafting original fiction about his home.* But *The Sketch Book* became a huge hit in America—and, even better, in Britain. "Everywhere I find in it the marks of a mind of the utmost elegance and refinement," admitted one London author, "a thing, as you know, that I was not exactly prepared to look for in an American."

Washington Irving became one of America's first renowned writers, which made him the perfect person for Henry Carey's fiction-driven plan. Henry recruited Irving and other promising Americans like James Fenimore Cooper, and the Careys published Cooper's *Last of the Mohicans* in 1826. Mathew, now in his sixties, would stop by the store and cluck about the changes. (Cooper's novel, he fretted, "will not prove a good speculation.") But Henry was right. *The Last of the Mohicans* became a big hit, and with the Careys leading the way, America's publishers started investing in novels written by their countrymen. In the 1820s, they published 128 such titles—more than had appeared in the country's first fifty years combined.

The number of homegrown novels doubled again in the 1830s, and American literature was off, at least in its biggest cities. There were more readers than ever, with the country's population topping 17 million in 1840. Many Americans now attended school until they were twelve or thirteen. Others resembled a future president, Andrew Johnson. He was born in North Carolina to poor, illiterate parents and apprenticed with a local tailor instead of getting an education. Tailors often paid someone to read aloud as they sat cross-legged in their shops, working their needles and thread, and Johnson found himself enchanted, listening to the poems, the stories, and especially the famous speeches like Washington's Farewell Address. Johnson began teaching himself to read and write, contributing to a literacy rate that, even for white Southerners like himself, now approached 90 percent.

A bigger audience meant room for different kinds of books. British imports still sold briskly, with foreign authors growing so frustrated

---

*"Rip Van Winkle," another story in Irving's *Sketch Book*, toyed with the theme of America's allegedly stunted culture. When Rip fell asleep, the sign at his village inn featured "a rubicund portrait of his Majesty George the Third." When Rip woke up twenty years later, the artwork had been altered in the least imaginative way: someone had hastily painted a tricorn hat over the king's crown and changed his coat from red to blue. At least there was a new title at the bottom of the portrait: "General Washington."

by the lack of progress on copyright legislation that they made plans to bribe the administration of James K. Polk. (Charles Dickens, who'd supplanted Scott as America's favorite author, agreed to contribute a hundred pounds to this scheme.) But American authors were thriving too. During this period, a whole syllabus's worth of important figures got their start: Emerson, Thoreau, Alcott, Poe. Many of them announced their desire to write books that were startling, original, and uniquely American. "If I feel physically as if the top of my head were taken off," Emily Dickinson wrote, "I know that is poetry." There were also books that left the reader's head comfortably intact—books like the so-called sentimental novels, which gained power from their predictability. These novels usually starred troubled young girls who, through a series of sympathy-stoking disasters, grew into moral and mature (and, ideally, married) young women.

Both kinds of author, the literary and the sentimental, could now earn an unprecedented level of fame. A clever businessman launched "The Game of Authors," a "Go Fish"–like diversion in which the cards featured images of writers like Washington Irving. By this point, Irving had returned to America and settled in as a senior man of letters. His imposing New York home, Sunnyside, served as the nation's second most famous residence, trailing only Washington's Mount Vernon. Irving hated it when tourists clipped ivy off his stone walls as a souvenir. Fans, however, could be more invasive. After finishing Walt Whitman's *Leaves of Grass*, one female reader sent him a letter that described the emotional power of reading it, of "an affinite soul blending harmoniously with mine." She was just getting started. "Know, Walt Whitman, that thou hast a child for me!" the fan wrote. "My womb is clean and pure. It is ready for thy child, my love." It was enough to scandalize even Whitman, who wrote "insane asylum?" on the letter.

While America's authors had become more visible than ever before, their profession remained unstable. Consider the actual career of Nathaniel Hawthorne, whose catalogue of fiction—what he sometimes called his "romances"—did as much as anyone's to kill the old query from the *Edinburgh Review*. When *The Scarlet Letter* appeared in Britain, a reader reported that it was "producing a greater sensation than any book since *Jane Eyre*." Who reads an American book? The answer, it seemed, was everyone. Yet Hawthorne's writing never made him rich, and he frequently relied on government jobs to support his family. It galled him to watch the latest sentimental novel outsell *The Scarlet Letter* by a factor of nine to one. "America," he wrote to his publisher, "is now wholly given over to a damned mob of scribbling women." Hawthorne knew his coun-

In *Little Women*, Jo March made a suggestion to her guests: "Let's have a sensible game of Authors to refresh our minds."

try had produced plenty of serious female authors, from Mercy Otis Warren to Margaret Fuller, but he wanted to whine. "I should have no chance of success," he wrote, "while the public taste is occupied with their trash."

Instead of sniveling, though, Hawthorne should have considered writing his own predictable, manipulative, and wildly popular book. In other words, he should have written a campaign biography.

THE POET-PRESIDENT

There were more opportunities than ever in America's increasingly democratic politics, even for its authors. As a young man, Washington Irving campaigned for the Federalists in New York's local elections. "I talked handbill-fashion with the demagogues," he wrote to a friend, "and I shook hands with the mob." Irving spent three days on the trail. "Truly," he concluded, "this saving one's country is a nauseous piece of business."

Whether the country was being saved or ruined depended on your politics, but either way the activity usually occurred on a local scale. In the first part of the nineteenth century, there were no organized national parties, no raucous conventions where partisans chose their presidential nominee. Instead, in busy cities and barely settled counties, one could find torchlight marches, barbecues drenched in free booze, and stump speeches made not by candidates but by charismatic citizens like Irving. No one knew this process better than John Quincy Adams, who spent his entire life in the muck of American politics. And yet Adams, with his sober and chilly temperament, could never quite embrace electioneering. He didn't want to be a candidate; he wanted to be a statesman. More than that, he wanted to be a poet.

Adams was born in 1767 and raised in a literary household, a place where his parents, John and Abigail, could debate their favorite passages from *Paradise Lost*. At the age of ten, John Quincy decided to tackle Milton's epic for himself. "I was mortified," he later wrote, "even to the shedding of solitary tears, that I could not even conceive what it was that my father and mother admired so much in that book." Adams was too ashamed to ask for his parents' help, so he tried a strategy he'd been using with another strange adult pleasure: cigars. Again and again, he smoked and read Milton until a taste for tobacco finally stuck, though an appreciation for *Paradise Lost* would elude him for many more years.

This bright but serious child tried forcing himself to appreciate Shakespeare as well, plowing guiltily through *As You Like It* and *King Lear*. Only *The Tempest* grabbed him. Perhaps it appealed to his sense of adventure. As a child, he also began accompanying his father on long diplomatic missions to Europe. John made time to nurture his son's talents. "Honored Mama," John Quincy wrote to Abigail, "my papa enjoins it upon me to keep a journal." The boy fretted about lacking the diligence to sustain a diary, about filling it with "my childish nonsense." But a few months after his twelfth birthday, John Quincy Adams opened a small volume and wrote on its first page, "A Journal By Me JQA." He would keep his diary, faithfully and revealingly, for the next sixty-eight years.

In 1785, after seven years abroad, John Quincy returned to America, went to Harvard, and became a lawyer. From his father, he had inherited stoutness, shortness, and, soon enough, baldness, though he attempted to combat the first of these through frequent walks. But there was an important difference between the two men: where John lived to lash out, John Quincy tried to stay calm and self-aware. One can see this difference in their writings—or in their public writings, at least, for John Quincy's anger and joy both seeped into the pages of his diary. After John wrote his *Defense of the Constitutions of Government of the United States of America*, and after his critics started smearing him as a monarchist, John Quincy defended his father in print under the pseudonym "Publicola." Most readers assumed this was actually John Adams defending himself, but Madison knew better. The author, he told Jefferson, had to be the son. "Publicola" wrote with a cleaner style and firmer sense of structure than the elder Adams had ever managed.

John Quincy became a political figure himself in 1794, when President Washington appointed him America's diplomat to the Netherlands. Adams, just twenty-six, viewed it as a temporary profession. He had already decided that practicing law was a solid way to support a family, but not much more. Even politics felt dull. What he wanted to do was read and write poetry—especially original, American poetry. Books had switched from duty to infatuation, and Adams now dreamed of doing something Hawthorne and Irving would not accomplish until decades later. "The Americans have in Europe a sad reputation on the article of literature," he wrote to his father, "and I shall purpose to render a service to my country by devoting to it the remainder of my life."

Adams was destined to serve in other ways. Over the next twenty years, he worked as a diplomat to Prussia and Russia and Britain, with stints as a state and US senator tucked in between; he married Louisa Catherine Johnson, who shared his transatlantic background and taste for serious books. Through all of it, Adams never stopped thinking about literature. He didn't stick to translating the classics and writing political essays, though he did both of those things. Adams also engaged in his era's biggest literary debates. In one essay, he considered the perennial question of whether authors should aim for pleasure or didacticism. The most successful writers, he believed, aimed for both. "Very few persons," he wrote, "can submit to the toil of reading for mere instruction."* In another essay—a lecture, technically, which Adams wrote after being asked to teach at Harvard—he

---

*Adams called this essay "Of Reading," though a better title would have been "Of Writing"—or, best of all, "A Father's Influence." John had encouraged his son to read widely and to start a diary, of course, but in his own writing, he'd struggled with confusing and exhausting readers. Now, in his essay, John Quincy considered the problem of writers who forget to keep their audience in mind. His real subject became clearer once he zeroed in on the *Monthly Review*, the same publication whose brutal review of his father's *Defense* had kept his mother up at night. "Note down the works of genuine merit upon which it has passed the censure of prejudice," John Quincy wrote of the *Review*. His point was that critics also fail their readers, but in this essay, it's just as easy to see a son grappling with his father's uneven books.

championed the pursuit of originality. Literature, he argued, should aspire "not merely to the praise of finding, but to the glory of creating."

These literary detours looped back, inevitably, to the desire that Adams had articulated to his father and that he continued to wrestle with in his diary: becoming a celebrated American poet. John Quincy Adams was always working on a poem. He wrote them on Sundays, during the preacher's sermons; he wrote them while sitting for a painter's portrait; he wrote them in his head while taking his long walks. The results were not always scholarly. Consider his bawdy and degrading ballad that alluded to Jefferson and Sally Hemings:

> Let dusky Sally henceforth bear
> The name of Isabella;
> And let the mountain, all of salt,
> Be christened Monticella.

Adams's larger goal, however, remained contributing to a new national literature—though with each year that goal seemed more likely to disappear under the demands of his political career.

While sitting for this portrait, which was finished in 1816, Adams wrote poetry to pass the time.

One such demand was that his poems appear anonymously, and not just the ones that meditated on the sex lives of presidents. "There is no small number of very worthy citizens," he explained to his brother, Thomas Adams, "irrevocably convinced that it is impossible to be at once a man of business and a man of rhyme."

How odd, then, that these fraternal letters led to John Quincy's first book. In 1800, he took advantage of a break in his diplomatic schedule and traveled to Silesia, an obscure province in central Europe. He'd planned to write Thomas quick missives from the road, but the correspondence consumed him. For one of the few times in his adult life, John Quincy let his diary lapse, putting all his energy into the letters—more than forty in total, a sunny but dense blend of history, geography, and present-tense observation. Together, the letters added up to a superb piece of travel writing, and Thomas convinced a Philadelphia magazine to publish them anonymously. But then a British printer gathered them into a book, *Letters from Silesia*, and put John Quincy and his famous last name on the cover; French and German editions soon followed. The whole thing surprised the author. He was happy to see the letters get a warm reception, happy they might make a small dent in America's literary trade deficit. But it was not the grand and poetic debut he'd spent so many years imagining. "If heaven should grant me life," he wrote to his wife, Louisa, "I hope at some future day to offer something of more value."

Adams's obstacle wasn't health but time. His political rise continued, and in 1817 James Monroe appointed him secretary of state. Adams excelled in the role, though he still found ways to squeeze in some literary activity, including the writing of a long and exuberant report on the metric system. ("Thank God," Louisa wrote when the report was finished, "we hear no more of weights and measures.") His success suggested an even busier role might loom in his future. After all, secretaries of state had a way of becoming presidents. Adams understood his flaws, in part because he'd spent so much time describing and probing them in his diary. "I am a man of reserved, cold, austere, and forbidding manners," he wrote in one piercing entry. "With a knowledge of the actual defect in my character, I have not the pliability to reform it." But he also believed his decades of service made a powerful and traditional case for a second Adams presidency. Nothing else needed to be said.

The problem was that many other Americans were starting to see politics differently. They had started speculating about the next president before Monroe began his second term, and while the craziest campaigning would

still happen locally—in states like Pennsylvania, which looked like a crucial battleground in 1824—there was room for candidates and their close
allies to work behind the scenes: by writing letters, providing information
to refute attacks, or carefully projecting an image of cagey enthusiasm.

Adams declined to do any of this. It demoralized some of his supporters and irritated others. Joseph Hopkinson, a powerful Pennsylvanian,
wrote to Louisa and begged her to help. "My dear madam," Hopkinson
wrote, "this won't do. The Macbeth policy—'If chance will make me king,
why chance may crown me'—will not answer where little is left to chance
or merit." Louisa agreed, showing the letter to her husband and urging him to be more active. By this point in his life, however, Adams had
become a supple reader of Shakespeare, Milton, and all the rest. He pulled
out his diary and began drafting a reply. "You say he never would have
been king?" Adams wrote of Macbeth. "True. And of course no tragedy."

OUTSOURCING THE CAMPAIGN BOOK

Andrew Jackson seemed more comfortable with the Macbeth skill set—
excellent general, ruthless murderer (well, "winning duelist"), and, ultimately, powerful ruler. It was one of many contrasts between him and
Adams. No one encouraged young Andrew to keep a diary. Instead, he
was an orphan at fourteen; his earliest surviving letter, which he wrote at
twenty-one, challenged another man to a duel. Details like this reinforce
the image of Jackson as an impulsive and illiterate frontier rascal, an image
his enemies appealed to constantly during his presidential campaigns. But
the truth is more complex. At several points during his rise, Jackson relied
on bookish tools to achieve his goals or brace his legacy. His greatest success was *The Life of Andrew Jackson*, a biography he authorized and then
carefully oversaw. It was an odd and draining process, as the book generated a body count to rival most Shakespearean tragedies. Yet Jackson
refused to give up because, more than most nineteenth-century politicians, he realized the power of literary persuasion.

Jackson was born in 1767, the same year as Adams, somewhere on
the border between North and South Carolina. His father died before
he was born, leaving his mother to raise him and his two older brothers. She managed to send Andrew to school for a few years, hoping he
might become a minister. When the Revolutionary War hit the Carolinas,
though, their precarious life turned impossible. Both the Tories and the

patriots engaged in brutal backwoods warfare, with colonist fighting colonist while British soldiers looted people's homes. At the age of thirteen, Jackson joined the Continental Army as a courier—then watched as one brother died, followed by the other, followed finally by his mother.

Once the war ended, Jackson bounced around the South, playing cards, racing horses, and causing trouble. For a while, he worked as a teacher; the thought of Jackson's classroom management strategies staggers the mind. He eventually decided to become a lawyer, and in 1788 he migrated to the frontier town of Nashville. Jackson fell in love with Rachel Donelson Robards, a woman technically (though unhappily) married to another man, and she and Jackson lived together for several years before she finalized the divorce. When a fellow Tennessean made a crack about Rachel's purity, among other insults, Jackson demanded a duel. Jackson let his opponent fire first, absorbing a bullet that shattered his ribs and stopped inches from his heart. Jackson then collected himself and killed the man with his first shot. "I should have hit him," he said defiantly, "if he had shot me through the brain."

Jackson's critics might have drawn a different lesson from that line, but the general was showing signs of settling down. He bought a plantation in Tennessee, the Hermitage, then expanded it to include a thousand acres and more than a hundred slaves. He became a notable son of the South, serving briefly as a US representative and US senator and more durably as a prosecutor and judge. Jackson was never a regular reader of books outside of practical or religious titles. And yet in his care for his children's education, one can see he grasped their value. "Tell my son how anxious I am that he may read and learn his book," Jackson wrote to Rachel. "Tell him that his happiness through life depends upon his procuring an education now."

Jackson's most important accomplishments before his presidency came on the battlefield. He served in the Tennessee militia and the US Army, fighting viciously against both British soldiers and Native Americans in the War of 1812. It was this latter conflict, and particularly the Battle of New Orleans, that made Jackson a national star. When he pulled off his stunning victory at the Crescent City, in January of 1815, neither side knew the war had already ended with the Treaty of Ghent. It was an example of how slowly news still circulated: although America's lead negotiator, John Quincy Adams, had signed the treaty on December 24, word of it did not reach Washington until February, about the same time the city heard of Jackson's triumph at New Orleans.

Regardless, the battle elevated Jackson to the rank of hero. During his long journey back to the Hermitage, in the spring of 1815, grateful citizens greeted him at various stops. They clamored for even a glimpse of the general—his long frame and longer face, his unnerving blue eyes, his thick white bristle of hair. "He is everywhere hailed as the savior of his country," noted John Reid, a handsome Virginian who'd served as Jackson's aide-de-camp. "Women, children, and old men line the road to look at him as they would at the elephant." Jackson had become the most talked-about man in America and done it so quickly that most of his countrymen still knew little about him. Even basic questions, like where he'd been born, could generate gossip. Had it been in England? Or was it Ireland? Maybe it was here, in one of the Carolinas, but which one?

A solid claim to natural-born citizenship would soon be essential to the general's goals. Even as he was traveling home, Jackson's supporters were strategizing about an authorized biography. The project made sense on several levels. The book might "find its way into Europe," as one of his colonels hoped, "[and] thus greatly increase the respectability of the American character throughout the civilized world." It would allow Jackson to shape his story, a key concern at a time when Americans were already mythologizing frontier figures like Daniel Boone. Finally, a book would help that story continue to spread, for Jackson and his supporters believed that he was, in the words of that same colonel, "destined to fill a still higher station in the dignity of the republic."

Jackson remained deeply and shrewdly involved with his book in a way that his previous biographers have overlooked. In fact, the initial plan called for him to do some of the writing himself. Perhaps he intended to write the whole thing, though the political dangers of this would have been obvious to all. Perhaps he intended to fashion a sketch the biographer might follow. Either way, Jackson started with New Orleans, spitting out forty-five handwritten pages on the battle, mostly in the third person. In his best letters and speeches, Jackson's writing resembled Washington's—sentences that galloped, ideas that overlapped, all of them churning toward some confident point. But in this format, and at this length, Jackson flailed. He captured some wonderful details: the slog of swamp warfare, the logic behind the Americans ransacking their own city for supplies, the look his men gave him before their goriest engagement—"cheerfulness," he wrote, "seen in all faces, with a determination to defend their line or bravely perish." Yet Jackson failed to render his own emotions, and in places his narrative became so jumbled it seemed almost stream of consciousness. Even today, the text reads like the trickiest parts of Faulkner or Woolf, and it requires just as much interpretation.

When Jackson finished the section on New Orleans, he quit. "It is certainly the most unpleasant task," he wrote to a friend, "for a man to become his own biographer." His allies quickly secured the perfect collaborator in Dr. David Ramsay. Ramsay, a South Carolinian, was one of the period's more talented part-time historians, a man who balanced his Charleston medical practice with the production of nonfiction tomes, including a biography of Washington and a history of his home state. This new project promised Ramsay his best material yet—not just Jackson's rowdy life story but access to his personal papers, which were crammed into several messy chests, plus interviews with his subordinates and even the general himself. Jackson, in short, was offering full cooperation, though that also meant full supervision.

Ramsay agreed to the terms, and by April he was compiling a list of topics for the book. Jackson, freed from the peril of generating more prose, put his time into other book-related tasks—organizing a network to sell subscriptions to the volume, securing an artist to make an engraving of him for its frontispiece, and courting potential publishers. Jackson wrote several letters to the country's best publisher, Mathew Carey. "Subscriptions to a very large amount have already been obtained," the general noted. "Various offers have been made." But Jackson was clearly angling for one more offer. "The work should issue to the world under the best auspices," he added—and eventually Carey did agree to publish the biography, in an ambitious edition of twenty-five hundred copies.

Late that spring, disaster struck. Once, in his role as doctor, Ramsay had served as an expert witness, testifying at a trial that the accused was insane. That man was now free, and on the morning of May 6, on one of Charleston's busiest streets, he shot Ramsay in the back. The doctor died two days later.

Suddenly the book needed a new author, and Jackson and his circle considered a number of options. They settled on John Reid, Jackson's old aide-de-camp. While Reid lacked Ramsay's experience—this would be his first book—he'd ghostwritten letters and reports for the general and organized many of his papers. Reid relocated to the Hermitage and went to work, with Jackson correcting his mistakes and pointing him to additional sources. The book was only growing in significance. By the fall, the general was receiving letters that urged him to run for president, letters that relayed enthusiastic endorsements from Ohio and Pennsylvania, Virginia and Kentucky. He never responded to these endorsements since even acknowledging them would open him to charges of vanity. In January 1816, though, Jackson wrote Reid a note that hinted at the stakes. "I need not say to you my anxiety for your success in your book," Jackson wrote. "There are many weighty reasons that create this anxiety."

That same month, Reid visited his family in Virginia. One morning, he woke up feeling a bit ill; eighteen hours later, he was dead. When Jackson heard the news, he was heartbroken—he'd lost a soldier and a friend, someone who left behind a pregnant wife and two small children. "The book must be finished for their benefit," Jackson told another supporter, and he seemed sincere in this desire. Yet it was also true that the book was transforming, however haltingly, into the first campaign biography. Jackson understood that it mattered to his future plans, and that meant a third search for an author.

The general decided on John Henry Eaton, a dark-haired Tennessean who would soon turn twenty-six but looked at least ten years younger. Eaton made his own move to the Hermitage, where he perused the general's papers and interviewed him at length. (One of last things his mother told him, Jackson confided, was basically *calm down*.) Eaton wrote seven more chapters to go with the four Reid had finished, and Jackson almost certainly reviewed every one of them. In the spring of 1817—the same year Mathew Carey promoted his son, Henry, to partner—Eaton traveled to Philadelphia with the manuscript. He kept Jackson updated on the paper quality, the typeface, and the edits that Carey suggested ("highly serviceable," Eaton admitted). Once he and Carey were happy with the chapters, they went to the printers. The book, finally, was finished.

The Life of Andrew Jackson should have been a fiasco, given its grisly development. And yet, thanks in large part to Jackson's own efforts, it turned out to be a solid nineteenth-century biography. The book sold well and drew admiring reviews, especially in the South. Both Eaton and Reid were competent stylists, and their subject's story offered many thrilling (and flattering) moments. The most memorable one came from his youth, when the colonies were at war. After some British soldiers captured Jackson, an officer told him to get down and wipe the mud off his boots. Jackson, barely a teenager, shot back that he was a prisoner of war and expected to be treated as such. The officer drew his sword and hacked at the boy—"a blow," his biographers wrote, "which would, very probably, have terminated his existence, had he not parried its effects by throwing up his left hand." Even with the parry, Jackson received a deep gash in his forehead, and he bore that scar for the rest of his life.

Stories like this one—the boy who wouldn't clean boots—proved surprisingly important when Jackson ran for president in 1824. Electioneering was changing. While previous races had featured character attacks and newspaper articles that summed up a candidate's life, they'd featured far more discussions of things like foreign policy. In 1824, though, the major candidates all ran as Democratic-Republicans. There were more voters than ever, and those two factors steered the election toward the superficial and the symbolic. In fact, there were times when the race seemed no deeper than this popular slogan:

John Quincy Adams
Who can write
Andrew Jackson
Who can fight

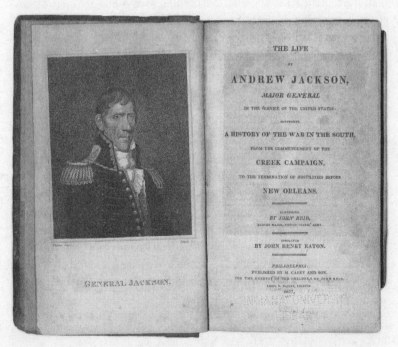

The 1817 edition of Jackson's *Life*—the one published by Mathew Carey—featured a portrait of the famous general as its frontispiece.

The irony, of course, was that Jackson was the one with a powerful book behind him. In the months before the election, and with the general's blessing, Eaton undertook a new edition of *Life*, making changes on nearly every page and transforming a positive book into an absurdly positive one. Jackson's teenaged capture became even more dramatic. ("To escape was impossible . . .") His flaws—his molten temper, say—transformed into strengths.*

The revised *Life*, printed on cheap paper and aimed at a wide audience, sold even faster than the first. Of course, in 1824, a book could sell only so fast. But the biography made an enormous impact. It was abridged and distributed in various pamphlet-sized editions; it also emerged as the go-to source for Jackson propagandists. The best example—and the election's most important piece of campaign literature—was a series of essays that ran in newspapers under the pseudonym "Wyoming." Wyoming was none other than John Eaton, and in one essay, he retold the story that his book had already made famous, the tale of the muddy boots. This time, Eaton added a Weems-like flourish: "Early dawnings often times evince the future character of the man." According to Wyoming, America's government and elites had been corrupted. The country needed a bold outsider, someone "directly from the people"—someone like Andrew Jackson. Who needed to know his views on a national bank when he'd stared down the British at fourteen?

John Quincy Adams declined to do any campaigning, though he did cooperate on a brief campaign biography, adapted from his own prose. Years before, he'd composed a first-person sketch for a historian; his supporters reworked it in the third person and distributed it widely, to counter the onslaught of Jacksonian prose. Adams asked his father, the family's autobiographical expert, to edit it. John cut the most self-serving elements—phrases like "my motives of conduct are pure and disinterested"—and in the end they created a dignified but dull document.

While Jackson was more active in private, he let his backers and his book carry the public message. The ideological overlaps between him and Adams—and their other main challengers, William Crawford and Henry Clay—ensured that the campaign frequently devolved into debates about

---

*It didn't take long for readers to realize that campaign biographies were partisan and exaggerated books. "I read the *Life of Andrew Jackson*," one Massachusetts man wrote in his diary, "and should have liked it better had the author told the whole story." But many of those same readers saw perusing these biographies—and, by extension, becoming better informed voters—as a democratic duty.

personality and character. Jackson's supporters slammed Adams for being intellectual and aloof, just like a previous generation had done with Jefferson. Between America's literary standing and Jackson's frontier roots, the opposite tack could also work, and Adams's supporters blasted Jackson for his ignorance. One pamphlet connected the general to the old question of who read American books. What, the pamphlet wondered, will "the *Edinburgh* and *Quarterly* reviewers, who have hitherto defamed even the best writings of our countrymen, say of a people who want a man to govern them who cannot spell more than about one word in four?"

In the end, Jackson won both the popular and electoral vote, but since none of the four contenders had secured a majority, the House of Representatives chose the next president. Adams and Clay both worked to defeat Jackson, a move that was almost immediately mythologized as the "corrupt bargain," though it can also be seen as Adams finally willing himself to do some electioneering. Either way, it got him the White House—and guaranteed that the next campaign would commence immediately. Like the rematch between Jefferson and John Adams, in 1800, the election of 1828 was nastier and noisier than its original incarnation. Jackson visited New Orleans on the anniversary of his great victory, a clever stunt that earned coverage in virtually every American newspaper. ("Pompous pageantry," John Quincy sniffed in his diary.) Before long, both sides were launching vicious attacks. Allies of Adams dredged up the complex marital status of Rachel, Jackson's wife. Allies of Jackson hit back with the revelation that Adams had spent taxpayer dollars on a White House billiard table. Things grew so petty that in an attempt to stoke further controversy, one congressman took the House floor and read Adams's old poem about Jefferson and Sally Hemings aloud.

It felt like a modern campaign, and it was fueled by a modern campaign book. During the development of *The Life of Andrew Jackson*, the general had sat for interviews, reviewed text, written a long memo, and remained obsessively in control—had done everything, in short, that many twenty-first-century candidates do when they "write" campaign books of their own. The biography had proven its worth, reaching readers through direct sales and parasitic pamphlets, and Jackson and Eaton agreed to bring it back in 1828. As he revised the third edition, Eaton decided to omit any material about the previous campaign—because, he told another supporter, readers might sense a "presidential motive." In the age of Jackson, presidential motives remained as dangerous as authorial ones. But the campaign biography let politicians leverage their nation's expanding literary talents in secret. This misdirection made everything else work, including the latest edition of Jackson's *Life*. "Country merchants," Eaton predicted, "will buy and scatter them every where and thus spread amongst the people the true character of Jackson."

LEARNING TO LOVE THE LOG CABIN

On March 4, 1829, Andrew Jackson took the presidential oath in Washington, DC. The capital had continued to expand, with its population passing thirty thousand people; impressive buildings now lined parts of Pennsylvania Avenue. Still, the city couldn't handle the crowds that arrived for the inauguration. While previous ceremonies had largely limited their audiences to congressmen and other officials, Jackson opened his to the people. He delivered the address outdoors, on the eastern side of the Capitol building, and so many Americans came to hear him that the cost of hotels, firewood, and food all tripled. By some estimates, the number of visitors exceeded the number of residents. Certainly the visitors were easy to spot—"walking arm in arm," one local noted, "gazing on all around them with the vacant stare of undisguised curiosity and wonder."

John Quincy Adams skipped the inauguration. He retreated to Peacefield, his family's estate, to the same study where his father had sulked at the start of his ex-presidency. The son added some bookshelves since he owned twice as many volumes as his father, but they couldn't soothe his spirits. "No such library exists in the hands of any other individual in the United States," he wrote in his diary. "But I have never had the enjoyment of it; nor can I expect to have it now." So he tried to find comfort in the same source his father had: authorship. John Quincy went to work in that study, writing so much that his grandchildren would later remember him as having a permanent ink stain on his right hand. He began working on a biography of John Adams, sifting through his father's records, his letters, even the manuscript of his autobiography. For whatever reason, John Quincy couldn't stick with the project. Louisa, his wife, grew so exasperated that she wrote her housemate a letter imploring him to focus. Adams wrote "good advice" on the back of it, but he finished only a couple chapters of the book.

In 1830, Adams found a new distraction when the citizens of Massachusetts asked him to run for Congress. While Adams told them he would not campaign, he won anyway and began a second life in the House of Representatives. He also continued to write. Back in Washington, he attempted a more pleasant project—a book-length poem set in medieval Ireland and starring a historical figure named Dermot MacMorrogh. On his morning walks, which sometimes passed Jackson's White House, Adams would compose the latest stanzas. In his hands, MacMorrogh became a fierce and irrational tyrant who steals another man's wife. In case someone (somehow) missed the subtext, Adams added this aside: "Such things have happened both before and since."

The poem appeared in 1832 and sold about two thousand copies—not bad for a poet, though not great for an ex-president. But Adams had enjoyed writing it, even if it didn't put an end to those diary passages where he reflected on his dreams of being a national poet. "Could I have carved out my own fortunes," he wrote in one such passage, "to literature would my whole life have been devoted. I have been a lawyer for bread and a statesman at the call of my country. . . . But the summit of my ambition would have been by some great work of literature to have done honor to my age and country." What Adams seemed to miss is that he did complete such a work, a few pages at a time. His diary would ultimately fill fifty-one volumes, providing not a dusty log of dates and names but a portrait of Adams as a father, a son, a reader, and a president—a great work of literature in his or any other American age.

In the White House, Andrew Jackson expanded executive power to an astonishing degree. Having won a new kind of campaign, he declared himself a new kind of president—one who spoke for the people and would act aggressively on their behalf. He vetoed more bills than all of his predecessors had, combined. He became the fiery leader of a new political party, the Democrats. He made his legislative priorities clear and then agitated for them, most notoriously in the Indian Removal Act of 1830, a brutal policy that culminated years later in the Trail of Tears.

These changes earned the president plenty of enemies in Washington, and one congressman planned a speech in which he would denounce the famous boot-cleaning anecdote as a fictionalized "electioneering story." When an adviser relayed the news, Jackson's old temper erupted. "That damned infernal scoundrel," he bellowed, before he started pulling at his hair. After locating the scar, he turned to his adviser and pointed: "Put your finger here."

Jackson, through his policies and his persona, reimagined the presidency, making it more active, more partisan, and more powerful. When Herman Melville decided to invoke the "great democratic God" in *Moby*

Dick, there was no question which of His children to cite: "Thou who didst pick up Andrew Jackson from the pebbles; who didst hurl him upon a war-horse; who didst thunder him higher than a throne!"

The presidents who came after Jackson rarely required much thunder. Instead, they chose to maintain or even diminish their office's executive power. Where they did expand on Jackson's legacy was his use of campaign biographies and superficial symbolism. The general's chosen successor, Martin Van Buren, won the presidency in 1836, then ran for reelection in 1840. The Whigs, the party that had emerged opposite the Democrats, ran William Henry Harrison, an elderly ex-general who'd spent years on the frontier. Democrats mocked Harrison as a withered mascot—a candidate who would probably be happier, one journalist joked, passing "the remainder of his days in his log cabin."

The Whigs responded with quick and choreographed outrage, decrying the out-of-touch Democrats and praising Harrison's connection to cabin-dwelling commoners. It was nonsense. (Harrison hailed from a prominent Virginia family and lived in a mansion.) But it worked. All around the country, Whigs began building log cabin floats, singing log cabin songs, and drinking whiskey out of log cabin–shaped bottles. Harrison embraced his new status as an everyman, becoming the first major candidate to hit the trail and deliver partisan speeches of his own. On the stump he wore a simple coat and a straw hat—looking, in the words of one credulous observer, like "a plain old farmer, just what he is."

Harrison won easily, showing that Jackson's style could apply to any party and nearly any candidate. He also borrowed Jackson's medium. During the election, Harrison's allies churned out more than twenty discrete campaign biographies and worked frantically to circulate them. In Illinois, a young Whig named Abraham Lincoln wrote to one of his friends at the capital: "Be sure to send me as many copies of the life of Harrison as you can spare." These books hit the usual highlights—Harrison was honest, patriotic, industrious, devout. They strained to compare him to the founders, with one author designating him the "Father of the Northwestern Territory," if not quite the Father of the Country. No one seemed too worried about the dissonance between being a powerful regional figure and a log cabin icon. The life of Andrew Jackson—and, just as much, *The Life of Andrew Jackson*—had taught future candidates how to run.

Over the next few decades, the campaign biography grew into a powerful and mandatory genre. Party officials at the state and county level bought each year's crop at bulk discounts. The biographies were sold in

In 1840, Harrison's supporters created many kinds of log cabin literature, including this lithograph that doubled as sheet music for a pro-Harrison song. Harrison stood in front of the cabin, shaking hands with a crippled veteran.

the streets of big cities; in pamphlets and newspapers, "Wyoming"-style writers synthesized the books' big themes. It was easy to see this tradition cynically. ("As soon as a man is nominated for the presidency," the *New York Times* noted, "three different biographies of him are immediately announced as being almost ready for publication.") But it also appealed to the American aspiration to learn, reason, and grow. "The campaign biography," observed a proud essayist, "does not form part of the election machinery of any other republic than this."

The genre began attracting better authors, including the historian George Bancroft, who wrote a campaign biography for Martin Van Buren, and the novelist Lew Wallace, who wrote one for Benjamin Harrison, the grandson of William Henry. "He did so well on *Ben-hur*," a Harrison booster noted, "that we can trust him with *Ben-him*."

In the end, even Nathaniel Hawthorne gave the genre a try. At Bowdoin, he'd befriended a fellow student named Franklin Pierce. Decades later, in 1852, Pierce became the Democratic candidate for president, and Hawthorne reached out to his old classmate and offered to write "the necessary biography." Once Pierce accepted, Hawthorne set aside his romances and started plotting how to portray the candidate—"a statesman in your proper life," he wrote to Pierce, "a gallant soldier in the hour of your country's need." The author turned to research and interviews, where he kept bumping into the stubborn contours of Pierce's life, with its privileged start and mediocre middle.

It wasn't much to work with, but this was the challenge Hawthorne had volunteered for, the challenge of campaign biographers everywhere, and he kept going. Pierce may have been born in a "mansion," the author wrote, but that mansion sat on the same land where his father had originally built smaller—had erected "a log hut," in fact. In each period of Pierce's life, Hawthorne tried to interpret, spin, and sell. He even managed to include Andrew Jackson, the patron saint for this sort of politics, in a deathbed scene, dubiously sourced, where the ailing general proclaimed that with Pierce, "the interests of the country would be safe." Writing a campaign biography, even for a professional like Hawthorne, took a long summer of work, but he did it. The book became a best seller, and Pierce became president. "The story is true," Hawthorne told a friend. "Yet it took a romancer to do it."

CHAPTER FIVE

"Abram" Lincoln Writes a Book

O ran Follett had spent several exhausting days aboard a train, with its crowded cars, its shrieking whistles, and its streams of smoke and soot. As he disembarked at the depot in Washington, DC, Follett could see that things weren't getting easier. When the depot had first opened a decade earlier, it seemed roomy and elegant and offered a nice view of the Capitol building. Now, in the fall of 1862, it just seemed chaotic. Everywhere you turned, there were passengers, pickpockets, giant piles of coal, and regiment after regiment of tired, blue-clad soldiers. Thanks to the Civil War, the number of freight cars rolling into the capital had spiked from eight per day to four hundred or more. There, in the middle of it all, stood Oran Follett. He was a stern-looking man, even by nineteenth-century standards, with a large head and large ears and a height of six-foot-three—nearly as tall as the president, the man he would soon meet.

Abraham Lincoln met with all sorts of citizens. Sometimes it seemed that he did little else. He listened to angry abolitionists, to Southern wives begging for their husbands' freedom, to authors like Hawthorne and Melville. ("Old Abe is much better looking than I expected," Melville observed. "He shook hands like a good fellow—working hard at it like a man sawing wood.") Follett was also a literary professional, running a small but successful publishing firm in Columbus, Ohio. But when he arrived at the White House, early on the morning of his third day in town, he found he would have to wait. The bloody battle of Antietam still haunted the city; a different kind of conflict loomed in the next week's many midterm elections. Just before lunch, Follett finally entered the president's cluttered office. Lincoln normally greeted visitors with a kind but direct "What can I do for you?" When he saw the publisher, though, he lit up. *I remember you*, Lincoln said. *Well, you ought to*, Follett boomed back, *given that our firm made you president!*

Lincoln could only smile at the confident publisher. Other people were always taking credit for his improbable rise. Before he became a famous novelist, William Dean Howells wrote a campaign biography of Lincoln; years later, he told Mark Twain, "You know I wrote the *Life of Lincoln* which elected him." There was more truth to Follett's claim. In the spring of 1860, his firm had published *Political Debates Between Hon. Abraham Lincoln and Hon. Stephen A. Douglas*, which reproduced the transcripts of the two men's famous debates. The book took more than a year to pull together. At the start of that process, few Americans saw Lincoln as a candidate for president; in the middle, they still considered him a mysterious figure, someone journalists kept referring to as "Abram"; by the end, they were ready to make him the Republican nominee. In the months before the general election, *Political Debates* sold an astonishing fifty thousand books—more than half a million copies, adjusted for today's population. Follett was right: in many ways, the book did make Lincoln president.

Follett got help from two key sources. The first was technology. The Industrial Revolution defined the nineteenth century, and that held for books as much as any other consumer good. By the time *Political Debates* appeared, steam engines weren't just powering locomotives; they were powering printing presses. Between 1820 and 1850, the publishing industry grew by 400 percent, and it really was becoming an industry, capable of producing national best sellers like *Uncle Tom's Cabin* by Harriet Beecher Stowe. When the novelist made her own visit to the White House, Lincoln reportedly said, "Is this the little woman who made the great war?" The 1850s was the first time that a book could reach enough readers to start a war—or win a presidency.

The second source of help was Lincoln himself. In fact, by any reasonable definition of the term, Lincoln was the author of *Political Debates*. It wasn't just that the book contained more than one hundred thousand of his words. Long before Follett (or anyone else) saw the project's potential, Lincoln was working by himself, gathering its materials and imagining its structure. It's a long and twisting story that the president's many biographers have missed. But Lincoln invented a new kind of campaign book— one in which the candidate oversaw not the work of a friendly biographer but the collection of his own prose.

That Lincoln achieved this should come as no surprise. When the president told Stowe that she and her book had started a war, he wasn't just giving her a compliment; he was revealing something about how he saw the world. Lincoln tended to think not of words or even speeches but of printed texts. Books, to him, meant power—the power to push a poor boy past his flat midwestern horizons or to present one's ideas directly to the American people. That's why Lincoln labored, unnoticed and alone, on *Political Debates*. That's why, when it came to his book, he became as anxious, as involved, and, ultimately, as proud as Stowe or Melville or any other great American author.

GOD WORKS IN INDUSTRIAL WAYS

In 1854, America's leading historian, George Bancroft, delivered a lecture celebrating his era's inventions and miracles and machines—"a half century," he said, "unequaled in its discoveries." Those discoveries often automated what had once been done by hand. In the book trade, for instance, craftsmen no longer set each line of type or made each piece of paper; machines completed those tasks with brisk efficiency. These changes didn't solve every problem of distribution or cost. (In southern Indiana, where Lincoln grew up, only one in five people owned a single book.) But they did transform the lives of many readers and writers. Like so much else in America's literary history, these innovations started in Europe, then crossed the Atlantic in the service of the highly capitalized devout. By this route, they amplified the printing press, which, to someone like Lincoln, was still the most important technology of all.

The key book in this was that faithful best seller, the Bible. In the first part of the nineteenth century, local groups known as Bible societies began purchasing the Good Book in bulk, then doling it out to their cities' poorest residents. In 1812, the members of the Philadelphia Bible Society tried something better: importing a set of stereotyped plates from Britain and printing the Bibles themselves. Stereotyping, in addition to birthing a metaphor still used today, let publishers print each full page with its own custom-made metal plate, no typesetting necessary. Europeans had spent a long time perfecting this technique. (In Paris, Jefferson had asked for a quote on printing his private run of *Notes* via stereotype—another clue that he was always imagining a larger audience.) Even now, stereotyping required an enormous investment, but that led to enormous gains in efficiency. A similar shift hit papermaking a few years later. The best method, which hailed from France, relied on a long, assembly line–like belt. After two Americans did some tweaking, they built their own version at a Connecticut paper mill, and industrial papermaking took off.

One of that mill's biggest clients was the American Bible Society. The ABS, which started in 1816, was itself a European knockoff. (The British and Foreign Bible Society, est. 1804.) From its base in New York City, the ABS cultivated a network of hundreds of "auxiliaries," or volunteer groups, in cities and towns all over the country. The auxiliaries bought ABS Bibles at a discount, then figured out how to distribute them throughout their regions. The ABS and its donors, which included some of this period's major capitalists, handled the manufacturing. After a Boston inventor spent time in London, studying the newest steam-powered presses, the ABS asked him to install some presses of his own design. By 1829, the organization was employing sixteen of these steam-powered devices, along with twenty of the older, arm-powered variety.

That same year, the ABS made a shocking announcement: over the next two years, they would put a Bible in every single one of America's 3 million households. This was less an act of ambition than of sheer imagination. In a country that didn't have national brands or even national political parties, the ABS wanted to make a national book—wanted to place identical copies of that book in the hands of the American walking

This nineteenth-century engraving depicts one of Harper & Brothers' many steam presses, which were powered by a basement boiler. Such presses were often fed by women, another new development in this period.

past their Manhattan offices *and* the American surviving on the fringes of the Western frontier. "The Most High is prompting his servants," the society argued. And while they didn't reach their goal, they still printed a million Bibles between 1829 and 1831, a number that seemed all the more impressive when compared to the output of secular publishers. After all, Harper & Brothers, which had replaced the Careys as America's leading literary firm, didn't acquire its first steam-powered press until 1833.

Commercial and celestial publishers both struggled to distribute books, especially on the frontier. Many pioneers chose not to bring a single volume with them, a choice that stemmed in part from simple, sensible priorities. Moving one's family to a dangerous and unfamiliar territory meant standing in front of a wagon and deciding what to pack. The question was less *What can I live without?* than *What will I need to stay alive?* Even after settling down, though, pioneers often showed little interest in books. The subscription library in Ohio, funded by furs, was an exception. The frontier remained a rough and untrusting place, with elements of violence, drunkenness, and superstition. Sometimes agents sent by the ABS would report that a rural church had rejected their offer of Bibles, believing it represented some kind of coastal scam.

The ABS persisted, pulling off gradual victories. A good example came in Princeton, Indiana, the seat of Gibson County, which sat one county over from the one where the Lincolns lived. Like many frontier towns, Princeton presented a mix of log cabins and frame houses, along with a tavern, a hotel, a wool mill, and a couple of general stores. In 1831, as part of the ABS's omni-household push, an agent came to ask for help in getting Bibles to "every destitute family in the south end of this state." After raising the money, ordering the Bibles, and identifying the families, the people of Princeton still had to deliver the books. In another Indiana county, a man on horseback handed out eleven Bibles one day and nine the next. This was seen as a blessed result.

The same challenges applied to secular books. Princeton's biggest general store operated in one of the town's rare brick buildings, under a sign with handsome gold lettering: "Robert Stockwell, Merchant." There, you could buy medicine, clothes, farm equipment, even panes of glass if you were wealthy enough to consider windows. At Stockwell's, you could also browse a tiny selection of books—mostly religious or practical titles, followed by a smattering of history and biography and a few novels or volumes of poetry. In the American interior, even cities lagged in their literary offerings. Indianapolis didn't get a stand-alone bookstore until 1833; once it opened, it offered some newer fiction like Washington Irving, Charles Dickens, and Mary Shelley's *Frankenstein*, but those books generally appeared a year or two after they'd hit bookstores in Philadelphia and New York.

What changed this, however haltingly, was transportation. In fact, transportation changed everything in the nineteenth century. It started with more and better roads, with canals and steamboats to chug through them. Then the locomotive arrived. In *The House of the Seven Gables*, Hawthorne described the psychology of riding the rails, of watching a once-static landscape whip by: "Everything was unfixed from its age-long rest." By 1860, America was latticed with more than thirty thousand miles of track. Trains didn't just create a new way to move books; they created a new place to read books. Before there was airport lit, there was railroad lit, and one clever publisher sold "Putnam's Railway Classics" in stalls at various depots, always in a handy pocket size.

The other thing that boosted book sales was falling prices. As stereotyping and steam-powered presses spread, the cost of the average book dropped by half. While a laborer still needed a full day's pay to buy a single volume, the upper and middle classes could now afford more books. All across the country, the residences of lawyers and doctors began to feature the same new room: a library.*

By the 1850s, America had a system that could produce and circulate certain books quickly and affordably—or, at least, could do so when compared to what had existed only a few years before. The system still couldn't launch a national best seller, not by itself. It needed a catalyst, something one could see in the reaction between slavery and Harriet Beecher Stowe.

---

*One residence that added a library was the White House. When Millard Fillmore moved in following Zachary Taylor's death in 1850, he found the president's home to be stark and dreary. (In one upstairs room, the carpet had turned brown from all the tobacco juice.) It didn't help that there were no books. While previous presidents had typically brought their own books from home, Taylor was not much of a reader. So Fillmore and his wife, Abigail, convinced Congress to devote $2,250 to stocking a standing White House library. The Fillmores remodeled that upstairs room, ripping out the carpet and adding beautiful mahogany bookshelves. The first couple also helped choose the books, and when the work was finished, Millard and Abigail (and their successors) could admire those new shelves, which held copies of many of the titles already discussed in this book: the multivolume edition of Jefferson's prose, edited by his grandson; the one of Washington's, edited by Jared Sparks; the one of John Adams's that contained long chunks from his autobiography; and *The Life of Andrew Jackson*, among others.

Slavery, of course, had become America's chief concern—politically, culturally, even historically. A far more malignant way to measure the legacy of Jefferson's *Notes on the State of Virginia* was to watch it inspire a national debate over the physical and mental inferiority of slaves. Abolitionists liked to cite the book's warnings about the evils of slavery. But they were countered by the Southerners who quoted Jefferson's demeaning descriptions. "Mr. Jefferson's remarks respecting us have sunk deep into the hearts of millions of the whites," wrote an African American named David Walker. *Notes*, he believed, had become "as great a barrier to our emancipation as any thing that has ever been advanced against us."

After the Fugitive Slave Law passed in 1850, Stowe decided to contribute a book of her own. Her sister-in-law had urged her to "write something that would make this whole nation feel what an accursed thing slavery is." The key word was *feel*, as Stowe lifted the techniques of the sentimental novel, crafting a story that balanced tense realism with wrenching pathos. Her controversial subject led at least one publisher to turn her down. Stowe ended up selling her book to a smaller firm in Boston, a firm that shared her beliefs though it rarely published fiction.

The novel appeared on March 20, 1852, and in abolitionist circles, it became an immediate hit. "Reader, buy *Uncle Tom's Cabin*," urged one newspaper. "Go after it, send for it by mail, send some way, any way, only get it." Soon the book reached all sorts of audiences, selling so many copies that Stowe's publisher had to hire extra help to print it. Three different paper mills churned out paper; three steam-powered presses worked around the clock. But these technologies meant that even a small publisher could meet the frenzied national demand. In San Francisco, where a gold rush continued to boom, miners paid a quarter to rent the novel; in Alabama, the citizens of Mobile ran a bookseller out of town for carrying it. By the end of its first year, *Uncle Tom's Cabin* had sold more than 300,000 copies—a feat not just of book selling but of book manufacturing and book distributing.

It was the best sign yet that America now boasted a powerful literary industry. It also suggested that industry was itself something like a steam engine. It came with plenty of complex parts: the boiler, the pipes, the fuel. Still, to get started, it needed an external flame, something to light that initial fire. Slavery certainly provided that flame, in the case of Stowe. And it would ignite many more fires to come.

A STUBBORN READER

Michael Floy rarely read novels. It wasn't that he disliked reading. In fact, all Floy did was read. He was the sort of person whose afternoon walks always seemed to end at one of New York City's dozens of bookstores—who, on train rides, would try to sneak a glimpse at the covers of other passengers' books. But Floy felt fiction didn't offer the same practical pay-off as nonfiction. "I find so many books daily published that are of real use," he wrote in his diary, "that all my leisure time is not sufficient for reading even them."

Floy lived in Manhattan, in a comfortable house with his family; their flower shop occupied the first floor. He was also an unyielding Methodist, and one October Sunday in 1833, he sketched out a new plan in his diary. It had been a dreary, rainy day, and Floy had already gone to church twice (and sang in the choir both times). Now, back at home, slowly drying out, slowly warming up, he decided to narrow his reading further. "I intend," he wrote, "to confine myself to reading biographies."

For the rest of the fall and much of the winter, that's exactly what he did, losing himself in the lives of George Washington and Napoleon Bonaparte and a host of famous preachers. It was a wonderful time to be an urban, middle-class reader. Books had become more accessible, and as an adult, Floy bought forty or fifty each year. Bookstores had become more inviting, with their latest volumes displayed in street-facing windows and their helpful clerks waiting inside. Thanks to newly affordable gadgets—a pair of eyeglasses, an oil lamp—you could read later and read longer.* You could say things like *I want to read nothing but nonfiction* or *I want to read nothing but biographies*. "I keep no money in my pocket very long," Floy confessed in his diary. "For when I see a book that takes my fancy, have it I must."

Abraham Lincoln was born in 1809, a year after Floy, but they lived in completely different worlds. Lincoln grew up, first in Kentucky, then in Indiana, without access to the books or education one might find in New

---

*Of course, every technology takes some getting used to. During one sermon, Floy's minister bumped into a lamp and spilled oil everywhere. The congregation tried not to laugh as he thrashed about the stage, praising the virtues of the humble candle.

An urban reader like Michael Floy had plenty of bookstores to choose from—
like this Baltimore store that specialized in nonfiction, shown here in a
nineteenth-century engraving.

York City, a place Lincoln didn't visit for the first time until 1857, when
he was a senatorial hopeful. While someone like Jefferson became president after a life of literary privilege, Lincoln became president after a life
of scrounging for books. At the beginning, at least, their contents barely
mattered. In a region that didn't appreciate him and in a family that didn't
understand him, Lincoln turned to books, any books, for identity, ambition, and escape.

From his mother, Lincoln got his looks and his temperament: tall, thin,
thoughtful, gloomy. He also got his first taste of reading. The Lincolns
owned a Bible at least, and his mother read it to him regularly. From his
father he got nothing. The man, Lincoln wrote years later, the resentment
still as fresh as a newly plowed field, "never did more in the way of writing than to bunglingly sign his own name." Lincoln's father approached
everything that way. He farmed just enough to live on. He kept his family's one-room house rustic, with dirt floors, no windows, and a few pieces
of splintery furniture. The Lincolns lived in contented poverty. This was
what a real log cabin candidate looked like.

In 1816, when Lincoln was seven, the family moved to Indiana. After
his mother died, two years later, his father remarried, and his new wife

pushed him to put down a floor and cut out windows, though the Lincolns covered them with stretched animal skins instead of glass. They remained poor. Frontier manners required offering gifts to any visitors, but that meant having something to spare. One early neighbor remembered stopping by the Lincolns', only to watch them scramble for some sweet potatoes, which they scraped clean before presenting.

While Lincoln's stepmother treated her new son with affection, she did not know what to make of him. When those neighbors came calling, the boy would sit there, mutely, until they left. Then came an outburst of questions. Lincoln needed, in his stepmother's words, to "understand everything, even to the smallest thing, minutely and exactly." Even after he pinned down a new idea, Lincoln would return to it, refining its logic and simplifying its expression. Sometimes he would examine the same idea for hours, keeping himself up late into the night or working himself into a near tantrum. This mental habit, as much as his memorable phrases or frontier wit, defined Lincoln's literary style. He possessed a remarkable ability to write simply and clearly without draining his subject of its philosophical complexity.

Southern Indiana, circa 1820, did not have much regard for this skill set. As Lincoln grew older, he nurtured a distaste for the region and for his father, though those feelings often intertwined. If a stranger who knew Latin passed through the state, Lincoln later recalled, "he was looked upon as a wizard." Even the local scholars failed to impress. "No qualification was ever required of a teacher," Lincoln remembered, "beyond readin', writin', and cipherin'." While he did several stints in those teachers' schools, they probably added up to less than a year combined.

Lincoln sought inspiration on his own, in books. One early title came from the library of Josiah Crawford, a neighbor who was doing better than the Lincolns, partly through his hard work and partly through his miserly approach. For the pioneers who did own books, the genres of history and biography ranked behind only religion in terms of popularity. Lincoln borrowed a small volume from Crawford: *The Life of Washington* by Mason Weems. Weems, of course, did not aspire to high literature. But his book struck the young Lincoln. While he loved its battles and heroics, he loved its ideas even more. "I recollect thinking," Lincoln said, decades later, "that there must have been something more than common that those men struggled for." Reading Weems encouraged him to mull issues like individual liberty and national unity—to turn his attention to something bigger than harvesting corn.

The corn still needed harvesting. While Lincoln was borrowing the Washington biography, a rainstorm hit his family's leaky cabin and water-logged the book. Somehow Crawford calculated that Lincoln would need to work multiple days in his cornfields to cover the damages. Lincoln had his own chores too. There were fields and livestock to tend to. There were logs to split into rails, something at which he proved particularly adept. There were errands to run on the family's gray horse. One time when he was a teenager, Lincoln went to Princeton, Indiana, to get his stepmother's wool carded. As he rode into town, he spotted the sign for "Robert Stockwell, Merchant"—the first time in his life he'd seen a sign with gold lettering. At the town mill, a clerk told him it would take several hours to finish his order. Lincoln spent a few minutes observing the mill itself, then headed one block west to the town square. He may have passed part of his afternoon in Stockwell's store, picking up and inspecting its latest books: a Bonaparte biography, a history of the Revolution. It would have been Lincoln's first chance to browse a (partial) bookstore.

Lincoln could not have afforded even one of those titles. Still, he discovered ways to read. Some of his wealthier acquaintances—an old judge, a merchant in another town—lent him more books and newspapers. And Lincoln would read anything, even if he didn't always read it all the way through: dusty classics, trashy best sellers, the textbooks and anthologies floating among the other children. (The local schools' books had value, at least, and it was there that he developed a fondness for poetry.) Lincoln had to find time to read, given his regular chores. He had to find places to read—an underrated challenge when as many as thirteen people crammed into the family's 360-square-foot cabin. Most of all, he had to face those who did not approve. His father would whip him for reading instead of working. But Lincoln refused to quit. His cousin, one of the people who lived in the cabin, remembered Lincoln like this: "He was a constant and, I may say, stubborn reader."

As a teenager, Lincoln also started to write. He began by copying passages from his favorite books—on paper when the family had it, on scraps of wood when they didn't. He experimented with original poetry, much of it delightfully coarse. One poem satirized the most prominent local family, people who saw their frontier royalty as some kind of prize. Long after the Lincolns left Indiana, folks still chuckled at this satire.

The Lincolns did leave, relocating to Illinois in 1830. Lincoln helped his father build another log cabin, but once he turned twenty-two, he left to pursue his own life. "If Abe don't fool away all his time on his books," his father declared, "he may make something yet." Yet books would be—had already been—the way Lincoln made something of himself. Over the next few years, he worked on a flatboat and in a general store; he split more rails. But at night he read, eventually teaching himself to be a lawyer. In 1837, Lincoln settled in Springfield, which would soon become the Illinois state capital. It was a town of thirteen hundred but growing fast—a town of neat white houses with shutters, a town with potential law partners, with potential marital partners, a town with a real bookstore, the first in the state. In Springfield, Lincoln met and married Mary Todd. They moved into one of those white houses, a ten-minute walk from the statehouse, less with Lincoln's long legs. Across from the statehouse sat Lincoln's law office and Johnson & Bradford, the bookstore and publishing firm run by two men who'd emigrated from the East Coast.

In this environment, Lincoln became a respected lawyer. He also became, for the first time, a more selective reader, submerging himself in poetry, in Shakespeare, in a medley of nonfiction. He never did develop a taste for fiction. His one exception was Edgar Allan Poe, whose mystery stories, with their dark atmospherics and logic-driven twists, gave his mind something new to ponder and revisit.

During the 1830s, Lincoln also launched his political career in the Whig Party, serving four terms in the state legislature and one in the US Congress. He became an ace surrogate for other, bigger candidates. A national political system had started to emerge, with tauter party networks and rowdy national conventions. In 1844, the Democrats met in Baltimore to decide that year's nominee; Samuel Morse and his newish invention, the telegraph, relayed instant updates to Washington.

Most presidential candidates still refused to campaign. Most presidential aspirants skipped their parties' conventions, and the winner would never take the floor to deliver a rousing acceptance speech. But a candidate's allies could campaign with more coordination than in the past. Lincoln wrote political essays for Illinois newspapers, usually under a pseudonym. During presidential elections, he stumped across the state on behalf of the nominee. When the Whigs splintered over slavery, Lincoln switched to the Republican Party, and his speeches in 1856 showed that the decades of reading, writing, and courtroom coaxing had paid off. In the middle of one such speech, an elderly Democrat stomped away, his cane thwacking the ground with each step: "He's a dangerous man, sir! A damned dangerous man! He makes you believe what he says, in spite of yourself."

In 1858, Lincoln decided to enter a major race of his own. Stephen Douglas was a Democrat running for reelection to the US Senate. He was also one of America's most widely known politicians, and Lincoln knew he faced serious disadvantages—in fame, in finances, and, according to most Illinois observers, in political talent. So Lincoln proposed a series of open-air debates.

It was a clever suggestion that harnessed the period's passion for communal events—revivals, circuses, and county fairs, but especially lectures and political gatherings. One of the most famous speakers was Ralph Waldo Emerson, who traveled across America and Europe. In fact, he gave three lectures in Springfield, with Lincoln almost surely in attendance for at least one. Activists, intellectuals, and authors all submitted to the lecturing craze. Charles Dickens added his own twist. At his events, which he held on both sides of the Atlantic, he would glide onstage and pick up his latest best seller. "Ladies and gentlemen," he'd say softly, "I am happy to have the honor of reading to you tonight." Then Dickens would do precisely that, providing perhaps the first instance of an author giving a public reading from his own work.

Charles Dickens was perhaps the first author to give public readings of his work, as illustrated in this nineteenth-century American engraving.

Political events were rarely that polite. On August 21, 1858, Lincoln and Douglas met for their first three-hour debate in Ottawa, Illinois. The candidates shared a specially built wooden stage. In front of them spread a crowd of as many as fifteen thousand people—men more interested in brawling or drinking, women breastfeeding their infants, peddlers hawking slices of watermelon, horses seeming spooked by the fireworks. There were plenty of informed voters as well, but even they turned unruly on the issue that was dividing Illinois and, indeed, the entire nation: slavery and whether it should carry over to America's newest territories. On the platform at that first debate, Douglas argued that those territories should decide for themselves. He also leaned heavily on Jefferson's ideas about the inferiority of black people.

Lincoln hedged on this issue, vowing that he didn't think slaves were his true equals. But he remained firm in his belief that slavery could grow no more. He preached from a different Jeffersonian text. "There is no reason in the world," Lincoln argued at Ottawa, "why the negro is not entitled to all the natural rights enumerated in the Declaration of Independence, the right to life, liberty, and the pursuit of happiness."

Lincoln and Douglas would grapple six more times that fall. Their debates became famous for their contrasts: the stubby Douglas, shouting in his deep baritone; the six-four Lincoln, speaking in his high-pitched Kentuckiana twang. One of the most meaningful contrasts, though, was that Lincoln saw the debates textually. The biggest newspapers in Illinois—like the *Chicago Times*, which favored Douglas, and the *Chicago Press & Tribune*, which favored Lincoln—sent correspondents with their preferred candidates. Instead of the boys on the bus, it was the boys on the train (or in the carriage or on the steamboat), and they filed dispatches soaked in partisan bias.* There was a second group of journalists: stenographers who recorded and published the transcripts of each debate, an innovative move in nineteenth-century journalism. Given that a gust of prairie wind could sweep away an entire spoken paragraph, this practice produced imperfect texts. (It also produced biased texts; if you didn't like a candidate, you could let that paragraph stay missing and leave him sounding addled.) Still, stenographers circulated the debates' texts to

*How biased were the journalists in this era? Here's how, a few years later, the *Chicago Press & Tribune* described Lincoln's Gettysburg Address: "The dedicatory remarks by President Lincoln will live among the annals of the war." Here's how the *Chicago Times* described the same speech: "The cheek of every American must tingle with shame as he reads the silly, flat, and dishwatery utterances."

readers throughout Illinois—and even across the country as some of the key coastal papers started printing the transcripts and summaries from this bitterly contested race.

Douglas failed to see the potential in this new form of coverage. His arguments were so repetitive that the stenographers from the *Chicago Times* sometimes paused for a break, knowing they could just copy his language from previous debates. But Lincoln understood that the printed texts would reach far more voters, and that those voters would devour the entire run of debates. He revised and extended his ideas carefully, focusing on how they'd read as much as on how they'd sound.

The *Chicago Press & Tribune*'s stenographer was a small man named Robert Hitt, and at the second debate, in Freeport, Lincoln stood up to give his opening speech. He noticed that his stenographer was missing from the platform.

"Where's Hitt?" Lincoln asked. "Is Hitt present?"

Hitt, it turned out, was trapped on the edge of another enormous crowd. "Here I am, Mr. Lincoln," he hollered.

There was only one thing to do: the farmers and millers and blacksmiths all hoisted him up and passed him forward until he reached the stage. Hitt, ever the professional, pulled out his notebook and pen. When his stenographer was ready, Lincoln began.

"UNDER MY OWN SUPERVISION"

Lincoln lost the race. Since US senators were still chosen by state legislatures and not by voters, his losing did not become official until January 5, 1859. On that day, Douglas's supporters swarmed the Springfield statehouse, packing its gallery and, once the vote concluded, loosing a rumbling cheer. Outside, the Democrats fired a ceremonial cannon. It seemed like a precarious occasion for someone who tended toward despair, and one of Lincoln's friends checked on him. After all, in his office or in his home, Lincoln would have heard the entire event. But that friend found a man who seemed less saddened than invigorated. In fact, Lincoln wanted to show him a new project—a scrapbook he'd spent the last few weeks frantically assembling. That scrapbook contained the newspaper transcripts from each of the Lincoln-Douglas debates, and it, along with his buoyant mood, suggested that Lincoln wasn't done running yet.

As soon as the Senate campaign had ended, there'd been rumblings that Lincoln should run for president in 1860, though those rumblings were fainter than cannon fire. Jesse Fell, another of Lincoln's friends, bumped into him at an Illinois courthouse, where he was restarting his legal career. (After months of stumping, Lincoln needed the money.) Fell had just returned from a trip to New England, where people were still buzzing about the debates. "Everywhere I hear you talked about," Fell told the recovering candidate. "Frequently I have been asked, 'Who is this man Lincoln, of your state?'"

Fell argued that it was time to consider a dark-horse presidential bid— and that the best way to prime such a bid would be for Lincoln to write an autobiographical sketch, something future campaign biographies might follow.

"I admit the force of much of what you say," Lincoln answered, "and admit that I am ambitious and would like to be president." But he didn't share his friend's optimism. There were too many Republicans with better name recognition and better support. "Besides," Lincoln added, "there is nothing in my early history that would interest you or anybody else."

Based on his private actions, Lincoln objected less to Fell's aims than to his methods. While Lincoln had circulated campaign biographies as a party regular, he distrusted the genre and the way it authorized other writers to speak on his behalf. So he decided to try a radical approach—preserving the debates himself, in a scrapbook, then using it to print a new kind of campaign book that would consist of only his and Douglas's words.*

It would be hard to overstate how obsessed Lincoln became with his scheme. On November 20, barely two weeks after losing the election, he sent a letter to one of the owners of the *Chicago Press & Tribune*. "I wish to preserve a set of the late debates," Lincoln wrote. "Send them to me by

---

*When it comes to presidential firsts, Lincoln has two potential precursors—Henry Clay and, of all people, Davy Crockett. Clay's contemporaries knew he was one of America's great orators, in addition to being a frequent candidate for president, and as he grew older, a handful of editors gathered his best speeches into books. (Lincoln actually owned the two-volume *Life and Speeches of Henry Clay*.) But while he worked assiduously to get his speeches into newspapers, Clay did not show the same interest in getting them into books. Crockett's case is more complicated. In the 1820s and 1830s, he served as a Tennessee congressman, eventually emerging as a presidential short-lister. One of his exploratory moves was publishing *Narrative of the Life of David Crockett, Written by Himself*. "I am ingaged in prepareing a worke that may be of little prophit to me [sic]," Crockett wrote to his son. As this raw prose suggests, Crockett needed some help. The *Narrative* was mostly ghostwritten, a campaign book that drew its power more from the life than from the words. Both Crockett and Clay lacked the innovation and dedication Lincoln used to publish *Political Debates*.

express, and I will pay you for the papers and for your trouble." It was an odd request, given that most people saw the transcripts as disposable—breaking news that had already broken. But Lincoln was determined. When the owner didn't respond, he wrote to a second contact. "I have no word from him on the subject," Lincoln said of the owner. It had been all of ten days.

In November and December, Lincoln sent or received at least nine letters about his potential book (and those are just the letters or replies that have survived). One of his concerns with the book—and from the very beginning, Lincoln imagined it as an affordable volume aimed at a mass audience—was appealing to readers from every political side. To be as fair as possible, Lincoln sought out two sets of transcripts: the *Chicago Press & Tribune*'s for his speeches and the *Chicago Times*'s for Douglas's. "I have hunted the city," wrote Lincoln's source for the *Times*. "I have found where they are." His contact at the *Press & Tribune* also came through, mailing Lincoln the elusive issues.

On Christmas Day, Lincoln confirmed that he'd received a bundle of newspapers. He couldn't have asked for a better present, and he wasted little time in getting to work. Lincoln liked to write at a table, and he would have needed space to spread out all of the copies. At some point, he'd purchased a large blank book, probably from Johnson & Bradford's bookstore in Springfield. Now he began cutting up the newspapers, column by column, the ink staining his hands. Lincoln pasted those transcripts, plus a few other speeches he and Douglas had given before the debates, into the blank book. It must have been a meticulous yet pleasant scene, like Jefferson laboring over his customized Bibles many years before. But Lincoln wasn't finished. He penciled in detailed captions for each of the speeches. While he refused to tamper with Douglas's prose, he carefully reviewed his own, comparing the texts of both newspapers and making more than thirty surgical edits. (On a paragraph that both papers had missed, he even substituted a clipping from a third outlet.) It must have taken many hours, given that the scrapbook ran to nearly two hundred pages. And yet, despite his legal work and court appearances and any time spent with his family, Lincoln appears to have completed his book by January 5, only eleven days after he'd acknowledged receiving the newspapers.

Lincoln's next step was to find a printer, though with the scrapbook finished, there was less need to rush. In the spring of 1859, he pitched the book to at least two Illinois firms. He tried the local shop, Johnson & Bradford; they politely but firmly declined. He also negotiated with William Ross, who lived in a town about seventy-five miles north of Springfield.

While Ross seemed enthusiastic at the start, he did not yet realize how demanding this author could be. The book, Lincoln explained in a long letter, needed to avoid "a one-sided and party cast." It needed to include no editorializing—nothing other than Lincoln's and Douglas's own words. It needed to follow the exact structure of Lincoln's scrapbook. And that led to his final condition: "to print it in Springfield, under my own supervision."

Ross replied with remarkable grace, agreeing to hire a Springfield printer so Lincoln could maintain total control. For whatever reason, though, the two chose not to proceed. While Lincoln continued preparing for a potential run in 1860, he directed most of his energy toward building contacts and giving speeches. He continued to criticize the evils of slavery. By the end of 1859, he'd traveled more than four thousand miles.

The most important trip, for both Lincoln and his book, was to Ohio. In September, William Bascom, an officer in Ohio's Republican State Central Committee, asked Lincoln to come to Columbus—to stump for local candidates but also to counter Douglas, who was delivering a speech there (and clearly doing some national strategizing of his own). Lincoln arrived at the city with his old friend Hitt, who would transcribe the speech for the paper back home. The Republicans lodged their guest at Columbus's finest hotel, the Neil House. Dickens had stayed there during one of his reading tours and praised its "excellent apartments."

Tucked away in Lincoln's luggage was his scrapbook. Perhaps he showed it to Bascom and the other Ohio Republicans in private; perhaps he explained his plan to publish it. Either way, they saw its value a bit later when, at the start of his speech, Lincoln pulled out the scrapbook and quoted a contentious passage from one of the debates.

Lincoln spoke again that evening. Over the next three days, he also spoke in Dayton, in Cincinnati, and, on the way home, in Indianapolis. At some point he realized he'd lost the scrapbook. Lincoln sent a panicked letter to Bascom, who headed straight to the Neil House. Thankfully, the hotel's manager, to whom Lincoln had sent a second panicked letter, had recovered the book. It was on its way back to Illinois.

That fall, Ohio's Republicans did marvelously in their elections, and many of them credited Lincoln more than they credited Salmon Chase, the state's governor and one of the party's presidential favorites, along with New York's William Seward. In December, the Buckeyes asked Lincoln if they could publish his scrapbook. "Prompt action is important for you," one of them urged, "and equally so for the general cause." Lincoln promptly said yes, with stipulations. "I wish the reprint to be precisely as the [scrapbook]," he wrote, "without any comment whatever." Just to make sure, he deputized a trusted clerk to escort the scrapbook to Columbus—and to report back to him on the print edition's progress.

While Lincoln must have hated ceding control, he had to see he was getting too busy to play printer. The same week he sent off the scrapbook, the Republican National Committee decided to hold their upcoming convention in Chicago in May. It gave Lincoln and his operatives home-field advantage. It also gave his printer a deadline. Bascom and the other Republicans had selected Oran Follett and his publishing firm, Follett, Foster, & Co., who agreed to print five thousand copies at his own expense. In January, Follett's team got to work, with the foreman—a Democrat, as it happened—slicing the scrapbook into pieces and handing them to his compositors, who made the proofs, or early, hand-set versions of the text, to check for mistakes.

The sight of his butchered scrapbook would not have bothered Lincoln, for his goal had always been to see it become a widely distributed book. One of the things keeping him busy was a trip to New York City, where he spoke at Cooper Union to an audience of intellectuals and elites. His speech kept the crowd so rapt that, as one member recalled, "you could hear the gentle sizzling of the gas-burners." But Lincoln cared most about the published version, and after the speech, he shared his handwritten text with a New York newspaper, then reviewed its proofs. Once he finished, Lincoln threw his handwritten document away. Whether it was his speech at Cooper Union or his scrapbook of the debates, Lincoln knew the biggest impact would come last, when his words appeared in print.

Lincoln kept checking on the book; Follett and his employees kept busy. They created stereotyped plates that would allow them to sell the clothbound book, which they'd titled *Political Debates Between Hon. Abraham Lincoln and Hon. Stephen A. Douglas*, at the bargain price of fifty cents. (A comparable edition of *Uncle Tom's Cabin* cost $1.50.) People were starting to understand the potential of Lincoln and his forthcoming book, and some of Chase's supporters applied behind-the-scenes pressure to bog the process down. Nevertheless, on March 20, 1860, Follett, Foster, & Co. announced that *Political Debates* was for sale—sixteen months to the day since Lincoln had sent his first strange letter asking after copies of old newspapers. While Lincoln had always maintained that he wanted no money for his work, Follett came up with something better than a royalty check: he shipped the author a hundred free copies of his book.

VOTE FOR LINCOLN

"A half century unequaled in its discoveries": a year or two after George Bancroft spoke that line in his lecture, Lincoln read it in a book. It became one of those ideas his mind liked to ponder and revisit. When did humans first achieve their various discoveries? Why did they achieve them? And why, as Bancroft pointed out, did the rate of discovery seem to be speeding up? Lincoln mulled these questions until, finally, he decided to write about them in a lecture of his own. He began drafting a wonky survey of humanity's greatest hits, from iron tools and woven clothing to the railroad and the telegraph.

On one topic, however, Lincoln's tone became surprisingly personal. It happened during his discussion of writing and, more important, of printing, which he called "the other half—and in real utility, the better half—of writing." Before printing, Lincoln argued, it had been incredibly difficult to share the other discoveries. In the dark ages, even in the early days of print, most people didn't realize how much their lives could improve. Although he was describing a historical problem, Lincoln slipped into a passionate and almost autobiographical voice. People without print, he wrote in his lecture, "looked upon the educated few as superior beings." *In Indiana, an educated outsider was looked upon as a wizard.* "Teachers," he wrote in his lecture, "were not very numerous, or very competent." *In Indiana, teachers knew little beyond readin', writin', and cipherin'.*

Lincoln's lecture—and Lincoln's life—didn't end there. Eventually books and pamphlets and newspapers reached larger masses of people. That's when everything changed. "To emancipate the mind from this false and under-estimate of itself," Lincoln wrote, "is the great task which printing came into the world to perform." Emancipation: it was not a metaphor he chose lightly, and it showed that print's transformative power was one of his most earnest beliefs. Books could change a life; books could change a nation. All you needed was printing, and also patience. "The effects could not come all at once," Lincoln wrote. "It required time to bring them out; and they are still coming."

Lincoln delivered versions of this lecture in 1858 and at least four more times in 1859 and 1860. In other words, he was working on it at the same time he was working on *Political Debates*. Lincoln's book proved his theory right. He distilled the debates, a series of crazy political carnivals, into a powerful and portable volume. While most voters never learned about his scrapbook or behind-the-scenes efforts, a stunning number of them read his words and ideas. Indeed, Lincoln's book spread across the country, its sales lit by the external flame of his presidential candidacy.

At first, Follett, Foster, & Co. handled the book like the small midwestern publisher it was, circulating copies throughout Ohio and its neighboring states. The firm got a boost from the approaching convention, where Lincoln was emerging as an intriguing alternative to Seward and Chase. He'd been an underdog before, in his race with Douglas, and that made *Political Debates* "a volume of extraordinary interest and value," according to one New York newspaper. East Coast Republicans started buying the book in bulk and giving it to their fellow partisans, the way they'd done with so many campaign biographies before. Lincoln welcomed regional and political sales alike. Even after Cooper Union, he needed the attention; another New York outlet promoted *Political Debates* as "the speeches of Stephen A. Douglas and the speeches of Abram Lincoln."

On May 16, the Republican convention kicked off in Chicago. It made the Lincoln-Douglas debates seem like a calm and mannered affair. While Lincoln and the other candidates did not attend, thousands of Republicans squeezed into the main hall; thousands more lingered outside. In this unruly atmosphere, Ohio's delegates threw the nomination to Lincoln on the third ballot.

Lincoln's nomination supercharged the sales of *Political Debates*. While the book had already helped his candidacy—it had sold well in Ohio, after all—in the general election it became a national sensation. Within a week of the convention, Follett was forced to order two more sets of stereotyped plates and two new steam-powered presses. The publisher hired additional outside bookbinders; it made distribution deals with major booksellers in Boston, New York, Chicago, Cincinnati, Pittsburgh, and Detroit. The Chicago partner was S. C. Griggs & Company, a hulking downtown store that readers referred to as "The Literary Emporium of the Prairie." One Friday morning, its clerks set out a stack of *Political Debates* that was seven feet high. By the end of the day, the stack was gone—and the store had sent to Columbus for more books.

Before long, *Political Debates* was selling five hundred copies a day. Perhaps the biggest factor was one Lincoln had always anticipated—this inexpensive and fair-minded volume appealed to readers on all sides. It made sense when a Republican paper claimed that Lincoln's book had "raise[d] him to the dignity of a full-grown statesman." But outlets that leaned Democratic also praised it, especially after Douglas secured their party's nomination. The *Boston Courier*, for instance, called it "a political textbook of sure value in the coming campaign." Then the *Courier* confessed that Lincoln came across as the better stylist. "There's a march of periods," the paper said of Lincoln's words, "a marshaling of sentences unsurpassed in the most brilliant speeches of American orators."

Like most other candidates, Lincoln tried to stay quiet. When people asked about his beliefs, he sometimes responded with a list of page numbers from his new book. He also begrudgingly accepted the rituals of electioneering, including Jackson-style campaign biographies and a catchy persona as the humble rail-splitter.* Supporters sent packages to Springfield—new steel wedges, like the ones used to split logs, and even chunks of rail Lincoln had once chopped (or so they hoped). Visitors descended on his office and his home, where Lincoln had filled the parlor with the stacks of *Political Debates* he'd received from Follett; some callers asked Lincoln to sign their own copies of the book. At least one was struck by a set of shiny, unscuffed wedges and wondered if they were the ones he'd used as a boy in Indiana.

"Are those the wedges, sir?" the visitor said.

Lincoln answered with a perfect pause: "These, sir, are the identical wedges—that were sent to me about a week ago."

By the end of June, *Political Debates* had sold close to thirty thousand copies. Lincoln had fun with its status as a best seller, making sure to send one of his author copies to Johnson & Bradford, the Springfield printer that had passed on the book. But *Political Debates* was making a serious impact. "This book," argued one paper, "should be in the hands of every voter." It sometimes felt like it was. Consider James Putnam, a lawyer, Shakespeare buff, and political enthusiast living in Buffalo, New York. Like a lot of voters in that state, Putnam was an old Fillmore supporter—someone who'd planned to stump for Seward but was now deciding between Lincoln and another candidate, John Bell. That summer, Putnam corresponded with Lincoln's boosters, but it was Lincoln's book that won him over. The candidate's prose, Putnam wrote in a blurb-worthy riff, exhibited "logical eloquence," a "clearness of statement," and "sincerity

---

*In 1860, publishers pushed out more than a dozen different campaign biographies of Lincoln. While he tried to assist some of the authors in private, he refused to authorize any of their books. An authorized biography, he explained to one publisher, was "a volume of hundreds of pages for adversaries to make points upon without end." It was one more instance of Lincoln seeing the power of print—and also evidence that he wanted his book, and his words, to stand alone.

While Lincoln disliked
campaign biographies,
a number of them
portrayed him in
1860—including
one published by
Follett, Foster, & Co.
that featured text by
William Dean Howells
and this engraving
based on a photograph
by Mathew Brady.

that commands your admiration and assent." He continued: "The truth is, I have read every thing I have been able to find he has written or said, and the ring of the best metal is in them all." When someone showed the letter to Lincoln, he copied out Putnam's praise to keep.

Political Debates eventually sold more than fifty thousand copies, but even that figure understates its effect. At Cooper Union, Lincoln spoke to a crowd of about 1,500; tens of thousands more read a transcript in the newspapers. But those transcripts appeared in viciously partisan contexts. They tended to be transient. (Lincoln could vouch for the challenge of tracking down old newspapers.) Lincoln's book, by contrast, could be studied and referenced and shared. Nineteenth-century journalists liked to claim that *Uncle Tom's Cabin* had "ten readers to every purchaser," and the same logic applied to Lincoln's book. In the months before the election, it became a site of social reading, the sort of reading Lincoln had relied on while growing up in Indiana. Voters like James Putnam of New York certainly valued the book. "You will be supported in this state by at least 75,000 men who in 1856 were supporters of Mr. Fillmore," he told Lincoln. "Your debates with Douglas they have studied." It's impossible to measure the accuracy of Putnam's estimate, or the number of New Yorkers who actually read *Political Debates*. But one thing is clear: Lincoln carried the crucial Empire State by just fifty thousand votes.

On February 11, 1861, the president-elect and his family boarded a special train for Washington. There would be so many ceremonies and celebrations that it would stretch into a twelve-day trip. One of the first came in Columbus, Ohio, where thousands of citizens greeted Lincoln at the depot. He was already tired of talking, but he headed to the statehouse to meet with more supporters. Someone had decided Lincoln should shake each person's hand, but there were so many who wanted to touch him, to bless him, that they crushed in—not angrily but with enthusiasm and hope. The line collapsed, and Lincoln found himself reaching out with both his right hand and his left, dispatching the crowd at a dizzying clip.

That night, he would head to the governor's house for a dinner, followed by another reception. The next day he would leave for another city. But at some point during this draining day, Lincoln made time to meet with some of the Republicans who'd helped him launch *Political Debates*. Their partnership had played a crucial role in winning the election. It had also allowed Lincoln, a lifelong lover of books, to publish a book of his own. While the fact that it was *his* book hadn't mattered in the campaign, it had mattered to him. In fact, when the Buckeyes had first asked to print the scrapbook, Lincoln could barely contain his joy. "I esteem the compliment paid me in this matter," he wrote, "as the very highest I have ever received." Now he could thank those people in person, could talk with them about what the next four or eight years might bring. One of the people he spoke with that day was William Bascom, the officer who'd first invited Lincoln to Ohio, and Bascom brought along his own copy of *Political Debates*. The author took the volume and autographed it on its flyleaf: "W. T. Bascom from A. Lincoln, Columbus, Ohio, February 13, 1861."

CHAPTER SIX

"General Grant, the People Are Moving En Masse upon Your *Memoirs*"

Abraham Lincoln needed a better general. The North had just won a bloody war's bloodiest battle, Gettysburg, a victory that cost the lives of twenty-three thousand Union soldiers. (The South lost even more.) But Lincoln's commanders—in this case, George Meade—continued to commit blunders of caution. While Meade had driven back Robert E. Lee and his attempt to invade north of the Potomac River, he'd failed to chase Lee farther. This approach, Lincoln told his general, seemed about as bold as "an old woman trying to shoo her geese across the creek." Yet Gettysburg still counted as a victory. Even Lincoln had to admit that, and one day, two weeks after the battle, he composed a silly and celebratory poem about it, like the ones he used to write in Indiana. It lasted only eight lines—a brief poem for a brief invasion. The most intriguing part was Lincoln's title: "Gen. Lee's Invasion of the North, Written by Himself."

Over the last 150 years, historians have credited the Civil War for all sorts of transformations—the end of slavery, the beginning of modern medicine, the decision to pursue another activity with industrial efficiency: war. It's time to add a new item to that list. In the conflict's aftermath, America's most prominent political and military figures began writing and publishing their life stories in real time. Decades before, Benjamin Rush, one of the only people with whom John Adams would discuss his autobiography, encouraged the ex-president: "No hand but your own must compose your voice from the tomb." Rush, Adams, and the many statesmen who followed shared the assumption that you wrote your autobiography to speak from the grave. The Civil War changed that. For the first time, generals and politicians published their own legacy books under their own names, then watched as sales soared—because of the authors' fame but also because of the readers' desire to learn, debate, and heal.

It's fair to wonder, given this rapid and remarkable shift, whether Lincoln would have attempted an autobiography. The president never stopped reading and writing; three months before his assassination, to take only one example, he talked about revising and publishing his old lecture on discoveries. While Lincoln loathed self-disclosure, he loved control. Writing a legacy book would have meant siding with the latter impulse, but that book—or even the output of Lincoln in retirement, echoing Jefferson and Adams in their literary puttering—would have left American literature incalculably richer. There are plenty of presidents who died before getting a chance to write or to write more. The loss of Lincoln hurts the most.

It's also fair to wonder whether Lincoln could have written a legacy book as good as Ulysses S. Grant's. Grant, of course, turned out to be the general Lincoln needed—a commander more worried about winning than not losing, even if those wins required terrible sacrifices. Grant eventually became America's eighteenth president and the author of *Personal Memoirs of U. S. Grant*, a classic that's been praised by everyone from Gertrude Stein to George W. Bush. *Personal Memoirs* captured the general's youth, defended his most controversial military decisions, and sold more copies than just about any other book in American history to that point. And yet for most of his life, Grant refused to think of himself as a potential author. A stunning bankruptcy forced him to start his book; a fatal form of cancer nearly kept him from finishing it. Instead of Lincoln's instant death, Grant faced a demise that was agonizing and slow and very, very public. Through all of it, the general continued to write—speaking, if not from the grave, then months, weeks, and finally days before entering it.

"WHAT LIKE A BULLET CAN UNDECEIVE"

One April evening in 1861, Walt Whitman went to the opera. After the show ended, he walked out into the warm Manhattan air—and into a world that had changed forever. The city's paperboys, he later wrote, were "yelling up the street, rushing from side to side even more furiously than usual." Whitman bought one of their nighttime editions and stopped to scan it under the bright lamps of the Metropolitan Hotel. Soon a crowd pressed silently around him, and one of them read the news aloud. The South had fired on Fort Sumter. The Civil War had begun.

Over the next four years, that conflict became the most disruptive in American history—something people experienced, in Whitman's words, "as by flashes of lightning." In 1860, the country's population stood at nearly 32 million people. By the war's end, more than a million had died or been grievously wounded. It made sense that something would change once writers began exploring those experiences. The first wave of authors, or at least some of them, tried to represent the bleakness and ambiguity of the war they'd just lived through. As time passed—and as more and more Americans called for healing and forgiveness—a second wave tried to justify their side's actions or to advance their historical agenda. In both cases, these authors embraced a new passion for realism. In fiction and nonfiction, in poetry and autobiography, they aimed for authenticity, telling their stories in a somber, documentary style.

The first place most Americans encountered this approach, outside of the battlefields themselves, was in newspapers and magazines. The war overpowered both media. A woman who lived in Louisiana, on her family's cotton plantation, described a typical periodical in her diary: "Nothing but 'War, War,' from the first to the last column." Northerners got the same news, but more of it. The Union enjoyed a huge advantage in manufacturing, and that included printing presses. (In 1860, there were 986 printers in the North but only 151 in the South.) Union publications produced better visuals, including engravings from the frontlines based on sketches by traveling artists or, increasingly, on photographs. The most iconic images came from Mathew Brady and his assistants. Since cameras required lengthy exposure times, the photographers depicted not war but its aftermath— scorched fences, muddy fields, swollen corpses. For the price of a novel, you could buy one of the pictures by mail or at one of Brady's galleries in Washington or New York. The level of detail, especially in the dead bodies and their faces, haunted Americans. "You can," one viewer shuddered, "identify not merely their general outline, but actual expression."

The North enjoyed another advantage: it billeted many more authors than did the South, and the war darkened their work. Hawthorne stopped writing romances and started writing skeptical reportage from Washington. Whitman, the poet who used to sing the body electric, now described the bodies of injured soldiers: "From the stump of the arm, the amputated hand, I undo the clotted lint, remove the slough, wash off the matter and blood."

Perhaps the best wartime writing came from Herman Melville, who decided to trade his career as a fizzling novelist for a new one, as a poet.

At Gettysburg, one of the photographers trained by Mathew Brady took this picture of dead soldiers. It was one of many examples where the war pushed artists toward realism.

In "Shiloh," a short lyric, Melville reflected on the Battle of Shiloh—the first of the war's Gettysburg-sized conflicts, in which Grant and his army defeated the South despite racking up an incomprehensible two-day death count. The poem opened with a quiet, pastoral scene:

> Skimming lightly, wheeling still,
> The swallows fly low
> Over the field in clouded days,
> The forest-field of Shiloh—

Yet Melville quickly began to unsettle that scene, to reveal the wounded bodies littering the field, "the parched ones stretched in pain." The poem seemed to recover, pivoting to nobler thoughts like the soldiers who respected their counterparts on the other side—until it shattered one last time in an eerie parenthetical: "(What like a bullet can undeceive!)."

Melville also fizzled as a poet. When *Battle-Pieces and Aspects of the War*, the collection that included "Shiloh," appeared in 1866, it sold only a few hundred copies. There was more of a market for simple, patriotic literature. The biggest market, though, centered on nonfiction. Historians and biographers wrote more rapidly than ever, something that bothered critics when it came to still-traumatic events like the assassination of Lincoln. "The body of the late president had not reached its final resting-place," complained one writer, "ere half-a-dozen biographers were engaged to write his life."* But readers responded, devouring instant best sellers like John S. C. Abbott's *History of the Civil War in America*.

Where readers seemed more hesitant was with Civil War autobiographies. While the genre had grown more stable and more secular since the age of Franklin, it remained highly democratic. Two-thirds of memoirs still came from religious figures or people on society's margins—sailors or thieves or pioneers abducted by Native Americans. In the nineteenth century, of course, no one was more marginal than an American slave, and black people wrote some of the period's most searing (and most widely read) autobiographies. More than sixty of these slave narratives appeared before the Civil War, including Solomon Northup's *Twelve Years a Slave* and Frederick Douglass's *Narrative of the Life of Frederick Douglass*, both of which quickly sold thirty thousand copies. These works drew their power from their first-person credibility—from their descriptions of flogged bodies, ruptured families, and harrowing escapes. Their plots, like those in the Puritans' spiritual autobiographies, turned on a series of conversions, and since many southern states had made it a crime to teach slaves to read and write, those conversions often revolved around books. "The more I read," Douglass wrote, "the more I was led to abhor and detest my enslavers."

The Civil War inspired new groups of marginal authors, including common soldiers and prisoners of war. (One POW started an autobiography while still imprisoned, sharpening a pencil with his fingernails and hiding the pages in his coat lining.) But the war made its biggest impact by empowering the powerful—by creating space for, say, the first president to publish a legacy book in his own lifetime.

That president was not Grant but James Buchanan. Buchanan's pre-

---

*Lincoln's death invigorated another classic political category: the kiss-and-tell book. The president's friends (and even his acquaintances) went on to publish volumes with titles like *Six Months at the White House*. One of the most fascinating was Elizabeth Keckley's *Behind the Scenes*, which appeared in 1868. Keckley was born a slave in Virginia, but her skillful sewing and grateful customers helped her buy her freedom. She emerged as one of Washington's most popular dressmakers, and after she did some work for Mary Todd, the two became friends. Keckley was at the White House for moments like the assassination's aftermath, when she tried to comfort the sobbing widow while Lincoln's children stood by. "Don't cry so, Mamma!" said the youngest, wrapping his arms around his mother. "Don't cry, or you will make me cry, too! You will break my heart."

decessors had, like the founders before them, felt the occasional autobiographical impulse. Like the founders, they had also pursued that impulse
cautiously. While Millard Fillmore wrote a short sketch of his life, it didn't
cover his presidency (and he sealed it until after his death). Martin Van
Buren started his story with two paragraphs on the White House before
promising he'd have "more to say hereafter." And yet, 1,247 handwritten
pages later, he still hadn't reached his presidency—or finished his book.

Buchanan's autobiography was different. Soon after leaving the White
House in 1861, he asked a friend to write a book about him, fortified with
access to his papers. Buchanan hoped it would rebut the many critics who
blamed him for the Civil War. (Slamming the ex-president had become
a rare activity that united North and South.) But the collaboration fell
through. "I shall now depend on myself," Buchanan told another ally, and
he started writing *Mr. Buchanan's Administration on the Eve of the Rebellion.*
The book, as its title suggests, dealt almost exclusively with his presidency, a
profound shift when compared to previous presidential titles. In most other
ways, though, Buchanan kept things conventional, writing in the third person and exhuming long passages from primary documents. He tried pin-
ning the war on abolitionists, on generals, on reporters—on everyone, in
short, but James Buchanan. When the book finally appeared in 1866, it
flopped. "Instead of trusting his enemy to write a book," the *New York Times*
marveled, "he deliberately writes the story of his own and his government's
dishonor himself!" The response turned so ugly that a few weeks after the
book's release, Buchanan asked supporters to stop sending him the reviews.

Readers needed to acclimate to real-time autobiographies—or at least
to ones written by lousy presidents. Still, the Civil War's questions and
causes inspired many prominent generals and politicians to pick up their
pens. The South struck first. A few months after he surrendered to Grant
at Appomattox, Robert E. Lee began hunting for documents. "It is my
purpose," he told a supporter, "to write the history of the campaigns in
Virginia." Lee knew the best way to ensure pro-Southern books was for
Southerners to produce them themselves, and he urged his former generals to join him. "Can you not occupy your leisure time in preparing
your memoirs of the war?" he wrote to James Longstreet. "Every officer
whose position and character would give weight to his statements ought
to do so." America's publishers certainly agreed, and a number of them
courted Lee, leading to buzz that his book would earn him $100,000. But
Lee never got the money because he never finished the book.

The Confederate defense fell instead to men like Jubal Early, who published the first autobiography by a Civil War general in 1866. Early emphasized the North's overwhelming advantages, the South's principled stand for states' rights, and the happy and loyal lives of black slaves—each one a fiction in the Confederacy's version of the Civil War, which quickly congealed into a myth known as the Lost Cause.

The North's response came slower, and it never developed into a durable and coordinated myth like the Lost Cause. *The Memoirs of General William T. Sherman* appeared in 1875. Like Lee and Grant and a few other postwar figures, Sherman had become quite famous. One time, he took a train from Hartford to West Point—Sherman was traveling by private car—and found a crowd at each stop, hoping to hear him speak. After yet another round of waving and declaiming, Sherman ducked inside his car and saw Mark Twain sitting there, smoking a cigar.

"Who told you you could go in this car?" Sherman asked the author, who was growing quite famous himself.

"Nobody," Twain replied.

"Do you expect to pay extra fare?"

"No, I don't."

"Then you'll work your way."

Sherman shrugged off his military coat and handed it to Twain, with the idea that, at the next stop, Twain could play Sherman and handle the crowd. When the train stopped, Twain marched onto the rear platform and greeted the people with a formal bow. They countered with a loud cheer—until one of them said, "Say, that ain't Sherman, that's Mark Twain." That just made everyone cheer a second time, and in the end Twain and Sherman both addressed the crowd.

Sherman's celebrity gave him the perfect platform for recounting his perspective on events like his infamous March to the Sea—and for rebutting the South's Lost Causers. When word leaked that he had retreated to St. Louis, to work on an autobiography, a New York editor put his son on the next westbound train. The son arrived at Sherman's home and received the following greeting: "I suppose you've come to make arrangements to publish my book."

The book was as blunt as its author, and its publication sparked a response so fiery the residents of Georgia must have smiled. The general found himself trapped in a two-front war: first, his fellow soldiers had their own interpretations, and all around the country everyone from Jefferson Davis to obscure Union privates wrote public letters disputing Sherman's account; second, many critics wondered whether someone in

Sherman's position should have written an autobiography at all. "Perhaps General Sherman's whole military career," the *Chicago Tribune* observed, "has not demonstrated so large a degree of courage as his recent publication of his personal memoirs."

Sherman knew that controversy meant sales. His *Memoirs* sold sixty thousand copies, and one of his early readers was James Garfield. The Ohio congressman and future president was bedridden with a bout of intestinal problems, but at least that gave him time to read. "There has been a great outcry among the newspapers against the book," Garfield noted in his diary, and he admitted he still wasn't sure what to think. Was it too soon for such a book? Should a soldier even write about a war he'd served in? Weren't autobiographies just exercises in ego? Garfield didn't know, but he did know that he wanted to keep reading. By the time he finished Sherman's second volume, a few days later, he'd made up his mind. Sherman had made a bold choice to tell an intimate story, but that intimacy made *Memoirs* a delightful and persuasive book. "He writes not a history of the war but his own experiences in the war," Garfield wrote. "This may not have been discreet but it is a fair and truthful picture of his own mind, and for that I love him."

THE FORGOTTEN EDITOR

A few months after reading Sherman's *Memoirs*, Garfield went to the White House to talk policy with its occupant, Ulysses S. Grant. Once they finished, the two chatted about Sherman and his book. Grant admitted that after the uproar, he'd expected to find it plagued with problems. In fact, when he first sat down to read the autobiography, he made sure to have a pencil and paper at hand, to log his specific complaints. When Grant finished, however, his paper remained unmarred. Sherman's *Memoirs* had impressed him as a work of fact and as a work of literature.

Sherman had impressed others too. More and more generals and politicians began opting to write their autobiographies, including Benjamin Butler and Philip Sheridan in the North and P. G. T. Beauregard and Joseph E. Johnston in the South.* Grant, who was always dutiful, espe-

---

*This is a very partial list. Another autobiographer—and, depending on how you define it, an American president—was Jefferson Davis. After the success of Sherman's book, the general's publisher offered Davis a hefty advance for his story. Davis agreed and started dictating passages and reviewing documents at Beauvoir, a lovely plantation on Mississip-

cially when it meant helping other soldiers, read many of these volumes after their publishers asked him to vet them. When those same publishers asked him to undertake a book of his own, though, Grant declined. "I have always distrusted my ability to write," he confessed to his friend Mark Twain. Soon enough, tragedy would drive Grant to authorship, with Twain famously serving as his editor and publisher. But the biggest influence on Grant's *Personal Memoirs* came from a different editor—someone who helped Grant realize what a wonderful writer he could be.

Grant was born in Ohio in 1822, the son of a tanner, a sweaty and pungent profession he hated. Still, Grant admired his father's intellectual zeal—the way that, much like Lincoln, he overcame poverty and the death of a parent by foraging for books and becoming, in Grant's words, "a constant reader." The child, a small, shy boy, became a reader as well, though his first love would always be horses. In 1839, and at his parents' urging, he headed to West Point. At five-foot-one and 117 pounds, he was the smallest cadet in his class.

One of the most remarkable qualities in Grant's *Personal Memoirs* is its directness, and he wrote honestly about the fact that he neither enjoyed nor excelled at his studies at West Point. "Much of the time, I am sorry to say, was devoted to novels," Grant recalled. Another of the book's qualities is its humor, often self-deprecating, and there's a flash of it in that "sorry to say." For Grant adored novels, to the point that he was America's first fiction-loving president. Jefferson and Adams read novels, but they did so sparingly, whether due to their own tastes or to a generational distrust of fiction. Grant showed no such restraint. West Point boasted a ten-thousand-volume library, and Grant galloped through its adventure stories and historical novels, plus the American classics of Washington Irving and James Fenimore Cooper. The cadet became so engrossed by reading that he once received demerits for lingering in the library.

After graduation, Grant set out on the life of an Army itinerant: Missouri, New York, Oregon, and other posts. That first stop happened to be close to the Dents, the family of a West Point roommate, and Grant

---

pi's Gulf Shore. After four years, however, the publisher discovered that Davis had made little progress on the actual book. While he'd hired a ghostwriter, Davis hadn't bothered to check on his scribe. "Strange as it may appear," Davis admitted to his editor, "I was but little better prepared than yourself to find how little had been done." The editor sent a more dynamic assistant, and after another year's work, Davis finally finished his book, *The Rise and Fall of the Confederate Government*. Though stilted and one-sided, it sold thousands of copies, mostly in the South.

started spending time with the daughter, Julia, who had thick hair and tanned skin from her many afternoons on horseback. They made an ideal match. Julia also loved to read, though an eye condition made it arduous, and when Grant moved to his next stop, they started swapping passionate literary missives. While stationed in Texas, Grant wrote a letter that revealed as much about his feelings toward his future wife as it did about his feelings toward fiction. Julia had just read a new novel, *The Wandering Jew*, and Grant borrowed a copy from another soldier, which came with that soldier's marginal notes. "How often I think of you while reading it," Grant wrote in his letter. "I think, 'Well, Julia has read the very same words that I am now reading and not long before me.' Yesterday, in reading the ninth [chapter], I saw a sentence marked around with a pencil and the word *good* written after it. I thought it had been marked by you, and before I knew it, I had read it over three or four times."

The couple married in 1848, but military life wore on them and, eventually, their children. In 1854, Grant resigned from the Army at the rank of captain. He tried and failed at farming; he tried and failed at other careers too. Finally, Grant found himself clerking at his family's store in Galena, Illinois. Like so many other Americans, he read the debates between Lincoln and Douglas and left them impressed by Lincoln. "I recognized then his great ability," Grant later remembered, and once the Civil War started, he returned to the army, this time to serve the president whose prose he'd so admired.

Neither his record nor his appearance suggested Grant as a future war hero. While he'd grown a few inches and filled out since his days as a cadet—he'd also cultivated a thick beard—Grant looked less like a general than like a rumpled quartermaster, a position he'd actually held during the Mexican-American War, though he'd also fought bravely. Now, in a time of crisis, a former quartermaster counted as seasoned, and Grant rose rapidly to general in the war's western theater. Early in 1862, he captured Fort Henry and Fort Donelson, two Confederate strongholds in Tennessee. They were the North's first major victories—and they made Grant a star. At Fort Donelson, his Confederate counterpart, Simon Buckner, tried to negotiate his surrender. "No terms except an unconditional and immediate surrender can be accepted," Grant replied. "I propose to move immediately upon your works." Those words ricocheted from newspaper to newspaper, providing the country with an ideal introduction to Grant and his literary style: calm, stubborn, concise.

Fort Donelson made one further contribution to Grant's newfound fame: cigars. While the general smoked them only occasionally, reporters spotted him puffing one during the battle. Once that detail followed "propose to move immediately" into the national consciousness, Grant's fans began sending him hundreds of boxes of cigars. Grant abandoned his pipe. He also continued to win, though at enormous human cost, until Lincoln promoted him to head of the Union forces. On April 9, 1865, Grant accepted Lee's surrender. He cut back on smoking, but only a bit. ("When I was in the field I smoked eighteen or twenty cigars a day," Grant joked to reporters. "Now I smoke only nine or ten.") In 1868, he ran as the Republican nominee for president, winning comfortably. After two terms, he and Julia embarked on a glamorous world tour, meeting with ambassadors in India and novelists in Europe until they finally returned in 1879.

The Grants didn't come home to Galena. Instead, they settled in New York. It was the height of the Gilded Age, a term Twain and a coauthor had coined in a satirical novel, and the city's elite reveled in the latest forms of wealth: lavish balls thrown by the Astors and the Vanderbilts; summer homes on the beach or in the mountains; and, in Manhattan's business district, buildings that crept slowly toward the sky. Grant went to work in one of those new buildings—2 Wall Street, the home of Grant and Ward, a brokerage run by one of his sons, Ulysses S. Grant Jr., and by a man named Ferdinand Ward. The general was nearing sixty, his body growing pudgy, his beard going gray, but he remained as resolute as ever. Each day he arrived at the office at ten, usually accompanied by a cigar, but one morning he was a few minutes late. Grant said nothing, and no one noticed anything amiss—until another of the building's tenants burst in. Was the general all right? It turned out that a few minutes before, Grant had been riding an elevator when the rope that supported it had snapped, causing the car to plunge several stories until a brake kicked in. Grant had seen no need to mention his near death. "We got nothing worse than a shaking up," he said.

Grant appeared well on his way to being a millionaire. He and Julia moved to an elegant brownstone on Sixty-Sixth Street, where the large windows provided a view of Central Park. In the spring of 1884, however, Grant and Ward collapsed. Ward, it seemed, had swindled everyone, starting with Grant and his son. But while the presence of an ex-president ensured national scandal—complete with implicating headlines like "Is Grant Guilty?"—Grant also lost everything himself. Suddenly he could not pay his pew fee at the Madison Avenue Congregational Church; he could not pay his grocer for the family's food. The general was now sixty-two years old, and he had failed and impoverished the people he loved.

Help came from an unlikely source: a magazine editor named Robert Underwood Johnson. Although Johnson was a young man, he carried himself like an old one, careful and neat, with a habit of constantly removing and polishing his glasses. He worked at the *Century*, a smart and well-known monthly that published poetry and fiction. (In fact, the magazine would soon serialize Twain's latest novel, *The Adventures of Huckleberry Finn*.) The *Century* also ran nonfiction, and Johnson and his colleagues were planning a sprawling, multiyear series on the Civil War—dozens of autobiographical essays by Northerners and Southerners alike.

The key, as in most military exercises, came in the recruiting. The *Century*'s staff approached the war's leading figures, many of whom had previously succumbed to the memoir trend. The biggest target was Grant. While the general had refused similar offers, always saying that he couldn't imagine himself as a literary author, Johnson hoped that now, with his financial problems compounding, Grant might relent.

It was June, and the Grants had retreated to their beach cottage on the Jersey shore. (At first, they'd tried to rent it, to bring in some income, but when that failed, they realized they could live there more cheaply than in Manhattan.) Johnson spent his summers in a nearby town, and he began to visit the general at his cottage, where they would sit on the porch and talk while the ocean sloshed in the distance. Before they addressed anything else, Grant insisted on explaining what he had and hadn't known about the failure of Grant and Ward; decades later, Johnson could still recall the general's anger and pain on the matter, "his dignified sorrow." But Johnson knew profit lurked in that pain, and he pitched Grant on the *Century*'s series, which would provide an opportunity to remind readers of his past victories—and also pay five hundred dollars per article, at a time when most magazine features might earn a writer fifty dollars.

At that price, Grant decided to give authorship a try. Johnson suggested he write four articles, starting with Shiloh, the bloody battle memorialized by Melville and so many others. On June 30, Grant submitted his first draft. There were hints of what would make *Personal Memoirs* a revered title—the clarity, the crisp descriptions, the candor. (The North's raw soldiers, Grant wrote, "were hardly able to load their muskets according to the manual.") On the whole, though, the article didn't work. Like so many of the presidential authors who'd preceded him, Grant had emphasized the public instead of the private. His article creaked under the weight of statistics and tiresome detail; it needed more of Grant's personality and perspective—needed, in Johnson's words, rescuing from "the blight of the deadly official report."

long subsequent to the close of the rebellion, and after public opinion had been most erroneously formed the subject of Shiloh Events had occurred before the battle, and others (occurred) subsequent to it, which determined me to make no report of that battle to my then Chief, further than was contained in a letter written immediately after the battle to his General Halleck, Commander of the Department, informing him that an engagement had been fought

In this early draft of Grant's Shiloh article, his first for the *Century*, one could see his hesitations and frustrations as a writer.

So the editor made another trip to Grant's summer cottage. Given the author's sensitivities about, well, authorship, Johnson needed to be careful. Before turning to the stodgy manuscript in his pocket, he asked Grant a few simple questions about the battle. The responses were detailed and energetic. Grant talked about his first night at Shiloh—how he suffered through torrential rain and an injured ankle until finally resting at a log cabin that had morphed into a makeshift hospital. "I couldn't stand the amputations," he admitted to Johnson, "and had to go out in the rain and sit for the most of the night against a tree."

As Grant continued to reminisce, Johnson jotted down notes. (He did so slyly in the margins of a newspaper, knowing that anything too official would render the general self-conscious.) After a while, he shared his notes with Grant—though in truth they were Grant's notes, based on his recollections and feelings. That immediacy was exactly what readers wanted, the editor explained, and Grant grasped the point immediately. Within two weeks, he finished a new draft, and this time everyone at the *Century* loved it, particularly the added passages like this one, which would become one of Grant's most celebrated after it appeared in the Shiloh section of his book:

> Some time after midnight, growing restive under the storm and the continuous pain, I moved back to the log-house under the bank. This had been taken as a hospital, and all night wounded men were being brought in, their wounds dressed, a leg or an arm amputated as the case might require, and everything being done to save life or alleviate suffering. The sight was more unendurable than encountering the enemy's fire, and I returned to my tree in the rain.

With Johnson's help, Grant made similar improvements throughout the article, cutting back on the military minutiae and rounding out supporting characters like Sherman. Grant discovered that the act of writing thrilled him. "Why, I am positively enjoying the work," he told Johnson. "I am keeping at it every day and night." Grant recruited another son, Frederick Grant, and a former aide, Adam Badeau, to check facts, dig up documents, and copy manuscripts.* With each completed article, he gained

---

*While Frederick and Badeau also read and commented on Grant's prose, their chief role was to help him write quickly. On Vicksburg, to take a small example, Grant wrote that it "was the first engagement of the war in which colored troops were used." When Frederick read the draft, he made a marginal correction: "Wrong, colored troops had been engaged before." In his next draft, Grant added an "important" before "engagement."

confidence. In his first attempt at Shiloh, one could see the frustration in his handwriting—in the aborted sentences and slashed-out phrases. Now Grant seemed like a natural, though he still insisted on punishing rounds of revision.

Summer was ebbing, and the Grants returned to their home on Sixty-Sixth Street. The general kept polishing his articles, working at a table, as he preferred, in a small room on the second floor. He talked about continuing the writing and even doing a full-scale memoir with the *Century*'s publishing arm. First, though, he needed to see a doctor about his throat, which had been bothering him for months. One day, while still at the cottage, Grant had taken a small bite of peach, then shot up from his chair in pain. Everyone's initial thought was that there'd been a stinging insect on the fruit, but when Grant rinsed his mouth the pain only increased. Even a sip of water, Julia remembered, "hurt him like liquid fire."

Grant declined to see a doctor until they returned to New York. On the afternoon of October 22, John Douglas, one of the city's top throat specialists, examined him. The inside of Grant's mouth was ghastly: three warts, an inflamed tonsil, and swelling at the base of his tongue that alternated between crusty and covered in mucus. "Is it cancer?" Grant asked. Dr. Douglas offered a euphemistic but unmistakable reply: "General, the disease is serious."

After seeing Dr. Douglas, Grant took a streetcar to the *Century*'s office. There, he met with Johnson's boss, Richard Watson Gilder, and talked at length about publishing his autobiography. Gilder's notes from the conversation don't mention anything strange about his visitor. ("General Grant has just been in, spent some time, and wants us to publish his book or books.") Outwardly, at least, Grant had defeated the shock of the doctor's news, had absorbed it as smoothly as that elevator dive a few years before. Inwardly, though, he saw the situation was grave. Grant's disease—his looming death—meant that everything in his life suddenly mattered more, starting with his book. What had once seemed like a way to fix a short-term financial problem would now be Grant's last chance to provide for his wife and children after he was gone. What had once seemed like a chance to remind the public of his better days would now be his final statement on his legacy.

So the general sat at his table and wrote. That fall, despite his ratcheting discomfort, he worked six days a week, supported by the ministrations of Dr. Douglas, who swabbed his throat with a mixture of cocaine and water, and of Robert Johnson, who continued to edit and encourage. As it happened, Mark Twain was also keeping busy, traveling the country on a series of lucrative lectures and launching a publishing firm of his own. In November, he entertained a large crowd in New York. Afterward, as he exited the hall, Twain spotted two men talking in the drizzling rain.

"Do you know General Grant has actually determined to write his memoirs and publish them?" one of them said.

Twain recognized the speaker was Richard Gilder, and when Gilder spotted Twain, he invited him over for a late supper. For more than an hour, the *Century* editor gushed about Grant—about how well he'd taken to writing and how serious he seemed with the book, though he and the *Century* had yet to sign anything official. Twain, despite his friendship with Grant, had not known the general's plans were this advanced, but he ate his meal quietly and listened. The very next day, he knocked on Grant's front door, and it wasn't long until the general had finalized plans to publish his book—not with the *Century* but with Twain.

WRITING AND DYING IN PUBLIC

A few weeks after Grant signed with Twain—a decision that, though it surprised and saddened Johnson and Gilder, made sense given Twain's literary clout (and given that his offer was at least twice as generous as the *Century*'s)—the general's new editor stopped by for another visit. It was a full house, with Julia, Dr. Douglas, Adam Badeau, and an assortment of sons and daughters-in-law. Grant was upstairs, taking one of his fitful naps. Everyone agreed he needed more of these breaks, between the book and the ways in which the cancer was making it harder to eat, drink, and breathe.

Twain didn't want to see the general. Instead, he wanted to see his image. A young sculptor Twain was supporting had recently started a clay bust of Grant, and they hoped to compare it to other versions of Grant and to get the family's feedback. Julia and the others loved the idea. They examined the in-progress bust and sent for other images: paintings, photographs, miniature portraits, and more. Each representation seemed to contradict the previous one, and the debate over Grant's features grew so spirited—over the nose, in particular—that Julia finally decided to summon the original. They found the general resting with his feet propped up, wearing a wool skullcap for warmth. Everyone squeezed into the room, and the debate continued. "I was sure his nose was so," said one family member. "Don't you think his head is so?" said another. Julia adjusted his posture, lovingly.

"Ulyss," she finally said, "Can't you put your feet to the floor?" The general silently, lovingly complied.

Grant's final months often resembled this surreal episode—the general simultaneously half living and half dead, half present and half past. The feeling flowed in large part from an army of journalists who, once they confirmed the true scope of his sickness in early 1885, tracked his every move. Up to that point, Grant had worked in peace, or at least in as much peace as the most famous man in America might expect. (On this count Twain was his only real rival.) Now Grant, his health, and his book became one of the nation's dominant news stories.

In February, the *Century* published Grant's first article, on Shiloh. It was a huge success, and Grant's further contributions, along with the other Civil War essays, nearly doubled the magazine's circulation, making it the most popular monthly in America. Just as readers got their first glimpse of Grant's *Personal Memoirs*, then, they learned its author was dying: "General Grant Very Ill," the headlines proclaimed. Dr. Douglas was now injecting morphine directly into his patient's swollen throat; Grant was subsisting on cold soup and milk, maybe a bit of oatmeal. Sometimes when the family gathered for dinner, a member other than Grant read the day's new pages aloud. The general couldn't eat, of course, but he also couldn't carve the meat or even sit through an entire meal. His agony grew too intense, leaving him to pace weakly in the library, trying to distract himself.

The country directed its full attention to Sixty-Sixth Street, and Grant's race to finish his book became a daily obsession in the way that, in the next century, people would obsess over a man flying across the Atlantic. Each morning while writing, Grant could look out his windows and see crowds of curious schoolchildren or tourists huddled in prayer. He could watch reporters competing for the smallest daily scoop—reporters not just from New York but from Boston, Washington, Chicago, St. Louis, San Francisco, and Los Angeles, plus the national news services. (One scribe tried bribing Grant's servants; another began wooing a chambermaid across the street to secure the view from her bedroom window.) Or Grant could simply wait until the next day to read the scoops himself: "General Grant Goes Out Twice," "General Grant More Hopeful," "General Grant

Depressed." The newspapers catalogued everything they could, often erroneously: Grant's sleep schedule, his diminishing weight, his decision to use a cane. "General Grant's Throat Irritable." "General Grant's Condition: He Finds Himself Constantly Growing Weaker, But Is Plucky."*

More than anything else, the papers reported on Grant's literary labor: "General Grant," went another headline, "at Work on His Book." His health kept deteriorating; in March, and again in April, he nearly died, coughing and choking on mouthfuls of blood. At least the writing, his family and physicians agreed, had given him purpose. There were certainly stretches where he felt too tired (or too depressed) to do much work. But they always passed, and most days it seemed nothing could keep Grant from his book. When the cancer left him too weak to write for extended periods, he dictated to a stenographer; when the fluids leaching into his throat made it too hard to speak, he whispered into his stenographer's ear. Grant marched from battle to battle, narrating each conflict with his mix of concrete particulars and private insights. What had once been seen as a single volume of five hundred pages now looked like it would stretch to two volumes, each of at least that size. Grant begged Twain for more pages, more revisions, more time. For someone who'd spent years claiming he wasn't a writer, the general was doing an awfully good authorial impression.

The most striking thing about Grant's commitment was that it was no longer strictly necessary. By the end of May, the first volume was in solid shape; even better, the publicity had generated more than sixty thousand preorders for his book. ("The people," an ex-soldier informed him, echoing that famous Fort Donelson line, "are moving en masse upon your memoirs.") The general's family would get plenty of money, and there was already plenty of book. Yet Grant kept expanding and revising. His book had blossomed into something he cared about fiercely and personally—a passion that became clear in his response to a scandalous charge of ghostwriting.

It started with a gossip column. Among other rumors, the article hinted that Grant had botched early attempts at writing his own story—"He is

---

*Dr. Douglas frequently conferred with reporters, and a side effect of Grant's decline was that it led to unprecedented coverage of cancer as a disease. Of course, even doctors had much to learn about cancer. While there's no way to prove Grant's cigars caused his affliction, it seems likely. Yet Dr. Douglas never considered it. One time, Twain asked him about the link between the general's habit and his cancer. "This is a warning to the rest of us," Twain suggested. "No, it isn't a warning to anybody," the doctor replied. "This is not a result of smoking. Smoking has never hurt General Grant, and it will never hurt you."

Grant frequently wrote on the porch of the Mount McGregor house, his body wrapped in blankets despite the summer heat.

not a writer. He does not compose easily"—and had decided to feed his material to the book's true author, Adam Badeau. Around the same time, Badeau, who may have planted the ghostwriting charge and who, at the very least, was unhappy in his role as a research assistant, demanded a raise. Grant responded forcefully. While many readers in 1885 would understand the realities of political authorship—the genesis of Washington's Farewell Address, after all, was now widely known—the pathos and publicity surrounding Grant's book made it different. The general fired Badeau and spent hours crafting a public letter that denied everything. The letter worked, with the accusations of ghostwriting only adding to the buzz around the book.

A second, private letter to Badeau suggested that Grant was fretting less about optics than authorship: "I do not want a book bearing my name to go before the world," Grant wrote, "which I did not write." The author still needed to finish, and in June his doctors advised that he escape the city's heat and congestion. And so, one year after his initial trip to the beach cottage, where he'd started his articles and first felt a stinging in his throat, Grant boarded a train for Mount McGregor, a rustic retreat in the Adirondacks.

One of Grant's supporters had offered him a summer house there, with room for the whole family plus a spacious porch encircled in maple and pine. Grant had returned to writing by hand—even whispering had become excruciating, to the point that he now did most of his communicating through scribbled notes—and he sat on that porch and wrote, bundled in blankets and gloves and his woolen cap despite the summer heat. Even with Mount McGregor's seclusion, Grant was visited by scores of journalists and photographers, by old generals from the North and South alike, and by an unceasing line of citizens who shuffled silently past the home. There, Grant said his final good-byes to Twain and to Robert Johnson, who was struck by the general's spirit during their visit—by the way he expressed his pain "with a patient, resigned expression, but not with a stricken look."

Throughout June and into July, Grant refined the second volume. He had grown so gaunt that his wedding ring no longer fit; his spasms of coughing echoed through the house, where his wife and children pretended not to hear. Grant reminded everyone that there were more details to add, more facts to check. But one day he paused to consider something more philosophical: the mysteries of "man's destiny," starting with his own soldierly trajectory. "I never thought of acquiring rank in the profession I was educated for," he wrote in a note to Dr. Douglas—and yet he became a decorated general. Grant continued:

> I certainly never had either ambition or taste for political life; yet I was twice President of the United States. If any one had suggested the idea of my becoming an author, as they frequently did, I was not sure whether they were making sport of me or not. I have now written a book.

LOST LEGACIES

Ulysses S. Grant died the way he lived: calm and resolute. On the morning of July 23, 1885, his family gathered around him at the house. He had made the final changes to his *Personal Memoirs* two days before; now he could let go. "Life passed away," Dr. Douglas remembered, "so quietly, so peacefully, that we had to wait a minute to be sure."

While Grant would never see his book in print, he died knowing that Twain would handle its publication. Twain had done little to shape the prose.* But he pulled off a sale with few precedents in American publishing (or American retail of any kind). Grant's book smashed every record for presidential sales, which makes it only stranger that one of its main legacies is showing that legacy books never seem to work the way their authors intended.

From their earliest discussions, Twain had argued that the general's renown would guarantee a huge hit—that it would provide the kind of external flame that had boosted other nineteenth-century best sellers like *Uncle Tom's Cabin*. Distribution remained the biggest challenge. "The factory hands and the farmers," Twain had once observed, "never go to a bookstore; they have to be hunted down." There were plenty of professionals living outside of bookstore range as well, and the best way to reach a truly mass audience was still by selling book subscriptions.

Twain hired a small army to push Grant's book, some of them veterans who had served with him in the Civil War. Each received a thirty-seven-page prospectus titled "How to Introduce the *Personal Memoirs* of U. S. Grant"—in other words, a script—and for much of 1885, the salesmen knocked on doors around the country. As soon as someone answered, they delivered their first line: "I called to give you an opportunity to see General Grant's book, of which so much has been said in the papers."

The first volume reached subscribers in December, and Twain needed forty-one steam presses to meet the demand. By the spring of 1886, the publisher and his agents had moved a stunning 325,000 two-volume sets. Grant's *Personal Memoirs* rewrote the very idea of what made a best-selling book. When *Uncle Tom's Cabin* had first appeared, Stowe received a royalty check for $10,300—a number the *New York Times* called "the largest sum of money ever received by any author, either American or European, from the actual sales of a single work in so short a period of time." When Twain presented Julia Grant with her first royalty check, it was for $200,000. She would eventually receive more than twice that, a figure that would easily top $10 million in today's dollars.

---

*A good example of Twain's hands-off editing—and of his promotional instincts—came when a friend asked about Grant's rumored taste for alcohol. "I wish I had thought of it!" Twain replied, long after the book had gone to print. "I would have said to General Grant: 'Put the drunkenness in the *Memoirs*—and the repentance and reform. Trust the people.'" Even if Twain had intervened, his author might have refused to discuss his drinking: "He was sore, there," Twain said.

Readers and reviewers raved about *Personal Memoirs*, though one could detect a geographical pattern in the enthusiasm. William Dean Howells was a proud Northerner, in addition to being an enthusiast for autobiography, democracy, and literature. Grant's book satisfied him on all fronts, especially in its unpretentious storytelling, its relentless narrative of attrition. "We have heard a lot about what the American was to be in literature when he got there," Howells wrote. "What if this were he?"

And yet as the nineteenth century gave way to the twentieth, Grant's reputation stumbled. There was a curious dearth of biographies and history books about him; as one critic put it in 1918, "We should doubtless have had, by this time, a greater number of serious attempts to represent [Grant]." Meanwhile, the Confederate backlist continued to swell. Robert E. Lee was emerging as a national hero, propped up by the Lost Cause and its countless pro-Southern histories, whose interpretations were seeping into novels like *Gone with the Wind*, movies like *The Birth of a Nation*, and textbooks in all sorts of schools. American culture was becoming softly, nostalgically Southern, which made it easier for everyone to ignore the real-world injustices of the Jim Crow South.

One way to elevate Lee was to tear down Grant—to turn the Union's best general into a vicious but clumsy foil, a leader who won only because of enormous advantages in materials and men. The Lost Cause's many tireless authors transformed the conflict into Lee the gentleman versus Grant the butcher, and Grant's book and its careful battlefield accounts couldn't do a thing to stop them. In its review of *Personal Memoirs*, the *Southern Historical Society Papers*, essentially the Lost Cause's house organ, had issued a warning: "The future historian who attempts to follow it will be led very far astray from the real truth." Many of those future historians did diverge from Grant's narrative, but that said more about the Lost Cause's influence than it did about Grant's accuracy. Authors still admired the style of *Personal Memoirs*. (Sherwood Anderson adored it—and the fact that his father had served as one of its traveling booksellers.) Politicians admired that it was admired. But in terms of defending Grant's military reputation, which had always been one of his chief concerns, the book was a bust.

Only now, as the twentieth century has given way to the twenty-first, has Grant's reputation been restored. The heroes have been academics and revisionist biographers, not the presidency's greatest memoirist. Even a legacy book as good (and as popular) as Grant's couldn't ensure a fair or favorable legacy. *Personal Memoirs*, to borrow an interpretive framework, was a saintly and chivalrous book. It just had the bad fortune of drawing a

cruel and bullying opponent, an opponent who triumphed thanks mostly
to superior resources.

AUTHOR TO AUTHOR

While *Personal Memoirs* failed to fortify Grant's reputation, it still touched
thousands and thousands of readers. One of them was Mark Twain.

Twain had slowed his own writing while helping with Grant's book.
There was one major exception—an essay for Robert Johnson's big series
in the *Century* that would be Twain's second attempt to write about the
Civil War.

The first had come in 1877, when the author gave a speech to the
Ancient and Honorable Artillery Company of Massachusetts, which
sounded like an organization from one of his short stories but was (and is)
a real thing. The company had invited Twain to its anniversary gala, and
in his remarks, he revealed his brief military past. "I, too, am a soldier!" he
told the crowd. "I have been through a stirring campaign, and there is not
even a mention of it in any history." Twain set out to fill this scholarly gap.
His campaign covered the two weeks he'd spent with the Marion Rangers,
a group of Missouri amateurs that, in Twain's telling, accomplished little
more than hassling farmers and finding reasons to skip picket duty. Their
greatest victory came when they holed up in a corncrib; their greatest
defeat came when, inside that corncrib, a Ranger was bitten by a rat.

Twain's speech seemed to mock everything about war: the bravery, the
hierarchy, and, most of all, the desire to memorialize its actors in histories
and autobiographies—in the sort of literature that, only two years after
Sherman's big book, was becoming increasingly popular. When Twain
took his second stab at depicting the Civil War, eight years later, he stuck
with the same plot. "You have heard from a great many people who did
something in the war," he wrote in the pages of the *Century*. "Is it not fair
and right that you listen a little moment to one who started out to do
something in it, but didn't?"

And yet something had changed between those two pieces of war
writing. Twain still wrote with humor. (How could he write otherwise?)
He still lampooned the Civil War's literary industry, which had grown
only more popular and pious. But this time, Twain didn't stop with these
points. Instead, near the end of his second essay, he added a somber scene.
One night, in the corncrib, the Rangers heard the enemy approaching.

The youthful Twain slid his rifle through a crack and fired at the first man he saw:

> Somebody said, hardly audibly, "Good—we've got him!—wait for the rest." But the rest did not come. We waited—listened—still no more came. There was not a sound, not the whisper of a leaf; just perfect stillness; an uncanny kind of stillness, which was all the more uncanny on account of the damp, earthy, late-night smells now rising and pervading it.

The scene mirrored Grant's description of his first night at Shiloh, and not just in its drizzly atmospherics. Twain devoted the rest of his essay to considering the folly of firing at a man he did not know, a man with a wife and children, a man who didn't deserve to die. The shooting allowed the author to examine war not just with satire but with realism and grace. The Twain of 1877 did not make room for such sentiments. The Twain of 1885—the one who'd spent months helping Grant and, just as much, reading Grant—did.

Twain's biographers (and he has attracted enough to make most presidents jealous) have frequently debated whether the shooting actually happened. Yet the reason Twain could invent it, if he did invent it, was his relationship with Grant. In the essay, Twain described cradling the head of the man he'd shot, and his descriptions—the ragged breathing, the darkening eyes—remain wrenchingly vivid. Could Twain have conjured something so real? Perhaps the better question is: Would he have needed to? After all, the entire time Twain was revising his essay, he was watching a good man die.

PART III

RUTHERFORD B. HAYES
TO
FRANKLIN D. ROOSEVELT

CHAPTER SEVEN

Head of the Class:
Roosevelt, Wilson, and
the Expansion of Executive Power

Theodore Roosevelt was used to being the hunter, but lately it seemed he was the prey. It was the spring of 1898, and the thirty-nine-year-old rancher, outdoorsman, old-moneyed New Yorker, multitime author, and now freshly appointed officer in the First US Volunteer Cavalry—an outfit that would soon be celebrated as the Rough Riders—was preparing to depart for Cuba, to serve in the Spanish-American War. But first Roosevelt needed to outlast an army of editors at home. Someone from the *Atlantic Monthly* was begging him to write for the magazine. Robert Underwood Johnson, Ulysses S. Grant's old editor, was trying to recruit him to the *Century*. ("If you hear of anything notable," Johnson wrote, "just slyly let us know.") In letters and in telegrams, book publishers were promising Roosevelt he could write whatever he wanted—a volume of memoir, of history, of anything really so long as it centered on Roosevelt himself. "I could make such an arrangement," Roosevelt replied to yet another editor, "provided neither the yellow fever nor a Mauser bullet catches me."

The sickness Roosevelt should have feared was a strain of cocky heroism, and his vibrant, swaggering life suggests he could catch that fever anywhere and any time. Roosevelt saw the world as a simple and dramatic place. Brave men. Big stakes. Patriotic pride. Each of these qualities infused the book he ultimately wrote about the Spanish-American War, *The Rough Riders*, along with the belief that its author always knew the right thing to do and the right man to do it. "If I was him," joked a contemporary, "I'd call the book *Alone in Cuba*."

This approach didn't stop with Roosevelt's words—his actions carried the same propulsive confidence. The many books he wrote provide a good way to gauge this. He insisted on drafting the chapters of *African Game Trails*, his most popular title, from the trails themselves, setting up a collapsible table, donning a mosquito net hood, and gripping the pen and paper through thick gloves. He completed book after book, some with multiple volumes, some with revised editions—as many as thirty-seven titles, depending on how you count. Shortly after his death in 1919, an editor analyzed his output and discovered that between the letters and essays and books Roosevelt had produced at least 18 million words, easily the equivalent of a long and robust career if he had been an author and nothing else.

Roosevelt was not the only literary president in this period. Woodrow Wilson struck many contemporaries as chilly, thoughtful, and restrained—precisely the demeanor one would expect from a man who, before he entered politics, was one of the most famous professors in America. Wilson loved history and literature, preferring in both cases practitioners of a British bent. (Once, on a trip to England, he took a bicycle to tour the haunts of his favorite poet, William Wordsworth: his home, his church, his grave.) But Wilson was also fiery and ambitious. He wrote twelve books, again depending on how you count, and faced his own horde of needy editors. He wrote essays and reviews for the nation's best periodicals. He lectured at events like the 1893 World's Fair. Whatever the format, Wilson addressed big audiences about big ideas: politics, art, nations, memory.

Yet the most interesting thing about Wilson and Roosevelt isn't their literary careers but their literary debuts. Long before they were prominent authors—and long before they were presidents—both men wrote fascinating first books. These books are fascinating for two reasons. First, both made measured but hugely influential arguments. Roosevelt and Wilson lived in an age of complexity and change. Between 1880 and 1920, America became bigger and messier—it tumbled through what the novelist Booth Tarkington called the "swiftest moving and most restless time the world has known." In response to this restlessness, America became more specialized. It was during this period that professionals started founding organizations like the American Library Association and the American Society of Mechanical Engineers. The country began to rely on experts and to revere scientific objectivity; Roosevelt and Wilson wrote books that demonstrated their objective expertise.

There's a second reason these volumes matter. Both books, in their commitment to context and nuance, provide a baseline for their authors' thinking. In fact, their debuts offer a way to mark and measure just how much Roosevelt and Wilson (and all presidents, really) evolve in their literary style—especially as they get closer and closer to real political power.

"HISTORY IS PAST POLITICS . . ."

One of the many professional organizations that bloomed in this period was the American Historical Association, which formed in 1884. For most of its existence, America had left the interpretation of its past to state societies, wealthy amateurs, and posthumously chatty presidents. Now the systems of modern historiography—scholarly monographs, national museums, best-selling books—were locking into place, and Americans showed more interest than ever in their history and how it should be taught, written, and read.

Not everything changed, and not all at once. The period's most popular historian was a forgotten figure named John Clark Ridpath, an improbable semischolar who blended a Weemsian flair for narrative with a Bancroftian belief in providence. Ridpath was born in 1840 in an Indiana log cabin. His father was a struggling farmer; he spent his childhood scrounging for books.

So far, so Lincoln, but as Ridpath grew older, he sought a new path: enrolling in one of the rapidly expanding colleges that were appearing all over the country. In 1840, America had somewhere around 10,000 undergraduates. By 1870, that number had jumped to 62,000, easily outpacing population growth; by 1920, there would be nearly 600,000 students.

Ridpath matriculated at Indiana Asbury University, a newish institution that would later be renamed DePauw. He was a motivated student. After a week of books and school, he studied more on Saturdays and then devoted Sundays to composing his own poetry and prose. His essays began running in local outlets before he'd finished his degree. "Today I . . . feel like an author," he wrote in his diary after seeing his name in print for the first time. "Just think of it."

After graduation in 1863, Ridpath turned to teaching, first at a high school and then at Asbury itself, where he covered literature and history and more. Still, he cared most about his writing, with his most significant work, *A Popular History of the United States of America*, appearing in 1876. The book was cheerful, patriotic, and constantly nodding toward an inevitable present. (In Ridpath's narrative, Native Americans essentially kept the continent warm for white people: "By flint and hatchet, the Red man supported his rude civilization and waited for the coming of the pale-faced races.") Ridpath didn't bother with originality or archival research; to understand George Washington, he skimmed a couple of biographies and the Farewell Address. Still, his books sold millions of copies, captivating young readers like Jane Addams and Thomas Wolfe. By the time he died in 1900, he'd grown so famous that fans sent him mail by addressing it to simply "Ridpath, the Historian."

Even as Ridpath reigned as the country's chief historian, its universities were redefining just what "historian" meant. They started by redefining the university itself, with two institutions driving this shift.

The first innovator was actually one of America's older establishments: Harvard. Most of its students still felt the Adams-Hawthorne dilemma: doctor, lawyer, minister. Whatever their choice, the curriculum in Cambridge and elsewhere stayed largely the same: Greek, Latin, religion. The methods remained tedious, with a focus on memorizing boring facts and then reciting them to bored professors.

That began to change in 1869 when Harvard hired a new president, Charles W. Eliot. Eliot, with his round glasses and carefully trimmed sideburns, looked more like a banker than a revolutionary. (In fact his grandfather had served as president of the Massachusetts Bank for years.) But at Harvard, Eliot reimagined the undergraduate experience. The university introduced him at a somber and formal event—a crowd of students and alumni squeezing into a Cambridge church, a choir singing a hymn by John Milton, a congratulatory address spoken entirely in Latin.

Then Eliot got up and delivered an address of his own. He rejected the idea that the world needed more Harvard gentlemen schooled in the clerics and classics—"the vulgar conceit," as he put it, "that a Yankee can turn his hand to anything." Instead, the university needed to teach a range of modern subjects. It needed its Yankees to specialize.

These reforms resulted in part from Eliot's own time as a chemistry professor. At Harvard and then at MIT, he had listened as students slogged through recitations. "I wish I could teach the science in which I am most interested," he complained at the time. Now as president, he could do something about it, scaling back language requirements, phasing out compulsory chapel, and expanding Harvard's elective system, which gave students the freedom to select more of the classes they would take. Eliot hired new faculty—a professor named William James to teach psychology; a professor named Henry Adams to teach history—and created modern, stand-alone departments like physics and English. Out went the recitations and drills; in came inspiring lectures and hands-on labs.

The second innovator was a new and experimental university, Johns Hopkins, which opened in 1876. Where Harvard had a traditional setting—the ivy-draped buildings, the elm-shaded Harvard Yard—Hopkins wedged its original location into downtown Baltimore, one of the nation's busiest cities. The campus consisted of converted row houses and hastily assembled buildings. Yet the oddest thing about it, by domestic standards at least, was its academic structure. It aspired to be America's first research university.

Hopkins borrowed this goal from Germany, where the professors focused on excavating fresh facts and training graduate students who would then produce the next generation of research. Those same priorities held at Hopkins, and the best spot to see them in action was the Seminary of Historical and Political Science, a weekly working group led by a professor named Herbert Baxter Adams. Adams was still in his twenties when he arrived in Baltimore, armed with a German doctorate and a drooping mustache that tried but failed to hide his youthful face. He was also sharp and meticulous, and at Hopkins he created a dynasty of future historians.

Adams settled his seminary on the third floor of the university library, in a big room that measured fifty-one by twenty-nine feet. (The professor was precise even when recording dimensions.) The walls were ringed with books, including multivolume editions of the writings of Washington, Jefferson, and Madison. Above them hung portraits and plaster busts of influential predecessors like George Bancroft and Jared Sparks. In the middle of the room sat a red table, big enough to accommodate twenty or more students, and on Friday night, starting at eight, they gathered to present and critique each other's latest research. Adams called his room a "laboratory," and during meetings hypotheses were tested and arguments were solved, often by the unfurling of a map or the grabbing of an old volume. At its best, the seminary felt like the making of American history in real time.

It really was American. "The historical seminary," Adams would later recall, "was founded upon a purely American basis, and devoted itself strictly to American history." Outside of that early stricture, though, students encountered lots of freedom. When a Wisconsin native named Frederick Jackson Turner wanted to research western expansion, a skeptical Adams signed off. In time Turner became one of the country's preeminent historians, thanks largely to his frontier thesis and its claim that

Herbert Baxter Adams taught at the large table inside his seminary
room at Johns Hopkins.

American identity—practical, independent, anxious—stemmed from the
shrinking vastness of the American West. It was the sort of vital and ambitious work Adams wanted the seminary to foster. On one wall of the main
room, there was a quotation painted in big, unsubtle letters: "History is
past Politics and Politics present History."

The reforms of Harvard and Hopkins spread. Charles W. Eliot became
America's most influential university president; PhDs trained by Adams
et al. fanned across the country, often landing at one of the land grant universities made possible by the Morrill Act of 1862. It took time—change
in academia always does. But universities were becoming more rigorous,
more professional, and more complex. America had perhaps two dozen
history professors in 1886; by 1910, it had nearly six hundred.*

Those professors often investigated narrow topics, but that created
more space (and more background reading) for a new kind of popular
historian. Instead of doctors or merchants writing state histories on the

---

*Those professors—and their students—were mostly male. That was changing, though
it also took time. In 1910, American men received 28,762 bachelor's degrees; women
received 8,437, and in the next few decades they would slowly shrink the gap. The whole
time, female authors continued writing significant works of history, frequently spotlight-
ing overlooked groups such as everyday Puritan women (Margaret Bell's *Women of the
Wilderness*) or African Americans on the Underground Railroad (Henrietta Buckmaster's
Let My People Go).

side, these were journalists and authors writing serious but sculpted best sellers, books with national scopes like James Truslow Adams's *Epic of America*. It was a sort of double specialization, on campus and off: the rise of academic disciplines and academic journals and, at the same time, the rise of public history and narrative-driven books. There were audiences enough for both. In Washington, DC, the Smithsonian and its National Museum Building were both drawing as many as 150,000 visitors per year.

Some historians spent their time getting angry and choosing sides, scholars versus storytellers. (Ridpath quit academia and groused about its "wrinkled sages.") But most saw these divisions as opportunities, as ways to create more options for readers and authors alike. While Carl Sandburg made his name as a poet, he'd always nurtured an obsession with Lincoln. One of the Lincoln-Douglas debates had occurred in his hometown, and as a young man he'd fallen in love with their text, reading a version based on Lincoln's original volume.

One day in 1923, Sandburg met with an editor to brainstorm his next book. The editor suggested a children's biography of Lincoln, short and accessible, and Sandberg warmed to it immediately. "A volume of 400 pages?" he said.

"Yes," the editor replied, "but it might run to a little longer."

Sandburg, of course, eventually completed a meandering six-volume biography, a mix of history and romance that still ranks as the most widely known life of Lincoln. No one would confuse its author with an academic, but Sandburg read deeply in the Lincoln literature before adding his own interviews and archival work. When his first volumes appeared in 1926, they became a literary sensation. One review came from Fanny Butcher, the excellent (and ominously named) critic at the *Chicago Tribune*. Butcher could just imagine her readers' reactions: "What," she wrote, "*another* life of Lincoln?" She believed Sandburg's epic had eclipsed the many that came before it. But it's worth pausing on her premise—that readers now lived in an age when they could grumble about not the absence of American history but the superabundance.

THE ETERNAL UNDERGRAD

As a biographical target, Theodore Roosevelt stands as one of Lincoln's only real rivals. Roosevelt's chroniclers have marveled at the breadth of his interests and opinions—and at his energy in sustaining every last one of them. Even his contemporaries marveled at it. Henry James once attended a White House reception and left it stunned by the president's vitality, calling him "a wonderful little machine: destined to be overstrained, perhaps, but not as yet, truly, betraying the least creak." Before he was a machine, though, Roosevelt was a confused college student. The man who would do everything didn't know what to do first, and the answer turned out to be something James would have admired: authorship.

Roosevelt was born in 1858 and blessed with every advantage—wealthy family, doting parents, private tutors—except one: his health. He spent his childhood in New York City battling asthma and other ailments, battles he won by remaking his body through stubbornness and hard work. The places to find him were in a rocking chair, reading, or outside in nature, observing.

The natural world enchanted Roosevelt and, more than anything else, shaped him as a writer. He loved studying its patterns, classifying its species, and hoarding its specimens (not all of them dead, to the family servants' chagrin). Even as a boy he began documenting all of this in dense diaries and notebooks, and this commitment to pure information, presented simply and cleanly, would never leave him.

A fine example came in his unpublished early essay, "Sou' Sou' Southerly." Roosevelt's title referred to the local nickname for a particular duck, *Clangula hyemalis*, and he opened by describing the Long Island Sound, where he and his brother Elliott would soon steer their sailboat to hunt the ducks:

> When the October weather begins to grow cool and sharp, and the northeast winds blow over the steel gray waters till they are tossed into long, foam-capped billows, then, for the first time, small parties of these birds appear, their bold, varied coloring and harsh but not unmusical clangor at once attracting the attention of anyone who may be out sailing over the autumn seas. On the clear fall days they can be seen a long distance off, and even before they can be seen can be heard the loud "ha'-ha'-we, ha'-ha'-wee."

Roosevelt engaged his reader's touch, hearing, and sight; he hinted at the voyage's possibilities, its inherent suspense. But he did this through detail. His prose rarely indulged in figurative language or ornate phrasing. Instead it charged forward with crisp specifics: the icicles hanging from the boat's rigging, the feathers floating in the water after a successful shot.

Roosevelt built all of his books this way, assembling each sentence and paragraph block by solid block.*

By the time he enrolled in college in the fall of 1876, Roosevelt believed he had a subject and a style. His family sent him north, to Harvard, where he planned to become a scientist, assembling a career out of observations even if they jumped from botany to biology to zoology and beyond. In Jefferson's time, this blend had been known as one subject, natural history. In Roosevelt's, however, it was headed toward being barely known at all. Thanks to Eliot's reforms, Harvard now treated subjects like biology as their own isolated fields, to be studied and taught by professors with PhDs. Instead of binoculars and a forest, one needed a microscope and a lab. Roosevelt rejected this approach but lacked a replacement. In his junior-year diary, he wrote, "I have absolutely no idea what I shall do when I leave college."

This uncertainty didn't stop him from enjoying his years on campus. He was a skinny but strong young man, with thick red side-whiskers and a defiant stare. He ditched the dorms to rent a room near the Charles River, which provided extra space for specimens, stuffed animals, and books. As a student, he took full advantage of Eliot's other changes, dodging the classics when possible and loading up on electives in newer fields (economics, for instance). During lectures, Roosevelt would interrupt and interrogate his professors. One resorted to pleading, "Now look here, Roosevelt, let me talk. I'm running this course." William James had a better tactic. "I can see [James] now," another student recalled, "in his double-breasted blue coat and flowing tie, settling back in his chair, in a broad grin . . . waiting for T. R. to finish."

Many of Roosevelt's important collegiate experiences came from books. He was a practical, literal reader. (As a boy, he'd rejected *The Swiss Family Robinson* because of its "wholly impossible collection of animals.") He had broad preferences—comedy over tragedy; classic over contemporary; American over European—but would page through almost anything.

Still, his most striking literary trait was the way that, every once in a while, he would grow obsessed with a topic, reading deeply and widely in it with clenched-jaw concentration. Classmates would notice him in

---

*What's missing in Roosevelt's nonfiction is introspection or analysis. Compare, for instance, his later essay "Hunting the Grizzly" with George Orwell's seminal "Shooting an Elephant." Orwell described shooting the titular elephant, then followed it with a meditation on imperialism and shame. Roosevelt described shooting the titular bear, then followed it with the shooting of another bear.

At Harvard, Roosevelt decided to forgo the dorms and rent this room instead, which offered more space for books.

the corner of a room full of rowdy undergrads, reading so briskly that his book's pages turned like the ticking of a clock. Roosevelt's life supplied a number of similar anecdotes: focusing on Plutarch's *Lives* during his epic stump tour in 1900, as William McKinley's candidate for vice president; blocking out a crowded hotel, during the GOP's raucous 1912 convention, to peruse the ancient historian Herodotus; passing time in the Brazilian wilderness, on a safari, with Gibbon's *Decline and Fall of the Roman Empire*. Reading, to him, was living. Once, in an essay, he considered the man who "is not fond of books." "I most sincerely commiserate with such a person," Roosevelt wrote, "but I do not know how to help him."

A bout of obsession led to Roosevelt's authorial debut. At some point during his Harvard years, he slipped into one of the libraries and borrowed the multivolume *Naval History of Great Britain*, first published in the 1820s and still considered a definitive work. Perhaps he chose the hefty title because of his taste for water; in addition to the many hours he'd spent afloat, from duck hunting on the Sound to canoeing in Maine's rivers, his maternal uncles had served in the Confederate Navy. (Roosevelt's mother, he later wrote, would "talk to me as a little shaver about ships, ships, ships, and fighting of ships, till they sank into the depths of my soul.") Whatever the impetus, the book exasperated him—especially in its biased, pro-British account of the War of 1812. It offended Roosevelt's sense of patriotism. But it also offended his sense of fairness. Soon he was reading exhaustively about the war; during classes, his mind would wander until he was picturing British and American ships, dueling at sea. Once he realized there were no objective and rigorous histories of the conflict's naval operations, he decided to write one himself. He finished the first chapter while still at Harvard. He could not have been older than twenty-one.

Roosevelt might have finished more chapters had he not been courting a local named Alice Lee. They married in the fall of 1880, a few months after his graduation. Their relationship was simultaneously intellectual—reading aloud together, imagining future travel—and adoring. Alice called him "Teddykins" or "Teedy," while he called her "my blessed little wife."

They eventually settled in a cozy Manhattan brownstone on Forty-Fifth Street, a twenty-minute walk from the house where, a few years later, Ulysses S. Grant would write much of *Personal Memoirs*, a book Roosevelt loved. For now, Roosevelt decided to enroll at Columbia's law school, though he wasn't thrilled by it. The law, like so many other professions, was changing, with aspiring counselors switching from apprenticeships or independent study to more specialized training. (The country had fifteen law schools in 1860; in 1890 there were sixty-one.) Roosevelt hoped a law degree would mean a stable career. It also kept a second, stealthier option open—"going into public life," as he confided in his diary.

What he cared about most were Alice and the book. For a title, he chose *The Naval War of 1812*, and Roosevelt spent most of his free time reading: posthumous memoirs by admirals; brittle seventy-year-old newspapers; books on navigation and tactics. Roosevelt didn't trust the war's previous historians, British or American—and besides, much of what he needed to know rested in sources no scholar had yet studied. So he kept digging and digesting, relying on the skills he'd refined as a naturalist. For major battles, he created taxonomic-like tables with the size and style of ships and the size and style of their cannons. (Then he went further, evaluating the foundries that made the specific guns.) He studied maps and reviewed weather patterns until he could draw meticulous diagrams by hand, tracing individual vessels through their battle-time dance. Alice would try to distract him, tickling his arm until his pen slipped and blotted the page. But Roosevelt continued to write, often late into the night. The couple developed a loving shorthand for the project: the author, they teased, was always "drawing little boats."

Writing a book as ambitious as *Naval War* forced Roosevelt to slow down, to experience self-doubt. "I have plenty of information now," he admitted to his sister, "but I can't get it into words; I am afraid it is too big a task for me. I wonder if I won't find everything in life too big for my abilities."

The only solution was to keep writing, even as he stayed busy with law school, the robust social calendar he shared with Alice, and the annual Harvard-Yale football game, which left him missing college and its camaraderie. In the spring of 1881 Roosevelt encountered his biggest distraction yet—a belated five-month honeymoon with Alice in Europe. Their party had three passengers: Alice, Theodore, and the manuscript of his unfinished book. In England the couple went to plays and visited with Roosevelt's Confederate uncles, who had moved there after the Civil War; Roosevelt spent much of the time quizzing them on naval topics. In France the couple sampled coffee and chocolate, but by the time they got to Germany, Roosevelt was meeting with another naval officer, an American who helped him secure access to rare documents at home. The War of 1812 hovered over their honeymoon. In Belgium, he and Alice toured art galleries, but even the paintings revived the author's anxieties. "They bring out the life of that period," he noted, "in a way no written history could."

In October the couple returned to America, and Roosevelt began his final scramble to finish the book. He had picked up a new distraction: a bid for the New York state legislature, which he won in November on the strength of his name (and with the help of some well-connected party operatives). But he continued to fret about *Naval War*, marshaling his concentration, writing next to the brownstone's row of bookshelves, standing on one leg and oblivious to everything around him, even Alice. The shorthand, as one friend witnessed, had become less loving. "We're dining out in twenty minutes," Alice exclaimed, "and Teedy's drawing little ships!" Roosevelt kept going, with one of his final tasks being a revision of the early chapter he'd written at Harvard. On December 3, 1881, he submitted the manuscript to his publisher, G. P. Putnam's Sons. He had yet to finish law school; his career as a legislator wouldn't start for a few more weeks. But Theodore Roosevelt had completed his first book.

A month later, Roosevelt was complaining that "my book seems to be getting on rather slowly"—an absurd charge for any book, much less one running to nearly five hundred pages and requiring a tricky design due to its many tables and diagrams. Yet *Naval War* was the product of a patient and scrupulous mind. It contained flashes of action and wit, but mostly it had wave after wave of information. (A sample sentence: "The Endymion

then had an armament of 28 long 24's, 2 long 18's, and 20 32-pound car-
ronades, making a broadside of 674 pounds"—followed by a footnote that
scolded another scholar for botching these figures.) It was the book of an
expert, and it showed its work.

It was also the book of a revisionist. Roosevelt's research had led him
to reevaluate the war's key episodes, especially the Battle of Lake Erie. To
most Americans this was really the Battle of Oliver Perry, the commander
who'd defeated the British in an important upset that was still commem-
orated around the country. Perry's legend had grown past the point of
the Navy naming ships after him; his fellow citizens had taken to naming
towns after him, from Perry, Ohio, to Perry, Georgia.

. After assessing the battle, however, Roosevelt decided that Perry
wasn't actually a hero—and that the battle wasn't actually an upset. While
the British ships had boasted more cannonry, an analysis of the guns and
their layout revealed that the Americans had about twice the effective fire-
power. Perry's victory at Lake Erie wasn't about his character or courage,
and it certainly wasn't about the flag flying at the top of his ship. Instead,
Roosevelt argued, it was a triumph of planning and resources, of factors
far more intricate than any individual and his actions. This cautious lesson saturated Roosevelt's book. "Something more than bravery is needed,"
he wrote, "before a leader can be really called great."*

When *Naval War* finally appeared in the summer of 1882, it earned
cheers on both sides of the Atlantic—and on both sides of the scholar-
storyteller divide. Reviewers praised its originality and objectivity. (Both
Harper's and the *Atlantic* celebrated its tone with a most un-Rooseveltian
adjective: "cool.") "If his conclusions stand," another critic added, "the
fame of some of our naval heroes will be seriously modified." The book
was a solid seller, going through nine editions in ten years, but that represented only part of its influence. Universities adopted *Naval War* as a
textbook, and the Navy mandated that every ship keep a copy on board.
The book introduced Roosevelt to admirals and politicians and surely

---

Naval War also revealed Roosevelt's persistent desire to reduce history to crude categories of ethnicity and race. This tradition, of course, stretched back to Jefferson's *Notes*
and beyond, and in his own book, Roosevelt casually stereotyped Portuguese and Italian
sailors as "treacherous" and "fond of the knife." Years later, in *Rough Riders*, he again used
degrading stereotypes to suggest that African American soldiers were "peculiarly dependent upon their white officers." As evidence, Roosevelt described a battle in which his black
comrades grew "uneasy" and tried to "drift to the rear"—until he pulled his revolver and
demanded that they stay. "The colored soldiers flashed their white teeth at one another as
they broke in broad grins," he wrote, "and I had no more trouble with them."

helped him become assistant secretary of the Navy; it earned him invitations to lecture and to write prestigious freelance assignments. And writing—its burdens and its possibilities—remained on Roosevelt's mind. "I should like to write some book that would really take rank as in the very first class," he told a friend a few years later. "But I suppose this is a mere dream."

THE ETERNAL GRAD STUDENT

It is difficult to imagine two presidents more different than Theodore Roosevelt and Woodrow Wilson—different in public, at least. While Roosevelt quivered with the enthusiasm of an undergraduate, Wilson displayed the quiet deliberation of a doctoral student. It was Wilson, in fact, who explicated their apparent contrasts better than anyone else. "He is a real, vivid person," Wilson explained to a friend while he and Roosevelt were facing off in the presidential election of 1912. "I am a vague, conjectural personality, more made up of opinions and academic prepossessions than of human traits." Yet Wilson omitted something important. In private, he could be as vivid and human, as arrogant and anxious, as Roosevelt or any other person. Whether it was in politics or literature or the places they overlapped, Wilson wanted success badly, and he wanted it on the biggest scale.

Wilson was born in 1856, the first son of the Reverend Joseph Wilson and his wife. The reverend watched over the First Presbyterian Church in Staunton, Virginia, but he kept an even closer eye on his boy. Before he learned the alphabet, Wilson had mastered the characters of Charles Dickens and James Fenimore Cooper—because of his father's willingness to read their novels aloud, but also because of Wilson's struggles with reading and writing, perhaps due to dyslexia or another developmental disorder. Once he caught on to the literary arts, Wilson's father coached him relentlessly. Most ministers took Mondays off, but the reverend devoted them to his son; at the end of a busy day, he would ask Wilson to write an essay about their activities and then read it aloud.

"Now," his father said when he had finished, "put down your paper and tell me in your own words what you saw."

The recitation was often brisker and better, which the reverend pointed out. "Write it down that way," he said.

This lesson in paternal style—and there were others, including the importance of directness and precise diction—stayed with Wilson the rest of his life. He would remain a slow and meticulous writer, a verbal stickler who could synthesize and analyze the most complex topics. Roosevelt piled up details and appealed to your senses; Wilson parsed ideas and appealed to your mind.

In 1873, Wilson enrolled at Davidson, a Presbyterian college, but he left after one year. He eventually switched to Princeton, where he excelled. "It was as natural for him as an undergraduate to talk about Burke," one classmate remembered, "as it was for the rest of us to allude to Cooper." Burke, of course, meant Edmund, and at Princeton, Wilson's Anglophilia fully emerged. He was also a slow and meticulous reader, and that forced him to focus, even as a student. ("Desultory reading," he opined in the *Princetonian*, "is worse than useless.") Although he enjoyed biographies, including Weems's life of Washington, he directed most of his energy toward political works like Walter Bagehot's *The English Constitution*. The more Wilson learned about British politics, the more he saw problems at home. America seemed plagued by corruption and closed-door politicking, and Wilson believed one solution would be to pivot toward a British-style parliamentary system—to encourage more open public debate, perhaps by seating some cabinet secretaries in Congress. During his senior year, Wilson gathered these ideas into an essay, "Cabinet Government in the United States," and sold it to a prestigious journal. He spent his small paycheck on a bookcase that would follow him all the way to the White House.*

Wilson's next step was law school, and he enrolled at the University of Virginia's in 1879. His ultimate goal was running for office, and, like Roosevelt, he hoped a legal career would help launch him. At Virginia, though, and at his first practice in Atlanta, Wilson often felt anxious and frustrated. Sometimes he worried that even with continued success at placing articles, he would never become a respected writer; sometimes he worried that he would never enter politics; sometimes he worried that no one could enter politics unless they came from independent wealth. The

---

*One of Wilson's worst episodes as president echoed this philosophy. He empowered cabinet secretaries who wanted to resegregate the federal workforce, and they divided black and white workers, revived separate bathrooms, and in general reversed many gains from Reconstruction. Wilson approved some of these policies personally and ignored the black community's outraged response. W. E. B. DuBois, one of the first African Americans to earn a PhD, wrote an open letter to the president about the effect of this policy: "It is no exaggeration to say that every enemy of the Negro race is greatly encouraged; that every man who dreams of making the Negro race a group of menials and pariahs is alert and hopeful."

real issue seemed to be that Wilson, in all his earnest agitation, couldn't decide what he wanted to be. In the end he abandoned his practice and applied to the PhD program at Johns Hopkins's department of history and political science. It seemed like a step away from power, not toward it. But at least it would give him more time to write. "What do I wish to become?" he asked a perplexed friend. "I want to make myself an outside force in politics."

Before departing Atlanta, Wilson met a young woman. Ellen Axson was everything he wanted: smart, cultured, Southern, Presbyterian. Still, a tricky family life kept her in Georgia, even as he left to spend the summer with his parents. They continued their courtship through passionate letters, and a few days before Wilson headed to Hopkins, he ran into her at a North Carolina hotel. On their last day together, he asked Ellen to marry him. On their first, though, he spent much of the time gushing about Walter Bagehot. Wilson had recently reread *The English Constitution*, and what struck him this time was the book's method. Bagehot had explored how politics worked not in theory but in grubby, fractious reality, and Wilson was starting to wonder whether someone might attempt a similar exploration of American politics. (Also: Ellen said yes.)

Wilson needed to acclimate to Hopkins before embarking on a new project. He arrived in Baltimore in the fall of 1883—still only twenty-six years old, despite his fretful self-seriousness, with piercing eyes and a jutting jaw, both of which conveyed the passion that burned behind them. Hopkins, which was starting its seventh year, still lacked sufficient housing options, and Wilson ended up in a boardinghouse near campus. From the beginning, he looked forward to Herbert Baxter Adams's Friday night seminary. "It is such a pleasant room," Wilson wrote to Ellen, and sitting at the red table he listened to papers on the Brook Farm utopia or to guest speakers like James Bryce, an Oxford professor who wrote on international politics.

The seminary was only part of the program. Wilson's first semester included graduate courses in economics, international law, colonial history, and the British constitution, and he bristled at the workload and the approach. In one letter, he started to tell Ellen about a course taught by Adams and then stopped: "I need not bore you about all this. I am sufficiently bored for both of us." Wilson was hardly the first PhD student to scoff at the customs of his field, but he may have been the first to almost immediately declare his department "weakly manned." He believed in the principles of scholarship. (Wilson dismissed Ridpath's *Popular History* for "its manifest crudeness.") But he hated archival research—"rummaging work," as he put it to Ellen, "which seemed very tiresome in comparison with the grand excursions among imperial policies I had planned for myself."

Wilson, to his credit, decided to do something about it. One day, a month into his first semester, he went to Adams and shared his frustrations—and his desire to pursue more contemporary political analysis. Adams, to his credit, listened. He had quickly identified Wilson as one of the best students he would ever teach, even if he did seem "a little over-intense," and the professor urged him to chase his ambitions. "[He] readily freed me," Wilson wrote to Ellen, "promising me all the aid and encouragement he could give me, and saying that the work I proposed was just such as he wanted to see done!"

There were still courses to attend, but Wilson ramped up his self-directed readings, taking careful notes and thinking about how to translate Bagehot's techniques to American life. By January 1, 1884, he had begun the book he would title *Congressional Government*. Wilson's previous writings had advocated for present-day reforms. With his book, he wanted to write something more permanent. He would describe how the federal government really worked, how it had developed historically, how it now relied not just on laws but on weighty layers of norms and precedents. The Constitution, he wrote in his first chapter, "is a corner-stone, not a complete building." His book would be a blueprint of the entire American edifice.

Wilson presented that first chapter to the seminary in May, to great excitement. (In his diary, a Hopkins professor called it "the ablest and maturest paper ever read there.") By August, Wilson had reached his fifth chapter, on the presidency. Even now, near the end of the nineteenth century, America's commanders in chief deferred to Congress; they focused on administrative tasks while the legislature debated the issues and dominated the capital's media coverage. Bryce, the Oxford don, described the president's job like this: "Four-fifths of his work is the same in kind as that which devolves on the chairman of a commercial company or the manager of a railway."

In his new chapter, Wilson summarized the state of the presidency, allowing for the wartime exception of Lincoln but mostly addressing the systemic ways in which the House and Senate checked executive power. If anything, Wilson suggested, the president had become weaker than the Constitution allowed, something you could see in the government's "very distressing paralysis in moments of emergency." Honestly, though, you could see it everywhere. There was a reason Wilson had titled his book *Congressional Government*, not *Executive Government*. As he put it in one of his crisp generalizations, "The business of the President, occasionally great, is usually not much above routine."

By September Wilson had finished his manuscript. The revisions had gone smoothly thanks to a recent purchase, a No. 2 Caligraph type-writer, with the "2" signifying that it could produce letters of both upper and lower case. Wilson had tested the gadget on a few personal missives. ("Don't write . . . me on that machine," a cousin replied. "We don't like it.") As he grew more comfortable, Wilson began typing up his handwritten first drafts, editing as he went. The whole process filled him with pleasure. "There is a keen satisfaction," he told Ellen, "in the act of creation."

Publication felt even better. Houghton Mifflin released *Congressional Government* in early 1885, with a first edition of one thousand copies, and it hit the world of ideas with a rare and enthralling force. Roosevelt's first book had been an influential volume; Wilson's first book was an intellectual event. The *Nation* called it "one of the most important books, dealing with political subjects, which have ever issued from the American press." Reviews of similar enthusiasm appeared around the country, and the publisher had to print two more editions before the end of the year. (By 1900, the book was on its fifteenth edition.) The academics agreed. Herbert Baxter Adams called it "the ablest contribution to American political science since the *Federalist*." James Bryce sent Wilson a private letter: "I know your *Congressional Government* so well and value it so highly that I seem to know you."

It was a remarkable compliment for any author, but especially for one who had written a scholarly treatise. Bryce was right: Wilson's mind had made it onto every page—his precise descriptions, his authoritative comparisons, his structural expertise. After mulling these topics for nearly a decade, Wilson had discovered at Hopkins the time, the libraries, and the motivation, positive and negative, to write his first and best book. Even now, though, he felt restless—torn between different kinds of writing, between different kinds of teaching, between his professional success and his not-quite-dormant desire to go into politics. Becoming an author, he admitted to Ellen, "has of course given me the deepest satisfaction and has cleared away a whole storm of anxieties. . . . But it has sobered me a good deal too. The question is, What next?"

main the adoption of the Constitution became, under the new division of parties, its champions, as sticklers for ~~its~~ a rigid and literal strictest and ~~narrowest~~ construction.

They were consistent enough in this, because ~~their~~ it was quite natural that their one-time fear of a strong central government ~~naturally~~ should passed into a dread of the still further expansion of the power of that government by a too loose construction of its charter; but what I would emphasize here is not the motives or the policy of the conduct of parties in our early national politics, but the fact that opposition to the Constitution as a constitution, and even hostile criticism of its provisions, ceased almost immediately upon its adoption; and not only ceased but gave place to an undiscriminating and almost blind worship of its principles and of that delicate dual system of sovereignty and that complicated scheme of administration which it had established. Admiration for that once so much traversed body of law became suddenly all the vogue, and criticism was estopped. From the first even down to the time immediately preceding the war the general scheme of the Constitution went unchallenged; nullification itself did not always wear its true garb of independent state-sovereignty, but masqueraded as a constitutional right; and the most violent policies took care to make show of at least formal deference to the worshipful fundamental law. The divine right of kings never ran a more prosperous course than did this un-

Wilson typed up his handwritten drafts of *Congressional Government*, editing as he went and then editing again by hand. He typed on a No. 2 Caligraph, similar to the model pictured here.

EVOLVING TOWARD THE MODERN PRESIDENCY

Soon after Theodore Roosevelt became president in 1901, Edith Wharton found herself in Washington with an invitation to lunch. Wharton and Roosevelt had moved in the same Manhattan circles; they had chatted about her fiction, which he admired. Now he had asked her to visit the White House, and as she entered the president's new home Wharton heard him roar happily: "Well, I am glad to welcome to the White House someone to whom I can quote *The Hunting of the Snark* without being asked what I mean!"

That day Roosevelt complained that no one in his administration knew *Alice's Adventures in Wonderland*, to say nothing of Lewis Carroll's lesser works. He had tried to joke with his secretary of the Navy, telling him, "Mr. Secretary, what I say three times is true." All he got in response was groveling. "Mr. President," the secretary replied, "it would never for a moment have occurred to me to impugn your veracity."

Washington was not a literary town, though to be fair, the presidency was not normally a literary position. But Roosevelt never stopped loving books. In the White House, he hounded his publishing friends and the librarian of Congress to keep him supplied with the latest works of history. He wrote less while president, but he still wrote. (During a feud with the Senate, he sequestered himself to write an essay on, of all things, ancient Irish poetry. "It took my mind off that caterwauling," he told his editor.) Roosevelt entered and exited the presidency as a literary eminence, someone whose past books were still discussed and whose future work was guaranteed a wide audience. The same applied to Woodrow Wilson. And yet something had changed for both men—had been changing for some time. Neither one ever wrote a book as good or useful as their first one, and it's worth considering why.

After *Naval War*'s publication in 1882, Roosevelt dabbled in various careers. The constant remained authorship. He averaged better than a book a year, in addition to penning innumerable magazine and newspaper articles. There were jaunty hunting narratives, essay collections, and biographies of American politicians like Thomas Hart Benton. But while the books sold better than ever, Roosevelt stopped working as hard. He never missed a deadline, in part because he often needed the money. Yet the author who had once used shipyard contracts to double-check the size of the American fleet now admitted to a friend that he didn't know much about the end of Benton's life—and wasn't even firm on the date of his death. ("Would it be too infernal a nuisance for you to hire someone," Roosevelt asked, "to look up, in a biographical dictionary or elsewhere, his life after he left the Senate in 1850?") To work faster, Roosevelt started dictating to stenographers, and this brought out the worst in his style; the waves of information became a tedious deluge. Working on a book still forced Roosevelt to slow down, to confess to his closest friends that he wasn't proud of his work, to promise that the next one would be better. But it never was.

Despite his run of mediocre titles, Roosevelt still dreamed of writing a masterpiece. His best chance, he decided, was a sprawling history of the southwestern frontier. "I realize perfectly," Roosevelt told his publisher, "that my chance of making a permanent literary reputation depends on how I do this big work." Roosevelt chose a big title: *The Winning of the West*. He finally returned to the archives, traveling from Kentucky to California and uncovering frontier letters and forgotten government documents. He published four fat volumes of *Winning* and planned at least two more.

With each volume, however, Roosevelt rushed the writing and tolerated huge gaps in his research, which forced him to lift from other scholars. The *New York Sun* accused him of plagiarism; at the very least, he was guilty of hasty paraphrasing. Frederick Jackson Turner, the frontier thesis professor (and a friendly acquaintance of Roosevelt), couldn't hide his frustrations in a review. While he praised Roosevelt's subject and style, Turner believed his book lacked "thoroughness of investigation" and "sobriety of judgment." In public Roosevelt defended his work and his honor. "I hereby offer a thousand dollars," he wrote in an open letter to the *Sun*, "to anyone who can show that ten lines . . . were written by anyone but myself." In private, though, he admitted his mistakes. "The book should have had careful revision," Roosevelt conceded to another disappointed reviewer. "But when I accepted the Civil Service commissionership I either had to get it out at once or wait several years; I ought to have done the latter, I suppose—but I didn't."

Near the end of his review, Turner diagnosed the key change in Roosevelt's post-*Naval* oeuvre: "While one can appreciate the energetic Americanism of Mr. Roosevelt, one can also lament that he finds it necessary to use his history as the text for a sermon to a stiff-necked generation." The problem wasn't just a slip in quality but a shift in ideas. In *Winning*, Roosevelt portrayed Daniel Boone and other explorers as "heroes of axe and rifle." In a chapter on Andrew Jackson's Battle of New Orleans, which he appended to later editions of *Naval War*, Roosevelt raved about the general's "rugged intellect and indomitable will." Roosevelt even cowrote a sloppy miscellany titled *Hero Tales from American History*. He no longer seemed interested in putting historical figures in their context, in evaluating and, if necessary, debunking their legacies, the way he'd done with Oliver Perry. Instead, Roosevelt seemed content to cheer on their bravery and patriotism. Late in life, he received a letter from another author who was putting together an informal syllabus of the best American history books. The author told Roosevelt he was including *Naval War*. "If you want anything from me," Roosevelt replied, "don't take the *War of 1812*, but take *Hero Tales*."

Wilson's literary career followed a similar arc, though he made more money along the way. In the years after *Congressional Government*, he began to flirt with different forms of writing, including literary essays and even fiction.* Unfortunately, his experimenting ended in the dullest possible outcome: college textbooks and bland volumes of history. Wilson didn't enjoy this sort of writing. (After finishing another "fact book," as he called them, he told Ellen, "I mean to be an author—never more a bookmaker.") But he kept doing it, taking on lucrative projects like a short, president-by-numbers biography of George Washington.

In 1902, Wilson published *A History of the American People*, which ushered its readers from Christopher Columbus through Grover Cleveland in five lavishly illustrated volumes. It was a massive hit, earning Wilson what at that point was one of the largest paychecks ever for an American work of narrative nonfiction: more than $50,000, or well over $1 million in today's dollars. The book was better than Ridpath's history, but that was the best one could say for it. Turner, who was also friendly with Wilson, found it superficial and slight. In another frustrated review, he criticized Wilson for ignoring the "deeper undercurrents of economic and social change."

Wilson had his defenses. The main one was that even though he was now a professor at Princeton, he had grown increasingly annoyed at academia and its specialized knowledge. Wilson preferred to address life's grander morals and themes. "I am not a historian," he told one editor. "I am only a writer of history." Roosevelt felt the same frustration, com-

---

*As a younger man Wilson had attempted some poetry. Now, in the late 1880s, he started a short story and a novel. He actually finished a second story, "The World and John Hart," and submitted it to the *Atlantic* and *Scribner's*. They both passed, perhaps because of moments like this: "'John,' she said, in a voice which, like herself, was of large plan but meager fiber, 'John,' she said, as she seated herself at the table, 'I heard from Mary today.'"

A

HISTORY

of the

AMERICAN

P E O P L E

by

WOODROW WILSON

WOODROW WILSON

(*Ph.D., Litt.D., LL.D., President of Princeton University*)

**A new, epoch-making work — the only complete narrative
history of the great Republic in existence to-day**

PRESIDENT WOODROW WILSON has devoted the best years of his
life to the preparation of his great work, "A History of the American People," from the earliest times to the accession of President Roosevelt. The
work is monumental in character and scope, represents the genius of the greatest historical writer of the present time, and is written in that delightfully flowing
style which translates historical facts into the romance of a nation. Hundreds
upon hundreds of new portraits, prints, maps (in colors), plans, and pictures
make the pictorial features alone tell their wonderful story — the birth and
growth of what is now the United States of America. There is a photogravure
frontispiece to each volume, and portraits in India tint and black. Dr. Woodrow
Wilson's is the first complete narrative history of the United States in existence.
  In order to meet the continued demand for this work, the publishers have
now in readiness a

NEW SUBSCRIPTION EDITION
WITH PHOTOGRAVURE PORTRAITS OF THE PRESIDENTS

After their first books Roosevelt and Wilson became
prominent literary figures, and their newest titles drew
reliable attention—including Wilson's *History of the
American People*, advertised here in the pages of the *Atlantic*.
Note the book was available by subscription, a method that
was slowing down but still alive.

plaining that the average academic was "a good enough day laborer"
who never quite realized he was merely gathering materials for "some
great master builder." (Even Roosevelt's ideal historian, it seemed, had
become a hero.) Wilson's reputation never suffered, and when Herbert
Baxter Adams retired, Hopkins tried to hire Wilson as his replacement.
But Wilson's writing declined. He seemed happy doing simpler books for
larger audiences—even though it meant ending his investigations into
the gnarled systems of politics, even though it meant never fulfilling the
promise of a young PhD student standing in front of the seminary table,
presenting his heady work in progress.

Like Roosevelt, Wilson blamed a busy life for his weakening authorial output. (Things got busier still when he became Princeton's president, a position that forced him to turn down potential biographies of Thomas Jefferson and Robert E. Lee.) But scheduling can't explain the entire reversal. After all, both men still made time to do something monumental—to be not just American presidents but transformational ones.

It was Roosevelt who took the first giant strides toward the modern presidency. To him, the president answered not to Congress but to the American people, and once he arrived at the White House, he inverted the legislator-executive dynamic. He began pushing his own political agenda, advocating for specific bills and leaving it to Congress to slow things down. Roosevelt realized that the president possessed powerful tools, including his own celebrity. When the Senate refused to regulate the railroads, for instance, Roosevelt turned a Rough Riders reunion into a national spectacle, giving a series of speeches and winning over the senators' voters (and thus their votes). Roosevelt didn't get everything he wanted. But he got more—and wanted more—than any previous president.

During Roosevelt's second term, Wilson ducked his campus duties long enough to deliver a rare lecture on politics, and his views on the presidency had changed: "The President is at liberty, both in law and conscience, to be as big a man as he can." When Wilson became president, he followed Roosevelt's activist example. A few weeks after his inauguration in 1913, Wilson delivered his first State of the Union address—not as a written report, as every president had done since Jefferson, but as a dramatic speech, delivered in person to a joint session of Congress. It was a powerful moment, and as Wilson's family rode back to the White House, they could tell he was pleased. "That's the sort of thing Roosevelt would have loved to do," Ellen said. "Yes," her husband replied. "I think I put one over on Teddy."

Perhaps what slowed Wilson and Roosevelt as writers, then, was the presidency itself—or rather, the way a president or presidential aspirant must perceive the world. In 1890, when he was still giving talks regularly, Professor Wilson wrote a lecture that considered this possibility. Like so much of his best writing, it started with a simple premise and then traced its subtleties. Why, he wondered, was there a "perennial misunderstanding between the men who write and the men who act"?

Wilson spent most of the lecture defining and refining his categories. He was interested in only the best examples of both: in someone who could change that world through politics, in someone who could write a book so good it would change that world by itself. "Men who write love proportion," he argued. "Men who act must strike out practicable lines of action and neglect proportion." Men who write must possess a sense of individualized empathy; men who act must concentrate on motivating the masses. Men who write must seek out new and challenging ideas. Men who act must search for simplicity, for ideas that are already primed to change. They seek, in Wilson's wonderful phrase, "the thoughts that are completed."

In the lecture Wilson never quite took a side. But he did make it clear that in an increasingly complicated world—what he called "the great maze of society"—the same person could not write a brilliant work of history *and* be a brilliant politician. It had nothing to do with intelligence or time; it had everything to do with each role requiring a radically different worldview.

If this was the lesson of Wilson's lecture, it was also the lesson of his life. Wilson and Roosevelt did something rare. In their first books—books of serious value, whose worth came not from their authors' platforms or personal experiences but from their ideas—they proved themselves to be men who write. In their presidencies, and particularly in their expansion of executive power, they proved themselves to be men who act. But in between those experiences, Wilson and Roosevelt changed—because they had to. It's hard to be a hero when you're skeptical about heroism; it's hard to transform a political system when you think systematically. The careers of Wilson and Roosevelt don't show how to be a man who writes and a man who acts. They show the impossibility of being, or doing, both.

CHAPTER EIGHT

Campaign Books Hit the Trail (Thanks to, of All Presidents, Calvin Coolidge)

A ndrew Carnegie loved books and he loved golf. When he hit the links with Frank Doubleday, the founder of a prestigious New York publisher, Carnegie got to enjoy both pursuits.

Carnegie was cheerful, competitive, and the richest man in America. One time he met Doubleday at the Saint Andrews Golf Club, just outside the city, after a tough negotiation with J. P. Morgan's associates; Carnegie played a round so relaxed that Doubleday didn't realize until weeks later that his partner that day had been in the process of selling his steel company for $480 million. The result of that deal, a new firm known as U.S. Steel, would become the world's first billion-dollar company.

Another time, again at Saint Andrews, Carnegie paused during their round to pose a question: "How much money did you make in your book business last month?"

Doubleday admitted he wasn't quite sure. American publishers circa 1900 were lucky to evaluate their finances once a year, much less once a month.

Carnegie considered this answer. "Do you know what I would do if I were in a business in which I couldn't tell the amount of monthly profit?" he asked.

"No," Doubleday replied. "What would you do?"

"I would get out of it."

America in this era—electrified, capitalized, urbanized, and interconnected—belonged to Carnegie more than to Doubleday. It belonged most of all to the new army of bankers, managers, advertising experts, and public relations specialists quietly conducting the business of business. The literary world tried, rather tepidly, to keep up. After that golf game, Doubleday updated his accounting practices, and his industry continued to stabilize and grow. (In 1925, the combined revenues of American publishers topped $200 million for the first time.) Still, most houses remained wary of the increasingly nationalized economy. Books, they believed, should stand apart from other consumer goods—should serve a civic purpose as much as a commercial one. George Mifflin, another important publishing executive, urged his employees to resist the marketing tactics being applied to everything from quack remedies to the latest brand of soap. "Our advertising," Mifflin said dismissively, must be "free from methods associated with patent medicine."

The political world had fewer reservations. It welcomed figures like Mark Hanna, a wealthy businessman who helped William McKinley win the presidency in 1896. "He has advertised McKinley as if he were a patent medicine," said Theodore Roosevelt, just as dismissively. But that didn't stop Roosevelt from running as McKinley's vice president in 1900 or from using the same techniques once he was at the top of the ticket. Campaigns were becoming as sprawling and proficient as America's biggest corporations. Politicians, and the experts behind them, were spinning reporters and spinning voters.

It's not surprising that a smart candidate found a way to fuse these approaches: the efficiency of business, the scale of politics, the gravity of books. But it is surprising that Calvin Coolidge was the one to do it. Historians (and history readers) have frequently overlooked America's thirtieth president. Every executive since has received an official, federally run presidential library, but not Coolidge. If he's known for anything, it's his demeanor—cold, distant, unfailingly terse—and a few fraying anecdotes that illustrate it. Once, at a society event, a woman accosted the man known as "Silent Cal": "I made a bet today that I could get more than two words out of you." His reply: "You lose."

That reply, however, contained not just concision but wit. As a writer and public speaker, Coolidge could be funny, imaginative, even rhetorically forceful when it served his ambitions, which were considerable. Like Roosevelt, he got his break as a running mate, to Warren Harding. But the way Coolidge secured his VP slot was unique. It's a story that's never been fully told—of a long-shot campaign built almost entirely around a candidate and his carefully packaged book. Coolidge and his allies decided that his best political weapon wasn't silence but its opposite: the words he wrote. And it worked. "Probably never before in the history of American politics," the Boston Globe observed, "has one lone book played so great a part in a nomination."

LITERARY DEPARTMENTS

James Corrothers didn't have toys, growing up as a bright and kind-faced boy in a small Michigan town. He didn't have a coat to protect him from the wind whipping in from Lake Michigan. He didn't have parents since his mother had died in childbirth and his father had mostly disappeared. So Corrothers, who was black, lived with his grandfather, who was white. Together they scrounged for driftwood to heat their home; they trimmed the old man's clothes until they fit the child. "I was," Corrothers remembered, "the most bepatched boy in town."

What Corrothers did have was books. He got them at the town's public schools, where he was often the only black pupil; he borrowed them from coworkers once he had to drop out to find a job. They weren't the newest books—Corrothers loved poetry, and he ended up studying a previous generation's greats: Longfellow, Whittier, Tennyson—and they weren't as numerous as he would have liked. But he studied them all the same.

Corrothers's second love was history, and as a teenager in the 1880s he went to a speech by Benjamin Butler, a retired Northern general. (He had read Butler's defense of his black soldiers: "The negro troops fought nobly.") Another time he attended a lecture by Frederick Douglass, who was still celebrated for his abolitionism and his autobiography. During the event, the hall's lights flickered out, leaving Douglass unable to see his manuscript. "Brethren," he bellowed from the stage, "let's turn this meeting into an old-fashioned Republican love feast"—and began riffing on whom the party should nominate in the next presidential election. While Corrothers disagreed with Douglass's short list, he reveled in the night's political turn. Corrothers read books for their ideas, their company, their insights into "the careers of American public men." "I labored at self-improvement," he later wrote. "I still recall the delight I found."

By the turn of the twentieth century, books were becoming more widely available, even to someone as marginalized as James Corrothers, living somewhere as marginalized as small-town Michigan. Between 1880 and 1920, the country's population doubled, to more than 106 million; more than 20 million were immigrants arriving at stations like Ellis Island. This explosion of potential readers ensured that more books could turn into big sellers (and not just exceptions like *Uncle Tom's Cabin*). It pointed a larger roster of authors toward reliable careers (and not just exceptions like Washington Irving). It energized what the *New York Times* called "this age of universal reading."

The literary industry reacted to these changes with predictable caution. Publishers continued to concentrate in New York, as smaller satellites like Ohio's Follett, Foster, & Co. shut down. The surviving companies continued to value prestige over profits. A good example was G. P. Putnam's Sons, the publisher of Roosevelt's *Naval War of 1812*. At the firm's Manhattan offices on Twenty-Third Street, the employees toiled pleasantly at rolltop desks, reading and writing under an oil portrait of George Palmer Putnam, who had founded the house in 1838.

Since Putnam's passing in 1872, the company had become more specialized. Its printing operation had moved to a dedicated facility outside the city, where workers set type with new and speedy Linotype-style machines instead of manufacturing stereotyped plates. But the company, now run by Putnam's son, remained genteel and calm. The editorial side stayed at Twenty-Third Street, on the second floor; on the first sat the Putnam's bookstore, with its big street-facing windows; in the basement workers sorted inventory and packed up books to ship out. The offices, an editor remembered, had a "pleasant air of disordered leisure."

That same air perfumed independent bookstores across the country, almost always in big cities or bustling college towns. In Northampton, Massachusetts, the Hampshire Bookshop occupied a brick building right downtown—perfect for luring townie readers or members of the nearby campuses of Amherst and Smith. The store's exterior was decorated with green flower boxes and red geraniums; its interior popped with one of the publishing industry's grudging innovations: dust jackets, which spattered the store in a broad palette of color. There were books everywhere—filling the bookshop's custom shelves and piled on its mismatched tables, each volume hand-chosen and frequently hand-sold by the store's two female owners. Customers often came to see literary celebrities: readings by Carl Sandburg or Amy Lowell, lectures by publishers like Frank Doubleday, naps by a gray-and-white shop cat named Folio. "You are one of the few bookshops in the world," Robert Frost told one of the owners, "where books are sold in something like the spirit they were written in."

The Hampshire Bookshop provided a haven for authors and dedicated readers, just like G. P. Putnam's Sons. In this period, however, both firms faced challenges. America's surging population meant that the ratio of bookstores to citizens was actually falling; the increased demand for books meant that publishers, most of them still family businesses, needed more

One of the owners of the Hampshire Bookshop, Marion Dodd,
stood in the store with Folio the cat.

capital. Many reorganized as private corporations: Harper in 1896, Scribner's in 1904, Houghton Mifflin in 1908.* But better financing couldn't fix
the perpetual problem of distribution. To reach new readers it would take
new retailers, namely department stores and mail-order catalogues.

Department stores like Macy's in New York were flourishing. Most
large cities—and more and more people were residing in those cities, with
the 1920 Census finding that for the first time, more Americans lived in
urban environments than in rural ones—had at least one. It would be a tall
and grand building, luxuriously lit and ventilated, with different depart-

---

*Putnam's solved its money troubles by taking on a silent partner: Theodore Roosevelt.
After the success of *Naval War*, Roosevelt wanted to learn more about publishing, and he
invested $20,000 from his inheritance. Putnam's happily took his money and gave him a
desk at their office—only to find that Roosevelt actually intended to use it. "He promptly
developed a full measure of original theories for the running of a publishing business,"
George Haven Putnam recalled, "theories which were always interesting but which in
most cases did not appear to be practicable." Roosevelt's daily enthusiasms wore on the
staff; the weeks he spent in Albany, attending to the state legislature, were a blissful break.
By the time his partner had cashed out, Putnam had learned his lesson: Roosevelt wasn't
capable of being a silent anything.

ments on different floors: furniture, jewelry, silverware, books. The clerks
sold their literary wares as aggressively as they sold everything else. They
ran constant promotions: buy six pairs of hose and get a book for a dime;
take home the season's hottest novel for half the retail price. Books made
an ideal loss leader since they drew upscale customers—and imbued the
store with intellectual cachet. While publishers and traditional bookstores
hated being undercut, the department stores didn't care. "We," said the
owner of Wanamaker's, in Philadelphia, "make our own prices."

During this period, department stores claimed a third or more of the
retail book market, and mail-order retailers were doing nearly as well.
Fat catalogues from Sears, Roebuck and Montgomery Ward emerged
as the one-per-farmhouse inheritors of Franklin's almanac, offering isolated customers a wider selection than any department store could. A
typical Sears catalogue bragged about having "the most complete book
department"—and backed it up with thirty-five tightly printed pages of
literary offerings. There were practical selections, including how-to volumes on hooking up electricity and indoor plumbing. There were also the
latest novels and nonfiction, plus a robust backlist: Hawthorne and Alcott;
a respected biography of John Quincy Adams; a multivolume set of Roosevelt's writings; and pages and pages more.

Macy's and Sears couldn't solve all of the book trade's issues. Shipping a book remained expensive. (Sears sold Ridpath's hefty *History of
the United States* for only $1.40—but charged another fifty-three cents in
postage.) But these retailers were good for readers, especially the ones
lucky enough to belong to America's growing middle class. Unskilled factory workers still needed to work a full day to buy a new novel, even at
department store prices, but they had fresh options too. Between 1880
and 1920, Andrew Carnegie and his fortune built 1,697 public libraries.
"It was my palace," one Russian immigrant wrote of her local branch.
"Mine, though I was born an alien."

These changes were also good for authors, who could finally count on
a chance at a steady career. To fight literature's old-fashioned approach,
these authors often hired a new kind of professional, the literary agent,
and these advisers proved equally valuable when navigating the world of
international copyright. After a long public debate—one in which authors
like Mark Twain and Frederick Douglass championed copyright legislation as a final step toward American literature thriving on the international stage—a comprehensive bill passed in 1891.

The end of cheap British reprints, the boom in American readers, the

SEARS, ROEBUCK & CO., Cheapest Supply House on Earth, Chicago. CATALOGUE No. 112. 119

BOOK DEPARTMENT

WE PRESENT TO YOUR NOTICE THE MOST COMPLETE BOOK DEPARTMENT, AND IF INTERESTED IN ANYTHING IN THIS LINE WE BELIEVE IT WILL PAY YOU TO CAREFULLY READ THE FOLLOWING PAGES.....

NOTE THE ILLUSTRATIONS AND DESCRIPTIONS AND PARTICULARLY THE PRICES.

WE FURNISH ONLY SUCH BOOKS AS ARE QUOTED ON THIS AND THE FOLLOWING PAGES.

'OU WILL FIND OUR BOOK DEPARTMENT MOST COMPLETE and we list every good standard book on the market.

IN TECHNICAL BOOKS ESPECIALLY OUR LINES ARE VERY COMPREHENSIVE.

,BOUT MAIL SHIPMENTS. WHEN BOOKS ARE TO BE SENT BY MAIL BE SURE TO ENCLOSE ENOUGH (TRA TO PAY POSTAGE. If you send too much we will immediately return e balance, but if you do not send enough we will be compelled to hold your der and write for the balance. DO NOT OVERLOOK THE NECESSARY POSTAGE ORDERING BOOKS BY MAIL.

OUR CLUB ORDER SYSTEM COMMENDS ITSELF TO BOOK BUYERS, for you will observe in looking over this catalogue that we have been able to figure our prices so low on many of the books that we can quote them to you at but little more than the cost of postage. For example, **our Argyle Series**, beautiful cloth bound books at 14 cents each, postage, 10 cents per volume.

It is therefore much cheaper to have books shipped by express or freight, **freight being preferable.** The transportation cost per volume is then reduced to next to nothing. **To take advantage of the lowest transportation rate**, it is desirable to make up a freight order. This you can do by getting your friends and neighbors to join with you and make up a club order.

/e always advise our readers to make their book orders large enough that we may ship by freight, but if one or more books are wanted by mail, the extra postage must be included.

AGRICULTURAL WORKS

AT A SAVING OF 50 PER CENT.

nder this heading we list Books on Butter, Cheese Making and the Dairy, Etc.

American Gardener's Assistant.

By Thos. Bridgeman. Contains practical direc- ons for the cultivation of vegetables, flowers, fruit ees and grape vines. Illustrated. Cloth.
No. 3T152 Our price.........80c
If by mail, postage extra, 12 cents.

ook of The Farm; or, The Handbook of Husbandry.

Full of practical information in regard to buy- g or leasing a farm, fences and farm buildings, arming implements, drainage, plowing, rotation f crops. Illustrated. Cloth.
No. 3T156 Our price.........75c
If by mail, postage extra, 14 cents.

Butter and Butter Making.

By Willis P. Hazard. How to color butter, milk- g and care of milk, skimming, churning, etc. Illus- ated.
No. 3T158 Our price.........20c
If by mail, postage extra, 3 cents.

Canning and Preserving.

By Mrs. S. T. Rorer. How to can and preserve uits and vegetables; and, also, the best method of aking marmalades, fruit butter and jellies, catsups, ickling. Oil cloth.
No. 3T160 Our price.........50c
If by mail, postage extra, 5 cents.

Common Sense Ideas for Dairymen.

By Geo. H. Blake. Contains the methods pursued y the most practical and successful dairymen in e Elgin district, embracing instructions in selec- on, feeding and care of dairy cattle; corn and lover culture; care of milk and cream; how to im- rove the farm, etc.
No. 3T164 Our price.........65c
If by mail, postage extra, 11 cents.

Farming by Inches.

A Practical Book, by Charles Barnard. Contain- g information about all kinds of vegetables, gar- en sass, time to seed and other information of value hich would assist in perfecting a garden. Cloth.
No. 3T166 Our price.........30c
If by mail, postage extra, 6 cents.

Flower Gardening.

By Charles Barnard. A valuable book for ama- ur or inexperienced gardeners. 166 pages. Illus- rated. Size, 5¼x7¾ inches. Cloth.
No. 3T178 Our price.........58c
If by mail, postage extra, 8 cents.

Fruit Gardening.

By Thomas Bridgeman. A valuable work treating the selection, propagation and cultivation of all inds of fruits, also information of value for fruit rowers, etc. Illustrated. Cloth.
No. 3T190 Our price.........35c
If by mail, postage extra, 10 cents.

Kitchen Gardening.

By Thomas Bridgeman. Contains instructions r the planting and care of all kinds of vegetables. lustrated.
No. 3T194 Our price.........42c
If by mail, postage extra, 8 cents.

ly Ten Rod Farm; or, How I Became a Florist.

By Charles Barnard. It tells just what to do and w to do it, also gives the exact experience of a idow left destitute who worked her farm to such a ed advantage that within a very short period it id her an income of $2,000 per year. Cloth.
No. 3T196 Our price.........30c
If by mail, postage extra, 7 cents.

Strawberry Garden.

By Charles Barnard. An interesting and prac- cal book, explaining the cost of conducting a straw- rry garden, also profits, etc. Cloth.
No. 3T198 Our price.........70c
If by mail, postage extra, 6 cents.

$2,000 a Year on Fruits and Flowers.

By Charles Barnard. An interesting book containing valuable information for all who are interested in flowers and the raising of vegetables in general, among which is the art of growing strawberries, etc. Cloth.
No. 3T200 Our special price.........70c
If by mail, postage extra, 13 cents.

Pasteurization and Milk Preservation.

By J. H. Monrad. With a complete chapter on selling milk. 70 illustrations; paper covers.
No. 3T202 Our price.........38c
If by mail, postage extra, 3 cents.

Potato Culture.

By C. C. Carpenter. This book has only been completed after years of experience. Mr. Carpenter has made a specialty of potato culture. He has carefully considered the suggestions of many seed growers, and is thoroughly convinced that there is a great lack of practical information among the average farmers upon this subject. Paper.
No. 3T206 Price.........15c
If by mail, postage extra, 2 cents.

ARCHITECTURE.

American Architecture; or, Every Man a Complete Builder.

Contains 104 pages; size, 11x14 inches, and consists of large 9x12 plates, giving detailed plans and instructions how to build seventy cottages, double houses, brick block houses, suitable for all sections of the country and costing from $800.00 to $6,500.00 each, etc. Bound in paper.
No. 3T250 Our price.........65c
If by mail, postage extra, 11 cents.

Barn Plans and Out Buildings.

250 illustrations. Bound in cloth. Size, 5½x7½ inches. Contains ideas, hints, suggestions, plans, etc., for the construction of barns and out buildings, by practical writers. A few chapters are devoted to the economic erection and use of grain houses, cattle and sheep barns, corn, smoke and ice houses, pig pens, granaries, etc.
No. 3T256 Our price.........80c
If by mail, postage extra, 12 cents.

Complete Housebuilder, with Hints on Building.

Contains 50 plans and specifications of dwellings, barns, churches, public buildings, etc. Adapted to all conditions of town and country, with accurate estimates of material and cost. Where to and how to build, and thousands of other subjects pertaining to material, help, etc. Bound in paper.
No. 3T264 Price.........17c
If by mail, postage extra, 2 cents.

Ideal Homes.

Latest and best book of its kind published. Complete in two volumes, illustrating 91 new houses, summer cottages, churches, barns and lumber sheds, etc., ranging in price from $550.00 to $8,500.00 each, giving all the comforts and conveniences, and suited to every taste, location, want, etc. If you contemplate building or altering and adding to your present home, you ought to have a copy of this book. The illustrations are printed from the best halftone cuts on enameled paper. Size, 7½x10¼ inches.
No. 3T270 Our price, for two volumes, complete.........75c
If by mail, postage extra, 12 cents.

Modern Carpentry.

A practical manual for carpenters and wood workers generally, by Fred T. Hodgson, author of Steel Squares, etc. A new complete carpenter's guide, containing over 100 quick methods of performing general carpenter work, such as laying roofs, rafters, stairs, joints and joining, timber splicing, moldings, bevels, hand railing, circular and splayed work, etc. Written in a very simple style, easily understood. The illustrations, of which there are many, are explanatory, making it possible for amateurs and carpenters generally to understand. This is the most complete, authentic and latest book on the subject published. It is thoroughly practical and reliable.
No. 3T282 Bound in cloth. Our special price..70c
If by mail, postage extra, 11 cents.

Palliser's New Cottage Homes.

Containing 160 new and original designs for cottages costing from $75.00 to $7,500.00 each, giving all the comforts and conveniences, and suited to every taste, location, want, etc. Fifty new designs for city brick block houses; 12 new designs for stable and carriage houses; 1,500 detailed drawings, covering the whole range of interior finish and exterior construction and ornamentation of plans; fences, summer houses, pavilions, conservatories, out buildings, etc. Bound in cloth, leather back. Size, 11x14 inches. Retail price, $4.00.
No. 3T300 Our price.........$2.75
If by mail, postage extra, 28 cents.

Palliser's Useful Details.

These details are, without exception, the best and cheapest lot of working drawings that have ever been offered to the workman. The whole series of 40 plates contain something like 1,100 separate designs. Bound in paper; portfolio style, 14x22 inches.
No. 3T302 Our price.........$1.40
If by mail, postage extra, 16 cents.

Practical Carpentry.

Guide to the correct working and laying out of all kinds of carpenters' and joiners' work; with the solutions of the various problems in hip roofs, gothic work, centering, splayed work, joints and joining, hingeing, dovetailing, mitering, timber splicing, hopper works, skylights, raising moldings, circular work, etc. Illustrated, over 300 engravings. Bound in cloth, gilt.
No. 3T306 Our price.........73c
If by mail, postage extra, 8 cents.

Reed's House Plans for Everybody.

It gives an estimate on the quantity of every article used in the construction and the cost of each article at the time the building was erected or the design made. Illustrated. Handsomely bound in cloth, black and gold. Size, 5¾x7¾ inches.
No. 3T316 Our price.........79c
If by mail, postage extra, 13 cents.

Stair Building Made Easy.

Simple, plain, and may be learned in an hour. A full and clear description of the art of building the bodies, carriages and cases for all kinds of stairs and steps, together with illustrations showing the manner of laying out stairs, forming treads and risers, building cylinders, preparing strings; with instructions for making carriages for common platform, dog-legged and winding stairs.
No. 3T320 Bound in cloth, gilt. Our price...70c
If by mail, postage extra, 10 cents.

The Sears, Roebuck catalogue promised its customers the nation's "most complete book department"—more than thirty pages of available titles, including popular histories like John Clark Ridpath's *History of the United States.*

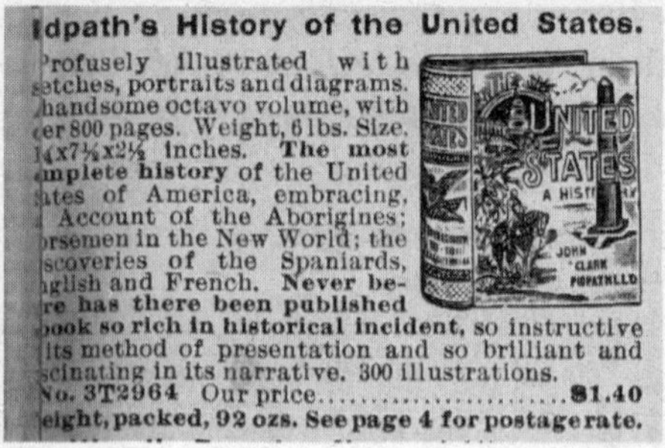

idpath's History of the United States.

'rofusely illustrated with etches, portraits and diagrams. handsome octavo volume, with er 800 pages. Weight, 6 lbs. Size. 14x7½x2½ inches. **The most mplete history** of the United ates of America, embracing, Account of the Aborigines; rsemen in the New World; the scoveries of the Spaniards, glish and French. **Never be- re has there been published ook so rich in historical incident,** so instructive its method of presentation and so brilliant and scinating in its narrative. 300 illustrations.
No. 3T2964 Our price.........$1.40
eight, packed, 92 ozs. See page 4 for postage rate.

rise of new retail channels: each of these contributed to "this age of universal reading." And yet, when a thing becomes universal, it loses its distinction. Books were more accessible than ever before. (In 1895 one magazine debuted an innovative ranking of "new books, in the order of demand"—in other words, best sellers.) But that also meant books were changing from symbols of high culture to something a general audience could enjoy. Like a lot of authors, Henry James worried about these trends. He also had reason for hope. "The public," he observed, "is really as subdivided as a chessboard, with each little square confessing only to its own kind of accessibility." James was right. In the span of only a few decades, American readers would see the development of science fiction, of hard-boiled detective stories, of superheroes battling in comic books—all alongside the academic canonization of literary fiction like Henry James's.*

Where there was turmoil, in other words, there was also opportunity, for readers and writers alike. One of those writers was James Corrothers, the boy from Michigan who grew up to be a journalist and poet. Corrothers was also a waiter and a preacher; it was tough to support himself when white colleagues would steal his prose and skim his paychecks. Eventually he realized that what readers wanted from a black poet was exaggerated dialect and minstrel-like imagery ("Way down in mah Southe'n home . . ."). Corrothers sold verse in this style to the *Century*, still one of the country's most prestigious magazines.

But he felt conflicted. He worked on nondialect poetry, wrote for black magazines, wrote for newspapers, wrote a book of short stories—took full advantage of his era's abundance of print. Finally, in 1912, he sold a nondialect poem to the *Century*, "The Negro Singer." It opened by acknowledging the prejudice that every black artist encountered, but this time instead of indulging that prejudice, Corrothers rejected it, blending classical allusions with African history and building to a proclamation that he would "sing":

---

*Many of these genres began as guilty pleasures, but detective fiction found a surprising defender in Woodrow Wilson. Wilson adored mysteries and wasn't afraid to admit it. "There are blessed intervals," he said at a press conference, "when I forget by one means or another that I am president of the United States. One means by which I forget is to get a rattling good detective story, get after some imaginary offender and chase him all over—preferably any continent but this." Wilson's comments were widely reprinted and helped change the genre's perception, from something puerile and pulpy to something a president might read. In 1930, one critic argued that two people were "responsible for the present vogue of mystery stories in America." The first was Arthur Conan Doyle. The second was Woodrow Wilson.

So shall men know me, and remember long,
Nor my dark face dishonor any song.

Corrothers was reclaiming his humanity in his authentic voice—and doing it in front of a national audience. It was the kind of protest poem that in a few years would inspire members of the Harlem Renaissance as they wrote their own authentic works, opening up even more squares on literature's chessboard, black and white.

THE MEN BEHIND THE MAN

Despite the extra readers and the uninvited assists from catalogues and department stores, the book trade struggled to match America's new assembly-line capitalism: fast, repetitive, relentless. One could see this when comparing the trade to more aggressive culture industries. While the number of new books in this period increased by 500 percent, the circulation of newspapers increased by 600 percent—and the circulation of monthly magazines increased faster still. The literary gap became even starker in the full consumer economy, which was thriving thanks to the rise of three intricately related fields: journalism, advertising, and public relations. Together they built a system that excelled at selling national brands on a national scale, including Campbell's soups, Kellogg's cereal, and, every four years, a handful of new candidates for president.

Magazines played a crucial role in developing this economy. Established outlets like the *Century*, which often had close ties to book publishers, were challenged by upstarts like *Cosmopolitan* and *McClure's*. S. S. McClure built his magazine around a simple mission: "articles of timely interest." He chased big stories ruthlessly. When he learned the *Century* was planning a retrospective on Napoleon, McClure recruited a promising journalist named Ida Tarbell to crash out a competing series, which *McClure's* puckishly launched the same month as its competitor. Tarbell's "Napoleon" simplified the story and homed in on the hero, "the greatest genius of his time, perhaps of all time." It was an enormous hit.

Readers loved *McClure's* for its articles—Tarbell's next big series, on a genius named Lincoln, pushed circulation well past 300,000, three times the *Century's*—but also for its price. At newsstands, the latest *Century* cost thirty-five cents; *McClure's* went for a dime. While that drop depended on speedy Linotype presses, it depended even more on ads. Editors like

McClure realized that by selling their magazines at a loss, they could sell their audiences' attention to a horde of hungry businesses. There were so many new products: automobiles, washing machines, refrigerators, plus nationalized brands in preexisting categories like baking powder and shoes. Together magazines, advertisers, and tens of millions of readers created a mass audience and, through it, a mass culture.*

Politicians operated in that same mass culture. The women's suffrage movement was demanding an expanded electorate. (During one New York protest, women who worked in bookstores and publishing marched together, brandishing copies of their favorite feminist titles.) Direct campaigning remained controversial, and most candidates still avoided their party's convention. Campaign biographies continued to appear, though their role was shrinking—replaced, as one reporter noted, by magazines and newspapers covering "all that is essential in the life of the candidate."

Electioneering did get some updates. A few nominees mounted "front porch" campaigns, devious technicalities where they could welcome supporters to their homes (and address them in front of the gathered press) while never quite going out to stump. Others continued to rely on surrogates who, in a sign of increasing party coordination, had started building their speeches around "campaign textbooks," affordable and fact-packed volumes issued by the national committees. In 1888, when Grover Cleveland's supporters were plotting his reelection, they chose a prominent ex-journalist named George F. Parker to write the textbook. Parker moved into the White House, where he discovered that he and Cleveland both liked working late at night. In the old mansion's halls, they would chat about the project. "You are certainly making campaigning easy for the average public speaker," the president said.

Cleveland lost, but his relationship to Parker was just beginning. Parker specialized in influencing his former colleagues in the press; his thinning hair and soft features made him look like a person you could trust, a useful

---

*While book publishers dabbled in advertising, they did so skeptically. "About the advertising of books," declared Walter Page, a colleague of Doubleday, "nobody knows anything." It was a fair point: each new title was different and difficult to predict in a way that wasn't true of, say, a new brand of crackers. But it was also another example of literature's lethargy. Publishers had some success with endorsements—Theodore Roosevelt read so many books, and talked about them with such gusto, that he became the industry's blurber in chief—but they struggled with other kinds of marketing. In fact, advertisers were far better at using books than books were at using advertising. Around a third of magazine ads featured books as props, adding a whiff of intellect and wealth to products as random as Jergens soap and Cream of Wheat.

impression in this emerging line of work. Parker showed the ex-president how to shape his coverage—editing one of his speeches, for instance, then devising a plan to get it reprinted in hundreds of newspapers. With Parker's help, Cleveland produced about seventy speeches and public letters over the next four years. "His smallest utterance," Parker later wrote, "was echoed from end to end of the country with a success never seen before." In 1892 Cleveland ran again. This time he won decisively.

It wasn't long before Parker and his behind-the-scenes boosterism had some competition. In 1896 the Republicans nominated William McKinley, whose front-porch campaign was compulsively managed by his friend Mark Hanna. Hanna had made his money in coal. He was a brilliant strategist, and once he took charge of the Republican National Committee, he began raising obscene amounts of cash—a quarter-million from Standard Oil; a quarter-million from J. P. Morgan—and synchronizing McKinley's nationalized campaign. In an election where just under 14 million Americans voted, the Republicans distributed more than 200 million pieces of campaign literature.

McKinley's opponent, William Jennings Bryan, knew he would be egregiously outspent. So he chartered a train and rammed it straight through tradition, traveling eighteen thousand miles and delivering hundreds of speeches himself. It wasn't enough. On election day, Hanna appeared calm and merry, his face still rosy from a shave. "I have carried on a war in Missouri that diverted their attention," he crowed to a reporter. "I have scared them in Nebraska and Tennessee." Hanna continued: "I have run the campaign as nearly as possible on business principles."

McKinley won, then beat Bryan again in 1900. During the rematch, however, the Republican boarded up his front porch. "The president," McKinley said, "should refrain from making a political canvass on his own behalf." The rules for campaigning were evolving, with one set for challengers, another for incumbents, and another for everyone else. McKinley's running mate that year, Theodore Roosevelt, gave hundreds of speeches. At rallies he would hold up a copy of *The First Battle*, a best-selling book Bryan had compiled after his loss in 1896. "This is an interesting book," Roosevelt would say to cheers from the crowd. "It is the best campaign book for the Republican party I know."

When Roosevelt ran as an incumbent president in 1904, he also refrained from campaigning. But that silence made his books stand out. The *Rough Riders* passage, where he threatened his black soldiers with a revolver, resurfaced and was widely condemned by black voters. (Roosevelt dismissed his critics, claiming they "have attempted to make a mountain out of a mole hill.") George Parker, who was still working for the Democrats, went further, scrutinizing everything Roosevelt had written. He and his staffers assembled a pamphlet titled *Roosevelt, Historian*, which used dozens of excerpts to argue that Roosevelt was too arrogant and contrarian to be president. The Democratic National Committee circulated hundreds of thousands of copies.

Political operatives were getting more and more sophisticated, which is a marketer's way of saying they were getting better at spin. One of Parker's colleagues was a young man named Ivy Lee, and after the election, they

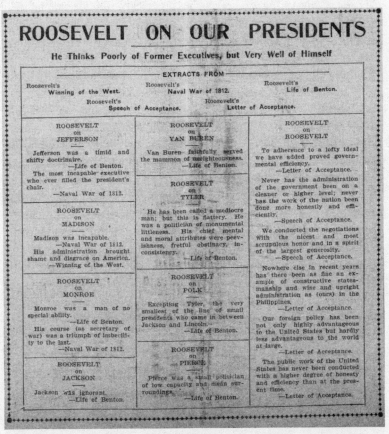

During the 1904 election, Roosevelt's books drew constant criticism. This advertisement, which ran in many newspapers, quoted his passages on previous presidents.

launched New York City's first public relations firm, Parker & Lee. They worked with railroads, coal mines, and other major industries, and eventually Lee started helping the Rockefellers manage their reputation, which had not yet recovered from a devastating *McClure's* investigation by Ida Tarbell. When the family made a big donation to Johns Hopkins University, Lee pitched the story to reporters with great success. "This was not really news," he admitted to John D. Rockefeller Jr. "This was wholly due to the manner in which the material was 'dressed up' for newspaper consumption. It seems to suggest very considerable possibilities along this line."

This time, at least, Lee wasn't overselling. By the start of World War I, there were more than a thousand public relations professionals in New York City alone. Advertising was growing just as quickly, with the amount spent on ads jumping from $200 million in 1880 to nearly $3 billion in 1920. More and more presidential candidates were traveling the country and making their own speeches, including William Howard Taft in 1908 and Woodrow Wilson in 1912. But the real revolution was happening backstage.

The best example came in 1920 when Albert Lasker sold voters on Ohio senator Warren Harding. Lasker was an advertising icon, a tall and twitchy man who spent his career marketing Kleenex and Kotex, among other brands. He had a gift for concocting pushy but positive campaigns, with his most famous work suggesting women should smoke Lucky Strike cigarettes to control their weight: "Reach for a Lucky instead of a sweet."

Lasker took the same approach with his Republican nominee. Harding revived the front-porch campaign, inviting supporters and journalists to his home on Mount Vernon Avenue. (Lasker didn't come up with that— that was just luck.) Meanwhile, in the house next door, Harding's advisers shaped his image, even his words. Lasker crafted a change-friendly slogan to slip into one of the candidate's speeches: "Let's be done with wiggle and wobble." He also shaped the slogan's reception. "We want it to appear that when the candidate wrote this sentence in his speech it was merely a passing sentence," Lasker noted in a private memo, "but that it was so forceful that it was spontaneously picked up." That's exactly what happened—even though by the time the speech occurred, Lasker had already arranged for his slogan to start appearing on billboards, on the sides of buses, and in magazine advertisements around the country.

"A PRETTY GOOD SPEECH, AFTER ALL"

Presidential campaigns began experimenting with another technique during this period: campaign books written by the candidates themselves. In 1891, more than three decades after Lincoln's lonely precedent, George Parker began gathering the materials that would make up *The Writings and Speeches of Grover Cleveland*, with Cleveland reviewing and approving the selections. In 1893, while McKinley and Hanna were planning their campaign, they worked closely with a publisher to release *Speeches and Addresses of William McKinley*. These speech collections resonated differently than campaign biographies or disposable pamphlets did, offering readers added intimacy and heft. The Democrats' *Roosevelt, Historian* summed up the power of authorship like this: "Roosevelt has written his own character into his work."

Such was the promise of campaign books, for critics and supporters alike, and each new title reinforced a growing tradition: Taft's *Present Day Problems*, Harding's *Rededicating America*, the *Speeches of Benjamin Harrison*.* During this period, publishing a collection was seen as clear evidence of someone's ambitions. McKinley's volume, noted the *Nation*, was "a presidential candidate's propitiation of his fellow citizens"—even though it appeared more than two years before the next presidential campaign.

These offerings didn't always succeed. (While the operative behind Harrison's book expected a big hit, he ended up with fifteen thousand unsold volumes stacked in his Washington home.) Still, their potential was obvious, and in 1920, Calvin Coolidge's *Have Faith in Massachusetts* finally made an impact on the level of Lincoln's *Debates*. Coolidge's book depended not on an obsessive candidate, working alone, but on the unseen efforts of moguls, bankers, and admen, plus a publishing house with its own professionals. And yet one thing made life easier on those experts, and arguably made *Have Faith* such a success: it was a really good book.

Calvin Coolidge was born in the tiny village of Plymouth Notch, Vermont, in a cottage that housed his family, a post office, and a general store; his father, John Coolidge, ran all three institutions with a strict and

---

*One offshoot of this tradition was the campaign recap, a book that assembled a president-elect's speeches to preview his agenda. These volumes boasted bland titles and staggering sales. Wilson's *New Freedom* was the fourth most popular nonfiction book in the country in 1913; Franklin Roosevelt's *Looking Forward* was the seventh most popular in 1933.

practical approach. The year was 1872, but Calvin's childhood resembled that of a boy born a century earlier. He tapped maple trees, pitched hay, and helped his father mend their stone fence. John Coolidge believed in civic duty—his son represented the family's fifth generation in Plymouth Notch—and he believed in hard work. Those values combined to make him a prominent Vermonter, and he eventually moved to a farmhouse nice enough to feature a sitting room decorated with gilt wallpaper. But John never eased up, especially on his son. "He had great faith," Coolidge later deadpanned, "in the advantage of early privation."

Calvin was quiet and thoughtful, a child who was uncomfortable around others and, just as much, was comfortable with silence. He was, in one neighbor's memory, "an odd stick." He read constantly and found plenty of sources, even in rural Vermont: leftover campaign literature, books sold by traveling booksellers, poetry anthologies intended for ornamentation but devoured by Coolidge all the same. The state was saturated in history, especially in the old-timers' stories stretching back to Andrew Jackson and related around the general store's stove. They inspired Coolidge to emphasize history and biography over fiction, a preference he never altered. Reading, he would tell his own children, was for "improving the mind." And yet to a shy and isolated boy, reading was also for comfort, and Coolidge maintained a lifelong devotion to prose. A friend once admitted that he didn't talk to Coolidge about important matters in person. When he really needed Coolidge to listen, he wrote him a letter.

After exhausting the opportunities at Plymouth Notch's one-room schoolhouse, Coolidge headed to boarding school and then to Massachusetts and Amherst College, where he enrolled in 1891. At each stop, teachers identified him as a skilled writer and diligent reader, particularly when the assignment involved Lincoln or the *Federalist Papers*. Coolidge remained reserved. ("The few who got in personal contact with him," one classmate recalled, "had to go the whole way.") But he also gained confidence, especially through Amherst's electives, in history and philosophy, and its campus oratory and debate. Coolidge developed habits that would never leave him— writing his speeches in pencil so he could rework them, polishing the prose until it was clever and concise. "Nothing in the world," he wrote to his father, "gives me so much pleasure as to feel that I have made a good speech."*

*Coolidge also found time to read a bit of fiction—at least according to "Margaret's Mist," a short story he published in Amherst's literary journal. The story recycled some of magazine fiction's most cherished clichés, starting with a chaste heroine who discovers her fiancé has led a double life: "'Waldo Martin,' said the emotionless Margaret, 'I need no

It's worth noting that Coolidge, in contrast to bookish peers like Roosevelt and Wilson, never appeared to contemplate a literary career. Perhaps his upbringing prevented it. Once, during an academic break, he read the passage in Franklin's *Autobiography* on the benefits of rewriting poetry as prose. He decided to try this regimen at home—until his father informed him that he spent plenty of time reading and writing at school and that summers and holidays were for chores on the farm.

Coolidge chose a more grounded application for his love of language and ideas: the law. While he considered attending one of America's new law schools, his father pushed for the old-fashioned method of aligning with a local firm and reading deeply in the field. Coolidge ended up at Hammond & Field in Northampton, Massachusetts, a city of around fifteen thousand. After a couple of months, one of the firm's partners, Henry Field, noticed Coolidge's name in the newspaper. He'd won a contest for the country's best collegiate history essay.

"Why didn't you say something?" Field asked him.

"I didn't want to brag about myself," Coolidge replied.

"Have you told your father about it?"

"No."

"Why not?"

"I didn't want to brag."

Coolidge eventually opened his own Northampton practice, Coolidge & Hemenway. He met Grace Goodhue, a teacher as warm as he was withdrawn, and they married in 1905. They moved into half a duplex on Massasoit Street, where they raised two boys and passed their evenings in the cozy living room with books and magazines and bay windows that gave Grace a view of the peaceful neighborhood while she knit. (One of the owners of Northampton's Hampshire Bookshop also lived on Massasoit, a couple of houses down.) The whole time, Coolidge pursued an orderly political ascent: city council, county clerk, state representative, and Northampton mayor, among other local offices.

It might seem odd that Coolidge had entered politics, much less that he was good at it. But it made sense. Another career he'd considered at Amherst was running his father's general store. "Would you like," he asked in a letter home, "to have me start in the store and live in Plymouth and

explanation. I know now. How I have loved you! How I've trusted you! Robber! Murderer! Betrayer!' " Why the young author conveyed emotionlessness with exclamation points is not immediately clear.

live for Plymouth?" The desire to live not just *in* a place but *for* it was pure Coolidge, just like his desire to live in and for language. Politics gave him a way to unite those desires, and their union made him a shockingly effective statesman. Coolidge didn't look like a politician: a small and severe man with his hair slicked back, his arms folded tight, his lips pressed into a thin grimace or, occasionally, a thin smile. But people liked and trusted him because of his strange demeanor. His reticence was authentic, and it was useful.

The other key to Coolidge's rise was his writing. He took speeches seriously, revising them for hours and sometimes even days. "None was ever wholly satisfactory to him at the time," Grace later recalled. "Afterward he would read one and say, 'That was a pretty good speech, after all.'" The labor produced a deceptively simple style: short sentences, elementary structures, and a gift for aphorism that Franklin would have liked. A fine example came in his first address as president of the Massachusetts state senate, which Coolidge delivered in 1914:

> Do the day's work. If it be to protect the rights of the weak, whoever objects, do it. If it be to help a powerful corporation better to serve the people, whatever the opposition, do that. Expect to be called a standpatter, but don't be a standpatter. Expect to be called a demagogue, but don't be a demagogue. . . . Don't hurry to legislate. Give administration a chance to catch up with legislation.

The full address was one of the shortest anyone could remember, but it marked its author as an instant star. In 1915 Coolidge was elected lieutenant governor—and governor three years after that.

Along the way Coolidge picked up an important ally, a Boston businessman named Frank Stearns. Stearns owned R. H. Stearns & Co., a majestic ten-story department store that sat on Boston Common, near the State House. With his waxed gray mustache and portly physique, Stearns looked like a gentle tycoon. But he'd made his fortune by being cagey and relentless, by understanding how to seize people's attention, and by controlling the smallest details—turning his store's basement, for instance, into the city's best toy department, with a twisting train track, a magic lantern show, and an enormous glass water tank where children could test out mechanical boats.

Now that he was approaching retirement, Stearns needed a new vocation, and he found it in Calvin Coolidge. The two were brought together not by idealism or ideology but something more common in state politics: a squabble over pipes. Amherst College wanted to connect to the local sewer system, so Stearns, a graduate and trustee, reached out to Coolidge. While Stearns knew it was technically too late in the session to address this, he figured a fellow alum might make an exception.

"Come up next year," Coolidge told him.

"We want this legislation now," Stearns insisted. "You being a graduate of Amherst we thought . . ."

He didn't get much further before Coolidge simply walked away. Stearns was struck by Coolidge's principles—and by the fact that next year, when the timing was right, the politician solved the problem by himself. He was also struck by Coolidge's speeches. Before anyone else saw him as presidential material, including the candidate himself, Stearns decided to be the Hanna to his McKinley. Stearns began talking up the governor to other Republicans and mailing them printed copies of that celebrated senate address. He also began mulling ways to use his money, his business connections, and his hustle to lift Coolidge to the White House.

By 1919, Stearns was planning Coolidge's presidential campaign. The most obvious play was a speech collection. "All right," said Coolidge, "but I'll have nothing to do with it." That wasn't entirely true, but Stearns did handle the particulars. He approached a traditional publisher, Boston's own Houghton Mifflin, which had its offices and company bookstore in a historic building just off the Common. Stearns connected with Roger Scaife, an editor there who'd come up through the advertising department and was known for his aggressive tactics and three-piece suits. By August, Scaife was finalizing plans for the speech collection, including a first run of three thousand copies, with Stearns and his allies promising to cover virtually all the costs of printing and distribution. "I think," Stearns told another supporter, "it will be money well spent."

That print run would prove far too modest. In September, Coolidge's reputation received an unexpected jolt when Boston's police officers went on strike. Their frustrations were fair, but in a country roiled by fears of labor radicalism, they were terribly timed. Coolidge responded harshly, scrawling out a telegram and sending it to a top union official (and to the Massachusetts press): "There is no right to strike against the public safety by anybody, anywhere, any time." Soon the strike—and the governor's sound bite—were dominating newspapers all over America.

Stearns was reviewing the book's proofs when the strike started, and he asked Scaife to add several relevant documents to the book, including Coolidge's full telegram. After cycling through several titles—*Bay State Orations, Occasional Addresses*—the editor had arrived at the more hortatory *Have Faith in Massachusetts*, a line from Coolidge's old senate address. That address would open the volume, and his telegram would end it. Everything in between rounded out the Coolidge worldview: cautious, nostalgic, pro-business, and idealistic about individual honor and freedom. Coolidge's ideas were often familiar—indeed, their familiarity was part of their appeal—but he expressed them freshly and convincingly. "Self-government means self-support"; "unless good citizens hold office, bad citizens will." *Have Faith* demonstrated his devotion to "Law and Order," a phrase that appeared on its dust jacket in type as large as the author's name.

There was a demand for these ideas, and also for insight into the unusual New England governor who had shut down that strike. When Houghton Mifflin released the book in the fall of 1919, Stearns had two goals for it: boosting Coolidge's national profile and influencing the Republican delegates who would choose a nominee next June. After strategizing with Scaife, Stearns invested thousands of dollars in a marketing campaign that placed simple, uniform ads in magazines and newspapers around the country. At the top, the ads announced, "Gov. Calvin Coolidge Says"; beneath that ran one of his best paragraphs and information on where to buy the book. Stearns began identifying important readers: judges, politicians, party officials, and especially potential delegates. He flooded Scaife with lists of people to send the book to: 483 names, 613 names, 785 names. Houghton Mifflin printed another five thousand copies, then five thousand more. Stearns didn't bother with hiring speakers or organizing events. The book was the campaign, and the campaign was the book.

Have Faith stood out in part because of its hesitant author. After the strike, Coolidge had received more than a thousand offers to give speeches or write essays; he'd turned them all down. In December, a Boston businessman asked Coolidge to sign his copy of *Have Faith*, then mentioned a connection to John T. Adams, an Iowan and the upcoming chairman of the Republican National Committee. "They don't know much about you out there in the middle west," the Bostonian explained, "and I'm wondering whether it would not be a good plan to send Mr. Adams a complimentary copy of this book."

"I thank you very much for thinking of me," Coolidge replied, "but inasmuch as I have never met Mr. Adams, I would not quite feel free to do what you suggest."

When this exchange reached Stearns, he groaned. "The big goose," he said, "he should have sent the book. I'll see that it's done at once." Yet Stearns also realized that his candidate had a plan. Several times that winter, Coolidge made firm statements about being focused on his job as governor, and, like so much else with Coolidge, this focus was simultaneously real and tactical. Coolidge was more involved with Stearns's efforts than either let on. (When Stearns attempted to arrange a campaign biography, Coolidge met with the author and reviewed some chapters; he also sent instructions through Stearns on how to punctuate the manuscript of *Have Faith*.) Both men understood that using one office to gain another would be unseemly, especially for a candidate whose character made up his charm.

In February, Stearns sent Scaife an urgent telegram asking him to rush out another ten thousand copies—and to prepare fifty thousand more soon after that. The convention was coming, and Stearns leaned on old business ties to secure enough paper on short notice; Scaife hired outside binders to keep up. "We have," Stearns wrote, "less than 100 days to use up all these books."

Thankfully, they had help. Dwight Morrow, a partner at J. P. Morgan's bank, was quietly raising money and selling Coolidge to his financial peers; Morrow also recruited Bruce Barton, an ad executive whose clients included General Motors and GE. For Coolidge, Barton provided both advertising and PR, helping journalists coordinate their coverage and then writing fawning features himself. Barton sharpened Coolidge's image—the rural boyhood, the frugal duplex, the fierce traditionalism. He also relentlessly plugged the book. "Here's Cal Coolidge as shown by his own words," Barton wrote in one of his features, a few weeks before the convention. "Let him sit down with you in your own home and tell you what he thinks about the country's problems."

Have Faith caught on better than anyone could have predicted. Meaty stories on the book ran in the *New York Times*, the *Los Angeles Times*, and the *Wall Street Journal*, among many other outlets, to say nothing of the innumerable excerpts, advertisements, and reviews. Stearns monitored the coverage (and mailed additional copies to sympathetic journalists and editors). But much of the excitement came from regular Republicans— people who read the book aloud at local events or passed a well-thumbed copy to their friends. These voters recognized that the collection wasn't simply Coolidge's book; it was his personality, his philosophy, his style, and they responded to all of it. In the end, Stearns distributed more than seventy-three thousand copies, or just under a quarter of a million books adjusted for today's population—and did it in a shockingly brief window. Roosevelt's *Rough Riders*, by comparison, took decades to sell seventy thousand copies.

By the time Stearns's hundred days were up, *Have Faith* had become a coast-to-coast hit. Back in Boston, Coolidge was staying quiet. He was also learning to drive. The man who lived in a duplex had never owned a car, but lately he'd been practicing with an Oldsmobile, and one day he went for a spin. The car stalled out at a busy Boston intersection, and a crowd began to gather. It got bigger when people realized the driver was their newly famous governor—and bigger still when he continued to stall. After another failed start, the crowd lapsed into an awkward silence, until someone yelled, "Have faith in the Oldsmobile, Cal." The governor smiled one of his thin smiles, and on the next try the vehicle started and slipped back into traffic, carrying its passenger forward, always forward, to his next stop.

CONVENTIONAL

By 1920, political conventions had become massive and nationalized events, with noisy crowds, jaded reporters, and a reliable chance for some kind of drama. At the previous convention, in the summer of 1916—long before *Have Faith* and the Boston police strike, back when Coolidge was still an obscure lieutenant governor—the GOP had gathered in Chicago. The convention eventually chose Charles Evans Hughes as its nominee, but early on, when everything was uncertain, a former senator ran into an old acquaintance, Northampton's Henry Field.

"I see your friend Frank Stearns is in town," the senator said.

"Yes," Field replied, "I saw him."

"Do you know who his candidate for president is?"

"Hughes, I imagine."

"You have a poor imagination. He's for Calvin Coolidge."

What was once a punch line was now a real possibility. For their 1920 convention, the Republicans returned to Chicago, and the Massachusetts delegation arrived by train on the afternoon of June 6. Over the next two days Stearns, Barton, Morrow, and their associates operated out of a hotel suite, working other delegates in the hallways or around the communal spittoons, trying to raise Coolidge's name above its current position of intriguing dark horse. While their candidate had remained in Boston, his book had traveled. Morrow shoved a copy at one man with the comment, "Coolidge is the man best fitted to be president." He was so excited he didn't recognize it was Herbert Hoover, himself a contender for the nomination.

On Tuesday, June 8, the convention began. The weather was inhumanely hot; inside the Chicago Coliseum, where the various delegations gathered under their states' signs, the skylights let in all of the sun and none of the breeze. Edna Ferber, there as a journalist, marveled at the crowd's pink-faced misery. Even in an age of top hats, she observed, "they shed collars, ties, even shoes." More than fourteen thousand attendees sat through long days of speeches and debates over the party platform. By Thursday, H. L. Mencken reported, any liquor smuggled past the Prohibition enforcers was gone.

Presidential nominations finally began on Friday, with each name accompanied by a rowdy floor demonstration that hinted at the support

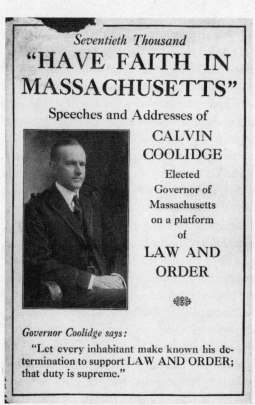

The *Have Faith* dust jacket stressed Coolidge's commitment to "Law and Order."

within the coliseum—forty-two minutes for General Leonard Wood, forty-six minutes for Governor Frank Lowden. Around three o'clock, a congressman nominated Coolidge. "Do you want a profound political thinker?" the congressman asked his fellow delegates. "Take the author of that inspiring volume *Have Faith in Massachusetts*. Do you want courage? Take the governor who just before an election sent the dauntless message: 'There is no right to strike against the public safety by anybody, anywhere, any time.'"

Coolidge's nomination earned three cheers from the crowd, though some of the excitement centered on the fact that a woman had seconded him, another marketing move arranged by Stearns. The actual voting didn't start until after five, with the first ballot featuring eleven candidates and an impasse at the top, Lowden versus Wood. Under the flags hanging lankly from the rafters, the delegates cast three more ballots before agreeing to adjourn until morning. "The hotels at midnight," wrote Mencken, "were bathed in the grisly quiet of a country village." One could blame the absence of alcohol or the presence of heat. The stillness also stemmed from the party leaders sequestering themselves in private meetings deep into the night, trying to find a solution.

Saturday brought six more ballots, with Warren Harding slowly gaining support as a compromise candidate. Late in the day, weighed down by the weather and the threat of paying for another night at a hotel, the delegates finally chose Harding, though not before rumors began spreading that his rise was being manipulated by party elites.

Coolidge had been receiving updates by phone, and he learned of Harding's victory around 7:30 p.m. He went for a walk through the Common and its surrounding streets; perhaps he paused by the windows of R. H. Stearns & Co. or Houghton Mifflin's bookstore.

Chicago had one last formality: selecting Harding's running mate. This time party leaders really did try to sway the outcome, sending word to various delegations to vote for Wisconsin senator Irvine Lenroot. Coolidge's supporters had given up; Frank Stearns had already headed back to his hotel to pack for the trip home.

After a fellow senator nominated Lenroot, the convention's presiding officer looked for a second. He spotted a tall and thin delegate from Oregon, standing on a chair and waving his hand.

That delegate was Wallace McCamant, a lawyer from Portland. McCamant was an enthusiastic partisan—this was his third national convention—but he'd never met Calvin Coolidge. Instead, he'd read *Have*

Faith. "Someone sent me Coolidge's book," McCamant later recalled, "and I read it through many times." In fact, Stearns and his supporters had sent McCamant the book on three separate occasions; one of the delegate's friends had also urged him to borrow his own copy. While McCamant had heard of Coolidge and the strike, it was the speeches that made him a fan—of Coolidge's character, of his literary precision, of his distinctly American values.

McCamant gave a short speech nominating not Lenroot but Coolidge, a man who "stood for law and order." This subversion thrilled the tired crowd, and delegates from all around the coliseum leaped up to second him—from Michigan and Maryland, Kansas and North Dakota. Coolidge had finished his walk by the time the phone rang with the news. "Nominated for Vice President," he told his wife.

Grace, who was used to her husband's teasing, gave an unmoved answer: "You don't mean it."

"Indeed I do."

Once the convention had finished, Mencken found himself in the passages under the coliseum, cooling off and sharing what felt like Chicago's last liquor with a member of the Boston press. The reporter was still stunned by Coolidge's nomination. "I know Cal Coolidge inside and out," he told Mencken. "He is the goddamn luckiest son of a bitch in the whole world."

Coolidge was lucky—even he would admit that. But he and his supporters had also prepared for years, whether it was the candidate revising his speeches or the supporters pushing the book. They were ready for luck, and now they turned to helping Harding in the fall. Coolidge agreed to stump in the South, though he insisted on writing the speeches himself. ("I must have time to do it in a thoughtful way," he told a Republican official.) Barton went to work with Al Lasker and the party's other admen. Still, he and Morrow and Stearns knew their favorite candidate. "We have decided to keep the committee together," Barton told Coolidge. "We think it has important work to do four years or eight years from now."

The work came sooner than that. One of the only famous moments from Coolidge's presidency is its start, in 1923. The vice president and his family had spent much of that summer in Plymouth Notch, trying to revive their once private life. On August 2, Coolidge hollowed out a tree that leaned precariously close to his father's house; the next day he planned to fill its trunk with cement.

That night, however, Harding died. John Coolidge's home still lacked plumbing, electricity, and a phone, so the news came in person, well after midnight. In the lamp-lit sitting room, where the gilt wallpaper had started to fade, John Coolidge read his son the oath of office. It was a simple and traditional scene, and standing there as president, Coolidge reflected on his new responsibilities and role. But one of the first things he thought about, Coolidge later admitted, was Wallace McCamant, the delegate who had nominated him after falling in love with *Have Faith*. "I knew the man who wrote those speeches was a patriot," McCamant told reporters after the convention. Now that man was president—because of his supporters and because of his luck, but also because of his book.

CHAPTER NINE

Legacy Books Get Personal
(Thanks to, of All Presidents, Calvin Coolidge)

O ne night in 1923, a few months before he became president, Calvin Coolidge took his wife on a date. It was a gala marking the centenary of a renowned Massachusetts piano manufacturer, and the schedule called for a formal dinner followed by a speech by the vice president himself. The Coolidges sat with the Stearnses, and after the meal, Calvin got up to deliver his address. Soon he was holding forth on the history of music, moving from composer to composer with graceful expertise—quite an achievement for someone who never even bothered to play the piano at the family's duplex. At first, Grace was astonished, but she quickly became amused. "When he joined us at the conclusion," she later wrote, "I burst into laughter in which he quietly joined, a little shamefacedly." Grace asked where he'd discovered so much rich detail; her husband, as usual, opted for a strategic silence.

That night was the first time Grace could remember Calvin using a ghostwriter—in this case, one of the manufacturer's PR specialists—and he clearly loathed it. When Stearns started compiling *The Price of Freedom*, Coolidge's next speech collection, timed for his presidential re-election, Coolidge insisted that it omit the piano address. Still, in the White House, he reluctantly pocketed his pencils and paper, dictating some speeches and deputizing aides to write others. In an era of new technology—the boxy radio sets residing in more and more homes, the timely newsreels playing before a movie theater's main event—politicians found themselves giving more speeches than in the past. When you factored in the executive branch's expanding profile, post-Roosevelt and post-Wilson, it seemed inevitable that presidents would get some help with their prose.

Technology was changing the lives of people everywhere. Movies and radio broadcasts shaped the way Americans talked, relaxed, and related to the world around them. (When Coolidge first became a national figure, a newspaper described him like this: "The governor looks like a typical Yankee of the movies.") They elevated a fresh generation of celebrities, from Babe Ruth to Charles Lindbergh, and stirred up frothy interest in their personal lives. Americans wanted more than ever to know their stars in public and in private—and now they got big doses of both, day by day and minute by minute.

This era saw the flourishing of a related innovation: the celebrity memoir. As early as 1900, an essayist had predicted that "an age of memoirs is upon us." He was right: Americans published nearly three times as many autobiographies between 1901 and 1940 as they had in the previous four decades, even though that earlier period had featured the surge in Civil War books. And these new autobiographies were different. They were more personal than historical, more gossipy than documentary, and readers adored them. Mark Twain earned so much from his memoirs' serial rights that he built a mansion—for a while he called it the "Autobiography House"—and such spoils were available even to lesser authors, so long as they could supply a big name and a big story. Actors, inventors, and athletes all wrote autobiographies with the help of ghostwriters. So did senators, cabinet members, first ladies, and presidents, who finally felt comfortable recounting their administrations soon after they ended. They felt so comfortable, in fact, that in this period, a tradition solidified. Writing legacy books switched from something former presidents did in secret to something they were supposed to do.

It really was an age of memoirs, in part because it was an age of ghosts. And yet despite the fruits of this partnership—namely, lots of bestselling books, some good, some bad, most in between—the ideal outcome remained a talented author reflecting on a fascinating life and then turning it into a fascinating book. That's precisely what happened with *The Autobiography of Calvin Coolidge*. As his presidency came to a close, Coolidge returned to his regimen of solitary writing, and his brief volume, which appeared less than a year after he left the White House, gave readers their first contemporary glimpse of the presidency and its human cost. It was an intimate and emotional book, a book that shocked many Americans, but maybe it shouldn't have. After all, the reason Coolidge cared about that piano speech—and the reason Grace could tease him—was that he wasn't just a celebrity. He was a writer.

FAMOUS AUTHORS, FAMOUS ARTHURS

The books of Bess Streeter Aldrich meant everything to Mary Brennan, mostly because they meant everything to her mother. From Aldrich's first major story—which ran in a 1911 issue of *Ladies' Home Journal*, America's first monthly magazine to hit a million subscribers—the author had crafted wholesome, homegrown fictions about life on the Great Plains. Brennan lived half a continent away, in the claustrophobic Bronx, but one day, she'd picked up a random book at her library, a novel by Aldrich. "The librarians soon realized," she explained in a letter to the Nebraska author, "the easiest way to get rid of me was to have one of your books on hand."

The real reason Brennan was writing, though, was to talk about her mother. She'd spent fifteen years caring for Mary and her siblings, clothing them, breastfeeding them, keeping them alive and content with what little money she had. Now that they were older, she finally had time for herself, time to read, and Aldrich's fiction had transformed her. "It seemed as though all those starved years," Brennan wrote, "were going to be made up immediately." Brennan's mother saved enough to buy each of Aldrich's books, and though she was normally the first person to share—"the soul of generosity in everything"—she kept her Aldrich volumes hidden, lest someone ask to borrow them. She wanted to savor those books herself. While discussing them, she opened up to her daughter about the burden of raising children, about how lonely and deadening it could be, about how fiction like Aldrich's might have helped. "That, Mrs. Aldrich, is why I am writing this letter," Brennan wrote. "I wonder if I am conveying to you just what your stories do."

Brennan's letter did convey that—through its understanding of Aldrich's work and, even more, its understanding of her mother's heart. Yet it ended on a lighter note: "I don't want to seem like some lovesick movie fan," Brennan wrote, "but my mother has been asking me for a picture of you."

Aldrich belonged to a new generation of celebrities, and each of them had to navigate their culture's shifting conception of fame. In the nineteenth century, fame had centered on one's didactic example—on duty, decorum, and public deeds. This form of eminence celebrated Nathaniel Hawthorne for his novels and Charles W. Eliot for his Harvard reforms. (It also kept presidential candidates off the trail.) In the twentieth century, however, fame began to shift to one's personality. Ideas and accomplishments still mattered, but what mattered just as much, and what was certainly more visible, were the dishy details from an individual's private life: the hobbies and hometowns and favorite cigarettes, all of which made a star seem more human, more real. This desire for personality swallowed entertainers and intellectuals alike. Mary Brennan didn't just ask Aldrich for a picture—she asked for "a snapshot of yourself taken in Nebraska."

This shift started with magazines and their mass audience, and radio stations and movie studios amplified it. In the 1920s, a town of even five thousand usually had its own movie theater, and each week tens of millions of Americans went to the movies—and frequently to the same movies, which unified audiences and exalted stars. "The smallest town," wrote a film critic in the *Atlantic*, "sees the same motion-picture players as the largest." That combination of universal consumer and individual celebrity drove radio broadcasts as well, and by the end of the decade, more than a third of households had a receiver. Most of those families tuned in every day, listening to programs like gossip columnist Louella Parsons's syndicated interview show, which promoted both its celebrity guests and its weekly sponsor, Sunkist Oranges.

Parsons's show had been cooked up by the ad agency of Al Lasker, and he also leveraged celebrity for his political clients. During the 1920 campaign, Lasker secured a glut of Harding endorsements, including ones from singers, stage actors, and movie stars. Al Jolson, the Jazz Age's most famous entertainer, answered to all of those titles, and he traveled to Ohio to perform with a brass band on Harding's front porch. The newsreel cameras captured Jolson singing and swaying while Harding lurked in the background, awkwardly embracing a tuba.

The power of celebrity energized even the creakiest industries, including literary ones. In 1927, when word arrived that Lindbergh and his *Spirit of St. Louis* had made it to Paris, an editor at Putnam's told his friend he wanted to publish Lindbergh's memoir. The friend laughed: "Indeed, you—and who else?"

Lindbergh had a book deal by the time he boarded the ship home, but it was magazines that really capitalized on the autobiographical boom. Editors like S. S. McClure loved putting famous names on their covers, and their ad revenues could pay far more than any book publisher to do it. McClure courted celebrities personally, planting the idea, hinting at a huge audience, and happily ceding editorial control. William Dean Howells might have called autobiography "the most democratic province," but democracy went only so far: an editor at *Ladies' Home Journal* dropped

$60,000 to buy and advertise Howells's memoirs, more than $1.5 million in today's dollars. "It is not expense," the editor explained, "it is investment. We are investing in a trademark. It will all come back in time."

Some of the period's best autobiographies came from writers. Gertrude Stein famously passed the 1920s in Paris with her fellow Modernists, including Hemingway, Picasso, and Pound, even as her own writing failed to catch on. (She'd struggled to sell even a hundred copies of her first book, the story collection *Three Lives*.) That changed with *The Autobiography of Alice B. Toklas*. It was a startling and inventive work, written in the third person not to create distance, as the technique had done for early autobiographers like Madison, but to create multiple selves, a past Stein and a present "Stein," who was technically a "Toklas," all merging into a deliberate mess of intention and exposure. Yet what made the *Autobiography* a sensation—first across four issues of the *Atlantic*, then as a best-selling book—was its smart-set gossip. "You are more discussed in Hollywood," a friend wrote, "than Greta Garbo." When Stein returned to America for a tour, her first visit in three decades, she was a star. At one event, a book signing at Chicago's Marshall Field's department store, the crowd grew so congested that fans couldn't exit the elevator.

Not all memoirists possessed Stein's linguistic skill. Once, before a Yankees game, a reporter chatted with Babe Ruth. "What books are you reading?" the reporter asked as they lingered by the batting cage.

"Reading isn't good for a ballplayer," Ruth replied. "Not good for his eyes."

"You must do some reading. Who are your favorite authors?"

"My favorite Arthurs? Nehf and Fletcher."

"Not Arthurs. Authors, writers."

"My favorite writer," the slugger said, "is Christy Walsh."

Ruth's answer meant, in a sense, that his favorite writer was Ruth himself—for Walsh ran a media syndicate that sold first-person columns and books by athletes, with Ruth as its star. "It involves no disrespect to Calvin Coolidge or to Charles W. Eliot," the *New York Times* observed, "to suggest that in the extent and immediacy of popularity the Home Run King is also the first citizen of the land." Millions listened to Ruth's World Series games on the radio, or saw his ads for underwear, or read his autobiographical prose, which he and Walsh produced with the support of a five-man rotation of ghosts.

In the 1920s, ghostwriting emerged as a common practice. The *Washington Post*'s sports desk watched a competing paper load up with Walsh's

When Babe Ruth donated the manuscript of his (ghostwritten) autobiography to Yale, he did so by handing it to the college team's first baseman. That player's name was George H. W. Bush.

clients, then responded with a motto that nodded to Lasker's Lucky Strike ads: "Reach for a *Post* instead of a Ghost." Elsewhere in the nation's capital, President Harding hired Judson Welliver, the White House's first modern speechwriter, and he stuck around to help Coolidge until he jumped to a more lucrative job in private sector PR. Magazine editors frequently connected their famous authors to diligent, sympathetic ghosts, with one contemporary estimating that perhaps two-thirds of the features with celebrity bylines were actually crafted by spectral pros.

Sometimes the way to tell a thing has arrived isn't in the thing itself but in the backlash. The published rebuttals to ghostwriting were vicious. A few journalists mocked it. ("Ghostwriters," wrote one, "are the crutches on which celebrity limps to authorship.") More often they lamented it as a sign of cultural erosion, the latest proof that politicians and celebrities could no longer think for themselves. Every few years—and, indeed, to this day—a major outlet ran a story with an alarming headline: "Survey of the Ghost Writers: They are increasing in numbers and importance—and the public is concerned as to the reason."

But those stories never offered evidence that the public actually cared. Even in the 1920s, insiders like Christy Walsh spoke honestly and uncontroversially about their methods. In 1929, the *New York Times* framed the practice of ghostwriting like this: "The public was at one time completely credulous on the point. Now it seems unlikely that it believes in any of the noted athletes, singers, or politicians who break out in print." What had been a major scandal for George Washington's reputation, and a minor one for Ulysses S. Grant's, was now simply a useful technique. The modern backlash to ghostwriting has never come from readers. It has come from writers.

Once the celebrity memoir could count on amenable editors, qualified assistants, and an enthusiastic audience, it thrived. "'To write or not to write one's autobiography?'" the *Washington Post* noted, "is the question the famous have to decide." A staggering number said yes. Autobiographies appeared from John Muir, Jane Addams, Frank Lloyd Wright, Louella Parsons, and Ida Tarbell. They came from Booker T. Washington and W. E. B. DuBois; from Andrew Carnegie and John D. Rockefeller; from Helen Keller and Henry Ford. Powerful politicians like Robert La Follette and Thomas Platt wrote memoirs packed with newsy nuggets. Helen Taft, the wife of William Howard Taft, wrote her autobiography, as did Edith Bolling Wilson, the second wife of Woodrow Wilson. In 1928, and in the afterglow of his movie *The Jazz Singer*, even Al Jolson decided to write his autobiography. He brought a ghostwriter with him on his honeymoon, a multiweek cruise. Jolson's book was never finished, but his marriage made it twelve years.

Many of these memoirs began as magazine serials; many of them relied on ghostwriters; many of them became best-selling books. They also aligned neatly with their era's new ideas about celebrity. In an internal memo, Edith Wilson's publisher proclaimed her autobiography "probably the most important book we have ever secured for our list." Yet the memo laid out a marketing plan that stressed its least important aspects: "Emphasize the entertainment value of the book, rather than its historical importance." This plan surely reflected some assumptions about Wilson's gender, just like the buzz surrounding Stein's *Autobiography*. But most celebrity memoirs were marketed and consumed in this fashion. The genre's goal was to entertain.

That made it surprising when the book industry passed on the period's most scandalous memoir: *The President's Daughter*, by Harding's mistress Nan Britton. Publishers were issuing plenty of titles packed with Washington dirt, including *The Mirrors of Washington* (so popular it earned a sequel, *Behind the Mirrors*) and *Washington Merry-Go-Round* (its sequel: *More Merry-Go-Round*). But Britton's memoir went further, recounting the couple's conception of a child in a Senate office and even their discussion on whether to seek an abortion. Respectable publishers like Knopf and Simon & Schuster rejected the manuscript. "We're passing up $100,000," one editor admitted to her, "and we know it!" Eventually Britton and a supporter, who had also helped her write it, decided to publish it themselves—though not before the New York Society for the Suppression of Vice sent in police officers to try and shut them down.*

The President's Daughter was an enormous hit, selling as many copies, and selling them as quickly, as Coolidge's *Have Faith*. It was also a terrible book. After the vice society's raid, Dorothy Parker quipped, "Those weren't policemen; they were critics of literature dressed up." But Parker's line obscured something important: many literary critics had surrendered their ability to call ghostwritten books good or bad because they'd dismissed them for being ghostwritten in the first place. The truth was, and is, that ghostwriting can be done scrupulously or hackishly. Instead of attacking the many memoirs S. S. McClure coaxed into existence, critics should have studied the memoir he wrote himself.

Technically, Willa Cather wrote it. McClure was an intense and inspiring leader; after Cather met him for the first time, for a career-making interview in 1903, she told a friend, "I feel as though I want to do well almost as much for him as for myself." She compared McClure's charisma to that of a powerful preacher, but she could have said a powerful politician too.

A decade later McClure found himself deeply in debt, and he turned to the frenzied memoir market to earn some cash. Cather, who had just finished *O Pioneers!*, agreed to help. Once a week, McClure arrived at her Manhattan apartment and said, "Now, where did I stop last time?" The room was underfurnished, and underheated as well, but McClure kept

---

*Harding's love life engendered another body of literature: his bawdy correspondence. He penned more than a hundred surviving letters to a second mistress, Carrie Fulton Phillips, and they remain shocking and vivid today. (Harding's pet name for his genitals: Jerry.) The president even attempted some poetry:

I love your poise
Of perfect thighs
When they hold me
in paradise. . . .

warm by pacing as he told and retold his life's story. Cather listened closely, absorbing his terse phrases and abrupt transitions, learning, as she later put it, to "work within the limits and color of that personality I knew so well."

My Autobiography began to appear in the fall of 1913, first as installments in *McClure's*, then in book form the following year, and in both versions, the author frankly acknowledged his "indebtedness to Miss Willa Sibert Cather." Cather, for her part, divulged her role in letters and to friends over tea. They were proud of their project, and they'd worked hard at it—Cather crafting a carefully realized character, McClure supplying as much honesty and detail as she needed, and both participants yielding to the other to make the best book they could. *My Autobiography* is indeed a fine book, and McClure, one of his era's best evaluators of literary talent, credited its quality to the collaboration. His coworkers, his college classmates, even his wife agreed, with all of them praising Cather for how well she captured his voice.

This kind of collaboration takes time, effort, and trust. What the ghostwriting scolds miss, in their solipsistic focus on the act of writing, is that while writing is important and difficult, it is hardly life's only important and difficult task. For those who struggle with translating their ideas and emotions into words—and here George Washington's example cuts a different way—ghostwriting makes sense as long as both partners take it seriously. There are many kinds of partner, from the talker-slash-editor, like McClure; to the politician who writes the first draft herself; to the celebrity who gives a couple of distracted interviews and then disappears until the book launch. The idea of ghostwriting, just like the idea of authorship, can impose a false uniformity on a range of outcomes, and each instance merits an evaluation on its own terms. The problem has never been ghostwriting—just bad ghostwriting.

THE EXPANSION OF THE EX-PRESIDENCY

F. Scott Fitzgerald had already written two novels, plus a string of stories for the magazines, which was where he made his real money. But in the early 1920s he became obsessed with the work he believed would make him a star: a stage play titled *The Vegetable, or From President to Postman*. It centered on a bored clerk named Jerry, no relation to Harding but someone who ascended to the White House all the same. Still, the play's real concern was its ideas: success, ambition, and the American dream. In

1923 it debuted with a disastrous one-week run; Fitzgerald's wife, Zelda, told a friend it "flopped as flat as one of Aunt Jemima's famous pancakes."

The playwright returned to fiction, eventually finding a way to write about American ambition without the presidency: a third novel, titled *The Great Gatsby*. Yet *The Vegetable* contained at least one joke worth preserving, in an exchange between Jerry and a bootlegger named Snooks:

> JERRY. Did you ever—did you ever have any ambition to be President?
> SNOOKS. Sure. Once.
> JERRY [ponderously]. You did, eh?
> SNOOKS. Once. I guess bootleggin's just as good, though. More money in it.

It was a reasonable look at Prohibition earning power except for one factor: the ex-presidency. Once they departed the White House, presidents merged with their culture's new model for celebrity. Should they use their fame to weigh in on current events? Would it be better if they essentially disappeared? "What," the *Century* asked in a big feature, "shall we do with our ex-presidents?" One answer was to have them write their memoirs, for better-than-bootlegger paychecks. During this era, America's presidents started a streak in which, with the partial exceptions of Taft and George H. W. Bush, each one who left the White House in good health went on to publish a legacy book. The president who inaugurated this streak was Theodore Roosevelt. After reading the *Century*'s feature, he told a friend, "They needn't worry about this ex-president. He'll take care of himself."

The autobiographical impulse seized Roosevelt and his peers more slowly than it did other celebrities. One reason was that the presidency failed to produce many stars. As the Oxford professor James Bryce put it, "Who now knows or cares to know anything about the personality of James K. Polk or Franklin Pierce?"

Another reason was a sincere attachment, common among ex-presidents, to the older conception of fame. Grover Cleveland and George Parker agreed that if anything, Cleveland received more attention as ex-president than he had as president. But Cleveland wanted to direct that attention toward the practical and the didactic. In 1905, three years before his death, he outlined his hope to another friend. "There are things in my life," he wrote, "that if set out, and read by the young men of our country, might be of benefit."

This was a tough sell in the new celebrity economy. That same year Cleveland turned down a Howells-sized check from *McClure's*. "Mr. McClure and all the forces about him," he explained, "have lately importuned me, in season and out of season, to write, say, twelve autobiographical articles." After thinking about it—"softened up," he admitted, "under the suggestion of duty and money"—Cleveland countered by proposing a series of edifying interviews. The editor wouldn't even consider it. What McClure wanted, Cleveland realized, was "the 'I,'" something to "attract the lovers of a 'snappy life.'"

So Cleveland wrote other books, including *Presidential Problems*, a collection of essays and university lectures that explored his ideas about the executive branch. Sometimes he illustrated those ideas with an anecdote or personal aside, but it fell well short of a "snappy life." Taft followed a similar formula in books like *Our Chief Magistrate and His Powers*, as did Benjamin Harrison in *This Country of Ours*. Each of these titles earned polite coverage, but little more. "Nothing," one reviewer said of Harrison's book, "has not been said before by others, but no one else has been able to treat the subject from the presidential point of view."

Theodore Roosevelt became an ex-president on March 4, 1909, when Taft, his chosen successor, was sworn in. Roosevelt went home to Sagamore Hill, his spacious home on Long Island. He'd designed it for his wife, Alice, and their future children, until she died after delivering their first in 1884. While her death had shattered Roosevelt—his diary that day read, simply, "The light has gone out of my life"—he eventually remarried, finishing the house and filling it with five more children. Now that he was in his fifties Sagamore Hill served as a book-strewn, wood-paneled sanctuary, a quiet spot to read and write. "The house," Edith Wharton remembered in her own autobiography, "was like one big library, and the whole tranquil place breathed of the love of books and of the country."

As promised, Roosevelt had already made plans to take care of himself. A few months before the end of his term, he started meeting with magazines and publishing houses, creating a frantic, auction-like atmosphere of private dinners, pleading editors, and literary buzz. He was leaving office as the biggest celebrity in the country and maybe the world, and a career-spanning autobiography seemed like the obvious choice—something more commercial and comprehensive than James Buchanan's largely ignored volume or Ulysses S. Grant's *Personal Memoirs*, which had stopped after the Civil War. But Roosevelt decided instead to write a series of articles and a book on the African safari he was planning. Even *African*

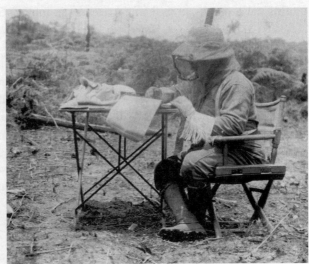

Roosevelt wrote *Through the Brazilian Wilderness* in the same way he wrote *African Game Trails*, donning a mosquito net hood and gripping his pen through thick gloves.

Game Trails, when it sold to Scribner's and its magazine, was front-page news. "It is believed that the story of the big hunt," the *New York Times* reported, "will sell as never a 'best seller' has sold before."

Perhaps Roosevelt put off his memoirs because he wasn't done with politics. By 1912 he'd soured on Taft, challenging him in that year's Republican primary and then running against him in the general as the Progressive Party's nominee, a bid that mostly just guaranteed Wilson's win.

Or perhaps Roosevelt didn't like the idea of writing his memoirs at all. That's what he told Lawrence Abbott, his editor at *Outlook* magazine, as they searched for Roosevelt's next major project in the weeks after the 1912 election. Around the same time, Roosevelt attended a dinner of prominent Progressives. It was a large group, gathered around a large table: authors, activists, and still more magazine editors. Roosevelt ended up next to Hamlin Garland, a lavishly bearded novelist who devoted much of the meal not to politics but to begging the ex-president to write an autobiography. Garland had been revising an autobiography of his own, and he and Roosevelt talked about the literary and historical value of a president telling his own story. They talked about other prominent memoirs, including Howells's and Twain's.

By the end of the evening, Roosevelt had warmed to the idea. "I am permanently out of politics," he admitted.

"Good!" Garland said. "Now you can write the book."

On November 30, 1912, *Outlook* announced that in the new year, it would start a series of autobiographical excerpts from the ex-president. "In these papers," it promised, "Mr. Roosevelt will talk with greater intimacy than he has on the platform [or] in his books." It was the language of celebrity, and it helped Roosevelt launch another bidding war for the book rights, which Macmillan won by offering an extravagant royalty of 50 percent. Almost immediately, journalists predicted Roosevelt's would be the most widely discussed memoir since Grant's.

Autobiography might have seemed like Roosevelt's most natural genre. Henry Adams, who wrote the era's defining memoir, recalled a dinner with the president: "We were overwhelmed in a torrent of oratory, and at last I heard only the repetition of I-I-I." Still, the writing tormented Roosevelt, slowing him down and stirring up uncertainty even more than his previous books had. A few days after Christmas, he wrote a letter to his sister-in-law. The family had shared a perfect holiday, with five of the six children returning to Sagamore Hill, just in time to see it blanketed in a deep and gorgeous snow. "The children acted as if it were fifteen years ago," he wrote. "They hung up their stockings, and came in and opened them on the bed next morning, and after breakfast trooped in to see their presents." Any seasonal cheer vanished, however, when he returned to his work. "I am having my hands full writing certain chapters of my past experiences," he confessed. "It is very difficult to strike just the happy mean between being too reticent and not reticent enough."

Roosevelt's narrative split into two halves: his life before politics and his life during. Both parts vexed him. Abbott tried to help with the first, showing up at Sagamore Hill with a stenographer and a list of questions about Roosevelt's childhood and Harvard years. Roosevelt dictated for hours, with Abbott patiently drawing out anecdotes, steering him toward a more personal tone, even reorganizing the resulting transcript—an example of the gray area between ghostwriting and authorship. Roosevelt continued to work with the stenographer and to revise each transcript strenuously. In some places, those early chapters approached his best writing, warm and teeming with details, like this description of the New York City spot where he got his start in party politics:

The Republican Association of which I became a member held its meetings in Morton Hall, a large, barn-like room over a saloon. Its furniture was of the canonical kind: dingy benches, spittoons, a dais at one end with a table and chair and a stout pitcher for iced water, and on the walls pictures of General Grant and of Levi P. Morton, to whose generosity we owed the room.

Still, the chapters were hardly intimate. Roosevelt omitted many memories and personal details, especially when they involved pain. He declined to explain the fortune he'd lost as a Badlands rancher; he skirted the alcoholism and death of Elliott, the brother with whom he'd hunted ducks; he didn't mention his first wife, Alice, at all.

Once the *Outlook* series started in 1913—and predictions about its popularity proved right, with each installment getting excerpted and analyzed in newspapers big and small—Roosevelt turned to writing about his political career. His narration remained selective, and its quality began to slip. The author was typically overbooked, balancing not just the autobiography but two other works in progress, *Life-Histories of African Game Animals* and *History as Literature*, plus a smattering of essays and reviews. Worse, he was bored. "I am working with heated unintelligence at my 'biography,'" he admitted to his daughter in April. "I fairly loathe it now." Roosevelt began delegating, asking at least seven former aides to write reports on their service. Gifford Pinchot, to take one example, submitted a long memo on conservation issues. This time it wasn't even a ghostly gray area: Roosevelt made a few tweaks and then folded Pinchot's prose directly into his book.

Roosevelt finally finished the manuscript in late spring. He had written more than six hundred pages in just over six months, and when reporters traveled with him that May—Roosevelt was suing a Michigan editor who had called him a drunk during the previous election—they noticed how tired he looked. The train to Michigan was packed with Roosevelt supporters, and one of his former aides brought an issue of *Outlook* to tease him.

"You made a slight mistake of detail," the aide said.

"I suppose I was intoxicated when I wrote it," was Roosevelt's deadpan reply.

Intoxicated is actually a fair description of *Theodore Roosevelt: An Autobiography*, a book whose political material is surly and mean-spirited, self-confident but not self-aware. "I have no desire to get even with anybody," Roosevelt had promised Hamlin Garland during their dinner. Once he started dictating, though, Roosevelt couldn't resist adding prickly insults and transparent defenses. He praised his administration for its "honesty" and "courage"; he compared himself to Lincoln. Roosevelt had finally written a book about his favorite hero: himself.*

Readers saw through it. "What this autobiography actually amounts to," wrote one frustrated reviewer, "[is] his justification of his career." While the book version sold tens of thousands of copies, Macmillan considered it a costly disappointment. Still, it established a precedent. Inside Woodrow Wilson's White House, staffers talked openly about their future memoirs; Wilson enjoyed citing John Quincy Adams's diaries and joking that their acidic tone now made more sense. In the aftermath of World War I, the president spoke to the Democratic National Committee about his anger at the Republicans trying to block the League of Nations. "I am going to begin to be a historian again," Wilson said, "and I am going to have the privilege of writing about these gentlemen without any restraints of propriety."

Wilson went on a grueling national tour to champion the League, but in the fall of 1919, just as the tour ended, he suffered a terrible stroke. It changed everything, including his desire and stamina to write. As an ex-president, he made a few authorial attempts, none of them good. A fellow historian urged Wilson to write his memoirs, even if he had to hire some help; a PR executive pointed out that someone was going to cash in on his fame—it might as well be Wilson himself. But he declined their offers. "Things are still a burden," Edith explained to the historian, "that have to be thought out."

That left the autobiographical onus on his advisers and aides. Edith wrote her memoirs, of course, but there were many others, especially after World War I increased demand. ("The prices of memoirs of conspicuous war figures," the *New York Times* noted, "have doubled.") Autobiographies appeared from Wilson's secretary of treasury and his secretary of state, among others. Joseph Tumulty, his press secretary, received a "fortune" for *Woodrow Wilson as I Knew Him*. Competition grew so hot that one aide plotted to steal a set of newsreels to use as a source for his memoirs, though he could never figure out how to get them off the White House grounds.

With better health, Wilson surely would have joined his supporters—

---

*Many of Roosevelt's insults were aimed at people who didn't share his expansive view of executive power, including Taft, who earned a comparison to Buchanan. In *Our Chief Magistrate and His Powers*, Taft responded. Roosevelt's memoir, he wrote, "suggests a story which a friend of mine told of his little daughter Mary. As he came walking home after a business day, she ran out from the house to greet him, all aglow with the importance of what she wished to tell him. She said, 'Papa, I am the best scholar in the class.' The father's heart throbbed with pleasure as he inquired, 'Why, Mary, you surprise me. When did the teacher tell you? This afternoon?' 'Oh, no,' Mary's reply was, 'the teacher didn't tell me—I just noticed it myself.'"

arguing with Republicans, arguing for his legacy, adding to the archive that future historians would sift. As he'd written many years earlier while still a young professor, "all correspondence and autobiography will repay perusal."

"IT COSTS A GREAT DEAL TO BE PRESIDENT"

Theodore Roosevelt: An Autobiography may have been a flawed memoir, but it was flawed in a Rooseveltian way: arrogant, vindictive, and brittlely certain. That, at least, was the case made by its friendly readers. As the legacy books began to pile up, however, it became clear that Roosevelt's memoir was actually flawed in a *presidential* way. Calvin Coolidge is proof that the genre doesn't have to be like this. When Coolidge published his first piece of writing after his presidency, a fragment of memoir that would form the heart of his *Autobiography*, it was perhaps the most celebrated magazine story in this magazine age. But what made it a phenomenon was its humility and honesty.

When Coolidge became president, he was not as big a celebrity as Roosevelt. But the machinery of celebrity had grown far bigger, and Coolidge manipulated it deftly. Photo ops, ghostwriters, newsreels, radio: he used each of them to shape his image as a simple, traditional American. On the day before the 1924 election, Coolidge delivered a radio address in which he marveled at his national audience—"including my father, up on the Vermont farm, listening in." Of course, Coolidge frequently visited that farm to work, in addition to slyly invoking it on air. That was his strength: he combined his era's older and newer versions of fame.

Voters loved him for it, reelecting him to his first full term by a healthy margin. They also loved his family. A few months before the election, Coolidge's youngest son, Calvin Jr., developed a small blister while playing tennis on the White House lawn. A fever followed, and soon it became clear that the blister was infected; in a time before antibiotics, the infection spread, killing him within a week. The death of Calvin Jr. devastated his parents, and the nation grieved with them. Radio stations carried memorial services. Reporters traveled to the burial in Plymouth Notch and described its heartbreaking scenes: the casket resting in the grave and covered in flowers, a mix of expensive bouquets and handpicked arrangements from the gardens of Northampton; the boy's mother lingering by the grave as the mourners walked to their cars, until she bent down and nestled his worn Bible in the flowers; the boy's father standing there silently, his lips pressed tight.

Three years later, Coolidge announced he would not seek a second full term, in part because he was content with his record of tax cuts and surpluses, in part because of his family's persistent sorrow. On March 4, 1929, Calvin and Grace attended Herbert Hoover's inauguration, then boarded an overnight train for Northampton. When they exited their car early the next morning, the whole town seemed to be there to welcome them, even the students from Smith with curlers still in their hair. There was also a platoon of photographers and newsreel cameras, and, since it was overcast, one of them set off some flash powder to illuminate the Coolidges. The explosion elicited a wave of shrieks, with one person crying, "I thought he was shot!" The residents of Northampton weren't used to flash photography.

The former residents of the White House were. They were excited to escape it, actually, to get back to their quiet home and quiet life. But it was four days before Coolidge could walk outside and pick up the paper without a photographer memorializing the moment. The tourists were worse. They gawked at the famous duplex and even peered through the bay windows, trying to glimpse the residents. The family's tree-lined street was besieged by cars with plates from all over the country. One of their neighbors started counting: a new car rolled past every six seconds. Coolidge couldn't outrun the attention either, since his father's remote farm had also become a destination, receiving as many as three hundred visitors a day. It discouraged the ex-president. He'd been happy to exploit his celebrity, but now he yearned for privacy. "What shall I do with him?" Grace asked Frank Stearns.

Things were about to get crazier still, mostly because of something Coolidge had done himself. When Coolidge had declined to run for reelection, nineteen months before, Ray Long had written immediately and urged him to write his autobiography—and to write it for Long's *Cosmopolitan*, a general interest magazine at the time. Long wasn't the only editor with this idea.* But he was the most persistent. He was a short, spectacled man with an outsized personality, and he'd pushed *Cosmopolitan*'s subscription base close to 2 million by wooing celebrity authors and making some headlines himself. Long considered Coolidge the most important pursuit of his career, and he followed up every few weeks: letters, phone calls, even visits when he could make it from New York to the White House.

---

*He wasn't even the first. Coolidge's father swore him in on August 3, 1923. By August 4, Roger Scaife, his old editor on *Have Faith*, was strategizing in an internal memo: "While it is too early to forecast whether Coolidge makes a good president or not, I think it is very important that we keep his friendship and interest in our concern as against future publications."

Coolidge wouldn't commit. He still hated the notion of chasing the next job while plying the current one. But he'd been thinking about writing something autobiographical for a while now—joking with Stearns about the surge of kiss-and-tell Wilson memoirs, or listening as Bruce Barton, his old friend in advertising, made suggestions on how to avoid Roosevelt's literary mistakes. Once Coolidge was ready, Barton helped him narrow the list of eager outlets to two: *Collier's* and *Cosmopolitan*. On the morning of January 25, 1929, Long finally got a shot at clinching the Coolidge deal. He arrived at the White House at 8:30 a.m. and met with the president in the Oval Office, a room that had been added during the Taft administration.

"Well, you're an early bird," Coolidge said when Long walked in.

"Mr. President, beneath this business suit beats the heart of a Canadian mounted policeman," Long replied. "I've come down to get my man."

Coolidge smiled, and they discussed a potential partnership. The key, of course, was money, and Long was willing to pay an unheard of twenty-five thousand dollars for a single autobiographical article. After an hour, he turned the room over to *Collier's*, whose editors had arranged for more than twenty businessmen and politicians to send Coolidge pro-memoir telegrams, in addition to getting another old friend, Dwight Morrow, to make the Oval Office pitch. Long headed to his hotel room and sat next to the phone, replaying their conversation in his head and wondering whether he should have offered more.

Finally, the phone rang. "Mr. Long," said Everett Sanders, Coolidge's secretary, "you are requested to come to the White House."

When the editor arrived, Sanders gave him the good news: Coolidge had signed his part of the contract. There was also a top-secret twist. "He insists that before you sign it, you read the manuscript," Sanders said. "If you are not satisfied, you are to feel perfectly free to withdraw your offer."

Long was stunned. Coolidge had said nothing about a manuscript, which he'd written recently and kept hidden from virtually all of his staff. Sanders led Long to the White House's vacant Cabinet Room, where he began to read it, a revealing account that started with Harding's death and continued through Coolidge's decision not to run. By the second page, he knew it was perfect.

That night, the editor hurried back to New York. The next day was a Sunday, but he called five staffers into *Cosmopolitan*'s empty offices, where they yanked their April issue's lead feature and replaced it with Coolidge's secret manuscript. Long didn't tell the advertising department about his new author; he told only two people at the printing plant, who split the text into small pieces so the other employees wouldn't understand what they were handling. Long's paranoia spiraled even deeper. He hired private detectives to monitor the plant during the two weeks it took to print the issue. A group of robbers with sawed-off shotguns actually broke into the building, but it was a fluke; once they cracked the safe, they grabbed the payroll cash, not realizing the real prize was a stack of typewritten pages.

Cosmopolitan announced Coolidge's article on the same day as Hoover's inauguration, a Monday. By Thursday, the April issue—"Mr. Coolidge's OWN STORY," the cover blared—was for sale. By Friday, there was literary chaos.

Readers responded to the article with unprecedented excitement for several reasons. The first was its surprise announcement, delivered on the same day Coolidge departed the White House. The second was their hunger for more insights into Coolidge's private life. ("No man of his august station," H. L. Mencken once said, "ever talked about himself less.") The third was the national esteem for Coolidge as a writer. During his presi-

Cosmopolitan's April issue sold out so quickly that the magazine received requests for extra inventory from more than nineteen hundred cities.

dency, the *New York Times Magazine* had analyzed his style and declared him "the most literary man who has occupied the White House since 1865." The claim drew approving letters from all over the country.

When Coolidge read that *Times* story, he wrote a letter himself. "I want," he told the journalist, "to express to you my appreciation." While the president clearly prided himself on his authorship, the close reading had unsettled him: "I am not conscious," Coolidge continued, "of having any particular style." And yet, conscious or not, his new *Cosmopolitan* article contained the same qualities as his best speeches—it was charming, self-deprecating, and stuffed with tangible detail. There were some bromides and back patting. ("In spite of [Harding's] remarkable record," he wrote, "much remained to be done.") But mostly there was the kind of prose that only looks easy to write. "I was awakened by my father coming up the stairs calling my name," Coolidge wrote of the night he became president. "I noticed that his voice trembled. As the only times I had ever observed that before were when death had visited our family, I knew that something of the gravest nature had occurred."

The most striking passage in Coolidge's article dealt with one of those deaths. Calvin Jr., he wrote, had been a perceptive and bookish boy. His parents wanted their young scholar to try some physical labor, and Coolidge shared a memorable story about summer jobs that made his paternal delight clear:

> The day before I became president he had just started to work in a tobacco field. When one of his fellow laborers said to him, "If my father was president I would not work in a tobacco field," Calvin replied, "If my father were your father, you would."

When it was time to describe Calvin Jr. on his deathbed, Coolidge was equally frank: "In his suffering, he was asking me to make him well. I could not." Coolidge admitted that he felt powerless—that, even five years later, he remained lacerated and unsure: "If I had not been president he would not have raised a blister. . . . I do not know why such a price was exacted for occupying the White House." As Coolidge put it in the article's final line, "It costs a great deal to be President."

On the morning that *Cosmopolitan*'s April issue went on sale, Grace headed out early to buy it at one of Northampton's newsstands. It was a good thing—by the end of the day the issue had essentially disappeared nationwide, even though Long had printed hundreds of thousands of extra copies. Scalpers were selling it for a dollar apiece; *Cosmopolitan* received requests for additional inventory from more than nineteen hundred cities. Eventually the magazine printed the feature as a pamphlet and offered it to anyone who would pay the postage. But that didn't help the people who wanted to read it, and especially its wrenching and widely discussed account of Calvin Jr., right now. "Calvin Coolidge," noted *Publishers Weekly*, "received more publicity in one day than George Bernard Shaw receives in three years." He eclipsed more than his fellow authors. Even during the first week of the Hoover administration, America was talking about its previous president more than its current one.

The article made Coolidge's life even more frantic. He was trying to revive his small-town routine: up early, oatmeal for breakfast, then a quick car ride—one of his only luxuries, as a still-spotty driver, was a chauffeur—to the same Northampton office he'd used for decades. Even there he encountered a rush of reporters and tourists. He added a second door so that when it got too crowded, he could slip out the back. Long asked how he was enjoying private life. "Fine," he replied, "if it could only be private."

Coolidge continued to write, at the office when possible and at home. It must have been one of the only elements in his new life that he enjoyed— no ghosts, no stenographers, just his paper, his pencil, and his memories. *Cosmopolitan* planned to run more articles, including two on his childhood in Vermont. Coolidge wrote the first drafts in longhand, and after a secretary typed them up, he made meticulous revisions. In a paragraph on the presidency and its incessant demand for public appearances, he changed "one of the most appalling tasks" to "one of the most appalling trials." He shortened many of his sentences. Every once in a while, he would make an addition in the margin, but even those had a way of calling for less: "A President cannot, with success, constantly appeal to the country. After a time he will get no response."

Long and his staffers were shocked by the cleanness of Coolidge's prose. (They seemed to spend more time passing his latest submission around the office than actually editing it.) They also wanted a book. On March 21, Coolidge and Frank Stearns took a train to New York for business meetings with *Cosmopolitan* and others. Reporters in Northampton watched them leave, then alerted their Manhattan colleagues that the ex-president was incoming. So many journalists swarmed his hotel that management installed a security guard at his door and refused to patch calls through to his room. Long brought Joseph Anthony, the head of *Cosmopolitan's* book division, to his meeting with Coolidge. "We feel," Long told the assembled reporters, "that he has much more to tell."

Coolidge was getting exasperated. "I'm trying to get back to private life," he pleaded with the press at Grand Central Station, waiting for his train home. "You fellows will have to help me." (Their response: when he finally boarded the train, someone wrote one last question on a piece of paper and pushed it against the window.) What Coolidge could control, and what was going well, was the writing. *Cosmopolitan* kept publishing autobiographical articles—"Mr. Coolidge's College Days"; "The Boston Police Strike"— and readers kept responding ecstatically.* Coolidge wrote about Grace: "I have seen so much fiction written on this subject that I may be pardoned for relating the plain facts. We thought we were made for each other." He wrote about the surreality of being a celebrity: "In public life it is sometimes necessary in order to appear really natural to be actually artificial."

In late April, Coolidge met with Long and Anthony again. This time they came to him to avoid the New York circus. He shared more manuscripts— chapters, really, because his book was mostly done. Once they'd read the entire thing, Coolidge drew up his own contract.

While Coolidge's story had already found an immense audience in its serial version—1929 was easily the best year of ad revenue in *Cosmopolitan*'s forty-three-year history—his book became a best seller. It sold for three dollars, though local outlets like Northampton's Hampshire Bookshop carried autographed copies for four, with the extra dollar going to Grace's favorite missionary society. Reviewers celebrated it as an important volume. Emily Newell Blair, a prominent suffragist, was no fan of Coolidge, but she was a fan of his book and praised it in the pages of *Good Housekeeping*. "Nothing could better educate us for choosing our public officials," Blair wrote, "than to read after each administration the ex-president's own interpretation of his life and experience. . . . It would make us understand our national characteristics, our national mind."

Coolidge's *Autobiography* made its author fabulously rich. The profits from it, plus his other writing gigs and a daily newspaper column—he

---

*There was one tiny controversy: a flimsy accusation of ghostwriting. A journalist named F. L. Lang—of course it was a writer—sent a letter to *Time*, speculating that "Long or one of his boys wrote the copy . . . and, like so many 'autobiographies' appearing in the popular magazines, that it was okayed by the subject." Long fired back with an affidavit, signed in front of a notary public: "No ghost writer," he promised, "could have put into a story the sincerity which Mr. Coolidge embodied." The editor continued: "Every line of the manuscripts . . . was written by Mr. Coolidge himself."

called it "Calvin Coolidge Says," a throwback to the advertising campaign for *Have Faith*—totaled more than half a million dollars at his death in 1933, or about $10 million in today's dollars.

The book also created a better potential model for presidential memoirs. Coolidge wrote a legacy book that barely defended his legacy, in part because he finished it before the Great Depression began. It presented a lasting portrait all the same. It was short. (The text ran to 45,000 words; Grant's *Personal Memoirs* topped 300,000.) It was modest. It was personal—less worried about theories of executive power than about what it felt like to be the executive. A president like Jefferson had tried in his autobiography to divide his public and private selves; a president like Roosevelt had refused to acknowledge his sadness. A person like Coolidge confessed that, especially in times of sadness, his public and private selves were the same.

FDR

Claude Bowers was one of the best practitioners in the burgeoning category of popular history, and in 1925 his latest book, *Jefferson and Hamilton*, popped up on plenty of Christmas shopping guides. It also received plenty of reviews, including one that December from a former politician named Franklin D. Roosevelt.

While Roosevelt had served as the Democrats' VP nominee in 1920—Coolidge's counterpart—his career had stalled after a strange illness left him partially paralyzed. Still, he remained obsessed with politics. In his review, he expertly sketched Bowers's big divide: on one hand, Hamilton the capable elitist, building a government for people like himself, and on the other, Jefferson the radical philosopher, trying to rouse regular Americans—"the scattered raw material of the working masses," Roosevelt wrote, "difficult to reach, more difficult to organize." As a writer, Roosevelt was so good at that kind of authoritative aside, making history feel thrilling and vibrant and, most of all, relevant; one part of his brain was always buzzing in the present. "Hamiltons we have today," Roosevelt noted near the end of his review, which is still one of the best pieces of prose ever written by a president. "Is a Jefferson on the horizon?"

Roosevelt became that Jefferson, but he never stopped dreaming about the life he might have led as a writer or editor. He'd grown up an ardent reader. (One early favorite was *The Naval War of 1812*, written by his distant cousin Theodore.) As an adult he owned some fifteen thousand volumes, though he sometimes seemed more a collector of books than a student of them. When he focused, as he did in the Bowers review, Roosevelt displayed real literary talent. Even after he returned to politics, winning New York's gubernatorial race in 1928, Roosevelt made time to talk with authors and editors, suggesting promising book ideas and vowing someday to write a few himself. "It strikes me," Roger Scaife wrote to him after one such meeting, "if you were not Governor of New York you should enter the field of publishing." If Roosevelt hadn't died in office, he possessed all of the skills to write a transformational legacy book.

Instead he settled for being a transformational president. When the Democrats nominated him in 1932, Roosevelt made the shocking choice to attend the convention and accept the nomination himself. He needed to demonstrate his health, of course, but he also wanted to exemplify the kind of change demanded by the Great Depression. "Let it be from now on the task of our party to break foolish traditions," Roosevelt proclaimed from the stage. "I pledge you, I pledge myself, to a new deal for the American people."

As president, Roosevelt developed and pushed an unprecedented agenda, leveraging his era's new tools of celebrity while also attending to the less flashy task of expanding the government. His speechwriting operation provided a good example of both approaches. Roosevelt recruited a broad network of ghosts, many of them experts on complex policies. He used their words—and his own massive fame, connecting personally with radio listeners through his friendly fireside chats—to radically expand executive power. The ghosts knew who was in charge. Roosevelt fretted over sentence constructions in the fireside chats; he purged abstractions. "Every word," remembered Robert Sherwood, who balanced writing speeches with writing Pulitzer-winning plays, "was judged not by its appearance in print but by its effectiveness over the radio."*

A bigger government meant a bigger stack of memoirs, and many of

---

*Another instance of FDR's presidential boldness centered on books. Publishers, in part because they lacked a centralized lobbying effort, still paid far more to mail their products than did their magazine peers. In 1938, the book trade decided to fix that by hiring Morris Ernst, a lawyer and old friend of Roosevelt. Ernst shipped two packages of equal weight to the White House—one a stack of books, including the Bible and Shakespeare's complete works, and one an assortment of dirty magazines. The books cost sixty cents; the magazines cost a quarter of that. Roosevelt loved the stunt and issued a proclamation lowering the postage rate for books, which fixed the problem until Congress finally passed a permanent solution in 1942.

Roosevelt's aides wrote books after leaving his administration. Eleanor Roosevelt became a best-selling autobiographer while still first lady; Charles Michelson, another of those speechwriters, titled his book *The Ghost Talks*. Roosevelt expected to join them, and in 1940 he signed a lucrative contract to become a contributor to *Collier's*, only to table it when he decided to run for a third term. His future plans stayed the same. "After he retired," recalled Samuel Rosenman, also a speechwriter, "he would spend his time taking care of his papers, writing his memoirs, and so forth."

While Roosevelt was never able to write his memoirs, he lived in an age when more Americans than ever could do so—and not just celebrities like S. S. McClure or presidents like Calvin Coolidge. One of the period's finest autobiographers was Richard Wright, whose *Black Boy*, a brutal look at life in the Jim Crow South, appeared in the spring of 1945. Like the authors of so many slave narratives that had come before, with their emphasis on learning to read and write, Wright slowed down for scenes with books. Even pulpy magazines could produce youthful epiphanies. "For the first time in my life," he wrote of his magazine reading, "I became aware of the life of the modern world, of vast cities, and I was claimed by it."

Black Boy was an immediate hit, and Wright spent that spring being a celebrity himself—giving interviews, going to readings, and signing lots and lots of books. He also braced for the backlash. On April 10, he learned that Mississippi had banned his book, and the bigotry escalated to the point that a US senator gave a floor speech, calling the book "a damnable lie from beginning to end. . . . It comes from a Negro, and you cannot expect any better from a person of his type."

On April 12, two days after the banning, Wright heard on the radio that Franklin D. Roosevelt was dead. "We are stunned," Wright wrote in his diary, "as though someone we know or who is related to us is dead." The news had spread from station to station in minutes—proof that the world was changing, that America was growing smaller, even as the presidency was growing larger. "Went to bed but did not sleep much at all," Wright wrote. "Thinking about Roosevelt."

HARRY S. TRUMAN
TO
DONALD TRUMP

CHAPTER TEN

Harry Truman's Histories

Harry Truman hated being alone in the White House, in part because he never felt truly alone. "Anyone with imagination can see old Jim Buchanan walking up and down," he wrote one day in his Oval Office diary. "Then there's Van Buren who inherited a terrible mess from his predecessor, as did poor old James Madison." Truman was nearly two years into his unpopular presidency, and messes were on his mind. The old mansion's pops and creaks, he decided, were the sounds of its most frustrated former inhabitants. The good presidents had all moved on. The bad ones—or at least the presidents "who were and are misrepresented in history"—they were the ones who lingered.

History had a way of haunting Truman, especially when he was contemplating his life's biggest moments. While he never graduated from a four-year college—the last president for whom this was true—he managed to read as deeply as any of his predecessors. Again and again, he would slip into past-tense reveries to grapple with present-day concerns: to calm his fears, to order his thoughts, to *think* his thoughts, to fortify his convictions. History guided him when he became Franklin D. Roosevelt's running mate and when he became his replacement after Roosevelt's death in 1945. History reassured him when his approval rating, a recent measure designed by the pollster George Gallup, tumbled to 23 percent. When Truman left the White House in 1953, he had plenty of reasons to write a legacy book: tradition, money, and a chance to convert the two-thirds of the country that still disapproved. Yet the most important reason to him was history. "I've always read a lot of history," he told a reporter, one year into the writing of his book, "and now I'm trying to write some myself. . . . I went through some important and tumultuous years and I think it's my duty to record them."

Truman had followed Roosevelt in expanding the modern presidency, in embracing its pressures and its powers, and this created enormous interest in his presidential memoirs. It helped that editors and readers had become increasingly charmed by timely nonfiction tomes. ("Down with fiction," *Publishers Weekly* reported, "and up with fact.") But the modern presidency also created challenges. The scale of its problems was different, starting with the Soviet Union and the atomic bomb. Even the scale of its documentation was different. At the end of George Washington's administration, his presidential papers ran to perhaps 40,000 pages. At the end of Truman's, his ran to nearly 6 million.

To write his two-volume *Memoirs*, Truman set up a small bureaucracy to review his years running a much larger one. More than a dozen people worked on the project, and at times it seemed that no more than two of them were actually capable—a number that included Truman himself. The book, hobbled by false starts, mishandled documents, and white-collar intrigue, took nearly three years to finish. "I'm not a writer," Truman often told his staffers. The trouble was neither were they.

The ex-president worked hard, toiling day after day on "the damned book" and "the cussed manuscript." The clichés about Truman—that he was decent and diligent and too quick to trust, all of which contributed to his image as a regular American—were also the truth about Truman. They were true of his book as well. And yet the defining trait, for both the autobiography and its author, would always be history. In the end, Truman became one of America's most beloved presidents. He also wrote a book that made a valuable contribution to his nation's archive, though not in the way he intended.

THE MIDDLEBROW PRESIDENT

Ramah Wofford was still a girl when her family headed north—her sharecropper parents and their seven children, each a member of the Great Migration's first wave. They ended up in Lorain, Ohio, a steel town on the shores of Lake Erie, and Wofford grew up there, marrying another native Southerner and starting a family of her own. Her husband worked for U.S. Steel while she worked on the side, cleaning houses and attending bathrooms, but there was never enough money, not in the depths of the Great Depression. Still, Wofford insisted on optimism, singing Ella Fitzgerald songs to her children and taking them to her African Methodist Episcopal church.

She also insisted on education. Although Lorain lacked a bookstore, it had a fine library, a Carnegie building stocked with the classics plus a children's room on the first floor. The Woffords were reliable patrons, but Ramah depended on one additional option: the Book-of-the-Month Club. It was the latest innovation to arise from outside the standard book trade, and the BOMC's discounts—and its deep customer data, courtesy of the same George Gallup—made it easy for subscribers like Wofford to purchase buzzy titles by mail. One of Wofford's children, a daughter named Chloe, remembered "the security I felt, the pleasure, when new books arrived."

The BOMC and its rivals—along with booms in paperback publishing and in Americans' free time and education—opened up a huge new audience for contemporary fiction and nonfiction. In 1925, American publishers had pulled in just over $200 million; in 1958, their revenues passed $950 million, easily outpacing population growth and inflation. The book trade redefined its idea of a big hit, from tens of thousands of copies sold to hundreds of thousands; the whole time, elite anxiety multiplied at roughly the same rate. Critics and journalists raced to name this new audience: *middlebrow*, *midcult*, and other words that implied middling. But readers like Ramah Wofford didn't seem to mind. They had their books, along with their knowledge that middlebrow readers could do great things. In fact, Wofford's daughter, Chloe, grew up to be a writer herself, though she published under a different name: Toni Morrison.

A middlebrow reader could also grow up to be president. Harry Truman was born in 1884 in a small Missouri town; his family bounced around the state before establishing itself in Independence, a slightly larger town near Kansas City. Truman considered it home the rest of his life.

It has become popular to see Truman as not only a regular American but a sensible midwesterner. This is a misreading of his childhood (and of the way places like Missouri experienced the Civil War). Truman was raised a Southerner, in a town and a family saturated with the Lost Cause's version of history. In Independence, they were still mad about Reconstruction and the War between the States. They still loathed Ulysses S. Grant, and they still worshipped Robert E. Lee, whose portrait adorned the walls of many local homes.

Growing up, Truman looked uncannily like his future self: the short, neat hair; the soft but serious features; the round face framed by round glasses. Those glasses were expensive but necessary, and to protect them he avoided baseball or wrestling and read instead. Like so many other readers in his era, he adored magazines like *Cosmopolitan* and *McClure's*. His mother, Martha Young Truman, had gone to college, and she loved books almost as much as she loved the Confederacy. She encouraged Truman's literary side, buying him the four-volume *Great Men and Famous Women* from a traveling bookseller, a Ridpathian collection that gathered short biographies from various authors. (Theodore Roosevelt had penned the entry on Winfield Scott.) Truman also relied on Independence's library. "He read more history than anybody," one of his schoolmates remembered. "I saw Harry go home many a time with two or three books on weekends, and I guess by Monday he had them all read."

Even as a student, Truman studied history in a particular way. His teachers would mention some tantalizing event and move on, leaving him to tromp to the library and locate more books about it. What he looked for—and this remained true for the rest of his life—were the individuals behind the event. "I saw that it takes men to make history, or there would be no history," Truman later recalled. "History does not make the man." He didn't examine the past for its ambiguity or ideas. He wanted its heroes, its lessons, and its parallels to contemporary life. Truman read for moral clarity—for marching orders.

Inspired by his studies, Truman planned to apply to West Point once he finished high school in 1901. It felt like his best shot at making some history himself, until he learned poor eyesight would disqualify him. He couldn't afford a civilian college, not after his father's finances began to implode, so Truman took a series of menial jobs: bank clerk, railroad timekeeper, and finally bookkeeper-slash-laborer on the family farm. He was now, in his own words, "a kind of good-for-nothing American farmer." But he remained a reader, self-motivated, self-directed, relentless.

One of the best ways to see this was in his courtship of Bess Wallace. While they'd grown up together in Independence, it wasn't until 1910 that they started writing frequent and revealing letters, with their reading lives a constant topic. He advocated for Missouri's own Mark Twain ("my patron saint in literature"). She countered with Charles Dickens, and after borrowing a copy of *David Copperfield*, he admitted he could see why she liked the author. They chatted about popular fiction—magazine stories and novels like Rex Beach's, best described as Jack London lite.

In his correspondence with Bess, Truman also demonstrated his style. He had the two qualities that can make anyone a passable writer: a strong voice—crisp, earthy, sincere—and a lifetime of reading. But Truman never mustered much confidence in his pen. In one letter, which he sent on June 22, 1911, he declared his feelings for Bess: "I've been crazy about you ever since we went to Sunday school together." Truman hinted at marriage, at a love story of their own, and while he was anxious about the question, he was also anxious about his ability to express it. "You said you were tired of these kind of stories in books," Truman continued, "so I am trying one from real life on you. You must bear in mind that this is my first experience in this line and also it is very real to me. Therefore I can't make it look or sound so well as Rex Beach."

It took a while, but Bess ultimately found his narration convincing. They were married in 1919, once Truman returned from serving bravely in France in World War I. The couple moved into Bess's family home, a dignified Victorian a few blocks from the Independence courthouse; they had their only child, a daughter named Margaret. Truman was already middle aged, an honest but mediocre businessman, when his war connections (and a shady political boss) lifted him into a role for which he finally seemed suited: politician. In 1922, he won a race to become a local judge, though in Missouri the role was closer to that of a county commissioner, and he began his slow climb in politics.

In 1934, the week after he turned fifty, Truman announced in Kansas City that he was running for the US Senate. He spent the night before in a downtown hotel, and at some point, unable to sleep, he grabbed a stack of hotel stationery and slipped into one of his historical reveries: "Tomorrow—today rather, it is 4 A.M.—I am to make the most momentous announcement of my life." Truman's mind drifted not to his remarks or his conflicted relationship with that boss, but to his childhood reading of *Great Men and Famous Women*: "When I was a very young boy, nine or ten years old, my mother gave me four large books. . . . In reading the lives of great men, I found that the first victory won was over themselves." As Truman rehearsed his favorite heroes and lessons—Hannibal and Cincinnatus, George Washington and Robert E. Lee—it became clear he was convincing himself he was good enough to run for the Senate. "Most of the really great ones never thought they were great," he wrote on the stationery. "[They] fought for what they thought was right and for their countries. They were patriots and unselfish. I could never admire a man whose only interest is himself."

Truman won the race and spent the next eighteen years in Washington. Along the way, he cultivated a taste for a certain kind of book: topical and serious nonfiction—what's often classified as current affairs. Many of his countrymen were falling for the same thing. The genre wasn't new. (*Notes on the State of Virginia* is in a very real sense a book of current affairs.) But the Depression invigorated it. "The shock of hard times," the *New*

York Times reported, "has made American book readers serious-minded."
After a surge in unemployment, libraries saw a surge in activity—but nonfiction borrowing increased twice as fast as fiction. Readers were turning
to biography and history but also to books covering the latest trends in
science, technology, politics, and business.

The Book-of-the-Month Club echoed this shift, upping its nonfiction
selections to include titles like Herbert Hoover's *Challenge to Liberty*. As
an author, Hoover matched Theodore Roosevelt and Woodrow Wilson in
enthusiasm, if not craft; he wrote more than thirty books, depending on
how you count, starting with specialized works in his field of mining and
then broadening to bigger questions. *The Challenge to Liberty* appeared
in 1934 as Hoover's first major statement as ex-president, an idea-driven
book that outlined his contenders for the most serious threats to the
American way of life: fascism, communism, and Franklin D. Roosevelt. It
became a solid hit as the BOMC's October selection, reaching subscribers
just before the midterms.*

World War II created even more demand for books on current affairs.
("This is a nonfiction war," the *Chicago Tribune* noted, "marked by serious books of many kinds.") Equally important was the paperback, which,
after a couple of stumbling attempts, was finally and permanently catch-
ing on. In 1939 an upstart called Pocket Books began selling mass-market
paperbacks for a quarter apiece; Flannery O'Connor sardonically called
them her "drugstore edition." You could buy them everywhere: tobacco
shops, lunch counters, bus depots, newsstands, and, yes, on wire racks
in drugstores. Pocket Books and its peers—including the Armed Service
Editions, which, along with the GI Bill, turned millions of soldiers into
readers—combined with other midcentury institutions like the BOMC to
democratize pulpy and brainy books alike. John Hersey, Rachel Carson,
and Richard Hofstadter gained huge audiences through these channels.

A new magnitude of readers guaranteed a new magnitude of angst,
and in 1949 *Harper's* published "Highbrow, Lowbrow, Middlebrow," an

---

*Hoover also loved autobiographies. During his term as president, he asked the Library of
Congress to restock the White House shelves with the best presidential memoirs and biographies. In the 1940s, Hoover began writing an autobiography of his own, though it was
closer to a vanity project than a modern presidential memoir. He declined royalties, subsi-
dized ad campaigns, and scoffed at edits. "This is the final manuscript," he informed Macmillan, his publisher. "In other words, it is a waste of time to suggest substantial changes."
Hoover ended up publishing three volumes on his presidency plus another four on his
time as famine relief administrator, all while laboring on other multivolume projects he
never completed—a literary career that produced more pages than readers.

In Baltimore, a
man looked at a
drugstore's display of
paperback books—
each one priced at
fifty cents.

arch taxonomy by Russell Lynes. Lynes, in a very highbrow move, chose to
complicate the notion of middlebrow by splitting it into upper and lower,
and his essay stirred up significant controversy. Even *Life* informed its millions of readers about Lynes, though the magazine did so with its trademark visual punch: a chart breaking down his brows by what they liked to
drink, wear, and read. According to *Life*, lower middlebrows read "book
club selections," while upper middlebrows went with "solid nonfiction."

That made Senator Truman an upper middlebrow, and he enjoyed his
era's literary bounty. In Kansas City he could browse the book department
at Kline's department store or the paperback racks at one of Missouri's
many Katz drugstores. But his favorite bookstore was run by Frank Glenn,
a local with a passion for pocket squares and antiquarian books. Glenn's
shop occupied a prime spot inside Kansas City's Muehlebach Hotel—a narrow room with fifteen-foot ceilings and bookshelves that scaled their full
height. At the front of the store, two windows peered into the hotel lobby,
previewing the newest releases; in the back, Glenn kept the rare stuff.

Despite his senatorial schedule—a schedule that only became busier
after Roosevelt chose him to be his running mate in 1944—Truman read
a stunning number of books. In Washington, especially during stretches

when Bess stayed home in Independence, he read at night until he fell
asleep; occasionally he decided to ignore his duties, like the morning he
escaped Capitol Hill to listen to an author lecture on Robert E. Lee. ("I
played hooky from the Appropriations Committee," Truman confessed
in his next letter home.) When he was in Independence, he preferred to
read in his study, in an easy chair next to a window and its natural light.
Both his friends and the journalists who covered him noted that Truman
always seemed to be in the middle of the latest big book: Carl Sandburg's
final volumes on Lincoln, a fresh account of World War II, even a new
military history on Ulysses S. Grant, whom Truman had softened on as he
studied the Civil War more closely.

In the spring of 1945, only a few days before Roosevelt's death, a
reporter interviewed Truman for a story. Even as vice president, Truman
had asked to keep his old Senate office. He was, the reporter wrote, "as
homespun as an old linsey quilt." The reporter described the many books
in Truman's office, including recent volumes on the British-Palestine relationship and on Florida's recovery since the Depression. "He is, to put it
mildly, an odd bookworm," the reporter concluded. But that got Truman
wrong. There was nothing odd about his devotion to the great men of
history or his desire to read about current affairs. All around the country,
people were making those same choices. Truman was more than just a
regular American—he was a regular reader too.

"SO-CALLED HISTORIANS"

Harry Truman nearly wrote a campaign book. In 1951, a friendly journalist named William Hillman secured a series of interviews with the president, and when he let Hillman access his letters and diaries, a book began
to coalesce. Hillman and his publisher, Farrar, Straus and Young, assembled the materials for what they stealthily referred to as their "statesman
book": expensive color photography of Truman at work, archival images of
his favorite predecessors, and hundreds of excerpts from his private documents, all bound together under the title *Mr. President*. It was a strange
and wonderful volume, half coffee-table book and half civics lesson. But
it was all Truman. Of *Mr. President*'s seventy-five thousand words, at least
sixty thousand came directly from Truman, and its publication generated
massive interest—an excerpt in *Reader's Digest*, an alternate selection by
the BOMC, a frantic scramble for the international rights—until Tru-

man surprised everyone, including his financially stretched publisher, by announcing he would not seek reelection in 1952.

Although *Mr. President* bombed, the literary world switched to buzzing about Truman's next book. In the days after Dwight Eisenhower's inauguration, there were rumors Truman might land a half-million-dollar advance, which was good since he needed the money. He was nearly seventy, with a monthly military pension of $112.56 as his and Bess's only consistent income. Ex-presidents had plenty of ways to make a buck—endorsement deals, consulting fees, marketing stunts—but Truman rejected all of them. He hated the thought of doing something that would exploit or demean the executive branch, and that standard applied to underfunded ex-presidents as well. "I'd rather starve," he said.

Truman didn't believe a legacy book would diminish the presidency. In fact, it struck him as a modern president's final duty. Instead of a standard contract with royalties, he sold his memoirs to *Life* for a staggering lump sum: $600,000, or nearly $6 million in today's dollars. The magazine had partnered with Doubleday, and the plan was for that house to publish a single 300,000-word volume, which *Life* would pillage first for excerpts. Still, the most important thing to Truman, as a lifelong reader of history,

Truman managed to read books even in the White House—here on the South Portico's famous second-floor balcony.

wasn't the money or the schedule. It was giving an honest account of why he'd made his decisions.

He also fretted about what history would give back. In the White House, he'd complained about his coverage by journalists and historians. "The lies are beginning to be solidified into historical 'facts,'" he wrote in 1950, one week after Joseph McCarthy had claimed the State Department was teeming with crypto-Communists. "I don't want a pack of lying, so-called historians to do to Roosevelt and to me what the New Englanders did to Jefferson." In his autobiography, Truman planned to defeat the so-called historians by becoming a historian himself—by overwhelming them with facts.

Over the next three years, those goals—preserving his perspective for history and defending himself with documents—clashed frequently, especially when Truman added his temper to the mix. In the opening months of 1953, however, the ex-president appeared excited and relaxed. The money hadn't changed him.* It did allow him to hire some help. Truman started by asking *Mr. President*'s William Hillman and another supporter named David Noyes to manage the project. They were an odd pair, Hillman bulky and extremely bald, with a journalist's habit of quietly observing; Noyes wiry and only mostly bald, with an adman's habit of chattering constantly. They worked with Truman on assembling a thorough outline for his book.

Since Hillman lived on the East Coast and Noyes on the West, they needed to station a chief ghostwriter in Kansas City. Truman tried recruiting Richard Neustadt, a Harvard PhD who'd served in his administration. Neustadt declined and wrote his own book instead—*Presidential Power*, a classic study of the modern presidency. Truman still coveted an academic, and Noyes recommended Robert Harris, a professor at UCLA. Once Harry and Bess finished a vacation to Hawaii in early May, the real work began.

Truman had rented some office space on the eleventh floor of the Federal Reserve Building in downtown Kansas City. It was a plain, three-room suite. (Even Truman's new letterhead was plain: "Harry S. Truman, Federal Reserve Bank Building, Kansas City 6, Mo.") The main flourishes were a Persian rug, a gift from a shah that Truman unfurled in his office,

---

*His one splurge: custom bookshelves for his study, which finally gave him a place to display his expanding library. Truman paid a carpenter $505.56 for the shelves, and he built them with a special kind of pine the local lumberyard ordered just for Truman. Afterward, the ex-president went to the lumberyard to thank the owners in person.

and the fifty or so padlocked filing cabinets that held his administration's most vital documents. Two secretaries tried to dam the flood of visitors and requests. Harris, a stenographer, and a pair of researchers rounded out the initial *Memoirs* team.

Each morning in Independence, Truman woke at 5:30 a.m. After his newspapers, a brisk walk, and breakfast, he drove himself to the Federal Reserve Bank Building around 8:00. It was the life of a normal citizen, except for the fact that he was driving on Truman Road.

At the office, he started by sitting down with Harris and the stenographer. The ghost had decided to tackle the outline's big political set pieces first—Truman relieving Douglas MacArthur during the Korean War, for instance—and he interviewed the ex-president for several hours. Sometimes Truman decided to write up an event himself. Sometimes he studied the contents of those file cabinets to refresh his memory: White House memos, private letters, and minutes from meetings, among other sources. In the afternoon, he switched to other tasks, such as planning the construction of his presidential library or taking a lunchtime meeting at the Muehlebach Hotel. Harris worked on turning the interview transcripts into narrative, making occasional trips to the tenth floor, where the staff had transformed another room into a research library. When Harris finished a draft, he gave it to Truman, who placed it in his briefcase to review that night with Bess. The ex-president always turned it around by the next morning.

When the famous magazine editor S. S. McClure reflected on his own *Autobiography*, he admitted that "Miss Cather is due the largest part of the literary success." But he knew he'd played an equally important part: "It is of course written exactly as I wanted it. I take great credit for the work from the standpoint of an editor." The same was true of Truman, who approached his edits and interviews seriously.

The problem was he didn't have a Cather or anyone close. Harris proved to be a vexing suitemate: bossy, paranoid, and uptight. (After one of their visits to Kansas City, Hillman and Noyes nicknamed him "small-fanny.") Worse, Harris was a poor writer, producing detail-free prose that sounded like a parody of a homespun president. It reminded Truman of the glib celebrity memoirs he'd read in magazines growing up. "I want none of it," the ex-president said. "I want history." On October 31, Harris penned an eight-page memo on editorial hierarchy and the sacrifices of Robert Harris. One week later, he was gone.

Harris had written about 150,000 words, none of them usable. "Good god," Truman penciled on one page, "what crap." Everyone hoped a new ghost would get things moving, and Hillman nominated a Columbia PhD named Morton Royce. But Royce went even more slowly, bogging down on specific topics. The biggest was Truman's decision to drop the atomic bomb. "What ethical considerations went through your mind as you made this decision?" Royce asked during an interview.

Truman gave an answer in the spirit of his *Memoirs'* final text: "I regarded the bomb as a military weapon and never had any doubt that it should be used."

Once the interview ended, Royce returned to his office; perhaps he did some research on the tenth floor. The next day, though, when he came back to speak with Truman, he revisited his question: "Mr. President, I've thought about what you told me yesterday, and it's just not possible that you didn't think about the ethical considerations. Now, *what* ethical considerations?"

Royce wasn't wrong to press, and it's worth noting that the bomb never seemed to prompt Truman into one of his extended historical reveries. But the ex-president didn't see things that way, and after a few sessions, he grew frustrated. "I did not ask for somebody to badger me to remember things that didn't happen," Truman said. By the end of April, Royce was gone too.

The *Memoirs* had now swallowed a full year of work, in addition to burning through tens of thousands of dollars in salary and overhead, all of it covered by Truman because of his lump-sum contract. Anticipation for the project remained keen. (One reporter cornered Truman in the building's men's room to press for updates.) But Doubleday and *Life* were getting nervous, and they weren't alone. One morning, a young staffer went to borrow a book from Truman's office and found him mixing a highball. "I fix one of these every morning to settle my nerves," Truman said. "But don't you follow my example."

Truman told Hillman and Noyes that they'd each tried and failed at picking a writer—and that this time he was going to choose one himself. The University of Missouri helped him find a third ghost, a graduate student named Herbert Williams. Although Williams had fallen far behind on his dissertation, he took the *Memoirs* gig anyway. He asked to work on the tenth floor by himself, and while he did better than Harris and Royce, he also announced at the end of 1954 that he was leaving for a job at Michigan State. Truman was surprised, but not as surprised as when, a couple months later, he received a letter from one of Williams's new colleagues praising his groundbreaking dissertation on Harry S. Truman. The ghost, it appeared, had been raiding the file cabinets.

That left Francis Heller, Truman's fourth and final writer. Heller, another academic, arrived a few weeks after Williams, once he'd finished his spring courses at the University of Kansas, and he took at least the third stab at drafting the book's opening pages. Heller finally got it right, following Vice President Truman through scenes like this:

> I reached the White House about 5:25 P.M. and was immediately taken in the elevator to the second floor and ushered into Mrs. Roosevelt's study. Mrs. Roosevelt herself, together with Colonel John and Mrs. Anna Roosevelt Boettiger and Mr. Early, were in the room as I entered, and I knew at once that something unusual had taken place. Mrs. Roosevelt seemed calm in her characteristic, graceful dignity. She stepped forward and placed her arm gently about my shoulder.
>
> "Harry," she said quietly, "the President is dead."
>
> For a moment I could not bring myself to speak. The last news we had had from Warm Springs was that Mr. Roosevelt was recuperating nicely. In fact, he was apparently doing so well that no member of his immediate family, and not even his personal physician, was with him. All this flashed through my mind before I found my voice.
>
> "Is there anything I can do for you?" I asked at last.
>
> I shall never forget her deeply understanding reply.
>
> "Is there anything we can do for you?" she asked. "For you are the one in trouble now."

Beginning the book with Roosevelt's death was an obvious choice, but it emphasized the *Memoirs'* great theme: the crushing and comprehensive weight of the modern presidency. As Truman put it in his preface, "The presidency of the United States carries with it a responsibility so personal as to be without parallel." The book's opening tracked Truman in real time, moving from Eleanor Roosevelt to his first cabinet meeting. At the end, the secretaries filed out wordlessly, except for Henry Stimson, his new secretary of war: in the empty room, he told Truman for the first time about the atomic bomb.

That sequence revealed the presidency's power and its burden. But Truman's narrative soon stumbled by reproducing three full pages from a diplomatic report. The *Memoirs* did this repeatedly, pausing to insert lengthy documents or the play-by-play of some minor meeting. A tran-

script of the first conversation between Truman and Winston Churchill proved riveting, until it dragged on for six pages. Each of Truman's
chapters contained material that was historic or personal or both. (When
he invited his Yankee-hating mother to the White House, she made one
thing clear: "If he puts me in the room with Lincoln's bed in it," she told
the family, "I'll sleep on the floor.") Yet Truman and his ghosts couldn't
stop wrestling with those so-called historians. Where Theodore Roosevelt
had lashed out at his critics, Truman tried to bury them in documents. A
book that was supposed to capture the presidency and its cost too often
captured the presidency and its paper trail.

It was a flawed approach, and also an exhausting one. Truman was up
for the work. On June 18, he took Bess to browse Frank Glenn's bookstore
and then to see a musical—only to have their night cut short when he began
experiencing excruciating stomach pains. Truman spent weeks in recovery
after doctors removed his gallbladder and appendix, but he demanded that
his staff bring the latest drafts for him to review at home. He asked his former aides to review drafts as well, and even to come to Kansas City where
they could submit to their own interviews. Truman sat in the room, for
instance, while Heller questioned former secretary of state Dean Acheson—
until the ex-president invariably jumped in, prompting Acheson, arguing
with him, and sharing his own anecdotes Acheson had brought to mind.

Truman wanted his book to be rigorous, but that was making it long
and late. The original contract had called for 300,000 words. By February
1955, the *Memoirs* team had drafted approximately 2 million words, most
of them dictated by Truman and reworked by Heller. Doubleday agreed
to go to two volumes, though even that meant paring the manuscript to
600,000 words. Hillman and Noyes started cutting, with the help of a representative from the publisher.* They were running out of time, but Truman wanted to add. He was still scheduling interviews with former aides
in April. He was also insisting that he, Heller, Hillman, and Noyes gather
in his office to read the final draft aloud, paragraph by paragraph, with the
stenographer taking notes as Truman suggested tweaks or added more
material. They were working crushing hours, and some nights Truman
stood up, said, "I just can't stand it anymore," and left. The next day, he
came back and did it all over again.

---

*In addition to the ghosts, the researchers and liaisons from Doubleday and *Life* created
extra headaches. One made so many long-distance phone calls that Truman got stuck with
a six-hundred-dollar bill; another got picked up by Kansas City's vice squad; a third ended
up in the hospital himself.

Finally, on June 30, Truman turned in the manuscript for his first volume, though he and Heller would need the fall to polish volume 2. Because his contract allowed for no royalties, Truman already knew the book was a financial failure. Between taxes and expenses, his $600,000 would dwindle to less than $40,000. "Sometimes I wish I hadn't undertaken these doggone memoirs," Truman told a reporter. "But I wanted to do this for history. . . . This country has given me a lot."

READER IN CHIEF

The first volume of Truman's *Memoirs* went on sale on November 2, 1955, a few weeks after excerpts started appearing in *Life*. To celebrate its publication, Truman agreed to autograph books for a few hours in Kansas City. As far as anyone could remember, it was the first time a former president had held a public book signing.

It took some convincing for Truman to submit to even this modest, home-cooked marketing. "I want the book sold on its merits," he told Doubleday. "If it cannot be sold that way, then it's not worth having." He eventually gave in, perhaps because of Frank Glenn's eager involvement. Such events usually occurred at bookstores like Glenn's, but Doubleday booked the ballroom at the Muehlebach Hotel in case they got a crowd.

On the day of the signing, Glenn's lobby-facing windows were filled with stacks of Truman's volume, along with a sign: "The Book of the Ages by the Man of the Ages." Truman was to autograph books from 10:00 in the morning until noon and then again in the afternoon, but people were lining up by 6:30 a.m. The press had turned out too—not just local media but reporters from *Life* and the *New Yorker*, plus television cameras from ABC, NBC, and CBS. Soon a line of hundreds of customers zigzagged across the ballroom. On the perimeter sat booths from Kansas City's book dealers, including Kline's department store, Katz drugstores, and, of course, Frank Glenn. In the middle stood a table surrounded by floodlights and six American flags, and when Truman walked in, wearing a dark suit and a plump carnation, he seemed thrilled. "I had no idea it would be anything like this," he said. He kept the smile all morning.

The schedule was packed with civic pageantry: a Girl Scout honor guard for Truman, an Air Force fighter zipping over the hotel, a local baker presenting a cake frosted to look like the book. Still, the crowd was there for the president. He was kind and attentive, signing each book "Harry

S. Truman" and ending each exchange with "Thank you very much." Because of the demand, he stayed for nearly three hours, then came back for an even longer session in the afternoon. Truman signed four thousand books that day—and Doubleday still had to turn people away. A reporter asked Truman if his hand had started to cramp. He answered with one of his vigorous handshakes: "Doesn't feel like it, does it?" The smile was still going strong.

Truman once claimed that book critics belonged "in the same class with people who criticize the actions of the President." But the *Memoirs'* first volume got tremendous reviews. There was highbrow enthusiasm, with the *New York Times Book Review* granting it one of its longest notices ever. Truman got positive coverage everywhere. Americans turning on their radios could hear a broadcaster declare the *Memoirs* "the most important publishing event of this year, and perhaps many years. . . . Truman seems to conceal nothing about what a president has to do." Americans opening their local papers could read that Truman "brings to the reader a realization that the president cannot be less than a superman or the sheer weight of work will crush him."

This executive branch intimacy thrilled and touched readers. While Roosevelt had died before he could write his legacy book, Truman had supplied the most detailed look so far at the American presidency, its expanding powers, and the past few years of global tumult. That may explain why so many lined up at the Muehlebach Hotel—to touch a modern president but also to make personal the modern world. Some of it was Missouri pride. (In the coming months, Glenn would sell close to ten thousand copies by himself.) But people were responding all over the country. Truman's first volume spent fifteen weeks on the *New York Times* best-seller list, finishing the year as one of 1955's ten best-selling nonfiction titles, though it hadn't appeared until late in the year. The second volume also did well—especially after the Book-of-the-Month Club made both volumes its March 1956 selection.

Truman's *Memoirs* was an imperfect book, a book with a better, slimmer volume lurking within. Not as slim as Coolidge's *Autobiography*—Truman was right to discuss more policy than his predecessor did, in part because he made more policy—but something closer to 200,000 words, with most of the cuts falling on the president's beloved documents. The book was a challenging read in the 1950s, as a few reviewers finally admitted while considering the second volume, and it became more challenging with each passing year. It did little to boost Truman's reputation. George

When the first volume of his *Memoirs* came out, Truman did a book signing at the Muehlebach Hotel. It had a fantastic turnout—not just of book buyers but of journalists and TV cameras as well.

Gallup had launched another measure of public approval, the "scalometer," and Truman's ratings from before the release of his *Memoirs* and from a few months after remained virtually unchanged. Future events would make him more appealing—the escalation of the Cold War, the cynicism of Watergate—but in polls, he continued to trail two other Democrats, Franklin D. Roosevelt and John F. Kennedy.

What made Harry a hero was a different book: David McCullough's massive biography, *Truman*. In the early 1980s, about a decade after Truman's death, McCullough's publisher suggested he write a book about Roosevelt. The author countered with a surprising subject: the president who followed him. McCullough spent the next decade researching and writing the first big biography of Truman, and in the summer of 1992, it became an enormous and unexpected hit—not just winning the Pulitzer Prize but making it on morning TV and outpacing more typical best sellers like Madonna's *Sex* and *The Juiceman's Power of Juicing*. *Truman* eventually moved more than a million hardcovers. "For this to happen to a $30, 1,100-page biography," McCullough told a reporter, "well, I won't call it unprecedented, but . . ." His voice went quiet. Even the historian couldn't find a precedent for his success.

Truman also popped up in the White House. During that year's presidential election, the candidates attempted to out-blurb each other, with Bill Clinton calling the book "magnificent" while George H. W. Bush went with "marvelous." Both men wanted to link themselves to the country's new favorite president (and the country's new favorite historian). Bush even used his incumbency advantage, inviting McCullough to Washington to give a lecture in the East Room. "Harry Truman," McCullough said to the crowd, "was exactly the kind of president that the Founding Fathers had in mind."

After Clinton won the battle of the *Truman* fans, Bush made a rare choice: he would not write an autobiography. Part of the reason was that, outside of election years, Bush had never been much of a reader. Part of it was that he hated talking about himself, a preference that ran so deep his staffers noticed he often elided the *I*s from his sentences. Instead of a memoir, Bush cowrote *A World Transformed*, a hybrid volume in which he and a former aide traded riffs on foreign policy. Disclosure didn't interest Bush. "Had my chance," he told a journalist. "We did a lot of things right, some wrong. I feel a little inhibited in trying to set the record straight. I have total confidence that objective scholars can do the job. The best example is Harry Truman. He left office lower than a snake's belly. Then historians like David McCullough took an objective look at him, and now he's respected because of his character."

Character really was the key. McCullough had written a big book—"a great American story," in the phrase he repeated during his promotional tour—but it returned again and again to its subject's integrity and charm. Truman's ideas hardly mattered, and the biography seemed as uninterested in the ethics of the bomb as the ex-president had been himself. To McCullough, character made Truman a great president. Certainly it made *Truman* an enchanting book. After all, the only way a political figure could appeal to both Clinton and Bush was if he was first emptied of politics.

Another factor in McCullough's success was a shift in academic history. While the divide between scholars and storytellers stretched back to Frederick Jackson Turner scolding Wilson and Theodore Roosevelt, it never felt wider than during the 1980s and 1990s. The track record of PhDs ghostwriting presidential memoirs may be bleak, but the academy proved prolific at producing a more specialized style of history, a style focused on political categories—labor, gender, race—and the regular Americans who populated them.

There is tremendous value in this approach. (Ramah Wofford, Morrison's mother, is also a great American story.) But even the most eloquent professors failed to win big, middlebrow audiences; sometimes the professors didn't seem to care, ceding the entire conversation to McCullough and his pop history peers. It was a new shift in nonfiction publishing: best-selling authors like Joseph Ellis and Doris Kearns Goodwin now wrote books that competed for shelf space with celebrity memoirs—that promised exciting protagonists and easy lessons. As Ellis put it in his smash hit *Founding Brothers*, "The old adage applies: men make history."

Harry Truman believed that adage until the day he died. And yet because he wanted to defend himself or because he hired bad help—or maybe because Ellis's adage just isn't true—Truman couldn't quite write a book that backed it up. He did something more important. The *Memoirs'* maximal process created 2 million words of narrative, with every insight and comma approved by Truman himself. It pushed Truman to write handwritten memos about key moments; it preserved diary entries and family letters that no longer exist in any other form; it initiated interviews with more than twenty members of Truman's administration. "I want to put you on the witness stand for the book," the ex-president told Dean Acheson, and he did. The conversations that followed aren't a chance to watch history being made. They are history, the thing itself.

Today, the *Memoirs* file at Truman's Presidential Library adds up to about forty thousand pages, pages rich with material for the professor and the popular biographer alike. These pages exist because of Truman's passion and persistence—because of his character. His respect for history and his capacity for hard work created an incredible archive, even if they didn't lead to an incredible book. Truman's *Memoirs* may not be the work of a skilled writer. But it is something just as important: the work of a faithful reader.

CHAPTER ELEVEN

The Writer Who Wouldn't Write

John F. Kennedy and Richard Nixon had both imagined themselves in the Oval Office. Now they were occupying it together. Only one of them was president, of course, as voters had narrowly chosen Kennedy in the election six months earlier. But in the spring of 1961 Kennedy asked his rival to come in for a private meeting. It had been three days since the disastrous Bay of Pigs invasion, and the president needed to talk it through.

They spoke for nearly an hour, and from the start, Nixon could see Kennedy wasn't his normal, vibrant self—he looked tired, angry, stooped. When they finished, Kennedy offered to escort his guest to a waiting White House car. As they walked through the Rose Garden, their conversation turned literary. The president's mood lifted. "I hope you'll take the time to write a book," he told Nixon. It didn't matter if the book sold well, Kennedy said, so long as it elevated one to the rank of intellectual. "There's something about being an author," he added, "which really builds the reputation of a political figure."

That comment inspired Nixon to write *Six Crises*, which became a best seller in 1962. The 1950s and 1960s were a golden age for political authors. Ghostwriting was not just accepted; it was institutionalized, with American University dedicating an entire course to it. Publishers, even small ones focused on fiction, were scrambling for campaign books. "Pick the right candidate," the *New York Times*'s Christopher Lehmann-Haupt advised the industry, "and you'd be in business." The candidates benefited most of all, with a few titles becoming enormous hits, including Barry Goldwater's *Conscience of a Conservative* and Kennedy's own *Profiles in Courage*.

Kennedy's book played an indispensable role in his ascent. It gave him celebrity, but it also gave him credibility—a brainy counterpoint to his good looks, glossy magazine covers, and famous televisual appeal. As Ted Sorensen, his most important ghostwriter, put it, Kennedy's writings were intended to "balance the flood" of superficial coverage. The plan would have worked perfectly except for one catch: the candidate wasn't content with a best-selling campaign book. Kennedy craved literary fame in a way that's never been fully appreciated. It wasn't just that he sweated his speech at the 1956 National Book Awards; it was that he personally and obsessively manipulated the reception of his ghostwritten book. Kennedy needed *Profiles* to be a political success *and* a literary success, even as he lacked the discipline to do literary work.

This psychic split got him into trouble at the worst possible time, and he feared it might destroy his bid for the presidency. What saved him was a classic Kennedy response: the ruthless leveraging of money, power, and spin, all of it driven by the family's focus on image over reality. As his father had told him many years before, when he was a twenty-three-year-old who'd just finished his first book, a published volume "will do you an amazing amount of good." It didn't matter if the book sold well, his father said, so long as it elevated one to the rank of intellectual. "You would be surprised," he added, "how a book that really makes the grade with high-class people stands you in good stead for years to come."

That line might have sounded familiar to Richard Nixon, walking through the Rose Garden. For even then, in a private moment when Kennedy was professing to be bookish, he was really just taking someone else's material and claiming it as his own.

"BY JACK KENNEDY"

Most Kennedy stories begin with the patriarch, and so it is with authorship. Joseph P. Kennedy was, in the description of the *New York Times*'s Arthur Krock, "tall, red-haired, red-faced"—a man simmering with "intelligence [and] forcefulness." Joseph's ambition wasn't money since he'd made plenty from his career in finance. It was power and influence, and books were a way to achieve that. He didn't find spiritual value in the acts of reading or writing. Books were blunt instruments, meant to persuade readers or impress elites.

In 1936 Joseph came up with a book idea of his own, a short volume defending the New Deal from the businessman's perspective. He burned through several ghostwriters before bringing in Arthur Krock. With his round glasses, slicked-back hair, and fleshy face, Krock looked like a veteran journalist, and he had the résumé to match: *Times* columnist, *Times* bureau chief, and two-time Pulitzer winner (with another one to come). But there was one gig he kept quiet: friendly embed within the Kennedy clan. Krock gave Kennedy's book a punchy title, *I'm for Roosevelt*, then edited and rewrote the whole thing. It appeared in the months before the presidential election, earning lots of coverage and a front-page story in Krock's paper. "I put down these few thoughts about our president, conscious only of my concern as a father for the future of his family," Joseph wrote. "I have no political ambitions for myself or my children."

The notion that Joseph had scribbled down his thoughts was surely the truest part of that passage. His ambitions were enormous, especially for his sons: Joe Jr., the most promising Kennedy until he died in World War II; John; Robert; and Ted. Their father was obsessed with getting them opportunities and guaranteeing them positive results. During family dinners, he channeled the conversation toward politics and news—and expected everyone to chime in. "Public life," Robert would later recall, "seemed really an extension of family life."

John F. Kennedy was born in 1917 in Brookline, a suburb of Boston. Jack, as the family called him, was a skinny and sickly child, fighting through measles, mumps, and scarlet fever—a cascading series of health problems that haunted him into adulthood, when he fought through stomach troubles, terrible back pain, and Addison's disease. His stints in hospitals or at home in bed gave him plenty of time to read. "He gobbled books," his mother, Rose Kennedy, remembered. Kennedy loved the various versions of King Arthur and the novels of Walter Scott—loved anything with romance and adventure. It's clear that he was the most literary of the Kennedy children. One of the family's cherished memories centered on a letter he wrote when he was about ten years old: "A Plea for a Raise / by Jack Kennedy." "Chapter I," like most of Kennedy's prose, got right to the point: "My recent allowance is 40 cents."

It's also clear, however, that Kennedy was not a particularly literary president. As he got older, he lost his taste for fiction, though his taste for romanticism never left. One can find plenty of generalizations about his adult reading: that he read quickly and with great curiosity, retaining everything and homing in on history and biography. But there are few solid examples—contemporary letters, marginalia, preserved discussions with friends—of Kennedy's actual encounters with books. As a reader, he did not measure up to Coolidge or Truman, much less to Wilson or Theodore Roosevelt. Kennedy studied the past for inspiration, for emotional uplift he could use in his own career. "I have an inquiring mind," he once told a reporter, "and I like history. After all, if you're an engineer, you like to read about engineers."

In the fall of 1935 Kennedy enrolled at Princeton, until health troubles forced him to drop out. The next year, he switched to Harvard. He was a popular youth in Cambridge: charming, easygoing, and bright, with a biting and self-deprecating sense of humor. He maintained his family's interests in politics and journalism—he'd started subscribing to the *Times* while in prep school—and those subjects, along with his restless energy, made Kennedy an engaging and rangy conversationalist. Around campus, he was always talking, always moving, his fingers drumming, his thick hair spilling forward, his face thin or gaunt, depending on his health at the moment. He refused to flaunt his money or name. One day during his freshman year, he and a classmate walked past a bookstore with stacks of *I'm for Roosevelt* in its windows. "Any relation?" the roommate asked. It seemed like a good quip until Kennedy said quietly, "My father," and kept walking.

Kennedy's diverse pursuits—and to current affairs he added football, convertibles, and young women—kept him busy. His studies did not. "Jack was not intellectual," Arthur Krock later said. "He was very intelligent, but not intellectual." Kennedy's best skill, his professors and classmates agreed, was writing, but even there, his effort underwhelmed. He submitted the occasional editorial to the *Harvard Crimson* and took electives in political science and economics. Late at night, when he and his roommates sat around plotting their futures, he usually said he wanted to be a writer.

While Kennedy was at Harvard, his father made his own career change, becoming America's ambassador to Britain. Jack joked about it, as he did everything else. ("I seem to be doing better with the girls," he wrote, "so before resigning give my social career a bit of consideration.") But it was a grave time in Europe. Adolf Hitler was looking to expand, and so far— most famously at a conference in Munich—Britain's leaders had let him, hoping to appease Germany and avoid the buildup to another bloody, costly war. In 1939, during the spring of his junior year, Kennedy traveled to Europe and witnessed the effects of appeasement up close, using his father's connections to visit the American embassies in Germany and France, among others.

Kennedy came back to Harvard a more sober young man; experiencing current affairs felt rather different than debating them. He also came back with an idea for his first major writing project, an honors thesis he titled "Appeasement at Munich: The Inevitable Result of the Slowness of

Conversion of the British Democracy from a Disarmament to a Rearmament Policy."

This thesis would eventually grow into Kennedy's first book, but before that came a lot of work—and a lot of help. On January 11, 1940, he sent a telegram to one of his father's top aides in London: "Send immediately pamphlets, etc., Conservative, Labor, Liberal, Pacifist." That aide, like the rest of the ambassador's staff, was living through a crisis: blackouts, shortages, Hitler. For the next two months, though, he picked up an extra duty as Jack's research assistant, shipping him boxes of books and compiling detailed statistics on Britain's defense budgets.*

Kennedy, to his credit, took the research seriously. "Dear Mother and Dad," he wrote, "am just in the process of finding out how little I know." His remedy was reading everything flowing in from the embassy, along with British periodicals and transcripts of parliamentary debates. Kennedy disliked typewriters, so his father paid for a secretary to type up his handwritten notes. Between his research and his observations from Europe, he developed a sophisticated argument—that Britain had failed to prepare for Germany not because of its dimwitted leaders but because democracy itself made such preparations difficult. In Britain, and in America, for that matter, politicians and voters seemed more worried about next year's tax rates than about outflanking an evil dictator. The argument offered an echo of *The Naval War of 1812*, which Theodore Roosevelt had started on that same Harvard campus sixty years before: where Roosevelt had shown that history could overrate its best leaders, Kennedy was showing it could overrate its worst leaders too.

It was shaping up to be an ambitious thesis, at least twice the usual length of seventy pages. It was also a mess. Kennedy did not appear to enjoy the patient and lonely work of writing. His father paid for a stenographer so he could dictate the actual text, but the help-wanted ad set off a scandal when dozens of female applicants showed up at the dormitory, on a campus still decades from going coed. (Kennedy's previous infractions in this realm earned him a university investigation; he ended up meeting with his stenographer at the library.) He was running out of time, and he asked at least two bookish classmates to help with revisions. Even then, the final thesis was cluttered with typos and factual blunders; Kennedy com-

*Kennedy kept the requests coming. On February 9, he cabled, "Rush pacifist literature." That one shocked the British agent charged with spying on the embassy, mostly because he failed to notice that the telegram's "Kennedy" was not the ambassador but his son. "Becoming a Pacifist!" the agent wrote in his notes.

piled helpful timelines, but in his rush, he stuck the wrong years with the wrong chapters. He made the deadline of March 15, but barely. "It represents more work," he admitted to his father, "than I've ever done in my life."

Kennedy needed a break, and that Easter, he headed to his family's waterfront compound in Palm Beach, Florida. As it happened, the *Times*'s Arthur Krock was staying a few mansions down, and Kennedy showed him the thesis. Krock said he should publish it, and Kennedy wrote his father to see if he agreed. Of course he agreed—a prestigious volume fit the family tradition. When Joe Jr. had visited Spain near the end of the Spanish Civil War, Joseph had urged him to write a book about it and even assigned another embassy aide to serve as ghostwriter. While that book was never published, the process worked. "Improve the writing," Joseph instructed Jack. "After you are satisfied with it, ask Arthur Krock to go over it again."

Krock's first task was finding a literary agent, an energetic insider named Gertrude Algase. Algase was thrilled to represent Kennedy—and eventually, she hoped, the entire family—and she tried to move quickly. But Jack seemed more interested in studying for finals or relaxing at the family's other waterfront compound, on Cape Cod. In late May, when Algase started shopping the manuscript to publishers, she was still circulating the unrevised thesis, though Krock had supplied a catchier title: *Why England Slept*, a riff on Winston Churchill's *While England Slept*. At least Algase's cover letter led with the book's main selling point: "Jack Kennedy . . . Ambassador Kennedy's son . . . is a client of mine."

Kennedy knew his thesis needed work. His professors had given it Harvard's lowest honors grade, pointing to its sloppy, repetitive prose. (It was so purely an undergraduate production that its conclusion began, "What conclusions can be drawn?") The bigger issue, as one professor put it in his comments, was that the "fundamental premise [was] never analyzed." The student had dutifully stacked citations and summaries; he hadn't explained what they meant.

Fixing that was a big job. And yet, in his letters from the spring and summer of 1940, Kennedy seemed curiously passive about it. "I suppose the best plan," he wrote to his father, "is that someone looks it over, suggests new ideas on how it can be improved, and then sends it back and I will work with someone around here as regards getting my English polished up." The same aide who'd worked on Joe Jr.'s volume gave Jack's a vigorous edit. More important, Kennedy spent time with Arthur Krock, visiting his Georgetown home and working with him in his library.

Why England Slept gained several chapters and a newly authoritative tone. While sentences from the thesis survived, virtually every paragraph was reworked. The book now boasted that missing analysis. ("Nations, like individuals, change their ideas slowly.") Joseph Kennedy convinced Henry Luce of *Time* to write a glowing foreword. He also sent his son a letter on what America might learn from Britain. "It seems to me," Kennedy wrote, "that this would be a good line to follow":

> We should profit by the lessons of England and make our democracy work. We must make it work right now. Any system of government will work when everything is going well. It's the system that functions in the pinches that survives.

Jack didn't just follow his father's line—he folded it and other paragraphs directly into his book.

After rejections from Harper's and Houghton Mifflin, Algase sold the revised version to a smaller firm, Wilfred Funk, Inc. One upside was that Funk could hurry, so that a manuscript finished in mid-June reached

After *Why England Slept* appeared, Kennedy was happy
to pose for promotional photos.

bookstores in late July. *Why England Slept* became a surprise hit, one of those volumes on current affairs that had thrived during the Depression and was thriving again as Europe collapsed. Joseph Kennedy helped the book along, talking it up to figures like Winston Churchill, promising them it was "already a best-seller." That was true, but only because the ambassador had made it so; as one of his secretaries would later admit, he directed his American employees to purchase thousands of copies.

Why England Slept was also widely discussed. Krock wrote a column championing it, though he never mentioned his involvement. Enthusiastic reviews appeared in the *Washington Post*, the *New Yorker*, and Luce's *Time*, among many other outlets, each of them highlighting the author's youth, the book's timeliness, and the uncanny maturity of its prose. As London's *Times Literary Supplement* put it, "*Why England Slept* is a young man's book; it contains much wisdom for older men."

It seems unlikely that this wisdom originated with the author. The John F. Kennedy Presidential Library has four manuscripts of *Why England Slept*, each of them a version of the original thesis; there is no known draft that documents the book's leap to its confident final form. Kennedy's surviving letters suggest he had three weeks—four at most—to complete this revision. He was an indifferent student who'd struggled to finish his thesis in the first place; his life after the book's appearance, with the exception of his brave service during World War II, followed a similar pattern. In 1945, for instance, Kennedy spent three months as a newspaper correspondent, a career punctuated by scenes like this: the aspiring journalist sprawled on a hotel bed, wearing his black tie best and phoning his editor with the message "Kennedy will not be filing tonight."

The simplest explanation is that Krock rewrote the book. When asked about his role, Krock usually stuck to verbs like "polish" and "amend." But just before his death in 1974, he gave an interview that was more revealing. After describing all the effort he'd put into Joseph Kennedy's *I'm for Roosevelt*, Krock turned to *Why England Slept*: "I did much more work on that."

While the historical record does not support John F. Kennedy's claim to have written *Why England Slept*, it does reveal two aspects about his relationship to books—aspects that would remain true for the rest of his life. The first is that Kennedy adored the public side of authorship. He posed for promotional photos, hunched over a typewriter he would never actually use; he gave winning interviews to reporters and radio hosts, recounting the hot twelve-hour days he spent finishing his book. During a trip to Hollywood, Kennedy leaned into his literary fame on the studio lots. ("A bestselling author," one stranger cooed, "my goodness.") He bought a green convertible with his royalties and kept its backseat stocked with author copies, which he would happily sign after propping one open on the steering wheel. Kennedy claimed *Why England Slept* sold eighty thousand copies, though his publisher's records suggest the real total, not counting his father's bulk buys, was closer to twelve thousand. Fifteen years later, Kennedy could still quote its notice in the *New York Times Book Review* from memory: "a notable text book for our times."

The second aspect is that Kennedy hated any hint that he did not deserve full credit for the book. When a journalist in 1940 asked about his father's influence on it, Kennedy shot back, "I haven't seen my father in six months." Like his pride, his defensiveness lingered. Years later, a Harvard classmate, one of the two who'd pitched in with revisions, tried to tease Kennedy about the thesis, theatrically promising never to reveal his role. Kennedy, the man who loved to joke, lashed out instead. "What do you mean?" he said. "You never did a goddamn thing on it. You never saw it."

JFK AND TCS

After his brief trial as a journalist, Kennedy switched to politics. In 1946 he won a Massachusetts congressional seat; his advisers based the campaign's slogan, "The New Generation Offers a Leader," on the positive responses to *Why England Slept*. By 1953 Kennedy had risen to US senator—still just thirty-five years old, but with a proven strategy for balancing his youth by building his intellectual reputation.

Kennedy believed books and articles could establish him as a politician, and he sought out all kinds of scholarly activities. During his first year as senator, for instance, the prominent historian Margaret Coit asked to interview him for her latest book. Coit wanted to discuss the period covered by *Why England Slept*; she also wanted to engage in some friendly flirting, and the senator encouraged both pursuits.

At the end of their third meeting, Kennedy offered to drive her home. His back pain had become agonizing—in person, Coit later recalled, he looked closer to forty-five—and he used crutches to exit the Senate Office Building. When they reached her apartment, she invited him in to rest. Kennedy collapsed on her couch. But then he tried to pull her down and kiss her.

That was not what Coit had in mind, and she pushed him away. "I made up my mind that I was not going to kiss you on the first date," she said.

"This isn't a first date," he replied. "We have been making eyes at each other three times now."

Kennedy grabbed at her again.

"I have standards just like your sisters," Coit pleaded. "You wouldn't want me to do anything you wouldn't want your sisters to do."

"I don't care what they do," he said, before grabbing at her a third time.

Coit started to cry, and Kennedy retreated, flipping back to bookish mode with frightening ease. "It was as if he had shifted gears," Coit later remembered. "It was the cold, machine-like quality that scared me so." Eventually Kennedy brought up her biography of John Calhoun, which had won a Pulitzer Prize. "You know," he said, "I would rather win a Pulitzer Prize than be president of the United States."

A senator's schedule made it difficult for Kennedy to indulge his appetites, but he usually found a way. Washington, DC, was growing more complicated. One of Kennedy's colleagues, Richard Neuberger from Oregon, wrote a frank essay on how little modern politicians were able to read. Between their committee work, constituent duties, and Senate sessions, they no longer had the time. Oregon's other senator—a former university dean—told Neuberger, "I feel that I am almost becoming book illiterate." An Idaho senator agreed: "[I] feel pretty much isolated from the books I used to have time to read as a lawyer in Boise." When Neuberger asked Kennedy about his reading, he called it "superficial."

And yet, paradoxically enough, there had never been a better time to be a political author. Publishing trends had moved from speech collections like *Have Faith in Massachusetts* to specially conceived, current affairs-ish books like Goldwater's *Conscience of a Conservative*. Supporters of the Arizona senator began planning that manifesto in 1959, and their reasons were obvious. A book, one explained in a private meeting, could "stimulate a popular movement for Senator Goldwater," even "secure the Republican nomination for him." Goldwater dictated a memo on *Conscience*'s key themes, each a variation on how the government was squelching individual liberty. L. Brent Bozell, a ghostwriter with ties to the *National Review*, studied that memo and the senator's speeches; the two met and spoke by phone, assembling a book that would sell millions and ultimately lift its author to the nomination in 1964. Before any of that, Goldwater had warned one of his backers, "My complete incapacity to be an author is well known." But that didn't matter—not in the book's creation and not in its impact.

Plenty of harried politicians attempted this plan in the 1950s and 1960s, including John F. Kennedy. He'd toyed with several book ideas since *Why England Slept*. One was a biography of fellow Catholic (and former presidential nominee) Al Smith, but Kennedy never got further than a title: *Al Smith, Public Servant*. To write his next book, he needed another collaborator, and he found an ideal one in Theodore C. Sorensen.

Sorensen, who was even younger than Kennedy, started working for the new senator in 1953. Before long, the tall and tidy Nebraskan was writing almost all of Kennedy's speeches, in addition to handling the press and digging into policy. (Sorensen almost certainly wrote the National Book Awards speech that Kennedy so carefully edited.) Kennedy called him "my intellectual blood bank," though from the outside their relationship appeared more vampiric. But Sorensen felt an intense loyalty to Kennedy, and Kennedy to him. Early on they discussed Sorensen's penning articles and books under Kennedy's name—and how to handle, as Sorensen cautiously put it, "the recognition of my participation." Both agreed that instead of sharing credit, they would share the profits from any such writings.

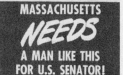

NEWSPAPERMAN AND AUTHOR OF BEST-SELLER

In addition to working as a news correspondent, Congressman Kennedy also wrote a best-selling book "Why England Slept." Of it the Boston Herald in August, 1940 said: "It is a book remarkable for its calm, its grasp of complex problems, its courageous frankness, its good manners and its sound advice."

MASSACHUSETTS NEEDS A MAN LIKE THIS FOR U.S. SENATOR!

In their campaign literature, Kennedy and his advisers emphasized his authorship to "balance the flood" of more superficial coverage.

This arrangement looked as if it would get its first test in the fall of 1953, when Kennedy pitched a book to Harvard University Press on reviving the New England economy. He and Sorensen had been targeting this topic in speeches and hoping it would turn the senator into a regional figure. Once Harvard expressed interest, Sorensen wrote an outline, did additional research, and met with an editor, updating Kennedy along the way. The senator seemed fine to delegate the literary work. When Sorensen confessed in a letter that some sample chapters weren't developing as he'd hoped, Kennedy didn't offer to help. Instead, he told Sorensen to send them to another Kennedy supporter to see if he could add some sparkle and punch."

While the senator ultimately abandoned his New England book, he and Sorensen used this method to produce a stream of Kennedy-bylined articles for outlets like the *New Republic* and the *New York Times Magazine*. In the spring of 1954, Kennedy came up with a new idea for an article, something historical that would examine political courage and the calculus behind it. He'd always been struck by the way John Quincy Adams, when he was a Massachusetts senator, had overruled his constituents to support Thomas Jefferson on several issues. "How about using this one and some other examples," Kennedy told Sorensen, "and put it together for *Harper's* or *Atlantic Monthly*?"

They mulled the article for the rest of 1954, and in the fall, Sorensen began working on a draft. Kennedy had other concerns. His back pain had become unbearable, with the most likely cause being the bone-weakening steroids he took to address other ailments. It was now a struggle to climb stairs or put on socks. On October 21, Kennedy submitted to a dangerous spinal surgery, then spent the next two months in a New York hospital, battling infection, falling into a coma, and coming so close to death that a priest gave him last rites. Just before Christmas, Kennedy relocated to his family's Palm Beach compound, but by February, he was back in New York for a second surgery. There were other hospitalizations as well, plus medications and checkups and physical therapy. Through much of it, Kennedy sported a gaping, eight-inch wound in his back. Sometimes he asked his friends to check on it: "Still oozing, Jack."

There's no question Kennedy was consumed by pain and recovery in late 1954 and early 1955. And yet that same period was when most of *Profiles in Courage* was written. On January 17, 1955, Sorensen mailed his draft of the courage article from Washington to Palm Beach. In a cover letter, the aide wondered if it might be the start of something more. "There is certainly a wealth of fascinating material which had to be boiled down," Sorensen wrote. He knew Kennedy had an in at Harper's with Michael Canfield, who'd married the sister of Jacqueline, the senator's wife. Would the house, Sorensen wondered, "be interested in a book along these lines?"

Sorensen's book idea thrilled Kennedy, to the point that even with his second surgery looming, he started negotiations with Harper's within the week. The publisher liked the pitch, and over the next few months, a book emerged, with each major chapter highlighting a historical senator and the bravery he showed during a tense moment. A volume that featured eight senators received input from at least nine different academics—not just citations and corrections but memos that ran twenty pages or more, each one packed with useful anecdotes and analysis.

By far the most important figure, even more than Kennedy, was Ted Sorensen. "My present suggestion," he wrote to the senator, "is that I might submit to you a manuscript of the approximate length desired . . . and we could then complete the editing (including some injection of your own philosophy, etc.) on a joint basis." Once Kennedy agreed, Sorensen got to work. The aide devoted seven days a week to the project, ignoring his young children and his very pregnant wife, pulling the best scholarship and popular history from the Library of Congress and writing at Kennedy's empty Senate office, often late into the night. By the end of February, Sorensen had finished a first draft—more than thirty thousand words written and researched in one month's time. In his dispatches and phone calls to Palm Beach, Sorensen spoke confidently about the book's audience, method, and themes. He labeled his chapters "working drafts" and expected Kennedy would pitch in with their "expanding" and "rewriting."

What Kennedy did instead was send a few of those chapters straight to Harper's. His reasons remain unclear, and the house was disappointed. On February 15, its chairman decided to kill the book. "I found in reading them that I got rather bogged down," he wrote in a reply to Kennedy. Two employees, Kennedy's brother-in-law and another editor named Evan Thomas, convinced the chairman not to send his letter. Harper's would give the senator a chance to work harder, with Thomas taking a special interest on the book.

Sorensen, of course, had always planned an extensive revision, and he gathered more material to guide it: memos from academics, fresh notes on the senators' personalities and motives, anything that would make the chapters more vivid and human, which was what Thomas and Harper's wanted.

On March 21, Sorensen headed to Palm Beach with this material. Just before the flight, he wrote a chapter-by-chapter summary of the book's status. Kennedy's name barely appeared. The entry for the chapter on Senator Daniel Webster, for example, read in full:

1. Daniel Webster—Chapter to be finalized on the basis of:
    a. Original draft of chapter
    b. Dean Landis's draft of chapter
    c. Memorandum containing additional notes on Webster
    d. Memorandum from Dr. Davids on Webster
    e. Books sent to Florida and Senator Kennedy's notes therefrom, etc.

The senator's notes must have frustrated Sorensen when he finally saw them in person. Kennedy had been convalescing in a pair of rooms that contained a hospital bed, a tape recorder, a telephone, and piles of those books from Washington. The senator had been reading and tweaking Sorensen's drafts. (Kennedy was a sharp line editor.) He had also filled several notebooks with his own prose. But those notebooks felt like a first attempt to make sense of the topic—light on structure and ideas, heavy on background and quotes from other books, a strange choice since Sorensen had sent those volumes only after mining them himself. A couple of handwritten passages from Kennedy's notebooks did show up in *Profiles*; the most extended one traced the political rise of Senator Lucius Q. C. Lamar. Even with Lamar, however, Kennedy was rewriting Sorensen's draft. Most of the senator's writing didn't make his book because most of it wasn't writing at all.*

During Sorensen's Florida visit and during a second visit in early May, he and Kennedy did work together. They revised several chapters into their final form, keeping long sections from Sorensen's drafts but adding

---

*Given the Kennedys' dedication to preserving their history, it seems significant that more evidence didn't survive. One must also consider the family's dedication to burying evidence. Near the end of his life, Sorensen admitted that Jacqueline Kennedy had asked him to destroy his draft of the "Ask not" inaugural. (Jack went even further, copying parts of the final typescript in his own hand and putting a false date on it.) Sorensen, as he once noted, "drafted anything of importance in longhand," and the Kennedy Library has handwritten drafts of several of Sorensen's other books. Yet not one of his handwritten *Profiles* drafts appears to have made it to the library. Sorensen may have disposed of his *Profiles* drafts, and he may have done so at the Kennedys' request.

catchy openings and fizzy, cliffhanger history. Perhaps Kennedy directed some of these revisions; perhaps he did more dictations as his health improved.

But the surviving evidence suggests that Kennedy's contributions were extremely limited. The four known recordings of his *Profiles* dictations, which total just over forty minutes, resemble his superficial, source-heavy notebooks. The Kennedy Library has thousands of pages of typed manuscripts relating to *Profiles*, many of them dated, and a comparison of those pages with Sorensen's files shows that the aide completed many of the major revisions while alone in Washington. Buried deep within these documents is a more revealing example of Kennedy's role. While perusing one of the memos Sorensen had brought to Palm Beach, Kennedy put brackets around an anecdote of Senator George Norris pulling a clever legislative trick. Kennedy wrote one word in the margin: "Begin." That anecdote became the opening to the Norris chapter, but Kennedy never bothered to write it himself. Instead, the new opening didn't materialize until a draft prepared weeks after the Florida trip. The senator, it seems, was waiting for someone else to do the work.

On May 24, Kennedy returned to Capitol Hill. The book was nearly done. Everyone understood that *Profiles*, with its uplifting subject and its bipartisan roster of senators, was simultaneously a historical and a political document. Joseph Kennedy read it and made one major suggestion: "Harper's should have an excellent editorial writer go over the whole book." Family habits die hard.

To ensure Harper's promoted the book correctly, Sorensen wrote a memo listing "the senator's own acts of political courage." He needn't have bothered, as Kennedy became heavily involved at the marketing stage. The senator weighed in on the book's cover, blurbs, flap copy, and author photo. (He requested a larger one.) He also wrote a brief preface that included his acknowledgments, and in it he failed to mention his chief collaborator. Based on their agreement, and based on Sorensen's superhuman efforts, Kennedy had paid him a bonus of six thousand dollars, roughly a third of Sorensen's annual salary. Perhaps Kennedy believed the money sufficed. When Sorensen edited the preface, though, he sent Kennedy four potential tweaks. The last one read: "4. TCS?"

Kennedy added a sentence thanking Sorensen "for his invaluable assistance and preparation of the material upon which this book is based." Meanwhile, Sorensen handled the book's tedious final details—its pictures and captions, its index and copyedits. Sorensen had also orchestrated a staggering campaign of magazine and newspaper serials, placing excerpts in *Harper's*, *Collier's*, and *Reader's Digest*, among many others. The book's publication date of January 1956 was approaching, and between the serial deals and the industry buzz, it looked like *Profiles* was going to be a big hit—and a boost to Kennedy's political standing.

Yet the senator was thinking about more than politics. On Christmas Eve, his editor, Thomas, was filling stockings with his wife when the phone rang. It was Kennedy, and he was in a rush: "I've really got to get this book out this year."

Thomas patiently explained that they were far too late in the process for that, but Kennedy wouldn't hear it. "We've got to get it out before the year turns," he said.

The two continued to talk past each other, and Kennedy grew frustrated. So did Thomas. (So, one suspects, did his wife.)

Finally the editor asked Kennedy why it mattered so much.

"Well," he said, "I've just been talking to Arthur Krock, and I understand it would win the Pulitzer Prize this year."

VOTE FOR KENNEDY

"The American writer in the middle of the 20th century," Philip Roth once wrote, "has his hands full." Novelists were struggling to capture the strangeness and sprawl of modern life. "The actuality," as Roth so famously put it, "is continually outdoing our talents."

What's less remembered is that Roth chose a specific example to illustrate this point: the Kennedy-Nixon debates, which were televised during the fall of 1960. Those debates, with their stagecraft, their squabbles over stagecraft, and their astounding and instant reach, summed up Roth's worries about midcentury America—about its dizzying distractions, but also its filtering of those distractions through TV. In 1950, one in ten American homes had a television; by 1960 it was nearly nine in ten, and 70 million people watched the first Kennedy-Nixon debate. *Profiles in Courage* sold a lot of copies, but it didn't sell 70 million.

Still, Kennedy's book became an unprecedented success, easily the most influential campaign book of the twentieth century. It resonated in the age of television, but it also resonated because of the age of television. The more Americans fretted about their future as readers, the more an inspiring title like *Profiles* appealed. It would have been the ideal outcome for Kennedy if he weren't so busy chasing the approval of writers like Philip Roth.

One thing that made *Profiles* inspiring was its ostensible backstory. Reviewers, columnists, and profile writers took turns rehearsing it: the back injury Kennedy misleadingly blamed on World War II; the risky surgeries; the convalescence he devoted to his book, which was usually illustrated by an anecdote about him lying flat in a hospital bed, his notebook pressed against a board above his head. "The book reflects Kennedy's own character," Evan Thomas told the *Boston Globe*. "He's quite a courageous guy."

This message sped across the country. "Most of us have stopped reading," complained a columnist in Greenville, Mississippi. "We just lazily loll before the TV." That's why *Profiles* and its heroic author seemed so refreshing. "Buy this book," the columnist urged, "read it, and pass it around." Between 1956 and 1957, *Profiles* spent eighty-eight weeks on the *New York Times* best-seller list. It morphed from a book into a phenomenon, a franchise, with Kennedy (and Sorensen) producing spinoffs such as a *McCall's* feature on three women who were themselves "profiles in courage."

Kennedy spent a lot of time in 1956 and 1957 signing copies of *Profiles*.

Kennedy rekindled his love for the public side of authorship, signing endless autographs and appearing at functions like the *Washington Post*'s Book and Author luncheon. ("I always used to wonder what the ladies did in Washington in the daytime," he joked.) *Profiles* earned him invites to TV shows like *Meet the Press*, where he was introduced as a senator and "an author"; it earned him gigs like the National Book Awards keynote. At that event, the senator ran into the historian Margaret Coit, though he didn't recognize her at first.

Even with these results, Kennedy remained fixated on his book, pestering Harper's for sales updates and panicking at the smallest slump in reorders. On June 25, 1956, he sent Thomas a letter: "Dear Evan: Just a note to let you know that neither the shop at the LaGuardia Airport nor the shop at the National Airport had a copy of my book."

Later that summer, Kennedy came within a few delegates of securing his party's nomination for vice president. During the convention, he stopped to see Truman at his hotel suite. What, a reporter wondered, had the ex-president asked about? "My book," Kennedy replied. Kennedy was still just a senator, but he was a far different senator than he'd been before the release of *Profiles*. Not even three years earlier, he'd been proposing a New England volume to a university press; now he and a different volume were national stars. In the weeks after the convention, the press continued to rave about *Profiles* and its author. "Our country," the *Philadelphia Tribune* noted in a column on the book, "[would be] in safe hands with such a political philosopher at the helm."

It's important to emphasize how much *Profiles* had accomplished by the start of 1957—how much Kennedy had to be thrilled with, to be content with. It was on track to accomplish even more, with Pocket Books preparing a paperback edition of 400,000 copies; Kennedy called the publisher directly to suggest spots where the books should be sold.

Yet Kennedy was also thinking about literary spoils and particularly the Pulitzer Prize. The Pulitzers were awarded each spring through a two-step process. First, a set of screeners, usually specialists, created a list of recommendations for their particular category; then the advisory board, made up of notable figures like the president of Columbia University and the publisher of the *Boston Herald*, chose the winners, typically but not always from the screeners' lists.

The process kicked off in January, and despite everything else he had to do, Kennedy made time to discuss the award personally with his father. On January 15, he followed up with a brief letter:

Dear Dad:

I am enclosing a list of the members of the Advisory Board for the Pulitzer Prize.

Joseph Kennedy—perhaps on his own, perhaps with his son's further direct involvement—enlisted Arthur Krock, who had recently finished a fifteen-year run on the advisory board, to persuade its current members to give *Profiles* the prize. "It is not even mentioned by the screeners," one member admitted to Krock. "Give me some reasons why the Kennedy book might be considered among the biographies." They must have been good reasons, for when the Pulitzers were announced on May 6, James Reston won for national reporting, Eugene O'Neill won for drama, and John F. Kennedy won for biography.

Kennedy's friends and family always said the Pulitzer made him happier than any other honor, including his World War II Purple Heart. But the award proved costly politically. In New York, journalists and editors had been gossiping about a ghost (and his cut of those royalties) since *Profiles* had first appeared, though none of them felt the need to report it. The Pulitzer changed that. On May 15, Gilbert Seldes wrote a column about the rumor in the *Village Voice*. "As no one else seems willing to do this," he began, "I will."

Seldes soon received a passionate denial from Kennedy, but the senator did not address the charge publicly, probably because no other outlets were willing to follow up. That month did see one other *Profiles* development: Joseph Kennedy's lawyers quietly drew up a document that paid Sorensen an additional and frankly astonishing sum of more than $100,000 (or $1 million in today's dollars).

The ghostwriting issue disappeared until December 7, when Drew Pearson went on *The Mike Wallace Interview*, a Saturday night show on ABC. Pearson was the author of the *Washington Merry-Go-Round* books and a popular column of the same name, and during a segment on Kennedy, he noted that the senator was "the only man in history that I know who won a Pulitzer Prize on a book which was ghostwritten for him." Pearson hadn't really planned to say this; as soon as he did, people in the ABC studio began worrying that Kennedy would sue.

They were right. On Sunday, Kennedy huddled with Sorensen; on Monday, he met with Clark Clifford, a former Truman speechwriter and now a pricey DC lawyer. Clifford thought Kennedy seemed surprisingly upset—until the phone rang: "I want you to sue the bastards," Joseph Kennedy roared, "for fifty million dollars."

Clifford pointed out that a lawsuit would only bring attention to Pearson's charge. (Given *Profiles'* paper trail, it might have also inadvertently exposed the truth.) The lawyer advised meeting with ABC instead, and Kennedy's staff assembled a list of loyal witnesses like Krock and Evan Thomas. They searched Kennedy's notebooks for the few handwritten passages that lined up with the book. Most important, Sorensen wrote an affidavit, sworn in front of a notary, in which he claimed that his only role was "to assist [Kennedy] in the assembly and preparation of research and other materials upon which much of the book is based."*

ABC didn't put up much of a fight, agreeing to an on-air retraction as long as Kennedy signed a document promising not to sue the network, the show, or their various corporate partners. Privately, though, the ghost-writing gossip persisted. During their ABC prep, Kennedy had said to Clifford, "You of course understand why this is so important."

Clifford admitted he did not.

"I will tell you in confidence," Kennedy said, "I am going to be a candidate for the Democratic nomination for president of the United States."

Kennedy worried that the rumors would capsize his upcoming candidacy. "We might as well quit if we let this stand," he told Sorensen. So the senator went on the offensive. When John Oakes, a journalist at the *Times*, half-joked with a Harper's employee about the matter, Kennedy sent Oakes a letter: "I have, on many occasions, directly and indirectly, formally and informally, stated unequivocally that I was the sole author of the book." The next time Oakes was in Washington, he met with Kennedy. The journalist tried to talk politics, but Kennedy refused. For a half hour, he made Oakes study the handwritten pages while he held forth on his authorship of the book.

It was quite a performance, and Kennedy delivered it again and again as he prepared to run for president. (While running for reelection to the Senate in 1958, Kennedy taped copies of those handwritten pages in the windows of his campaign headquarters.) There is no reason to trust any of it. During his defenses, Kennedy lied easily and prolifically. He pointed to *Why England Slept* as proof he could buckle down on a book. He claimed he had pocketed all profits from *Profiles*, with no mention of Sorensen's two separate bonuses. He claimed the Pulitzer—both the award itself and

---

*Later in the affidavit, Sorensen added that his assistance had been "very generously acknowledged by the Senator in the Preface." It was a breathtaking bit of loyalty—citing the credit in the preface that existed only because Sorensen had reminded Kennedy that he hadn't credited him at all.

his willingness to accept it—was proof of his authorship. The lies became cover for the lies.

The lies worked. Kennedy didn't just win the presidency—he won it with a literary aura, a valuable resource in a televisual age. After his victory, it became fashionable to claim that culture once again had a friend in the White House. The *Washington Post* tasked a reporter with totaling up the books written by Kennedy appointees; she got to 110, "not counting the president's own." Kennedy and Jacqueline threw lavish, salon-like parties, like the one that occurred in the spring of 1962.

More than 150 guests attended the event, including painters, musicians, and of course authors: Saul Bellow, Thornton Wilder, Tennessee Williams, and Robert Lowell. At one point, Kennedy bumped into Edmund Wilson and mentioned he'd seen a review of his Civil War book, *Patriotic Gore*. What, Kennedy asked, had Wilson made of the conflict? Wilson replied that the Civil War was too complex to discuss in a setting like this; he told Kennedy to read the book. The president walked away puzzled. "He said something," Wilson wrote in his journal, "about it being unusual for an author not to want to talk about his book."

A few weeks later, Lowell confessed to Wilson that the entire event had felt fraudulent. "Everyone there seemed addled with adulation at having been invited," Lowell wrote in a letter. "It was all good fun but next morning you read that the president . . . might have invaded Cuba again." Lowell believed that Kennedy's party had been distracting and demeaning—that America's intellectuals should have known better. "We should be windows," he wrote, "not window-dressing."

PRESIDENTS AND PULITZERS

McMillan Lewis would never forget that day at the White House, when he was a boy of eleven or twelve, standing in line to meet the president. It was 1915, and Lewis and his father had come all the way from St. Louis to see Woodrow Wilson. Three years before, they'd watched Wilson deliver one of his tradition-bending stump speeches while running for president; now Lewis was going to shake Wilson's hand.

That day, Lewis felt a deep connection to politics and history. He grew up, went to college, started selling insurance and never really stopped. But he also kept participating in local politics and reading about America's past, and in his forties, Lewis decided to go back to school and become a high school history teacher instead. He wrote his master's thesis on Wilson, and during the research, he noticed a scholarly gap regarding Wilson's time as a professor. So Lewis wrote letters to four thousand Princeton alums, asking for their memories of Wilson, interviewing faculty members, and compiling the responses into a fine book he published with a regional press.

Lewis eventually landed a job at a high school in St. Louis. He taught into his seventies, advising the student government club, serving as an officer in the Missouri Historical Society, and living in a ranch house in the suburbs, which had a library lined with custom bookshelves. Lewis still loved to read, especially titles in history and current affairs. One day in 1956, after finishing his latest book, the recently published *Profiles in Courage*, he wrote a letter to its author. "Dear senator," Lewis wrote, "I have never met you but feel I know you." Lewis explained how much he admired the book, how he was already planning to assign it to his students. "I wrote a small book," he admitted near the letter's end. "I understand the work and research that went into your book."

When John F. Kennedy lied about *Profiles in Courage*, he wasn't just lying to elites—he was lying to readers like McMillan Lewis. The book's structure, research, first draft, and most of its second came from Ted Sorensen. Even the book's idea came from Sorensen. When Kennedy's biographers speculate on his motives (Did he convince himself that he truly wrote the book?) or debate the semantics of authorship (Doesn't he deserve at least some credit?), they miss the obvious point. Kennedy wrote *Profiles* the way most politicians write their books, and one can locate his efforts on an authorial continuum: he did more than Goldwater but less than Truman. The problem came in his quest for literary fame, particularly the Pulitzer.

Kennedy's readers grasped this point better than his lawyers, his intellectuals, and his biographers. When Drew Pearson raised the rumor on ABC, readers didn't worry about ghostwriting; they worried about integrity. The librarian writing to ask Kennedy what she should tell her patrons; the woman wondering about the post-Pulitzer charge that "the book was ghostwritten (all right in itself)"; the man reminding Kennedy that "you accepted a high honor"—each of them wanted to believe the senator, but they also wanted the truth. It was not a complicated question, though it was a question of character.

CHAPTER TWELVE

Reagan and the Rise
of the Blockbuster

At seventy-nine, Ronald Reagan could still sell a role. It was the fall of 1990, and Simon & Schuster had just published his presidential memoir, *An American Life*. For years, insiders had predicted it would be "the major memoir of the nineties," and the book had the marketing campaign to match: TV appearances, excerpts in *Time*, and industry buzz over an advance of $5 million or $7 million—either way, a new nonfiction record. Reagan even traveled to Simon & Schuster's Manhattan headquarters, where he played the part of author. As the photographers and television crews followed along, Reagan and his editor, Michael Korda, leaned over a thick sheaf of blank paper, each man holding a pen and pretending to jot down comments or queries, both of them thinking, nodding, conferring. After everyone got what they needed, Reagan headed for the door. Just before exiting, he turned and said, "I hear it's a terrific book! One of these days I'm going to read it myself."

Reagan was poking fun at his reputation—at the idea that he was, in Clark Clifford's phrase, "an amiable dunce." During his political career, Reagan's opponents, and some of his allies, frequently dismissed him as a mere actor. He might be able to deliver lines convincingly, the thinking went, but they were still just lines, fed to him by party officials or pricey campaign pros.

Reagan was also poking fun at his publisher. In the 1980s, publishing went through an unprecedented mutation. Big, publicly traded companies were buying and consolidating independent houses; chains like Waldenbooks were slashing prices and staking out suburban malls. Together they radically expanded the market for books, and especially for blockbuster hardcovers. In fiction, that meant authors whose brands were as carefully managed as a car company's (and who produced a new volume every model year): Stephen King, Michael Crichton, Danielle Steel. In nonfiction, it meant celebrities who now got their biggest checks not from magazines like *McClure's* but from book publishers themselves. The best example was Lee Iacocca, who ran an actual car company; the Chrysler CEO's autobiography sold millions of copies before it reached the paperback racks.

These blockbusters were often speedy, assembly-line products—books where one could joke about their authors not bothering to read them. But plenty of people bought them. After years of steady growth—American publishers topped $2 billion in revenues in 1972—the industry erupted in the 1980s, becoming a $10 billion-a-year business. "The prevailing atmosphere," complained an editor at W. W. Norton, one of the last big independents, "is very much one of high capitalism characteristic of the late Reagan era."

It would be a mistake, however, to merge Reagan's authorship and Reagan's economy. Throughout his life, he devoted long stretches to reading and writing, usually working alone with a yellow legal pad and one of his favorite fountain pens. Reagan drafted and researched all of his speeches until he became governor of California (and continued writing many of them until he became president). In his cramped cursive, he penned hundreds of articles, hundreds of radio commentaries, and thousands of letters, almost all of them polished and personal.

In other words, Reagan left behind a far stronger record of authorship than Clark Clifford's most famous client, John F. Kennedy. And it is more than the record of a mere communicator. Reagan's writings reveal him shaping his political ambitions, and his political imagination, long before any advisers showed up. The place to see this is not in *An American Life* but in his first and largely forgotten book, a strange and beguiling memoir that reveals much about Reagan, and maybe about blockbuster publishing as well.

"MY LITERARY EPIC"

The plot points of Reagan's life before the presidency are well known: the tanned lifeguard in high school; the smooth sportscaster in Iowa; the handsome movie star in Hollywood; and finally the slick TV pitchman for General Electric and then for Barry Goldwater, which primed Reagan's own political ascent.

And yet, alongside each of these moments, there runs a steady subplot of Reagan reading, writing, and thinking. He didn't just serve as a lifeguard; he wrote a thoughtful essay about it, "Meditations of a Lifeguard," which ran in his high school yearbook. He didn't just broadcast baseball; he penned a weekly sports column for the *Des Moines Dispatch*. He didn't just act in Hollywood; he spent his downtime reading, earning a reputation around the lots for being a bookworm (and for boring costars with his latest facts). After Reagan delivered his famous speech in support of Goldwater's presidential campaign in 1964, a fan sent him a letter: "I don't know whether or not you wrote it, nor do I care, but it was the finest speech I ever heard." In the margin, Reagan scribbled three words: "I wrote it."

Reagan was born in 1911 in the small town of Tampico, Illinois. His family moved five times before he turned ten, ultimately settling in Dixon, Illinois. There was a lot about his life that felt unsettled. His father, Jack, struggled with alcoholism; there was never enough money, which meant the Reagans couldn't afford a radio, though they caught the occasional movie at the Dixon Theatre. In a difficult situation Reagan's mother, Nelle, leaned on reading and religion, and Reagan joined her in both pursuits. He got a library card their first year in Dixon, and during his visits, he often read one book at the library so he could check out a second one to read at home. Reagan loved the legends of King Arthur so much he named his cat Sir Lancelot. He loved modern myths as well: the westerns of Zane Grey, the river tales of Mark Twain, the science fiction of Edgar Rice Burroughs. "The joy of reading has always been with me," he later recalled. "I believe I was probably as regular a patron as the library ever had."

In Dixon, Reagan also read Calvin Coolidge's *Autobiography*. The story of Calvin Jr. working hard in the tobacco fields stuck with him— "If my father were your father . . ."—and Reagan told and retold it the rest of his life. But he never mentioned the book's account of Calvin Jr.'s sickness and death. Reagan was an optimist, something he also got from his mother, and that optimism extended to his reading. "As I look back," he later noted, "I realize that all my reading left an abiding belief in the triumph of good over evil. There were heroes who lived by standards of morality and fair play." Perhaps there were, but the books he grew up with included other elements. Reagan, like most readers, found in them what he wanted to find.

A high school teacher encouraged Reagan to try out for student plays—and also to experiment with his passion for writing. Reagan kept it up at Eureka College, taking a dozen courses on literary topics: crea-

On a set in 1949, Reagan read the recently published *The Negro in Films*,
a book that critiqued Hollywood and the stereotyped roles
it offered black actors.

tive writing, feature writing, the Romantics.* After graduation he started
working as a sportscaster, and in 1937 he headed to California to cover
spring training. While there, he did a screen test for Warner Brothers.
Soon he was a rising star.

Reagan was brainier than most other actors, though that never seemed
to compromise his cheerful, All-American appeal. He read obsessively in
current affairs. He got involved in the Screen Actors Guild, eventually
serving as president during a tense and complex period where Hollywood
dealt with labor strikes and Communist blacklists. Reagan's literary side

*Reagan's presidential library has preserved more than a dozen prose pieces from his high
school and college years, in addition to the lifeguard essay, and they display a genre writer's
gifts for nervy phrasing and evocative detail. A train pulling into town lets out "a gasping,
panting roar"; a minor character makes a memorable debut: "Marjory something or other,
who was very cool and very blonde and talked from the corner of her scarlet mouth."
Taken together, Reagan's youthful stories suggest that had he wanted to, he could have
written a few blockbuster novels himself.

even popped up in his movies. In 1952, he starred in *She's Working Her Way through College*, a musical about a burlesque dancer trying to get an education (and to overcome some ugly stereotypes). Reagan played a professor who gives a speech denouncing bias in all its forms, and when he didn't like the speech in the script, he rewrote it himself. Studio head Jack Warner couldn't believe it. "What's this I hear," he demanded of the director, "about you letting a damned actor write his own speeches?" Then Warner watched Reagan's version: "You win."

The most striking thing about the speech—"a precedent which may lead tomorrow to the barring of students because they go to the wrong church, come from the wrong side of the tracks, or were born in the wrong country"—is that it doesn't sound like a professor's. It sounds like a politician's. Reagan's movie career was slowing down, and in 1954 he started hosting (and occasionally acting in) a television show, *General Electric Theater*. He also began visiting GE's plants and giving real speeches, which he based on his reading in conservative economics. While he'd grown up a loyal Democrat, voting for Franklin Roosevelt and Harry Truman, Reagan had moved rightward as he'd studied volumes like Friedrich Hayek's *Road to Serfdom* and Henry Hazlitt's *Economics in One Lesson*. He read those books the same way he read everything else, sorting their ideas into good and evil, identifying their exemplary anecdotes, and finding simple morals in even the most ambiguous issues.

General Electric Theater became one of the country's biggest shows, behind only *I Love Lucy* and *The Ed Sullivan Show*, and its success allowed Reagan to build a sprawling midcentury home in Pacific Palisades, where he lived with his children and his second wife, an actress named Nancy Davis. GE transformed the house into an infomercial, installing the latest gadgets—an electric iron, an electric waffle maker—and filming ads where Ron and Nancy breezily demoed the "Home of the Future." But Reagan was growing more focused on the antigovernment, anti-Communist manifesto he delivered at factories and Rotary suppers around the country. "When I'd get back from school in the afternoon," his son Michael remembered, "I'd toss my books and go into the master bedroom to say hello. Dad had a big desk there, and he was always at the desk, writing. Not almost always. Always."

In the spring of 1962, GE canceled Reagan's show—because, he believed, he'd become too political. Reagan tried going back to movies but discovered there wasn't much demand for an aging actor. A new possibility swiftly emerged: a New York publisher asked Reagan if he wanted to write a book, "a dramatic first-hand narrative," in the words of his editor, that focused on "the excision of the communist cancer in Hollywood."

The idea must have appealed to a lifelong reader like Reagan. He also saw its political potential. *Profiles in Courage, The Conscience of a Conservative*, and *Six Crises*, the last of which came out that same spring, had proven that campaign books could stir interest and shape images, and Reagan was beginning to think in those terms. While California conservatives wanted him to challenge the state's moderate Republican senator in a primary, Reagan's ambitions ran higher. In 1962, his daughter, Maureen, told him in a letter that he could be governor. "Well, if we're talking about what I *could* do," he replied, "I could be president." It might have been a joke, but, like all of Reagan's jokes, it worked because it contained some truth.

Whatever he ran for, Reagan knew he had two weaknesses—the charge that he was a mere actor and the charge that he was a far-right extremist. Once he started the actual writing of his book, early in 1963, he switched it from a story about Hollywood to a broader autobiography that cleverly addressed both concerns.

Reagan had help from Richard Hubler, a mildly frustrated fiction writer who also wrote screenplays, magazine stories, and as-told-to autobiographies. They made an excellent pair. Both were in their fifties. Both shared the same sense of humor. (Hubler called the book "the saga of Reagan"; Reagan called it "my literary epic.") And both took the project quite seriously. Reagan and Hubler would meet at the "Home of the Future," where the ghost rarely needed to prompt or guide his partner's dictations. If anything, Hubler needed Reagan's help—in sorting out, say, the history of a particularly knotty Hollywood strike. "Dear Dick," Reagan wrote in a follow-up letter. "Of course you are confused—we were all confused while it was going on. Anyway, here is the schedule: in the summer of '45 . . ." The narrative went on for three pages, with Reagan drawing a dense time line in the margin.

They decided to title the autobiography *Where's the Rest of Me?* a reference to one of Reagan's most celebrated roles in *King's Row*. But the book made clear that Hollywood had never fulfilled him. There were plenty of *Photoplay*-style tidbits, including Reagan's advice for delivering an on-screen kiss. (The secret: don't go full smooch, which "shoves her face out of shape.") There was much more on Reagan's life before and after his acting peak. "I was eleven years old the first time I came home to find my father flat on his back," he wrote. Reagan described his feelings of shame and guilt, his mother's message that alcoholism was a "sickness," his father's snoring as he grew damp in the snow. "I bent over him," Reagan continued, "smelling the sharp odor of whiskey from the speakeasy. I got a fistful of his overcoat. Opening the door, I managed to drag him inside."

Such prose—and *Where's the Rest of Me?* is a remarkably rich campaign book—came from Reagan and Hubler's diligent revisions. They worked hardest on the final pages. The book had already traced Reagan's political evolution, from "a near-hopeless hemophilic liberal" who "bled for 'causes'" to a free market conservative. Now, at the end, Reagan needed to show that his new beliefs fit comfortably within America's mainstream, and he went through at least two major drafts to get the sentences just right. He added a paragraph invoking Lincoln. He noted that when he'd attacked Eisenhower's big government, it was "a nonpartisan viewpoint." Only after a Democrat took the White House did these views morph into "an expression of right wing extremism."

Reagan's defense was debatable, of course, but the most interesting thing is that he was making it by himself. He and Hubler had finished their manuscript by the end of 1963, and it lacked the sanitizing touch of an experienced political handler. *Where's the Rest of Me?* can also be a remarkably odd campaign book. Consider its opening:

> The story begins with the close-up of a bottom in a small town called Tampico in Illinois, on February 6, 1911. My face was blue from screaming, my bottom was red from whacking, and my father claimed afterward that he was white when he said shakily, "For such a little bit of a fat Dutchman, he makes a hell of a lot of noise, doesn't he?" . . . Ever since my birth my nickname has been "Dutch" and I have been particularly fond of the colors that were exhibited—red, white, and blue.

If you squint, even the opening had a purpose, framing Reagan as a homey and patriotic foil to thundering conservatives like Goldwater. (It certainly sounded like Reagan.) While the publisher was startled by how much the book had changed, it agreed to publish it after the presidential election. Reagan campaigned for Goldwater and delivered his sensational speech on October 27, 1964. Republicans lost the White House in a rout, but Reagan's star was rising a second time.

Early in 1965, Reagan met with Stu Spencer at a ritzy Los Angeles club. Spencer's firm, Spencer-Roberts & Associates, belonged to the booming field of political consultants—not admen with a political itch, like Bruce

Barton, but specialists who did campaigns and nothing else. In 1960, according to one count, 188 campaigns had relied on some kind of a professional campaign manager; by 1968, that number would swell to 658.

It was an interview of Reagan as much as of Spencer. The consultant was worried about the actor's right-wing reputation, but found him to be smart, funny, and restrained. Spencer agreed to help Reagan explore a run for governor, though the candidate had one more surprise. "I wrote a book," he said. "It's going to come out this spring. How's that going to fit?"

Rather nicely, it turned out. Spencer wanted Reagan to meet more voters, and book signings provided the perfect cover. The consultant checked in on an early event at a Los Angeles bookstore, where Reagan arrived straight from his horse ranch. "He showed up in his English riding gear, breeches, boots, everything but the whip," Spencer remembered. Reagan still charmed the crowd, signing books and chatting with housewives, aspiring actors, Illinois transplants, and elderly readers. He did events for *Where's the Rest of Me?* all over California—San Francisco, Irvine, Long Beach. He was still in leading man shape, just over six feet tall with dark brown hair and hazel eyes, and he was a natural at retail politics. That year, Spencer-Roberts scheduled more than a hundred speaking engagements for Reagan in addition to his book signings. At one of those signings, a reporter asked Reagan whether he'd found the rest of him. "I've found it," he replied, "in politics."

The official campaign announcement came in 1966, and Reagan's book, which would sell 200,000 copies by early 1968, provided a valuable foundation. "It was a nice background piece," Spencer said, "showing who he was and where he came from."

Reagan's chief opponents—George Christopher in the primary, Pat Brown in the general—saw it as a vulgar weakness. Lou Cannon, who covered the race as a reporter, was offered the book by one of Reagan's staffers. "I already got my copy from your opponents," Cannon replied, and they both had a good laugh. Yet the attacks proved less sophisticated than the book itself. Christopher brought an underlined copy to interviews so he could show that Reagan had once belonged to organizations with Communist leanings. "Where's the rest of me?" Brown would ask on the stump. "Just dig out the old Goldwater speeches and you'll find the answer." All these charges did, though, was remind voters of Reagan's most celebrated achievements (and of the fact that he'd written a well-reviewed book about them).

Reagan ignored the criticisms, projecting the image of a cool and disciplined moderate. He thumped Christopher and Brown, then won an easy reelection in 1970. Spencer ran that campaign too, along with Reagan's presidential runs in 1980 and 1984. *Where's the Rest of Me?* didn't join them, dropping out of print in 1970; given passages like its opening close-up, Reagan's handlers surely didn't mind. Still, the book made a difference during his initial bid for governor, and today it makes Reagan's instincts and independence clear. During that first run, he'd given Spencer a copy of his book. "To Stu," he wrote inside it. "Who probably has an idea about what the rest of me should look like." But that wasn't right. Reagan already grasped what he needed to look like. The proof was right there in the book he'd just inscribed.

HOUSES OF THE FUTURE

In the preface to his *Memoirs*, Harry Truman lamented America's lack of legacy books. "I have often thought in reading the history of our country," he wrote, "how much is lost to us because so few Presidents have told their own stories." Like a lot of readers, Truman didn't seem familiar with the autobiographies of Adams, Jefferson, Madison, Monroe, and so many others. But the second half of the twentieth century brought a surge of new titles that was impossible to miss. Indeed, Truman's lament soon felt out of date, thanks in part to Truman's example.

In the summer of 1963, while Reagan was working on his campaign book, Dwight Eisenhower was working on his legacy one. Eisenhower had previously written *Crusade in Europe*, a crisp memoir of his service in World War II; it sold more than a million copies and remained a boon when he ran for president in 1952.

Now that he was done with politics, he promised to write a "personal memoir." Unfortunately, the output of Eisenhower and his peers would render this one of the emptiest promises in politics. In public and in private, America's ex-presidents could diagnose the problems with their burgeoning genre; each of them vowed to write a better book, a book that wouldn't worry about settling scores or history's final verdict, a book that would humbly capture their point of view. Then they all wrote the same stale autobiography, justifying their actions and ahem-ing their future historians, in part through the threat of being crushed by the published volume's heft. To write his two-volume memoirs, Eisenhower commandeered an old brick house in Gettysburg, Pennsylvania, where he read research digests prepared by his staff, then dictated according to their outlines. The process lacked Truman's devotion to history, and the author lacked Truman's pungent style. While Eisenhower's editors and aides also diagnosed the book's problems, no one wanted to challenge an ex-president. At the end, everyone sat around a long table, briskly reviewing the proofs.

"I suppose I'm going to have to go along with these split infinitives," Eisenhower said.

"They're your split infinitives," an editor said.

"Let's get some of them out of here," the author replied, reaching for his pencil.

Eisenhower's first volume appeared in the fall of 1963, two weeks before John F. Kennedy's assassination. The book was widely discussed, including at the White House, where Kennedy chuckled at its self-righteous tone. "Apparently he never did anything wrong," the president told an aide. "When we come to writing the memoirs of this administration, we'll do it differently."

Kennedy never got the chance, but his successor, Lyndon B. Johnson, also pledged a "personal" book. Johnson used a similar setup to Eisenhower's, with staffers sifting files and creating outlines, then letting him dictate while a reel-to-reel recorder whirled. "President Johnson was at his best, his hill-country best," recalled Harry Middleton, one of the ghosts. Johnson would pace around the office, sharing blunt stories and barbed appraisals of his contemporaries, sometimes with impressions, always in his profane style. The writers squeezed as much of that as possible into the early chapters, only to have Johnson reject them. His real criterion, it turned out, wasn't "personal" but another word, ominous and ill defined: *presidential*. Once the writers cut everything Johnson deemed unworthy of his former office, they were left with the usual mash of names, schedule summaries, and self-defenses. "I got used to that," Middleton said, "doing the chapter over, eliminating the folksy stuff. Later on, I didn't even try to include it."

After Watergate, Richard Nixon's memoirs drew more interest than any legacy book thus far. The media scrapped over scoops. There was the advance: $2.5 million, or more than $13 million in today's dollars. The length: just under twelve hundred pages. The title: *RN*. Inside his San Clemente compound, Nixon dictated well over a million words, nearly as many as Truman. "We just started from the birth," said Ken Khachigian, one of the ghosts, "and went to resignation." That left Watergate for last, and staffers created a detailed chart tracking the timeline, the personalities, and the major events—"the key to *Finnegans Wake*," one of them cracked. Even the chart couldn't inspire Nixon to full transparency, and when his book appeared in the spring of 1978, it drew numerous protests. A group of Washington twenty-somethings, led by Tom Flanigan, founded the Committee to Boycott Nixon's Memoirs, selling bumper stickers and pale blue shirts featuring the slogan "Don't Buy Books by Crooks." It felt like one last howl from the counterculture, and the group dissented on *Good Morning America* and *Saturday Night Live*. But in truth, even they were looking to cash in. "From the very beginning," Flanigan later admitted, "we were trying to make money off it."

There was a lot of money to be made in the 1970s and 1980s. Hollywood was rolling out record-breaking movies like *Jaws*, a $470 million blockbuster that didn't drift from the cities out to the suburbs but opened everywhere, all at once. TV and its three networks loomed larger than ever, now in color. (One key to the *Jaws* opening was the ads that ran during *The Waltons* and *Sanford and Son*.) American culture was becoming nationalized in ways a *McClure's* reader would have never imagined, and these changes were finally hitting the book trade with similar speed and scale. *Jaws*, after all, began as a book.

Its author, Peter Benchley, had done a stint as a speechwriter in Johnson's White House. ("This is the worst thing I ever read," the president once told him, "all these chicken shit writers giving me names I can't pronounce.") Now, years later, Benchley got a modest advance for his novel; he made his real money when the publisher sold the paperback rights to another house. Even celebrity authors abided by this fragmentary and underfunded process, including Truman, who had his hybrid deal with Doubleday and *Life*, and Eisenhower, who, in addition to his book, sold a separate interview series to CBS—what the network's chief would eventually style as selling one's "electronic memoirs."

That all changed with blockbuster publishing. It started with a spate of mergers. In 1965, for instance, G. P. Putnam's Sons acquired a paperback publisher, Berkley Books; a decade later, MCA, Inc., a synergistic behemoth with holdings in movies and music, acquired Putnam's itself. Suddenly Putnam's, a house that had once relied on Theodore Roosevelt as an eccentric investor, was part of a rigid, rationalized conglomerate. At an editorial meeting, an executive made the new agenda clear: "The emphasis will be on entertainment." In 1975, Putnam's pulled in $23 million in revenue; by 1989, it was closing in on $200 million per year.

This consolidation was occurring all over publishing, and soon the

Orders for 1-6 dozen t-shirts can be filled at the convention.

WHOLESALE PRICE LIST
Effective May 25, 1978

Bumper Stickers

1-2 doz.	$ .65 ea.
3-6 doz.	$ .55 ea.
6-12 doz.	$ .45 ea.
12-100 doz.	$ .35 ea.
over 100 doz.	inquire

Heat Transfers (Decals)

1-2 doz.	$1.00 ea.
3-6 doz.	$ .85 ea.
6-12 doz.	$ .65 ea.
12-100 doz.	$ .45 ea.
over 100 doz.	inquire

T-Shirts

1-2 doz.	$3.75 ea.
3-6 doz.	$3.25 ea.
6-12 doz.	$3.00 ea.
12-100 doz.	$2.75 ea.
over 100 doz.	inquire

Posters

1-2 doz.	$1.00 ea.
3-6 doz.	$ .85 ea.
6-12 doz.	$ .65 ea.
12-100 doz.	$ .45 ea.
over 100 doz.	inquire

Buttons

1-2 doz.	$ .60 ea.
3-6 doz.	$ .55 ea.
6-12 doz.	$ .50 ea.
12-100 doz.	$ .45 ea.
over 100 doz.	inquire

BUMPER STICKERS

THE BOOK STOPS HERE — A

BOYCOTT Nixon's memoirs — B

ERASE the memoirs — C

DON'T BUY books by crooks — D

For immediate orders, call (800) 336-4645.

Shipment guaranteed in 4 to 10 calendar days.

All orders shipped U.P.S., C.O.D., unless otherwise specified, certified check or money order.

For other items, i.e. bookbags, backpacks and custom shirts, please inquire.

The Committee to Boycott Nixon's Memoirs
P.O. Box 57300, Washington, D.C. 20037

The Committee to Boycott Nixon's Memoirs sold stickers, buttons, and other merchandise; Dan Aykroyd brandished one of the group's T-shirts during an episode of *Saturday Night Live*.

Jimmy Carter wrote *Keeping Faith* on a Lanier word processor that he leased; the machine retailed for close to $12,000.

To promote *Surviving at the Top*, his sequel to *The Art of the Deal*, Donald Trump attended a book signing at a Waldenbooks.

companies left standing were involved with the hardcover, the mass-market paperback, the trade paperback—even the TV or movie rights if they had a parent company like MCA, Inc. Bookselling was consolidating at the same time. Waldenbooks and B. Dalton, two chains that had launched in the 1960s, were flourishing as the trade's dominant retailers. They built their stores where America was growing, in suburban malls and shopping centers, and arranged them to welcome casual readers: wide aisles, standardized layouts, bright and bold signs. For better or worse, the chains made buying a book feel like buying a sweater or a VHS tape, and that applied behind the scenes as well, where their corporate offices used computers to track inventory and project sales.* By 1981, there were more than seven hundred Waldenbooks stores and more than five hundred B. Daltons, with both chains adding fifty or more locations per year.

The chain stores, which typically stocked eight or ten thousand titles, boosted all sorts of books. In 1989, literary works like Amy Tan's *Joy Luck Club* and John Irving's *Prayer for Owen Meany* each sold more than 200,000 hardcovers—sold more copies, in other words, than *Jaws* had sold in 1974, when it finished as that year's third biggest novel. Still, the most significant shift came at the top. The best-selling novel in 1989, Tom Clancy's *Clear and Present Danger*, moved 1.6 million hardcovers.

Consolidated publishers and consolidated bookstores both needed blockbusters—needed "big books," or books designed for bigness before anything else. "This is a business of self-fulfilling prophecies," said Mort Janklow, an agent who specialized in blockbuster clients like David McCullough and Danielle Steel. The houses now had more money for advances; they also had owners demanding fatter profit margins and predictable growth. The chains depended on volume, which they achieved by discounting best sellers by as much as 50 percent. In fiction, the big books came from big novelists, a lucrative club of automatic million sellers that was nearly impossible to crack. Clancy achieved it through a pres-

---

*Computers made it easier not only to sell books but to write books. By 1984, the American Association of Publishers estimated that perhaps half of all authors were using word processors or personal computers. Blockbuster writers seemed particularly passionate about their devices, including Michael Crichton, Stephen King—and Jimmy Carter. When he left the White House in 1981, Carter promised "a highly personal book," then wrote a legacy book with the standard flaws. His innovation was being the first president to write his memoirs on a word processor, a bulky Lanier with a cathode ray monitor and magnetic disks that could save thirty pages of typed text. "It's much easier to compose on," Carter told a reporter. "You can . . . add words or sentences, delete sections or move paragraphs around."

idential endorsement. One day in 1984, Reagan's staffers noticed that he seemed tired. "I was up until four o'clock," the president said, "reading this book." It was *The Hunt for Red October*, and when *Time* mentioned Reagan's fondness, the novel quickly crashed the *New York Times* best-seller list—and, more important, secured Clancy one of those perpetual slots as a top-ten novelist.

In nonfiction, the big books came from celebrities. Once Iacocca's autobiography hit—"the fastest-selling hardcover ever," *Publishers Weekly* purred in 1985—the book trade pursued stars more aggressively than ever. Some of them offered a good story, and all of them offered a massive platform to promote their books. Publishers signed up Roseanne Barr, Michael Jackson, Jim McMahon, and many, many more. As one publicist put it, "We all want the next Iacocca."

The houses wanted this so literally that they handed book deals to all sorts of businessmen, including a New York developer named Donald Trump. Before meeting with Trump, Peter Osnos, then an editor at Random House, took a Russian novel off his shelf and had the art director wrap it in black paper. Across the front, they added "TRUMP" in shiny gold letters. "Trump was very pleased," Osnos recalled, to the point that the developer didn't even try to negotiate better terms. He accepted a six-figure advance and split it with a ghostwriter who did most of the work, though Trump gave him fabulous access. When he reviewed the final text, Trump made only a few changes. One was to cut a jab at Lee Iacocca.

Political memoirs fit blockbuster publishing as snugly as a Stephen King novel. While the genre had thrived since the Wilson administration, its authors had observed certain rules of decorum and delay. Most titles resembled Ted Sorensen's reverential *Kennedy*. When Emmet John Hughes, a speechwriter for Eisenhower, wrote his critical *The Ordeal of Power*, he didn't publish it until seven years after he'd left the administration—and his timing still created controversy.

The 1980s shattered these standards. Political books became a trendy product line, just like magnate memoirs after Iacocca. Trump's editor, Osnos, received a directive straight from the company that owned Random House: "Stop losing all these big name political books." So Osnos entered the next auction and bought the memoirs of Speaker of the House Tip O'Neill for a million dollars.

The richest deals went to anyone exiting the Reagan administration. David Stockman, for instance, got a $2.4 million advance. A few years before, he might have gotten $50,000 or $100,000. But political books, especially ones in the kiss-and-tell tradition, were different now—faster, newsier, more searing and superficial. Reagan's family and staff combined to produce more than twenty major memoirs; one of them, Alexander Haig's *Caveat,* appeared so quickly it actually beat titles from Carter's cabinet members to the stores. "This outpouring of books," Frances FitzGerald observed in the *New Yorker,* "is extraordinary."

Each of these Reagan authors came with a platform, even if it mostly depended on their proximity to the president. They, and their publishers, knew something else drove sales: a combustible piece of news. Don Regan, a former chief of staff, sold his book for a million dollars. He might have gotten more if his brief proposal had mentioned Nancy Reagan's consultations with an astrologer, which she used to determine, say, the best times for Reagan to meet with foreign leaders. To placate the first lady, Regan had kept a color-coded schedule: green for good days, red for bad ones.

Once Regan and his ghostwriter finished the first few chapters, they asked their editor, Daphne Merkin, to come to Washington to read them.

"So," Regan said, "what do you think?"

"My god," Merkin replied, "this country is run by colored magic markers."

Merkin hurried back to New York to share this "amazing detail" with her bosses. Everyone agreed to speed up the book's production, and once the astrology tidbit leaked, Regan's memoir became the biggest story in the country. The coverage grew so frenzied that Lynn Goldberg, Regan's publicist, would call up television bookers and say simply: "Regan—yea or nay?"

The Reagan books kept coming, though no one in Washington or New York seemed too concerned about their contents, outside of that one amazing detail. Political authors and blockbuster publishers brought out the worst in each other. Soon after Reagan left the White House in 1989, former Attorney General Edwin Meese sold his memoirs for a Trump-sized advance. Meese had worked with Reagan since his time as governor, and his publisher, Henry Holt & Company, had big plans for the book. At that year's American Booksellers Association convention, an event that would later be renamed BookExpo, Holt feted its author with a cocktail party; Meese made the usual promises about a detailed diary, a thousand pages of progress, about really getting "in the swing of it now." The publisher's fall catalogue featured *Witness to History,* a "behind-the-scenes account of what's *really* been going on in the executive branch."

Meese missed his first deadline, then another after that. Finally, in the spring of 1990, Holt canceled the contract. "Nothing was ever delivered," an editor admitted. He was talking about *Witness to History*, but that comment applied to plenty of blockbuster books.

JAWS: A MEMOIR

Between Nixon's resignation in 1974 and his own defeat in 1976, Gerald Ford didn't get much time to shape the presidency. He saved his real influence for the ex-presidency. Once he departed the White House, Ford quickly became a board member (or well-paid consultant) at more than a dozen companies. He signed a fat contract with NBC and started doing private speeches at fifteen thousand dollars a pop, all while pulling in pensions as both ex-president and ex-congressman. In only a couple of years, Ford was worth millions—a feat he hadn't exactly attained through popularity. Ford's memoirs had generated so little interest that he ended up doing a joint deal with his wife, Betty, where they got another million for both of their books. On Ford's birthday, Betty gave him a T-shirt that read, "I bet my book outsells yours." It was one of those jokes that contained some truth. Selling seemed to be the only thing on Gerald Ford's mind.

When Reagan became an ex-president, he embraced the same options, though his 63 percent Gallup approval rating ensured him fifty thousand dollars per speech. But in 1989 there was now another possibility—the newly supercharged publishing industry. The Reagans signed with Mort Janklow, a star agent. "They came to me," Janklow said. He sold Nancy's memoir to Peter Osnos and Random House for around $2 million.* He sold Ron's to Simon & Schuster, which was now owned by Paramount Communications, for around $7 million, or more than $14 million in today's dollars. Reagan's book went to Michael Korda, a star editor. ("No one," a rival said, "is better attuned to what Americans will want to read.") Truman had written the first modern presidential memoir; now Reagan would write the first blockbuster one.

He would, of course, have help. While Reagan and Richard Hubler had talked several times about doing more books together, Hubler died in 1981. Simon & Schuster nominated a new ghost, Robert Lindsey, a respected and bespectacled journalist who'd once flown on Reagan's campaign plane. In the spring of 1989, Janklow took Lindsey to the Reagans'

---

*The resulting book, which they titled *My Turn*, picked so many fights with former staffers like Don Regan that it earned the nickname *My Burn*.

home—not the "Home of the Future," which they'd sold after relocating
to the White House, but a new and more opulent residence in Bel Air.
After they were greeted by a uniformed maid, and by the Secret Service,
Janklow and Lindsey walked in. Off to the side, Lindsey saw someone in a
green leprechaun hat, dancing a vigorous jig. It was St. Patrick's Day, and
it was Ronald Reagan.

Lindsey and Reagan agreed to collaborate, with most of the work taking place in Reagan's new penthouse office in the Fox Plaza building, the
skyscraper Bruce Willis had recently defended in *Die Hard*. Korda sent
along some notes before they started. (Emulate Grant's prose; emphasize
the log cabin beginnings.) In a memo, the editor even proposed an opening focused on Reagan's first thoughts as ex-president: "what goes through
his mind as he flies back across the country," the memo read, "passing
over this vast country, thinking about . . . what he has achieved in these
past eight years."

Other than that, the ghost was on his own. Since Lindsey lived in
Northern California, he flew to LA once a week and worked with Reagan
from Monday to Thursday, interviewing him each morning from ten until
noon. The rest of the time Lindsey labored alone, trying to turn Reagan's
answers into narrative. It was difficult. While the ex-president remained
charming and cheerful, even on days that did not involve St. Patrick, he
didn't seem invested in his book. Around the office, Reagan referred to
the project as "the monkey on my back." He couldn't remember details he
should have; he would repeat the same stories three or four times. With
Korda's memo in mind, Lindsey asked Reagan again and again about his
plane ride home but got nothing. At some point—perhaps before the
White House; certainly in it—Reagan appeared to have lost his instinct to
read and think deeply.

By the end of his third or fourth trip, Lindsey was starting to fret. "I'm
trying to write the memoirs of a guy who doesn't have much of a memory,"
he told his wife. Things got worse the closer they got to the presidency.
While Reagan had kept a diary in the White House, he refused to analyze
his decisions after the fact. Lindsey could have supplemented by studying
Reagan's papers, but that was hard to pull off as a one-man operation. Reagan's staffers didn't seem very invested in the book either, which forced
Lindsey to go to an off-site warehouse himself, where he requested a handful of specific letters but never mounted any kind of systematic review.

Given the Alzheimer's diagnosis Reagan would receive a few years later,
it's fair to wonder whether his cognitive health contributed to his apathy.

(Both Korda and Janklow reject this idea.) Whatever the reason, Reagan simply didn't care about his book. One theme that ran through his administration's kiss-and-tell corpus was Reagan's detachment from the day-to-day White House—"circling his own presidency like a lost satellite," as the novelist Don DeLillo once put it. Now he was circling his legacy book.

Lindsey kept going, and by October, he'd largely completed his interviews with Reagan. That same month, the ex-president took a well-publicized trip to Japan—well publicized because he received $2 million to deliver a couple of speeches. The backlash to that trip, along with the persistence of Iran-Contra and other scandals, eroded Reagan's approval rating. While Nancy had long obsessed over her husband's reputation, she grew even more protective. "It was a pain for me," Lindsey remembered, "and for Reagan." Once the ghost finished the draft, he spent five days reviewing it with Ron, Nancy, and a handful of aides. Nancy demanded the most cuts, usually motivated by her vision of Reagan as a great statesman. That vision also explained why she didn't want Lindsey's name on the cover of the book. "A shared writing credit," Korda said, "was not presidential."

In the spring of 1990, Korda came to California for his own review. It was the first time he'd interacted with Reagan since the initial deal. Korda had remained remarkably hands-off with his $7 million asset. He hadn't even bothered to read *Where's the Rest of Me?* "All Simon & Schuster wanted to know," recalled Mark Weinberg, a longtime aide to Reagan, "was, 'What's the news?'"

On Korda's first morning in LA, he and Lindsey sat down with Reagan at his office—only to find the ex-president had scheduled a golf date at noon. Reagan suggested they tackle the book's major problems together, with Korda handling the rest by himself. They decided on the title, *An American Life*. They decided that Reagan did need to mention his first wife, Jane Wyman. (Reagan's reluctance, the editor sensed, was Nancy's.) That left the book's opening, and there Reagan finally offered a suggestion of his own: swapping the plane ride for the Geneva Summit, where he'd met with the Soviet Union's Mikhail Gorbachev. Reagan began recounting the story of how he and Gorbachev sat down by themselves, like two grandfathers, and talked. By the time he finished, there were tears in his eyes. Korda loved the idea, though he wondered to a staffer how such a meeting took place without interpreters and security. "They weren't alone," came the reply. "That's just the way the president likes to remember it."

With the addition of a few more people, Reagan's Geneva Summit story did become his book's opening passage:

Nancy and I awoke early on the morning of November 19, 1985, and, at the first glimmer of daylight, we looked out from our bedroom at the long gray expanse of Lake Geneva. There were patches of snow along the edge of the lake and in the gardens of the magnificent lakeside eighteenth-century residence that had been loaned to us for a few days. In the distance we could see the majestic high peaks of the Alps.

The lake was shrouded in mist that gave its rippled surface the look of burnished pewter. Above, the sky was a dull curtain of dark clouds.

It was a dreary, yet strikingly beautiful panorama.

I had looked forward to this day for more than five years. For weeks, I'd been given detailed information about political currents in the Soviet Union, the complexities of nuclear arms control, and the new man in the Kremlin. In my diary the night before, I wrote: "Lord, I hope I'm ready."

This time, there was no bottom close-up. In its place were clichés, contrived tension, description for description's sake—pure blockbuster prose. Worse than the style, though, was the stilted self-presentation. Reagan went on to describe how poorly he slept, and his unedited diary entry offers a hint as to why: "Lord, I hope I'm ready and not over-trained." Here was something interesting—a sitting president anxious not only about an enormous international test, but also about being overprepared, about getting too much advice from too many directions. And yet in his legacy book, Reagan elided this concern, blaming his insomnia instead on "jet lag."

When *An American Life* came out in the fall of 1990, it received a blockbuster rollout. Reagan made an unprecedented five straight appearances on *Good Morning America*, in addition to doing TV interviews with William F. Buckley, Larry King, and more. One of Reagan's first appearances was a pretaped conversation with Barbara Walters and *20/20*, and Nancy did everything she could to prepare him. "The interview with Barbara is in a few days," she told Weinberg, the aide. "You have to make sure he sees the book before it." When Weinberg tried to hand Reagan a finished copy, he found him to be strangely and grumpily resistant. Reagan did not want to spend time reviewing his book. After several attempts, Weinberg finally held the copy up to its irritated author.

"Mr. President, do you *see* this book?" he asked.

Reagan nodded.

"So if anyone in Bel Air asks if you've seen the book, you can say yes?" Reagan smiled and said yes.

Much of the promotion for *An American Life* felt similarly detached. Waldenbooks advertised the book aggressively, discounting it at 25 percent off, just like the latest from Stephen King. But executives at Simon & Schuster had to pressure Reagan to do those TV interviews. There was nothing they could do to convince him to go on a book tour—not after the Japan controversy, not when a long line of autograph seekers struck the Reagans as tacky. "Both Ron and Nancy," Korda remembered, "did not want to be seen as selling a book." Reagan did approve one event, a rally in Dixon, Illinois. On that trip, he visited his childhood home, skipped rocks at the spot where he'd once been a lifeguard, and spoke to thousands of supporters inside a local gym. It was at a new high school; the old one, where Reagan had pursued his first experiments as a precocious writer, had been torn down a long time ago.

In the twentieth century, many presidential memoirs have lost money for their publishers, including Eisenhower's, Johnson's, and Ford's. Most of the Reagan era's kiss-and-tell books flopped too. *An American Life* also lost money, though not as much as people would later claim. Nixon's *RN* had sold 262,000 hardcovers in its first eight months; *An American Life* sold around 400,000 hardcovers in its first two months. In the age of the blockbuster, this was what failure looked like: the best-selling presidential memoir of all time.

And yet Reagan's book did fail. There were plenty of reasons for that, none of them as simple as jet lag, but the best way to see them is to compare his second book to his first. The difference between *Where's the Rest of Me?* and *An American Life* is the difference between good ghostwriting and bad ghostwriting. It's the difference between an author exerting himself and an author surrendering to the indifferent momentum of blockbuster publishing. It's the difference between writing a book before you're president and writing a book after.

CHAPTER THIRTEEN

The Literary Candidate

Josh Kalven loved walking through Hyde Park—across the University of Chicago's campus, past his university-affiliated high school, and along the Lake Michigan shore. Those strolls guaranteed him some teenage freedom; they also got him to his part-time job at 57th Street Books, an independent bookstore that belonged to the neighborhood's Seminary Co-op.

One day in the spring of 1996, Kalven walked past a yard sign on Lake Park Avenue. It was odd that he noticed it; most teenagers tune out bids for the state senate. It was even odder that he recognized the name. Where had he seen that name, Obama? *Oh yeah*, Kalven remembered, *that guy's a member at the bookstore.*

Barack Obama first joined the Co-op in 1986, and for many years he would duck into 57th Street's basement location, wearing a leather jacket in the winter and shirtsleeves rolled up in the summer, browsing quietly while the shop echoed with the sounds of the apartment dwellers above. Obama often came at night, just before closing, circling the new releases table in the front, studying the staff selections along the back, and usually leaving with a small stack of novels and nonfiction. At the counter, he would spell his name to get the member discount—a treasured and anonymous ritual unless your name was strange enough, and your visits frequent enough, that a clerk might remember you.

Obama's anonymity ended for good in 2004, when he gave his iconic keynote at the Democratic National Convention. During his rise from state senator to US senator to president, one of the most obvious things about him was that he was literary. His two books, *Dreams from My Father* and *The Audacity of Hope*, combined to sell more than 6 million copies, making them the most successful campaign books of the twenty-first century. Obama nabbed endorsements from highbrow authors like Philip Roth and Toni Morrison. The narrative of his life, told in his books and best speeches, often felt like the key to his appeal. "We're not running against a real person," one of Hillary Clinton's staffers complained in 2008. "We are running against a story."

That was true enough, especially since Obama himself frequently appealed to the idea of stories. But it also misses something important. Obama was not just literary in the sense of crafting his policy speeches or campaign books. He was literary in the sense of reading fiction—of *needing* fiction, with its prickly characters, its poetic language, its self-conscious complexity, and its cautious pace. Obama's presidency spanned a period when American culture became less bookish. (In 1992, the year Bill Clinton was elected, 54 percent of adults claimed they'd read a work of literature in the previous twelve months; by 2015, near the end of Obama's second term, that number had fallen to 43 percent.) It spanned a period when publishing became even hungrier for blockbusters, as houses got bought by international conglomerates while Waldenbooks gave way to Barnes & Noble, Costco, and Amazon.

Barack Obama stood apart from these trends and from the presidents who came before him. Grant enjoyed novels; Wilson devoured detective stories. But Obama read more fiction than any previous president, and that reading shaped his mind, his books—even, in the end, his politics.

"THE FICTIVE IMAGINATION"

Confident and *smooth*—those were the words to describe Obama while he was running for president. Even his biography seemed confident and smooth. "My father was from Kenya," he would say in his mild midwestern accent, "which is where I got the name. . . . My mother was from Kansas, which is why I talk the way I do." Obama believed his background could point toward a less cynical, less divided future. As he put it in his keynote speech, "I stand here knowing my story is part of the larger American story." Residents of red states and blue states could work together if they opened themselves to hard work and hope—"the hope," he continued, "of a skinny kid with a funny name who believes that America has a place for him, too."

This persona, however, was a creation, a character, the result of the years Obama spent writing (and failing to write) *Dreams from My Father*. "Writing a book," he later said, "forced me to be honest about myself, about where I had been. . . . It was good training for the kind of politics I try to practice now." Even when that book seemed destined to be a respectable but forgotten flop—and that was its fate for nearly a decade—

Dreams mattered as an act of self-discovery. Obama-the-writer came before Obama-the-candidate because he had to.

Barack Obama was born in 1961, in the recently formed state of Hawaii. His childhood was marked by displacement. His mother, Ann Dunham, was a bright and passionate bookworm; she met his father, a talented exchange student named Barack, in a class at the University of Hawaii. While Obama was still a baby, his father left the island; his mother moved him to Indonesia while he was still a child. At ten, Obama returned to Hawaii by himself, where he lived with his maternal grandparents while attending an elite prep school. During each of these changes, changes he rarely controlled, Obama relied on books—starting with Dr. Seuss, graduating to Spider-Man and science fiction, ending in high school with the novels of James Baldwin and Ralph Ellison. "I loved reading," he would later say. "The idea of having these worlds that were portable, that were yours, that you could enter into, was appealing to me."

In 1979, Obama headed to Occidental College, a liberal arts school in Los Angeles. Like many of his era's bookish undergrads, he encountered two approaches to literature: reading for empathy and reading for ideology. Another way to define this divide was reading like a novelist and reading like an English professor. Toni Morrison had offered a good example of the first approach only two years earlier, in an interview about her new novel, *Song of Solomon*, which was also her first novel to feature men as major characters. Morrison described how hard she'd worked to enter the minds of those men—"to become that intimate with a character," she said, "to try to feel what it was really like."

This act of imagination—in creating characters and, increasingly, in reading someone else's characters, in entering their minds a second time and empathizing with their point of view—had become central to the teaching of creative writing. At Occidental, Obama sought out that literary crowd. "There was a strong circle of supportive but competitive writers," recalled Tom Grauman, a classmate of Obama. "Basically, we all wanted to be in Paris between the wars." Instead they found themselves in The Cooler, the campus's cinderblock diner, where they talked earnestly about their writing and reading. Obama enrolled in a seminar where he workshopped poems; he submitted two of them to *Feast*, an ambitious campus magazine that Grauman and others had launched. The whole time, Obama continued to read on his own. The book that shaped him the most, he later said, was *Song of Solomon*.

In The Cooler, Obama, Grauman, and their friends also talked about the intersection of literature and politics. Obama got even more of that after he transferred to Columbia University in 1981. He remained a committed student. "Hey," a roommate would ask, "what did you do today?" Obama's answers were so monotonous—reading, writing, maybe a run—that eventually the roommate quit asking. While Obama had decided to major in political science, his English electives hit similar themes: a lecture with Edward Said that analyzed fiction through a postcolonial lens, a seminar with Lennard Davis that looked at the ideologies embedded in Dickens and Defoe. This form of reading also resonated with Obama. "I recommend *Marxism and Literature* by Raymond Williams," he wrote to a friend during his senior year. "It generally has a pretty good aim at some Marxist applications of cultural study."

And yet in the end, Obama sided not with the English professors but with the novelists. Consider a passage from early in *Dreams*, where Obama chatted with two black classmates at Occidental, one of whom, Marcus, condemned the "racist tract" Obama was carrying, Joseph Conrad's *Heart of Darkness*:

Regina smiled and shook her head as we watched Marcus stride out the door. "Marcus is in one of his preaching moods, I see."

I tossed the book into my backpack. "Actually, he's right," I said. "It is a racist book. The way Conrad sees it, Africa's the cesspool of the world, black folks are savages, and any contact with them breeds infection."

Regina blew on her coffee. "So why are you reading it?"

"Because it's assigned." I paused, not sure if I should go on. "And because—"

"Because . . ."

"And because the book teaches me things," I said. "About white people, I mean. See, the book's not really about Africa. Or black people. It's about the man who wrote it. The European. The American. A particular way of looking at the world. If you can keep your distance, it's all there, in what's said and what's left unsaid. So I read the book to help me understand just what it is that makes white people so afraid. Their demons. The way ideas get twisted around. It helps me understand how people learn to hate."

Obama's classmate, Marcus, was echoing Chinua Achebe, who a few years earlier had described Conrad and his book as "bloody racist." At

Obama joined Chicago's Seminary Co-op in 1986 and frequently shopped
at its 57th Street Books location, pictured here.

first Obama seemed to agree—or, at the very least, to strain for some
kind of consensus between the empathy and ideology sects. Ultimately,
though, he chose to focus less on politics than on people. Obama read fiction because he wanted to experience psychological interiority—in Conrad's characters, in Conrad's readers, in Conrad himself—and because he
had faith in his ability to interpret it.*

After graduation, Obama felt torn between several possible futures,
including one that was vaguely literary, in which he would try to write
fiction, and one that was vaguely political, in which, drawing from a different strain of his reading, on the history of civil rights, he would try to
make a difference. By 1985, politics seemed to be winning. Obama applied
for a job as a community organizer in Chicago, and when he interviewed

*For Obama, and for many other literary readers, interpretation never really stops. One
example of his future intellectual celebrity was the excitement that greeted each title he
cited in an interview or slipped on a vacation reading list; when President Obama mentioned Richard Price's *Lush Life*, the novel's sales doubled. During his second term, Obama
dropped by Politics and Prose, the celebrated Washington, DC, bookstore, and purchased
a large stack of books. His daughters, now teenagers themselves, went with him, and one
book the family chose was the same title Obama had grappled with in college: *Heart of
Darkness*.

with his prospective boss, Jerry Kellman, he emphasized his idealism and his desire to help black communities. And yet, once Obama got the job and moved to Chicago's South Side, he and Kellman had a second conversation, this one while walking along the shore of Lake Michigan. "He talked about having a deep interest in writing fiction," Kellman recalled. "He hadn't decided whether he wanted to pursue it."

Over the next few years, Obama worked hard at organizing, meeting with local residents and building support for issues like asbestos removal. He also continued to write. Sometimes he wrote journal entries that recorded overheard dialogue and vivid city scenes. Sometimes he wrote fiction, eventually finishing several stories he shared with friends from Occidental and Columbia and with his fellow organizers. "Take a look at this," he said to Kellman, a bit embarrassed, before handing him a draft about a storefront preacher. The stories showed promise, particularly in the relationships between their characters. "Write outside your own experience," Obama urged another friend in a letter, though only after he urged him to cut back on the adverbs. "Write a story about your Grandmother in Armenia, or your sister in college; I find that this works the fictive imagination harder."

In 1988 Obama enrolled at Harvard Law School. He wanted a more practical way to make a difference, though he kept writing as well. In fact, he and a classmate, Rob Fisher, began working on an academic manuscript, *Promises of Democracy: Hopeful Critiques of American Ideology.* The coauthors completed more than two hundred pages, even as Obama was winning an internship at Sidley Austin, one of Chicago's best firms; there he met and started dating a lawyer named Michelle Robinson. In 1990, the *Harvard Law Review* elected Obama as its new president, making him the first African American to hold that spot. The choice was covered by the *New York Times* and the *Chicago Tribune*, among many other outlets, with each story hitting the same Obama beats: his historic first, his unusual biography, and his political ambitions. "Down the road," the *Los Angeles Times* noted, "he plans to run for public office."

When Jane Dystel saw those stories, she decided to give Obama a call. Dystel was a fiery literary agent who'd spent a year in law school herself, and she promised Obama there was a book in all this buzz. Obama admitted he'd considered writing a novel, though never nonfiction, and he came to Manhattan to discuss it further. "We both said," Dystel later recalled, "it should be a memoir."

That genre was thriving in the 1980s and early 1990s, led by new

classics like Maxine Hong Kingston's *The Woman Warrior*. Kingston
applied the novelist's tools of character and empathy to her actual life. She
depicted real people and real events but did so by reconstructing dialogue
and rehearsing family lore—all with the aim of capturing what it felt like
to be a daughter, to be confused, to be simultaneously Chinese and American. This kind of narrative, which aspired to emotional as much as documentary truth, was emerging as a vibrant presence in bookstores, literary
journals, and creative writing workshops, where memoir taught as easily
as minimalism. "Our usual idea of biography is of time-lines, of dates and
chronological events," Kingston explained to an interviewer. "I am certainly more imaginative than that; I play with words and form."

Dystel helped Obama craft a proposal for the memoir they were calling *Journeys in Black and White*. In the proposal, Obama listed his literary
models, including *The Woman Warrior*. "Such works take on the narrative force of fiction," Obama wrote, "and invite the reader to share in the
hopes, dreams, disappointments and triumphs of individual characters,
thereby soliciting a sense of empathy and universality that is absent in too
many works on race in America."

In the fall of 1990, Dystel shopped Obama's proposal to a number of
publishers before selling it at an auction to Poseidon Press, an imprint of
Simon & Schuster, for around $125,000. Obama's contract called for an
initial payment of $40,000, with another coming when he turned it in and
a third when Poseidon published it; the due date was June 15, 1992.

This outcome thrilled Obama, and once he returned to Chicago, he
talked excitedly about the book deal, about being done with law school
and having a way to pay down some of his student loans. He was twenty-
nine years old, and for the first time in a while, his literary side seemed to
have a shot at winning.

The writing proved difficult, which left the author eager for distraction. He spent more and more time with Michelle Robinson. To Poseidon's irritation, he agreed to run a voter registration drive during the 1992
election—what was in many ways a campaign in miniature. "Do you want
to write this memoir," someone from the drive asked, "or rescue democracy?" Obama, as usual, wanted to do both. While meeting with activists
and voters, he carried a bag that held his handwritten drafts and the boxy
laptop he used to type and revise them. When Obama finally submitted
a long chunk of the book, it was months late. "The manuscript came in,"
recalled Ann Patty, then Poseidon's editorial director, "and it was not at all
Dreams from My Father."

On October 3, 1992, Barack and Michelle were married. On October 20, Poseidon canceled the contract. Part of the blame fell on blockbuster publishing, as Simon & Schuster appeared anxious to streamline its smaller expenses. (The next year, it folded Poseidon. "It was a simple case," a Paramount executive said, "of the numbers not adding up.") Part of the blame fell on Obama, who had blown not only his deadline but the structural balance of his book. While parts of it traced his life, drawing on his rich journals and letters, in too many places it sounded like that dense manuscript he'd abandoned at Harvard. Even Fisher, his old coauthor, agreed. "The best story here," he told Obama, "is you."

That was also the hardest story. One of the things Obama loved about writing was the way it forced him to clarify what he thought and felt about something. In this case, though, that meant clarifying his fractured identity—and the anger he harbored at his white family and his absent black father. He no longer had a publisher. (It was worse than that: he now owed Simon & Schuster forty thousand dollars.) But with Dystel's encouragement, he started a second major draft. Obama tried all sorts of tricks to focus, writing late at night, escaping to a cabin in Wisconsin, spending a few weeks at a cottage in Indonesia. He tried reading for inspiration.

One of the books he studied during this period was Kingston's *Woman Warrior*, and it shows. In its final form, *Dreams* was fully a literary memoir, built out of characters, epiphanies, and cinematic scenes. Obama was tough on himself, admitting to past drug use: "Pot had helped, and booze; maybe a little blow when you could afford it." He was tough on his family, using his grandparents' racial blind spots to demonstrate the realities white people often miss. Yet Obama also captured his grandparents' complexity—their struggles and sacrifices and love. In *Dreams*, their racism was only one of the things that made them human.

In the spring of 1993, Dystel called Henry Ferris, an editor at Times Books, an imprint of Random House. Once Ferris agreed to look at Obama's revised manuscript, it arrived by messenger service, an oversized box stuffed with hundreds of pages—and that was just the first two sections, on Hawaii and Chicago. "I was like, 'What am I taking on here?'" Ferris recalled. "But before I was at the bottom of the first page, I was convinced I had to buy the book."

Ferris went to his boss, Peter Osnos, and found him an easy sell. It helped that the book was a memoir; it helped that it was cheap. (Dystel, who'd already whiffed with other houses, asked for a flat forty thousand dollars, to pay off the Simon & Schuster debt.) Osnos wanted to meet

Obama, to determine whether he'd finish the book, and their encounter went well. "He had a clear vision for what he wanted the book to be," Osnos said.

Osnos approved the deal, which meant the same editor who signed *The Art of the Deal* also signed *Dreams from My Father*. Ferris showed Obama where to trim, and the author proved so responsive that the third, not-yet-written section, on a trip to Kenya, came in much tighter. Obama continued to collect distractions, including a full-time position at a Chicago law firm and a part-time gig at the University of Chicago. But he finished the book.

Dreams appeared in August 1995. On its publication day, Obama sent flowers to the offices of Times Books. He was proud of his book. A few weeks earlier, he'd dropped by 57th Street Books and asked if the store would host a reading. It was a bit odd, if only because such requests usually came from the publisher, but Jack Cella, the Co-op's longtime general manager, was happy to help a local author and loyal member. On the night of the reading, about thirty people showed up, most of them familiar faces from community organizing and the University of Chicago. When Obama introduced the book, he seemed slightly awkward, a little

In his office at the firm of Davis, Miner, Barnhill & Galland, Obama revised parts of *Dreams*, propping his feet on the desk and editing on his computer.

abstract. Once he started reading, though, he transformed. That night he gave a confident authorial performance, drawing out words, slipping into accents, and choosing the perfect pauses—a reminder that he mastered his style as a writer long before he mastered his style as an orator.

The memoir got good reviews, and Obama did a modest book tour beyond Chicago. Still, he sold only ten thousand or so hardcovers. Times Books failed to generate internal interest in a paperback, so it sold the rights to a smaller firm, Kodansha. Deborah Baker, then an editor at the house, asked Obama about his next project. "He mentioned he was torn between writing a novel or going into politics," Baker remembered. "I encouraged him to write a novel."

Politics won—finally, decisively—a few weeks after Obama's book tour ended, when he announced he was running for state senate. His campaign literature never cited the recently published *Dreams*, and while local journalists vetted the memoir, it mostly faded away, one more line on Obama's impressive résumé. At least it was easy to find, though that was only because Powell's Books, the independent that had started in Chicago before expanding to Portland, had purchased four thousand remaindered paperbacks.

Obama remained proud of his book. As a new state senator, he toured southern Illinois for the first time in 1997, a trip that would play a crucial role in his future ambitions since it convinced him he could connect with rural voters—with white people who reminded him of his grandparents. On that trip, Obama brought along copies of *Dreams*. "He would give one to someone he really connected with," said Dan Shomon, his aide at the time. It was an intimate gesture, not a political one.

It was an intimate book. While Obama had told many people about his desire to run for office, including the journalists who'd covered his rise at the *Harvard Law Review*, he worked far too obsessively on his manuscript and its revisions for it to be some sort of long-term political gambit. *Dreams* is not revealing because Obama wrote it before he had electoral ambitions. It's revealing because he wrote it *after* he had them—because even at that point, he couldn't help but write a book that was stubborn, poetic, confessional. Obama didn't do it for money. (As Ferris put it, "He essentially wrote *Dreams* for us for free.") He did it because books had always mattered to him and because writing this book helped him understand himself.

In that sense *Dreams* did produce a political benefit. Writing it helped Obama see that his life was itself a story—that his character could be emphasized and adjusted, could be shaped to seem radical and angry (reading *Heart of Darkness*, seeing "demons" in white people) and yet, by the end of that same chapter, could be shaped to seem unifying and hopeful (cataloguing the lessons he'd learned, including many "from my grandparents"). *Dreams* didn't just form Obama. It formed his rhetorical style. As he put it in 1995 during one of the few interviews he did for his book, "My family is an example—and hopefully I am an example—of the possibility of arriving at some common ground."

BLOCKBUSTER II: THE SEQUEL

A few years later, in the summer of 2001, Knopf announced that it had signed Bill Clinton to write his presidential memoirs. As usual, the book industry began gossiping about how much Knopf, the house of Morrison and Hofstadter, had spent. Was it ten million dollars? Twelve? Clinton's advance, it turned out, was fifteen million dollars, a new nonfiction record. The industry pivoted quickly to critique, predicting the deal would lose millions, just like the deals of Reagan and many of his kiss-and-tell foes. "Publishing books by famous politicians is an ego trip for publishers," Roger Straus told a reporter. He spoke from experience, given how badly he'd exposed Farrar, Straus and Young while publishing Truman's *Mr. President*.

Yet something was shifting in the 1990s and 2000s. America's publishers continued to thrive, bringing in $27 billion in 2004, the year Clinton's *My Life* finally came out. It was a cheerful figure, though adjustments for inflation and population showed that the industry's revenues had remained essentially flat since the 1980s. Where things had changed, once again, was at the top. The biggest books were bigger than ever, and that included political ones. Legacy books, campaign books, even legacy books masquerading as campaign books: they could all make money now—so much money, in fact, that sometimes it seemed as if that was their only reason to exist.

Publishers continued to consolidate during these decades. Consider a brief history of Clinton's Knopf, which can also serve as a brief history of the modern book trade. In 1960, the house founded by Alfred Knopf Sr. was sold to Random House; in 1965, Random House was sold to RCA, which eventually sold it to Advance Publications; in 1998, Random House and its Knopf-sized components were sold to the German conglomerate, Bertelsmann AG, at a price of more than a billion dollars.

That last transaction contained a certain irony, a global twist for an industry that had emerged in this country with Mathew and Henry Carey taking patriotic risks on American books. Still, most publishers ended up in Knopf's spot, as small pieces at one of a handful of multinational, multibillion-dollar corporations. Computerized printing and central-ized warehouses helped things move faster. Blockbuster publishing—star authors, trendy boomlets, predictable profits, ceaseless growth—intensified. In 1999, one editor watched two of his novelists win spots on Oprah Win-frey's televised book club, a fantastic bit of luck, twice. The editor felt no joy in this. "Now my bosses," he told a colleague, "are going to expect me to do better next year."

Bookselling followed a similar pattern: the same, but more. A chain like Waldenbooks yielded to a chain like Barnes & Noble and its so-called superstores, enormous, boxy buildings with wood paneling, comfy chairs, maybe a coffee shop, and ten times as many titles to choose from. At their peak, Barnes & Noble and its rival, Borders, combined for more than twelve hundred such locations.

The superstores had plenty of competition. Discount stores like Wal-mart and warehouse clubs like Sam's Club attempted to out-chain the chains, offering fewer titles with bigger discounts and faster turnover. While they focused on commercial fiction or celebrity memoirs, they carried the occasional serious surprise. Costco discovered a hit in David McCullough's *John Adams*, which at one point was selling ten thousand copies a week at that chain alone. "That one," said Pennie Ianniciello, Costco's book buyer, "went on and on."

Then there was Amazon, launched by Jeff Bezos in 1995. Bezos chose to devote his site to books not because he loved them but because there were so many titles to sell—and because, after centuries of frustration, the book trade had finally developed an efficient and centralized distribution system. The Sears catalogue had once claimed to be the country's "most complete book department"; now Amazon was boasting about being "Earth's biggest bookstore."

Almost immediately, Amazon began poaching sales from bookstores, especially independent bookstores, and not just the in-person variety. At Obama's beloved Seminary Co-op and 57th Street Books, two people stayed busy handling the orders and friendly questions that arrived by email. Then one Friday, one of them went to Jack Cella and said, "I think I'm going to leave early today. I don't have anything to do." Cella didn't believe it until he checked the numbers himself. The store's correspond-

Even on its early home pages, like this one from 1995, Amazon called itself "Earth's biggest bookstore."

ence had dropped dramatically, and its mail-order business, which had been closing in on $1 million per year, soon fell to half that.

The promise of Amazon, or of a Barnes & Noble that stocked 100,000 titles, was size. Soon a theory emerged—sometimes called the "long tail" or, as Bezos dubbed it in a BookExpo speech, "the hard middle"—that this surfeit of choice would help small artists and even medium artists find an audience, particularly online. The theory flopped for several reasons. One was that media companies and their partners realized it was more profitable to prioritize the most likely hits. (A superstore required a superlease, and best-seller foot traffic remained the easiest way to pay rent.) Another was that consumers seemed to prefer those hits, something one could track in iTunes charts and box office totals and *Publishers Weekly* sales figures. As Anita Elberse, a professor at Harvard Business School, put it, "Now you need to make bigger bets."

So that's what publishing did. In 1989, Tom Clancy's *Clear and Present Danger* had topped the charts with 1.6 million hardcovers; in 2004, Dan Brown's *The Da Vinci Code* sold 4.3 million hardcovers—and that was in its second year of publication, following a 5.7 million 2003. It wasn't always possible to predict a blockbuster. (Brown's first three novels had fizzled.) But once the book trade realized what it had, it responded with more speed and force than ever. With *The Da Vinci Code*, Brown's publisher, Doubleday, circulated ten thousand advance reader's editions—

more copies than any of his previous books had actually sold—and got him a dinner with key executives from Border's. The novel debuted at number one on the *New York Times* best-seller list, creating momentum that helped it excel in airports and Targets and independent bookstores.

This splashy, star-powered approach worked especially well with political titles. Colin Powell, former chairman of the Joint Chiefs of Staff, got $6 million to write his memoirs. He studied the autobiographies of Iacocca and Grant and worked diligently with his ghostwriter. But the thing that supercharged his sales—and turned his book into a huge moneymaker—was the buzzy rollout. When *My American Journey* appeared in 1995, Powell did TV interviews with Jay Leno and Larry King, among many others. His publisher scheduled a book tour so aggressive that Powell had to travel by private jet; at each stop, he encountered long lines of fans, held in place by temporary metal fencing, and clusters of friendly reporters. Again and again, the reporters asked whether Powell was planning a run for president, and plenty of people in line, waving their homemade "Powell '96" signs, hoped he'd say yes.

Powell's tour was not a happy coincidence, as Reagan's had been with *Where's the Rest of Me?* It was designed to work like this—to measure his appeal, to jam his name into the news, to boost his book sales and political prospects at the same time. While Powell ultimately chose not to run, he sold more than 1.5 million hardcovers, a number that caught the attention of publishers and politicians alike. Both camps were relying less on literary agents like Mort Janklow and more on a man named Robert Barnett, a Washington lawyer who wore vintage cuff links and charged hundreds of dollars per hour; he was also, in the words of Bob Woodward, "the last bargain in Washington." Barnett seemed to know everyone in politics, publishing, and the media, and he could help politicians auction their books, then coach and choreograph their publicity, often by reaching out to TV anchors he also represented. The best part, strangely enough, was that opulent hourly rate—a bargain only when compared to a literary agent's 15 percent cut of a multimillion-dollar deal.

Barnett sold legacy books and campaign books, Republican books and Democratic books, Dan Quayle's autobiography and Hillary Clinton's too. Another client was Bill Clinton. "When I was a young man," the ex-president once said, "one of the goals I had in life was to write a great book." He began planning his memoirs at the start of his first term, asking Taylor Branch, a Pulitzer-winning historian and personal friend, to visit the White House and interview him in secret. The two talked seventy-nine times over eight years, and once he left Washington, Clinton organized similar interviews with another historian, Edward Widmer, to dig into his early life.

Those transcripts formed the foundation of *My Life*, which Clinton wrote in longhand, filling more than twenty notebooks. Unfortunately, Clinton was doing many other things at the same time—giving so many paid speeches, for instance, that he made more than $25 million in fees between 2001 and 2003. When he did have time to write, Clinton cluttered his prose with the names and stories of everyone he wanted to mention. "You're not running for anything," teased his editor, Robert Gottlieb. But Gottlieb eventually saw that Clinton, like Johnson and Reagan and so many other ex-presidents, would be running for something until the day he died.

A few weeks before his deadline, Clinton asked Branch to review what he'd written. The historian could hardly believe it—even at this late stage, even with all those notebooks, the author was only now starting the chapters on his presidency. Clinton scrambled to finish his legacy book. To keep him focused, Gottlieb spent multiple nights on his author's couch. On May 24, 2004, they submitted the final text file. It topped a thousand pages, but thanks to the technology and scale of twenty-first-century publishing, *My Life* still hit its pub date of June 22.

That same month, Clinton addressed a large and elated crowd at Book-Expo. The ex-president made a familiar promise: his would be a "personal" book. It wasn't. *My Life* was rushed and unruly—less a first draft of history than the free writing of it. But Knopf and Clinton knew how to promote it, hopping from Oprah to *Good Morning America*, from a book signing at an Arkansas Walmart to one at an iconic independent like Seattle's Elliott Bay Book Company. On June 22, a few stores opened at midnight, the way they did for a *Harry Potter* release, and by the end of the year, *My Life* had sold more than 2 million hardcovers, trailing only *The South Beach Diet* and *The Purpose-Driven Life* as 2004's best-selling nonfiction title.

Clinton's memoir turned a hefty profit, an outcome that in recent years many political books have matched, even if their authors can't equal the raw fame and raw sales of a president. Barnett got Sarah Palin and Ted Kennedy advances of around $8 million; both books were hits. Blockbuster publishing appears to be working well for publishers. Even the busts—Barnett securing Andrew Cuomo a rumored $1 million, for instance, only to see the volume sell at an early Dan Brown clip—can be understood as bets that someone's profile might rise.

Blockbuster publishing also works for big-time authors. During their

In 2004, Clinton held a number of signings for *My Life*—including this one at a Costco in Washington State, where fans began lining up a full day before he arrived.

book tours, politicians gauge their support. They gain unfiltered access to voters who buy the book—and low-risk access to those who don't through television interviews that arrive with an easy setup and a sturdy escape hatch: *Well, I cover that in the book.* Most of all, they make money. During the 2012 campaign, Herman Cain was accused of running for president to boost his book sales. "If you know Herman Cain, you know nothing is further from the truth," he replied. "And if you don't believe me, I invite you to get a copy of my new book, *This Is Herman Cain!* If you can find one, because they are selling like hotcakes." It was a shameless line, but it was also a true one: that same month, Cain's book debuted in fourth place on the *New York Times* best-seller list.*

It's less clear that blockbuster publishing works for readers. One might

*Some candidates give themselves a further lift by purchasing their own books at a discounted rate—or by letting super PACs do it, which allows them to collect the full royalties. In 2016 Donald Trump and his allies funneled hundreds of thousands of dollars to this practice, bulk-buying copies of *The Art of the Deal* and his latest volume, *Crippled America: How to Make America Great Again.*

counter that these books aren't really intended for readers—that in Washington, they exist for index checks, to see if you got mentioned, and that in the rest of the country, they exist as souvenirs for a candidate's keenest fans. If anything, this goes too easy on the nation's capital, a city that specializes in treating books in the least bookish way possible, in extracting a few amazing details and then moving on to the next one.

Americans elsewhere deserve better. For more than two centuries, they've cared about history, democracy, and books. (And, yes, about celebrity, though a reader motivated by celebrity is a reader all the same.) Modern political books prey on this tradition. For each thoughtful volume—Colin Powell's is one example; John McCain's *Faith of My Fathers* is another—there are dozens that cynically exploit the author-reader relationship. The content of these books scarcely matters, something made clear by Rand Paul's *Government Bullies*, a book that lazily plagiarized five consecutive pages from a think tank—and Paul is hardly the only politician-author who's seen this happen.

Only a few thousand people bought *Government Bullies*, a publishing bet that didn't pay off. But they still paid money, and some of them still read it, and most of them expected a decent book. Decent books are at best a by-product of blockbuster publishing, but because the system benefits everyone who's not a reader it seems likely to continue. Even its critics eventually submit. David Plouffe, who ran Obama's campaign in 2008, liked to grumble in private that Robert Barnett was an unctuous insider. And yet when Plouffe decided to write a memoir, there was no question whom he would call. Barnett arranged an auction with more than a dozen bidders, and Plouffe's book ultimately won an advance of around $2 million.

There is one upside to blockbuster publishing. It might not cultivate decent books, but if a decent book somehow materializes, blockbuster publishing can circulate it—print it quickly, place it in all sorts of retailers, help it reach every possible reader. While Barnett was working with Plouffe, he set up meetings with the potential publishers, and one of them employed Henry Ferris, the editor who'd taken a second chance on Obama and *Dreams*. Plouffe sat down with Ferris and five or six others, including folks from editorial, publicity, and marketing, and they began by going around the conference table to do introductions.

"I'm Henry Ferris," the editor said, "and I was the editor of *Dreams from My Father*."

Before the next person could speak, Plouffe jumped in. "That book," he said, "got Obama elected."

THE LITERARY PRESIDENT

On January 4, 2007, Neva Durand logged on to Amazon and ordered two books: John McCain's *Faith of My Fathers* and Barack Obama's *Dreams from My Father*. Despite growing up in Washington, DC, Durand had never been a fan of political titles. "I'm always reading," she said. "I just can't read politicians' books." Durand preferred novels for their language and characters; she usually got her political news from the *New Yorker*. But the upcoming election, and its potential candidates like McCain, Obama, and Hillary Clinton, felt different. "I wanted to read more about them," Durand said. "I was very engaged."

By that point, Durand had moved to Washington State, where she was finishing a graduate program in computer science. She adored independent bookstores, and a few times a year, she went to Seattle to browse at Elliott Bay. She also bought a lot of books from Amazon, for the convenience, rating the ones she finished on a website called Goodreads. Durand's account shows that during her electoral regimen, she was also reading John Fowles's *The Magus*, Philip Roth's *American Pastoral*, and Jane Austen's *Northanger Abbey* (three stars; "Not Jane Austen's best book").

Durand didn't finish McCain's *Faith*; she didn't vote for him either. *Dreams* and its author won her over. "This is a fantastic memoir," she wrote on Goodreads, "paced like a novel." To Durand, Obama's style revealed something about his mind. "I liked his book," she said, "liked his temperament, liked that he saw things in shades of gray. What came through to me really strongly in the book is that he has a nuanced view of the world."

Dreams and its follow-up, *The Audacity of Hope*, helped Obama reach a shocking number of readers and voters during the 2008 election. In fact, their success shocked Obama himself.

The author hadn't forgotten his book. In 2001, for instance, he gave a talk about it at a brown-bag lunch in Springfield, Illinois, where he was still serving as a state senator. Sitting in front of a small library crowd, his hair still black, his smile still boyish and wide, Obama reflected on *Dreams*. "This book's been out for five years now," he said, before correcting himself: "six—I'm getting older." He admitted that the memoir had flopped, that he sometimes wondered whether it had been worth the work. ("Stephen King," he joked, "isn't losing any sleep.") But Obama explained that writing it had helped him sort through his jumbled identity. "The thing I'm happiest about," he added, "is having this for my children."

Soon after that talk, Obama began sketching out his bid for the US Senate. *Dreams* never factored in the planning for the 2004 campaign. When he learned that Powell's was ready to toss its last few hundred remaindered copies, Obama bought them for a buck apiece and stashed them in a closet at his campaign headquarters. But no one considered them an asset for outreach. Obama never mentioned the book in his ads on TV. "It had nothing to do with anything in the campaign," remembered Jim Cauley, the campaign manager. The only time *Dreams* came up was when Cauley and his candidate got into one of their good-natured spats. Whenever Obama tried to blame something on Cauley—telling Michelle, for instance, that the aide was why he'd missed a parent-teacher conference—Cauley responded by looking at his boss and reciting the memoir's most embarrassing passage: "Pot had helped, and booze; maybe a little blow when you could afford it."

On March 16, 2004, Obama won a five-way Democratic primary. It looked like he would face a tough general election, until the Republican was felled by a sex scandal. Suddenly Obama had plenty of time, and he started drafting a second, more political book. ("He was writing that book all summer," Cauley said.) In early July, Bill Clinton came through Chicago on his big *My Life* book tour; while in town, he also held a fundraiser for Obama and praised his political future.

"My life would probably be a lot better if I was just finishing up this book tour," Obama replied.

"I'd trade places with you any day of the week," Clinton said.

There was movement in Obama's own literary career soon enough, though he wasn't the one to spark it. After reading about his primary win, Rachel Klayman, an editor at Crown, remembered hearing something years ago about an Obama book. She went on Amazon and discovered a listing for the out-of-print *Dreams*. Klayman tried buying a copy everywhere before asking Obama's agent, Jane Dystel. Dystel didn't have a copy either, but Obama was happy to send one of his remainders. Klayman loved the book and decided to reissue it as a trade paperback, a plan that proved fairly simple since, due to one of publishing's never-ending mergers, Crown's parent company Random House now owned the book's rights.

On July 14, John Kerry announced that Obama would deliver the keynote at the Democratic Convention. When interest surged in the candidate and his soon-to-be-reissued book, blockbuster publishing was ready. Crown sped up the release date; Barnes & Noble bumped its initial order to twenty thousand copies. Then came the speech itself, an event whose impact can be measured in many ways, including in the affection of America's publishers. Almost instantly, there were rumors of a second book and a seven-figure advance. "We're already talking about it," Dystel told a reporter, "and this one should make some money."

First was the *Dreams* reissue, which hit the *Times* best-seller list on August 29 and stayed there for years. Its impact surprised everyone. While Obama and his staff clearly had big plans, they'd never expected that a nine-year-old book would help achieve them. Now it was, and Obama continued to promote *Dreams* on television: Letterman, *The View*, even Oprah. On her show, Obama read the passage on drug use—Oprah directed him right to it: "Page 93"—and talked about how he'd grown from the experience. "He is really more than a politician," Oprah told her viewers. "He's the real deal, and I wanted him here because his personal story is so remarkable. I wanted everybody to hear it."

Once the 2004 election ended—not even forty-eight hours after it ended, actually—Obama replaced Dystel with Robert Barnett. It was a ruthless move, but Barnett secured a $1.9 million deal for Obama's next three books. During 2005, Obama lowered his profile, as sure a sign of his ambitions as linking up with Barnett. The new senator turned down the Sunday morning shows to focus on town halls in southern Illinois; he wanted to add substance to his celebrity, something his second book could help with. Obama decided to title it *The Audacity of Hope*, and he wrote it the same way he'd written *Dreams*: working late at night, writing in longhand, revising while typing, filling it with dialogue and scenes. He returned to his themes of imagination and empathy. "I am obligated to try to see the world through George Bush's eyes," Obama wrote, "no matter how much I may disagree with him."

In truth, *Audacity* was a book in search of agreement—incremental, even-handed, a bit dry. It was a well-executed campaign book, in other words, as shaped by its genre as *Dreams* was by the literary memoir. Once the author finished, his staff and his publisher planned a flashy tour to promote it, though Obama requested that the first event occur at 57th Street Books. On the morning of October 17, 2006, fans were lining up by 5:00 a.m. "I have to be loyal to my bookstore," Obama said when he arrived, and after signing close to five hundred books, he headed to a second Chicago event at a Borders on Michigan Avenue.

That fall Obama toured the country, and thousands turned out for

Obama asked that the
first event for his *Audacity*
tour take place at
57th Street Books.

each event, chanting "2008" and buying so many copies of *Audacity* that
they pushed it to the top of the *Times* best-seller list, above new titles from
John Grisham and Bill O'Reilly. Back in 1995, during his brief tour for
Dreams, Obama happened to have a library event in Boston on the same
day Colin Powell hit the city for one of his *American Journey* jamborees.
Obama opened his reading with a joke: "We were going to coordinate our
tours. He was a little worried that I'd siphon off the crowd, but it looks like
he did okay." Now, eleven years later, Obama and *Audacity* were drawing
bigger crowds than Powell ever had.

It was the best example yet of a star politician, a decent book, and
blockbuster publishing all working together. Based on the book tour, Slate
declared, "Obama, not Hillary, will be the de facto Democratic front-
runner the day he declares."

That day came on February 10, 2007, and during his presidential run
Obama finally embraced his literary candidacy. He remained a reader.
While campaigning in Iowa, for instance, he carried a copy of *Gilead*, a
novel by one of his favorite authors, Marilynne Robinson; Obama would
read about her small and fictional Iowa town while traveling between the

state's small and real ones. "I saw those people every day," he later said. "The interior life she was describing that connected them—the people I was shaking hands with and making speeches to—it connected them with my grandparents."

For the first time in his political career, though, Obama decided to run as a writer. Each night, when he was done with his events, he would sign fifty or a hundred books for the campaign to distribute. *Dreams* and *Audacity* guided his message. "There were speeches," recalled Adam Frankel, one of Obama's speechwriters, "where whole sections were adapted from those books." Newly hired staffers listened to the audiobooks as they drove toward the campaign's Chicago headquarters. In New Hampshire, aides organized official Obama book clubs. The first assignment: *Dreams from My Father*.

Obama's books, and Obama's story, helped him beat Hillary Clinton in the Democratic primary, then John McCain in the general. The books caused him some trouble on the trail, much of it misleading. There were email forwards with fabricated quotes. (Nowhere in *Audacity* did he write, "I will stand with the Muslims.") There were coordinated partisan attacks. Conservative bloggers tried to prove that a radical figure named Bill Ayers was *Dreams'* real author. A top editor at Fox News sent an internal memo listing "Obama's references to socialism, liberalism, Marxism and Marxists in his autobiography, *Dreams from My Father*." Not even ninety minutes later, those references were being debated on air.*

And yet, once Obama got to the White House, his reading mattered more than his writing. That Fox News memo had highlighted *Dreams'* description of college, of Obama listening to "Marxist professors and structural feminists." But that got Obama wrong. His literary reading had always meant more than any other influence. Beginning with empathy, considering each side of a question, pushing past stereotypes (red state, blue state): those traits didn't originate in college or at Harvard Law

---

*The silliest scandal waited until 2012, when Obama was running for reelection. It started when a biographer showed that several characters in *Dreams*—including Regina, the girl with whom he discussed *Heart of Darkness*—were composites. Someone at Politico tried to turn this into a microscoop about Obama and scandalous cover-ups. It seemed unlikely that this reporter had ever read a literary memoir like Maxine Hong Kingston's; in fact, he'd never even read Obama's book, in which the author clearly explained his reliance on "composites of people I've known." Politico's much-corrected story still pinged around right-wing media, from the Drudge Report to Rush Limbaugh. The whole affair revealed something about the conservative loathing of Obama—and also about Washington's inability to appreciate books.

School. They developed while Obama was reading Morrison and Conrad, and they were reinforced every time he walked into a place like 57th Street Books. Near the end of his presidency, Obama sat in the Oval Office and talked with Michiko Kakutani, a book critic for the *New York Times*. The president reflected on how novels had helped him: "I found myself better able to imagine what's going on in the lives of people throughout my presidency because of . . . reading fiction. It exercises those muscles."

It was the same idea Obama had expressed in a private letter, decades before: *it works the fictive imagination*. But this time he was saying it after eight years of Republican obstruction. He was saying it in a nation more divided than at any point in its recent history, which is to say a nation more stereotyped—the gun owner more likely than ever before to vote conservative, the immigration supporter more likely than ever to vote liberal. After two terms in the White House, terms his supporters had often experienced with frustration, Obama still held on to his commitment to complexity and interiority. It was less clear that this commitment made one an effective president in a partisan age.

Or in any age. In his 1890 lecture on men who write and men who act, Woodrow Wilson had considered this very issue. Wilson decided that literary empathy—what he called, in the language of an earlier era, the "subtle power of sympathy"—created a real obstacle for elected officials. They didn't need to imagine "a thousand individual motives." They needed to simplify and fight.

Wilson drew his examples from the writing side of the author-reader equation. "No popular leader could write fiction," he insisted. But if Wilson was right, that presidents could not write fiction, a second question follows: Could, or should, they read it?

Epilogue

Early in 2008, a few days before Presidents Day, George W. Bush headed to Africa. The press was fixated on Barack Obama and Hillary Clinton, battling for the Democratic nomination, but Bush was still president, and he wanted to continue his work to slow the spread of malaria and HIV/AIDS.

On the long flight home, Bush asked his favorite speechwriter, Chris Michel, to come to the front of Air Force One. He wanted to talk presidential memoirs. Bush had been thinking about his for a while, about how to make it less defensive and more readable than his predecessors'. Now Michel pitched him on a potential structure—not a comprehensive memoir but a book that focused on a handful of his presidency's biggest decisions. Bush loved it. So did Condoleezza Rice, who was sitting beside him. They began to brainstorm an outline, until Michel got booted back to his old seat. (The president had to call the prime minister of Turkey.) Soon enough Michel was summoned back to the front, to map out more of the book's key decisions. "By the end of the flight," Michel said, "we more or less had the list."

Bush's successor, Obama, was inaugurated on January 20, 2009. The ex-president began working on *Decision Points* the very next day, writing with the same discipline and dogmatic certainty that he did everything else. He kept Michel as a collaborator, and they completed their draft of the book, which had received an advance rumored to be $7 million, just over a year later. When the memoir appeared in the fall of 2010, Bush promoted it with a prime-time special on NBC, followed by Oprah, CNN, and a suite of Fox News hits, each of them orchestrated by his lawyer, Robert Barnett. It was pure blockbuster publishing, and *Decision Points* became the year's best-selling book, moving more than 2.5 million hardcovers. To land the prime-time special, NBC admitted it had lobbied Bush's staff "for the better part of a year." That meant the network spent nearly as much time getting the author interview as Bush spent authoring the book.

Just before the inauguration of his successor, Donald Trump, Obama did his Oval Office interview with Michiko Kakutani. "It was important to pick up the occasional novel during the presidency," he told her. "Fiction . . . was a way of seeing and hearing the voices, the multitudes of this country." It's easy to list the differences between Obama and Trump, and one of the starkest is their attitudes toward books. While Trump has written more than a dozen volumes, he's also someone who, when asked for the last book he read, replied, "I read passages, I read areas." Late one night in 2014, a sportswriter named David Roth wrote a satirical, Trump-inspired tweet: " 'I was never one who looked at success as bad. For me, success was always good. I loved it, and still do.'—Donald Trump, WINNING, pg. 27." Not even an hour later, @realDonaldTrump retweeted it—which meant the future president was up at 1:00 a.m., manually searching his name on Twitter and retweeting quotes from books he'd never written because they'd never actually existed.

The fact that Obama and Trump both won the White House suggests voters aren't looking for a strictly literary president. It's not even clear that being literary makes one an effective president. In the twenty-first century, and arguably earlier, presidents have struggled to persuade voters with soaring speeches; using the bully pulpit to endorse a specific policy might motivate your side, but it also motivates your opponents. Both Obama and Trump bumped against these partisan limits, though they also expanded the vitality and cultural visibility of the presidency. During his second term, Obama said he was done "waiting for legislation. I've got a pen." But he wasn't talking about being a writer—he was talking about being a president, signing executive orders.

If executive power has shifted, literary power has too. Some of those shifts have been less sweeping than predicted; e-book sales spiked, until they didn't.* Amazon now aspires to be the world's biggest store, period. While Borders has declared bankruptcy, Barnes & Noble has survived. Independent bookstores have thrived, boosted by the same blend of booksmarts and quirks that helped the Hampshire Bookshop succeed so long ago. Publishers have continued to consolidate, most notably in the merger of two enormous and internationally owned companies: Penguin and Random House. The book trade has become only more blockbuster

---

*According to Michel, Bush was one of the White House's earliest Kindle adopters. "He'd read it all the time on Air Force One," the speechwriter recalled, usually choosing a book of biography or history. *Decision Points* also benefited from the early e-book boom, selling more than 300,000 digital copies in its first few months.

compatible. The agent Andrew Wylie, a blockbuster figure himself, predicted that Barack and Michelle Obama might get $30 million for their memoirs. In the end, Penguin Random House paid them more than twice that figure.

With paydays and profits like that, why change a thing? Because by most other measures, modern political books disappoint. The history of these books—from Jefferson and Adams to Obama and Bush—is more complicated and rewarding than a reader of *This Is Herman Cain!* might expect. But that's an indictment of the present as much as it's a celebration of the past.

Political books can be better. Their history also shows that campaign books tend to make a bigger impact, while legacy books tend to excite a larger number of readers. Both traditions should play to their strengths. When writing their legacy books, too many presidents try to cover everything and, worse, to justify everything. They hire competent ghostwriters—a smart choice by itself; Bush and Michel's teamwork did make *Decision Points* one of the more readable presidential memoirs—and promise a personal book. Then they do the opposite, even as their editors and ghosts strain to save them. Something about the office, or the kind of person who pursues the office, interferes. At the start of his deadening and defensive memoir, Lyndon Johnson wrote, "This is a book that only a president could have written." The author was admitting more than he knew.

Imagine a different approach, in two steps. First, the ex-president could use part of that inevitable blockbuster advance to hire a team of researchers and collaborators. Together, they could document and defend every one of the administration's major choices—because there is value in justification, in seeing what presidents thought and how they saw themselves. This process would generate millions of words, which belong in a presidential library where biographers and historians can study them. The second step would be to set those words aside and write a shorter book that readers will actually enjoy, a book that tries to capture the human side of the presidency.

This approach doesn't require that much imagination. Truman completed the first step with his *Memoirs*—and with the thousands of extra pages that make up his library's *Memoirs* file. Coolidge completed the second with his *Autobiography*, especially its passages on his son's early death. Other presidents have written revealing and relatively brief titles after finishing their ponderous memoirs: Truman's *Mr. Citizen*, Eisenhower's *At Ease*, Carter's *An Hour Before Daylight*. Perhaps those books could come first. If Grant's legacy book could not guarantee a favorable legacy, no legacy book can. Show what it felt like to be president and leave the full story to the historians. Do the Truman work, then write the Coolidge book.

Improving campaign books is simpler, if not necessarily easier. Politicians and their collaborators could just write decent books, books with a purpose beyond making their authors rich or landing them on TV. That doesn't mean trying to be Thomas Jefferson. Jefferson lived in an age that was more hierarchical and less complex—an age when one person (or, more precisely, one white man) could be a president and an expert scientist and his country's best prose stylist too. But that was also an age without antibiotics, and Coolidge's *Autobiography* recorded the downsides of that. Presidential candidates don't need to aim for *Notes on the State of Virginia*. Writing their *Where's the Rest of Me?* would be good enough.

There are plenty of reasons to write a decent campaign book, or a decent legacy book, but the most important one is doing right by America's readers—readers like Hiram Harwood in Vermont, James Corrothers in Michigan, and Mary Brennan in New York. If they were still alive, each of them would surely tell their twenty-first-century counterparts that it's a wonderful time to be a book lover. Consider one last presidential comparison, between Obama and Lincoln. It's easy to list their similarities, in part because Obama and his supporters have been listing them for a long time. (When Obama described the White House in *The Audacity of Hope*, the occupants he mentioned were Kennedy and Lincoln.) Both were lanky lawyers who ended up in Illinois. Both won the presidency in part by writing two of the most successful campaign books in American history.

From a reader's perspective, though, the most interesting thing about Obama and Lincoln are the differences: the difference between riding a horse to Robert Stockwell, Merchant, to buy whatever book you can find, and driving a car to Barnes & Noble to buy the book you want; the difference between the efficiency of the steam press and the efficiency of downloading an e-book; the difference between transporting books by train and distributing them through centralized, computerized warehouses. A reader buys a book and begins to read—it's a familiar act, a personal act, an act with its own history and an act that's never been easier. Those are all incentives for a politician or any author to make their book as good as it can be.

Appendix I:
A Presidential Reading List

During the decade I spent writing this book about presidents and their books, I got used to two reactions. When optimists learned about the project, they'd say, "Grant's is good, right?" Everyone else would shudder and ask, "Are any of them worth reading?"

The answers are yes and yes, and in this appendix, I offer a practical guide for anyone interested in more presidential prose. I have no desire to list every presidential book—because of the definitional nightmares that would entail (Is a collection of lectures a book? Is a pamphlet?), and because for most readers, the only value in knowing that Herbert Hoover wrote a mining textbook is the strangeness of that fact. Completists should consult *Presidents of the United States—Their Written Measure: A Bibliography*, compiled by James Sayler (Washington, DC: Library of Congress, 1996), a heroic reference that is itself not quite complete.

My recommendations here focus less on what was historically significant than on what is enlightening or enjoyable to read today, though of course those categories overlap. But I have one more thing to say about the mechanics of reading. Thanks to resources like Google Books, HathiTrust, the Internet Archive, and the National Archives' Founders Online, a lot of the texts I mention in this appendix are available for free online—and not just texts that are out of copyright. (Sayler's bibliography, for instance, is available at catalog.hathitrust.org/Record/003094422.) Resources like JSTOR, along with a growing number of enterprising academics, have also made scholarship easier to find, and much of it rewards lay reading.

Still, in the time I've worked on this book, some things about reading and researching online have actually gotten worse. Google, for instance, has abandoned its attempt to digitize old magazines and newspapers while also deciding to quietly and bizarrely limit the searches for many volumes on Google Books to a maximum of five results. There was a time when it was easy to root for Google, especially if you were writing a book that relied on very obscure books, but it's getting harder to be a digital utopian. Not everything is online, not everything online is improving, and there's nothing stopping one of the digital citations that follow from vanishing by the time you read this.

Thomas Jefferson's *Notes on the State of Virginia*

It's best to approach Jefferson's volume with clear expectations—about its committed racism, and also about its challenging structure. Like many pieces of early American prose, *Notes* can seem unwelcoming to modern readers. Take the ending, where Jefferson offers not a rousing peroration on American vitality but a pages-long list of Virginia's major laws, treaties, and deeds. Still, there is much that rewards patient study. The easiest version to find is in *Thomas Jefferson: Writings* (New York: Library of America, 1984), a collection that also includes Jefferson's *Autobiography* and his career-launching *A Summary View*. In addition to the Queries discussed in chapter 1, make time to read the end of Query V, with its description of Virginia's Natural Bridge, and the beginning of Query XI and the middle of Query XIV, with their analysis of the state's Native Americans—an analysis that, relatively speaking, is far more generous than the one Jefferson grants the state's slaves. In the end, though, the best way to experience *Notes* is to page through it. Jefferson goes on many startling tangents, jumping between his pet issues like agrarianism and religious tolerance, sometimes in the same sentence: "Those who labor in the earth are the chosen people of God, if ever he had a chosen people" (290). Reading *Notes*, you never know where the next tart line or skeptical riff will pop up.

John Adams's *Autobiography*

Editors at the Adams Papers have transcribed the *Autobiography*'s full manuscript and put it online (www.masshist.org/digitaladams/archive /autobio). While the structural caveats about Jefferson's book apply to Adams's, his childhood reminiscences remain a joy to read. After that, search for the character sketches. ("The whole time I sat with him in Congress," he writes of Jefferson, "I never heard him utter three sentences together. The most of a speech he ever made in my hearing was a gross insult on religion, in one or two Sentences, for which I gave him immediately the reprehension which he richly merited.") There are several stretches of sustained narrative, with my favorite being Adams's account of a treacherous sea voyage to France. Beginning at part 2, sheet 2, in the Adams Papers' pagination, Adams describes the storms that left him and his young son, John Quincy, trapped below deck, listening to "a constant cracking night and day, from a thousand places in all parts of the ship." One more thing: if Adams inspires you to search out more early auto-biographies, the place to start is *American Lives: An Anthology of Auto-biographical Writing*, edited by Robert F. Sayre (Madison: University of Wisconsin Press, 1994)—assuming, of course, that you've already read Franklin's *Autobiography*. If not, start there.

John Quincy Adams's Abandoned Biography of His Father

John Quincy's diaries are astonishing—and very accessible in two new volumes from the Library of America, with the excerpting and editing handled expertly by David Waldstreicher. But the Adams text I think about most is the biography of his father he started soon after losing the White House to Andrew Jackson. While John Quincy never finished this book, his son, Charles Francis Adams, included two of its chapters in his own biography that makes up the first volume of *The Works of John Adams* (Boston: Little, Brown, 1856). This volume is easy to find online. (The first John Quincy chapter begins, "In tracing the short and simple annals of the paternal ancestors of John Adams . . ."; his contributions end at page 89.) It's a biography written by a poet—John Quincy parallels his father's rise to Gray's famous "Elegy"—but it's also a presidential biography written by a president and a family biography written by a son. Nearly two centuries later, George W. Bush wrote *41: A Portrait of My Father* (New York: Crown, 2014), which led his publisher to boast that "never before has a President told the story of his father, another President." But that's not true. The Adamses got there first and then, as always, got overlooked.

Abraham Lincoln's Speeches (All of Them)

The Library of America offers an affordable and handsome paperback titled *Abraham Lincoln: Selected Speeches and Writings* (New York: Library of America, 1992). While perusing it, pay attention to Lincoln's careful invocations of history—his use of "the patriots of seventy-six" to sell his early ideas (17), or his frequent attempts to claim Jefferson for the antislav-ery side. Savor his language and rhetoric; as Obama once said, "I'd put the

Second Inaugural up against any piece of American writing" ("President Obama's Reading List," *New York Times*, January 18, 2017). But also make time to read Lincoln's "Lecture on Discoveries and Inventions," a brainy and earnest reminder that his curiosities went past politics. And if, like Lincoln, you have a deep belief in the power of print, do track down *Perspectives on American Book History: Artifacts and Commentary*, edited by Scott E. Casper, Joanne D. Chaison, and Jeffrey D. Groves (Amherst: University of Massachusetts Press, 2002). Despite its stuffy title, the book is a delight—a mix of accessible essays on the history of America's book trade and quirky primary sources that illustrate that history: title pages, diary entries, daguerreotypes, and old excerpts that will make you feel what it was like to be a reader in the age of Lincoln and many other presidents.

Ulysses S. Grant's *Personal Memoirs* (Some of It)

The thing about Grant's so-called presidential memoirs is that it does not cover his presidency. His accounts of growing up and going to West Point are wonderful (pages 17–35 in *Ulysses S. Grant: Memoirs and Selected Letters* [New York: Library of America, 1990]). But his descriptions of the Civil War's major battles feel a bit dry to me—pure military history, though military history of a very high grade—and unless you're a fan of that genre, you might agree. My suggestion is to read the book selectively. Grant's clarity and King James prose come through on every page, so don't worry about missing that. Search instead for the epiphanies and emotions that would anchor a more modern memoir: Grant's realization about the mind-set of his Confederate counterparts, for instance, on page 164. Search, again, for the character sketches, especially the one of Lincoln on page 469, which captures his graciousness, and the one of Robert E. Lee on page 732, which captures Grant's. If you find yourself warming to military history, seek out William Sherman's *Memoirs of General W. T. Sherman* (New York: Library of America, 1990)—a book that would be more beloved if not for the eclipsing excellence of Grant's volumes. One last thought: look for *Hearts Touched by Fire: The Best of Battles and Leaders of the Civil War*, edited by Harold Holzer (New York: Modern Library, 2011), which gathers the best entries from the *Century*'s series of Civil War essays. It's an enthralling reminder of how this conflict, at great cost, created a new flowering of American autobiographical prose.

Theodore Roosevelt's *Autobiography* (Just One Chapter)

Roosevelt wrote a lot, and most of it is revealing, at least in how it discloses his cocky, curious, restless persona. Whether most of it makes for good reading is another question. His nature writing, much of it collected in out-of-copyright books, is usually quite good—the kind of description that came effortlessly to Roosevelt. Of particular interest is *Outdoor Pastimes of an American Hunter* (New York: Scribner's, 1905), which he worked on in the White House. "It isn't customary for presidents to publish a book during office," he told his editor, "but I am going to publish this one" (*Impressions of Theodore Roosevelt* [New York: Doubleday, 1920], 174). Other styles of writing came harder to Roosevelt, and it shows. His *Naval War*, while excellent, makes the battles in Grant's *Memoirs* seem breezy. Roosevelt's grudges and boasting overwhelm his *Autobiography* (New York: Macmillan, 1913)—except for its ninth chapter, "Outdoors and Indoors." There Roosevelt makes a relaxed case that "the love of books and the love of outdoors, in their highest expressions, have usually gone hand in hand" (328). As evidence he examines his life, his favorite poets, and his library spilling through the rooms of his home, Sagamore Hill. It's warm and learned and sincere. The next chapter, titled "The Presidency," isn't half as good.

Woodrow Wilson's *Congressional Government*

Before Wilson's books, here's a fascinating book about Wilson: *The Ordeal of Woodrow Wilson*, written by none other than Herbert Hoover. Hoover's book, which provides another forgotten precedent to Bush's *41*, was a best seller when it first appeared in 1958. It's worth reading today as an example not only of one president analyzing another, but of two presidents with very different ideologies falling into a kind of conversation. In terms of Wilson's oeuvre, it's worth sampling one or two of his belletristic essays. ("Every man who writes ought to write for immortality, even though he be of the multitude that die at their graves": *Mere Literature* [Boston: Houghton Mifflin, 1896], 56.) But *Congressional Government* remains his best and most absorbing title, and it's easy to find online—a helpful format if you want to use search terms to locate specific topics in this highly browsable book. The trick (for now) is to Google "Woodrow Wilson AND 'preface to fifteenth edition.'" That preface, which opens the edition Houghton Mifflin published in 1901, allows Wilson to reflect on the country's rapid changes since he first wrote the book. "New leadership of the executive," he argues, "will have a very far-reaching effect upon our whole method of government. . . . It may put this whole volume hopelessly out of date" (xiii). Wilson finished his preface on August 15, 1900. One year later, William McKinley was shot, Theodore Roosevelt became president, and the outdating of Wilson's book began.

Calvin Coolidge's "Books of My Boyhood"

Coolidge's *Autobiography* (easy to read at www.archive.org) holds up better than *Have Faith in Massachusetts*, which has aged as even the best campaign literature must. In book form, the *Cosmopolitan* article that caused such a stir is the fifth chapter, but the entire book merits a speedy read. My favorite piece of Coolidge prose is much harder to find—another *Cosmopolitan* essay he wrote a few years after the *Autobiography* called "Books of My Boyhood" (October 1932). Coolidge reflects on how his rural upbringing shaped his literary tastes. "If there was little to suggest progress," he writes of his youth, "there was much to suggest history." He describes the traveling bookseller who convinced his father to subscribe to a biography of James Garfield shortly after that president's assassination. He explains how even now, living in a luxurious new home paid for by his authorial earnings, he has reserved a shelf for the small and eclectic set of books he read as a boy in Vermont. "I do not expect anyone else ever to have much understanding of them," he writes, "or cherish them as I do." But Coolidge also knew that lifelong readers would feel something similar when they reflected on their own stack of eclectic childhood books.

Harry S. Truman's *Memoirs*

There are good moments in every presidential book—private glimmers that biographers will use in their own work, even as they mock the book they grabbed it from. Truman's *Memoirs* has more good moments than most, though they're broken up by his primary documents and laborious lists. In the first volume, *Year of Decisions* (New York: Doubleday, 1955), he slows down and devotes 111 pages to his first days taking over for Franklin D. Roosevelt. It's a powerful choice that captures the burden of the modern presidency. Starting at page 112, though, the narrative flashes back to Truman's early life, and as historian Robert Ferrell has detailed, Truman wrote most of these passages himself. They're wonderful: his youthful reading of history (118–119); the teacher who helped him prepare to apply to West Point (122—this is one of those moments biographers always lift); and the modifications he made to his roadster while driving around as a local politician (137). In addition to the *Memoirs'* two volumes, you can find more of Truman's first-person prose in a slim but rich book Ferrell assembled from the president's other writings, including memos he wrote for *Mr. President: The Autobiography of Harry S. Truman* (Boulder: Colorado Associated University Press, 1980).

Jimmy Carter's *An Hour Before Daylight*

Carter's *Why Not the Best?*, first published by a religious press and then as a mass-market paperback by Bantam Books, gave his dark-horse candidacy a huge boost during the primaries of 1976. It sold more than 300,000 copies that year, and it contains some vivid and surprising moments—most notably Carter's frank descriptions of his father's racial discomfort in their small Georgia community (32–33 in the Bantam edition). Still, Carter's best book by far is a later one, a brief memoir of his early years, *An Hour Before Daylight* (New York: Simon & Schuster, 2001). Despite his attempts in other literary genres—Carter has written a historical novel and a volume of poetry, among many other books—his memoir does not strain for lyricism. In simple, Coolidgean sentences, he recalls his rural childhood: ordering essentials from the Sears, Roebuck catalogue; splurging to see Al Jolson at the movies; going outside to catch and kill a chicken for dinner after his mother says, "Jimmy, go get me a big broiler" (89). Carter subtly connects his story to broader political forces: the Great Depression, the lingering Lost Cause bitterness, the cruelty of the Jim Crow South. And yet his personal, perspective-driven style could work just as well in a more purely political book. "It is difficult for me to explain why the town of Plains is so attractive to Rosalynn and me," he writes (129). But Carter doesn't need to explain it because *An Hour Before Daylight* reveals the town as Carter sees it, feels it, remembers it. It's too bad he (and most other presidents) failed to write about the White House in the same way.

Ronald Reagan's *Where's the Rest of Me?*

There are lots of options for the Reagan reader, from the edited volumes like *Reagan: A Life in Letters* (New York: Simon & Schuster, 2003) and

Reagan, in His Own Hand (New York: Simon & Schuster, 2001) to the excerpts from a winning letter he once wrote about his childhood reading ("I'm a Sucker for Hero Worship," *New York Times*, August 30, 1981). Still, I find Reagan's first book, *Where's the Rest of Me?* (New York: Duell, Sloan and Pearce, 1965), to be the best one—because it captures his voice and self-image and remarkable personal story, but also because he worked so hard on it. Reagan's collaboration with Richard Hubler is a classic example of good ghostwriting, and their labors mean you can really lean on the language. Take Reagan's infamous tendency to distort the line between fiction and reality, to the point that he once claimed he'd visited Nazi concentration camps, despite spending World War II in California as a member of the Army's motion picture unit. In *Where's the Rest of Me?* Reagan dwells frequently on "legend" and "reality" (90), "truth" and "fiction" (94). It's clear that he understands these distinctions; it's equally clear that he doesn't care about them when a larger idea is at stake. This may explain why Reagan never read much history or biography. He would regularly appeal to the past, with a good example being the story he told during a commencement speech at Eureka College. It centered on the debate over the Declaration of Independence, and Reagan draws out its drama and emphasizes Jefferson's authorship: "Then, Jefferson writes, a voice was heard coming from the balcony" (*Your America Be Free* [privately printed by Eureka College, 1957], 4). That voice belonged to a mysterious figure, a man who'd slipped past the guards at Independence Hall, and Reagan describes him delivering a speech that overwhelmed the founders—then vanishing by the time they'd finished signing the document. The story is utterly fanciful, with no known source in Jefferson's writings. ("Among other problems," James McClure of the *Papers of Thomas Jefferson* told me, "it ignores the fact that the decision to issue the Declaration and the signing of it did not take place on the same day.") But Reagan liked the story enough to tell it again and again. If the cause was just—American patriotism, peace in Geneva—legend was good enough.

Barack Obama's *Dreams from My Father*

Like Reagan with *Where's the Rest of Me?* Obama wrote *The Audacity of Hope* carefully enough to sustain careful analysis. It certainly captures its author's mind-set and mode of argument; when the book first appeared, the journalist Joe Klein counted "no fewer than 50 instances of excruciatingly judicious on-the-one-hand-on-the-other-handedness" ("The

Fresh Face," *Time*, October 23, 2006). In the end, though, it's still a modern campaign book, and readers should choose Obama's best speeches over *Audacity*—and *Dreams from My Father* over them both. Obama's on-the-other-handedness, which might also be called empathy, makes his first book another where the character sketches stand out. Here, on page 55 in Three Rivers Press's 2004 reprint, he describes his grandfather, a salesman who could never quite settle down: "Sometimes I would tiptoe into the kitchen for a soda, and I could hear the desperation creeping out of his voice, the stretch of silence that followed when the people on the other end explained why Thursday wasn't good and Tuesday not much better, and then Gramps's heavy sigh after he had hung up the phone, his hands fumbling through the files in his lap like those of a cardplayer who's deep in the hole." That simile hints at Obama's literary ambitions, circa 1995, and those ambitions make *Dreams* a book that will feel only stranger with time, as Obama becomes a more purely historical figure. Before he wanted to be president, he wanted to be a novelist—a dream he felt with such artistic intensity that, among America's presidents, only John Quincy Adams can compare.

Appendix II: An Essay on Sources and Methods

This book could not have been written fifteen years ago, for two reasons. First, every single page is built on a foundation of terrific recent scholarship, especially the edited papers of individual presidents and erudite overviews like the five-volume, multiauthor *History of the Book in America*. Second, many of the details come from new, digitized databases that allow searching for something specific—say, *Truman AND Memoi?*—across thousands of periodicals, from small-town papers to trendy but forgotten magazines. *Author in Chief* emerged from the blending of these sources, the grand synthesis and the granular detail.

While working on this book, I visited more than a dozen archives, interviewed more than a hundred sources, and read tens of thousands of articles from those databases (some of which contradicted other articles; the tricky part is the interpretation). One thing I realized early on was that presidential books had made a far bigger impact than most people realize. There are plenty of places to see this—in the way Coolidge's biographers have missed the sensation his *Autobiography* caused in serial form, or in the way Lincoln's have overlooked his private quest to assemble *Political Debates*—but nothing is starker than numbers. When Reagan's *American Life* appeared in 1990, the *Wall Street Journal* surveyed the ostensibly limp history of presidential memoirs; according to the paper, Eisenhower's contribution had sold "a respectable but not remarkable 60,000 to 70,000 [copies]" (Meg Cox, "Reagan Memoirs Could Run Up a Deficit," *Wall Street Journal*, November 26, 1990). Yet documents in the postpresidential files at Eisenhower's presidential library reveal that the memoir's first volume, *Mandate for Change*, quickly sold more than three times that figure: in its first few months, the volume sold 89,000 copies through retail channels, plus another 135,000 copies through the Literary Guild, a popular book club.

When it comes to presidential titles, this sort of derisive underestimating pops up everywhere. A few years later, while promoting his own memoir, Reagan's editor, Michael Korda, described *An American Life* as "probably the largest disaster of modern publishing," adding that it "sold 15,000 or 20,000 in the end" ("Another Life: A Memoir of Other People," *Booknotes*, C-SPAN, July 11, 1999). That's quite a contrast to the numbers Korda's own company provided *Publishers Weekly* in 1990; for the magazine's year-end sales roundup, Simon & Schuster reported that the book had sold just under 400,000 copies. In an interview, I asked Korda about the discrepancy, but he stuck with his original comments. "Given the advance," he told me, "those might as well be the real numbers."

Rediscovering this tradition of presidential books—and telling a story about that tradition, about its writers and readers and effects—has always been my goal in *Author in Chief*. To keep the story relatively focused, I've ignored other bookish politicians. (Consider the Senate: Henry Cabot Lodge, Albert Beveridge, Richard Neuberger, Paul Douglas, Daniel Patrick Moynihan, and Jim Webb, among many other talented authors.) I've glossed over important aspects of political and publishing history. I don't mention the rise of book returns during the Great Depression or the rise of direct primaries after McGovern-Fraser because those developments didn't directly serve the story I was trying to tell, though of course they influenced it in important ways.

In the rest of this essay, and in the notes that follow, I'll point readers toward specialized sources in case they want to dig deeper. More important, these citations will acknowledge my profound debts to the authors, their research, and their expertise. Many of the names I mention answered follow-up questions by email or phone—too many to name, in most cases, so I hope the citations of their work will suffice. In that same spirit, I've written topical mini-essays for each of the thirteen chapters, along with the introduction and epilogue; after each mini-essay are citations for that chapter's quotations.

Academics have done surprisingly little work on presidential books or political books of any kind—one more way to gauge the neglect that's greeted this literary tradition. A few exemplary studies show the potential for taking these books seriously, especially Jonathan Arnold's "Publishing Theodore Roosevelt, 1882–1919" (PhD diss., University of London, 2010); Priscilla Coit Murphy's " 'Books Are Weapons': Books in Twentieth-Century Presidential Campaigns" (presentation at the Association for Education in Journalism and Mass Communication annual convention, Washington, DC, August 1995); and Mitchell S. Ross's *The Literary Poli-*

ticians (New York: Doubleday, 1978). I learned a lot from several unpublished dissertations on this subject, though strangely they all focused on legacy books while ignoring the more impactful campaign books: see Starr Jenkins, "American Statesmen as Men of Letters" (PhD diss., University of New Mexico, 1973); Allen F. Cole, "The President's Pen: A Literary History of American Presidential Autobiographies" (PhD diss., University of Maryland, 2010); and Kevin L. Jones's "American Post-Presidential Memoirs and Autobiographies" (PhD diss., University of Arkansas, 2011). Other useful sources include Ben Gibran, "Books as a Political Communication Medium in the United States," *Publishing Research Quarterly* 22, no. 2 (2006): 38–48; Gil Troy, "Stumping in the Bookstores: A Literary History of the 1992 Presidential Campaign," *Presidential Studies Quarterly* 25, no. 4 (1995): 697–710; and John Maxwell Hamilton, "Dear Mr. Politician," in his book *Casanova Was a Book Lover* (Baton Rouge: Louisiana State University Press, 2000), 196–229. Some of the most insightful work has come from historians writing about these books for popular outlets, including David Greenberg, "Reading the Candidates," *Dissent* 54, no. 4 (2007): 41–50, and Jill Lepore, "Confessions of a Presidential Candidate," *New Yorker*, May 13, 2019. These books have also attracted a number of independent scholars and collectors, and they've taught me a lot, particularly Jim Hier and his "Checklist of the Published Writings and Speeches of President Jimmy Carter" (unpublished manuscript).

There has been even less research on political books from a comparative perspective. Two important exceptions are Sean Scalmer's *On the Stump: Campaign Oratory and Democracy in the United States, Britain, and Australia* (Philadelphia: Temple University Press, 2017) and George W. Egerton's work, whether his own writing or the groundbreaking collection he edited: *Political Memoir: Essays on the Politics of Memory* (London: Frank Cass, 1994). Egerton's scholarship, along with George Misch's *A History of Autobiography in Antiquity*, trans. E. W. Dickes (Cambridge, MA: Harvard University Press, 1951), and G. P. Gooch's *Studies in Diplomacy and Statecraft* (London: Longman, Green, 1942), shows just how old the impulse for leaders to record their legacies is—an impulse that surfaced not just in Greece and Rome but in Egypt, India, and other cultures.

In the West, there are a number of significant early legacy books, including Edward Hyde's *History of the Rebellion* (written in the 1640s, published in the 1700s) and Otto von Bismarck's *Memoirs* (published after his death in 1898). In addition, Europe has produced a series of public intellectuals who also happened to be politicians, from Britain's Benjamin

Disraeli to Spain's Pablo Iglesias. (The most famous example is, of course, Winston Churchill; see David Reynolds's *In Command of History: Churchill Fighting and Writing the Second World War* [New York: Random House, 2005].) America has no real equivalents outside of Theodore Roosevelt and Woodrow Wilson—and they could keep it up for only a book apiece. Still, a handful of intellectuals is not the same thing as a broad range of politicians writing popular campaign books and legacy books, and both genres emerged as mass traditions in America first. Today the rest of the world has mostly caught up: see George Egerton, "Political Memoir as Polygenre," *Biography* 15, no. 3 (1992): 221–242; Sean Scalmer, "The Rise of the Insider: Memoirs and Diaries in Recent Australian Political History," *Australian Journal of Politics and History* 56, no. 1 (2010): 82–104; and Francis Beckett, "Author Versus Author," *Guardian*, March 31, 2007. A special thanks to a few professors who discussed these comparative issues with me: Stephen Levine, Steven Kale, and Eoin O'Malley, along with Egerton and Scalmer.

One last international point: the most revealing profile of a political author I've read comes from an odd source, the preface to Charles Moore's authorized biography of Margaret Thatcher. In his first volume, *Margaret Thatcher: From Grantham to the Falklands* (London: Allen Lane, 2013), Moore explains why interviewing Thatcher was so difficult, even though she'd approved the project—her distaste for introspection, her tendency to see every interview as a political battle, her perpetual desire to pivot to the broader point. Before agreeing to Moore's biography, Thatcher wrote her own two-volume memoirs, and Moore's description of them could stand as its own broader point: "They could never quite overcome the problem that they were the autobiography of someone who did not think autobiographically" (xii).

To better understand the history of American electioneering, as I now can't help but call it, I've relied on Robert J. Dinkin, *Campaigning in America: A History of Election Practices* (Westport, CT: Greenwood Press, 1989), and Gil Troy, *See How They Ran: The Changing Role of the Presidential Candidate* (New York: Free Press, 1991). Also insightful were Robert Westbrook's "Politics as Consumption: Managing the Modern Election," in *The Culture of Consumption: Critical Essays in American History, 1880–1980*, ed. Richard Wightman Fox and T. J. Jackson Lears (New York: Pantheon Books, 1983), and Richard Jensen's "Armies, Admen and Crusaders: Types of Presidential Election Campaigns," *History Teacher* 2, no. 2 (1969): 33–50. Richard J. Ellis has written a number of important essays on this topic, including "Accepting the Nomination: From Martin Van Buren to Franklin Delano Roosevelt," in *Speaking to the People: The Rhetorical Presidency in Historical Perspective*, ed. Richard J. Ellis (Amherst: University of Massachusetts Press, 1998); and (with Mark Dedrick) "The Presidential Candidate, Then and Now," *Perspectives on Political Science* 26, no. 4 (1997): 208–216. Along with Seth Cotlar, Ellis has also edited a fine essay collection that touches on several presidential books: *Historian in Chief: How Presidents Interpret the Past to Shape the Future* (Charlottesville: University of Virginia Press, 2019).

Ellis's *The Development of the American Presidency*, 3rd ed. (New York: Routledge, 2018) was a crucial source for understanding the presidency itself, along with Sidney M. Milkis and Michael Nelson's *The American Presidency: Origins and Development, 1776–2018*, 8th ed. (Los Angeles: Sage/CQ Press, 2019). On the evolution of executive power, see Edward S. Corwin, *The President, Office and Powers* (New York: New York University Press, 1948); Clinton Rossiter, *The American Presidency* (New York: Harcourt, Brace, 1956); Gene Healy, *The Cult of the Presidency: America's Dangerous Devotion to Executive Power* (Washington, DC: Cato Institute, 2008); Richard J. Ellis, "The Joy of Power: Changing Conceptions of the Presidential Office," *Presidential Studies Quarterly* 33, no. 2 (2003): 269–290; and James T. Patterson, "The Rise of Presidential Power before World War II," *Law and Contemporary Problems* 40, no. 2 (1976): 39–57.

I drew details and analysis from a number of wide-ranging books on the presidency. See Tevi Troy's *Intellectuals and the American Presidency: Philosophers, Jesters, or Technicians* (Lanham, MD: Rowman & Littlefield, 2002) and *What Jefferson Read, Ike Watched, and Obama Tweeted: 200 Years of Popular Culture in the White House* (Washington, DC: Regnery, 2013); Robert Schlesinger's *White House Ghosts: Presidents and Their Speechwriters* (New York: Simon & Schuster, 2008); Sean McCann's *Pinnacle of Feeling: American Literature and Presidential Government* (Princeton: Princeton University Press, 2008); Jodi Kanter's *Presidential Libraries as Performance: Curating American Character from Herbert Hoover to George W. Bush* (Carbondale: Southern Illinois University Press, 2016); and David Greenberg's *Republic of Spin: An Inside History of the American Presidency* (New York: Norton, 2016).

The history of publishing and authorship has been blessed by many wonderful studies, typically from English professors and historians writing under the banner of "the history of the book." Such studies often (and understandably) focus on literary titans like Nathaniel Hawthorne or

Edith Wharton, though that has changed in the past few decades. Still, the best guides to what most Americans actually read come from an earlier generation: James D. Hart, *The Popular Book: A History of America's Literary Taste* (New York: Oxford University Press, 1950); Frank Luther Mott, *Golden Multitudes: The Story of Best Sellers in the United States* (New York: Macmillan, 1947); and Alice Payne Hackett, *80 Years of Best Sellers, 1895–1975* (New York: Bowker, 1977). Other important sources of publishing data include Keith L. Justice, *Bestseller Index: All Books, by Author, on the Lists of Publishers Weekly and the New York Times through 1990* (Jefferson, NC: McFarland, 1998), the *Bowker Annual* (now known as *The Library and Book Trade Almanac*), and the US Census's tracking of the "Printing and Publishing" category. (Thanks to Albert Greco for helping me analyze the Census data and compare its shifting terminology across the decades.) There has never been a good history of America's nonfiction canon and tastes, but one can piece the story together from other important overviews, including John Tebbell, *A History of Book Publishing in the United States*, 4 vols. (New York: Bowker, 1972–1980), and Hellmutt Lehmann-Haupt et al., *The Book in America: A History of the Making and Selling of Books in the United States* (New York: Bowker, 1951).

The mini-essays that follow, which appear at the start of the notes for each chapter, detail scholarship that helped me understand specific presidents and specific topics in printing, bookselling, and other literary topics. (They also pointed me toward many of the regular readers I portray.) But I want to say one more time how essential the overviews were; it's easy to take these works for granted, but they saved me again and again as I crashed from era to era. Some of the best, which you can find at any good research library, include multivolume series like *The Dictionary of American Biography*, *The American National Biography*, *The Biographical Directory of the American Congress*, *The Oxford History of the Novel in English*, *The Cambridge History of American Literature*, and *The Dictionary of Literary Biography* (especially its entries on minor American historians). The many entries in Blackwell's "companion to" series, which cover everything from presidents to literary periods, deserve special praise for their clear surveys and robust bibliographies. Whenever I encountered one of those in the stacks—even Rutherford B. Hayes gets part of one (*A Companion to the Reconstruction Presidents, 1865–1881*, ed. Edward O. Frantz [Malden, MA: Wiley Blackwell, 2014])—I breathed a sigh of relief.

Notes

Introduction

One of the most important contentions in this book is necessarily subjective: that Americans have wanted to read presidential books and also that they actually have read presidential books. There's been excellent (objective) research on reading more broadly, with most of it suggesting a slight downturn in the number of readers; Caleb Crain smartly summarizes these findings in "Twilight of the Books," *New Yorker*, December 24, 2007. (See also Crain's online sequel, "Why We Don't Read, Revisited," newyorker.com, www .newyorker.com/culture/cultural-comment/why-we-dont-read-revisited, and the supplemental posts on his blog Steamboats are Ruining Everything.) And yet, once you turn to more specific forms of reading—autobiographies, say, or books on current affairs—the data mostly disappear. The default view has been that presidential books sell because of blockbuster publishing or partisan loyalty. The most famous articulation of this view is a fun (but faux rigorous) experiment run by Michael Kinsley, in which he slipped vouchers for five dollars inside the back half of popular Washington books without ever getting any nibbles ("The Myth of Books," *New Republic*, June 17, 1985). Honestly, I've been guilty of pushing this line myself ("The Decider as Memoirist," *New York*, November 15, 2010). When it comes to big political books, the jokes write themselves.

I hope the main counter to this is the book I've written, especially its collection of regular readers. But there are also some related questions and answers that suggest—to me, at least—that Kinsley's cynicism is misguided, at least when applied outside the Washington metro area. The first question is: How many people know about these books? Here, blockbuster publishing proves its might. During the week Michael Wolff's *Fire and Fury* was published, Morning Consult polled 1,988 registered voters. "As you may know," went one of the questions, "journalist Michael Wolff is releasing a book that covers President Trump's candidacy and first year in office. Based on what you know, how credible do you find this book?" Only one in five responded with some version of "I haven't heard of this book" (morningconsult.com/wp-content/uploads/2018/01/180102_crosstabs_POLITICO_v1 _AP-2.pdf).

The second question is: How many people read these books? Again, it's hard to answer this objectively, but one can find reasons for optimism in the National Endowment for the Arts (NEA) figure I cite in the introduction—that 68 million Americans read at least one volume of history, biography, or memoir in 2017. (The NEA's report, "U.S. Trends in Arts Attendance and Literary Reading: 2002–2017," can be read at www.arts.gov/sites/default /files/2017-sppapreviewREV-sept2018.pdf; thanks to Victoria Hutter and Sunil Iyengar for pulling custom numbers out of the data for me.)

The third question is: How many people are being honest? That's the hardest one to answer; even the NEA figure is extrapolated from a self-reported survey of 27,969 respondents. But FiveThirtyEight recently crunched data from audiobooks.com to see just how far listener-readers made it through a few big political titles, and there are more reasons for optimism. For Obama's *Dreams from My Father*, which in audiobook form is just over seven hours long, the average listener made it 57 percent of the way through. For Bush's *Decision Points*, which is more than twenty hours long, the average listener made it nearly 60 percent of the way through. See Walt Hickey, "Politicians Write Lots of Books. Here's How Far into Them People Read," FiveThirtyEight, fivethirtyeight.com/features /politicians-write-lots-of-books-heres-how-far-into-them-people-read.

One last note on the numbers: it's difficult to compare data between countries because of cultural variations, but also because the few surveys that exist often don't measure the same precise things. That said, American readers do exhibit some tentative differences. Consider a large survey commissioned by the United Kingdom's BookTrust (www.djs research.co.uk/Free/published/1576-booktrust-reading-habits-report-final.pdf). When British readers were asked to respond to a group of positive statements about books, the reason "I read to learn new things" finished third. Now compare that to Pew's Book Reading 2016 survey (www.pewinternet.org/2016/09/01/book-reading-2016), which found that American readers listed the pragmatic "To research specific topics of interest" as their top reason to read. In the Booktrust survey, 16 percent of readers listed "history" as one of their favorite genres. That makes quite a contrast to the NEA data, which, when presented in percentage form, suggest that just under 30 percent of Americans read a book of history, biography, or memoir in 2017.

The idea that Americans have a special relationship to their nation's past is also subjective. The underlying causes make sense: a relatively recent founding, a concentrated burst of civic creation, and a final product built less on a language or ethnicity than on a set of ideas. America is still using that political system two-plus centuries later—not a long span in global terms—and its founding documents and personalities have been vigilantly preserved, as I detail in chapter 3. For that reason the nation's history is, or at least feels, relevant. Daniel J. Boorstin has argued that America and its citizens are unique, with the possible exception of Israel's modern state, in the way they "use their history not only as a source of myth and an object of filial piety, but as a substitute for political theory" (Boorstin, *The Genius of American Politics* [Chicago: University of Chicago Press, 1953], 8). For similar arguments, see C. Vann Woodward's brief lecture, *American Attitudes toward History* (Oxford: Clarendon Press, 1955); J. R. Pole's "The American Past: Is It Still Usable?," *Journal of American Studies* 1, no. 1 (1967): 63–78; and Gordon S. Wood's "Founders and Keepers," *New York Review of Books*, July 14, 2005.

The best recent work on American voters and their international "attitudinal advantage" comes from Russell J. Dalton, especially his *Participation Gap: Social Status and Political Inequality* (New York: Oxford University Press, 2017) and *Citizen Politics: Public Opinion and Political Parties in Advanced Industrial Democracies*, 7th ed. (Los Angeles: Sage/CQ Press, 2020). On Republican efforts to restrict voting access—and after reading Berman's book, one might argue that this effort is sadly all too American—see Ari Berman, *Give Us the Ballot: The Modern Struggle for Voting Rights in America* (New York: Farrar, Straus and Giroux, 2015). For a thoughtful overview of the research on democracy and participation, see Yoni Appelbaum, "Americans Aren't Practicing Democracy Anymore," *Atlantic*, October 2018.

The John F. Kennedy presidential library has at least six typescript drafts of the National Book Awards keynote, in Kennedy's Pre-Presidential Papers, Senate Files, box 894. In its online finding aid, the library suggests there are "several drafts with notations by the Senator" (www.jfklibrary.org/asset-viewer/archives/JFKSEN/0894/JFKSEN-0894-033), but the majority of the notations—and surely the first major draft—came from Theodore Sorensen. I explore Sorensen and Kennedy's relationship more fully in chapter 11, but on this speech they seemed to edit in concert, and it is often difficult to tell which person made which handwritten comment or cut. In the introduction I focus on the contributions Kennedy made to the keynote's second major draft, in part because it's easier to differentiate that one since Kennedy edited first with a pen before Sorensen followed up with a pencil. It's worth noting that Kennedy never gave these drafts as much attention as Sorensen did. (On the second draft, Sorensen made more than one hundred significant edits, while Kennedy made far fewer.) Still, Kennedy's decision to have Sorensen working so hard on the keynote was itself a reflection of the senator's desire to impress a literary crowd.

Kennedy's biographers never mention the keynote as more than an aside; to reconstruct it I've relied on the Kennedy library's holdings and on contemporary reports such as Rochelle Girson, "Among the Books and Authors," *Ottawa Citizen*, February 11, 1956, and "The 7th National Book Awards," *Publishers Weekly*, February 18, 1956. The NEA last asked about voting and reading in "To Read or Not to Read" (www.arts.gov/sites/default /files/ToRead.pdf), though this finding has been echoed in more recent Pew surveys on voting and newspaper reading. On the autobiographical riffing of Howells, a writer who's easy to quote but hard to explicate, I relied on Anthony M. Dykema-VanderArk, "'This Most Democratic Province of the Republic of Letters': Autobiography and Periodical Publishing in Turn-of-the-Century America" (PhD diss., Michigan State University, 1998).

ix *Epigraphs*: Bess Truman's quotation appears in Inez Robb, "Mrs. Truman Credited with Swim Suit Veto," *Atlanta Constitution*, July 5, 1952. Marilynne Robinson's appears in *The Paris Review Interviews, IV* (New York: Picador, 2009), 465.

x *A Note on Quotations*: Truman sent this letter to Bess on February 13, 1912—the Roosevelt in question is Theodore—and it can be found in *Dear Bess: The Letters from Harry to Bess Truman, 1910–1959*, ed. Robert H. Ferrell (Columbia: University of Missouri Press, 1983), 73.

1 *"That a United States Senator"*: *Christian Science Monitor*, January 5, 1956.

1 *"political action"*: This undated draft can be found in the Papers of John F. Kennedy, Pre-Presidential Papers, Senate Files, box 894, John F. Kennedy Presidential Library.

2 *"The only fiction"*: Kennedy's quotes come from his actual address, audio of which can be heard at "1956 National Book Awards, Part 2," WNYC, www.wnyc.org/story /1956-national-book-awards-part-2-senator-john-f-kennedy.

3 *"The brave words"*: Francis Brown, "Mr. Landon States His Principles," *New York Times*, September 27, 1936.

3 *"attitudinal advantage"*: G. Bingham Powell Jr., "American Voter Turnout in Comparative Perspective," *American Political Science Review* 80, no. 1 (1986): 17–43, at 18.

4 *"Need for more reading"*: Richard Reeves, *President Nixon: Alone in the White House* (New York: Simon & Schuster, 2001), 23.

4 *"the peculiarly American version"*: Pole, "The American Past: Is It Still Usable?" 63.

4 *"a good citizen is a good reader"*: Carl Solberg, "You, Citizen-Reader in a Democracy," in *The Wonderful World of Books*, ed. Alfred Stefferud (Boston: Houghton Mifflin, 1953), 125.

4 *"Of course it must not appear"*: Lincoln to Jesse W. Fell, Enclosing Autobiography, December 20, 1859, *Collected Works of Abraham Lincoln*, ed. Roy P. Basler (New Brunswick: Rutgers University Press, 1953–1955), 3:511.

5 *"most democratic province"*: William Dean Howells, "Editor's Easy Chair," *Atlantic*, October 1909.

5 *"A message in book form"*: Roger Scaife to Franklin Roosevelt, September 24, 1928, Houghton Mifflin Publishing Company Correspondence and Records, 1832–1944, Houghton Library, Harvard University.

5 *"I struggle and plunge"*: Roosevelt to Brander Matthews, June 27, 1892, *Letters of Theodore Roosevelt*, ed. Elting E. Morrison (Cambridge, MA: Harvard University Press, 1951–1954), 1:288.

Chapter One: In and Out of Control: Thomas Jefferson and the First Campaign Book

Any student of Jefferson must start with the *Papers of Thomas Jefferson*, the *Papers of Thomas Jefferson: Second Series*, and the *Papers of Thomas Jefferson: Retirement Series*, all published by Princeton University Press. And what a fortunate place to start: since the first volume's publication in 1950—an early copy was presented to President Truman at the Library of Congress—the various editors of the *Papers* have completed more than fifty volumes, each one packed with insightful essays and footnotes, and they have many more to go. Those volumes, along with many documents that have been transcribed but not yet fully edited, can also be read at the National Archives' Founders Online (founders. archives.gov).

The best look at Jefferson's life during the years he was writing *Notes* remains Marie Kimball's *Jefferson: War and Peace, 1776 to 1784* (New York: Coward-McCann, 1947). Other valuable books include Robert M. S. McDonald, *Confounding Father: Thomas Jefferson's Image in His Own Time* (Charlottesville: University of Virginia Press, 2016); Jay Fliegelman, *Declaring Independence: Jefferson, Natural Language, and the Culture of Performance* (Stanford: Stanford University Press, 1993); Pauline Maier, *American Scripture: Making the Declaration of Independence* (New York: Knopf, 1997); and Garry Wills, *Inventing America: Jefferson's Declaration of Independence* (New York: Doubleday, 1978). On Jefferson's custom bookshelves, see Jack McLaughlin's *Jefferson and Monticello: The Biography of a Builder* (New York: Holt, 1988). On Jefferson's reading more broadly, see William Peden's "Thomas Jefferson: Book Collector" (PhD diss., University of Virginia, 1942); E. Millicent Sowerby's multivolume *Catalogue of the Library of Thomas Jefferson* (Washington, DC: Library of Congress, 1952–1959); and Kevin J. Hayes's *The Road to Monticello: The Life and Mind of Thomas Jefferson* (New York: Oxford University Press, 2008). Hayes has also edited the excellent *Jefferson in His Own Time: A Biographical Chronicle of His Life, Drawn from Recollections, Interviews, and Memoirs by Family, Friends, and Associates* (Iowa City: University of Iowa Press, 2012). On the Mecklenburg controversy, itself a sign of the increasing salience of authorship in this period, see Elizabeth M. Renker's "'Declaration-Men' and the Rhetoric of Self-Presentation," *Early American Literature* 24, no. 2 (1989): 120–134.

Annette Gordon-Reed has written two revolutionary books on Jefferson's life—and, more important, on the lives of Sally Hemings and her family: *Thomas Jefferson and Sally Hemings: An American Controversy* (Charlottesville: University of Virginia Press, 1997) and *The Hemingses of Monticello: An American Family* (New York: Norton, 2008). On Jefferson's racism, see Lucia Stanton's *"Those Who Labor for My Happiness": Slavery at Thomas Jefferson's Monticello* (Charlottesville: University of Virginia Press, 2012), and Ibram X. Kendi's *Stamped from the Beginning: The Definitive History of Racist Ideas in America* (New York: Nation Books, 2016).

Kendi understandably echoes Jefferson's biographers in seeing *Notes* as an accidental publication: "With no intention to publish," Kendi writes, "Jefferson unabashedly expressed his views on Black people" (108). A few academics have started to challenge this "accidental" view, and I've relied on and extended their analysis. They include Douglas L. Wilson's "The Evolution of Jefferson's *Notes on the State of Virginia*," *Virginia Magazine of History and Biography* 112, no. 2 (2004): 98–133, which also traces Jefferson's revisions to the sections on race in *Notes*; and Dustin Gish and Daniel Klinghard's *Thomas Jefferson and the Science of Republican Government: A Political Biography of Notes on the State of Virginia* (Cambridge: Cambridge University Press, 2017), which also shows how *Notes* responded to contemporary political pressures.

The Massachusetts Historical Society has created a wonderful website where readers can explore one of Jefferson's handwritten manuscripts for *Notes*, including his many revisions and additions (www.masshist.org/thomasjeffersonpapers/notes). Other useful sources on *Notes* include Pamela Regis, *Describing Early America: Bartram, Jefferson, Crèvecoeur, and the Rhetoric of Natural History* (De Kalb: Northern Illinois University Press, 1992), and David W. Lewes, "In Parisian Salons and Boston's Back Streets: Reading Jefferson's *Notes on the State of Virginia*" (master's thesis, College of William and Mary, 2002). On the book's French edition, see Dorothy Medlin, "Thomas Jefferson, André Morellet, and the French Version of *Notes on the State of Virginia*," *William and Mary Quarterly* 35, no. 1 (1978): 85–99, and Gordon S. Barker, "Unraveling the Strange History of Jefferson's *Observations sur la Virginie*," *Virginia Magazine of History and Biography* 112, no. 2 (2004): 134–177. Special mention must be made of Coolie Verner's bibliographical surveys: *A Further Checklist of the Separate Editions of Jefferson's Notes on the State of Virginia* (Charlottesville: Bibliographical Society of the University of Virginia, 1950); "Mr. Jefferson Distributes His *Notes*: A Preliminary Checklist of the First Edition," *New York Public Library Bulletin* 56 (1952): 159–186; and "Mr. Jefferson Makes a Map," *Imago Mundi* 14 (1959): 96–108.

There are many places to see the impact of Jefferson's book. The best is still Merrill D. Peterson's *The Jefferson Image in the American Mind* (New York: Oxford University Press, 1960). Frank Shuffleton traces the circulation of excerpts in contemporary periodicals in "Binding Ties: Thomas Jefferson, Francis Hopkinson, and the Representation of the *Notes on the State of Virginia*," in *Periodical Literature in Eighteenth-Century America*, ed. Mark L. Kamrath and Sharon M. Harris (Knoxville: University of Tennessee Press, 2005), 255–276. Edward T. Martin traces the book's reception in scientific circles in *Thomas Jefferson: Scientist* (New York: Henry Schuman, 1952). Examples of regular readers who owned Jefferson's book can be found in Michael Hope Harris, "The Availability of Books and the Nature of Book Ownership on the Southern Indiana Frontier, 1800–1850" (PhD diss., Indiana University, 1971), and Harold Holmes Dugger, "Reading Interests and the Book Trade in Frontier Missouri" (PhD diss., University of Missouri, 1951). For more on *Notes'* role in the debate over slavery, see my mini-essay for chapter 5.

There are a number of helpful sources on Jefferson's presidential campaigns, though none of them have documented the full impact of the candidate's book. On the religious issue in 1800, see Daniel Dreisbach, *Thomas Jefferson and the Wall of Separation between Church and State* (New York: New York University Press, 2002). On the campaign more generally, see Charles O. Lerche, "Jefferson and the Election of 1800: A Case Study in the Political Smear," *William and Mary Quarterly* 5, no. 4 (1948): 467–491; Edward J. Larson, *A Magnificent Catastrophe: The Tumultuous Election of 1800, America's First Presidential Campaign* (New York: Free Press, 2007); and Susan Dunn, *Jefferson's Second Revolution: The Election Crisis of 1800 and the Triumph of Republicanism* (Boston: Houghton Mifflin Company, 2004). For *Notes'* (far smaller) role in the 1796 election, see Jeffrey L. Pasley, *The First Presidential Contest: 1796 and the Founding of American Democracy* (Lawrence: University Press of Kansas, 2013).

English and history professors have produced many important studies on America's early literary culture. In addition to the first volume in *A History of the Book in America: The Colonial Book in the Atlantic World*, ed. Hugh Amory and David D. Hall (New York: Cambridge University Press, 2000), foundational works include Cathy Davidson, *Revolution and the Word: The Rise of the Novel in America* (New York: Oxford University Press, 1986); Michael Warner, *Letters of the Republic: Publication and the Public Sphere in Eighteenth-Century America* (Cambridge, MA: Harvard University Press, 1992); Larzer Ziff, *Writing in the New Nation: Prose, Print, and Politics in the Early United States* (New Haven, CT: Yale University Press, 1991); Trish Loughran, *The Republic in Print: Culture in the Age of U.S. Nation Building, 1770–1870* (New York: Columbia University Press, 2009); and Benjamin Spencer, *The Quest for Nationality: An American Literary Campaign* (Syracuse, NY: Syracuse University Press, 1957).

More focused works were also crucial to my research. On the transatlantic nature of eighteenth-century publishing—and *Notes*, a book written in America but first published in Paris and London, is a perfect transatlantic case study—see Joseph M. Adelman, "Trans-Atlantic Migration and the Printing Trade in Revolutionary America," *Early American Studies* 11, no. 3 (2013): 516–544. On the development of authorship, see Martha Woodmansee, "The Genius and the Copyright: Economic and Legal Conditions of the Emergence of the 'Author,'" *Eighteenth-Century Studies* 17, no. 4 (1984): 425–448; Karen A. Weyler, *Empowering Words: Outsiders and Authorship in Early America* (Athens: University of Georgia Press, 2013); and Michael J. Everton, *Grand Chorus of Complaint: Authors and the Business Ethics of American Publishing* (New York: Oxford University Press, 2011). On the ubiquity of the almanac and other pragmatic texts, see Patrick Spero, "The Revolution in Popular Publications: The Almanac and New England Primer, 1750–1800," *Early American Studies* 8, no. 1 (2010): 41–74. On the shipping of early books, see Richard B. Kielbowicz, "Mere Merchandise or Vessels of Culture?: Books in the Mail, 1792–1942," *Papers of the Bibliographical Society of America* 82, no. 2 (1988): 169–200. On Mathew Carey and Mason Weems, see James N. Green's essential *Mathew Carey, Publisher and Patriot* (Philadelphia: Library Company of Philadelphia, 1985), and James Gilreath's "Mason Weems, Mathew Carey and the Southern Booktrade," *Publishing History* 10 (1981): 27–49, in addition to the Washington-centric Weems scholarship mentioned in my mini-essay for chapter 3. On early printing and bookselling more broadly, see Lawrence C. Wroth's *The Colonial Printer* (New York: Grolier Club, 1931), Rosalind Remer's *Printers and Men of Capital: Philadelphia Book Publishers in the New Republic* (Philadelphia: University of Pennsylvania Press, 1996), and James N. Green and Peter Stallybrass's *Benjamin Franklin: Writer and Printer* (Philadelphia: Library Company of Philadelphia, 2006). On reading and literacy in early America, see Jennifer Monaghan's definitive *Learning to Read and Write in Colonial America: Literacy Instruction and Acquisition in a Cultural Context* (Amherst: University of Massachusetts Press, 2005). On books in Jefferson's Virginia, see William S. Simpson's "A Comparison of the Libraries of Seven Colonial Virginians, 1754–1789," *Journal of Library History* 9, no. 1 (1974): 54–65; and Joseph F. Kett and Patricia A. McClung's "Book Culture in Post-Revolutionary Virginia," *Proceedings of the American Antiquarian Society* 94, no. 1 (1984): 97–147.

Throughout this book, I've keyed all population adjustments to the US Census Bureau's January 2019 estimate of America's population: 328,231,337. For pre-Census data, see Evarts Boutell Greene and Virginia Draper Harrington, *American Population Before the Federal Census of 1790* (New York: Columbia University Press, 1932). I've keyed all inflation adjustments to Bureau of Labor Statistics' Consumer Price Index (https://data.bls.gov /cgi-bin/cpicalc.pl), also as of January 2019. For pre-1913 data, I've relied on Robert Sahr's equivalents (liberalarts.oregonstate.edu/spp/polisci/research/inflation-conversion-factors).

9 *"The country is"*: Adams to Jefferson, May 22, 1785, *Papers of John Adams*, ed. Robert J. Taylor et al. (Cambridge: Harvard University Press, 1977–), 17:116; hereafter cited as *PJA*, followed by volume and page number.

9 *"It is our meditation"*: *PJA* 17:117.

10 *"The American states"*: Charles Brockden Brown, "A Sketch of American Literature, for 1806–7," *The American Register, or General Repository of History, Politics, and Science* 1 (1807): 173–86, at 174.

11 *"Philosophy, rhetoric"*: "The Autobiography of the Reverend Devereux Jarratt, 1732–1763," *William and Mary Quarterly* 9, no. 3 (1952): 346–393, at 366. Jarratt eventually became an important minister, and his preaching and physical appearance are described in William Buell Sprague, *Annals of the American Pulpit* (New York: Robert Carter & Brothers, 1859), 5:221.

11 *"As I had no candle"*: "Autobiography of the Reverend Devereux Jarratt," 374.

11 *"I myself used"*: Madison to William Bradford, January 24, 1774, *Papers of James Madison*, Congressional Series, ed. William T. Hutchinson et al. (Chicago: University of Chicago Press, 1962–1977; Charlottesville: University Press of Virginia, 1977–1991), 1:105.

12 *"Early to bed"*: Franklin, *Autobiography, Poor Richard, and Later Writings* (New York: Library of America, 1987), 458.

12 *"a native of America"*: *A Dissertation on the Canon and the Feudal Law*, *PAJ* 1:118.

12 *"the trifling narrow"*: Abigail Adams to John Adams, June 30, 1778, *Adams Family Correspondence*, ed. Lyman H. Butterfield et al. (Cambridge, MA: Harvard University Press, 1963–), 3:52; hereafter cited as *AFC*, followed by volume and page number.

13 *"the difficulty of getting"*: *A History of the Work of Redemption* (Edinburgh: Printed for W. Gray and J. Buckland and G. Keith, 1774), iii.

13 *"My store"*: Mathew Carey, *Autobiography* (Brooklyn: E. L. Schwaab, 1942), 25.

14 *"Seduction!"*: Davidson, *Revolution and the Word*, 84.

14 *"Roused from sweet"*: Weems to Carey, October 15, 1796, in *Mason Locke Weems: His Works and His Ways*, ed. Emily Ellsworth Skeel (New York: Private printing, 1929), 2:47.

15 *"Behold, the antidote"*: Lawrence C. Wroth, *Parson Weems: A Biographical and Critical Study* (Baltimore: Eichelberger Book Company, 1911), 47.

15 *"Our country is"*: Weems to Carey, March 25, 1809, in *Mason Locke Weems: His Works and His Ways*, 2:397.

16 *"No man is"*: Warner, *Letters of the Republic*, 114.

16 *"Mr. Jay"*: Sowerby, *Catalogue of the Library of Thomas Jefferson*, 3:228.

16 *"If writing"*: Tyler to Joseph Nancrede, February 15, 1800, in *The Prose of Royall Tyler*, ed. Marius B. Péladaut (Montpelier: Vermont Historical Society, 1972), 457.

16 *"We have few"*: Letter from Joel Barlow to the Continental Congress (1783), Primary Sources on Copyright (1450–1900), ed. L. Bently and M. Kretschmer, www.copyrighthistory.org.

17 *"I cannot live"*: Jefferson to John Adams, June 10, 1815, *Papers of Thomas Jefferson*, Retirement Series, ed. J. Jefferson Looney (Princeton: Princeton University Press, 2004–), 8:523; hereafter cited as *PTJRS*, followed by volume and page number.

17 *"A correct classical"*: Jefferson, *Autobiography*, in *Thomas Jefferson: Writings* (New York: Library of America, 1984), 4.

17 *"a constant reader"*: Sarah Randolph, *The Domestic Life of Thomas Jefferson* (New York: Harper, 1871), 43.

17 *"Time wastes"*: *Papers of Thomas Jefferson*, ed. Julian P. Boyd et al. (Princeton: Prince-

ton University Press, 1950–), 6:196; hereafter cited as *PTJ*, followed by volume and page number.

18 *"I told him"*: William Peden, "A Book Peddler Invades Monticello," *William and Mary Quarterly* 6, no. 4 (1949): 631–636, at 632.

18 *"After using"*: Jefferson to James Ogilvie, January 31, 1806, Founders Online, founders .archives.gov/documents/Jefferson/99-01-02-3156.

18 *"the first American"*: Chastellux's account is reprinted in translation in *Jefferson in His Own Time*, 2–8.

18 *"books of a handy"*: *PTJ* 13:650.

18 *"Sometimes . . . [he] would"*: *Memoirs of a Monticello Slave* (Charlottesville: University of Virginia Press, 1951), 27. The slave's name was Isaac.

19 *"The God who"*: *PTJ* 1:135.

19 *"a very hasty"*: Jefferson to Edmund Pendleton, August 13, 1776, *PTJ* 1:491.

19 *"peculiar felicity"*: Adams to Timothy Pickering, August 6, 1822, Founders Online, founders.archives.gov/documents/Adams/99-02-02-7674.

19 *"Mr. Jefferson's"*: *Papers of George Washington*, Colonial Series, ed. W. W. Abbot et al. (Charlottesville: University of Press Virginia, 1983–1995), 10:139.

19 *"Yesterday, the famous"*: Samuel Ward to Henry Ward, June 22, 1775, *PTJ* 1:676.

21 *"You shall"*: Adams to Timothy Pickering, August 6, 1822, Founders Online, founders .archives.gov/documents/Adams/99-02-02-7674.

21 *"We hold"*: Walter Isaacson, *Benjamin Franklin: An American Life* (New York: Simon & Schuster, 2003).

21 *"mutilations"*: *PTJRS* 13:463.

21 *"life, liberty"*: Wills, *Inventing America*, 229.

21 *"pursuing and obtaining"*: Wills, *Inventing America*, 240.

21 *"I have often"*: Hayes, ed., *Jefferson in His Own Time*, 96.

22 *"act of the united"*: David Ramsay, *History of the American Revolution*, 2 vols. (Philadelphia: Robert Aitken, 1789), 1:340–41. Ramsay was the first historian offered the chance to write Andrew Jackson's life, as discussed in chapter 4.

22 *"I am at present"*: Jefferson to D'Anmours, November 30, 1780, *PTJ* 4:168.

23 *"most rare"*: Jefferson to Thomas Cooper, January 16, 1814, *PTJRS* 7:128.

23 *"more fully handled"*: Jefferson to Charles Thomson, December 20, 1781, *PTJ* 6:142.

23 *"The present is"*: Monroe to Jefferson, May 11, 1782, *PTJ* 6:183.

23 *"degenerated"*: *Buffon's Natural History*, 10 vols. (London: H. D. Symonds, 1797), 8:154.

23 *"Let both parties"*: *PTJRS* 13:464.

24 *"I killed"*: N. A. to Jefferson, October 12, 1783, in Kimball, *Jefferson: War and Peace*, 272.

24 *"All prospects"*: Jefferson to Chastellux, November 26, 1782, *PTJ* 6:203.

24 *"He was never"*: Randolph, *Domestic Life*, 63.

24 *"And every time I"*: *PTJ* 6:196.

24 *"as dead to"*: Jefferson to Chastellux, November 26, 1782, *PTJ* 6:203.

25 *"In war"*: Jefferson, *Notes on the State of Virginia*, in *Thomas Jefferson: Writings* (New York: Library of America, 1984), 190.

25 *"Nature had not"*: Jefferson to Maria Cosway, April 24, 1788, *PTJ* 13:104.

25 *"worth a voyage"*: *Notes*, 143.

26 *"Nature has hidden"*: *Notes*, 170.

26 *"great political"*: *Notes*, 214.

26 *"has waged"*: *PTJ* 1:426.

26 *"I tremble"*: *Notes*, 289.

26 *"removed beyond"*: *Notes*, 270.

26 *"which gives them"*: *Notes*, 265.

26 *"I advance it"*: *Notes*, 270.

26 *"The parent storms"*: *Notes*, 288.

27 *"I have lately"*: Jefferson to Chastellux, January 16, 1784, *PTJ* 6:467.

27 *"I devoted"*: Jefferson to Samuel H. Smith, September 21, 1814, *PTJRS* 7:682.

27 *"Answer me soon"*: Jefferson to Madison, May 11, 1785, *PTJ* 8:148.

28 *"I fear the terms"*: Jefferson to Monroe, June 17, 1785, *PTJ* 8:229.

28 *"the circumstances under"*: Verner, "Mr. Jefferson Distributes His *Notes*," 163.

28 *"not yet to be"*: Adams to Richard Cranch, March 11, 1786, *AFC* 7:85.

28 *"Make any extracts"*: Jefferson to Chastellux, June 7, 1785, *PTJ* 8:184.

29 *"hireling translator"*: Jefferson to Madison, February 8, 1786, PTJ 9:265.

29 *"mutilated"*: Jefferson, *Autobiography*, 55.

29 *"I have got"*: Jefferson to William Stephens Smith, January 15, 1787, *PTJ* 11:46.

29 *"I am now"*: Jefferson to Madison, February 8, 1786, *PTJ* 9:265.

29 *"a tittle altered"*: Jefferson to John Stockdale, February 1, 1787, *PTJ* 11:107.

29 *"Mr. Jefferson's concubine"*: Gordon-Reed, *Hemingses of Monticello*, 264.

30 *"ingenious author"*: *Monthly Review*, May 1788.

30 *"one of the small"*: *Mercure de France*, June 2, 1787.

30 *"Our interest will"*: *Notes*, 300.

30 *"We are flattered"*: Jefferson from Joel Barlow, June 15, 1787, *PTJ* 11:473.

30 *"Notes on Virginia will"*: George Washington to Richard Henderson, June 19, 1788, *Papers of George Washington*, Confederation Series, ed. W. W. Abbot (Charlottesville: University of Press Virginia, 1992–1997), 6:342. The Scotsman had first asked the question to Henderson, who did not share his name with Washington.

31 *"Attempting to gain"*: Robert J. Dinkin, *Campaigning in America: A History of Election Practices* (Westport, CT: Greenwood Press, 1989), 13.

32 *"a signal"*: Matthew Spalding and Patrick J. Garrity, *A Sacred Union of Citizens: George Washington's Farewell Address and the American Character* (Lanham, MD: Rowman & Littlefield, 1996), 58.

32 *"Party spirit"*: Adams to John Quincy Adams, November 11, 1796, *AFC* 11:401.

32 *"Hamilton harangues"*: Ron Chernow, *Alexander Hamilton* (New York: Penguin, 2004), 608.

32 *"Do not let"*: Jefferson to Monroe, February 11, 1799, *PTJ* 31:24.

33 *"Happily for truth"*: *The Voice of Warning, to Christians, on the Ensuing Election of a President of the United States* (New York: G. F. Hopkins, 1800), 8. The author was John Mason.

33 *"to theorize about"*: *Connecticut Courant*, July 12, 1800.

33 *"The legitimate powers"*: *Notes*, 285.

33 *"the most serious"*: *Serious Considerations on the Election of a President: Addressed to the Citizens of the United States* (New York: John Furman, 1800), 17. The author was William Linn.

33 *"Ponder well"*: *Voice of Warning*, 19.

33 *"Could a man"*: *Centinel of Liberty*, October 24, 1800.

33 *"their judgments"*: *Notes*, 273.

34 *"He told me"*: *Jefferson in His Own Time*, 34.

34 *"should have been extensively"*: *Observations upon Certain Passages in Mr. Jefferson's Notes on Virginia* (New York: n.p., 1804), 5.

34 *"On horseback"*: Henry Adams, *History of the United States of America during the Administrations of Thomas Jefferson* (New York: Library of America, 1986), 1251.

34 *"one of the standing"*: Isaac Riley to Jefferson, October 16, 1809, *PTJRS* 1:600.

35 *"Experience has not"*: Jefferson to John Melish, December 10, 1814, *PTJRS* 8:134.

35 *"You know my"*: Jefferson to Samuel H. Smith, September 21, 1814, *PTJRS* 7:682.

35 *"You ask how"*: Jefferson to George Watterston, March 2, 1816, *PTJRS* 9:531.

35 *"And great multitudes"*: *The Jefferson Bible, Smithsonian Edition: The Life and Morals of Jesus of Nazareth* (Washington, DC: Smithsonian Books, 2011).

36 *"Do you intend"*: Carey to Jefferson, October 22, 1816, *PTJRS* 10:480.

36 *"Certainly not"*: Jefferson to Carey, November 11, 1816, *PTJRS* 10:518.

36 *"I write now"*: Jefferson to Hugh Paul Taylor, October 4, 1823, Founders Online, founders.archives.gov/documents/Jefferson/98-01-02-3789.

36 *"Books were"*: Randolph, *Domestic Life*, 340.

Chapter Two: Autobiography's Founding Father: John Adams and the First Legacy Book

John Adams's biographers haven't paid enough attention to his books and other writings. The best sources here are more specialized. On the content and impact of *Defense*, which was spelled *Defence* in early editions, see Gordon S. Wood, *Creation of the American Republic, 1776–1787* (Chapel Hill: University of North Carolina Press, 1969); Robert Roswell Palmer, *The Age of the Democratic Revolution: A Political History of Europe and America, 1760–1800* (Princeton: Princeton University Press, 1964); John R. Howe, *The Changing Political Thought of John Adams* (Princeton: Princeton University Press, 1966); and C. Bradley Thompson, *John Adams and the Spirit of Liberty* (Lawrence: University Press of Kansas, 1998). On Adams's autobiography, see Bernard Bailyn, *Faces of Revolution: Personalities and Themes in the Struggle for American* (New York: Knopf, 1990); Peter Shaw, *The Character of John Adams* (Chapel Hill: University of North Carolina Press, 1976); Earl N. Harbert, "John Adams' Private Voice: The Diary and Autobiography," *Tulane Studies in English* 15 (1967): 89–105; and Herbert Sloan, "Presidents as Historians: John Adams and Thomas Jefferson," in *John Adams and the Founding of the Republic*, ed. Richard Alan Ryerson (Boston: Massachusetts Historical Society, 2001), in which Sloan also makes trenchant points about political memoir taking off far more quickly in America than elsewhere. On Adams's letters to Jefferson, see David Haven Blake, " 'Posterity Must Judge': Private and Public Discourse in the Adams-Jefferson Letters," *Arizona Quarterly* 50, no. 4 (1994): 1–30.

The best scholarship on Adams's autobiography lives within the editorial apparatus of the Adams Papers, published by Harvard University Press. When the first volumes appeared, in 1961, John F. Kennedy hosted a luncheon for the editors from the Massachusetts Historical Society. "Four volumes out," the president joked, "and only eighty or a hundred more to go" (Bailyn, *Faces of Revolution*, 3). Kennedy actually undershot it, as the Adams Papers has grown into a massive undertaking that will ultimately reproduce documents by John, Abigail, John Quincy, Louisa Catherine, and Charles Francis, among other Adamses. Thankfully, for my purposes, those first four volumes included the first full reprinting of John Adams's diary and autobiography, though they were later supplemented by *The Earliest Diary of John Adams*, ed. L. H. Butterfield et al. (Cambridge, MA: Harvard University Press, 1966). As with Jefferson, many of the Adams documents that have been transcribed but not yet fully edited can be read at the National Archives' Founders Online (founders.archives.gov).

On Adams's life, see John Ferling's *John Adams: A Life* (Knoxville: University of Tennessee Press, 1992), and David McCullough's *John Adams* (New York: Simon & Schuster, 2001). On Adams as a reader, see Zoltan Haraszti's *John Adams and the Prophets of Pro-*

gress (Cambridge, MA: Harvard University Press, 1952), and Alfred Iacuzzi's *John Adams, Scholar* (New York: F. S. Vanni, 1952). On Adams's escritoire, see Wilhelmina S. Harris's "Furnishings Report of the Old House, Adams National Historic Site," typescript (Washington, DC: National Park Service, 1966–1974). On John Mein and his London Bookstore, which also served as Boston's first circulating library, see John R. Alden, "John Mein: Scourge of Patriots," *Colonial Society of Massachusetts, Publications* 34 (1943): 571–99.

There are a number of studies on the relationship between autobiography and America, though it's worth noting that this idea existed long before scholars took it up. In *The Life Stories of Undistinguished Americans, as Told by Themselves* (New York: James Pott, 1906), Edwin Slosson argued that "the ordinary man under ordinary circumstances" was the link between democracy and autobiography. "In politics," Slosson wrote, "he has gained his rights and in history and literature he is coming to be recognized" (4). Academics who would agree include James Olney, in his essays and edited volumes like *Autobiography: Essays Theoretical and Critical* (Princeton: Princeton University Press, 1980); James M. Cox, *Recovering Literature's Lost Ground: Essays in American Autobiography* (Baton Rouge: Louisiana State University Press, 1989); G. Thomas Couser, *Memoir: An Introduction* (New York: Oxford University Press, 2011); and Robert Sayre, "Autobiography and the Making of America," *Iowa Review* 9, no. 2 (1978): 1–19. The problem with these studies, as more recent scholarship has pointed out, is that they tend to freeze ideas like "American" and "autobiography"—a problem made only more troubling by the fact that many early autobiographies were written by authors whose race or gender moved them outside their period's definition of what was "American."

Research on autobiographies written in early America breaks into two categories: Benjamin Franklin and everyone else. For Franklin, *The Papers of Benjamin Franklin* and its editorial apparatus provide the best starting point. A fine recent analysis is Christopher A. Hunter, "'A New and More Perfect Edition': Reading, Editing, and Publishing Autobiography in America, 1787–1850" (PhD diss., University of Pennsylvania, 2009). In *The Unfinished Life of Benjamin Franklin* (Baltimore: Johns Hopkins University Press, 2012), Douglas Anderson argues that Franklin's *Autobiography* originally had five parts, with the fifth (and often overlooked) piece being the "sample" he shared with Jefferson. For Franklin's life, see J. A. Leo Lemay's *The Life of Benjamin Franklin* (Philadelphia: University of Pennsylvania Press, 2006–2009) and Walter Isaacson's *Benjamin Franklin: An American Life* (New York: Simon & Schuster, 2003).

One can see the number of not-Franklins in Louis Kaplan's *Bibliography of American Autobiography* (Madison: University of Wisconsin Press, 1961), a rough but impressive compilation of the thousands of autobiographies published before 1945. For a more qualitative perspective, see Ruth A. Banes, "The Self in Context: A History of American Autobiography" (PhD diss., University of New Mexico, 1970); Susan Clair Imbarrato, *Declarations of Independency in Eighteenth-Century American Autobiography* (Knoxville: University of Tennessee Press, 1998); Stephen Carl Arch, *After Franklin: The Emergence of Autobiography in Post-Revolutionary America, 1780–1830* (Lebanon: University Press of New England, 2001); and William L. Andrews, *To Tell a Free Story: The First Century of Afro-American Autobiography, 1760–1865* (Urbana: University of Illinois Press, 1986). On spiritual autobiographies, see David Hall, *Worlds of Wonder, Days of Judgment: Popular Religious Belief in Early New England* (Cambridge, MA: Harvard University Press, 1989); Sacvan Bercovitch, *The Puritan Origins of the American Self* (New Haven, CT: Yale University Press, 1975); Edmund Sears Morgan, *Visible Saints: The History of a Puritan Idea* (New York: New York University Press, 1963); Patricia Caldwell, *The Puritan Conversion Narrative: The Beginnings of American Expression* (New York:

Cambridge University Press, 1983); and Daniel B. Shea, *Spiritual Autobiography in Early America* (Princeton: Princeton University Press, 1968). On the shifting meanings of *memoir* and *autobiography*, see Julie Rak, "Are Memoirs Autobiography? A Consideration of Genre and Public Identity," *Genre* 37, no. 3–4 (2004): 483–504.

There are a number of fine books on the Constitutional Convention and the development of the executive branch. I learned the most from Catherine Drinker Bowen's *Miracle at Philadelphia: The Story of the Constitutional Convention* (Boston: Little, Brown, 1966) and Charles Thach's *The Creation of the Presidency, 1775–1789* (Baltimore: Johns Hopkins Press, 1922)—still an important title and a product, like Wilson's *Congressional Government*, of the famous Johns Hopkins graduate training. On Adams's use of executive power, see Jean S. Holder, "The Sources of Presidential Power: John Adams and the Challenge to Executive Primacy," *Political Science Quarterly* 101, no. 4 (1986): 601–616. On the "bear-garden scene" of colonial newspaper and pamphlet publishing, see Marcus Daniel's *Scandal and Civility: Journalism and the Birth of American Democracy* (New York: Oxford University Press, 2009), and Mel Laracey's *Presidents and the People: The Partisan Story of Going Public* (College Station: Texas A&M University Press, 2002).

37 *"Who shall write"*: Adams to Jefferson, July 30, 1815, Founders Online, founders .archives.gov/documents/Adams/99-02-02-6497.

37 *"I have never"*: Adams to Benjamin Rush, August 28, 1811, Founders Online, founders .archives.gov/documents/Adams/99-02-02-5678.

37 *"On the subject"*: Jefferson to Adams, August 10, 1815, *Papers of Thomas Jefferson*, Retirement Series, ed. J. Jefferson Looney (Princeton: Princeton University Press, 2004–), 8:657.

38 *"if I am cold"*: John Adams to Abigail Adams, December 25, 1786, *Adams Family Correspondence*, ed. Lyman H. Butterfield et al. (Cambridge, MA: Harvard University Press, 1963–), 7:412; hereafter cited as *AFC*, followed by volume and page number.

38 *"the torment"*: *Diary and Autobiography of John Adams*, ed. L. H. Butterfield (Cambridge, MA: Harvard University Press, 1961), 3:290; hereafter cited as *DAJA*, followed by volume and page number.

39 *"Thus I was"*: Morgan, *Visible Saints*, 92.

39 *"what need I"*: *The Diary of Samuel Sewall 1674–1729*, ed. M. Halsey Thomas (New York: Farrar, Strauss & Giroux, 1973), 1:44.

40 *"Some may think"*: *A Brief and General Account of the Life of the Reverend Mr. Geo. Whitefield* (Philadelphia: B. Franklin, 1740), i–ii. Franklin was reprinting a British book, which was titled *A Short Account of God's Dealings with the Reverend Mr. Whitefield*.

40 *"I silently resolved"*: *The Autobiography of Benjamin Franklin: A Genetic Text*, ed. J. A. Leo Lemay and P. M. Zall (Knoxville: University of Tennessee Press, 1981), 105.

40 *"Sin and Dangers"*: Imbarrato, *Declarations of Independency*, 6.

40 *"an unnatural compound"*: Paul M. Spurlin, *Rousseau in America, 1760–1809* (Tuscaloosa: University of Alabama Press, 1969), 98.

41 *"there was scarcely"*: Adams to Boston Patriot, November 8, 1810, Founders Online, founders.archives.gov/documents/Adams/99-02-02-5574.

41 *"gratify my own"*: Franklin, *Autobiography*, 2.

41 *"three great puffy"*: Franklin, *Autobiography*, 24.

41 *"plan for self-examination"*: Franklin, *Autobiography*, 86.

42 *"I cannot say"*: Jefferson, *Autobiography*, in *Thomas Jefferson: Writings* (New York: Library of America, 1984), 99.

42 *"All that has happened"*: Franklin, *Autobiography*, 185–186.
42 *"Whenever I sit"*: Adams to Jefferson, July 9, 1813, Founders Online, founders
    .archives.gov/documents/Adams/99-02-02-6098.
42 *"dissipated"*: Abigail Adams to John Adams, December 30, 1782, *AFC* 5:61.
42 *"My child is too young"*: John Adams to Abigail Adams, January 22, 1783, *AFC* 5:75.
43 *"Montezillo"*: Adams explained the reference to Richard Rush in a letter dated November
    24, 1814, Founders Online, founders.archives.gov/documents/Adams/99-02-02
    -6353.
43 *"like a short"*: Adams to William Tudor Sr., March 29, 1817, Founders Online, founders
    .archives.gov/documents/Adams/99-02-02-6735.
43 *"I am now entering"*: *DAJA* 1:35.
43 *"Another year is now"*: *DAJA* 1:168.
43 *"I am just entered"*: *DAJA* 1:169.
43 *"Vanity . . . is my"*: *DAJA* 1:25.
43 *"The universal object"*: *Works of John Adams*, ed. Charles Francis Adams (Boston: Little and Brown, 1850–1856), 6:240.
44 *"I have spent"*: John Adams to Abigail Adams, June 29, 1774, *AFC* 1:114.
44 *"Sensible!"*: Haraszti, *John Adams and the Prophets of Progress*, 103.
44 *"Curious!"*: Haraszti, *John Adams and the Prophets of Progress*, 102.
44 *"A pen is"*: *DAJA* 1:168.
45 *"Humphrey Ploughjogger"*: See *Papers of John Adams*, ed. Robert J. Taylor et al. (Cambridge, MA: Harvard University Press, 1977–), 1:58–61; hereafter cited as *PJA*, followed by volume and page number.
45 *"a bear-garden scene"*: Jefferson to Uriah McGregory, August 13, 1800, *Papers of Thomas Jefferson*, ed. Julian P. Boyd et al. (Princeton: Princeton University Press, 1950–), 32:99; hereafter cited as *PTJ*, followed by volume and page number.
45 *"Here is one"*: Abigail Adams to Mary Smith Cranch, December 12, 1784, in *AFC* 6:18.
48 *"painful and distressing"*: Adams to Jefferson, July 13, 1813, Founders Online, founders
    .archives.gov/documents/Adams/99-02-02-6101.
48 *"I tell him"*: Abigail Adams to Mary Smith Cranch, October 8, 1787, *AFC* 8:187.
48 *"Had the book"*: *Monthly Review*, May 1787.
49 *"The spirit of"*: *DAJA* 4:73.
49 *"the commonest carpenter"*: Weems to Carey, March 8, 1811, in *Mason Locke Weems: His Works and His Ways*, ed. Emily Ellsworth Skeel (New York: Private printing, 1929), 3:38.
49 *"I see well"*: Margaret M. O'Dwyer, "A French Diplomat's View of Congress, 1790," *William and Mary Quarterly* 21, no. 3 (1964): 408–444, at 435.
49 *"extremely pleased"*: Jefferson to Jonathan B. Smith, April 26, 1791, *PTJ* 20:290.
50 *"My unpolished writings"*: Adams to Thomas Jefferson, July 29, 1791, Founders Online, founders.archives.gov/documents/Adams/99-02-02-1255.
50 *"Do you ask"*: *To the Freemen of Rhode Island* (Providence: n.p., 1800), 2. The author was Jonathan Russell.
50 *"a considerable pause"*: *Papers of James Madison*, ed. Henry D. Gilpin (Washington, DC: Langtree & O'Sullivan, 1840), 2:762.
51 *"It squints"*: Thomas S. Kidd, *Patrick Henry: First among Patriots* (New York: Basic Books, 2011), 199.
52 *"I feel very much"*: *David Humphreys' Life of General Washington with George Washington's Remarks*, ed. Rosemarie Zagarri (Athens: University of Georgia Press, 1991), 50.
52 *"Jefferson thinks"*: John Adams to John Quincy Adams, January 3, 1793, *AFC* 10:3–4.

52   *"In republican government"*: *The Federalist Papers*, ed. Clinton Rossiter (New York: Signet Classic, 2003), 318.

52   *"A peck of"*: John Adams to Abigail Adams, December 13, 1798, Founders Online, founders.archives.gov/documents/Adams/99-03-02-0246.

53   *"I am weary"*: John Adams to Abigail Adams, February 10, 1796, *AFC* 11:172.

53   *"The mind which"*: "Madame de Staël, the Vain Woman: John Adams's Opinion of Her and Her Book," *Bulletin of the Boston Public Library* 1 (1926): 101–105, at 104.

53   *"Books and agriculture"*: Haraszti, *John Adams and the Prophets of Progress*, 104.

54   *"the delicate subject"*: Edward Gibbon, *Memoirs of My Life* (New York: Penguin, 2006), 104.

54   *"From the memoirs"*: John Adams to Benjamin Rush, December 4, 1805, Founders Online, founders.archives.gov/documents/Adams/99-02-02-5110. While the editors of the Adams Papers have not finalized the text of this letter, it is sometimes transcribed as "the memories of individuals." In the previous sentence, however, Adams discusses "private memoirs of the American Revolution"—either way, his meaning is clear.

54   *"The lives of philosophers"*: *DAJA* 3:253.

54   *"What would you"*: *DAJA* 3:257.

56   *"I was of an amorous"*: *DAJA* 3:260.

56   *"a connection which"*: *DAJA* 3:280.

56   *"My children"*: *DAJA* 3:261.

56   *"Whitefield . . . To France"*: Franklin, *Autobiography*, 202–205.

56   *"So convenient"*: Franklin, *Autobiography*, 35.

57   *"My excellent father"*: *DAJA* 3:269.

57   *"would set me"*: John Adams to John Quincy Adams, December 6, 1804, Founders Online, founders.archives.gov/documents/Adams/99-03-02-1354.

57   *"a star of"*: *DAJA* 3:330.

57   *"suffer my character"*: *DAJA* 3:435.

57   *"Franklin kept"*: *DAJA* 4:119.

58   *"Mr. Adams"*: *DAJA* 4:35–38.

58   *"To be wholly"*: *Works of John Adams*, 6:239.

58   *"More, much more"*: *DAJA* 4:147.

58   *"You advise me"*: John Adams to Benjamin Rush, April 12, 1809, Founders Online, founders.archives.gov/documents/Adams/99-02-02-5339.

59   *"the late President Adams"*: Shaw, *Character of John Adams*, 209.

59   *"for reasons which"*: Haraszti, *John Adams*, 267.

59   *"Constitution of U.S."*: Haraszti, *John Adams*, 267.

59   *"a book that has"*: John Adams to John Taylor, April 15, 1814, Founders Online, founders.archives.gov/documents/Adams/99-02-02-6278.

59   *"I have no"*: Abigail Adams to Harriet Welsh, March 3, 1815, Founders Online, founders.archives.gov/documents/Adams/99-03-02-2796.

59   *"As you are"*: John Adams to Thomas Jefferson, January 1, 1812, Founders Online, founders.archives.gov/documents/Adams/99-02-02-5735.

59   *"We consider a sheep"*: Jefferson to John Adams, January 21, 1812, *Papers of Thomas Jefferson*, Retirement Series, 4:428.

60   *"The world does not"*: *Collected Works of Ralph Waldo Emerson*, ed. Robert E. Spiller et al. (Cambridge, MA: Harvard University Press, 1971–2013), 7:168.

60   *"inexpressible comfort"*: *DAJA* 3:276.

61   *"I should be"*: John Adams to John T. Watson, July 23, 1818, Founders Online, founders.archives.gov/documents/Adams/99-02-02-6939.

61 *"The just always"*: John Adams to Charles Holt, September 4, 1820, Founders Online, founders.archives.gov/documents/Adams/99-02-02-7396.

Chapter Three: Primed and Cocked:
American History Finds Its Readers

One of the most essential areas of scholarship for writing this book has been historiography, and in this chapter I relied on many excellent studies of America's early historians. See especially David D. Van Tassel, *America's Past: An Interpretation of the Development of Historical Studies in America, 1607–1884* (Chicago: University of Chicago Press, 1960); Gerald Danzer, "America's Roots in the Past: Historical Publication in America to 1860" (PhD diss., Northwestern University, 1967); George H. Callcott, *History in the United States, 1800–1860: Its Practice and Purpose* (Baltimore: Johns Hopkins Press, 1970); Arthur H. Shaffer, *The Politics of History: Writing the History of the American Revolution, 1783–1815* (Chicago: Precedent Publishing, 1975); and Eileen Cheng, *The Plain and Noble Garb of Truth: Nationalism and Impartiality in American Historical Writing, 1784–1860* (Athens: University of Georgia Press, 2008).

On the broader culture's burgeoning interest in history, see Scott Casper's authoritative *Constructing American Lives: Biography and Culture in Nineteenth-Century America* (Chapel Hill: University of North Carolina Press, 1999); Walter Whitehill's *Independent Historical Societies* (Boston: Boston Athenaeum, 1962); Josh Lauer's "Traces of the Real: Autographomania and the Cult of the Signers in Nineteenth-Century America," *Text and Performance Quarterly* 27, no. 2 (2007): 143–163; and Teresa Barnett's *Sacred Relics: Pieces of the Past in Nineteenth-Century America* (Chicago: University of Chicago Press, 2013). Hiram Harwood's story—and I offered only a small taste—can be found in Robert E. Shalhope, *A Tale of New England: The Diaries of Hiram Harwood, Vermont Farmer, 1810–1837* (Baltimore: Johns Hopkins University Press, 2003). On Mason Weems's biography of Washington, see Christopher Harris, "Mason Locke Weems's *Life of Washington*: The Making of a Bestseller," *Southern Literary Journal* 19, no. 2 (1987): 92–101, plus the work on Washington's legacy mentioned below. The best edition for modern readers is *The Life of Washington: A New Edition with Primary Documents and Introduction*, ed. Peter S. Onuf (New York: M. E. Sharpe, 1996); Onuf bases his text on Weems's ninth edition, which appeared in 1809.

Oddly enough, there's never been a study that compares the autobiographies of Adams, Jefferson, Madison, and Monroe. On Jefferson's text, see Kevin J. Hayes, *The Road to Monticello: The Life and Mind of Thomas Jefferson* (New York: Oxford University Press, 2008); James M. Cox, *Recovering Literature's Lost Ground: Essays in American Autobiography* (Baton Rouge: Louisiana State University Press, 1989); and Robert M. S. McDonald, "Thomas Jefferson and Historical Self-Construction: The Earth Belongs to the Living?", *Historian* 61, no. 1 (1999): 289–310. As McDonald notes, one way to see what Jefferson withheld is to compare his narrative to his granddaughter Sarah Randolph's more intimate book: *The Domestic Life of Thomas Jefferson* (New York: Harper & Brothers, 1871). In *Affairs of Honor: National Politics in the New Republic* (New Haven, CT: Yale University Press, 2002), Joanne B. Freeman suggests that Jefferson intended the *Anas* to be read alongside the *Autobiography* as a single narrative, with the *Anas* serving as the nationalized equivalent to the Virginia history Jefferson subbed in for his years as governor.

For an analysis of Madison's memoir, along with the text itself, see Douglass Adair, "James Madison's Autobiography," *William and Mary Quarterly* 2, no. 2 (1945): 191–209. Mary Sarah Bilder's important *Madison's Hand: Revising the Constitutional Convention*

(Cambridge, MA: Harvard University Press, 2015) demonstrates that Madison revised his *Notes on the Debates in the Federal Convention* much more extensively than previously understood. The best edition for reading Monroe's autobiography is *The Autobiography of James Monroe*, 2nd ed., ed. Stuart Gerry Brown (Syracuse, NY: Syracuse University Press, 2017). Lucius Wilmerding's *James Monroe: Public Claimant* (New Brunswick, NJ: Rutgers University Press, 1960) offers background on Monroe's earlier publication, the *Memoir of James Monroe*. For Hamilton's attempts to reveal the authorship of the *Federalist Papers*, see *The Papers of Alexander Hamilton*, ed. Harold C. Syrett (New York: Columbia University Press, 1961–1987), 4:287–301.

There are many clues that Jefferson, Adams, and their peers expected the documents they were gathering would see publication. During his retirement, for instance, Jefferson wrote a short preface to his *Summary View*, and the last sentence appears to hail future editors: "Here follow my proposition, and the more prudent one which was adopted" (*Papers of Thomas Jefferson*, ed. Julian P. Boyd et al. [Princeton: Princeton University Press, 1950–], 1:671).

While digital databases allowed me to trace the full impact of Jefferson's *Memoirs* for the first time, scholars have written about the edition before, and I learned a great deal from Joseph Carroll Vance, "Thomas Jefferson Randolph" (PhD diss., University of Virginia, 1957); Lisa A. Francavilla, "Jefferson's Grandchildren and the Creation of the Jefferson Image" (presented at the annual Society for Historians of the Early American Republic conference, Worcester, MA, July 2007); Francis Cogliano, *Thomas Jefferson: Reputation and Legacy* (Charlottesville: University of Virginia Press, 2006); and Merrill D. Peterson, *The Jefferson Image in the American Mind* (New York: Oxford University Press, 1960). Peterson mentions a possible predecessor to Jefferson's groundbreaking edition: *The Memoirs of the Life and Writings of Benjamin Franklin*, which saw its first volume appear in 1818. A few other publications revealed the private founders, like the *Correspondence between the Hon. John Adams, Late President of the United States, and the Late Wm. Cunningham* (Boston: E. M. Cunningham, 1823). But versions of Franklin's *Autobiography* had been circulating for decades when his edition appeared, and he was not a president; the edition of Adams's letters was a small (and unauthorized) selection. Jefferson's multivolume edition was something different—and the best way to see that is in its rapturous reception.

George Washington might be a terse figure in the national imagination, but several scholars have shown he was an active reader and writer, especially Kevin J. Hayes, *George Washington: A Life in Books* (New York: Oxford University Press, 2017), and Troy O. Bickham, "Sympathizing with Sedition? George Washington, the British Press, and British Attitudes during the American War of Independence," *William and Mary Quarterly* 59, no. 1 (2002): 101–122. Jill Lepore offers an excellent overview of Washington's editors and biographers in "His Highness," *New Yorker*, September 20, 2010. I also relied on Robert L. Brunhouse, "David Ramsay, 1749–1815: Selections from His Writings," *Transactions of the American Philosophical Society* 55, no. 4 (1965): 1–250. The pages Humphreys actually finished were published in Jedidiah Morse's *American Geography*; today they can be read in *David Humphreys' Life of General Washington with George Washington's Remarks*, ed. Rosemarie Zagarri (Athens: University of Georgia Press, 1991).

For Washington's Farewell Address, the starting point remains Victor Hugo Paltsits's *Washington's Farewell Address, in Facsimile . . .* (New York: New York Public Library, 1935; hereafter cited as *WFA*), though editors at the Washington Papers and the Hamilton Papers also offer important evaluations. The incredible response to the address is charted in Jeffrey J. Malanson, *Addressing America: George Washington's Farewell and the Making of National Culture, Politics, and Diplomacy, 1796–1852* (Kent, OH: Kent State University Press, 2015); Matthew Spalding and Patrick J. Garrity, *A Sacred Union of Citizens: George*

Washington's Farewell Address and the American Character (Lanham, MD: Rowman & Littlefield, 1996); and Gerald Kahler, "Washington in Glory, America in Tears: The Nation Mourns the Death of George Washington, 1799–1800" (PhD diss., College of William and Mary, 2003). On the controversy over the address's authorship, I learned a lot from Palsits and from Malanson's " 'If I Had It in His Hand-Writing I Would Burn It': Federalists and the Authorship Controversy over George Washington's Farewell Address, 1808–1859," *Journal of the Early Republic* 34, no. 2 (2014): 219–242; Malanson deftly connects that controversy to the era's contemporary political concerns. On the explosion of books and biographies that appeared after Washington's death, including Weems's, see Edward G. Lengel, *Inventing George Washington: America's Founder, in Myth and Memory* (New York: HarperCollins, 2011), and François Furstenberg, *In the Name of the Father: Washington's Legacy, Slavery, and the Making of a Nation* (New York: Penguin, 2006).

62 *"a lover of books"*: John C. Hamilton, *The Life of Alexander Hamilton* (New York: Halsted and Voorhies, 1834), 1:3.
63 *"American history"*: Madison to Edward Everett, March 19, 1823, *The Papers of James Madison*, Retirement Series, ed. David B. Mattern et al. (Charlottesville: University of Virginia Press, 2009–), 3:16–17.
63 *"wished I had"*: Shalhope, *A Tale of New England*, 59.
63 *"tide of anger"*: Shalhope, *A Tale of New England*, 36.
64 *"I have nothing"*: Rosemarie Zagarri, *A Woman's Dilemma: Mercy Otis Warren and the American Revolution* (Wheeling, IL: Harlan Davidson, 1995), 142.
64 *"peculiar province"*: Cheng, *The Plain and Noble Garb*, 62.
64 *"I long to"*: David Ramsay to Benjamin Rush, May 1, 1787, in Brunhouse, "David Ramsay, 1749–1815," 112.
65 *"Every child"*: Shaffer, *Politics of History*, 41.
66 *"I laugh at"*: William Buell Sprague to Thomas Raffles, April 13, 1832, in Lauer, "Traces of the Real," 155.
66 *"very busy among"*: *Collected Works of Edgar Allan Poe*, ed. Thomas Ollive Mabbott (Cambridge, MA: Harvard University Press, 1969–), 2:280.
66 *"I've something"*: Weems to Carey, January 12 (or possibly 13), 1800, in Furstenberg, *In the Name of the Father*, 106.
67 *"an aged lady"*: Weems, *Life of Washington*, 7–10.
67 *"The following anecdote"*: Weems, *Life of Washington*, 9.
67 *"It is not"*: Weems, *Life of Washington*, 2.
67 *"down off the"*: Henry S. Randall to Nicholas P. Trist, May 4, 1856, in Francavilla, "Jefferson's Grandchildren."
67 *"the same kind"*: William Short to Jefferson, March 27, 1820, Founders Online, founders.archives.gov/documents/Jefferson/98-01-02-1180.
68 *"Writing the history"*: Jefferson to Skelton Jones, July 28, 1809, *Papers of Thomas Jefferson*, Retirement Series, ed. J. Jefferson Looney (Princeton: Princeton University Press, 2004–), 1:383.
68 *"very voluminous"*: Jefferson to James Madison, June 22, 1817, *Papers of Thomas Jefferson*, Retirement Series, 11:461.
68 *"A.H. condemning"*: *Papers of Thomas Jefferson*, ed. Julian P. Boyd et al. (Princeton: Princeton University Press, 1950–), 22:8.
68 *"We are not"*: *Papers of Thomas Jefferson*, Retirement Series, 12:417.
68 *"At the age"*: Jefferson, *Autobiography*, in *Thomas Jefferson: Writings* (New York: Library of America, 1984), 3.

68 *"I am already"*: Jefferson, *Autobiography*, 43.

68 *"Being now"*: Jefferson, *Autobiography*, 45.

69 *"the cherished companion"*: Jefferson, *Autobiography*, 46.

69 *"first political writer"*: Galliard Hunt, *Life of James Madison* (New York: Doubleday, Page, 1902), 316.

69 *"He gave me"*: Ralph L. Ketcham, "An Unpublished Sketch of James Madison by James K. Paulding," *Virginia Magazine of History and Biography* 67, no. 4 (1959): 432–437, at 435–436.

69 *"a chronicle"*: Madison to Noah Webster, October 12, 1804, *Papers of James Madison*, Secretary of State Series, ed. Mary A. Hackett et al. (Charlottesville: University of Virginia Press, 1986–), 8:162.

69 *"When sleep"*: Madison's youthful poetry is collected in *The Papers of James Madison*, Congressional Series, ed. William T. Hutchinson et al. (Chicago: University of Chicago Press, 1962–1977; Charlottesville: University Press of Virginia, 1977–1991), 1:61–68.

70 *"I feel the"*: Madison to James K. Paulding, April 1, 1831, Founders Online, founders .archives.gov/documents/Madison/99-02-02-2317.

70 *"The biography of"*: "James Madison's Autobiography," 209.

70 *"I think your"*: Daniel C. Gilman, *James Monroe* (Boston: Houghton, Mifflin, 1883), 192–193.

71 *"My pursuits at"*: Monroe to General Lafayette, May 2, 1829, in *Writings of James Monroe*, ed. Stanislaus Murray Hamilton (New York: G. P. Putnam's Sons, 1896–1903), 7:201.

71 *"the public"*: Monroe to General Lafayette, May 2, 1829, in *Writings of James Monroe*, 7:201.

71 *"The night was"*: *Autobiography of James Monroe*, 30.

71 *"Is this self-written?"*: Bentham to John Herbert Koe, August 21, 1817, in *The Collected Works of Jeremy Bentham*, ed. Stephen Conway et al. (New York: Oxford University Press, 1968–), 1:47.

71 *"the hand that"*: Robert M. S. McDonald, "Thomas Jefferson's Changing Reputation as Author of the Declaration of Independence: The First Fifty Years," *Journal of the Early Republic* 19, no. 2 (1999): 169–195, at 181.

72 *"These volumes will"*: *Virginia Literary Museum and Journal*, July 8, 1829.

73 *"The negroes are"*: *Richmond Enquirer*, November 3, 1826.

73 *"perfect authenticity"*: Madison, "Preface to Jefferson Memoir, August 1826," Founders Online, founders.archives.gov/documents/Madison/99-02-02-0716.

73 *"backwardness"*: Madison to Nicholas P. Trist, November 25, 1826, Founders Online, founders.archives.gov/documents/Madison/99-02-02-0805.

73 *"almost exclusively"*: The description comes from an undated draft of a letter by Randolph; see Vance, "Thomas Jefferson Randolph," 131.

73 *"treason . . . to alter"*: Martha Jefferson Randolph to Thomas Jefferson Randolph, February 29, 1828, in Vance, "Thomas Jefferson Randolph," 132.

73 *"considerable memoir"*: *Niles Weekly Register*, July 15, 1826, reprinting an earlier item from the *Richmond Enquirer*.

73 *"sought by every"*: *Louisiana Advertiser*, August 16, 1828.

74 *"exploded so near"*: *American Quarterly Review*, March–June 1837.

74 *"We are friendly"*: *Christian Advocate*, February 1, 1830.

74 *"one of the most"*: *Westminster Review*, October 1830.

74 *"It is a luxury"*: *North American Review*, April 1830.

75 *"unusually severe"*: *Memoirs of John Quincy Adams, Comprising Portions of His Diary . . .* , ed. Charles Francis Adams (Philadelphia: Lippincott, 1874–1877), 8:308.

75 *"There are no"*: *Memoirs of John Quincy Adams*, 8:270.

75 *"There it ends"*: *Memoirs of John Quincy Adams*, 8:272.

75 *"No one can"*: "New Publications," *New York Tribune*, September 1, 1851.

76 *"every lover of"*: *Ohio State Journal*, March 31, 1841.

76 *"Ah! Woe's me"*: *Papers of George Washington*, Colonial Series, ed. W. W. Abbot et al. (Charlottesville: University of Press Virginia, 1983–1995), 7:47.

76 *"letters of compliment"*: Washington to Henry Knox, January 5, 1785, *Papers of George Washington*, Confederation Series, ed. W. W. Abbot (Charlottesville: University of Press Virginia, 1992–1997), 2:253.

76 *"They ought"*: Washington to James McHenry, July 29, 1798, *Papers of George Washington*, Retirement Series, ed. W. W. Abbot (Charlottesville: University Press of Virginia, 1998–1999), 2:473.

76 *"I have not leisure"*: Washington to David Humphreys, July 25, 1785, *Papers of George Washington*, Confederation Series, 3:149.

77 *"They then"*: *David Humphreys' Life*, 12–13.

77 *"Earnestly requested"*: *David Humphreys' Life*, xxxviii.

78 *"If I could persuade"*: Adams to Benjamin Rush, August 28, 1811, Founders Online, founders.archives.gov/documents/Adams/99-02-02-5678.

78 *"a direct address"*: Madison to Washington, June 20, 1792, in *Papers of James Madison*, Congressional Series, 14:319–320.

78 *"If you form one anew"*: Washington to Alexander Hamilton, May 15, 1796, Founders Online, founders.archives.gov/documents/Washington/99-01-02-00521.

78 *"You must be"*: *Papers of Alexander Hamilton*, 20:173.

79 *"a precious treasure"*: *Christian Watchman*, November 18, 1825.

79 *"its illustrious author"*: WFA 68.

79 *"sentiments will be"*: WFA 66.

79 *"May God"*: Edward Lynch to George Washington, September 1796, WFA 57.

79 *"the last letter"*: Weems, *Life of Washington*, 113.

79 *"That man does"*: *Papers of Alexander Hamilton*, 20:173.

79 *"Fondness for"*: Peters to John Jay, April 11, 1811, in WFA 272.

80 *"It was never"*: Madison to Thomas Jefferson, June 27, 1823, *Papers of James Madison*, Retirement Series, 3:80–81.

80 *"If I had"*: Richard Peters to John Jay, February 14, 1811, WFA 263.

80 *"falling into"*: Rufus King to Charles King, November 26, 1825, *Life and Correspondence of Rufus King*, ed. Charles R. King (New York: G. P. Putnam's Sons, 1894–1900), 6:618.

80 *"to menace me"*: Rufus King to John A. Hamilton, May 28, 1825, *Life and Correspondence of Rufus King*, 6:616; this letter survives only in draft form, and it is not clear that King sent it.

80 *"the Hamilton papers"*: *Torch Light and Public Advertiser*, November 9, 1826, and *Brattleboro Messenger*, December 24, 1825, among many others.

81 *"It is a vile"*: *Christian Watchman*, November 18, 1825.

81 *"the charm of"*: Madison to Thomas Jefferson, June 27, 1823, *Papers of James Madison*, Retirement Series, 3:80–81.

82 *"Washtub"*: Lengel, *Inventing George Washington*, 34.

82 *"speaks the very mind"*: Howard Binney, *An Inquiry into the Formation of Washington's Farewell Address* (Philadelphia: Parry & McMillan, 1859), 170.

82 *"George Washington as"*: "University Club Banquet," *Washington Post*, February 18, 1906.

82 *"which he did"*: Henry Beach Needham, "Woodrow Wilson's Views: An Interview," *Outlook*, August 26, 1911.

82 *"A majority of"*: " 'A Smart Aleck' Is Amusing, Instructive—But Dangerous," *New York Journal*, March 5, 1912.

Chapter Four: The Poet, the President Who Couldn't Spell,
and the Campaign Biography

Strangely enough, campaign biographies have received far better scholarly treatment than presidential campaign books. I depended on William Burlie Brown, *The People's Choice: The Presidential Image in the Campaign Biography* (Baton Rouge: Louisiana State University Press, 1960); M. J. Heale, *The Presidential Quest: Candidates and Images in American Political Culture, 1787–1852* (London: Longman, 1982); and William Miles, *The Image Makers: A Bibliography of American Presidential Campaign Biographies* (Metuchen, NJ: Scarecrow Press, 1979). One can find lively overviews of the genre in Jill Lepore, "Bound for Glory," *New Yorker*, October 13, 2008, and James D. Hart, "They Were All Born in Log Cabins," *American Heritage*, August 1956. In *Lincoln's Campaign Biographies* (Carbondale: Southern Illinois University Press, 2014), Thomas A. Horrocks details Lincoln's relationship to the genre. In "The Two Lives of Franklin Pierce: Hawthorne, Political Culture, and the Literary Market," *American Literary History* 5, no. 2 (1993): 203–230, Scott E. Casper does the same for Hawthorne and Pierce. Only infrequently does this scholarship dwell on the campaign biography's American origins. In addition to the items mentioned in my essay on sources and methods, the best discussions are themselves historical—Brander Matthews, a close associate of Theodore Roosevelt, saying "the campaign biography, so far as I know, does not form part of the election machinery of any other Republic" ("Changing Fashions in Presidential Campaigns," *New York Times*, October 10, 1920), or a London critic calling the genre "a characteristic variety of American literature" (*Saturday Review of Politics*, November 4, 1876).

The Adams Papers and the Massachusetts Historical Society are editing John Quincy Adams's papers and correspondence, to their usual high standards. They've already put every page of his diary online, though the pages are not currently transcribed (www .masshist.org/jqadiaries/php). I found the best biography to be Paul C. Nagel's *John Quincy Adams: A Public Life, a Private Life* (New York: Knopf, 1997); Louisa Adams was also a talented memoirist, something you can glimpse in Louisa Thomas's excellent *Louisa: The Extraordinary Life of Mrs. Adams* (New York: Penguin, 2016). There have been a few studies of Adams as a writer, all of them useful, including Earl N. Harbert, "John Quincy Adams and His Diary," *Tulane Studies in English* 18 (1970): 81–93, which in truth provides a good overview of Adams's entire oeuvre; S. D. Stirk, "John Quincy Adams's *Letters on Silesia*," *New England Quarterly* 9, no. 3 (1936): 485–499; Linda K. Kerber and Walter John Morris, "Politics and Literature: The Adams Family and the *Port Folio*," *William and Mary Quarterly* 23, no. 3 (1966): 450–476; and Jacqueline Kaye, "John Quincy Adams and the Conquest of Ireland," *Éire-Ireland* 16, no. 1 (1981): 34–53.

The Papers of Andrew Jackson has also put many documents online (trace.tennessee .edu/utk_jackson). Thanks to the *Papers'* Thomas Coens for his help with historical questions and enigmatic handwriting. Coens has delivered a fascinating conference paper, "Andrew Jackson and the Press" (presented at the annual Society for Historians of the Early American Republic conference, Philadelphia, July 2014), that opens another angle on the idea I raise in the chapter—that Jackson was more literary than previous scholars have realized. Coens presents striking examples of Jackson actually writing anonymous essays for newspapers. Another example of Jackson's literary mind is his desire to draw together Eaton's "Wyoming" letters: "These pieces," Jackson wrote, "I intend having collected in due time and published in pamphlet form" (Jackson to Andrew Jackson Donelson, April 4, 1824, *Papers of Andrew Jackson*, ed. Sam B. Smith et al. [Knoxville: University of Tennessee Press, 1980–], 5:389; hereafter cited as *PAJ*, followed by volume and page number). Another example comes from John Spencer Bassett's still valuable *Life of Andrew Jackson* (New York: Doubleday, Page, 1911), which shows how Jackson carefully preserved his papers and even wrote on some, "To be kept for the historian" (v).

Other useful biographies of Jackson include Robert V. Remini's classics—*Andrew Jackson: The Course of American Empire, 1767–1821* (New York: Harper & Row, 1977), *Andrew Jackson: The Course of American Freedom, 1822–1832* (New York: Harper & Row, 1981), and *Andrew Jackson and the Course of American Democracy: 1833–1845* (New York: Harper & Row, 1984)—and Jon Meacham's *American Lion: Andrew Jackson in the White House* (New York: Penguin, 2008). I relied on Gabriel L. Lowe Jr., "John H. Eaton, Jackson's Campaign Manager," *Tennessee Historical Quarterly* 11, no. 2 (1952): 99–147. The best reading edition of Eaton and Reid's book is *The Life of Andrew Jackson*, ed. Frank Owsley Jr. (Tuscaloosa: University of Alabama Press, 1974), which reprints the 1817 text. Jackson's attempt to write a possible early draft appears in Remini's "Andrew Jackson's Account of the Battle of New Orleans," *Tennessee Historical Quarterly* 26, no. 1 (1967): 23–42.

In addition to the broader scholarship cited in my essay on sources and methods, I relied on a few specific works to understand this period's shifts in campaigning and voting. Sean Wilentz's *The Rise of American Democracy: Jefferson to Lincoln* (New York: Norton, 2005) and Daniel Walker Howe's *What Hath God Wrought: The Transformation of America, 1815–1848* (New York: Oxford University Press, 2007) provide context. Lynn Hudson Parsons's *The Birth of Modern Politics: Andrew Jackson, John Quincy Adams, and the Election of 1828* (New York: Oxford University Press, 2009) and Colin McCoy's "Democracy in Print: The Literature of Persuasion in Jacksonian America, 1815–1840" (PhD diss., University of Illinois, 2001) are more focused. Donald Ratcliffe's important *The One-Party Presidential Contest: Adams, Jackson, and 1824's Five-Horse Race* (Lawrence: University Press of Kansas, 2015) revises the mistaken idea of a "corrupt bargain." John Lawrence's "Politics and Personality: The Development of the Counter-Image of Andrew Jackson" (PhD diss., Indiana University, 1970), shows that even Jackson's enemies used his campaign biography to fuel their pamphlets. Roger A. Fischer's *Tippecanoe and Trinkets Too: The Material Culture of American Presidential Campaigns, 1828–1984* (Urbana: University of Illinois Press, 1988) summarizes many of the other campaign techniques that flourished in this period. In *Washington: A History of Our National City* (New York: Basic Books, 2015), Tom Lewis shows how these changes changed the capital itself.

There are many fine studies of authorship in this period, but the first person I need to acknowledge is James N. Green, who alerted me to the undiscovered Jackson documents at the Historical Society of Pennsylvania, cited below, and also helped clarify the size of Carey's edition of the Jackson *Life*. (Thanks also to the society's Kaitlyn Pettengill.) In addition to Green's scholarship, cited in the mini-essay to chapter 1, I learned about Mathew and Henry Carey's growing business from David Kaser's *Messrs. Carey & Lea of Philadelphia* (Philadelphia: University of Pennsylvania Press, 1957) and Emily Bishop Todd's "The Transatlantic Context: Walter Scott and Nineteenth-century American Literary History" (PhD diss., University of Minnesota, 1999). William Charvat's works—*Literary Publishing in America* (Philadelphia: University of Pennsylvania Press, 1959) and *The Profession of Authorship in America* (Columbus; Ohio State University Press, 1968)—remain vital. Two scholars who've done wonderful work exploring issues that Charvat raised are Meredith

McGill, *American Literature and the Culture of Reprinting, 1834–1853* (Philadelphia: University of Pennsylvania Press, 2003), and Leon Jackson, *The Business of Letters: Authorial Economies in Antebellum America* (Stanford: Stanford University Press, 2008). I also relied on James J. Barnes, *Authors, Publishers and Politicians: The Quest for an Anglo-American Copyright Agreement, 1815–1854* (Columbus: Ohio State University Press, 1974); Grantland S. Rice, *The Transformation of Authorship in America* (Chicago: University of Chicago Press, 1997); Melissa J. Homestead, *American Women Authors and Literary Property, 1822–1869* (New York: Cambridge University Press, 2005), and Susan S. Williams, *Reclaiming Authorship: Literary Women in America, 1850–1900* (Philadelphia: University of Pennsylvania Press, 2006). Michael Winship surveys the Hawthorne-sentimental spat in "Hawthorne and the 'Scribbling Women': Publishing The Scarlet Letter in the Nineteenth-Century United States," *Studies in American Fiction* 29, no. 1 (2001): 3–11.

85 *"I have not"*: Hawthorne to Elizabeth Manning Hawthorne, March 13, 1821, *Centenary Edition of the Works of Nathaniel Hawthorne*, ed. William Charvat et al. (Columbus: Ohio State University Press, 1962–), 15:138–39; hereafter cited as *CENH*, followed by volume and page number.

85 *"I feel as if"*: Williams, *Reclaiming Authorship*, 52.

86 *"Candidates for"*: Robert Remini, *The Election of Andrew Jackson* (Philadelphia: Lippincott, 1963), 62.

87 *"born and bred"*: *Edinburgh Review*, January 1820. The author was Sydney Smith.

87 *"the bookseller in"*: James N. Green, *Mathew Carey, Publisher and Patriot* (Philadelphia: Library Company of Philadelphia, 1985), 23.

88 *"There is nothing"*: Henry Carey to Mathew Carey, December 8, 1832, in Kaser, *Messrs. Carey & Lea*, 50.

88 *"hasten the"*: Hugh L. Hodge, *On Diseases Peculiar to Women* (Philadelphia: Henry C. Lea, 1868), 256.

89 *"a rubicund"*: Washington Irving, *History, Tales, and Sketches* (New York: Library of America, 1983), 772, 779.

89 *"Everywhere I find"*: William Godwin to James Ogilvie, September 15, 1819, in Brian Jay Jones, *Washington Irving: An American Original* (New York: Arcade Publishing, 2008), 183.

89 *"will not prove"*: Kaser, *Messrs. Carey & Lea*, 80.

90 *"If I feel"*: *The Letters of Emily Dickinson*, ed. Thomas H. Johnson and Theodora Ward (Cambridge, MA: Harvard University Press, 1958), 474.

90 *"an affinite soul"*: Horace Traubel, *With Walt Whitman in Camden*, ed. Sculley Bradley (Philadelphia: University of Pennsylvania Press, 1953), 4:312–313.

90 *"producing a greater"*: Nathaniel Hawthorne to Louisa Hawthorne, July 10, 1851, *CENH* 16:454.

90 *"America is now"*: Nathaniel Hawthorne to William D. Ticknor, January 19, 1855, *CENH* 15:304.

91 *"I talked"*: Jones, *Washington Irving*, 64.

92 *"I was mortified"*: *Memoirs of John Quincy Adams, Comprising Portions of His Diary . . .* , ed. Charles Francis Adams (Philadelphia: Lippincott, 1874–1877), 8:157; hereafter cited as *MJQA*, followed by volume and page number.

92 *"Honored Mama"*: John Quincy Adams to Abigail Adams, September 27, 1778, *Adams Family Correspondence*, ed. Lyman H. Butterfield et al. (Cambridge, MA: Harvard University Press, 1963–), 3:92; hereafter cited as *AFC*, followed by volume and page number.

92 *"A Journal"*: Nagel, *John Quincy Adams*, ix.

93 *"The Americans have"*: John Quincy Adams to John Adams, November 25, 1796, Founders Online, founders.archives.gov/documents/Adams/99-02-02-1804.

93 *"Very few persons"*: "Of Reading," *Port Folio*, January 22, 1803.

94 *"not merely to"*: *Lectures on Rhetoric and Oratory* (Cambridge, MA: Hilliard and Metcalf, 1810), 1:165. This was the book Adams sent to Jefferson to break their long silence.

94 *"Let dusky Sally"*: "The Discoveries of Captain Lewis," *Boston Review and Monthly Anthology*, March 1807.

95 *"There is no"*: John Quincy Adams to Thomas Boylston Adams, March 21, 1801, Founders Online, founders.archives.gov/documents/Adams/99-03-02-0919.

95 *"If heaven should"*: John Quincy Adams to Louisa Adams, September 23, 1804, Founders Online, https://founders.archives.gov/documents/Adams/99-03-02-1323.

95 *"Thank God"*: Thomas, *Louisa*, 266.

95 *"I am a man"*: *MJQA* 4:388.

96 *"My dear madam"*: Joseph Hopkinson to Louisa Adams, January 1823, in Burton Alva Konkle, *Joseph Hopkinson, 1770–1842* (Philadelphia: University of Pennsylvania Press, 1931), 239.

96 *"You say he"*: *MJQA* 6:132.

97 *"I should have"*: Bassett, *Life of Andrew Jackson*, 64.

97 *"Tell my son"*: Jackson to Rachel Jackson, March 16, 1824, *PAJ* 5:376.

98 *"He is everywhere"*: Remini, *Andrew Jackson: The Course of American Empire*, 318.

98 *"find its way"*: A. P. Hayne to John Reid, May 5, 1815, in *Index to the Andrew Jackson Papers* (Washington, DC: Library of Congress Manuscript Division, 1967), vi–vii.

98 *"destined to fill"*: Hayne to Reid, September 13, 1815, in *Index to the Andrew Jackson Papers*, vii.

98 *"cheerfulness . . . seen"*: Remini, "Andrew Jackson's Account," 35.

99 *"It is certainly"*: Jackson to Edward Livingston, July 5, 1815, *PAJ* 3:371.

99 *"Subscriptions to"*: Jackson to Mathew Carey, November 19, 1815, Lea & Febiger Records, Historical Society of Pennsylvania.

100 *"I need not"*: Jackson to Reid, January 15, 1816, *PAJ* 4:4.

100 *"The book must"*: Jackson to Nathan Reid Jr., February 8, 1816, *PAJ* 4:8.

100 *"highly serviceable"*: Eaton to Jackson, March 20, 1817, *PAJ* 4:104.

100 *"a blow"*: Eaton and Reid, *Life of Andrew Jackson*, 12.

101 *"John Quincy Adams"*: *Pittsburgh Mercury*, February 10, 1824.

102 *"To escape was"*: John Henry Eaton, *The Life of Andrew Jackson* (Philadelphia: Samuel F. Bradford, 1824), 12.

102 *"I read the"*: *Diary of Christopher Columbus Baldwin* (Worcester, MA: American Antiquarian Society, 1901), 169.

102 *"Early dawnings"*: *The Letters of Wyoming, to the People of the United States, on the Presidential Election* (Philadelphia: S. Simpson & J. Conrad, 1824), 93.

102 *"directly from"*: *Letters of Wyoming*, 51.

102 *"my motives"*: Samuel Flagg Bemis, *John Quincy Adams and the Union* (New York: Knopf, 1956), 19.

103 *"the Edinburgh"*: *An Impartial and True History of the Life and Services of Major General Andrew Jackson* (n.p., n.d.), 40.

103 *"Pompous pageantry"*: *MJQA* 7:479.

103 *"presidential motive"*: Eaton to John Coffee, March 28, 1828, in Lowe, "John H. Eaton," 139–140.

104 *"walking arm"*: Parsons, *Birth of Modern Politics*, xi.
104 *"No such library"*: Walter J. Morris, "John Quincy Adams's German Library, with a Catalog of His German Books," *Proceedings of the American Philosophical Society* 118, no. 4 (1974): 321–333, at 321.
104 *"good advice"*: Nagel, *John Quincy Adams*, 373.
105 *"Such things"*: *Dermot MacMorrogh; or, The Conquest of Ireland* (Boston: Carter, Hendee, 1832), 22.
105 *"Could I have"*: *MJQA* 5:219–220.
105 *"electioneering story"*: Remini, *Andrew Jackson: The Course of American Democracy*, 150.
105 *"That damned"*: Remini, *Andrew Jackson: The Course of American Democracy*, 150.
105 *"great democratic"*: *Moby-Dick, or The Whale*, ed. Harrison Hayford, Hershel Parker, and G. Thomas Tanselle (Evanston, IL: Northwestern University Press, 1988), 117.
106 *"the remainder of"*: Fischer, *Tippecanoe and Trinkets Too*, 35.
106 *"a plain old"*: Robert Gray Gunderson, *The Log-Cabin Campaign* (Lexington: University Press of Kentucky, 1957), 165.
106 *"Be sure to"*: Lincoln to John T. Stuart, January 20, 1840, *Collected Works of Abraham Lincoln*, ed. Roy P. Basler (New Brunswick, NJ: Rutgers University Press, 1953–1955), 1:184.
106 *"Father of the"*: S. J. Burr, *The Life and Times of William Henry Harrison* (New York: L. W. Ransom, 1840), 76.
107 *"As soon as"*: "Campaign Lives," *New York Times*, August 28, 1880.
107 *"The campaign biography"*: Charles Wolcott Balestier, "Campaign Biographies," *Critic: A Literary Weekly*, August 2, 1884.
107 *"He did so"*: Harry J. Sievers, *Benjamin Harrison* (New York: University Publishers, 1952–1959; Indianapolis: Bobbs-Merrill, 1968), 2:370.
107 *"the necessary biography"*: Hawthorne to Pierce, June 9, 1852, *CENH* 16:545.
107 *"a statesman"*: Hawthorne to Pierce, July 5, 1852, *CENH* 16:561.
108 *"mansion . . . log hut"*: *Life of Franklin Pierce* (Boston: Ticknor, Reed, and Fields, 1852), 47, 8.
108 *"the interests of"*: *Life of Franklin Pierce*, 28.
108 *"The story is"*: Hawthorne to Horatio Bridge, October 13, 1852, *CENH* 16:605.

Chapter Five: "Abram" Lincoln Writes a Book

Lincoln's historical significance—and his early death, which jump-started the memorialization process—led to an enormous and contradictory body of contemporary testimony. Here's a small example: while most childhood acquaintances said the Washington biography he borrowed was Weems's, Lincoln's cousin claimed it was David Ramsay's. Thankfully, such testimony has itself led to a rigorous body of scholarly sifting, and I've tried to trust the experts, like the pro-Weems Robert Bray in "What Abraham Lincoln Read—An Evaluative and Annotated List," *Journal of the Abraham Lincoln Association* 28, no. 2 (2007): 28–81.

And yet, because *Political Debates* has received so little attention, I've had to do a lot of sifting myself, and I think it's worth walking through three of the knottiest puzzles. The first is how much of the scrapbook assembly came from Lincoln. The evidence clearly points to him doing it entirely by himself. In "The Unfinished Text of the Lincoln-Douglas Debates," *Journal of the Abraham Lincoln Association* 15, no. 1 (1994): 70–84, Douglas L. Wilson reviews the surviving scrapbook, now at the Library of Congress, and counts thirty-three edits made in Lincoln's handwriting. The edits (and Lincoln's sequential captions) both demonstrate the kind of personalized, hyperprotective attention Lincoln lavished on the finished scrapbook, and it's almost impossible to imagine him trusting another person in Springfield to slice up the back issues he'd worked so hard to acquire.

The second puzzle is when Lincoln finished the scrapbook. On December 25, 1858, he wrote to his good friend Henry C. Whitney to thank him for two sets of the *Press and Tribune*, which he'd just received (*Collected Works of Abraham Lincoln*, ed. Roy P. Basler [New Brunswick: Rutgers University Press, 1953–1955], 3:331; hereafter cited as *CW*, followed by volume and page number). On January 8, 1859, Lincoln mentioned the scrapbook in another letter: "By dint of great labor since the election, I have got together a nearly, (not quite) complete single set to preserve myself" (*CW* 3:359). How could Lincoln have finished the scrapbook by January 5, as I suggest in my chapter, if he was still waiting on a (small) part of the complete set? It's one of the many contradictions in the Lincoln record, and I've sided with the memories of Whitney, who vividly recounts Lincoln showing him the scrapbook in Springfield on January 5—surely a memorable day for both men, due to the celebrations of Douglas's supporters—"with considerable satisfaction" (*Life on the Circuit with Lincoln* [Boston: Estes and Lauriat, 1892], 458). Perhaps Lincoln showed Whitney a version that was only nearly complete. Perhaps in his January 8 letter—addressed to a Republican printer he did not know—Lincoln was understating his effort and ambitions, employing his era's preferred stance of humility as he would do again with his previously mentioned autobiographical sketch: "Of course it must not appear to have been written by myself" (*CW* 3:511).

The third puzzle is when the published version appeared. Most of what scholarship there is on *Political Debates* has come from early twentieth-century bibliographers, and most of them have doubted that the book appeared early enough to make an impact on the Republican convention, which met from May 16 to May 18. By far the best analysis of *Political Debates*—and a book I've depended on frequently—is David Henry Leroy's *Mr. Lincoln's Book: Publishing the Lincoln Douglas Debates* (New Castle, DE: Oak Knoll Press, 2009; hereafter cited as *MLB*). Leroy, for instance, argues convincingly that Lincoln's book sold fifty thousand copies and not thirty thousand, as many of the bibliographers had believed. I also appreciate his answering follow-up questions.

Even Leroy, though, is equivocal on whether *Political Debates* made a difference at the convention. Thanks to new digitized databases, I can say confidently that the book was circulating widely in the Midwest and along the East Coast by mid-May. To be fair, newspaper reports contain their own contradictions, with the *Press and Tribune* claiming on February 25 that *Political Debates* was published and then running an ad for preorders in March. But once Follett, Foster, announced the book's publication, on March 20, the mentions that implied a strong familiarity with (or availability of) the book began to pile up. A quick sampling, in addition to the instances cited in the chapter, follows: a bookstore ad in Cincinnati promising "fresh supplies of . . . Douglas and Lincoln's Debate" (*Cincinnati Daily Press*, April 25, 1860); a Boston bookseller promoting it (*Boston Daily Advertiser*, April 26, 1860; on the same page is an ad for Whitman's *Leaves of Grass*); a paper in Lexington, Illinois, giving a local official "our thanks for a copy of the Debates between Douglas and Lincoln" (*Weekly Globe*, April 26, 1860); a Connecticut paper calling the book "a very valuable political document" (*Hartford Courant*, May 7, 1860).

Even after the convention, a New York paper praised the book's advance impact: "We had repeatedly urged Republicans to buy and circulate this discussion—had ourselves procured and sold some hundreds of copies of it—before we ever dreamed that Mr. Lincoln would be our candidate for President" (*New York Daily-Tribune*, May 26, 1860). Citations like this, in addition to the copies Lincoln personally signed and dated before the convention, which are inventoried in *MLB*, make it clear that the book was being read and discussed in April and May. Common sense also makes this clear. Follett, Foster, said that by the middle of June, it had sold close to thirty thousand copies, and that it was moving as many as five hundred copies a day. Even wildly generous assumptions—selling five hundred copies a day, every single day in June—mean as many as fifteen thousand copies were moved in March, April, and May. *Political Debates* had an enormous impact on Lincoln's presidential bid before *and* after the convention, even if his biographers and historians have largely failed to notice it.

The rest of Lincoln's life, thankfully, has been more enthusiastically documented. Other than Basler's *Works*, the indispensable and authoritative Lincoln book is Michael Burlingame's *Abraham Lincoln: A Life*, 2 vols. (Baltimore: Johns Hopkins University Press, 2008; an even longer version lives at www.knox.edu/about-knox/lincoln-studies-center /burlingame-abraham-lincoln-a-life). I wish every president had a biography as exhaustive as this one. If you're obsessed with Lincoln, this is the next book you should read.

I've also relied on Douglas Wilson's wonderful books *Honor's Voice: The Transformation of Abraham Lincoln* (New York: Knopf, 1998) and *Lincoln's Sword: The Presidency and the Power of Words* (New York: Knopf, 2006), though we diverge in that Wilson sees Lincoln as obsessed with writing where I see him as obsessed with printing. In *Lincoln: The Biography of a Writer* (New York: Harper, 2008), Fred Kaplan illuminates Lincoln's reading life. In addition to Bray's "What Abraham Lincoln Read," an essential work for separating reality from myth is *Recollected Words of Abraham Lincoln*, ed. Don E. Fehrenbacher and Virginia Fehrenbacher (Stanford: Stanford University Press, 1996). For Lincoln's time in Indiana, see Louis A. Warren, *Lincoln's Youth: Indiana Years* (Indianapolis: Indiana Historical Society, 1991). In the 1840s and 1850s, Lincoln published political essays in Illinois newspapers, usually under a pseudonym; see Burlingame, "Lincoln Spins the Press," in *Lincoln Reshapes the Presidency*, ed. Charles M. Hubbard (Macon, GA: Mercer University Press, 2003), 65–78. For Lincoln's "Discoveries and Inventions" lecture, see Wayne C. Temple, "Lincoln the Lecturer, Part I," *Lincoln Herald* 101, no. 3 (1999): 94–110, and "Lincoln the Lecturer, Part II," *Lincoln Herald* 101, no. 4 (1999): 146–163. For Lincoln's presidential campaign, see Melvin L. Hayes, *Mr. Lincoln Runs for President* (New York: Citadel Press, 1960). I also depended on Harold Holzer's *Lincoln at Cooper Union: The Speech That Made Abraham Lincoln President* (New York: Simon and Schuster, 2004) and Daniel J. Ryan's *Lincoln and Ohio* (Columbus: Ohio State Archaeological and Historical Society, 1923).

For Lincoln's scrapbook, start with Leroy's *Mr. Lincoln's Book*. After that, it's odds and ends. Follett recounts his meeting with Lincoln, which came near the end of a trip that stretched from Columbus to Boston to Washington, in *Sketches of the Ball and Follett Families*, comp. Alice E. Ball (privately printed but available at the Library of Congress), 80–90; Lincoln also appears to have had a friendly White House meeting with Follett's partner, Frank Foster (*CW* 4:556). David C. Mearns has edited a helpful facsimile of the scrapbook: *The Illinois Political Campaign of 1858: A Facsimile . . .* (Washington, DC: Library of Congress, n.d.). Leroy surveys the earlier bibliographical scholarship; I found the most helpful to be Gerald McMurtry, "The Different Editions of the 'Debates of Lincoln and Douglas,' " *Journal of the Illinois State Historical Society* 27, no. 1 (1934): 95–107. While Lincoln's involvement with the book did not help or hurt his candidacy in any material way, a few people must have known about it because, as McMurtry points out, a few early copies of the Follett version included a letter Lincoln had sent the Ohio Republicans. This must have exasperated Lincoln, and Stephen Douglas tried to make a scandal out of it, suggesting the letter proved the book was "partial and unfair," though his real motive was surely trying to slow a book that was helping his opponent more than himself (101).

On publishing's industrialization, see the second and third volumes of *A History of the Book in America: An Extensive Republic: Print, Culture, and Society in the New Nation, 1790–1840*, ed. Robert A. Gross and Mary Kelley (Chapel Hill: University of North Carolina Press, 2010), and *The Industrial Book, 1840–1880*, ed. Scott E. Casper et al. (Chapel Hill: University of North Carolina Press, 2007). I also relied on Ronald J. Zboray's masterful *A Fictive People: Antebellum Economic Development and the American Reading Public* (New York: Oxford University Press, 1993); Gillian Silverman's *Bodies and Books: Reading and the Fantasy of Communion in Nineteenth-Century America* (Philadelphia: University of Pennsylvania Press, 2012); David Paul Nord's *Faith in Reading: Religious Publishing and the Birth of Mass Media* (New York: Oxford University Press, 2004); and the essays in *Getting the Books Out: Papers of the Chicago Conference on the Book in 19th-Century America*, ed. Michael Hackenberg (Washington, DC: Library of Congress, 1987). On Stowe's best seller, see Michael Winship's "'The Greatest Book of Its Kind': A Publishing History of Uncle Tom's Cabin," *Proceedings of the American Antiquarian Society* 109, no. 2 (1999): 309–332, and Claire Parfait's authoritative *The Publishing History of Uncle Tom's Cabin, 1852–2002* (Aldershot: Ashgate, 2007). Thanks to Winship for answering my questions about the operations and presses at Follett, Foster.

To understand Lincoln's bookish backdrop, read Michael Harris's still unsurpassed "The Availability of Books and the Nature of Book Ownership on the Southern Indiana Frontier, 1800–1850" (PhD diss., Indiana University, 1971), which calculates the figure that only one in five Hoosier estate inventories listed any books; also useful is Howard Peckam's "Books and Reading on the Ohio Valley Frontier," *Mississippi Valley Historical Review* 44, no. 4 (1958): 649–663. For Lincoln's Springfield, see J. C. Power, *History of Springfield* (Springfield, IL: Springfield Board of Trade, 1871). For the bookstores of New York City—the stores Michael Floy loved to visit—see Kristen Doyle Highland's valuable and methodologically innovative "At the Bookstore: Literary and Cultural Experience in Antebellum New York City" (PhD diss., New York University, 2015). For the nineteenth-century lecturing craze, see Susan L. Ferguson, "Dickens's Public Readings and the Victorian Author," *SEL* 41, no. 4 (2001): 729–749, and Bonnie Carr O'Neill, "'The Best of Me Is There': Emerson as Lecturer and Celebrity," *American Literature* 80, no. 4 (2008): 739–767. For the fascinating history of the White House library, see *The First White House Library: A History and Annotated Catalogue*, ed. Catherine M. Parisian (University Park: Pennsylvania State University, 2010). For the American Bible Society, see Creighton Lacy, *The Word Carrying Giant: The Growth of the American Bible Society* (Pasadena, CA: William Carey Library, 1977).

The nineteenth-century influence of Jefferson's *Notes* is charted in Merrill D. Peterson, *The Jefferson Image in the American Mind* (New York: Oxford University Press, 1960), and Winthrop D. Jordan, *White over Black: American Attitudes toward the Negro, 1550–1812* (Chapel Hill: University of North Carolina Press, 1968). Two recent dissertations have dug even deeper: Cara J. Rogers, "Jefferson's Sons: Notes on the State of Virginia and Virginian Antislavery, 1760–1832" (PhD diss., Rice University, 2018), and Kelly M. Payne, "The Image of Jefferson in Nineteenth-Century U.S. Literature, 1826–1871" (PhD diss., University of Nebraska, 2018). On Crockett and Clay, see James Atkins Shackford, *David Crockett: The Man and the Legend* (Chapel Hill: University of North Carolina Press, 1956), and Robert V. Remini, *Henry Clay: Statesman for the Union* (New York: Norton, 1993).

109 *"Old Abe is"*: Melville to Elizabeth Melville, March 24 or 25, 1861, *Correspondence*, ed. Lynn Horth (Evanston, IL: Northwestern University Press, 1988), 365.

109 *"What can I"*: Burlingame, *Abraham Lincoln*, 2:253.

110 *"You know I"*: Howells to Twain, August 5, 1876, *Mark Twain-Howells Letters: The Correspondence of Samuel L. Clemens and William D. Howells*, ed. Henry Nash Smith and William M. Gibson (Cambridge, MA: Harvard University Press, 1960), 2:142.

110 *"Is this the"*: Daniel R. Vollaro, "Lincoln, Stowe, and the 'Little Woman/Great War' Story," *Journal of the Abraham Lincoln Association* 30, no. 1 (2009): 18–34, at 20. While Vollaro lists several somewhat contradictory versions of the anecdote, he presents enough contemporary evidence that when one factors in Lincoln's commitment to print, it seems clear that some version of the exchange occurred. I quote the earliest (printed) version of the exchange, from 1896.

111 *"a half century"*: *Literary and Historical Miscellanies* (New York: Harper, 1857), 481.

113 *"The Most High"*: Nord, *Faith in Reading*, 83.

113 *"every destitute family"*: Harris, "The Availability of Books," 59.

113 *"Robert Stockwell"*: Warren, *Lincoln's Youth*, 138.

114 *"Everything was unfixed"*: *Centenary Edition of the Works of Nathaniel Hawthorne*, ed. William Charvat et al. (Columbus: Ohio State University Press, 1962–), 2:256.

114 *"Putnam's Railway"*: Kevin J. Hayes, "Railway Reading," *Proceedings of the American Antiquarian Society* 106, no. 2 (1998): 301–326, at 306.

115 *"Mr. Jefferson's remarks"*: David Walker, *Walker's Appeal . . .* (Boston: David Walker, 1830), 31–32.

115 *"write something"*: Joan D. Hedrick, *Harriet Beecher Stowe: A Life* (New York: Oxford University Press, 1994), 207. The sister-in-law's name was Isabella Beecher.

115 *"Reader, buy"*: Parfait, *Publishing History*, 91.

116 *"I find so"*: *The Diary of Michael Floy, Jr.: Bowery Village, 1833–1837*, ed. Richard A. E. Brooks (New Haven, CT: Yale University Press, 1941), 7.

116 *"I intend"*: *Diary of Michael Floy*, 6.

116 *"I keep no"*: *Diary of Michael Floy*, 7.

117 *"never did more"*: Burlingame, *Abraham Lincoln*, 1:10.

118 *"understand everything"*: Warren, *Lincoln's Youth*, 132.

118 *"he was looked"*: *CW* 3:511.

118 *"No qualification"*: *CW* 3:511.

118 *"I recollect"*: *CW* 4:236.

119 *"He was a"*: Wilson, *Honor's Voice*, 58.

119 *"If Abe don't"*: Burlingame, *Abraham Lincoln*, 1:10.

120 *"He's a dangerous"*: Wilson, *Lincoln's Sword*, 280.

121 *"Ladies and gentlemen"*: Ferguson, "Dickens's Public Readings," 734.

122 *"There is no"*: *CW* 3:16.

122 *"The dedicatory . . . The cheek"*: Harold Holzer, *Lincoln and the Power of the Press: The War for Public Opinion* (New York: Simon & Schuster, 2014), 454.

123 *"Where's Hitt?"*: *The Lincoln-Douglas Debates of 1858*, ed. Edwin Erle Sparks (Springfield, IL: Illinois State Historical Library, 1908), 79. Burlingame documents a second (very similar) version of this story in *Abraham Lincoln*, 1:502.

124 *"Everywhere I hear"*: *Lincoln Memorial: Album-Immortelles* (New York: G. W. Carleton, 1882), 473.

124 *"I admit the"*: *Lincoln Memorial*, 476.

124 *"I am ingaged"*: Shackford, *David Crockett*, 264.

124 *"I wish to"*: Lincoln to Charles H. Ray, November 20, 1858, *CW* 3:341.

125 *"I have no"*: Lincoln to Henry C. Whitney, November 30, 1858, *CW* 3:343.

125 *"I have hunted"*: *MLB* 7. The letter is dated December 11, providing further evidence that Lincoln would finished the scrapbook by January 5, 1859.

126 *"a one-sided"*: Lincoln to William A. Ross, March 26, 1859, *CW* 3:372.

126 *"to print it"*: Lincoln to Ross, March 26, 1859, *CW* 3:373.

126 *"excellent apartments"*: *American Notes, for General Circulation* (London: Chapman and Hall, 1842), 2:161.

126 *"Prompt action"*: Samuel Galloway to Lincoln, December 13, 1859, *MLB* 45.

126 *"I wish the"*: Lincoln to George M. Parsons, December 19, 1859, *CW* 3:510.

127 *"you could hear"*: Hayes, *Mr. Lincoln Runs*, 28.

128 *"the other half"*: *CW* 3:362.

128 *"looked upon. . . . Teachers were"*: *CW* 3:362.

128 *"To emancipate"*: *CW* 3:363.

128 *"The effects could"*: *CW* 3:362.

129 *"a volume of extraordinary"*: *New York Independent*, April 19, 1860.

129 *"the speeches of"*: "Book-list for the Week," *New York Saturday Press*, April 21, 1860.

129 *"The Literary Emporium"*: Hellmutt Lehmann-Haupt et al., *The Book in America: A History of the Making and Selling of Books in the United States* (New York: Bowker, 1951), 247.

129 *"raise[d] him"*: *Chicago Press and Tribune*, June 7, 1860, but reprinting an earlier, undated story from the *Daily Union* of Auburn, New York.

130 *"a political textbook"*: The *Boston Courier* review is quoted in J. Q. Howard, *The Life of Abraham Lincoln* (Columbus: Follett, Foster, & Co., 1860), 112.

130 *"a volume of hundreds"*: Lincoln to Galloway, June 19, 1860, *CW* 4:80.

130 *"Are those the"*: Burlingame, *Abraham Lincoln*, 1:652.

130 *"This book . . . should"*: *Randolph County Journal*, April 12, 1860.

130 *"logical eloquence"*: James O. Putnam to Leonard Swett, June or July 1860, *CW* 4:84.

131 *"ten readers"*: Parfait, *Publishing History*, 103.

131 *"You will be"*: James O. Putnam to Abraham Lincoln, September 25, 1860, Abraham Lincoln Papers, Library of Congress, microfilm reel 9.

132 *"I esteem"*: Lincoln to Galloway, December 19, 1859, *The Collected Works of Abraham Lincoln: Supplement, 1832–1865* (New Brunswick, NJ: Rutgers University Press, 1974), 47.

132 *"W. T. Bascom"*: *MLB* 154.

Chapter Six: "General Grant, the People Are Moving En Masse upon Your *Memoirs*"

Grant's *Personal Memoirs* is generally seen as the best presidential book, and it boasts the best secondary literature of any presidential volume as well. The best biographies are William S. McFeely's *Grant: A Biography* (New York: Norton, 1981) and Ron Chernow's *Grant* (New York: Penguin, 2017), though both should be read alongside Joan Waugh's magnificently meta *U.S. Grant: American Hero, American Myth* (Chapel Hill: University of North Carolina Press, 2009). The thirty-two-volume *Papers of Ulysses S. Grant*, ed. John Y. Simon et al. (Carbondale: Southern Illinois University Press, 1969–2012; hereafter cited as *PUSG*, followed by volume and page number) makes it easy to dig deeper. The *PUSG* editors have also produced the best edition of Grant's book, *The Personal Memoirs of Ulysses S. Grant: The Complete Annotated Edition*, ed. John F. Marszalek (Cambridge, MA: Harvard University Press, 2017); my citations of the published volumes follow this edition, though I supplemented it by studying Grant's various article and book drafts in the Ulysses S. Grant Papers, which are held at the Library of Congress.

About the only critique one can aim at Grant's biographers is that they give Mark

Twain too much credit, though his charm makes this an understandable slip. (Between them, McFeely and Chernow award Robert Underwood Johnson, Grant's most important editor, only a few paragraphs.) On Grant's race to finish his book, see Thomas M. Pitkin, *The Captain Departs: Ulysses S. Grant's Last Campaign* (Carbondale: Southern Illinois University Press, 1973), and Charles Bracelen Flood, *Grant's Final Victory: Ulysses S. Grant's Heroic Last Year* (New York: Da Capo Press, 2011). I also relied on delightful memoirs from Johnson (*Remembered Yesterdays* [Boston: Little, Brown, 1923]) and his colleague L. Frank Tooker (*Joys and Tribulations of an Editor* [New York: Century, 1924]), along with a shorter one from Grant's stenographer, N. E. Dawson (*Philadelphia Inquirer*, February 6, 1894). In *The Man Who Saved the Union: Ulysses Grant in War and Peace* (New York: Doubleday, 2012), H. W. Brands gives Grant's reading special attention. Ishbel Ross's *The General's Wife* (New York: Dodd, Mead, 1959) captures Julia Grant's life marvelously; Lloyd Lewis's *Captain Sam Grant* (Boston: Little, Brown, 1950) does the same for Grant's youth, with additional context on his reading coming from *Cadet Life before the Mexican War*, ed. Sidney Forman (West Point: United States Military Academy Library, 1945).

For the selling of Grant's book—and here Twain does deserve credit—see Walter A. Friedman, *Birth of a Salesman: The Transformation of Selling in America* (Cambridge, MA: Harvard University Press, 2004). Twain's business sense, along with post–Civil War shifts in American publishing, receive excellent treatment in Bruce Michelson, *Printer's Devil: Mark Twain and the American Publishing Revolution* (Berkeley: University of California Press, 2007). Justin Kaplan's wonderful biography of Twain, *Mr. Clemens and Mark Twain: A Biography* (New York: Simon & Schuster, 1966), offers a longer analysis of how Grant influenced the death scene in Twain's second Civil War essay. On that essay and its precursor, see Fred W. Lorch, "Mark Twain and the 'Campaign That Failed,'" *American Literature* 12, no. 4 (1941): 454–470.

The Civil War's impact on American letters has also received thorough study. See Alice Fahs's *The Imagined Civil War: Popular Literature of the North and South, 1861–1865* (Chapel Hill: University of North Carolina Press, 2001); Cynthia Wachtell's *War No More: The Antiwar Impulse in American Literature, 1861–1914* (Baton Rouge: Louisiana State University Press, 2010); Randall Fuller's *From Battlefields Rising: How the Civil War Transformed American Literature* (New York: Oxford University Press, 2011); and Daniel Aaron's groundbreaking *The Unwritten War: American Writers and the Civil War* (New York: Knopf, 1973). My reading of Melville's "Shiloh" owes much to Michael Warner's in "What Like a Bullet Can Undeceive?" *Public Culture* 15, no. 1 (2003): 41–54. For Whitman learning about Fort Sumter, a memory the poet garbled a bit, see Mark Caldwell, *New York Night: The Mystique and Its History* (New York: Scribner, 2005).

Scholars have been slower to appreciate how the Civil War transformed the conventions governing legacy books by generals, politicians, and other famous Americans. A small way to see the increase in such books is to chart how many volumes Grant agreed to review in manuscript form. (There are numerous examples in the Records of the D. Appleton-Century Company at the Lilly Library, Indiana University, Bloomington.) A larger way is to look at the creation and reception of James Buchanan's and William T. Sherman's legacy books. See Philip S. Klein, *President James Buchanan: A Biography* (University Park: Pennsylvania State University Press, 1962); Stephen Patrick O'Hara, "'The Verdict of History': Defining and Defending James Buchanan through Public Memorialization" (master's thesis, Virginia Tech, 2012); John F. Marszalek, *Sherman: A Soldier's Passion for Order* (New York: Free Press, 1993); and Gerard Wolfe, *The House of Appleton* (Metuchen, NJ: Scarecrow Press, 1981). On the *Century*'s efforts to popularize Civil War autobiography, see Stephen Davis, "'A Matter of Sensational Interest': The *Century* 'Battles and Leaders' Series,"

Civil War History 27, no. 4 (1981): 338–349; and Timothy Paul Caron, "'How Changeable Are the Events of War': National Reconciliation in the *Century Magazine*'s 'Battles and Leaders of the Civil War,'" *American Periodicals* 16, no. 2 (2006): 151–171; the magazine also produced a four-volume book collecting its best essays, which sold about seventy-five thousand copies.

In addition to the factors mentioned in this chapter, one more thing suggests that an aging Lincoln might have tried to write his presidential memoirs. Several of his contemporaries noticed how little the president knew about his family's past—and how much he spoke about wanting to learn more. "I heard him say on more than one occasion," Lincoln's secretary of the navy recalled, "that when he laid down his official life he would endeavor to trace out his genealogy and family history" (Gideon Welles, "Administration of Abraham Lincoln," *Galaxy*, January 1877). Van Buren's autobiography appeared posthumously as *The Autobiography of Martin Van Buren* (New York: Augustus M. Kelley, 1969); as ex-president he wrote another posthumously published book, *Inquiry into the Origin and Course of Political Parties in the United States* (New York: Hurd and Houghton, 1867), though in it Van Buren seemed more interested in the political battles of the founders than in the ones he actually participated in. Fillmore's autobiographical sketch can be found in the first volume of the *Millard Fillmore Papers*, ed. Frank H. Severance (Buffalo: Buffalo Historical Society, 1907). In the Papers of James Garfield at the Library of Congress, there is a long document, partially written and partially dictated, in which Garfield recounts much of his life "for the benefit of biographers." See the Garfield Papers, series 17D, along with Garfield's excellent and underappreciated diary: *The Diary of James A. Garfield*, ed. Harry James Brown and Frederick D. Williams (East Lansing: Michigan State University Press, 1968–1981). Thanks to Scott Casper for alerting me to Garfield's autobiographical dictations.

On autobiographies by less famous figures, see Ann Fabian's *The Unvarnished Truth: Personal Narratives in Nineteenth-Century America* (Berkeley: University of California Press, 2000), and William Best Hesseltine's *Civil War Prisons: A Study in War Psychology* (Columbus: Ohio State University Press, 1930), which documents the explosion in prisoner memoirs. A good overview of nineteenth-century autobiography is Lawrence Buell, "Autobiography in the American Renaissance," in *American Autobiography: Retrospect and Prospect*, ed. Paul John Eskin (Madison: University of Wisconsin Press, 1991), 47–69. On slave narratives, see William L. Andrews, *To Tell a Free Story: The First Century of Afro-American Autobiography, 1760–1865* (Urbana: University of Illinois Press, 1986), and Christopher Hager, *Word by Word: Emancipation and the Act of Writing* (Cambridge, MA: Harvard University Press, 2013). Many of these narratives, along with informative introductions, can be read online at the invaluable North American Slave Narratives website (docsouth.unc.edu/neh/chronautobio.html).

I learned a lot about the Lost Cause from two edited collections: *The Memory of the Civil War in American Culture*, ed. Alice Fahs and Joan Waugh (Chapel Hill: University of North Carolina Press, 2004), and *The Myth of the Lost Cause and Civil War History*, ed. Gary W. Gallagher and Alan T. Nolan (Bloomington: Indiana University Press, 2000). William A. Blair explores how Grant and his book fared in "Grant's Second Civil War: The Battle for Historical Memory," in *The Spotsylvania Campaign: Military Campaigns of the Civil War*, ed. Gary Gallagher (Chapel Hill: University of North Carolina Press, 1998), 223–254.

133 *"an old woman"*: Michael Burlingame, *Abraham Lincoln: A Life* (Baltimore: Johns Hopkins University Press, 2008), 2:512.

133 *"Gen. Lee's"*: Burlingame, *Abraham Lincoln*, 2:515.

133 *"No hand but"*: Rush to John Adams, September 4, 1811, Founders Online, founders
.archives.gov/documents/Adams/99-02-02-5680.

134 *"yelling up"*: *Memoranda During the War*, ed. Peter Coviello (New York: Oxford University Press, 2004), 108.

135 *"as by flashes"*: *Poetry and Prose of Walt Whitman*, ed. Louis Untermeyer (New York: Simon and Schuster, 1949), 516.

135 *"Nothing but 'War'"*: Fahs, *Imagined Civil War*, 18.

135 *"You can"*: Emily Godbey, "'Terrible Fascination': Civil War Stereographs of the Dead," *History of Photography* 36, no. 3 (2012): 265–74, at 271.

135 *"From the stump"*: *Poetry and Prose of Walt Whitman*, 285.

136 *"Skimming lightly"*: *Published Poems: The Writings of Herman Melville*, ed. Robert C. Ryan et al. (Evanston, IL: Northwestern University Press, 2009), 46.

137 *"The body"*: "History by the Yard," *Nation*, November 23, 1865.

137 *"Don't cry"*: Keckley, *Behind the Scenes* (New York: G. W. Carleton & Co., 1868), 192.

137 *"The more I read"*: Frederick Douglass, *Autobiographies* (New York: Library of America, 1994), 227.

138 *"more to say"*: Van Buren, *Autobiography*, 8.

138 *"I shall now"*: Buchanan to Harriet Lane, November 6, 1861, *Works of James Buchanan*, ed. John Bassett Moore (Philadelphia: J. B. Lippincott, 1908–1911), 11:226.

138 *"Instead of trusting"*: "Mr. Buchanan and His Book," *New York Times*, December 1, 1865.

138 *"It is my purpose"*: Lee to William B. Reid, November 10, 1865, in Allen W. Moger, "General Lee's Unwritten *History of the Army of Northern Virginia*," *Virginia Magazine of History and Biography* 71, no. 3 (1963): 341–363, at 345.

138 *"Can you not"*: Lee to James Longstreet, March 8, 1866, in Longstreet, *From Manassas to Appomattox: Memoirs of the Civil War in America*, 2nd ed. (Philadelphia: Lippincott, 1908), 655.

139 *"Who told you"*: Albert Bigelow Paine, *Mark Twain: A Biography* (New York: Harper, 1912), 2:710–711.

139 *"I suppose"*: Wolfe, *The House of Appleton*, 156.

140 *"Perhaps General"*: *Chicago Tribune*, May 16, 1875.

140 *"There has been"*: *Diary of James A. Garfield*, 3:101. Sherman would have sold at least twice as many copies had he not forbid his publisher from selling the book by subscription. The general "had a horror of book agents," his editor, James C. Derby, recalled (*Fifty Years Among Authors, Books and Publishers* [New York: G.W. Carleton, 1884], 184).

140 *"He writes not"*: *Diary of James A. Garfield*, 3:103.

141 *"Strange as"*: Davis to James C. Derby, February 14, 1880, in Derby, *Fifty Years Among Authors*, 496.

141 *"I have always"*: Grant to Twain, January 14, 1881, *PUSG* 30:118.

141 *"a constant reader"*: *Personal Memoirs*, 9.

141 *"Much of the time"*: *Personal Memoirs*, 21.

142 *"How often I"*: Grant to Julia Grant, October 1845, *PUSG* 1:60.

142 *"I recognized"*: *Personal Memoirs*, 473.

142 *"No terms except"*: Grant to Simon Buckner, February 16, 1862, *PUSG* 4:218.

143 *"When I was"*: *Hartford Courant*, June 4, 1866.

143 *"We got nothing"*: *New York Herald*, December 19, 1909.

143 *"Is Grant Guilty?"*: McFeely, *Grant*, 492.

144 *"his dignified sorrow"*: Johnson, *Remembered Yesterdays*, 213.

144 *"were hardly able"*: Ulysses S. Grant Papers, Library of Congress, microfilm reel 5. This sentence survived in the published book, at page 235.

144 *"the blight of"*: Johnson, *Remembered Yesterdays*, 214.

146 *"I couldn't stand"*: Johnson, *Remembered Yesterdays*, 215.

146 *"Some time after"*: *Personal Memoirs*, 239.

146 *"Why, I am"*: Johnson, *Remembered Yesterdays*, 215.

146 *"was the first"*: *Index to the Ulysses S. Grant Papers* (Washington, DC, 1965), ix.

147 *"hurt him"*: Julia Grant, *Personal Memoirs of Julia Dent Grant*, ed. John Y. Simon (New York: G. P. Putnam's Sons, 1975), 329.

147 *"Is it cancer?"*: Pitkin, *The Captain Departs*, 24.

147 *"General Grant has"*: Flood, *Grant's Final Victory*, 85.

148 *"Do you know"*: *Autobiography of Mark Twain*, ed. Harriet E. Smith et al. (Berkeley: University of California Press, 2010–2014), 2:60.

149 *"I was sure his"*: *Mark Twain's Notebooks and Journals*, ed. Frederick Anderson et al. (Berkeley: University of California Press, 1975–1979), 3:107; *Autobiography of Mark Twain*, 1:89.

149 *"General Grant Very"*: Waugh, *U.S. Grant*, 173.

149 *"General Grant Goes"*: The headlines in this paragraph come from Waugh, *U.S. Grant*, 174, except for "General Grant's Condition," which ran in the *Washington Post*, June 22, 1885.

150 *"This is a warning"*: *Autobiography of Mark Twain*, 2:66.

150 *"General Grant at Work"*: Waugh, *U.S. Grant*, 192.

150 *"The people . . . are"*: Edward Henry to Grant, June 22, 1885, *PUSG* 31:369.

150 *"He is not"*: Pitkin, *The Captain Departs*, 36–37.

151 *"I do not want a book"*: Grant to Badeau, May 5, 1885, *PUSG* 31:355.

152 *"with a patient"*: Johnson, *Remembered Yesterdays*, 223.

152 *"man's destiny"*: *PUSG* 31:414–415.

152 *"Life passed"*: Ross, *The General's Wife*, 311.

153 *"I wish I"*: Twain to Henry Ward Beecher, September 11, 1885, in *Mark Twain's Letters*, ed. Albert Bigelow Paine (New York: Harper & Brothers, 1917), 2:460.

153 *"The factory hands"*: Richard S. Lowry, *"Littery Man": Mark Twain and Modern Authorship* (New York: Oxford University Press, 1996), 21.

153 *"I called to"*: Friedman, *Birth of a Salesman*, 46.

153 *"the largest sum"*: *New York Times*, July 12, 1852.

154 *"We have heard"*: Howells, "Editor's Study," *Harper's*, August 1886.

154 *"We should doubtless"*: *Dial*, January 17, 1918.

154 *"The future historian"*: *Southern Historical Society Papers*, January–December 1886.

155 *"I, too, am"*: *Mark Twain's Civil War*, ed. David Rachels (Lexington: University of Kentucky Press, 2007), 30.

155 *"You have heard"*: *Mark Twain's Civil War*, 47.

156 *"Somebody said"*: *Mark Twain's Civil War*, 72.

Chapter Seven: Head of the Class: Roosevelt, Wilson, and the Expansion of Executive Power

It would almost be easier to list the turn-of-the-century memoirs that don't have a good Theodore Roosevelt story than ones that do. In his own contribution to the field, Finley

Peter Dunne depicted the ex-president pacing and dictating frantically while working on a magazine story. "When you are dealing with politics," Roosevelt explained, "you feel that you have your enemy right in front of you and you must shake your fist and roar the gospel of righteousness in his deaf ear" (*Mr. Dooley Remembers* [Boston: Little, Brown, 1963], 185).

Roosevelt the politician has been the subject of numerous studies. I relied the most on Edmund Morris's *The Rise of Theodore Roosevelt* (New York: Coward, McCann & Geoghegan, 1979), *Theodore Rex* (New York: Random House, 2001), and *Colonel Roosevelt* (New York: Random House, 2010). Roosevelt the writer has also received ample analysis. There's Morris's essay on the topic, collected in *This Living Hand* (New York: Random House, 2012), along with more sustained treatments such as Jonathan Arnold, "Publishing Theodore Roosevelt, 1882–1919" (PhD diss., University of London, 2010); Thomas Bailey and Katherine Joslin, *Theodore Roosevelt: A Literary Life* (Lebanon, NH: University Press of New England, 2018); Aviva F. Taubenfeld, *Rough Writing: Ethnic Authorship in Theodore Roosevelt's America* (New York: New York University Press, 2008); Aloysius A. Norton, *Theodore Roosevelt* (Boston: Twayne, 1980); and Lawrence J. Oliver, *Brander Matthews, Theodore Roosevelt, and the Politics of American Literature, 1880–1920* (Knoxville: University of Tennessee Press, 1992), the last of which thoroughly documents Roosevelt's John Quincy Adams–like passion for fostering a distinctly American literary tradition. In "The Lasting Influence of Theodore Roosevelt's *Naval War of 1812*," *International Journal of Naval History* 1, no. 1 (2002): n.p., Michael J. Crawford traces the influence of Roosevelt's first book, an idea also explored in Richard W. Turk's *The Ambiguous Relationship: Theodore Roosevelt and Alfred Thayer Mahan* (Westport, CT: Greenwood, 1987). Meredith Hindley's "Roosevelt the Revisionist," *Humanities*, September–October 2013, also discusses the creation of Roosevelt's first book.

In *The Life of Theodore Roosevelt* (Philadelphia: John C. Winston, 1919), William Draper Lewis documents Roosevelt's reading life. Important sources for Roosevelt's time at Harvard include Donald George Wilhelm, *Theodore Roosevelt as an Undergraduate* (Boston: J. W. Luce and Company, 1910); J. Laurence Laughlin, "Roosevelt at Harvard," *Review of Reviews*, October 1924; and Michael R. Canfield, *Theodore Roosevelt in the Field* (Chicago: University of Chicago Press, 2015). For Roosevelt's response to the rapidly specializing field of law, see Robert B. Charles, "Theodore Roosevelt, the Lawyer," in *Theodore Roosevelt: Many-Sided American*, ed. Natalie Naylor, Douglas Brinkley, and John Allen Gable (Interlaken, NY: Heart of Lakes Publishing, 1991), 121–139.

The best look at Woodrow Wilson as a politician is John Milton Cooper's *Woodrow Wilson: A Biography* (New York: Random House, 2009). The best look at Wilson as a writer is Henry Wilkinson Bragdon's *Woodrow Wilson: The Academic Years* (Cambridge, MA: Harvard University Press, 1967). Both approaches benefit from the incredible sixty-nine-volume resource that is the *Papers of Woodrow Wilson*, ed. Arthur S. Link (Princeton: Princeton University Press, 1967–1994; hereafter cited as *PWW*, followed by volume and page number). The editorial headnotes illuminate all sorts of topics—Wilson's unfinished opus "Philosophy of Politics," or his early attempts to write fiction.

Other useful looks at Wilson's writings include John M. Mulder, *Woodrow Wilson: The Years of Preparation* (Princeton: Princeton University Press, 1978); Niels Aage Thorsen, *The Political Thought of Woodrow Wilson, 1875–1910* (Princeton: Princeton University Press, 1988); and David Anderson, *Woodrow Wilson* (Boston: Twayne, 1978). Stockton Axson's "Brother Woodrow": A Memoir of Woodrow Wilson* (Princeton: Princeton University Press, 1993) has a vivid account of Wilson's reading for pleasure. W. Barksdale Maynard's "More Than a Mere Student," *Johns Hopkins Magazine*, September 2007, surveys Wilson's time at Adams's seminary.

While Roosevelt and Wilson both revolutionized the presidency, there's a case to be made that William McKinley and Grover Cleveland—the latter a favorite subject of Wilson's writing—were important and active precursors. The presidential scholarship I cite in my essay on sources and methods covers this thoroughly, but I also learned from period-specific research, especially Peri Arnold's *Remaking the Presidency: Roosevelt, Taft, and Wilson, 1901–1916* (Lawrence: University Press of Kansas, 2009); George Juergens's *News from the White House: The Presidential-Press Relationship in the Progressive Era* (Chicago: University of Chicago Press, 1981); and David Ryfe's "'Betwixt and Between': Woodrow Wilson's Press Conferences and the Transition toward the Modern Rhetorical Presidency," *Political Communication* 16, no. 1 (1999): 77–93.

In addition to the historiography mentioned in my mini-essay for chapter 3, I relied on a number of works to understand the twinned rise of history professors and pop historians. The most valuable were Ian Tyrrell's *Historians in Public: The Practice of American History, 1890–1970* (Chicago: University of Chicago Press, 2005), Robert B. Townsend's *History's Babel: Scholarship, Professionalization, and the Historical Enterprise in the United States, 1880–1940* (Chicago: University of Chicago Press, 2013), and Gregory M. Pfitzer's *Popular History and the Literary Marketplace, 1840–1920* (Amherst: University of Massachusetts Press, 2008). Other useful studies—and these also touch frequently on this period's fondness for specialization and expertise—include John Higham, *History: Professional Scholarship in America* (New York: Harper & Row, 1973), Ellen Fitzpatrick, *History's Memory: Writing America's Past, 1880–1980* (Cambridge, MA: Harvard University Press, 2002), Pero Dagbovie, *The Early Black History Movement, Carter G. Woodson, and Lorenzo Johnston Greene* (Urbana: University of Illinois Press, 2007); Ray Allen Billington, *Frederick Jackson Turner: Historian, Scholar, Teacher* (New York: Oxford University Press, 1973); William H. Jordy, *Henry Adams: Scientific Historian* (New Haven, CT: Yale University Press, 1952); Susan Katcher, "Legal Training in the United States: A Brief History," *Wisconsin International Law Journal* 24 (2006): 335–375; and Roger L. Geiger, *The History of American Higher Education: Learning and Culture from the Founding to World War II* (Princeton: Princeton University Press, 2014). For Ridpath, see Louis Christian Smith, "John Clark Ridpath—U.S. Popular Historian" (PhD diss., University of Illinois, 1972). For Sandburg, see Penelope Niven, *Carl Sandburg: A Biography* (New York: Scribner's, 1991), and James Hurt, "Sandburg's Lincoln within History," *Journal of the Abraham Lincoln Association* 20, no. 1 (1999): 55–65.

159 *"If you hear"*: Johnson to Roosevelt, May 7, 1898, in Arnold, "Publishing Theodore Roosevelt," 63.
159 *"I could make"*: Roosevelt to Robert Bridges, May 21, 1898, *Letters of Theodore Roosevelt*, ed. Elting E. Morrison (Cambridge, MA: Harvard University Press, 1951–1954), 2:832; hereafter cited as *LTR*, followed by volume and page number.
159 *"If I was"*: The contemporary was Dunne, and he put the joke in the mouth of his popular satirical character who pronounced it "Cubia." See *Mr. Dooley Remembers*, 275.
160 *"swiftest moving"*: Tarkington, *The World Does Move* (New York: Doubleday, 1928), 290.
161 *"Today I"*: Pfitzer, *Popular History*, 128.
162 *"By flint"*: Ridpath, *A Popular History of the United States of America* (New York: Nelson & Phillips, 1878), xxxvii.
162 *"Ridpath, the Historian"*: Smith, "John Clark Ridpath," 22–23.
162 *"the vulgar conceit"*: *Addresses at the Inauguration of Charles William Eliot* (Cambridge, MA: Sever and Francis, 1869), 39.

162 *"I wish I"*: Eliot to Charles Eliot Norton, September 18, 1860, in Henry James, *Charles William Eliot* (Boston: Houghton Mifflin, 1930), 1:87.

163 *"laboratory"*: Adams, "Seminary Libraries and University Extension," *Johns Hopkins University Studies in Historical and Political Science* 11 (1887): 443–469, at 455.

163 *"The historical seminary"*: Herbert Baxter Adams, *The Study of History in American Colleges and Universities* (Washington, DC: Government Printing Office, 1887), 171.

164 *"History is past"*: Adams, *Study of History*, 185.

165 *"wrinkled sages"*: Pfitzer, *Popular History*, 146.

165 *"A volume of"*: *A Tribute to Carl Sandburg at Seventy-five*, ed. Harry E. Pratt (Chicago: Abraham Lincoln Bookshop, 1953), 397.

165 *"What, . . . another life?"*: Fanny Butcher, "Sandburg Writes Beautiful, Great Lincoln Biography," *Chicago Tribune*, January 30, 1926.

166 *"a wonderful little"*: James to Edith Wharton, January 16, 1905, *Henry James: Selected Letters*, ed. Leon Edel (Cambridge, MA: Harvard University Press, 1974), 360.

166 *"When the October"*: D. J. Philippon, "Theodore Roosevelt's 'Sou'-Sou'-Southerly': An Unappreciated Nature Essay," *North Dakota Quarterly* 64 (1997): 83–92, at 86–87.

167 *"I have absolutely"*: Canfield, *Theodore Roosevelt*, 121.

167 *"Now look here"*: Wilhelm, *Theodore Roosevelt*, 35.

167 *"I can see"*: Ralph Barton Perry, *The Thought and Character of William James* (Boston: Little, Brown, 1936), 2:247.

167 *"wholly impossible"*: Roosevelt, *Theodore Roosevelt: An Autobiography* (New York: Macmillan, 1913), 21.

168 *"is not fond"*: Roosevelt, *A Book-Lover's Holidays in the Open* (New York: Scribner's, 1916), 259.

168 *"talk to me"*: Ferdinand Iglehart, *Theodore Roosevelt: The Man as I Knew Him* (New York: Christian Herald, 1919), 122.

169 *"Teddykins . . . Teedy . . . my blessed"*: These descriptions appear in the letters gathered in Michael Teague's "Theodore Roosevelt and Alice Hathaway Lee: A New Perspective," *Harvard Library Bulletin* 33, no. 3 (1985): 225–238.

169 *"going into"*: Morris, *Rise of Theodore Roosevelt*, 117.

169 *"drawing little"*: See the letters in Teague, "Theodore Roosevelt and Alice Hathaway Lee."

170 *"I have plenty"*: Roosevelt to Anna Roosevelt, August 21, 1881, *LTR* 1:50.

170 *"They bring out"*: Roosevelt to Corinne Roosevelt, August 24, 1881, *LTR* 1:51.

170 *"We're dining"*: Owen Wister, *Roosevelt: The Story of a Friendship, 1880–1919* (New York: Macmillan, 1930), 24.

170 *"my book seems"*: Arnold, "Publishing Theodore Roosevelt," 31.

170 *"The Endymion"*: Roosevelt, *Naval War of 1812* (New York: G. P. Putnam's Sons, 1882), 56.

171 *"Something more"*: Roosevelt, *Naval War*, 271.

171 *"treacherous . . . fond"*: Roosevelt, *Naval War*, 36.

171 *"peculiarly dependent"*: Roosevelt, *The Rough Riders* (New York: Scribner's, 1899), 143–45.

171 *"cool"*: "Editor's Literary Record," *Harper's*, November 1882; "Books of the Month," *Atlantic*, July 1882.

171 *"If his conclusions"*: *Literary World*, June 3, 1882.

172 *"I should like"*: Roosevelt to Jonas S. Van Duzer, January 15, 1888, *TLR* 1:136.

172 *"He is a real"*: Wilson to Mary A. Hulbert, August 25, 1912, *PWW* 25:56.

172 *"Now . . . put down"*: Cooper, *Woodrow Wilson*, 20.

173 *"It was as natural"*: David Lawrence, *The True Story of Woodrow Wilson* (New York: George H. Doran, 1924), 330.

173 *"Desultory reading"*: *PWW* 1:276.

173 *"It is no"*: W. E. B. Du Bois, "Another Open Letter to Woodrow Wilson," *The Crisis*, September 1913.

174 *"What do I"*: Wilson to Robert Bridges, May 13, 1883, *PWW* 2:358.

174 *"It is such"*: Wilson to Ellen Axson Wilson, November 27, 1883, *PWW* 2:551.

174 *"I need not"*: Wilson to Ellen Axson Wilson, October 27, 1884, *PWW* 3:379.

174 *"weakly manned"*: Wilson to Ellen Axson Wilson, November 27, 1883, *PWW* 2:552.

174 *"its manifest"*: Wilson to Henry Mills Alden, January 22, 1900, *PWW* 12:82–83.

175 *"rummaging work"*: Wilson to Ellen Axson Wilson, October 16, 1883, *PWW* 2:479–80.

175 *"a little over-intense"*: Edith Gittings Reid, *Woodrow Wilson: The Caricature, the Myth, and the Man* (New York: Oxford University Press, 1934), 38.

175 *"[He] readily"*: Wilson to Ellen Axson Wilson, October 16, 1883, *PWW* 2.480.

175 *"is a cornerstone"*: Woodrow Wilson, *Congressional Government: A Study in American Politics* (Boston: Houghton Mifflin, 1885), 9.

175 *"the ablest and"*: *John Franklin Jameson and the Development of Humanistic Scholarship in America*, ed. Morey Rothberg and Jacqueline Goggins (Athens: University of Georgia Press, 1993), 320.

175 *"Four-fifths"*: James Bryce, *The American Commonwealth* (New York: Macmillan, 1889), 1:76.

175 *"very distressing"*: Wilson, *Congressional Government*, 282.

176 *"The business"*: Wilson, *Congressional Government*, 254.

176 *"Don't write"*: Jessie Bones Brower to Wilson, July 15, 1883, *PWW* 2:367.

176 *"There is a keen"*: Wilson to Ellen Axson Wilson, July 28, 1884, *PWW* 3:264.

176 *"one of the most"*: *Nation*, February 13, 1885.

176 *"the ablest contribution"*: Adams, *Study of History*, 226.

176 *"I know your"*: Bryce to Wilson, February 25, 1884, *PWW* 5:707.

176 *"has of course"*: Wilson to Ellen Axson Wilson, December 2, 1884, *PWW* 3:506–507.

178 *"Well, I am glad"*: Edith Wharton, *A Backward Glance* (New York: Appleton-Century, 1934), 311.

178 *"Mr. Secretary"*: Wharton, *Backward Glance*, 312.

178 *"It took my"*: Maurice Francis Egan, "Theodore Roosevelt in Retrospect," *Atlantic*, May 1919.

179 *"Would it be"*: Roosevelt to Henry Cabot Lodge, June 7, 1886, *LTR* 1:102.

179 *"I realize perfectly"*: Roosevelt to George Haven Putnam, January 13, 1890, *LTR* 1:211.

179 *"thoroughness of"*: Frederick Jackson Turner, *American Historical Review* 2, no. 1 (1896): 171–176, at 176.

179 *"I hereby offer"*: Roosevelt to Charles Anderson Dana, September 25, 1889, *LTR* 1:191. Dana was the editor of the *Sun*.

179 *"The book should have had careful revision"*: Roosevelt to William Frederick Poole, October 27, 1889, in George B. Utley, "Theodore Roosevelt's the Winning of the West: Some Unpublished Letters," *Mississippi Valley Historical Review* 30, no. 4 (1944): 495–506, at 499.

179 *"While one can"*: Turner, *Winning* review, 175.

179 *"heroes of axe"*: Roosevelt, *Winning of the West* (New York: G. P. Putnam's Sons, 1889–1896), 1:155.

180 *"rugged intellect"*: Roosevelt, *Naval War of 1812 . . . to Which Is Appended an Account of the Battle of New Orleans* (New York: G. P. Putnam's Sons, 1902), 204.

180 *"If you want"*: Lawrence Fraser Abbott, *Impressions of Theodore Roosevelt* (New York: Doubleday, Page, 1920), 182.

180 *" 'John,' she said"*: *PWW* 5:568.

180 *"fact book"*: Wilson to Ellen Axson Wilson, March 9, 1889, *PWW* 6:139.

180 *"deeper undercurrents"*: Frederick Jackson Turner, *American Historical Review* 8, no. 4 (1903): 762–765, at 762.

180 *"I am not"*: Wilson to Richard Watson Gilder, January 28, 1901, *PWW* 12:84.

181 *"a good enough"*: Roosevelt to George Trevelyan, January 23, 1904, LTR 3:708.

182 *"The President is"*: Wilson, *Constitutional Government in the United States* (New York: Columbia University Press, 1908), 70.

182 *"That's the sort"*: Cooper, *Woodrow Wilson*, 214.

182 *"perennial misunderstanding"*: The text of Wilson's address can be found in *PWW* 6:644–71. Wilson delivered an early version of the lecture in 1889, then delivered this version multiple times in the 1890s.

Chapter Eight: Campaign Books Hit the Trail
(Thanks to, of All Presidents, Calvin Coolidge)

The success of Coolidge's *Have Faith* is one way to track the growing significance of books to this period's campaigns, and other politicians and their allies gave the medium a try. William E. Russell's *Speeches and Addresses* (Boston: Little, Brown, 1894) was a minor hit—and might have been a major one had its author, a very successful and very youthful governor, not died at thirty-nine. Letters that show how involved McKinley and Hanna were in the publication of *Speeches and Addresses of William McKinley* can be found in the Appleton-Century mss., box 15, Lilly Library, Indiana University. ("The retail price of the book," McKinley stipulated in a letter on June 23, 1893, "is to be two dollars.") For the *Speeches of Benjamin Harrison*, see "A Disgusted Republican," *New York Times*, November 7, 1892; for Bryan's *First Battle*, see Michael Kazin, *A Godly Hero: The Life of William Jennings Bryan* (New York: Knopf, 2006).

Another way to track the significance of such books is to look at the attacks they elicited—especially the many titles by Roosevelt and Wilson. In this chapter, I mention the pamphlet *Roosevelt, Historian* and black voters' anger at *Rough Riders*. (For more on the second controversy see "An Address," *Valentine Democrat*, September 27, 1900; and "Teddy, the Terrible," *Hopkinsville Kentuckian*, October 9, 1900.) There were plenty of others. In 1912, a US senator mocked Wilson for suggesting in *History of the American People* that an economic downturn improved only after a "Republican administration came in" ("Burton Cites Wilson's Book," *Chicago Tribune*, October 12, 1912). In another passage from *History*, Wilson deployed ugly Hungarian and Italian stereotypes while discussing immigration; when the passage drew criticism, Wilson dodged by claiming it was "very unfortunate if I have been so awkward in my way of expressing what I had to say" (Edward N. Saveth, *American Historians And European Immigrants, 1875–1925* [New York: Columbia University Press, 1948], 143). Wilson's writings generated enough controversy that Democratic National Committee operatives had to help in the response: "Governor Wilson is running for President on his record as a public man," one said, "rather than what he wrote as an historian" ("Daniels Defends Wilson," *New York Tribune*, August 6, 1912).

As even his earliest biographers have noted, Coolidge is a difficult person to decipher. "His secretiveness," wrote Claude M. Fuess, one of those early biographers and still Coolidge's best, "is almost unparalleled among American statesmen" (*Calvin Coolidge: The Man from Vermont* [Boston: Little, Brown, 1940], 469). Of course, that makes Coolidge's books even more valuable for understanding him. Other works I depended on include Hendrik Booraem's splendid *The Provincial: Calvin Coolidge and His World, 1885–1895* (Lewisburg, PA: Bucknell University Press, 1994); John L. Blair's authoritative "The Governorship of Calvin Coolidge, 1919–1921" (PhD diss., University of Chicago, 1971); Arthur F. Fleser's *Rhetorical Study of the Speaking of Calvin Coolidge* (Lewiston, NY: Edwin Mellen Press, 1990); Kerry W. Buckley's "A President for the 'Great Silent Majority': Bruce Barton's Construction of Calvin Coolidge," *New England Quarterly* 76, no. 4 (2003): 593–626; Thomas W. Kilmartin's "The Last Shall Be First: The Amherst College Days of Calvin Coolidge," *Historical Journal of Massachusetts* 5, no. 2 (1977), 1–12; and David Greenberg's *Calvin Coolidge* (New York: Times Books, 2006).

Fuess also predicted that "no one will ever publish a volume of the letters of Calvin Coolidge. They are too few in number and tell too little about the essential man" (349). Thankfully, he wasn't entirely right. *Your Son, Calvin Coolidge,* ed. Edward Lathem (Montpelier: Vermont Historical Society, 1968), collects many of Coolidge's early letters and a few diary extracts. For his adult letters, I've relied on the holdings of the Coolidge Presidential Library at the Forbes Library in Northampton, Massachusetts—technically not a presidential library because it lacks federal recognition and funding, but a wonderful place to research all the same—and the Houghton Mifflin Papers at Harvard's Houghton Library. Both archives have documents from Stearns, Scaife, Barton, Grace Coolidge, and other key players, and those helped me trace for the first time the full story of the publication and impact of *Have Faith*.

To understand this period's literary culture, I started with *A History of the Book in America*'s fourth volume, *Print in Motion: The Expansion of Publishing and Reading in the United States, 1880–1940,* ed. Carl F. Kaestle and Janice A. Radway (Chapel Hill: University of North Carolina Press, 2009). Also helpful were Megan Benton, "'Too Many Books': Book Ownership and Cultural Identity in the 1920s," *American Quarterly* 49, no. 2 (1997): 268–297; Catherine Turner, *Marketing Modernism between the Two World Wars* (Amherst: University of Massachusetts Press, 2003); Christopher Wilson, *The Labor of Words: Literary Professionalism in the Progressive Era* (Athens: University of Georgia Press, 1985); James L. W. West III, *American Authors and the Literary Marketplace since 1900* (Philadelphia: University of Pennsylvania Press, 1988); and—British in focus but invaluable in ideas—Leah Price, *How to Do Things with Books in Victorian Britain* (Princeton: Princeton University Press, 2012). For Northampton's (and the Coolidges') best bookstore, I depended on Barbara A. Brannon's meticulous and invaluable "'No Frigate like a Book': The Hampshire Bookshop of Northampton, 1916–1971" (PhD diss., University of South Carolina, 1998). For an analysis of popular books in the twentieth century, including a chapter on the best-selling religious titles by a very busy Bruce Barton, see Erin Smith, *What Would Jesus Read? Popular Religious Books and Everyday Life in Twentieth-Century America* (Chapel Hill: University of North Carolina Press, 2015). For the period's department stores, see Susan Porter Benson, *Counter Cultures: Saleswomen, Managers, and Customers in American Department Stores, 1890–1940* (Urbana: University of Illinois Press, 1986). For the authorial career of James Corrothers, see Kevin Gaines, "Assimilationist Minstrelsy as Racial Uplift Ideology: James D. Corrothers's Literary Quest for Black Leadership," *American Quarterly* 45, no. 3 (1993): 341–369. For the *Black Mask*, a detective magazine and fine example of this era's proliferating genres, see the letters of its editor: *Letters of H. L. Mencken* (New York: Knopf, 1961). In one missive, written near the end of the Wilson administration, Mencken joked with a friend: "The *Black Mask* is a lousy magazine—all detective stories. I hear that Woodrow reads it" (216).

To understand the rise of America's mass culture, and of the advertising and PR experts who quickly learned to exploit it, start with Richard Ohmann's seminal *Selling Culture: Magazines, Markets, and the Class at the Turn of the Century* (New York: Verso, 1996). I also relied on Harold S. Wilson, *McClure's Magazine and the Muckrakers* (Princeton: Princeton University Press, 1970); Peter Lyon, *Success Story: The Life and Times of S. S. McClure* (New York: Scribner's, 1963); Ray E. Hiebert, *Courtier to the Crowd: The Story of Ivy Lee and the Development of Public Relations* (Ames: Iowa State University Press, 1966); and Scott M. Cutlip, *The Unseen Power: Public Relations: A History* (Hillsdale, NJ: Erlbaum, 1994). Nell Irvin Painter's *Standing at Armageddon: United States, 1877–1919* (New York: Norton, 1987) helped me understand the era from the perspective of regular Americans. John A. Morello's *Selling the President, 1920: Albert D. Lasker, Advertising, and the Election of Warren G. Harding* (Westport, CT: Praeger, 2001) helped me connect mass culture to mass campaigning, as did Lasker's own brief volume, *The Lasker Story: As He Told It* (Chicago: Advertising Publications, 1953). I also learned from more specific studies of campaigning and politics, including Gordon Moon, "George F. Parker: A 'Near Miss' as First White House Press Chief," *Journalism Quarterly* 41, no. 2 (1964): 183–190; R. Hal Williams, *Realigning America: McKinley, Bryan, and the Remarkable Election of 1896* (Lawrence: University Press of Kansas, 2010); Daniel Klinghard, *The Nationalization of American Political Parties, 1880–1896* (New York: Cambridge University Press, 2010); and Michael E. McGerr, *The Decline of Popular Politics: The American North, 1865–1928* (New York: Oxford University Press, 1986), in which McGerr details an innovation related to the bookish ones discussed in my chapter: "literary bureaus" run by the national committees that focused on churning out campaign literature.

184 *"How much money"*: Doubleday, *The Memoirs of a Publisher* (New York: Doubleday, 1972), 58–59.

185 *"Our advertising"*: Ellen B. Ballou, *The Building of the House: Houghton Mifflin's Formative Years* (Boston: Houghton Mifflin, 1970), 426.

185 *"He has advertised"*: Thomas Beer, *Hanna* (New York: Knopf, 1929), 165.

185 *"I made a bet"*: Ishbel Ross, *Grace Coolidge and Her Era: The Story of a President's Wife* (New York: Dodd, Mead, 1962), 67.

185 *"Probably never before"*: "Book of Speeches Put Coolidge Over," *Boston Globe*, June 14, 1920.

186 *"I was"*: Corrothers, *In Spite of the Handicap: An Autobiography* (New York: George H. Doran, 1916), 24.

186 *"The negro troops"*: Corrothers, *In Spite of the Handicap*, 35.

186 *"Brethren, . . . let's"*: Corrothers, *In Spite of the Handicap*, 66.

186 *"the careers of"*: Corrothers, *In Spite of the Handicap*, 58.

187 *"this age of"*: "Literary Presidents," *New York Times*, July 18, 1920.

187 *"pleasant air of"*: George Palmer Putnam, *Wide Margins: A Publisher's Autobiography* (New York: Harcourt, Brace, 1942), 14.

187 *"You are one of"*: Frost to Marion Elza Dodd, May 16, 1921, in *The Letters of Robert Frost*, ed. Donald Sheehy et al. (Cambridge, MA: Harvard University Press, 2014–2016), 2:163.

188 *"He promptly developed"*: George Haven Putnam, *Memories of a Publisher, 1865–1915* (New York: G. P. Putnam's Sons, 1915), 137.

189 *"We . . . make our"*: *Publishers Weekly*, September 2, 1882.

189 *"the most complete"*: *Sears, Roebuck, & Co. Catalogue* no. 112.

189 *"It was my"*: Mary Antin, *At School in the Promised Land* (Boston: Houghton Mifflin, 1912), 95.

191 *"new books"*: Frank Luther Mott, *Golden Multitudes: The Story of Best Sellers in the United States* (New York: Macmillan, 1947), 204.

191 *"The public . . . is"*: *The American Essays of Henry James*, ed. Leon Edel (Princeton: Princeton University Press, 1956), 200.

191 *"There are blessed"*: *Papers of Woodrow Wilson*, ed. Arthur S. Link (Princeton: Princeton University Press, 1967–1994), 29:364.

191 *"responsible for"*: Heywood Broun, "Sherlock Holmes and the Pygmies," *Woman's Home Companion*, November 1930.

191 *"Way down in"*: Corrothers, " 'Way in de Woods, an' Nobody Dar," *Century*, April 1899.

192 *"So shall men"*: Corrothers, "The Negro Singer," *Century*, November 1912.

192 *"articles of timely"*: Wilson, *McClure's Magazine and the Muckrakers*, 104.

192 *"the greatest genius"*: Ida M. Tarbell, "Napoleon Bonaparte," *McClure's Magazine*, April 1895.

193 *"About the advertising"*: Algernon Tassin, "The Story of Modern Book Advertising," *Bookman*, May 1911.

193 *"all that is"*: Willis Abbot, "Big Job to Get Illinois," *Chicago Tribune*, September 10, 1908.

193 *"You are certainly"*: Parker, *Recollections of Grover Cleveland* (New York: Century, 1909), 120.

194 *"His smallest utterance"*: Parker, "Grover Cleveland: Estimate of His Character and Work," *Saturday Evening Post*, October 25, 1924.

194 *"I have carried"*: William Shaw Bowen, "At the M'Kinley Home," *Chicago Tribune*, November 4, 1896.

194 *"The president . . . should"*: Gil Troy, *See How They Ran: The Changing Role of the Presidential Candidate* (New York: Free Press, 1991), 109.

194 *"This is an interesting"*: "Bryan's Book," *Cincinnati Enquirer*, October 12, 1900.

195 *"have attempted to"*: "The Colored Soldiers and Roosevelt," *Troy Daily Times*, October 31, 1900.

196 *"This was not"*: Lee to Rockefeller Jr., July 6, 1914, in Hiebert, *Courtier to the Crowd*, 114.

196 *"Let's be done"*: McGerr, *Decline of Popular Politics*, 170.

196 *"We want it"*: Morello, *Selling the President*, 66.

197 *"Roosevelt has written"*: Roosevelt, *Historian*, 1.

197 *"a presidential candidate's"*: "Three American Orators," *Nation*, February 8, 1894.

198 *"He had great"*: Coolidge, "Books of My Boyhood," *Cosmopolitan*, October 1932.

198 *"an odd stick"*: Booraem, *The Provincial*, 10.

198 *"improving the mind"*: *Meet Calvin Coolidge: The Man Behind the Myth*, ed. Edward Lathem (Brattleboro, VT: Stephen Greene Press, 1960), 65–66.

198 *"The few who"*: Fuess, *Calvin Coolidge*, 71.

198 *"Nothing in the"*: Coolidge to John Coolidge, January 27, 1895, *Your Son*, 63.

198 *" 'Waldo Martin' "*: Fuess, *Calvin Coolidge*, 62.

199 *"Why didn't you"*: M. E. Hennessy, "Coolidge as Neighbors Know Him," *Boston Globe*, June 2, 1918.

199 *"Would you like"*: Coolidge to John Coolidge, April 26, 1894, *Your Son*, 56.

200 *"None was ever"*: *Meet Calvin Coolidge*, 69.

200 *"Do the day's work"*: Coolidge, *Have Faith in Massachusetts* (Boston: Houghton Mifflin, 1919), 7–8. This is the "second edition enlarged," as its title page reads, with seven additional speeches added after the telegram and other strike material.

201 *"Come up next"*: M. E. Hennessy, "Senate No Graveyard for Him," *Boston Globe*, November 25, 1920.

201 *"All right"*: Fuess, *Calvin Coolidge*, 235.

201 *"I think . . . it"*: Stearns to W. Murray Crane, November 20, 1919, Calvin Coolidge Papers, Governor series, Forbes Library.

201 *"There is no"*: Coolidge, *Have Faith*, 223.

202 *"Self-government means"*: Coolidge, *Have Faith*, 5.

202 *"unless good citizens"*: Coolidge, *Have Faith*, 271.

202 *"Gov. Calvin Coolidge"*: On April 29, 1920, for instance, the ad ran in the *Chicago Tribune*, the *Cincinnati Enquirer*, the *New York Tribune*, and the *Los Angeles Times*, among many other papers and many other dates.

202 *"They don't know"*: Fuess, *Calvin Coolidge*, 242.

202 *"The big goose"*: Fuess, *Calvin Coolidge*, 243. The Houghton Mifflin correspondence shows that Stearns and Coolidge ultimately abandoned the campaign biography mentioned in this paragraph.

203 *"We have . . . less"*: Stearns to Scaife, March 11, 1920, Houghton Mifflin Publishing Company Correspondence and Records, 1832–1944, Houghton Library, Harvard University. The telegram asking for ten thousand more copies can be found in the same collection, with a date of February 28, 1920.

203 *"Here's Cal Coolidge"*: Barton, "He Refuses to Talk about Himself," *Oxnard Daily Courier*, May 22, 1920. Like the "Coolidge Says" ads, Barton's various features were syndicated across the country.

204 *"Have faith in"*: "Coolidge Smiles When His Oldsmobile Stalls," *Philadelphia Inquirer*, September 18, 1921. Despite the dateline, the anecdote in this story occurred during Coolidge's time as governor, sometime after the publication of his book. While the story claims Coolidge owned the Oldsmobile, his biographers agree he did not own a car at this time.

204 *"I see your friend"*: M. E. Hennessy, "The Man behind Coolidge," *Boston Globe*, November 25, 1920.

205 *"Coolidge is the man"*: Fuess, *Calvin Coolidge*, 409.

205 *"they shed collars"*: Edna Ferber, *A Peculiar Treasure* (New York: Doubleday, Doran, 1939), 251.

206 *"Do you want"*: *Official Report of the Proceedings of the Seventeenth Republican National Convention* (New York: Tenny Press, 1920), 120.

206 *"The hotels at"*: Mencken, "G.O.P Ticket Triumph for Old Bosses," *Baltimore Sun*, June 13, 1920.

207 *"Someone sent me"*: "Here Is the Man Who Nominated Coolidge," *Boston Globe*, June 27, 1920. For more on McCamant, see Robert Brady, "Man Who Put Coolidge Over Wins Reward," *Boston Post*, July 9, 1920; M. E. Hennessy, " 'Couldn't Get Lodge, So Took Coolidge,' " *Boston Globe*, December 3, 1920; and McCamant's letter to Fuess, reprinted in Blair, "Governorship of Calvin Coolidge," 307–308.

207 *"stood for law"*: *Boston Herald*, June 13, 1920.

207 *"Nominated for"*: Fuess, *Calvin Coolidge*, 264.

207 *"I know Cal"*: Mencken, "Coolidge," *American Mercury*, April 1933.

207 *"I must have"*: Coolidge to James B. Reynolds, October 1, 1920, in Fleser, *Rhetorical Study*, 31.

207 *"We have decided"*: Barton to Coolidge, August 19, 1920, in Buckley, "A President for," 612.

208 *"I knew the"*: "Here is the Man Who Nominated Coolidge." For Coolidge's thinking

that night, see his November 12, 1923, letter to McCamant, reprinted in Blair, "Governorship of Calvin Coolidge," 511.

Chapter Nine: Legacy Books Get Personal
(Thanks to, of All Presidents, Calvin Coolidge)

Coolidge's *Autobiography* has never been adequately studied, as a piece of writing and as a multimedia phenomenon. There's a rich record of contemporary coverage. (Indeed, the surge in articles like "How Coolidge Article Was Kept a Secret," *Franklin News-Herald*, March 12, 1929, is another indicator of Coolidge's popularity.) But that coverage can be tricky because journalists would breathlessly recount the writing of a chapter—the one drafted during a presidential train ride to Florida, for instance—only to produce an account that, on closer examination, was almost entirely misleading because of the way *Cosmopolitan* split those chapters into multiple articles. The Coolidge Presidential Library at the Forbes Library in Northampton, Massachusetts, has typescripts of the book chapters with Coolidge's edits, but it has very few letters relating to the project. In addition to the Coolidge sources cited in my mini-essay to chapter 8, I also relied on Alan Schenker, "Calvin Coolidge in Retirement: Public Life of a Private Citizen," *Presidential Studies Quarterly* 18, no. 2 (1988): 413–426, and Robert E. Gilbert *The Tormented President: Calvin Coolidge, Death, and Clinical Depression* (Westport, CT: Praeger, 2003). Grace Coolidge wrote her own popular and revealing magazine articles, later gathered in *Grace Coolidge: An Autobiography*, ed. Lawrence E. Wikander and Robert H. Ferrell (Worland, WY: High Plains Publishing, 1992).

I also relied on studies of this era's many other political memoirs. Some of the best include George W. Egerton, "The Lloyd George 'War Memoirs': A Study in the Politics of Memory," *Journal of Modern History* 60, no. 1 (1988): 55–94; Daniel Scroop, "A Life in Progress: Motion and Emotion in the Autobiography of Robert M. La Follette," *American Nineteenth Century* 13, no. 1 (2012): 45–64; Jack L. Hammersmith, "In Defense of Yalta: Edward R. Stettinius's Roosevelt and the Russians," *Virginia Magazine of History and Biography* 100, no. 3 (1992): 429–454; and Milan Kedro, "Autobiography as a Key to Identity in the Progressive Era," *History of Childhood Quarterly* 2, no. 3 (1975): 391–407. In *The Learned Presidency: Theodore Roosevelt, William Howard Taft, Woodrow Wilson* (Rutherford, NJ: Fairleigh Dickinson University Press, 1988), David H. Burton analyzes Roosevelt's *Autobiography*. Jonathan Arnold shows that, despite its flaws, the book sold more than eighty thousand copies in its first two decades—a decent number that may not even include the sales from the first Macmillan edition of 1913 ("Publishing Theodore Roosevelt, 1882–1919" [PhD diss., University of London, 2010]). Carl Anthony Sferrazza's *Nellie Taft: The Unconventional First Lady of the Ragtime Era* (New York: Morrow, 2005), Maurine H. Beasley's *Eleanor Roosevelt and the Media: A Pubic Quest for Self Fulfillment* (Urbana: University of Illinois Press, 1987), and Phyllis Lee Levin's *Edith and Woodrow: The Wilson White House* (New York: Scribner, 2001), perceptively cover the writing careers of their subjects as first ladies. Late in life, Edith's husband frequently and firmly denied any possibility of writing his own autobiography. "I have no intention whatever," he wrote, "of writing or publishing 'memoirs'" (Wilson to Joe Skidmore, November 18, 1920, *Papers of Woodrow Wilson*, ed. Arthur S. Link [Princeton: Princeton University Press, 1967–1994], 66:387; hereafter cited as *PWW*, followed by volume and page number). Wilson's biographers, much like Jefferson's, have taken him at his word. But those denials all occurred after his stroke, and before his health problems Wilson talked just as frequently about his desire to write one or more legacy books.

Another way to see the popularity of Coolidge's *Autobiography* is in *The John Rid-*

dell Murder Case (New York: Scribner's, 1930), which parodied various best-selling forms, from detective stories to Dreiser to the *Autobiography* of Calvin Coolidge. In satirizing Coolidge, it was also satirizing its era's affection for celebrities and their personal stories, and a number of scholars have pinpointed this period as the one when the idea of celebrity shifted, from Richard Dyer's distinction between "stars-as-special" and "stars-as-ordinary" (*Stars* [London: British Film Institute, 1979]) to Leo Lowenthal's between "idols of production" and "idols of consumption" ("Biographies in Popular Magazines," in *Radio Research, 1942–43,* ed. Paul F. Lazarsfeld and Frank Stanton [New York: Duell, Sloan, and Pearce, 1944], 507–548). The work I found most helpful on this shift was Charles L. Ponce De Leon, *Self-Exposure: Human-Interest Journalism and the Emergence of Celebrity in America, 1890–1940* (Chapel Hill: University of North Carolina Press, 2001). Valuable studies of the era's celebrity memoirs include Lise Jaillant, "Shucks, We've Got Glamour Girls Too! Gertrude Stein, Bennett Cerf and the Culture of Celebrity," *Journal of Modern Literature* 39, no. 1 (2015): 149–169; Rod Rosenquist, "The Ordinary Celebrity and the Celebrated Ordinary in 1930s Modernist Memoirs," *Genre* 49, no. 3 (2016): 359–383; and Ellery Sedgwick, "Magazines and the Profession of Authorship in the United States, 1840–1900," *Papers of the Bibliographical Society of America* 94, no. 3 (2000): 399–425. In " 'Song of Ourselves': A Quantitative History of American Autobiographies," *Gerontologist* 36, no. 4 (1996): 448–453, Jeffrey S. Levin and Thomas R. Cole quantify the genre's explosion. A good example of multiple magazine editors pursuing a prominent figure can be seen in the fifth volume of the *Booker T. Washington Papers,* ed. Louis Harlan (Urbana: University of Illinois Press, 1972–1989)—a pursuit that ultimately resulted in Washington writing his *Up from Slavery.*

While there isn't much scholarship on ghostwriting, the many writers scandalized by the practice have produced a lot of useful journalism. See Alva Johnston, "The Ghosting Business," *New Yorker,* November 23, 1935, in which Christy Walsh says of his clients, "I wouldn't insult the intelligence of the public by claiming they write their own stuff"; Graves Glenwood Clark, "The Ghost Writer and His Story," *Editor,* February 25, 1920; *The Puppet-Show on the Potomac* (New York: R. M. McBride & Co., 1934); and Joseph Fulling Fishman, E. B. White, and Ralph Ingersoll, "Nan Britton," *New Yorker,* October 14, 1927. (On Britton, see also Philip G. Payne, *Dead Last: The Public Memory of Warren G. Harding's Scandalous Legacy* [Athens: Ohio University Press, 2009].) Willa Cather's stint as a ghost has been sharply analyzed by Matthew J. Lavin, "Reciprocity and the 'Real' Author: Willa Cather as S. S. McClure's Ghostwriter," *a/b* 31, no. 2 (2016): 233–260, and in the editorial apparatus to Willa Cather, *The Autobiography of S. S. McClure,* ed. Robert Thacker (Lincoln: University of Nebraska Press, 1997).

For the entertainment trends in this era, I depended on David Nasaw, *Going Out: The Rise and Fall of Public Amusements* (Cambridge, MA: Harvard University Press, 1999). For the pressures that ensure modern presidents give ever-more speeches, see Samuel Kernell, *Going Public: New Strategies of Presidential Leadership* (Washington, DC: CQ Press, 1986). For Franklin D. Roosevelt's fireside chats, see Robert S. Fine, "Roosevelt's Radio Chatting: Its Development and Impact during the Great Depression" (PhD diss., New York University, 1977). Bennett Cerf and Random House tried to publish an elaborate edition of Roosevelt's speeches during his presidency, and the edition failed in some interesting ways; see Cerf's oral history at the Columbia Center for Oral History, along with "Writing for Pay Brings Attack On Roosevelt," *New York Herald-Tribune,* February 26, 1938.

209   *"When he joined"*: For Grace's story, see *Meet Calvin Coolidge: The Man behind the Myth,* ed. Edward Lathem (Brattleboro, VT: Stephen Greene Press, 1960), 69. Although she described the event as occurring while Coolidge was governor,

contemporary documents suggest Grace misremembered the timing. See David Suisman, *Selling Sounds: The Commercial Revolution in American Music* (Cambridge, MA: Harvard University Press, 2012), 178–179, along with contemporary reporting like "Coolidge to Speak at Chickering Dinner," *Boston Globe*, April 16, 1923.

210 *"The governor looks"*: "Coolidge Is Typical Hard Working Yankee," *Wyoming State Tribune*, November 22, 1919.

210 *"an age of"*: "The Decline of Memoir," *Living Age*, April 1900.

210 *"Autobiography House"*: *Autobiography of Mark Twain*, ed. Harriet E. Smith et al. (Berkeley: University of California Press, 2010–2014), 3:446.

211 *"The librarians soon"*: Mary Brennan to Bess Streeter Aldrich, November 10, 1935, Bess Streeter Aldrich Papers, Nebraska State Historical Society Library, Lincoln, Nebraska. I first learned about Brennan in Melissa J. Homestead's exceptional article, "Middlebrow Readers and Pioneer Heroines: Willa Cather's *My Antonia*, Bess Streeter Aldrich's *A Lantern in Her Hand*, and the Popular Fiction Market," in *Crisscrossing Borders in the Literature of the American West*, ed. Reginald Dyck and Cheli Reutter (New York: Palgrave-Macmillan, 2009), 75–94. Thanks to Homestead for sharing her transcription of this letter.

212 *"The smallest town"*: Walter Prichard Eaton, "Class-Consciousness and the 'Movies,'" *Atlantic*, January 1915.

212 *"Indeed, you"*: George Palmer Putnam, *Wide Margins: A Publisher's Autobiography* (New York: Harcourt, Brace, 1942), 231.

212 *"the most democratic"*: William Dean Howells, "Editor's Easy Chair," *Atlantic*, October 1909.

213 *"It is not"*: Edward Bok, *The Americanization of Edward Bok* (New York: Scribner's, 1921), 202.

213 *"You are more"*: Max Ewing to Stein, September 19, 1933, in Janet Hobhouse, *Everybody Who Was Anybody: A Biography of Gertrude Stein* (New York: Doubleday, 1975), 139.

213 *"What books are"*: Robert Creamer, *Babe: The Legend Comes to Life* (New York: Simon & Schuster, 1974), 316.

213 *"It involves no"*: "Are We Forgetting Nature?" *New York Times*, April 12, 1925.

214 *"Reach for a Post"*: "The World Series and The *Post*," *Washington Post*, September 28, 1933.

214 *"Ghostwriters . . . are the"*: Frederick F. Van De Water, "The Ghost Writers," *Scribner's*, March 1929.

214 *"Survey of the Ghost Writers"*: The article, by Harry Gilroy, ran in the *New York Times* on March 27, 1949.

215 *"The public was"*: "Fame for Ghost Writers," *New York Times*, February 27, 1929.

215 *" 'To write or' "*: Elisabeth E. Poe, "Books," *Washington Post*, January 12, 1930.

215 *"probably the most"*: D. L. Chambers, internal memo, November 11, 1938, Bobbs-Merrill mss., 1885–1957, box 190, Lilly Library, Indiana University.

216 *"We're passing up"*: Britton, *Honesty or Politics* (New York: Elizabeth Ann Guild, 1932), 62.

216 *"I love your"*: Jordan Michael Smith, "All the President's Pen," *New York Times Sunday Magazine*, July 13, 2014.

216 *"Those weren't policemen"*: Dorothy Parker, "Recent Books," *New Yorker*, October 15, 1927.

216 *"I feel as"*: Cather to Will Owen Jones, May 7, 1903, in *The Selected Letters of Willa Cather*, ed. Andrew Jewell and Janis Stout (New York: Knopf, 2013), 72.

216 *"Now, where did"*: Cather, *The Autobiography of S. S. McClure*, x.

217 *"work within the limits"*: Cather to Will Owen Jones, May 20, 1919, in *Selected Letters of Willa Cather*, 278.

217 *"indebtedness to Miss"*: Cather, *The Autobiography of S. S. McClure*, xiv.

218 *"flopped as flat"*: Zelda Fitzgerald to Sandy Kalman, November 1923, in *Some Sort of Epic Grandeur: The Life of F. Scott Fitzgerald* (New York: Harcourt Brace Jovanovich, 1981), 219.

218 *"JERRY. Did you"*: F. Scott Fitzgerald, *The Vegetable, or, From President to Postman* (New York: Collier Books, 1987), 47.

218 *"What . . . shall we"*: Robert Underwood Johnson, *Remembered Yesterdays* (Boston: Little, Brown, 1923), 389.

218 *"They needn't worry"*: Johnson, *Remembered Yesterdays*, 389.

218 *"Who now knows"*: James Bryce, *The American Commonwealth* (New York: Macmillan, 1889), 1:100.

218 *"There are things"*: Cleveland to Richard W. Gilder, January 28, 1905, in *Letters of Grover Cleveland, 1850–1908*, ed. Allan Nevins (Boston: Houghton Mifflin, 1933), 592.

219 *"Mr. McClure and"*: Cleveland to Gilder, January 28, 1905, *Letters of Grover Cleveland*, 592.

219 *"Nothing . . . has not"*: *Congregationalist*, November 11, 1897.

219 *"The light has gone"*: Edmund Morris, *The Rise of Theodore Roosevelt* (New York: Coward, McCann & Geoghegan, 1979), 230.

219 *"The house . . . was"*: Wharton, *A Backward Glance* (New York: D. Appleton-Century, 1934), 316.

220 *"It is believed"*: "Scribner's to Print the Roosevelt Hunt," *New York Times*, July 9, 1908.

220 *"I am permanently"*: Garland, *Companions on the Trail; A Literary Chronicle* (New York: Macmillan, 1931), 506.

221 *"In these papers"*: "An Announcement Concerning Mr. Roosevelt," *Outlook*, November 30, 1912.

221 *"We were overwhelmed"*: Adams to Elizabeth Cameron, January 10, 1904, in *The Selected Letters of Henry Adams*, ed. Newton Arvin (New York: Farrar, Straus and Young, 1951), 241.

221 *"The children acted"*: Roosevelt to Emily Tyler Carow, January 4, 1913, *Letters of Theodore Roosevelt*, ed. Elting E. Morrison (Cambridge, MA: Harvard University Press, 1951–1954), 7.689.

221 *"The Republican Association"*: Roosevelt, *Theodore Roosevelt: An Autobiography* (New York: Macmillan, 1913), 63–64.

222 *"I am working"*: Roosevelt to Ethel Roosevelt Derby, April 1, 1913, in Edmund Morris, *Colonel Roosevelt* (New York: Random House, 2010), 275.

222 *"You made a"*: "Roosevelt Intends to Lay Bare His Life," *New York Times*, May 26, 1913.

222 *"I have no"*: Garland, *Companions on the Trail*, 507.

223 *"honesty . . . courage"*: Roosevelt, *Theodore Roosevelt*, 305 and 265, among many others.

223 *"suggests a story"*: Taft, *Our Chief Magistrate and His Powers* (New York: Columbia University Press, 1916), 144.

223 *"What this autobiography"*: "Books for Christmas," *Detroit Free-Press*, December 14, 1913.

223 *"I am going"*: Joseph P. Tumulty, *Woodrow Wilson as I Know Him* (New York: Doubleday, Page, 1921), 378.

223 *"Things are still"*: Edith Wilson to William E. Dodd, May 22, 1921, *PWW* 67:288.

223 *"The prices of"*: "Biggest Money Makers among Past Memoirs," *New York Times*, September 24, 1922.

223 *"fortune"*: "Biggest Money Makers."

224 *"all correspondence"*: *PWW* 5:403.

224 *"including my father"*: David Greenberg, *Calvin Coolidge* (New York: Times Books, 2006), 104.

225 *"I thought he"*: "Homecoming of Coolidges Modestly Gay," *New York Herald-Tribune*, March 6, 1929.

225 *"What shall I"*: Ishbel Ross, *Grace Coolidge and Her Era: The Story of a President's Wife* (New York: Dodd, Mead, 1962), 260.

225 *"While it is"*: Roger Scaife, internal memo, August 4, 1923, Houghton Mifflin Publishing Company Correspondence and Records, 1832–1944, Houghton Library, Harvard University.

226 *"Well, you're an early"*: "Power, Glory Died With Son, Coolidge Writes," *Washington Post*, March 8, 1929. George Palmer Putnam offers a similar account of this exchange in *Wide Margins*.

226 *"Mr. Long, . . . you"*: Putnam, *Wide Margins*, 185.

226 *"He insists that"*: Putnam, *Wide Margins*, 186.

227 *"Mr. Coolidge's OWN STORY"*: *Cosmopolitan*, April 1929.

227 *"No man of"*: Mencken, "Editorial," *American Mercury*, March 1929.

228 *"the most literary man"*: Charles Willis Thompson, "Another Calvin Coolidge Is Introduced," *New York Times Sunday Magazine*, December 28, 1924.

228 *"I want . . . to"*: Coolidge to Thompson, December 29, 1924, Calvin Coolidge Papers, Library of Congress, reel 148.

228 *"In spite of"*: Calvin Coolidge, *Autobiography* (New York: Cosmopolitan Book Service, 1929), 181. In the passages quoted in this chapter, though not in the entire *Autobiography*, the text of the book version and the magazine version is identical.

228 *"I was awakened"*: Coolidge, *Autobiography*, 173–174.

228 *"The day before I"*: Coolidge, *Autobiography*, 189–190.

228 *"In his suffering"*: Coolidge, *Autobiography*, 190–192.

229 *"Calvin Coolidge . . . received"*: Samuel Moore, "The Business of Ideas," *Publishers Weekly*, December 7, 1929.

229 *"Fine . . . if it"*: "No Such Thing as Privacy, Says Calvin Coolidge," *Atlanta Constitution*, March 23, 1929.

229 *"one of the most"*: undated typescript, Calvin Coolidge Papers, Autobiography series, Forbes Library.

230 *"We feel . . . that"*: "Mr. Coolidge's Literary Plans His Topic Here," *New York Herald-Tribune*, March 22, 1929.

230 *"I'm trying to"*: "Coolidge, Leaving, Pleads for Privacy," *New York Times*, March 23, 1929.

230 *"Mr. Coolidge's College Days"; "The Boston Police Strike"*: These chapters ran in the August 1929 and November 1929 issues.

230 *"Long or one"*: Lang's letter, and Long's affidavit in response, can be found in *Time*, April 22, 1929.

230 *"I have seen"*: Coolidge, *Autobiography*, 93.

230 *"In public life"*: Coolidge, *Autobiography*, 20.

230 *"Nothing could better"*: Emily Newell Blair, "Books I Am Glad I Have Read," *Good Housekeeping*, January 1930.

231 *"Calvin Coolidge Says"*: Greenberg, *Calvin Coolidge*, 152.

231 *"the scattered raw"*: "Is There a Jefferson on the Horizon?" *New York World*, December 3, 1925.

232 *"It strikes me"*: Roger Scaife to Franklin Roosevelt, February 2, 1931, Houghton Mifflin Publishing Company Correspondence and Records, 1832–1944, Houghton Library, Harvard University.

232 *"Let it be"*: *The Public Papers and Addresses of Franklin D. Roosevelt*, ed. Samuel Rosenman (New York: Random House, 1938), 1:657–659.

232 *"Every word"*: Sherwood, *Roosevelt and Hopkins: An Intimate History* (New York: Harper, 1948), 265.

233 *"After he retired"*: Samuel I. Rosenman oral history, Harry S. Truman Presidential Library, Independence, Missouri.

233 *"For the first"*: Richard Wright, *Later Works: Black Boy (American Hunger); The Outsider* (New York: Library of America, 1991), 123.

233 *"a damnable lie"*: Hazel Rowley, *Richard Wright: The Life and Times* (New York: Henry Holt, 2001), 319.

233 *"We are stunned"*: Rowley, *Richard Wright*, 313.

Chapter Ten: Harry Truman's Histories

Truman's ghostwriters were active (and often counterproductive) figures in the writing of his book. In this book, I've suggested that regular readers saw ghostwriting as a nonissue almost from the moment they first learned about it, whether during the Farewell Address controversy or the celebrity memoir boom. So why did Truman, a consummate regular reader, insist during the early months of working on his *Memoirs* that he would write it himself? It had less to do with vanity than taxes. During the press conference where Truman announced his book deal, a reporter asked if he would write the prose himself. "Of course," Truman replied, but his more revealing comment came later: "I am entering the field as Harry S. Truman, private citizen" ("*Life* Magazine Buys Truman Memoir Rights for $600,000," *Baltimore Sun*, February 22, 1953). During this era, nonprofessional writers sometimes got their book earnings taxed as capital gains instead of as income, though Congress was making this harder to pull off. For an advance the size of Truman's, it was the difference between a tax rate of about 25 percent and one of 65 percent or higher, and a few years earlier, as president, Truman had helped get Dwight D. Eisenhower the lower rate for *Crusade in Europe*. Now Eisenhower was president, but there's no record at either presidential library that he even attempted to return the favor, and Truman ended up paying the income tax. When he announced the deal, though, he didn't know how this would play out—so he very deliberately presented himself as the writer of his book *and* as a nonprofessional writer, "Harry S. Truman, private citizen."

One thing Truman's ghosts were good at was writing their own memoirs, and I relied on Herbert Lee Williams's "I Was Truman's Ghost," *Presidential Studies Quarterly* 12, no. 2 (1982): 256–259, and Francis H. Heller's "Harry S. Truman: The Writing of His Memoirs," in *Political Memoir: Essays on the Politics of Memory*, ed. George Egerton (London: Frank Cass & Co., 1994), 257–273. The best way to get a taste of Truman's role in the process is through his updates to Acheson, reprinted in *Affection and Trust: The Personal Correspondence of Harry S. Truman and Dean Acheson, 1953–1971*, ed. Ray Geselbracht and David C. Acheson (New York: Knopf, 2010). I also relied on the archives at Truman's presidential library, and I appreciate Tammy Williams and Randy Sowell answering questions and confirming the value of the *Memoirs* file. The Glenn Bookshop Records at the State Historical Society of Missouri, Kansas City, include valuable information on Frank Glenn and on Truman as a reader and bookstore customer.

Because of Truman's royalty-free arrangement with Doubleday and *Life*, his presidential library does not have many records on the sales of his book. Still, I find estimates that it sold perhaps 60,000 copies (for example, Meg Cox, "Reagan Memoirs Could Run Up a Deficit," *Wall Street Journal*, November 26, 1990) to be wildly low. The first volume's first print run exceeded 100,000 copies (Harvey Breit, "In and Out of Books," *New York Times*, November 27, 1955)—and that was before the Book of the Month Club got involved. A rough but fair estimate is that a club like the BOMC, which had more than half a million subscribers in 1950, would often at least double a book's retail sales; hence the first volume of Eisenhower's memoirs selling 89,000 copies through retail and 135,000 through the Literary Guild, as I mention in my essay on sources and methods. Another example is Richard Wright's *Black Boy*, which by the end of 1945 had sold 195,000 retail copies and 351,000 BOMC copies. (See Lawrence Jackson, *The Indignant Generation: A Narrative History of African American Writers and Critics, 1934-1960* [Princeton: Princeton University Press, 2011]; Jackson also explores how the BOMC censored Wright.) I would guess Truman's two-volume book sold well over 200,000 copies, though it's only a guess. While books were a mass medium by the 1950s, Truman's story reached even more readers through expansive serialization deals with the *New York Times* and the *St. Louis Post-Dispatch*.

The most helpful biographies on Truman are David McCullough, *Truman* (New York: Simon & Schuster, 1992), and Robert H. Ferrell, *Harry S. Truman: A Life* (Columbia: University of Missouri Press, 1994). Another enormously popular Truman book—and one could make the case that it began to perk up Truman's reputation before McCullough fully revived it—is Merle Miller's *Plain Speaking: An Oral Biography of Harry S. Truman* (New York: G. P. Putnam's Sons, 1974); Miller's book, however, should not be trusted, as Ferrell and Heller explain in "Plain Faking?" *American Heritage*, May–June 1995. In "Truman: On and Off the Record," in Egerton's *Political Memoir*, 274–284, Ferrell makes a strong case that Truman was a strong writer. For Truman's relationship to history, see Ethan S. Rafuse's incisive "'Far More Than a Romantic Adventure': The American Civil War in Harry Truman's History and Memory," *Missouri Historical Review* 104, no. 1 (2009): 1–20, and Samuel W. Rushay's "Harry Truman's History Lessons," *Prologue* 41, no. 1 (2009): 24–34. For Truman's home library, see Ron Cockrell, "Historic Structures Report: History and Significance, Harry S. Truman National Historic Site" (Omaha, NE: National Park Service, 1984). For Truman's presidential library, see Raymond H. Geselbracht, "Creating the Harry S. Truman Library: The First Fifty Years," *Public Historian* 28, no. 3 (2006): 37–78. For the *Mr. President* flop, see Boris Kachka, *Hothouse: The Art of Survival and the Survival of Art at America's Most Celebrated Publishing House, Farrar, Straus, and Giroux* (New York: Simon & Schuster, 2013).

In addition to the Macmillan company's records, housed at the New York Public Library, the best place to learn about Herbert Hoover as a writer is in the editorial apparatus for the two posthumous (and memoir-like) volumes edited by George H. Nash: *Freedom Betrayed: Herbert Hoover's Secret History of the Second World War and Its Aftermath* (Stanford, CA: Hoover Institution Press, 2011) and *The Crusade Years, 1933–1955: Herbert Hoover's Lost Memoir of the New Deal Era and Its Aftermath* (Stanford, CA: Hoover Institution Press, 2013). I also learned a lot from Timothy Walch's research, especially "The Ordeal of a Biographer: Herbert Hoover Writes about Woodrow Wilson," *Prologue* 40, no. 3 (2008): 12–19.

On the flourishing of nonfiction and the rise of the current affairs book, the place to start is the formidable scholarship of Priscilla Coit Murphy, especially *What a Book Can Do: The Publication and Reception of Silent Spring* (Amherst: University of Massachusetts Press, 2005) and "'Down with Fiction and up with Fact': *Publishers Weekly* and the Postwar Shift to Nonfiction," *Publishing Research Quarterly* 14, no. 3 (1998): 29–52. (In "The Article as Art," *Harper's*, July 1958, Norman Podhoretz describes a similar chronological evolution in magazine publishing.) There have been many other fine works on this period's literary culture, and I relied on Charles Lee, *The Hidden Public: The Story of the Book-of-the-Month Club* (New York: Doubleday, 1958); Kenneth C. Davis, *Two-Bit Culture: The Paperbacking of America* (Boston: Houghton Mifflin, 1984); Joan Shelley Rubin, *The Making of Middlebrow Culture* (Chapel Hill: University of North Carolina Press, 1992); Janice Radway, *A Feeling for Books: The Book-of-the-Month Club, Literary Taste and Middle-Class Desire* (Chapel Hill: University of North Carolina Press, 1997); Beth Luey, *Expanding the American Mind: Books and the Popularization of Knowledge* (Amherst: University of Massachusetts Press, 2010); Kathy Roberts Forde, "Profit and Public Interest: A Publication History of John Hersey's *Hiroshima*," *Journalism and Mass Communication Quarterly* 88, no. 3 (2011): 562–579; and Kristin L. Matthews, *Reading America: Citizenship, Democracy, and Cold War Literature* (Amherst: University of Massachusetts Press, 2016). This more subjective scholarship pairs nicely with Daniel M. G. Raff's economic analysis of the BOMC, including his compelling "The Book-of-the-Month Club: A Reconsideration" (presented at the Yale Economic History Workshop, November 2017). For the expansion of higher education, see Keith W. Olson, *The G.I. Bill, the Veterans, and the Colleges* (Lexington: University Press of Kentucky, 1974). For the life of Toni Morrison, see Stephanie Li's fine *Toni Morrison: A Biography* (Santa Barbara, CA: Greenwood Press, 2010) and Morrison's own autobiographical writings, most notably "A Slow Walk of Trees (as Grandmother Would Say) Hopeless (as Grandfather Would Say)," *New York Times*, July 4, 1976.

For my discussion of the widening gap between academic and popular historians, I relied on Timothy Paul Donovan, *Historical Thought in America: Postwar Patterns* (Norman: University of Oklahoma Press, 1973), Andrew Shocket, *Fighting over the Founders: How We Remember the American Revolution* (New York: New York University Press, 2015), David Greenberg, "That Barnes & Noble Dream," Slate, slate.com/news-and-politics/2005/05/academics-historians-vs-popularizers.html; Jeffrey L. Pasley, "Federalist Chic," Common-place, www.common-place-archives.org/publick/200202.shtml; David Waldstreicher, "Founders Chic as Culture War," *Radical History Review* 84 (2002): 185–194; and Erik Christiansen, *Channeling the Past: Politicizing History in Postwar America* (Madison: University of Wisconsin Press, 2013), the last of which also offers several case studies of the current affairs boom. The popularity of McCullough and other pop historians is also related to the rise of blockbuster publishing, which I discuss in chapters 12 and 13. McCullough was right—there is simply no precedent for the sales numbers hit by a handful of hefty biographies that began appearing in the 1990s. In 1938, to offer one comparison, Carl Van Doren's *Benjamin Franklin*, by contemporary reports a biographical smash, sold 42,000 copies.

237 *"Anyone with imagination"*: The entry is from January 6, 1947. The Harry S. Truman Library has made the diary transcript available at https://www.trumanlibrary.org/diary/index.html.

237 *"I've always read"*: Drew Pearson, "Truman Pays Tribute to Herbert Hoover," *Tuscaloosa News*, January 8, 1954.

238 *"Down with fiction"*: "Fiction Titles Were Fewer in 1948," *Publishers Weekly*, January 22, 1949.

238 *"I'm not a writer"*: McCullough, *Truman*, 937.

238 *"the damned book . . . the cussed manuscript"*: Truman to Dean Acheson, July 9, 1955, in *Affection and Trust*, 92.

239 *"the security I felt"*: Claudia Dreifus, "Chloe Wofford Talks About Toni Morrison," *New York Times Magazine*, September 11, 1994.

240 *"He read more"*: Henry P. Chiles oral history, Harry S. Truman Library.

240 *"I saw that"*: Harry S. Truman, *Memoirs* (New York: Doubleday, 1955–1956), 1:120.

240 *"a kind of"*: Truman to Bess Truman, June 22, 1911, in *Dear Bess: The Letters from Harry to Bess Truman, 1910–1959*, ed. Robert H. Ferrell (Columbia: University of Missouri Press, 1983), 39.

240 *"my patron saint"*: Truman to Bess Truman, January 10, 1911, in *Dear Bess*, 20.

240 *"I've been crazy"*: Truman to Bess Truman, June 22, 1911, in *Dear Bess*, 39.

241 *"Tomorrow—today"*: Harry S. Truman Papers, President's Secretary's Files, box 283, Harry S. Truman Library.

241 *"The shock of"*: "Book Industry Thrives Despite Depression," *New York Times*, August 31, 1931.

242 *"This is the final"*: Hoover to H. S. Latham, January 15, 1951, Macmillan Company records, box 57, New York Public Library, Manuscripts and Archives Division.

242 *"This is a nonfiction"*: "Margaret Banning Finds This Is a Nonfiction War," *Chicago Tribune*, December 5, 1943.

242 *"drugstore edition"*: Flannery O'Connor to "A," February 11, 1956, in *The Habit of Being*, ed. Sally Fitzgerald (New York: Farrar, Straus and Giroux, 1980), 137.

242 *"Highbrow, Lowbrow"*: Lynes's article ran in *Harper's* February 1949 issue.

243 *"book club selections . . . solid nonfiction"*: *Life*, April 11, 1949.

244 *"I played hooky"*: Truman to Bess Truman, February 11, 1937, Papers of Harry S. Truman, Pertaining to Family, Business, and Personal Affairs, box 9, Harry S. Truman Library.

244 *"as homespun as"*: Edward A. Harris, "Harry S. Truman," in *Public Men in and out of Office*, ed. J. T. Salter (Chapel Hill: University of North Carolina Press, 1946), 3–21, at 5.

244 *"He is, to put it"*: Harris, "Harry S. Truman," 3.

244 *"statesman book"*: See for example Paul Palmer (of *Reader's Digest*) to Roger Straus, December 6, 1951, Farrar, Straus & Giroux, Inc. Records, box 156, New York Public Library, Manuscripts and Archives Division. "This is one of the most exciting pieces of publishing that I have ever had anything to do with," Palmer wrote.

245 *"I'd rather starve"*: Clarence Johnson, "Being Ex-President Is Wearing," *Washington Post*, January 30, 1955.

246 *"The lies are beginning"*: Truman to George Elsey, February 15, 1950, in J. Garry Clifford, "President Truman and Peter the Great's Will," *Diplomatic History* 4, no. 4 (1980): 371–385, at 371.

246 *"Harry S. Truman, Federal Reserve"*: See the correspondence in Harry S. Truman Papers, Post-Presidential Papers, Harry S. Truman Library.

247 *"Miss Cather is due"*: McClure to Martha Young Rice, April 6, 1914, in *The Autobiography of S. S. McClure*, ed. Robert Thacker (Lincoln: University of Nebraska Press, 1997), xiv.

247 *"smallfanny"*: Hillman to Noyes, November 5, 1953, Harry S. Truman Papers, Post-Presidential Papers, William Hillman File, box 632, Harry S. Truman Library.

247 *"I want none"*: Francis Heller oral history, in Monte Poen Papers, box 3, Harry S. Truman Library.

247 *"Good god"*: Heller, "Harry S. Truman," 272.

248 *"What ethical considerations"*: Francis Heller oral history, in Monte Poen Papers, box 3, Harry S. Truman Library.

248 *"I regarded"*: Truman, *Memoirs*, 1:419.

248   *"Mr. President"*: Francis Heller oral history, in Monte Poen Papers, box 3, Harry S. Truman Library.

248   *"I did not ask"*: Francis Heller oral history, in Monte Poen Papers, box 3, Harry S. Truman Library.

248   *"I fix one"*: Williams, "I Was Truman's Ghost," 259.

249   *"I reached"*: Truman, *Memoirs*, 1:5.

249   *"The presidency of"*: Truman, *Memoirs*, 1:ix.

250   *"If he puts"*: Truman, *Memoirs*, 1:220.

250   *"I just can't"*: Webster Schott, "How the Memoirs Were Written," *New Republic*, March 19, 1956. Schott was the reporter who confronted Truman in the bathroom.

251   *"Sometimes I wish"*: Drew Pearson, "Truman Pays Tribute."

251   *"I want the book"*: Philip Hamburger, "Good of You to Do This for Us, Mr. Truman," *New Yorker*, November 19, 1955.

251   *"The Book of"*: Hamburger, "Good of You."

251   *"I had no idea"*: Hamburger, "Good of You."

252   *"Thank you"*: Truman's small talk can be heard in recordings made by Randall Jessee of Kansas City's WDAF, SR66-30, 66-31, 66-32, in the Sound Recordings Collection, Harry S. Truman Library.

252   *"Doesn't feel like"*: "Truman Autographs 1000 Books to Launch Sales," *Los Angeles Times*, November 3, 1955.

252   *"in the same class"*: Truman, interview transcript for *American Weekly* article, William Hillman Papers, box 5, Harry S. Truman Library.

252   *"the most important"*: *The World Around Us*, WCAU-FM, Philadelphia. The broadcaster was Charles Shaw.

252   *"brings to the reader"*: "Extreme Candor Contained in *Memoirs* of Mr. Truman," *Indianapolis Star*, December 11, 1955.

254   *"scalometer"*: For Truman's reputation, as measured by Gallup and other means, see Sheldon Appleton, "Public Perceptions of Truman," in *Harry S. Truman: The Man from Independence*, ed. William F. Levanstrosser (New York: Hofstra University Press, 1986), 169–185.

254   *"For this to"*: Harry Levins, "Wild about Harry," *St. Louis Post-Dispatch*, June 28, 1992.

254   *"magnificent . . . marvelous"*: Carol McCabe, "Harry Truman, American Original," *Providence Journal*, September 20, 1992.

254   *"Harry Truman . . . was exactly"*: Donnie Radcliffe, "George, Taking Heart from Give-'em'-Hell Harry," *Washington Post*, July 29, 1992.

254   *"Had my chance"*: Paul Burka, "The Revision Thing," *Texas Monthly*, November 1997.

255   *"a great American story"*: Jocelyn McClurg, "McCullough Says Truman Gave Him Lots to Work With," *Hartford Courant*, June 13, 1993.

255   *"The old adage applies"*: Joseph J. Ellis, *Founding Brothers: The Revolutionary Generation* (New York: Knopf, 2000), 4.

255   *"I want to put you on"*: Truman to Acheson, October 14, 1954, *Affection and Trust*, 60.

Chapter Eleven: The Writer Who Wouldn't Write

Profiles in Courage has probably drawn more attention for its ghostwriting than any ghostwritten book in history, and this attention has stemmed in part from Kennedy's own efforts to create a literary myth. I've focused on revealing the full extent of this myth-making for the first time, including Kennedy's personal intervention in his family's Pulitzer push, but I've also tried to document how both of his books were assembled, relying on letters, memos, drafts, and contemporary recordings.

Such documentation is important because many accounts of Kennedy's authorship, whether flattering or critical, simply don't hold up. Consider a critical one: Late in life, Harvey Klemmer, a former embassy aide to Joseph Kennedy, told Peter Collier and David Horowitz that he essentially rewrote *Why England Slept*. "When I got it, it was a mish-mash, ungrammatical," he said. "It was a very sloppy job, mostly magazine and newspaper clippings stuck together" (*The Kennedys: An American Drama* [New York: Warner, 1984], 444). But the typescript with Klemmer's markings is at Kennedy's presidential library, in the Personal Papers, box 26, and it shows Klemmer's contributions amounted to a vigorous copyedit. Klemmer also claimed he "put in a little peroration" (444)—but that is clearly not true since the ending of the published book is largely made up of full paragraphs lifted from a letter by Joseph Kennedy. John F. Kennedy didn't write *Why England Slept*, but Harvey Klemmer didn't either.

Such documentation is also important because—almost unbelievably—a few recent Kennedy books have tried to revise the earlier consensus, based on Herbert Parmet's authoritative *Jack: The Struggles of John F. Kennedy* (New York: Dial Press, 1980), that Kennedy didn't contribute much to his books. In *Ask Not: The Inauguration of John F. Kennedy and the Speech That Changed America* (New York: Holt, 2004), Thurston Clarke argues that Kennedy's role in *Profiles* has been underrated, supporting this claim with a paraphrase of an interview with Sorensen's secretary: "Although Sorensen contributed a lot of research, much of the book is based on Kennedy's dictation to her" (103). In *An Unfinished Life: John F. Kennedy, 1917–1963* (New York: Little, Brown, 2003), Robert Dallek points to dictations—to his credit he cites ones that actually survive, the Dictabelt recordings 25A, 25B, 26, and 27A at the John F. Kennedy Library—to offer a similarly soft evaluation: "Jack did more on the book than some later critics believed, but less than the term *author* normally connotes" (199). Dallek graciously helped me with a number of questions, but I've listened to these recordings and cannot see how he considers them "conclusive evidence of Jack's involvement" (199). There is other evidence of his involvement—in the handwritten Lamar pages I discuss in this chapter, which can be found in Kennedy's Personal Papers, box 29. (That box also includes Sorensen's initial version of the chapter; compare both drafts to *Profiles in Courage* [New York: Harper & Row, 1956], 154 and following.) In fact, there are just enough of these handwritten pages that I suspect they were the sample Kennedy and his supporters showed again and again to *Profiles* skeptics, though the pages also represent a small part of the book's real labor. Finally, and most baffling, is Michael O'Brien's conclusion in *John F. Kennedy: A Biography* (New York: Thomas Dunne, 2005): "Kennedy deeply believed he wrote enough of *Profiles* to claim real authorship. He may have been mistaken in his judgment, but there is no evidence he tried to deceive. He could accept the Pulitzer prize with a clear conscience" (339).

In addition to Parmet—and to Dallek, who misfires on *Profiles* but offers the best account of Kennedy's health problems—I depended on Joan and Clay Blair's *The Search for JFK* (New York: Berkley, 1976), and Nigel Hamilton's *JFK: Reckless Youth* (New York: Random House, 1992). I also reviewed and benefited from some of the research materials that Parmet, Hamilton, and the Blairs preserved. Kennedy's authorial side earned frequent contemporary coverage, with Kennedy's frequent encouragement: see Fletcher Knebel, "Joe Jr. Was Politician; Jack Started as a Writer," *Boston Globe*, January 5, 1960, and Harry Muheim, "When J.F.K. Was Rich, Young, and Happy," *Esquire*, August 1966, among many others. I've also relied on the reminiscences of key figures, including Clark Clifford, *Counsel to the President: A Memoir* (New York: Anchor, 1992); Mike Wallace, *Between You and Me: A*

Memoir (New York: Hyperion, 2005); and *Washington Merry-Go-Round: The Drew Pearson Diaries, 1960–1969*, ed. Peter Hannaford (Lincoln: University of Nebraska Press, 2015). John Hellman's *The Kennedy Obsession: The American Myth of JFK* (New York: Columbia University Press, 1997) applies the literary critic's tools to Kennedy and his books, with insightful results; David Haven Blake's *Liking Ike: Eisenhower, Advertising, and the Rise of Celebrity Politics* (New York: Oxford University Press, 2016) examines the precursors to the Kennedys' PR blitz. For an account of Kennedy's reading life—and the accounts rarely get more detailed than this—see Arthur Schlesinger's *A Thousand Days: John F. Kennedy in the White House* (Boston: Houghton Mifflin, 1965): "History was full of heroes for him, and he reveled in the stately cadences of historical prose. His memory of what he read was photographic. Situations, scenes, and quotations suck in his mind for the rest of his life" (80).

For the life of Joseph Kennedy, see Richard Whalen, *Founding Father: The Story of Joseph P. Kennedy* (New York: New American Library, 1965), and Ronald Kessler, *The Sins of the Father: Joseph P. Kennedy and the Dynasty He Founded* (New York: Warner, 1996). For details on his time as ambassador, see Alison Holmes and J. Simon Rofe, *The Embassy in Grosvenor Square: American Ambassadors to the United Kingdom, 1938–2008* (New York: Palgrave-Macmillan, 2012). For the Fordist assembly of Goldwater's *Conscience of a Conservative*—and the original plan for it to also serve as a clever campaign finance workaround—see Rick Perlstein, *Before the Storm: Barry Goldwater and the Unmaking of the American Consensus* (New York: Hill & Wang, 2001); Lee Edwards, *Goldwater: The Man Who Made a Revolution* (Washington, DC: Regnery, 1995); and Nicole Hemmer, *Messengers of the Right: Conservative Media and the Transformation of American Politics* (Philadelphia: University of Pennsylvania Press, 2016).

257 *"I hope you'll"*: Jonathan Aitken, *Nixon: A Life* (Washington, DC: Regnery, 1993), 347.

257 *"Pick the right"*: Christopher Lehmann-Haupt, "The Publishing of Politics," *New York Times*, June 2, 1968.

258 *"balance the flood"*: Sorensen, *Counselor: A Life at the Edge of History* (New York: HarperCollins, 2008), 145.

258 *"will do you"*: Joseph Kennedy to John F. Kennedy, August 2, 1940, in *Hostage to Fortune: The Letters of Joseph P. Kennedy*, ed. Amanda Smith (New York: Viking, 2001), 453.

258 *"tall, red-haired"*: Krock, *Memoirs: Sixty Years on the Firing Line* (New York: Funk & Wagnalls, 1968), 330.

259 *"I put down"*: Joseph P. Kennedy, *I'm for Roosevelt* (New York: Reynal & Hitchcock, 1936), 3

259 *"Public life"*: Schlesinger, *A Thousand Days*, 79.

259 *"He gobbled"*: Rose Kennedy, *Times to Remember* (New York: Doubleday, 1974), 104.

259 *"A Plea for"*: O'Brien, *John F. Kennedy*, 27.

259 *"I have an inquiring"*: Ralph G. Martin and Ed Plaut, *Front Runner, Dark Horse: A Political Study of Senators Kennedy and Symington* (New York: Doubleday, 1960), 122.

260 *"Any relation?"*: Gerald Walker and Donald A. Allan, "Jack Kennedy at Harvard," *Coronet*, May 1961.

260 *"Jack was not"*: Transcript of interview with Arthur Krock, in the Clay Blair Papers, American Heritage Center, University of Wyoming, Laramie, Wyoming.

260 *"I seem to be"*: Kennedy to Joseph Kennedy, n.d., in Blair and Blair, *Search for JFK*, 71.

260 *"Appeasement at Munich"*: The thesis drafts, including one Algase sent out to publish-

ers, can be found in the Papers of John F. Kennedy, Personal Papers, box 26, John F. Kennedy Library.

261 *"Send immediately"*: Hamilton, *JFK*, 307.

261 *"Rush pacifist . . . Becoming a"*: *Hostage to Fortune*, 232.

261 *"Dear Mother and Dad"*: John F. Kennedy to Rosemary and Joseph Kennedy, n.d., Joseph P. Kennedy Personal Papers, box 5, John F. Kennedy Library.

262 *"It represents more"*: John F. Kennedy to Joseph Kennedy, n.d., in Blair and Blair, *The Search for JFK*, 80.

262 *"Improve the writing"*: Joseph Kennedy to John F. Kennedy, May 20, 1940, in *Hostage to Fortune*, 435.

262 *"Jack Kennedy . . . Ambassador"*: Algase to Alfred Harcourt, June 20, 1940, Nigel Hamilton Papers, box 2, Massachusetts Historical Society. The ellipses are Algase's.

262 *"What conclusions"*: Papers of John F. Kennedy, Personal Papers, box 26, John F. Kennedy Library.

262 *"fundamental premise"*: Blair and Blair, *The Search for JFK*, 81.

262 *"I suppose the"*: John F. Kennedy to Joseph Kennedy, n.d., *Hostage to Fortune*, 444.

263 *"Nations, like individuals"*: Kennedy, *Why England Slept* (New York: Wilfred Funk, 1940), 3.

263 *"It seems to me"*: Joseph Kennedy to John F. Kennedy, May 20, 1940, *Hostage to Fortune*, 434–435. Compare to *Why England Slept*, 231.

264 *"already a best-seller"*: Joseph Kennedy to Winston Churchill, August 14, 1940, in *The Letters of John F. Kennedy*, ed. Martin W. Sandler (New York: Bloomsbury, 2013), 11.

264 "Why England Slept *is*": "Lessons of England's Sleeping Years," *Times Literary Supplement*, October 12, 1940.

264 *"Kennedy will not"*: Arthur Krock oral history, John F. Kennedy Library.

264 *"polish and amend"*: Arthur Krock oral history, John F. Kennedy Library.

264 *"I did much more"*: Transcript of interview with Arthur Krock, in the Clay Blair Papers, American Heritage Center, University of Wyoming.

265 *"A bestselling author"*: Hamilton, *JFK*, 380.

265 *"a notable text book"*: John F. Kennedy to Sorensen, John F. Kennedy Personal Papers, box 32, John F. Kennedy Library. Although the letter is undated, it clearly references the promotional planning for *Profiles*, which took place in the second half of 1955.

265 *"I haven't seen"*: Hamilton, *JFK*, 335.

265 *"What do you"*: Ralph G. Martin, *A Hero for Our Times: An Intimate Story of the Kennedy Years* (New York: Macmillan, 1983), 128.

265 *"The New Generation"*: Kenneth P. O'Donnell et al., *Johnny, We Hardly Knew Ye; Memories of John Fitzgerald Kennedy* (Boston: Little, Brown, 1972), 55.

266 *"I made up"*: Margaret L. Coit oral history, John F. Kennedy Library.

266 *"I feel that"*: Richard L. Neuberger, "For Our Senators, Reading Time Is Stolen from Hours of Sleep," *New York Times*, July 21, 1957.

266 *"stimulate a popular"*: Edwards, *Goldwater*, 117.

266 *"My complete incapacity"*: Goldwater to Stephen Shadegg, September 7, 1959, in John W. Dean and Barry M. Goldwater Jr., *Pure Goldwater* (New York: Palgrave Macmillan, 2008), 110.

267 *"Al Smith, Public Servant"*: See the undated telegram Kennedy sent to Algase's office in Papers of John F. Kennedy, Pre-Presidential Papers, House of Representative Files, box 73, John F. Kennedy Library.

267 *"my intellectual blood bank"*: Theodore White, *The Making of the President, 1960* (New York: Atheneum, 1961), 55.

267 *"the recognition of"*: Sorensen to John F. Kennedy, October 9, 1953, Theodore C. Sorensen Personal Papers, box 6, John F. Kennedy Library.

268 *"add some sparkle"*: Sorensen to James Landis, December 18, 1953, Theodore C. Sorensen Personal Papers, box 6, John F. Kennedy Library. Sorensen was paraphrasing Kennedy's instructions.

268 *"How about using"*: Martin and Plaut, *Front Runner*, 200.

268 *"Still oozing"*: Geoffrey Perret, *Jack: A Life Like No Other* (New York: Random House, 2001), 213.

268 *"There is certainly"*: Sorensen to John F. Kennedy, January 17, 1955, Theodore C. Sorensen Personal Papers, box 7, John F. Kennedy Library.

269 *"My present suggestion"*: Sorensen to John F. Kennedy, January 25, 1955, Theodore C. Sorensen Personal Papers, box 15, John F. Kennedy Library.

269 *"working drafts . . . expanding . . . rewriting"*: Sorensen to John F. Kennedy, February 8, 1955, Theodore C. Sorensen Personal Papers, box 7, John F. Kennedy Library.

269 *"I found in"*: Cass Canfield to John F. Kennedy, February 15, 1955, Harper & Row, Publishers Records, 1935–1973, box 117, Columbia University Libraries, Rare Book and Manuscript Library.

270 *"1. Daniel Webster"*: "Worksheet on Political Courage Book," n.d. (but probably written on March 17, 1955), Theodore C. Sorensen Personal Papers, box 7, John F. Kennedy Library.

270 *"drafted anything of"*: Sorensen, *Kennedy* (New York: Harper & Row, 1965), 60.

271 *"Begin"*: Papers of John F. Kennedy, Personal Papers, box 29, John F. Kennedy Library; the memo was by Jules Davids of Georgetown University.

271 *"Harper's should"*: Joseph Kennedy to Sorensen, August 15, 1955, *Hostage to Fortune*, 669.

271 *"the senator's own"*: Sorensen to Thomas, October 7, 1955, Papers of John F. Kennedy, Personal Papers, box 31, John F. Kennedy Library.

271 *"4. TCS?"*: Papers of John F. Kennedy, Personal Papers, box 27, John F. Kennedy Library.

271 *"for his invaluable"*: Kennedy, *Profiles*, xiv.

272 *"I've really got"*: Evan Thomas oral history, Columbia Center for Oral History.

272 *"The American writer"*: Roth, "Writing American Fiction," *Commentary*, March 1961.

273 *"The book reflects"*: John Harris, "Editor Tells How Bay State Senator Wrote of Nation's Great Leaders," *Boston Globe*, December 26, 1955.

273 *"Most of us"*: Charles Cason, "Stimulating Book Written by Young Massachusetts Senator," *Delta Democrat-Times*, February 26, 1956.

273 *"profiles in courage"*: Kennedy, "Three Women of Courage," *McCall's*, January 1958.

274 *"I always used"*: Liz Hillenbrand, "Authors Air Problems of Craft," *Washington Post*, February 9, 1956.

274 *"an author"*: See the transcripts of his appearances on October 28, 1956, and January 3, 1960, among others, in Papers of John F. Kennedy, Pre-Presidential Papers, Senate Files, box 920, John F. Kennedy Library.

274 *"Dear Evan"*: John F. Kennedy to Evan Thomas, June 25, 1956, Harper & Row, Publishers Records, 1935–1973, box 117, Columbia University Libraries, Rare Book and Manuscript Library.

274 *"My book"*: "Historians Truman and Kennedy Chat," *Boston Globe*, August 15, 1956.

274 *"Our country"*: William Harrison, "Massachusetts' Junior Senator Author of Great Book on Famous Americans," *Philadelphia Tribune*, September 4, 1956.

275 *"Dear Dad"*: Kennedy to Joseph Kennedy, January 15, 1957, Papers of John F. Kennedy, Pre-Presidential Papers, Senate Files, box 521, John F. Kennedy Library.

275 *"It is not even"*: Robert Choate to Krock, March 11, 1957, Arthur Krock Papers, box 21, Seeley Mudd Library, Princeton University.

275 *"As no one else"*: Gilbert Seldes, "The Lively Arts," *Village Voice*, May 15, 1957.

275 *"the only man"*: Clark Clifford Personal Papers, box 1, John F. Kennedy Library.

275 *"I want you"*: Clifford, *Counsel to the President*, 307.

276 *"to assist [Kennedy]"*: Clark Clifford Personal Papers, box 1, John F. Kennedy Library. The affidavit is dated December 14, 1957.

276 *"very generously"*: Clark Clifford Personal Papers, box 1, John F. Kennedy Library.

276 *"You of course"*: Bill Moyers, "Clark Clifford," A Second Look with Bill Moyers, PBS, May 28, 1989. Clifford recounts a similar version of this exchange in *Counsel to the President*, in which Kennedy says of the ghostwriting charge, "It could have destroyed my candidacy" (310).

276 *"We might as well"*: Theodore C. Sorensen, *Kennedy* (New York: Harper & Row, 1965), 69.

276 *"I have, on many"*: Kennedy to John B. Oakes, January 30, 1958, Theodore C. Sorensen Personal Papers, box 7, John F. Kennedy Library. For a similar exchange—and there were many like this—see Kennedy's defensive correspondence with Emma Sheehy in the John F. Kennedy file, U.S. Senate Library. (Thanks to John T. Shaw for alerting me to these letters.)

277 *"not counting the"*: Rasa Gustaitis, "Official Family of President Prolific Writers and Editors," *Washington Post*, February 5, 1961.

277 *"He said something"*: *The Sixties: The Last Journal, 1960–1972*, ed. Lewis M. Dabney (New York: Farrar, Straus and Giroux, 1993), 80.

277 *"Everyone there"*: Lowell to Edmund Wilson, May 31, 1962, in Ian Hamilton, *Robert Lowell: A Biography* (New York: Random House, 1982), 299.

278 *"Dear senator"*: Lewis to John F. Kennedy, May 20, 1956, Papers of John F. Kennedy, Pre-Presidential Papers, Senate Files, box 507, John F. Kennedy Library.

278 *"the book was"*: Mrs. Lawrence Anderson to Kennedy, November 23, 1957, Theodore C. Sorensen Personal Papers, box 7, John F. Kennedy Library. The librarian letter came from Marion V. Leahy of the Deborah Cook Sayles Public Library in Pawtucket, Rhode Island, December 11, 1957, also in box 7.

278 *"you accepted"*: Charles J. McCue to Kennedy, December 19, 1957, Theodore C. Sorensen Personal Papers, box 7, John F. Kennedy Library.

Chapter Twelve: Reagan and the Rise of the Blockbuster

A key source for this book has been memoirs by publishers, politicians, and staffers, and I've tried to remember that these books are imperfect (and to evaluate their claims accordingly). Here's a small example: two completely opposed recollections of why, when it came time to sell *An American Life*, Reagan found himself already under contract with Simon & Schuster. The cause was an older, unfulfilled book deal, and the two sides renegotiated it on a blockbuster scale. Reagan's first literary agent, Bill Adler, recalled in his autobiography that Simon & Schuster had actually tried to wriggle out of the deal before Reagan became president; in a "rather terse phone call," Adler wrote, Simon & Schuster CEO Richard Snyder demanded that "we should get our money back with interest," until Adler gamely convinced him to stick with his client (*Inside Publishing* [Indianapolis: Bobbs-Merrill, 1982], 143–144). Korda, by contrast, remembered that Snyder "shrewdly refused to take back the money for many years, trusting in Reagan's star" (Korda, "Prompting the President," *New Yorker*, October 6, 1997).

Memory can distort even across shorter distances. In a fascinating article, "John Dean's Memory: A Case Study," *Cognition* 9, no. 1 (1981): 1–22, Ulric Neisser covers the controversy surrounding Dean, Richard Nixon's former White House counsel. During his Watergate Senate testimony—and later in his kiss-and-tell book—Dean offered an astonishing number of details about his recent past with Nixon: dates, meetings, dialogue. Reporters dubbed Dean "the human tape recorder," until Nixon's actual tape recordings surfaced. As Neisser carefully demonstrates, Dean got many of his specifics wrong, even as he got his larger points right, a pattern psychologists have often noted while studying memory.

For this reason, the most valuable sources for revealing Reagan's intellectual side are contemporary documents. While Reagan's presidential library has still not made his most important personal papers available, I learned a lot reviewing the Richard G. Hubler Papers at Boston University, an archive that Reagan's many biographers have neglected. I confirmed Reagan's increasing political savvy—and Nancy's as well—by studying their 1960s correspondence with William F. Buckley at Yale University. (Thanks to Christopher Buckley for granting permission to review those letters.) I also relied on Matthew Dallek's superb *The Right Moment: Ronald Reagan's First Victory and the Decisive Turning Point in American Politics* (New York: Oxford University Press, 2000); Garry Wills's *Reagan's American: Innocents at Home* (New York: Doubleday, 1987); and Edmund Morris's *Dutch: A Memoir of Ronald Reagan* (New York: Random House, 1999)—still a wonderful source on Reagan's life, despite Morris's frustrating authorial choices. I felt it necessary to contact Reagan's presidential library to confirm Morris's quotations of Reagan's juvenilia, and I'm sure many historians share my unease.

The best traditional biographies of Reagan come from Lou Cannon, particularly *President Reagan: The Role of a Lifetime* (New York: Simon & Schuster, 1991) and *Governor Reagan: His Rise to Power* (New York: Public Affairs, 2003). Some of Reagan's prose has been published in two useful volumes: *Reagan, in His Own Hand*, ed. Kiron K. Skinner et al. (New York: Simon & Schuster, 2001) and *Reagan: A Life in Letters*, ed. Kiron K. Skinner et al. (New York: Simon & Schuster, 2003); see also the authorship analysis performed by Edoardo M. Airoldi, Stephen E. Fienberg, and Koron K. Skinner in "Whose Ideas? Whose Words? Authorship of Ronald Reagan's Radio Addresses," *PS: Political Science and Politics* 40, no. 3 (2007): 501–506. There are excellent accounts of Reagan's reading in Stephen Vaughn's *Ronald Reagan in Hollywood: Movies and Politics* (Cambridge: Cambridge University Press, 1994)—especially its chapter on Reagan and black actors, which provides a rich and overlooked example of Reagan reading deeply on current affairs—and Burstein's *Democracy's Muse: How Thomas Jefferson Became an FDR Liberal, a Reagan Republican, and a Tea Party Fanatic, All the While Being Dead* (Charlottesville: University of Virginia Press, 2015). In 1977, a librarian named Dallas Baillio asked various celebrities about their reading lives, and much of Reagan's response is reprinted in Jerry Griswold, "'I'm a Sucker for Hero Worship,'" *New York Times*, August 30, 1981. Baillio told me Reagan's was easily the most detailed and reflective one he received. Stories like that make Reagan's later attitudes toward reading and writing stand out. For Reagan's role in *An American Life*, see Robert Lindsey, *Ghost Scribbler: Searching for Reagan, Brando, and the King of Pop* (self pub., CreateSpace, 2012). For a suggestive analysis of Reagan's impromptu speaking, see Visar Berisha et al., "Tracking Discourse Complexity Preceding Alzheimer's Disease Diagnosis: A Case Study Comparing the Press Conferences of Presidents Ronald Reagan and George Herbert Walker Bush," *Journal of Alzheimer's Disease* 45, no. 3 (2015): 959–963.

Three scholars have done essential work on blockbuster publishing: John B. Thompson, *Merchants of Culture: The Publishing Business in the Twenty-First Century*, 2nd ed. (New York: Polity, 2013); Laura J. Miller, *Reluctant Capitalists: Bookselling and the Culture of Consumption* (Chicago: University of Chicago Press, 2007); and Albert Greco, *The Culture and Commerce of Publishing in the 21st Century* (Stanford, CA: Stanford Business Books, 2007), and, with Jim Milliot and Robert M. Wharton, *The Book Publishing Industry*, 3rd ed. (New York: Routledge, 2014). I also relied on the final volume in *A History of the Book in America*, *The Enduring Book: Print Culture in Postwar America*, ed. David Paul Nord, Joan Shelley Rubin, and Michael Schudson (Chapel Hill: University of North Carolina Press, 2009). In addition to conducting interviews, I reviewed contemporary media coverage—coverage that was often professionally fact-checked in a way that renders it more rigorous than, say, an editor's memoirs. Some of the most insightful features and essays include Patricia Morrisroe, "Mega-Mort: Superagent Janklow's Blockbuster Life," *New York*, February 2, 1987; Ted Solotaroff, "The Literary-Industrial Complex: How the Corporate Mentality Has Undermined the Profession of Publishing," *New Republic*, June 8, 1987; Christopher Buckley, "Washington Memoirs: Bombshell or Bust," *New York Times*, October 1, 1989; Edwin Diamond, "The Book of Trump," *New York*, July 16, 1990, and Jane Mayer, "Donald Trump's Ghostwriter Tells All," *New Yorker*, July 18, 2016; Jacob Weisberg, "Rough Trade: The Sad Decline of American Publishing," *New Republic*, June 17, 1991; Roger Cohen, "Dick Snyder's Ugly Word," *New York Times*, June 30, 1991; and Peter Ross Range, "David Stockman's $2 Million Book Contract," *Washington Post Magazine*, November 24, 1985, which boasts an early appearance by Robert Barnett, who shows up in the last chapter in this book but was still a mysterious presence when he helped Stockman land his deal. ("I told him to get a good agent," one editor told Range, "which he didn't.") I owe this chapter's "blockbuster" terminology to Thomas Whiteside's wonderful *New Yorker* series that was collected in *The Blockbuster Complex: Conglomerates, Show Business, and Book Publishing* (Middletown, CT: Wesleyan University Press, 1980), though Whiteside's fears about the movie business commandeering the book business proved misplaced.

I also relied on contemporary coverage of politics and campaigns. For Reagan's rise, see Jessica Mitford, "The Rest of Ronald Reagan," *Ramparts*, November 1965; William F. Buckley, "Ronald Reagan: A Relaxing View," *National Review*, November 28, 1967; Jack Langguth, "Political Fun and Games in California," *New York Times Magazine*, October 16, 1966; and Jules Witcover and Richard Cohen, "Where's the Rest of Ronald Reagan?" *Esquire*, March 1976, in which Reagan himself credited his reading and writing as the main forces behind his rightward shift: "Eventually what happened to me was, because I did my own speeches and did the research for them, I just woke up." David Lee Rosenbloom's *Election Men: Professional Campaign Managers and American Democracy* (New York: Quadrangle Books, 1973) offers excellent ideas and data. For Eisenhower's legacy book, see Phillip Hamburger, "Notes for a Gazeteer," *New Yorker*, April 4, 1964. For Carter's, see the reminiscences of his assistant Steven Hochman, "With Jimmy Carter in Georgia," in *Farewell to the Chief: Former Presidents in American Public Life*, ed. Richard Norton Smith and Timothy Walch (Worland, WY: High Plains, 1990), 123–136. For Lyndon Johnson's, see Edwin Diamond, "The Johnson Version," *New York*, September 28, 1970, and Doris Kearns Goodwin, *Leadership: In Turbulent Times* (New York: Simon & Schuster, 2018); the postpresidential files at Johnson's presidential library contain transcripts of some of his unfiltered dictations, before his ghosts gave up on trying to elicit that side of him, and Michael Beschloss has published one in "Lyndon Johnson on the Record," *Texas Monthly*, December 2001. For Nixon's legacy book, see Robert Sam Anson's terrific *Exile: The Unquiet Oblivion of Richard M. Nixon* (New York: Simon & Schuster, 1984). For a good example of an ex-president critiquing his predecessors' legacy books, see Jonathan Alter's interview with Bill Clinton ("Writing the Book of Bill," *Newsweek*, August 19, 2001).

279   *"the major memoir"*: Edwin Diamond, "Memoir Mania," *New York*, November 11, 1985.
279   *"I hear it's"*: Michael Korda, *Another Life: A Memoir of Other People* (New York: Random House, 1999), 475.
279   *"an amiable dunce"*: James M. Perry, "For the Democrats, Pam's Is the Place for the Elite to Meet," *Wall Street Journal*, October 8, 1981.
280   *"The prevailing atmosphere"*: Gerald Howard, "Mistah Perkins—He Dead: Publishing Today," *American Scholar*, Fall 1989.
281   *"Meditations of"*: *Dixonian*, 1928.
281   *"I don't know"*: Sue Ragland Diggle to Reagan, June 22, 1966, in *Reagan: A Life in Letters*, 288.
281   *"I wrote it"*: *Reagan: A Life in Letters*, 288.
281   *"The joy of reading"*: Reagan to Hellen P. Miller, September 3, 1981, *Reagan: A Life in Letters*, 7.
281   *"As I look back"*: Griswold, " 'I'm a Sucker for Hero Worship.' "
282   *"a gasping, panting" and "Marjory something"*: Morris, *Dutch*, 93, 104.
283   *"What's this I hear"*: "Five Former Co-Stars Rate Reagan as a Leading—and Sometimes Misleading—Man," *People*, August 10, 1981.
283   *"a precedent which"*: *She's Working Her Way Through College*, directed by Bruce Humberstone (Warner Bros., 1952), DVD.
283   *"When I'd get"*: David T. Byrne, *Ronald Reagan: An Intellectual Biography* (Lincoln: University of Nebraska Press, 2018), 89.
284   *"a dramatic first-hand"*: Charles A. Pearce to Reagan and Hubler, November 27, 1963, Richard G. Hubler Papers, box 70, Howard Gotlieb Archival Research Center, Boston University. Despite the date of this letter, the Hubler collection contains several letters from June and July 1962, showing the project was already underway—the November 1963 letter is Pearce's description of what he'd expected as compared to the manuscript he'd just received, a manuscript Reagan had ensured was far different from what they'd originally agreed on.
284   *"Well, if we're"*: Reagan to Maureen Reagan, in Cannon, *Governor Reagan*, 133. Cannon does not provide the letter's date.
284   *"the saga of Reagan"*: Hubler to Anne (no last name), July 19, 1963, Richard G. Hubler Papers, Box 70, Howard Gotlieb Archival Research Center, Boston University.
284   *"my literary epic"*: Reagan to Lorraine and Elwood Wagner, July 25, 1963, in *Reagan: A Life in Letters*, 753.
284   *"Dear Dick"*: Reagan to Hubler, n.d., Richard G. Hubler Papers, Box 27, Howard Gotlieb Archival Research Center, Boston University. For Hubler's own description of Reagan's diligence, see Ray Walters, "Paperback Talk," *New York Times*, July 12, 1981.
284   *"shoves her face"*: *Where's the Rest of Me?* (New York: Duell, Sloan and Pearce, 1965), 80.
284   *"I was eleven"*: *Where's the Rest of Me?*, 7–8.
285   *"a near-hopeless"*: *Where's the Rest of Me?*, 139.
285   *"a nonpartisan viewpoint"*: *Where's the Rest of Me?*, 271–272.
285   *"The story begins"*: *Where's the Rest of Me?* 3.
286   *"I wrote a book"*: Interview with Spencer.
286   *"He showed up"*: Interview with Spencer.
286   *"I've found it"*: Marry Ellis Carlton, "Actor Reagan Finds Answer in Politics," *Long Beach Independent*, July 29, 1965.

286 *"It was a nice"*: Interview with Spencer.

286 *"I already got"*: Interview with Cannon.

286 *"Just dig out"*: "Brown Intensifies Tour Campaigning by Airplane," *Redlands Daily Facts*, June 4, 1966.

287 *"To Stu"*: Spencer shared pictures of his inscribed book.

287 *"I have often thought in reading"*: Harry S. Truman, *Memoirs* (New York: Doubleday, 1955–1956), 1:ix.

287 *"personal memoir"*: "A Week's Miscellany," *New York Times*, June 16, 1963.

288 *"I suppose I'm"*: Lewis Nichols, "In the Literary Vineyards of Gettysburg, an Author Labors On," *New York Times*, July 7, 1963.

288 *"Apparently he never"*: Arthur M. Schlesinger, *Journals: 1952–2000* (New York: Penguin, 2007), 202.

288 *"'personal' book"*: *The Vantage Point: Perspectives of the Presidency, 1963–1969* (New York: Holt, 1971), ix.

288 *"President Johnson was"*: Interview with Middleton. Tom Johnson shared similar experiences in a separate interview.

288 *"I got used"*: Interview with Middleton.

288 *"We just started"*: Interview with Khachigian.

289 *"the key to"*: Anson, *Exile*, 180.

289 *"Don't Buy Books"*: Mary McGrory, "Nixon's Book Runs into a Boycott Campaign," *Boston Globe*, April 26, 1978, among many other stories.

289 *"From the very"*: Interview with Flanigan.

289 *"This is the worst"*: Ted Morgan, "Sharks . . . and Then, and Then, and Then," *New York Times Magazine*, April 21, 1974.

289 *"electronic memoirs"*: Les Brown, "CBS Schedules Haldeman Interviews," *New York Times*, March 13, 1975.

289 *"The emphasis will"*: Whiteside, *Blockbuster Complex*, 153.

292 *"a highly personal book"*: Jimmy Carter, *White House Diary* (New York: Farrar, Straus and Giroux, 2010), 521.

292 *"It's much easier"*: Edwin McDowell, "'No Problem' Machine Poses a Presidential Problem," *New York Times*, March 24, 1981.

292 *"big books"*: See Thompson's chapter of the same title in *Merchants of Culture*.

292 *"This is a business"*: Trip Gabriel, "Call My Agent!" *New York Times Magazine*, February 19, 1989.

293 *"I was up"*: Kenneth Adelman oral history, Miller Center Oral History Program.

293 *"the fastest-selling"*: Daisy Maryles, "The Year's Bestselling Books," *Publishers Weekly*, March 15, 1985.

293 *"We all want"*: Joshua Hammer, "Shoot-Out on Publishers' Row," *Newsday*, January 11, 1987.

293 *"Trump was very"*: Interview with Osnos.

293 *"Stop losing"*: Interview with Osnos.

294 *"This outpouring"*: Frances FitzGerald, "Memoirs of the Reagan Era," *New Yorker*, January 16, 1989.

294 *"So, . . . what do"*: Buckley, "Washington Memoirs."

294 *"Regan—yea"*: Interview with Goldberg.

294 *"in the swing"*: Charles Trueheart, "Meese Memoirs Bought," *Washington Post*, February 1, 1989.

294 *"behind-the-scenes"*: Charles Trueheart, "Meese Book Contract Dropped," *Washington Post*, April 17, 1990.

294 *"Nothing was ever"*: Elizabeth Mehren, "The Case of the Bookless Book Party," *Los Angeles Times*, July 1, 1990. Meese eventually published his memoirs in late 1992 with the conservative house Regnery: *With Reagan: The Inside Story* (Washington, DC: Regnery, 1992).

295 *"I bet my"*: Marjorie Hunter, "Betty Ford's Renaissance," *New York Times*, November 10, 1978.

295 *"They came to me"*: Interview with Janklow.

295 *"No one . . . is better"*: Josh Getlin, "The Man in the Middle," *Los Angeles Times*, February 16, 1989.

296 *"what goes through"*: Korda, *Another Life*, 468–469.

296 *"the monkey"*: Interview with Mark Weinberg.

296 *"I'm trying"*: Interview with Lindsey.

297 *"circling his own"*: DeLillo, "American Blood: A Journey Through the Labyrinth of Dallas and JFK," *Rolling Stone*, December 8, 1983.

297 *"It was a pain"*: Interview with Lindsey.

297 *"A shared writing"*: Interview with Korda.

297 *"All Simon & Schuster"*: Interview with Weinberg.

297 *"They weren't alone"*: Korda, *Another Life*, 471.

298 *"Nancy and I"*: Ronald Reagan, *An American Life* (New York: Simon & Schuster, 1990), 11.

298 *"Lord, I hope I'm ready and not"*: *The Reagan Diaries*, ed. Douglas Brinkley (New York: HarperCollins, 2007), 369.

298 *"jet lag"*: Reagan, *An American Life*, 11.

298 *"The interview with Barbara"*: Interview with Weinberg. Weinberg tells a similar version of this story in his *Movie Nights with the Reagans: A Memoir* (New York: Simon & Schuster, 2018).

299 *"Both Ron and Nancy"*: Interview with Korda.

Chapter Thirteen: The Literary Candidate

There have been many insightful profiles of Obama—because he's a great story and because journalists tend to fall hard for him. (Even in Illinois politics, his fellow writers were a crucial audience for his first book.) To understand his ascent, I relied on Hank De Zutter, "What Makes Obama Run?" *Chicago Reader*, December 7, 1995; William Finnegan, "The Candidate," *New Yorker*, May 31, 2004; Mary Mitchell, "Memoir of a 21st-century History Maker," *Black Issues Book Review*, January–February 2005; the *Chicago Tribune*'s "Making of a Candidate" series, which started in the March 25, 2007, edition; Todd Purdum, "Raising Obama," *Vanity Fair*, March 2008; Ryan Lizza, "Making It," *New Yorker*, July 21, 2008; and especially Janny Scott, "The Story of Obama, Written by Obama," *New York Times*, May 18, 2008, and Robert Draper, "Barack Obama's Work In Progress," *GQ*, November 2009. I also relied on four significant Obama biographies: David Mendell, *Obama: From Promise to Power* (New York: HarperCollins, 2007); David Remnick, *The Bridge: The Life and Rise of Barack Obama* (New York: Knopf, 2010); David Maraniss, *Barack Obama: The Story* (New York: Simon & Schuster, 2012), which first identified *Dreams'* Regina as a composite; and David Garrow, *Rising Star: The Making of Barack Obama* (New York: HarperCollins, 2017)—the last one edited, in a fun twist, by Henry Ferris.

While Obama's life as a writer has been well analyzed, his life as a reader has not. Thoughtful exceptions include David Samuels, "Invisible Man," *New Republic*, October 22, 2008; Michiko Kakutani, "How Reading Nourished Obama during the White House

Years," *New York Times*, January 16, 2017; and James Kloppenberg, *Reading Obama: Dreams, Hope, and the American Political Tradition* (Princeton: Princeton University Press, 2010). One glimpse of Obama talking like a reader comes in the interview he did with Marilynne Robinson, which the *New York Review of Books* split between its November 5, 2015, and November 19, 2015, issues. Reading novelists like Robinson really did shape Obama's writing, which shaped everything else—made that writing lyrical and empathetic, instinctually scenic and character-rich. You can see this in Obama's juvenilia, like the dry essay he wrote at Columbia that conjures a scene where there is none, pivoting from antiwar platitudes to a riff on "the taste of war—the sounds and chill, the dead bodies" (Obama, "Breaking the War Mentality," *Sundial*, March 10, 1983). You can see it in the equally dry essay he wrote while a community organizer, which opens with a public school employee dressing him down in snappy dialogue (Obama, "Why Organize?" in *After Alinsky*, ed. Peg Knoepfle [Springfield: Sangamon State University, 1990], 35–40). So it makes sense that you can also see it in his mature writing, especially when that writing is a literary memoir.

The excitement that surrounded this genre in the 1990s can still be felt while reading James Atlas's "Confessing for Voyeurs," *New York Times Magazine*, May 12, 1996. Jeremy Rosen helpfully surveys concepts like contemporary fiction, literary fiction, and genre fiction in "Literary Fiction and the Genres of Genre Fiction," *Post45: Peer Reviewed* (August 2018), post45.research.yale.edu/2018/08/literary-fiction-and-the-genres-of-genre-fiction. To understand Obama's literary context I also relied on Julie Rak, *Boom! Manufacturing Memoir for the Popular Market* (Waterloo: Wilfrid Laurier University Press, 2013), Mark McGurl, *The Program Era: Postwar Fiction and the Rise of Creative Writing* (Cambridge, MA: Harvard University Press, 2009), and Matthew G. Kirschenbaum, *Track Changes: A Literary History of Word Processing* (Cambridge, MA: Harvard University Press, 2016). Someone should write a historical and sociological account of the rise of literary empathy—as a creative writing tenet and as a defense for literature—but until then it's worth noting that both strains have a long history, even if their terminology sometimes shifts. Obama's 1990 book proposal is part of that history, as is Wilson's 1890 lecture. Empathy also saturates Kingston's writing and interviews—in this line, for instance, from a conversation in 1996: "Writing has to do with how to get out of one's own narcissism and solipsism in order to imagine another human being and the rest of the universe" (*Conversations with Maxine Hong Kingston*, ed. Paul Skenazy [Jackson: University of Mississippi Press, 1998], 221).

In addition to the works cited in my mini-essay to chapter 12, the best way to track the book trade is to read its beat reporters, especially Jeffrey Trachtenberg at the *Wall Street Journal* and Alexandra Alter (and, before her, Julie Bosman) at the *New York Times*. In "The End," *New York*, September 22, 2008, Boris Kachka captures the industry's postdigital anxiety. In "Why Big Books Still Matter," *Big Money*, October 4, 2009, Marion Maneker explains the logic of blockbuster political titles—a logic that applies to the industry's other product lines such as, say, the comedian memoir, where Tina Fey and *Bossypants* served as kind of a funnybone Iacocca.

There's been a lot of coverage about recent Washington books, though it rarely considers those books' merits as books. (Barnett, for instance, is a key character in Mark Leibovich's *This Town* [New York: Blue Rider Press, 2013], which also details Plouffe's distaste for the lawyer.) The best writer on modern political books is Andrew Ferguson, and I learned a lot from his cranky triptych: "The Literary Obama," *Weekly Standard*, February 12, 2007; "What Does Newt Gingrich Know?" *New York Times Magazine*, June 29, 2011; and "The Groaning Shelves," *Weekly Standard*, October 8, 2018. Other useful articles include Jon-

athan Rauch, "Robert Reich, Quote Doctor," Slate, slate.com/news-and-politics/1997/05
/robert-reich-quote-doctor.html, and "Reich Redux," Slate, slate.com/news-and-poli
tics/1998/02/reich-redux.html; David S. Bernstein, "Romney Rewrites," *Boston Phoenix*,
thephoenix.com/BLOGS/talkingpolitics/archive/2011/02/10/romney-rewrites-sampler.
aspx; Andrew Kaczynski, "Three Pages of Rand Paul's Book Were Plagiarized from Think
Tanks," Buzzfeed, www.buzzfeednews.com/article/andrewkaczynski/entire-section-of
-rand-pauls-book-copied-verbatim-from-case (note that in the print edition it's five pages:
130–135); Dan Amira, "Herman Cain Set for Huge Payday After Campaign," *New York*,
nymag.com/intelligencer/2011/11/herman_cain_money_business_plan.html; Gabriel
Sherman, "The Revolution Will Be Commercialized," *New York*, May 3, 2010; McKay
Coppins, "Killing Conservative Books," Buzzfeed, www.buzzfeednews.com/article/mc
kaycoppins/killing-conservative-books-the-shocking-end-of-a-publishing; Olivia Nuzzi
and Ben Collins, "Donald Trump Used Campaign Donations to Buy $55,000 of His Own
Book," *Daily Beast*, www.thedailybeast.com/donald-trump-used-campaign-donations
-to-buy-dollar55000-of-his-own-book; Alex Shephard, "Art of the Steal," *New Republic*,
newrepublic.com/article/144541/art-steal-trump-boosted-book-sales-gamed-new-york
-times-best-seller-list; and Jason Zengerle, "The Escape Artists," *New York Times*, March
31, 2019.

For America's increasing partisanship and polarization, see Pew's "The Partisan Divide
on Political Values Grows Even Wider" (www.people-press.org/wp-content/uploads
/sites/4/2017/10/10-05-2017-Political-landscape-release-updt..pdf). The most convincing
explanation I've seen for why this is happening is Lilliana Mason's *Uncivil Agreement: How
Politics Became Our Identity* (Chicago: University of Chicago Press, 2018). For Powell's
American Journey, see Elizabeth Taylor, "Generally Speaking," *Chicago Tribune*, August 25,
1996, and Powell's own discussion with Brian Lamb ("My American Journey," *Booknotes*,
C-SPAN, January 7, 1996); Newt Gingrich's 1995 book tour is an important analogue to
Powell's (see Katharine Q. Seelye, "Gingrich, by the Book," *New York Times*, August 16,
1995). For Clinton's *My Life*, see Robert Sam Anson, "Bill and His Shadow," *Vanity Fair*,
June 2004. When Clinton ran in 1992, his book with Al Gore, *Putting People First*, was a
best seller, as was Ross Perot's *United We Stand*, but both were bland and hastily assembled
manifestoes—assembled by Peter Osnos and staff, in Clinton's case. They echo earlier titles
like Wilson's *New Freedom* and Roosevelt's *Looking Forward*, except sped up to match the
metabolism of blockbuster publishing.

300   *"We're not running"*: Glenn Thrush and Dylan Byers, "The Dangerous New Obama
       Book," Politico, www.politico.com/story/2012/05/davids-new-goliath-barack-
       obama-075865.
301   *"My father was"*: Noam Scheiber, "Race against History," *New Republic*, May 31,
       2004.
301   *"I stand here"*: Obama's convention speech is reprinted in *We Are the Change We Seek:
       The Speeches of Barack Obama*, ed. E. J. Dionne Jr. and Joy-Ann Reid (New York:
       Bloomsbury, 2017).
301   *"Writing a book"*: Melissa Merli, "Obama Book a Reflection on Family, Race, Iden-
       tity," *News-Gazette*, July 18, 2004.
302   *"I loved reading"*: This quote comes from a transcript of Michiko Kakutani interview-
       ing Obama: "Obama on Books That Guided Him," *New York Times*, January 16, 2017.
302   *"to become that intimate"*: Morrison gave the quote in a 1977 interview on WTTW,
       a PBS station in Chicago. Part of the interview can be viewed online at www.pbs.org
       /video/toni-morrison-empathy-and-storytelling-lfmkla.

302 *"There was a strong circle"*: Interview with Grauman. To get a feel for that circle, see the tribute Grauman and several others built for Chuck Jensvold, a writer who overlapped with Grauman and Obama at Occidental and to whom Obama mailed several short stories for critique even after he left for Columbia: jensvold.specialcollections .oxycreates.org/remembering-charles-jensvold/index.

303 *"Hey . . . what did"*: "The Choice 2012," PBS Frontline, www.pbs.org/wgbh/pages /frontline/oral-history/choice-2012/coming-of-age. The roommate's name was Sohale Siddiqi.

303 *"I recommend Marxism and Literature"*: Obama to Alex McNear, February 10, 1983, in Garrow, *Rising Star*, 156. McNear was also a founder of *Feast*.

303 *"Regina smiled"*: *Dreams from My Father: A Story of Race and Inheritance* (New York: Times Books, 1995), 103. All citations come from the Crown 2004 reprint.

303 *"bloody racist"*: Chinua Achebe, "An Image of Africa," *Massachusetts Review* 18, no. 4 (1977): 782–794, at 788.

305 *"He talked about"*: Interview with Kellman.

305 *"Take a look"*: Interview with Kellman.

305 *"Write outside"*: Obama to Phil Boerner, November 20, 1985, in Maraniss, *Barack Obama*, 279.

305 *"Down the road"*: Tammerlin Drummond, "Barack Obama's Law," *Los Angeles Times*, March 12, 1990.

305 *"We both said"*: Cindy Adams, "Obama's Memoir's Really 18 Years Old," *New York Post*, June 9, 2008.

306 *"Our usual idea"*: *Conversations with Maxine Hong Kingston*, 75. The interview was conducted in 1986.

306 *"Such works take"*: Maraniss, *Barack Obama*, 596.

306 *"Do you want"*: Remnick, *The Bridge*, 221.

306 *"The manuscript came"*: Interview with Patty.

307 *"It was a simple case"*: Sarah Lyall, "Book Notes," *New York Times*, July 7, 1993.

307 *"The best story"*: Garrow, *Rising Star*, 483.

307 *"Pot had helped"*: Obama, *Dreams*, 93.

307 *"I was like"*: Interview with Ferris.

308 *"He had a clear"*: Interview with Osnos.

309 *"He mentioned he"*: Deborah Baker, email to the author. Philip Turner, then of Kodansha, shared similar memories in an interview.

309 *"He would give"*: Interview with Shomon.

309 *"He essentially wrote"*: Interview with Ferris.

310 *"from my grandparents"*: Obama, *Dreams*, 110.

310 *"My family is"*: "Dreams from My Father," *Bill Thompson's Eye on Books*, August 9, 1995. Thompson has put a transcript online at http://www.eyeonbooks.com/obama _transcript.pdf.

310 *"Publishing books by"*: John H. Fund, "Bill's Book Deal," *Wall Street Journal*, August 8, 2001.

311 *"Now my bosses"*: Kachka, "The End."

311 *"That one . . . went"*: Matthew Rose, "Pennie Ianniciello Picks Books for Costco, Where Stacks Go Fast," *Wall Street Journal*, April 10, 2002.

311 *"most complete"*: Sears, Roebuck, & Co. Catalogue no. 112.

311 *"Earth's biggest bookstore"*: Another early motto was "Earth's Largest Bookstore." See Brad Stone, *The Everything Store: Jeff Bezos and the Age of Amazon* (New York: Little, Brown, 2013).

311 *"I think I'm"*: Interview with Cella.

312 *"long tail"*: Anderson coined the concept in "The Long Tail," *Wired*, October 2004.

312 *"the hard middle"*: James Marcus, *Amazonia: Five Years at the Epicenter of the Dot .Com Juggernaut* (New York: New Press, 2004), 89.

312 *"Now you need"*: Interview with Elberse.

313 *"Powell '96"*: Susan Baer, "Powell Is a Popular Not-Quite Candidate," *Baltimore Sun*, September 17, 1995.

313 *"the last bargain"*: D. D. Guttenplan, "The Go-Between," *Financial Times*, October 25, 2008.

313 *"When I was"*: Clinton previewing *My Life* at the 2004 BookExpo, broadcast on C-SPAN on June 3, 2004.

314 *"You're not running"*: Robert Gottlieb, *Avid Reader: A Life* (New York: Farrar, Straus and Giroux, 2106), 253.

314 *"personal"*: Caroline Daniel, "Clinton Touts Memoirs at Top-Billed BookExpo," *Financial Times*, June 5, 2004.

315 *"If you know Herman"*: T. A. Frank, "On the Ropes with Herman Cain," *New York Times Magazine*, November 6, 2011.

316 *"I'm Henry Ferris"*: Interview with Ferris.

316 *"That book . . . got"*: Interview with Ferris.

317 *"I'm always reading"*: Interview with Durand.

317 *"Not Jane Austen's"*: Durand logged her review of *Northanger Abbey* on April 19, 2007: www.goodreads.com/review/show/792377.

317 *"This is a fantastic"*: Durand logged her review of *Dreams* on March 21, 2007: www .goodreads.com/review/show/363654.

317 *"I liked his"*: Interview with Durand.

317 *"This book's been"*: Obama, "Booked for Lunch," Illinois State Library, March 7, 2001. The Illinois Center for the Book has a DVD of Obama's talk, which is the source of this paragraph's quotations.

318 *"It had nothing"*: Interview with Cauley.

318 *"Pot had helped"*: Interview with Cauley.

318 *"He was writing"*: Interview with Cauley.

318 *"My life would"*: John Heilemann and Mark Halperin, *Game Change: Obama and the Clintons, McCain and Palin, and the Race of a Lifetime* (New York: HarperCollins, 2010), 21.

319 *"We're already talking"*: Cindy Adams, "Dem's Rising Star Barack a Writer Too," *New York Post*, August 5, 2004.

319 *"He is really more"*: "Living the American Dream," *The Oprah Winfrey Show*, January 19, 2005.

319 *"I am obligated"*: Obama, *The Audacity of Hope: Thoughts on Reclaiming the American Dream* (New York: Crown, 2006), 68.

319 *"I have to be"*: Max Corey, "Obama Kicks Off Tour on Home Turf," *Chicago Maroon*, October 20, 2006.

320 *"We were going"*: Obama book reading, Cambridge Public Library, September 20, 1995. *22-CityView* has posted video of this event online at www.youtube.com /watch?v=w5JlqDnoqlo.

320 *"Obama, not Hillary"*: Jacob Weisberg, "Obama's New Rules," *Slate*, slate.com /news-and-politics/2006/10/in-the-past-10-days-obama-has-turned-american-poli tics-upside-down.html.

321 *"I saw those people"*: "Obama on Books That Guided Him."

321 *"There were speeches"*: Interview with Frankel.

321 *"I will stand"*: Emi Kolawole, "Obama's 'Dreams of My Father,'" FactCheck.org, www
.factcheck.org/2008/06/obamas-dreams-of-my-father.

321 *"Obama's references"*: David Brock and Ari Rabin-Havt, *The Fox Effect: How Roger
Ailes Turned a Network into a Propaganda Machine* (New York: Anchor Books,
2012), 5–9.

321 *"composites of people"*: Obama, *Dreams*, xvii. The Politico story can be found at www
.politico.com/blogs/media/2012/05/obama-new-york-girlfriend-was-composite
-122272.

321 *"Marxist professors"*: Obama, *Dreams*, 100.

322 *"I found myself"*: "Obama on Books That Guided Him."

322 *"subtle power of sympathy"*: *Papers of Woodrow Wilson*, ed. Arthur S. Link (Princeton:
Princeton University Press, 1967–1994), 6:648.

Epilogue

In my research, I found no parallels to Truman's *Memoirs* files—no examples, in other
words, of other presidents working so diligently to preserve their perspective on every
decision. The closest analogue is probably Clinton's interviews with Taylor Branch and
Edward Widmer, which produced thousands of pages, now at the Clinton library (though
still not open to researchers). But this remains a much smaller archive, and Clinton did not
work as hard as Truman to check his views against those of his cabinet members. I asked
Joanne Drake, the Chief Administrative Officer at Reagan's library, if she knew of anything
similar at her institution. "Unfortunately," she told me, "I just don't think there is a treasure
trove like at the Truman Library." Nor did Chris Michel know of any similar caches created
by Bush during the work on *Decision Points*.

For Bush as a writer and reader, see Susan Baer, "Gone Fishing," *Washingtonian*,
January 2010; Bryan Curtis, "Bush's Ghostwriter," *Daily Beast*, www.thedailybeast.com
/bushs-ghostwriter; and Karl Rove, "Bush Is a Book Lover," *Wall Street Journal*, December 26, 2008. During his first run for president, Bush commissioned a well-known author
named Mickey Herskowitz to ghostwrite a campaign book, but their relationship fractured
in fascinating ways; see Wendy Benjaminson, "Bush Pulls Writer from His Book," *Houston
Chronicle*, October 1, 1999, and Russ Baker, "Candidate Bush was Already Talking Privately About Attacking Iraq, According to His Former Ghost Writer," GNN.tv, October 28,
2004. Once in office, Bush inspired a number of kiss-and-tell books, and Trump seems on
pace to top him. "Is Everyone in Washington Writing a Political Tell-All?" asked a headline
in the February 17, 2019, issue of the *New York Times Book Review*. The sales of volumes
like James Comey's *A Higher Loyalty* suggest the answer is probably yes.

For the expansion and partisan limits of the modern presidency, see George Edwards,
On Deaf Ears: The Effect of Presidential Rhetoric (New Haven, CT: Yale University Press,
2003); Frances Lee, *Beyond Ideology: Politics, Principles, and Partisanship in the U. S. Senate*
(Chicago: University of Chicago Press, 2009); and the work of Brendan Nyhan, including
"Our Unrealistic Hopes for Presidents," *New York Times*, December 14, 2014, and "Obama
and the Myth of Presidential Control," *New York Times*, www.nytimes.com/2014/07/25
/upshot/obama-and-the-myth-of-presidential-control.html.

The following work was especially helpful in understanding the book trade's recent
shifts: Julie Bosman, "Penguin and Random House Merge, Saying Change Will Come
Slowly," *New York Times*, July 2, 2013; Alexandra Alter, "The Plot Twist: E-Book Sales Slip,
and Print Is Far From Dead," *New York Times*, September 23, 2015; Alex Shephard, "Pulp

Friction," *New Republic*, newrepublic.com/article/133876/pulp-friction; Ryan Raffaelli, "Reframing Collective Identity in Response to Multiple Technological Discontinuities: The Novel Resurgence of Independent Bookstores" (Harvard Business School extended abstract, November 2017); Alter and Tiffany Hsu, "Barnes & Noble Turmoil Falls On Its Founder," *New York Times*, August 12, 2018; Jim Milliot and Rachel Deahl, "What's the Matter with Fiction Sales?," *Publishers Weekly*, October 26, 2018; Jeffrey Trachtenberg and Ellen Gamerman, "Stakes High for Obama Memoir," *Wall Street Journal*, November 12, 2018; and Alter, "In Consolidation Move, Penguin Random House Closes Prestigious Imprint," *New York Times*, January 28, 2019.

323 *"By the end"*: Interview with Michel.
323 *"for the better"*: Joe Coscarelli, "Matt Lauer Teases Upcoming George W. Bush Interview," *Los Angeles Times*, latimesblogs.latimes.com/showtracker/2010/10/about-late -last-night-matt-lauer-george-w-bush.html.
324 *"It was important"*: "Obama on Books that Guided Him," *New York Times*, January 16, 2017.
324 *"I read passages"*: Emily Temply, "Hillary Clinton vs. Donald Trump: What Do They Read?" LitHub, lithub.com/hillary-clinton-vs-donald-trump-what-do-they-read.
324 *"'I was never'"*: David Roth, "I Made Up a Fake Donald Trump Quote, and He Retweeted It," SB Nation, www.sbnation.com/2014/6/10/5797056/donald-trump -fake-quote-twitter.
324 *"waiting for legislation"*: James Surowiecki, "The Perils of Executive Action," *New Yorker*, August 8 and 15, 2016.
324 *"He'd read it"*: Interview with Michel.
325 *"This is a book"*: Johnson, *The Vantage Point: Perspectives of the Presidency, 1963–1969* (New York: Holt, 1971), ix.

Acknowledgments

As a child, Thomas Jefferson supposedly read every book in his family's library. I wanted to read only one. Thanks to my parents for reading *Three Little Pigs* a million times—and for reading my kids *Little Excavator* a million times more. Mom and Dad, this book would not exist without your own passion for books. Thanks to my grandparents, sisters, and in-laws, who were quick to encourage (and to help with the kids). Thanks to those kids, Henry and Maisie, for reminding me that some things matters more than presidents and books.

Thanks to Dr. Kearns, Dr. Darrell, Dr. Jaquess, and Dr. Bloom at the University of Southern Indiana, where I got my start thinking and writing seriously. At Yale, Michael Warner, Caleb Smith, and my fellow grad students provided wonderful company and sharp ideas. Thanks again to the many academics who answered my questions, most of whom are cited in my endnotes. I do want to single out a few who offered feedback on part or all of the manuscript: Scott Casper, Richard Ellis, Chris Hunter, and Jonathan Arnold.

Thanks to the libraries upon which a book like this is built. That includes the librarians, of course, who also answered many questions. I relied on generous research grants from the Truman Library Institute, the Eisenhower Foundation Abilene Travel Grants Program, and the John F. Kennedy Library Foundation.

Thanks to my friends, many of whom read parts of this book: Dustin Sinclair, Nikki Sinclair, Tony Domestico, Megan Eckerle, Andrew Heisel, and Andrew Seal. Thanks to my agent, Edward Orloff, who saw the potential in this project earlier than anyone. (He also gave timely advice on building bookshelves.)

Thanks to everyone at Simon & Schuster who helped make this a book: Carolyn Reidy, Jonathan Karp, Wendy Sheanin, Leah Hays, Felice Javit, Alison Forner, David Gee, Jessica Chin, Bev Miller, Erich Hobbing, Brigid

Black, Amanda Mulholland, Julie Ficks, and Laura Ogar. Thanks also to everyone at Avid Reader: Ben Loehnen, Meredith Vilarello, Jordan Rodman, Allie Lawrence, Morgan Hoit, and Julianna Haubner. Thanks, most of all, to Jofie Ferrari-Adler and Carolyn Kelly. Carolyn helped with many tricky issues, especially the images that appear throughout. Jofie was an ideal editor and a reliable source of good cheer. If we ever invent time travel, let's send him to play a round with Frank Doubleday and Andrew Carnegie at Saint Andrews—he's earned it.

Thanks, finally, to my wife and first reader. Candice, you know better than anyone how much I hate cutting archival tidbits, so I'll squeeze one more in here. When Woodrow Wilson received his first copies of *Congressional Government*, he sent one to Ellen, along with a note thanking her for her patience and help. "Everything in the book was yours already," he wrote, "having been written in the light and under the inspiration of your love. . . . Every word of it was written as if to you, with thoughts of what you would think."

Index

Page numbers in *italics* refer to photographs.

413

Image Credits

117   Detail of advertisement for Cushings & Bailey, Booksellers and Stationers. Courtesy of the Library of Congress.

121   *Harper's Weekly*, December 7, 1867. Courtesy of the Library of Congress.

131   *Lives and Speeches of Abraham Lincoln and Hannibal Hamlin* (Columbus, OH: Follett, Foster, & Co., 1860). Courtesy of the Lilly Library, Indiana University, Bloomington.

136   *A Harvest of Death, Gettysburg, Pennsylvania.* Courtesy of the Library of Congress.

145   Ulysses S. Grant Papers. Courtesy of the Library of Congress.

151   *Gen. U. S. Grant Writing His Memoirs, Mount McGregor, June 27th, 1885.* Courtesy of the Library of Congress.

164   Copyright JHU Sheridan Libraries / Getty Images.

168   No. 520.11. Courtesy of the Theodore Roosevelt Collection, Houghton Library, Harvard University, Cambridge, Massachusetts.

177   Typescript page from the Woodrow Wilson Papers. Courtesy of the Library of Congress. Typewriter illustration from *Scientific American*, March 6, 1886. Courtesy of the Herman B. Wells Library, Indiana University, Bloomington.

181   *Atlantic*, June 1904. Courtesy of the University of Michigan Library.

188   Courtesy of Smith College Special Collections, Northampton, Massachusetts.

190   Sears, Roebuck Catalogue no. 112. Courtesy of the Winterthur Museum Library.

195   *St. Paul Globe*, October 5, 1904. Courtesy of the Library of Congress.

205   Calvin Coolidge. *Have Faith in Massachusetts* (Boston: Houghton Mifflin, 1919). Courtesy of George Ayerego and Ayerego Books, Toronto, Ontario.

214   Courtesy of the National Archives.

220   Courtesy of the Library of Congress.

227   *Cosmopolitan*, April 1929. Courtesy of the Paper-Jungle eBay store.

243   Marjory Collins. *Night Shift Worker Waiting. . . .* Courtesy of the Library of Congress.

245   *Harry S. Truman Reading on the Balcony of White House.* Courtesy of the National Archives.

253   Harry Barth. *Harry Truman and Gene Bailey at Autograph Party.* Courtesy of Truman presidential library.

253   Harry Barth. *Harry Truman and Gene Bailey with Others at Party.* Courtesy of Truman presidential library.

263   Copyright Kennedy presidential library / Alamy.

267   Courtesy of the Kennedy presidential library.

273   Copyright Kennedy presidential library / Alamy.

282   Mary Evans. Copyright Studiocanal Films Ltd. / Alamy.

290   Committee to Boycott Nixon's Memoirs illustrations courtesy of Tom Flanigan.

291   Carter photograph copyright *Time Magazine*, May 24, 1982. Trump photograph copyright Getty Images / Newsday LLC.

304   Pierre Gratia. Courtesy of 57th Street Books.

308   Copyright Marc PoKempner.

312   Courtesy of Amazon.

315   Copyright ZUMA Press, Inc. / Alamy.

320   Courtesy of 57th Street Books.